ENCYCLOPEDIA OF NATIVE AMERICAN TRIBES

REVISED EDITION

CARL WALDMAN

Illustrations by
MOLLY BRAUN

Facts On File, Inc.

Encyclopedia of Native American Tribes, Revised Edition

Text copyright © 1999, 1988 by Carl Waldman
Illustrations copyright 1999, 1988 by Molly Braun

Checkmark Books
An imprint of Facts On File, Inc.
132 West 31st Street
New York, NY 10001

Library of Congress Cataloging-in-Publication Data

Waldman, Carl.
Encyclopedia of Native American tribes / Carl Waldman; illustrations by Molly Braun.—Rev. ed.
p.   cm.
ISBN 0-8160-3963-1.—ISBN 0-8160-3964-X (pbk.)
1. Indians of North America—Encyclopedias, Juvenile. [1. Indians of North America—Encyclopedias.] I. Braun, Molly.
II. Title.
E76.2.W35 1999
970.004'97'003—dc21 98-50263

Checkmark Books are available at special discounts when purchased in bulk quantities for businesses, associations, institutions or sales promotions. Please call our Special Sales Department in New York at (212) 967-8800 or (800) 322-8755.

You can find Facts On File on the World Wide Web at http://www.factsonfile.com

Text design by Cathy Rincon

Printed in China

Creative/Hermitage 10 9 8 7 6 5 4

(pbk) 10 9 8

This book is printed on acid-free paper.

For Chloe and Devin

CONTENTS

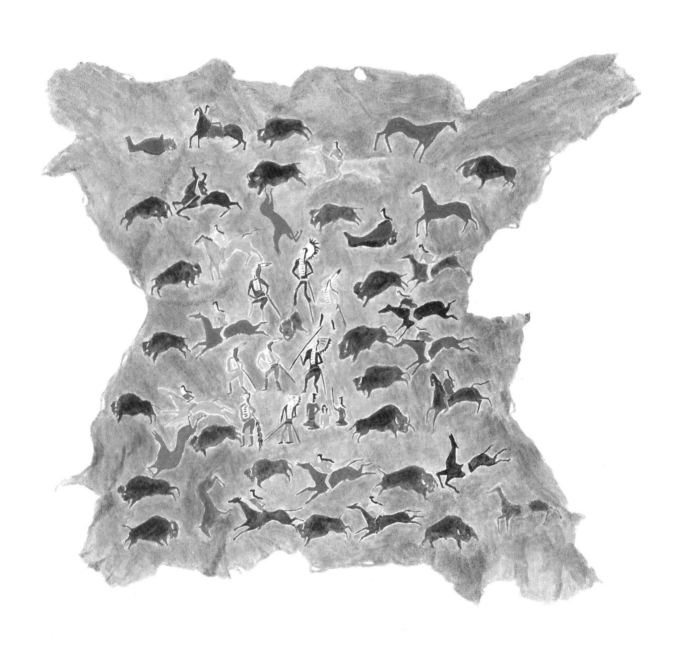

INTRODUCTION

The *Encyclopedia of Native American Tribes* is designed to tell part of the story of native North Americans—a subject matter that, although central to the story of the Americas, receives all-too-little emphasis in public education. The book tries to give in an accessible format an overview of historical events while imparting some of the rich culture of the First Nations. It also attempts to show that the story is ongoing, with Indians a vital part of the contemporary scene.

Any single volume covering such a vast topic has to limit itself somewhat arbitrarily as well as impose a somewhat arbitrary system of organization and classification. As such, this book focuses its attention only on some of the hundreds of North American Indian tribes, while including a number of cultural groupings to give a broader picture.

As for the concept of *tribe* in the title, the term is used in many different ways to indicate varying kinds of social organization. In some cases, it refers to a group of local bands or villages with common ancestry, culture, and language. It also sometimes refers to groups of peoples spread over a wider area but united politically in what is called a confederacy. In still other cases, *tribe* refers to just one village. Furthermore, scholars do not always agree on how to classify a particular people. Some may define a group of people as a distinct tribe while others consider the same people a *band* or *subtribe*.

In addition to the word *band*, there are other terms that scholars sometimes use interchangeably or as a subgrouping of *tribe*. The term *chiefdom* sometimes is used in reference to Southeast Indians, and *tribelet* in reference to California Indians. In Mexico and Central America, some native peoples are said to have been organized into *city-states* or *civilizations*. Many contemporary Native Americans prefer the term *nation* rather than *tribe* because it implies the concept of political sovereignty, indicating that their people have goals and rights like other nations, leading to the phrase now applied to Canadian tribes, *First Nations*. In the study of prehistoric Indians, the term *culture* rather than *tribe* is used for groups of people.

This book lists different Indian tribes or peoples alphabetically. Most of the names that head the various sections are considered names of tribes. But other headings are more general cultural names: MISSION INDIANS, MOUND BUILDERS, PREHISTORIC INDIANS, PUEBLO INDIANS, and SOUTHWEST CULTURES. Other headings apply to Mesoamerican civilizations: AZTEC, MAYA, OLMEC, and TOLTEC. Still others apply to language families: ALGONQUIANS and ATHAPASCANS, since it is helpful to discuss these groupings as specific categories. The IROQUOIS (HAUDENOSAUNEE) heading applies to a confederacy of tribes.

There is another category of headings in this book: "culture areas." A culture area is a geographic region where the various Indian peoples had lifeways in common. The system of culture areas has been devised by scholars to make Native American studies easier. With the system, students can get a sense of cultural patterns. One can see, for example, that the tribes of the Great Plains lived differently than those of the Great Basin did. The culture area entries in this book include the following: ARCTIC PEOPLES, CALIFORNIA INDIANS, GREAT BASIN INDIANS, NORTHEAST INDIANS, NORTHWEST COAST INDIANS, PLAINS INDIANS, PLATEAU INDIANS, SOUTHEAST INDIANS, SOUTHWEST INDIANS, and SUBARCTIC INDIANS. A map showing all the culture areas is included in the front matter. Each culture area entry is accompanied by a map showing general locations of those tribes with entries. An additional culture area is included for clarification—PRAIRIE INDIANS—although this author uses the system of 10 culture areas for what now is territory in the United States and Canada. In addition to offering cross-references to those tribes having their own entries, the culture area entries list other tribes placed by scholars in that particular region.

Three lists follow this section to give the reader a frame of reference: The first is an alphabetical listing of all the entries in the book, with some alternate spellings and names included parenthetically. The second is a list of entries organized by culture areas (as well as by miscellaneous categories). The third is a listing of entries organized by culture areas and languages, including other tribes mentioned in the text.

The system of language phyla, language families, and language isolates as presented in this third list is based for the most part on a classification by C. F. Voegelin and F. M. Voegelin as found in Harold Driver's *Indians of North America.* It should be kept in mind that linguistic studies involve a certain amount of guesswork, so readers may encounter other language groupings in other readings.

Throughout the text, cross-references lead the reader to different levels of organization (the cross-references are set in small capital letters the first time they appear in an entry). For example, as stated, within each culture area entry there are cross-references to all the tribes of that culture area listed in this book. And for each tribe with an entry, a culture area is cited, so that by turning to the culture area entry, the reader can get an overview of the entire geographic region and all its peoples. Moreover, other tribes within the entries are cited that have a special relationship historically or culturally with the given tribe. Serious students should follow the cross-references to where they lead for a better understanding of the complex information.

This book has space enough to cover only a selection of tribes. South American peoples are not covered. Those tribes selected are especially relevant historically in relations with non-Indians or are representative of a way of life. Yet those not having entries, even extinct tribes, are no less important in Native American studies. As stated, tribes without their own entries are mentioned in the culture area entries. Others are mentioned in tribal entries. In some instances, bands, or subtribes, also are discussed in tribal entries.

Certain tribes have alternate names or alternate spellings for their names. Some of these are given in the text (or, as stated, they are given parenthetically in the alphabetical list of entries). The pronunciations of the primary names are given. (These are the pronunciations in use today and not necessarily the historical pronunciations.) In some instances, deciding which primary name to use as the heading is problematic because, although a name might be the most familiar one to a reader, it now has fallen out of favor. (*Eskimo,* for example, is no longer used by native peoples although it still appears in popular culture.) To help the reader find his or her way, some of the more common alternate names, as well as branch tribes or cultural subgroupings, are cross-referenced between entries.

The illustrations in the book convey a great deal about Native American life. Most are drawings of ancient objects; those drawn from objects made by 20th-century Indians are identified as such. Some of the objects shown are reconstructions if no original has been found or photographed. The scenes, of course, give hypothetical views of Native American life. Some are based on early or contemporary photographs.

There are many unfamiliar terms used in Native American studies—for cultural and political concepts, for natural phenomena, and for various objects. A glossary at the end of the book defines some of them.

Keep in mind that each tribe has a detailed history to be further explored. Each has individuals who have made or who are making a contribution to their own people or to the general society through leadership and in art and literature. Also keep in mind that each tribe has its own worldview and ceremonials. A selected bibliography will help the reader further pursue Native American studies. Those books listed are for the most part general titles, especially helpful in giving an overview of the subject. It is hoped that the reader will pursue these titles and other more specialized ones to achieve a greater understanding of North America's first citizens.

LISTING OF ENTRIES

Alphabetical List of Entries with Alternate Spellings and Alternate Names

Note: headings are in boldface.

The Indian Culture Areas, showing one system of categorizing Indian peoples by culture and geography

Entries Organized by Culture Areas

Note: headings are in boldface.

Potawatomi
Powhatan
Roanoke
Sac
Shawnee
Susquehannock
Wampanoag
Wappinger
Winnebago

NORTHWEST COAST CULTURE AREA
(Northwest Coast Indians)

Chinook
Haida
Kwakiutl
Makah
Nootka
Tlingit
Tsimshian

PLATEAU CULTURE AREA
(Plateau Indians)

Cayuse
Coeur d'Alene
Flathead
Kalispel
Klamath
Kootenai
Modoc
Nez Perce
Palouse
Umatilla
Spokan
Walla Walla
Yakama

SOUTHEAST CULTURE AREA
(Southeast Indians)

Alabama
Apalachee
Caddo
Calusa
Catawba
Chitimacha
Choctaw
Coushatta
Creek
Lumbee
Natchez

Seminole
Timucua
Tunica
Yamasee
Yazoo
Yuchi

SOUTHWEST CULTURE AREA
(Southwest Indians)

Akimel O'odham (Pima)
Apache
Havasupai
Hopi
Hualapai
Mojave
Navajo
Pueblo Indians
Tohono O'odham (Papago)
Yaqui
Yavapai
Yuma (Quechan)
Zuni

SUBARCTIC CULTURE AREA
(Subarctic Indians)

Beothuk
Carrier
Chipewyan
Chippewa (Ojibway)
(most Chippewa bands part of
Northeast Culture Area)
Cree
Kutchin
Montagnais
Naskapi

MISCELLANEOUS CATEGORIES

CARIBBEAN TRIBES
Arawak (Taino)

LANGUAGE FAMILIES
Algonquians
Athapascans

MESOAMERICAN CIVILIZATIONS
Aztec
Maya

Entries, plus Other Tribes or Groups Mentioned in Text, Organized by Culture Areas and Language Families

Note: headings are in boldface.

CULTURE AREAS AND LANGUAGE FAMILIES

ARCTIC CULTURE AREA
(Arctic Peoples)

Eskimaleut Language Family
(American Arctic/Paleo-Siberian Phylum)
Aleut
Inuit

CALIFORNIA CULTURE AREA
(California Indians)

Algonquian Language Family
(Macro-Algonquian Phylum)
Wiyot
Yurok

Athapascan Language Family
(Na-Dene Phylum)
Bear River
Cahto (Kato)
Chilula
Hupa
Lassik
Mattole
Nongatl
Sinkyone
Tolowa (Smith River)
Wailaki
Whilkut

Chimariko Language Isolate
(Hokan Phylum)
Chimariko

Chumashan Language Family
(Hokan Phylum)
Chumash

Esselen Language Isolate
(Hokan Phylum)
Esselen

Karok Language Isolate
(Hokan Phylum)
Karok

Maidu Language Family
(Penutian Phylum)
Maidu

Miwok-Costanoan Language Family
(Penutian Phylum)
Costanoan
Miwok

Palaihnihan Language Family
(Hokan Phylum)
Achomawi (Pit River)
Atsugewi (Pit River)

Pomo Language Family
(Hokan Phylum)
Pomo

Salinan Language Family
(Hokan Phylum)
Salinas

Shastan language Family
(Hokan Phylum)
Konomihu
Okwanuchu
Shasta

Uto-Aztecan Language Family
(Aztec-Tanoan Phylum)
Alliklik (Tataviam)
Cahuilla
Cupeño
Fernandeño
Gabrieliño
Juaneño

Kitanemuk
Luiseño
Nicoleño
Serrano
Tubatulabal (Kern River)
Vanyume

Wintun Language Family
(Penutian Phylum)
Nomlaki (subgroup of **Wintun**)
Patwin (subgroup of **Wintun**)
Wintu (subgroup of **Wintun**)
Wintun

Yanan Language Family
(Hokan Phylum)
Yahi
Yana

Yokutsan Language Family
(Penutian Phylum)
Yokuts

Yukian Language Family
(undetermined phylum)
Huchnom
Wappo
Yuki

Yuman Language Family
(Hokan Phylum)
Akwaala
Diegueño (Ipai)
Kamia (Tipai)

GREAT BASIN CULTURE AREA
(Great Basin Indians)

Uto-Aztecan Language Family
(Aztec-Tanoan Phylum)
Bannock
Chemehuevi
Kawaiisu
Mono
Paiute
Panamint
Sheepeater (subgroup of **Bannock** and
Shoshone)
Shoshone
Snake (subgroup of **Paiute**)
Ute

Washoe Language Isolate
(Hokan Phylum)
Washoe

GREAT PLAINS CULTURE AREA
(Plains Indians)

Algonquian Language Family
(Macro-Algonquian Phylum)
Arapaho
Blackfeet
Blood (subgroup of **Blackfeet**)
Cheyenne
Gros Ventre
Piegan (subgroup of **Blackfeet**)
Plains Cree (see **Cree**)
Plains Ojibway (see **Chippewa**)

Athapascan Language Family
(Na-Dene Phylum)
Kiowa-Apache (see **Apache**)
Sarcee

Caddoan Language Family
(Macro-Siouan Phylum)
Arikara
Kichai
Pawnee
Tawakoni
Tawehash
Waco
Wichita
Yscani

Kiowa-Tanoan Language Family
(Aztec-Tanoan Phylum)
Kiowa

Siouan Language Family
(Macro-Siouan Phylum)
Assiniboine
Crow
Hidatsa
Ioway
Kaw
Mandan
Missouria
Omaha
Osage
Otoe
Ponca

Quapaw
Sioux (Dakota, Lakota, Nakota)

Tonkawan Language Isolate
(Macro-Algonquian Phylum)
Tonkawa

Uto-Aztecan Language Family
(Aztec-Tanoan Phylum)
Comanche

NORTHEAST CULTURE AREA
(Northeast Indians)

Algonquian Language Family
(Macro-Algonquian Phylum)
Abenaki
Algonkin
Amikwa (Otter)
Chippewa (Ojibway) (see also Subarctic Culture
Area)
Chowanoc
Conoy
Coree (Coranine) (probably Algonquian)
Fox (Mesquaki)
Hatteras
Illinois
Kickapoo
Kitchigami
Lenni Lenape (Delaware)
Machapunga
Mahican
Maliseet
Manhattan (subgroup of **Lenni Lenape** or
Wappinger)
Massachuset
Mattabesec
Menominee
Miami
Micmac
Mohegan
Montauk
Moratok
Nanticoke
Narragansett
Nauset
Niantic
Nipmuc
Noquet
Ottawa
Pamlico (Pomeiok)

Passamaquoddy
Paugussett
Penacook
Penobscot
Pequot
Pocomtuc
Poospatuck (subgroup of **Montauk**)
Potawatomi
Powhatan
Raritan (subgroup of **Lenni Lenape**)
Roanoke
Sac
Sakonnet
Secotan
Shawnee
Shinnecock (subgroup of **Montauk**)
Wampanoag
Wappinger
Weapemeoc

Iroquoian Language Family
(Macro-Siouan Phylum)
Erie
Honniasont
Huron (Wyandot)
Iroquois (Haudenosaunee)
Cayuga
Mohawk
Oneida
Onondaga
Seneca
Tuscarora
Meherrin
Mingo (subgroup of **Iroquois**)
Neusiok (probably Iroquoian)
Neutral (Attiwandaronk)
Nottaway
Susquehannock
Tobacco (Petun)
Wenro

Siouan Language Family
(Macro-Siouan Phylum)
Winnebago

NORTHWEST COAST CULTURE AREA
(Northwest Coast Indians)

Athapascan Language Family
(Na-Dene Phylum)
Chastacosta

Chetco
Clatskanie
Coquille (Mishikhwutmetunne)
Dakubetede
Kwalhioqua
Taltushtuntude
Tututni (Rogue)
Umpqua

Chimakuan Language Family
(undetermined phylum)
Chimakum
Quileute

Chinookian Language Family
(Penutian Phylum)
Cathlamet
Cathlapotle
Chilluckittequaw
Chinook
Clackamas
Clatsop
Clowwewalla
Multomah (Wappato)
Skilloot
Wasco
Watlala (Cascade)

Haida Language Isolate
(Na-Dene Phylum)
Haida

Kalapuyan Language Family
(Penutian Phylum)
Ahantchuyuk
Atfalati
Chelamela
Chepenafa (Mary's River)
Kalapuya
Luckiamute
Santiam
Yamel
Yoncalla

Kusan Language Family
(Penutian Phylum)
Coos
Miluk

Salishan Language Family
(undetermined phylum)
Bella Coola
Chehalis

Clallam
Comox
Cowichan
Cowlitz
Duwamish
Lumni
Muckleshoot
Nanaimo
Nisqually
Nooksack
Puntlatch
Puyallup
Quaitso (Queets)
Quinault
Sahehwamish
Samish
Seechelt
Semiahmoo
Siletz
Skagit
Skykomish
Snohomish
Snoqualmie
Songish
Squamish
Squaxon (Squaxin)
Stalo
Suquamish
Swallah
Swinomish
Tillamook
Twana

Takelman Language Isolate
(Penutian Phylum)
Latgawa
Takelma (Rogue)

Tlingit Language Isolate
(Na-Dene Phylum)
Tlingit

Tsimshian Language Isolate
(Penutian Phylum)
Gitskan (Kitskan)
    (subgroup of **Tsimshian**)
Nisga (Niska)
    (subgroup of **Tsimshian**)
Tsimshian

Wakashan Language Family
(undetermined phylum)
    Haisla (subgroup of **Kwakiutl**)
    Heiltsuk (Heitsuk)
      (subgroup of **Kwakiutl**)
    Kwakiutl
    Makah
    Nootka

Yakonan Language Family
(Penutian Phylum)
    Alsea
    Kuitsh
    Siuslaw
    Yaquina

PLATEAU CULTURE AREA
(Plateau Indians)

Athapascan Language Family
(Macro-Algonquian Phylum)
    Stuwihamuk

Cayuse Language Isolate
(Penutian Phylum)
    Cayuse

Chinookian Language Family
(Penutian Phylum)
    Wishram

Klamath-Modoc Isolate
(Penutian Phylum)
    Klamath
    Modoc

Kutenai Language Isolate
(Macro-Algonquian Phylum)
    Kootenai

Molalla Language Isolate
(Penutian Phylum)
    Molalla

Sahaptian Language Family
(Penutian Phylum)
    Klickitat
    Nez Perce
    Palouse
    Pshwanwapam
    Skin (Tapanash)
    Taidnapam
    Tenino

    Tyigh
    Umatilla
    Walla Walla
    Wanapam
    Wauyukma
    Yakama

Salishan Language Family
(undetermined phylum)
    Chelan
    Coeur d'Alene
    Columbia (Sinkiuse)
    Colville
    Entiat
    Flathead
    Kalispel
    Lake (Senijextee)
    Lillooet
    Methow
    Ntlakyapamuk (Thompson)
    Okanagan
    Sanpoil
    Shuswap
    Sinkaietk
    Sinkakaius
    Spokan
    Wenatchee

SOUTHEAST CULTURE AREA
(Southeast Indians)

Atakapan Language Isolate
(Macro-Algonquian Phylum)
    Akokisa
    Atakapa
    Bidai
    Deadose
    Opelousa
    Patiri

Caddoan Language Family
(Macro-Siouan Phylum)
    Adai
    Caddo
    Eyeish (Ayish)

Chitimachan Language Isolate
(Macro-Algonquian Phylum)
    Chawasha (subgroup of **Chitimacha**)
    Chitimacha
    Washa (subgroup of **Chitimacha**)

Iroquoian Language Family
(Macro-Siouan Phylum)
Cherokee

Muskogean Language Family
(Macro-Algonquian Phylum)
Acolapissa
Ais
Alabama
Amacano (probably Muskogean)
Apalachee
Apalachicola
Avoyel
Bayogoula
Calusa (probably Muskogean)
Caparaz (probably Muskogean)
Chakchiuma
Chatot
Chiaha
Chickasaw
Chine (probably Muskogean)
Choctaw
Coushatta
Creek
Cusabo
Guacata (probably Muskogean)
Guale
Hitchiti
Houma
Ibitoupa (probably Muskogean)
Jeaga (probably Muskogean)
Kaskinampo
Miccosukee (subgroup of **Seminole**)
Mobile
Muklasa
Napochi
Oconee
Okelousa
Okmulgee
Osochi (probably Muskogean)
Pasacagoula (probably Muskogean)
Pawokti
Pensacola
Quinipissa
Sawokli
Seminole
Tamathli
Tangipahoa
Taposa
Tawasa

Tekesta (probably Muskogean)
Tohome
Tuskegee
Yamasee

Natchesan Language Isolate
(Macro-Algonquian Phylum)
Natchez
Taensa

Siouan Language Family
(Macro-Siouan Phylum)
Biloxi
Cape Fear (probably Siouan)
Catawba
Cheraw (Sara)
Congaree (probably Siouan)
Eno (probably Siouan)
Keyauwee (probably Siouan)
Lumbee (perhaps Algonquian and Iroquoian
dialects as well)
Manahoac
Monacan
Moneton
Nahyssan
Occaneechi
Ofo
Pee Dee
Santee (Issati)
Saponi
Sewee
Shakori
Sissipahaw
Sugeree
Tutelo
Waccamaw
Wateree
Waxhaw
Winyaw
Woccon
Yadkin (probably Siouan)

Timucuan Language Family
(undetermined phylum)
Timucua

Tunican Language Family or Isolate
(Macro-Algonquian Phylum)
Griga
Koroa
Tiou
Tunica
Yazoo

Yuchian Language Isolate
(Macro-Siouan Phylum)
   Yuchi

SOUTHWEST CULTURE AREA
(Southwest Indians)
Athapascan Language Family
(Na-Dene Phylum)
   Apache
   Navajo

Coalhuitecan Language Isolate
(Hokan Phylum)
   Coahuiltec

Karankawan Language Isolate
(undetermined phylum)
   Karankawa

Keresan Language Isolate
(undetermined phylum)
   Keres (**Pueblo Indians**)

Kiowa-Tanoan Language Family
(Aztec-Tanoan Phylum)
   Piro (**Pueblo Indians**)

Uto-Aztecan Language Family
(Aztec-Tanoan Phylum)
   Akimel O'odham (Pima)
   Hopi
   Jumano (Shuman) (probably Uto-Aztecan)
   Sobaipuri
   Tewa (**Pueblo Indians**)
   Tiwa (**Pueblo Indians**)
   Tohono O'odham (Papago)
   Towa (Jemez) (**Pueblo Indians**)
   Yaqui

Yuman Language Family
(Hokan Phylum)
   Cocopah
   Halchidhoma
   Halyikwamai
   Havasupai
   Hualapai
   Kohuana
   Maricopa
   Mojave

   Yavapai
   Yuma (Quechan)
Zunian Language Isolate
(Penutian Phylum)
   Zuni

SUBARCTIC CULTURE AREA
(Subarctic Indians)

Algonquian Language Family
(Macro-Algonquian Phylum)
   Chippewa (Ojibway) (see also Northeast
      Coast Culture Area)
   Cree
   Montagnais
   Naskapi

Athapascan Language Family
(Na-Dene Phylum)
   Ahtena (Copper)
   Beaver (Tsattine)
   Carrier
   Chilcotin
   Chipewyan
   Dogrib (Thlingchadinne)
   Eyak
   Han
   Hare (Kawchottine)
   Ingalik
   Kolchan
   Koyukon
   Kutchin
   Nabesna
   Nahane (Nahani)
   Sekani
   Slave (Slavey, Etchaottine)
   Tahltan
   Tanaina
   Tanana
   Tatsanottine (Yellowknife)
   Tsetsaut
   Tutchone (Mountain)

Beothukan Language Isolate
(Macro-Algonquian Phylum)
   Beothuk

MISCELLANEOUS CATEGORIES

CARIBBEAN TRIBES

Arawakan Language Family
  (Andean-Equatorial Phylum)
    Arawak (Taino)

LANGUAGE FAMILIES

  Algonquians
  Athapascans

MESOAMERICAN CIVILIZATIONS

  Aztec
  Maya

  Olmec
  Toltec

OTHER GROUPINGS

  Métis
  Mission Indians
  Mound Builders
  Prairie Indians
  Southwest Cultures

Tribes and Peoples

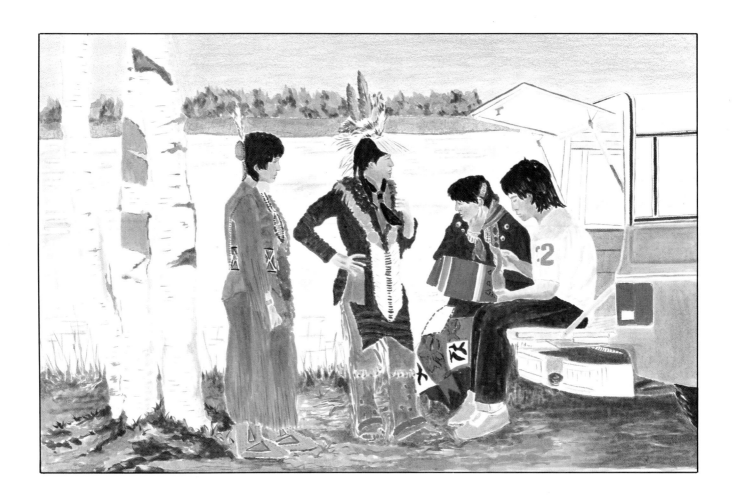

ABENAKI

Abenaki, pronounced AB-eh-nah-kee, can be translated from the Algonquian language as "those living at the sunrise," "people of the dawn land," or "easterners." (The Algonquian word itself is *wapanahki;* alternative spellings include *Abnaki, Wabanaki,* or *Wapanaki.*) Those people classified under this name occupied ancestral territory in what now is the state of Maine, the easternmost of all the states, as well as parts of present-day New Hampshire, Vermont, and Massachusetts.

The Abenaki actually were an alliance of many Algonquian-speaking tribes or bands—the Abenaki Confederacy—consisting of the Abenaki proper, along with other groups in Maine, the PASSAMAQUODDY and the PENOBSCOT, as well as the MALISEET and MICMAC to the north in present-day Canada and the PENNACOOK to the west in present-day New Hampshire. The Abenaki sometimes are discussed as the Eastern Abenaki and the Western Abenaki. The Penobscot, living along the Penobscot River in Maine, and other bands, such as the Pequawket (Pigwacket) and Norridgewock, living along the Androscoggin, Kennebec, and Saco Rivers, are considered Eastern Abenaki. The Passamaquoddy are sometimes placed in the eastern subdivision although their closest relatives linguistically are the Maliseet. The Western Abenaki classification, based on a particular dialect, includes bands living along the upper Connecticut River valley in New Hampshire, Vermont, and Massachusetts, as well as the Missiquoi (Missiassik) on Lake Champlain in northwestern Vermont. The Pennacook in New Hampshire and bordering parts of Maine, Massachusetts, and Vermont are sometimes grouped with them as well.

The Abenaki way of life resembled that of other NORTHEAST INDIANS, combining some farming with hunting, fishing, and gathering. Yet the Abenaki were less dependent on agriculture than were ALGONQUIANS living farther south, because of less favorable growing conditions. Furthermore, unlike most other New England Algonquians, the Abenaki generally built cone-shaped wigwams rather than dome-shaped wigwams. Some bands built IROQUOIS (HAUDENOSAUNEE)–style longhouses as well. They used birch-bark and elm-bark mats over sapling frames to shape these woodland dwellings. Like the tipis of PLAINS INDIANS, the wigwams had holes in the top to let out the smoke from cooking fires. The bark mats could be rolled up and carried to new village sites or camping sites during long hunting, fishing, or warring expeditions. In the winter, tribal members lined the interior walls of the wigwam with bear or deer skins for insulation. They also built walls of upright logs—referred to as palisades—around their villages for protection.

After King Philip's War of 1675–76, involving the WAMAPANOAG, NARRAGANSETT, and NIPMUC living to the south of the Abenaki, some Abenaki bands began moving north to French Canada, eventually settling at St. Francis Mission and Bécancour in Quebec. During the French and Indian wars, the French and their Indian allies fought against the English and their Indian supporters. These various conflicts for control of North America lasted almost 100 years—from 1689 to 1763—and are further organized in history books as the following: King William's War (1689–97), Queen Anne's War (1702–13), King George's War (1744–48), and the French and Indian War (1754–63). The Abenaki allied themselves with the French. They launched many raids

Abenaki conical wigwam with elm-bark covering

against British settlements in New England—sometimes collectively referred to as the Abenaki Wars.

The Abenaki first became involved in the fighting through their friendship with a Frenchman, Jean Vincent de l'Abadie, baron de St-Castin. St-Castin established a fur-trading post at the site where Castine, Maine, now stands. His marriage to the daughter of a chief sealed his friendship with many of the Abenaki bands. When British troops raided and plundered his trading post and home in 1688, Abenaki warriors sought revenge against the settlers. British settlements were at risk over the following years. Saco in Maine, Dover and Salmon Falls in New Hampshire, Haverhill and Deerfield in Massachusetts, along with many other villages, were attacked.

In 1724, the Abenaki stronghold known as Norridgewock on the Kennebec River fell into British hands. Many families withdrew to Quebec, where they made new homes among other Abenaki. A number of militant Abenaki surrendered their weapons in 1754 and relocated as well. European diseases, especially smallpox, killed more Abenaki than did warfare.

Both Eastern and Western Abenaki now live in Quebec—at Odanak (St. Francis) and Wollinak (Becancour). The Passamaquoddy and Penobscot have reservation lands in Maine. There also is a community of Western Abenaki in the Highgate-Swanton-St. Albans area of northern Vermont: the St. Francis–Sokoki Band of the Abenaki Nation. They are applying for federal recognition as a tribe.

Joseph Bruchac of Abenaki and Slovak ancestry has written about Abenaki legends (as well as those of other tribes) in a number of books, including *The Wind Eagle and Other Abenaki Stories as Told by Joseph Bruchac* (1985) and the novel *Dawn Land* (1995).

ADENA *see* MOUND BUILDERS

AKIMEL O'ODHAM (Pima)

The Akimel O'odham have been known by non-Indians as the Pima. The Pima name, pronounced PEE-mah, is derived from the native phrase *pi-nyi-match,* which means "I don't know." It came to be applied to the tribe when the Indians used it in response to questions by early Spanish explorers. Their Native name, pronounced AH-kee-mul-oh-OH-tum, means "river people," to distinguish themselves from the TOHONO O'ODHAM or "desert people," their kin also known as Papago. Their related dialects are of the Uto-Aztecan language family, sometimes grouped together as Piman.

The Akimel O'odham occupied ancestral lands now mapped as part of southern Arizona and northern Sonora, a state of Mexico. They were divided into two major groups—called historically the Pima Alto, or Upper Pima, and the Pima Bajo, or Lower Pima. The Upper Pima lived along the Gila and Salt Rivers. The Lower Pima, or Nevone, as they are known in Mexico, lived along the Yaqui and Sonora Rivers much farther south. The Tohono O'odham lived to the immediate west of the Upper Pima. Both Akimel O'odham and Tohono O'odham are classified by scholars as SOUTHWEST INDIANS.

It is thought that the ancient ancestors of both peoples were the Hohokam Indians. *Hohokam* is an Akimel O'odham word, meaning "vanished ones." Hohokam Indians constructed advanced irrigation systems in the Gila and Salt River valleys (see SOUTHWEST CULTURES).

Lifeways

The Akimel O'odham, villagers and farmers, irrigated their fields by diverting water from rivers. They grew corn, squash, pumpkins, kidney beans, tobacco, cotton, and, after the whites brought the seeds to them, wheat and alfalfa. The men were the farmers and the fishermen, as well as the hunters of small game, such as rabbits. The men also did all the building. Houses were small, round, flat-topped, pole-framed structures, covered with grass and mud. Their villages also contained a number of ramadas, rectangular structures similarly built but with no walls at all or just one wall as a windbreak. The ramadas were used as clubhouses. Small square huts were used for storage.

The women gathered wild plant foods, such as saguaro cactus fruits and mesquite seeds. Women made baskets from willow and other plants and shaped and

Akimel O'odham house

polished red-and-black pottery. They also made clothing—cotton breechcloths for men and outfits of shredded bark for themselves, as well as hide sandals and cotton and rabbit-skin blankets for both sexes. Men wove cotton on a horizontal loom.

The Akimel O'odham had an overall tribal chief, elected from among the various village chiefs. He presided over councils. The responsibilities of the village chiefs under him included overseeing communal farm projects and defending against APACHE raiders. Each village had a ceremonial leader as well, known as the Keeper of the Smoke. Each village was organized into two clans—the Red Ant and White Ant clans—who opposed each other in games. Unlike in some tribes, members from the same clan were allowed to marry. Every fourth harvest, the tribe held a festival, called the Viikita, to celebrate continuing tribal well-being and ensure future good fortune. In the Akimel religion, the most powerful gods were the Earthmaker and Elder Brother. The prevalent man-on-the-maze pattern on their baskets represents Elder Brother preparing to journey through the maze of life.

Contacts with Non-Indians

The Spanish explorer Father Marcos de Niza visited the Akimel O'odham in 1589. Father Eusebio Kino entered their territory on several occasions more than a century later from 1694 to 1698. He grouped the Indians in missions and introduced them to livestock and wheat. Another Spanish explorer, Father Francisco Garcés, traveled deeper into Akimel O'odham country from 1768 to 1776.

Although the Akimel O'odham could be warlike—as the Apache who mounted raids against them well knew—they were generally friendly toward the Spanish. During the 1600s, Spanish officials organized Pima territory into the district of Pimería Alta, establishing missions, presidios (forts), ranches, and mines among them. And the Spanish began imposing taxes on the Indians,

demanding a percentage of their crops as well as labor from them. In 1695, the Lower Pima rebelled, carrying out some violence against missionaries as well as looting and burning of Spanish property. Spanish officials sent in soldiers, who quickly put down the rebellion. Some Lower Pima, however, escaped northward and joined the Upper Pima on the Gila and Salt Rivers.

Some of the descendants of the rebels revolted again in 1751. An Akimel O'odham by the name of Luis Oacpicagigua, who served the Spanish as a captain-general against other Indians, began to resent Spanish treatment of his people. He saw that the Spanish ranching and mining frontier was expanding northward into Upper Pima country, and he knew that more and more forced labor would follow. He plotted a rebellion, sending word to neighboring tribes—Tohono O'odham, Apache, and Sobaipuri—to join his cause.

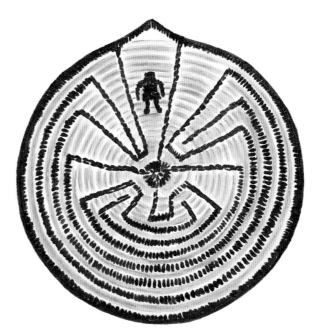

Akimel O'odham basket with labyrinth design

On the night of November 20, the rebels struck. Luis and his war party attacked and killed 18 Spaniards at the settlement of Saric. A missionary managed to escape and spread word of the uprising. Still, small groups of Akimel O'odham and Tohono O'odham plundered a number of other missions and ranches. The Apache and Sobaipuri did not join the fight, however. And the majority of insurgents, fearful of Spanish reprisals, refrained from violence.

Spanish officials ordered presidio captains and troops into the field. They quelled the revolt in several months, executing some of the rebels. Luis Oacpicagigua saved himself by agreeing to supervise the rebuilding of churches destroyed in the uprising.

After that, the Akimel O'odham generally were peaceful toward whites. During the California gold rush, when starting in 1849, many Anglo-Americans passed through their territory, they even provided food and supplies for weary travelers.

Tribal territory came under United States authority with the Gadsden Purchase from Mexico in 1853. In the following years, many Euroamerican farmers began settling along the Gila River. The settlers, despite friendly overtures from of the Akimel O'odham, took advantage of them. They appropriated the best farmland. They diverted the tribe's water supply for use on their own crops. A reservation on the Gila River was established in 1859. Nevertheless, many Gila River inhabitants ended up resettling to the north on the Salt River, where a reservation was established in 1879.

Contemporary Akimel O'odham

The Akimel O'odham share the Gila River and Salt River Reservations with the Maricopa (Pee-Posh). The Maricopa, a Yuman-speaking people, originally migrated to Akimel O'odham country from the west during the 1700s because of attacks on them by the warlike YUMA (QUECHAN). There also are some Akimel O'odham living among the Tohono O'odham on the Ak Chin Reservation. An Akimel O'odham by the name of Ira Hayes, a marine in World War II, was one of six men who helped raise the flag on Iwo Jima, a famous event on the Pacific front. He died in 1955.

The Akimel O'odham recently have taken greater control of their economic development with investments at both Gila River and Salt River, such as community farming, sand and gravel mining, industrial parks, and a casino. The Gila River Arts and Crafts Center helps preserve traditional customs. A persistent problem affecting tribal members is the high rate of diabetes, among the highest in the world, resulting from the change of diet in the 20th century.

ALABAMA

The name of the Alabama people, pronounced al-uh-BAM-uh, has been passed to the state. Also spelled *Alibamu,* it probably means "I clear the thicket" or "weed gatherers," although some linguists give the meaning as "to camp." The Alabama share ancestry, culture, and language—similar dialects of the Muskogean language family—with the CREEK and CHOCTAW. They were allied with the Creek in what is called the Creek Confederacy. All three peoples are classified as SOUTHEAST INDIANS, that is, part of the Southeast Culture Area.

For most of their history, the Alabama lived along the upper Alabama River in what now is the center of the state bearing their name. When the Spanish expedition led by Hernando de Soto encountered them in 1540, they might have been living farther to the north. In the 18th century, the Alabama became allies of the French, who founded Mobile on Mobile Bay in 1710 and, three years later, built Fort Toulouse in Alabama territory. When France lost its holdings in North America in 1763 to Britain, after the French and Indian War, many Alabama left their homeland. Some joined the SEMINOLE in Florida. Others resettled north of New Orleans on the banks of the Mississippi River and later moved to western Louisiana. The majority of this same band eventually moved to Texas, where they were later granted state reservation lands along with the COUSHATTA. Those who stayed behind in Alabama fought alongside the Creek in the Creek War of 1813–14. In the 1830s, some Alabama bands were resettled in the Indian Territory along with their Creek allies.

The Alabama, along with the Coushatta, presently maintain tribal identity as the Alabama-Coushatta Tribe on a shared reservation in Polk County, Texas. Both the Alabama and Coushatta dialects of Muskogean are still spoken. Tourism is important to the reservation's economy: The Alabama-Coushatta Tribe maintains a museum and camping facilities and sponsors a powwow every June. Alabama and Coushatta in Oklahoma, near Weleetka, although having administrative ties to the Muskogee Creek Nation, maintain their identity as the Alabama-Quassarte Tribe of Oklahoma.

ALEUT

Almost 100 in number, the Aleutian Islands extend westward about 1,200 miles into the Pacific Ocean from the tip of the Alaska Peninsula. They are really a partly submerged continuation of the Aleutian Range, a volcanic mountain chain. The climate of the islands is cold and damp, with thick fog. Few trees grow in the rocky soil, only bushes, grasses, and marsh plants called sedge.

These rugged, barren islands were the ancestral homeland of the Aleut. The name, pronounced a-LOOT or AL-ee-oot, may have been either a native word meaning "island" or a Russian word meaning "bald rock." The name *Alaska* was taken from an Aleut phrase, *alaeksu* or *alaschka,* meaning "mainland." The Aleut native name is *Unangan* or "the people."

The Aleut dialects resemble those of the numerous INUIT bands, indicating a close relationship between the two peoples. But the Aleut dialects are different enough for scholars to classify them as a distinct group. Dialects of both peoples are considered part of the Eskimaleut (or Eskaleut) language family.

Some scholars do not use the word *Indian* for Aleut and Inuit but apply the phrases *native peoples, indigenous peoples,* or *Native Americans,* because, in terms of their ancestry, both the Aleut and the Inuit are more closely related to Siberian peoples in Russia than to the other Native American peoples in this book. The Aleut and Inuit came to the Americas much later than did the other native peoples, from about 2500 B.C. to 1000 B.C., and they came by boat and not over the Bering Strait land bridge (see PREHISTORIC INDIANS).

Two main groups of Aleut established permanent villages on the Aleutian Islands' coasts: the Unalaska, closer to the mainland, and the Atka, farther west.

Lifeways

Aleut culture resembles that of the Inuit, and scholars classify the two peoples in the Arctic Culture Area (see ARCTIC PEOPLES). But because of their location, the Aleut also had cultural traits in common with NORTHWEST COAST INDIANS. The Aleut traded objects and shared ideas with these neighbors.

Aleut economy was based on the sea. Aleut hunted the mammals of the ocean, such as sea otters, seals, sea lions, walruses, and whales, and they fished, especially for salmon and shellfish. They also hunted birds and gathered roots and berries.

The Aleut lived in *barabaras,* large communal houses built over pits, with roof beams made from driftwood or whale bones and walls made from chunks of sod. The smokehole in the roof or a separate passageway facing east served as a door. The houses were heated and lighted with stone oil lamps.

Aleut kayaks, or *baidarkas,* were made much like Inuit kayaks—oiled walrus or seal skins stretched over light wood frames. They were short, with the bow curved upward and the stern squared off. Sometimes the bows were shaped like a bird's open beak. Usually there were two cockpits—the rear one for the paddler and the front one for the harpooner. The harpooner used a throwing board for extra leverage in flinging the harpoon in addition to a stabbing harpoon on the prey.

Aleut clothing was efficient for rain and cold. It came in double layers and was made mostly from gut—especially seal intestines—as well as from hide. Hooded parkas of varying lengths—from the hip to below the knee—served as outer garments. Hunters wore wooden helmets with long visors that were decorated with ivory

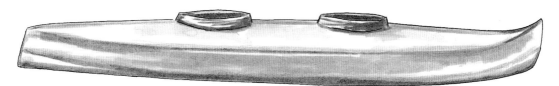

Aleut *baidarka* (skin-covered boat)

and sea lion whiskers. The Aleut added intricate decorations to their clothing by using hair bristles and animal skin dyed different colors.

The Aleut also crafted elegant baskets, as did the Northwest Coast Indians, using rye grass growing on the beaches. The stems of the grass were split with the fingernails to make threads, and some of the threads were dyed to make intricate woven designs.

Another cultural trait that the Aleut had in common with Northwest Coast Indians was their type of social organization. The Aleut were more concerned with rank and wealth than the Inuit were. The *toyons,* or village chiefs, and the nobles under them demonstrated their importance through their possessions, such as shells or amber. Under the chiefs and nobles were commoners and slaves. Unlike the Northwest Coast Indians, the Aleut did not practice the potlatch, an elaborate feast during which gifts were exchanged.

The Fur Trade

Russian traders and trappers forever altered the Aleut way of life. In 1741, Vitus Bering, a Danish navigator in the service of Russia's czar, Peter the Great, carried out his famous voyage of exploration, sailing from eastern Russia to the Bering Sea, Aleutian Islands, and Gulf of Alaska. Bering's reports of plentiful sea mammals in the region soon brought the sailing ships of the *promyshlenniki* (Russian for "fur traders and trappers"). They had previously worked their way across Siberia, trapping animals for their pelts. Now they had a whole new domain to exploit. They came first to the Aleutians, which were especially rich in sea otters. And they took advantage of the Aleut to make their fortunes in fur.

The traders would sail to a native village; take hostages by force; pass out traps to the Aleut men; then demand furs in exchange for the release of the women and children. The women and children also were forced to work, cleaning the furs the men brought in. In the men made any effort to rebel or failed to deliver furs, the traders might execute individuals or destroy entire villages.

The *promyshlenniki* worked eastward along the Aleutian chain. The first organized resistance came from the Unalaska Aleut on the Fox group of islands. In 1761, they wiped out a party of traders. The next year, they managed to destroy a fleet of five ships. The Russians responded in 1766 with an armada of warships, manned by European mercenaries and armed with cannon. They bombarded many of the Aleut villages, destroying houses and killing many.

Aleut resistance was only sporadic after that. The *promyshlenniki* established their first permanent post in North America at Three Saints on Kodiak Island in 1784.

Russian officials and businessmen began regulating and restricting the behavior of the traders more and more, leading to somewhat better treatment. Supposedly the Aleut and Inuit were to get paid for their work. But the traders consistently cheated them by charging them fees for food, protection, and other kinds of made-up expenses. In 1799, the czar granted the charter of the Russian American Company, creating a monopoly that competed in the 1800s with the Hudson's Bay Company for the world fur market.

Those Aleut who had survived the violence of the past years and the diseases carried to them by Europeans were essential to this huge fur operation. They were, after all, some of the best sea-mammal hunters in the world. Another people, the TLINGIT, would take up the mantle of resistance against the Russians.

Russian missionaries would further change the culture of the Aleut. In 1824, the Russian Orthodox priest Veniaminoff began his work among the Indians. The Aleut came to trust him and converted to his religion because he fought for their rights.

In 1867, Russia sold the territory of Alaska to the United States, and the native peoples came under American control.

Aleut in the Twentieth Century

World War II proved a trying time for Aleut peoples. The Japanese attacked the Aleutians and captured the island of Attu in 1942, removing the villagers to Japan. The United States regained control the next year and evacuated Aleut families from other islands to abandoned canneries on the mainland. Without enough food or fuel for heating or medical attention, many died. On returning, Aleut survivors found most of their villages destroyed or their possessions stolen by U.S. military personnel.

The majority of Aleut now live in protected native villages, many on the mainland. These have been organized, along with a number of Inuit villages, into native regional corporations to manage money and land conveyed by the Alaska Native Claims Settlement Act of 1971. Many Aleut work as commercial fishermen or in fish canneries. The oil spill of 1989 of the *Exxon Valdez* tanker in Alaska's coastal waters proved a major economic setback for those Aleut peoples depending on the sea. Some Aleut still practice the Russian Orthodox religion. Aleut elders are working to teach the young their traditional songs, dances, and crafts.

ALGONKIN

The application of tribal names can be confusing. In the case of the terms *Algonquian, Algonquin, Algonkian,* and *Algonkin,* for example, different writers use different spellings. Moreover, the varying spellings sometimes are used to discuss one small Canadian tribe, the people who originally held the name. But at other times they are used to denote many different tribes who spoke a common language but who were spread throughout much of North America. One might see the phrase *Algonquian proper* to distinguish the original tribe from other Algonquian-speaking peoples. This book uses *Algonkin* for the original tribe and *Algonquian* for the whole language family of tribes (see ALGONQUIANS and NORTHEAST INDIANS).

As for the Algonkin (pronounced al-GON-kin and possibly meaning "at the place of spearing fish"), in addition to being the first bearers of the now widespread name, they are important historically as early allies and trading partners of the French.

Samuel de Champlain, a French explorer and fur trader, came to North America in 1603 and helped establish New France in what is now the eastern part of Canada. He had extensive contact with the Algonkin. He was the first European to lead expeditions along the Ottawa River, which now forms part of the border between Quebec and Ontario. The Ottawa River is named after another Indian tribe, the OTTAWA. But the river and some of its northern tributaries flowed through Algonkin territory too.

Samuel de Champlain and his men alienated the powerful IROQUOIS (HAUDENOSAUNEE) nations to the south by attacking some of their people. So the Iroquois became allies of the enemies of the French in North America—first the Dutch, then the English. The Iroquois made raids into the north against the French and their Indian allies and drove the Algonkin and other tribes from their homelands. Some Algonkin joined other Algonquian tribes, such as the Ottawa. Others eventually returned to their original territory, where their descendants live today in various Canadian Indian bands.

In their heyday, the Algonkin lived like other northern Algonquians—little farming and much hunting, fishing, and gathering. They left their villages to track game when necessary for survival. Their houses were usually cone-shaped like tipis rather than dome-shaped like New England wigwams. They also built rectangular houses. In the summer, they traveled in birch-bark canoes; in the winter, they used snowshoes and toboggans.

Algonkin religious beliefs resembled those of other Algonquian peoples of the northern forest. For them Manitou, sometimes referred to as the Great Spirit, was the primary force of nature and life, a supernatural power inherent in all living and nonliving things. As such, Manitou had many manifestations. One Algonkin man, for example, claimed that the most important religious possession or totem he had was a hair that he had pulled from the mustache of Manitou. He kept the hair wrapped in duck down, which was placed in a leather pouch decorated with porcupine quills, which was placed in another pouch, which was placed in still a third pouch. This man claimed that Manitou's mustache hair had saved him from drowning and from sickness and had led him to moose when he was hunting.

Like Native Americans all over the continent, the Algonkin danced ceremonially. In their Feast of the Dead, for example, they entertained visiting tribes with a dance depicting warfare. In one such dance, a warrior would chase another with a warclub, but would lose the advantage and almost be killed by the enemy. By weaving and bobbing, all in time to the beat of the drum, he would eventually manage to outmaneuver his opponent and win the day.

There are currently nine Algonkin bands with reserve lands in Quebec, and one band in Ontario. The Abitibi, with one band in Ontario and one in Quebec, are considered a subtribe of the Algonkin.

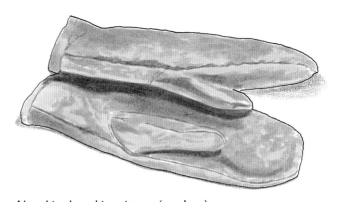

Algonkin deerskin mittens (modern)

ALGONQUIANS

Many different Native American languages have existed—perhaps more than 2,000 in all of the Americas, with about 300 in North America. The Algonquian (pronounced al-GON-kee-in) language is really a language family made up of many different dialects, or regional variations. Algonquian dialects had vocabulary, grammar, and pronunciation in common. But they still had many differences. In fact, Native Americans speaking one Algonquian dialect might not understand those speaking another and might need sign language to communicate.

Much can be learned about the early histories of tribes by studying their languages. It can be discovered, for example, that two tribes might have been one group in earlier times and then divided before Europeans came to the Americas. Yet in studying Indian culture, geography is usually more important than language. Even if tribes spoke similar languages, they would have different ways of life if they lived in different environments—Plains people would live differently than woodland people, for instance, whether they spoke the same language or not.

In some cases, however, when tribes of the same language family lived in the same environment, it is convenient to study them together. The family of tribes known as Algonquians is one such grouping. Most Algonquian peoples lived in the woodlands of the Northeast and they had much in common (see NORTHEAST INDIANS). Yet because of varying lifeways and different histories, many Algonquian tribes are listed in this book by their individual names. This section will examine what the various Algonquian tribes had in common.

Sometimes the Algonquians are divided into more specific groups: (1) New England Algonquians, such as ABENAKI, MASSACHUSET, MOHEGAN, NARRAGANSETT, NIPMUC, PASSAMAQUODDY, PENNACOOK, PENOBSCOT, PEQUOT, and WAMPANOAG; (2) Hudson River Algonquians, such as MAHICAN and WAPPINGER; (3) Middle-Atlantic Algonquians, such as LENNI LENAPE (DELAWARE) and MONTAUK; (4) Southern Algonquians, such as POWHATAN and ROANOKE; (5) Great Lakes Algonquians, such as CHIPPEWA (OJIBWAY), MENOMINEE, OTTAWA, and POTAWATOMI; (6) Prairie Algonquians, such as ILLINOIS, MIAMI, and SHAWNEE; (7) Combined Great Lakes/Prairie Algonquians, such as FOX (MESQUAKI), KICKAPOO, and SAC; (8) Canadian Woodland Algonquians, such as ALGONKIN, MALISEET, and MICMAC; and (9) Canadian Subarctic Algonquians, such as CREE, MONTAGNAIS, NASKAPI, and some Chippewa (Ojibway) bands (studied as SUBARCTIC INDIANS).

Other Algonquian peoples lived in the East. Among the New England Algonquians were the Mattabesec, Nauset, Niantic, Pocumtuc, and Sakonnet. Among the Middle-Atlantic Algonquians were the Conoy and Nanticoke. Among the Southern Algonquians were the Chowanoc, Coree (probably Algonquian), Hatteras, Machapunga, Moratok, Pamlico, Secotan, and Weapemeoc. Among the Great Lakes Algonquians were the Noquet. Other Algonquians migrated westward to the Great Plains, such as the ARAPAHO, BLACKFEET, CHEYENNE, and GROS VENTRE. But they are usually studied as PLAINS INDIANS. And people speaking what is thought to be an Algonquian-related dialect, such as the YUROK and Wiyot, lived on the Pacific Coast but are studied as CALIFORNIA INDIANS. It is the eastern tribes that historians generally refer to when they use the name *Algonquian*—the Algonquians who played such an important part in American and Canadian early history, from colonial times until about 1830.

Since so many Algonquians lived along the Atlantic seaboard, they were among the earliest Native Americans having contact with European explorers and settlers, such as the Jamestown colonists, the Pilgrims, and the founders of Quebec and Montreal. From the Algonquian language have come such familiar English words as *hickory, hominy, moccasin, moose, papoose, powwow, sachem, squash, squaw, succotash, tomahawk, totem, wigwam,* and *woodchuck.*

Many Algonquians were scattered or pushed westward soon after the arrival of Europeans in the colonial years. The Algonquians of the Great Lakes region lasted longer in their original homelands, but by the early 1800s, most of them had also relocated. Many of these peoples ended up in Oklahoma.

In general, the Algonquians were friendly with the French and often fought as their allies against the British and their allies, the IROQUOIS (HAUDENOSAUNEE). Then in later years, many Algonquians fought against Americans. The tribes' histories are summarized under individual entries. This entry looks of cultural traits organized by the following categories: social organization and political systems; food; shelter; transportation; clothing; other arts and crafts; and religion, rituals, and legends. Some of these same subjects will also be discussed under individual tribal entries.

Social Structure

Concerning their intertribal organization, the Algonquians commonly formed confederacies, such as the Abenaki Confederacy, the Wappinger Confederacy, and the Powhatan Confederacy. These alliances were not as structured as the Iroquois League, which had an intricate system of laws governing tribal interaction, but rather loose networks of villages and bands; they traded together and helped one another in times of war. These confederacies typically had a grand sachem with greater authority than regular sachems. Sometimes the lesser sachems in charge of a particular village or band were known as sagamores. In some instances, the grand sachem served as little more than a mediator between the sagamores during intertribal councils. In other cases, as with the Powhatan of Virginia, the grand sachem was more like a king, having absolute power.

But not all Algonquian tribes were part of a confederacy with a grand sachem. In the Great Lakes area, it was more common to have two chiefs for each tribe, the peace chief and the war chief. The first was usually a hereditary position, passed on from father to son. The second was chosen for his military prowess in times of war. Some tribes also had a third leader, the ceremonial leader. He was the tribe's shaman, or medicine man, and was in charge of religious rituals.

For the Algonquian tribes of northern Canada, the band was the most important political unit. These peoples moved around so much in small hunting groups that they had little social organization other than the extended family—parents, brothers and sisters, cousins, and in-laws. Many of these bands met with one another once a year for a communal celebration, and then their various leaders met as equals.

The family played an important part in Algonquian society. Many tribes were organized into clans, clusters of related families traced back to a common ancestor. Tribes tracing descent through the female line are called matrilineal; those tracing back through a male line are called patrilineal. Clans usually had favorite animals as names and symbols to distinguish them from one another; these are called totems. The animal totems were thought of as spiritual guardians or supernatural ancestors.

Tribes often organized their clans into two different groups, called moieties, meaning "halves." These moieties would be responsible for different duties and chores. They would also oppose each other in sporting events. Clans, totems, and moieties were common to Indians all over North America, not just to Algonquians.

Food

Most of the year, in spring, summer, and fall, Algonquians lived in villages, typically located along rivers, where they grew crops. Corn was the staple food for the farming tribes; beans and squash also provided nourishment. In the wintertime, Algonquians left the villages in small bands to track game. For some of the Algonquian peoples of Canada, the soil was too rocky to break up with wood, bone, or antler digging sticks. They had to depend on hunting, fishing, and gathering wild plants for all their food. These northern peoples covered greater distances than their kin to the south. The Algonquians did not raise domestic animals for meat or wool as modern farmers do, but they did have trained dogs who helped them hunt.

Algonquians hunted whatever game they could, large or small. All the Algonquians hunted deer, rabbit, squirrel, beaver, and various birds, such as turkey, partridge, duck, and goose. Algonquians in the northern woods also hunted moose, elk, and bear. Some lived far enough north to track caribou herds as well. And some Algonquians living near the prairies of the Mississippi River valley hunted buffalo.

Before Europeans brought the horse to North America, Native Americans had to hunt on foot. In addition to spears, arrows, and clubs, they used traps, snares, and deadfalls, which are devices that drop heavy objects on the prey. And they sometimes used disguises, such as animal skins; animal calls, such as a birch-bark instrument to lure moose; and fire, to drive herds into an ambush.

Algonquians also fished the rivers, streams, lakes, and ponds in their territory. They used harpoons, hooks, nets, traps, and weirs (fencelike enclosures placed in the water). Algonquians living along the Atlantic Coast depended on shellfish for part of their warm-weather diet. A common method of preserving both fish and meat was hanging it over a fire and letting smoke penetrate it for a long time. Fish and meat smoked this way could be kept through the winter or taken on long journeys.

All Algonquian peoples ate wild plants: berries, nuts, roots, stalks, and leaves. Algonquians living in maple country collected the sap from the trees in early spring and boiled it down into maple syrup and sugar. Some tribes living along the Great Lakes gathered the grain of a tall grass plant known as wild rice.

Many of the foods of the Algonquians were unknown to Europeans before they came to North America. From the Algonquians, non-Indians first learned to eat corn, pumpkin, maple sugar, wild rice, cranberries, blueberries, lobster, clams, and oysters.

Houses

Algonquians lived in many different types of structures, but the dwelling most often associated with them is the wigwam. The typical wigwam frame consisted of small trees bent and tied together in a dome shape and covered with strips of birch bark that were sewn together. But some Algonquians did not round off the framework; rather, they propped the saplings together to form a cone resembling a small tipi. And where birch bark was not available, they might use another bark, such as elm, to make the coverings. Or they might weave some other plant matter, such as cattail reeds, into mats that also served to keep out rain, snow, and wind. Or they might use animal skins as the Plains Indians did on their tipis. Or they would use various combinations. The men usually built the framework, then the women added the coverings.

Algonquian wigwam

Swampgrass and animal furs made good insulation for the wigwams. Branches covered with hides served as floors and beds. All the different-shaped Algonquian dwellings had holes in their roofs to let smoke out.

Some Algonquians also constructed large rectangular buildings similar to the Iroquoian longhouses. These might serve as places where the tribal council met. Or a family might choose to use one of these roomy and airy structures as their home. On the trail, of course, the smaller, portable structures with removable coverings were more practical. Algonquian villages often had palisades of upright logs surrounding them for protection.

Like other Indian peoples, Algonquians had special buildings for sweating. These sweathouses were often dome-shaped like a wigwam. Water would be poured over hot rocks to make steam for the purpose of purifying the body and spirit. Afterward, the individual would typically take a dip in a stream, lake, or snowbank.

Transportation

The Algonquians have a special place in the Native American legacy because of their birch-bark canoes (other peoples in western Canada also used birch-bark canoes). These remarkably light, swift, and graceful craft are probably, along with the Plains Indians tipi, warbonnet, and peace pipe, the most well known of all Indian objects. Using the network of rivers and lakes, Algonquians could travel throughout their territory to hunt, fish, trade, and make war. They could use more than one waterway by portaging their light canoes overland from one body of water to another. And on the trail, the canoes could be used as makeshift lean-tos to provide shelter from the elements.

These canoes were made in a variety of sizes, materials, and styles: with a low bow and stern, offering little wind resistance, for calm waters; or with high ends, which could slice through large waves, for rough waters (such as the Great Lakes). They differed in size: A small river canoe could be paddled by one or two persons; whereas large lake canoes could be handled by eight or 10 persons, four or five to a side. Cedar, which could be split easily and evenly and which held up well in water, was normally used for the framework. Then the bark of the paper birch would be peeled off the tree in large sheets. The paper birch had few imperfections on its surface. Moreover, birch bark did not shrink or stretch. The pieces of bark would be sewn together with spruce roots and shaped around the cedar frame. Then the resins of spruce trees would be spread on the seams to waterproof them. Maple was the wood of choice for the thwarts, the braces that extended from side to side and held the gunwales, or sides, together. Maple was also used to make paddles.

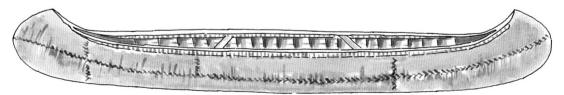

Algonquian (Chippewa) birch-bark canoe

When birch bark was not available, Algonquians sometimes used the heavier elm bark or spruce bark on their boats, or even moose hide. Or they hollowed out the trunk of a single tree to make a dugout canoe. Large dugouts proved more durable in the open sea for those Algonquians along the Atlantic Coast who went on whaling expeditions.

In wintertime, Subarctic Algonquians used toboggans. Unlike Inuit sleds with runners, toboggans have platforms for people or possessions resting directly on the snow. The platform was made of smooth planks curved upward at the front end. Northern Algonquians also used snowshoes to travel in deep snow. Spruce, birch, or willow was usually used to make the snowshoes' oval-shaped frame, with rawhide webbing strung in between.

Clothing

Algonquians made use of buckskin more than any other material for clothing, especially the hide of the white-tailed deer. Moose, elk, and caribou, also of the deer family, provided some tribes with materials for their garments. The hides were cured to make soft leather. Men wore shirts, breechcloths, leggings, and moccasins. Women wore either skirts and blouses or dresses, plus moccasins. Algonquian clothing often had short fringes hanging from the seams and edges. Both men and women wore fur robes for extra warmth in the winter. They also wore belts and sashes of cured leather or woven plant material.

Both men and women decorated their clothing with quillwork. The quills of the porcupine would be soaked and softened in water and then dyed with vegetable coloring. Paint, feathers, shells, and moosehair embroidery were also used to add color and designs to clothing. After Europeans came, the Algonquians began using glass beads in addition to quills and shells. Beadwork also replaced stone and shell in the making of some jewelry.

Women often wore their hair in braids and decorated it with a small cap or a band of shells. Men usually went bareheaded in order to show off their hair. They wore their hair in a variety of styles, depending on individual taste. Hair for Algonquians, as for other Native Americans, was a symbol of selfhood and strength.

Other Arts and Crafts

The discussions of food, shelter, transportation, and clothing have shown the wide range of Algonquian tech-nology. The Algonquians, like other Native Americans, ingeniously used the materials at hand to shape tools, weapons, and ceremonial objects. They used wood and bark, other plant materials, stone, clay, hide, bone, antler, shells, quills, and feathers for their artifacts. And some Great Lakes Algonquians used copper to make metal objects. After the arrival of Europeans, the Indians adapted their crafts to new materials, using metals, glass beads, and strips of cloth in original ways.

The Algonquian use of a variety of materials to make containers shows the extent of their ingenuity. Some Algonquians favored birch bark. Some of these birch-bark containers, like the mocuck, were watertight, their seams smeared with pitch, and were used for carrying and storing water. Others were used as bowls, dishes, and trays, or for winnowing (separating chaff from grain) wild rice.

Algonquian birch-bark mocuck (modern)

Algonquians also carved containers out of wood. The burls or knots of birch, elm, and maple, or some other hardwood, were charred in a fire to soften for scraping with stone or bone tools. Wood was also used to make the mortars and pestles needed for grinding corn.

Wood splints and sweet grass were utilized in basketry, the wood splints to make plaited baskets and the sweet grass to make coiled baskets.

Pottery was also used to make containers for cooking, carrying, and storing. Although Algonquians in the Northeast did not develop techniques in ceramics to the extent that Indians of the Southeast and Southwest did, some tribes crafted pottery containers for cooking, carrying, and storing. Algonquians had one main practical design. They made elongated clay pots for cooking with rounded or pointed bottoms and a neck at the top. They shaped the clay into pots without a potter's wheel, then smoothed the outside with a cord-wrapped paddle before firing. The pots were unpainted but had geometric designs from tapping, pressing, or scratching objects into the clay either before or after firing.

Algonquians applied this same sort of ingenuity to the making of weapons for hunting and warfare. They used wood, stone, bone, and, after the whites began to trade with them, metal, to make spears, clubs, and bows and arrows. Some among them also used wood for armor and shields.

Both the eastern Algonquians and neighboring Iroquois used wampum for ceremonial purposes. They made wampum from seashells, especially of the quahog clam, grinding the raw material into purple and white beads, then stringing the beads on a belt. They used wampum belts as tribal records and to commemorate special events, such as a peace treaty or a festival. They also exchanged wampum belts as gifts or as trade goods. In later years, the Indians used European glass beads to make wampum. Dutch and English settlers also began manufacturing wampum from glass beads in order to trade with the Indians. Wampum thus became a form of money.

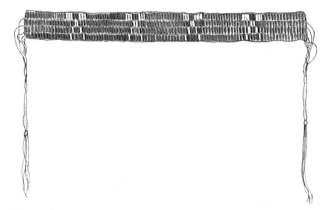

Algonquian wampum

An item common to the western Algonquians was the peace pipe. Because these pipes were used for other types of ceremonies as well, such as councils of war, *ceremonial pipes, sacred pipes,* and *calumet,* a French word referring to the long stems of the pipes, are more fitting terms.

Indians of the Great Lakes and the nearby prairies originally used calumets. In later years, the practice spread onto the Great Plains. A particular pipe passed down through the generations often was a tribe's most valued object. A pipe might also serve as a passport through hostile territory. Sometimes white explorers and traders carried them to show their peaceful intentions.

The bowl of the calumet was carved from pipestone. This kind of stone is also known as catlinite after 19th-century frontier painter George Catlin, who lived among a number of tribes. The red, pink, or gray stone is found in Great Lakes country. It can be carved with a knife when first quarried, but then it turns hard after being exposed to the air. The pipestems were made from light wood or reeds and were often carved with intricate designs. The pipes were usually decorated with feathers. White feathers meant peace; red feathers meant war. Quillwork or beadwork might be wrapped around the stem.

Algonquians grew tobacco to smoke in their pipes. They also smoked a concoction called *kinnikinnik,* or "mixture," consisting of dried plant matter, such as willow bark, mixed with tobacco leaves.

Algonquian sacred pipe

Religion

The Algonquians believed that a Great Spirit pervaded all existence, called Gitche Manitou, or simply Manitou or a variation. But Manitou had many manifestations. That is, the Great Spirit was found in all things—animals, plants, water, rocks, and other natural phenomena, such as the Sun, Moon, weather, or sickness. Lesser individual manifestations of the Great Spirit may also be called manitous or may have other names, such as Thunderbird, Bringer of Rain.

Shamans were supposed to be able to control these spirits, found in all living and nonliving things. Some tribes also had secret medicine societies, such as the Midewiwin Society of the Great Lakes whose members all supposedly could make contact with the spirit world.

The belief in Manitou was common to Algonquian peoples. Different tribes had different mythologies and legends, with varying supernatural beings. Some of these beings were heroes or guardian spirits, such as Manibozho (or Manabush), the Great Hare, who, according to Chippewa and other Great Lakes peoples, remade the world after bad spirits destroyed it with a flood. Others were demons, such as windigos of the northern forests who, according to the Montagnais and other Subarctic peoples, ate people.

Although Algonquian tribes had varying rituals and festivals, they all celebrated with singing, drumming, and dancing. Some rituals had to do with hunting; others, such as the Green Corn Festival, related to farming; others concerned peacemaking or warfare; others were to cure illness; still others were for rites of passage, such as a boy passing to manhood.

As a rite of passage into adulthood, both boys and girls were sent into the woods to fast and pray for a vision. If the child were fortunate, a spirit, usually in the form of an animal, would come to promise protection and to give the child his or her own special identity.

For a fuller sense of Algonquian culture and history, see those tribes indicated earlier as having their own entries.

Algonquian beaded medicine bundle, used to hold personal talismans

ANASAZI *see* SOUTHWEST CULTURES

ANISHINABE *see* CHIPPEWA (OJIBWAY)

APACHE

On hearing the name *Apache* (pronounced uh-PATCH-ee), many people think of the chief Geronimo, along with the warlike nature of the tribe. Throughout most of their history, the Apache raided other tribes for food and booty. The ZUNI, who feared them, gave them the name *apachu,* meaning "enemy." The Apache also stubbornly resisted Spanish, Mexican, and Anglo-American expansion. But there was of course much more to Apache culture than warfare. Like all Indian peoples, the Apache had a well-defined society and a complex mythology. Different versions of the Apache native name include *Tineh* (*Tinneh*), *Tinde, Dini, Inde* (*N'de*), *Deman,* and *Haisndayin* for the "people."

The Apache ancestral homeland was located on the region of North America referred to as the Southwest Culture Area, and they are classified as SOUTHWEST INDIANS. The numerous Apache bands roamed far and wide in this region—territory that now includes much of New Mexico and Arizona, as well as northern Mexico, western Texas, southern Colorado, western Oklahoma, and southern Kansas.

The various Apache peoples migrated to the Southwest later than other Indians. Before Europeans reached North America, Athapascan-speaking bands broke off from other ATHAPASCANS in present-day western Canada and migrated southward, probably about 1400 (although some scholars have theorized as early as A.D. 850), and became known as the Apache. Other Athapascans who migrated to the region became known as the NAVAJO.

The Apache can be organized by dialects into the following groups, each made up of various bands: San Carlos, Aravaipa, White Mountain, Northern Tonto, Southern Tonto, and Cibecue in Arizona; Chiricahua and Mimbreno in Arizona and New Mexico; Mescalero in New Mexico and Mexico; Lipan in Texas and Mexico; Jicarilla in New Mexico and Colorado; and Kiowa-Apache in

Oklahoma. Members of these different groups intermarried or were placed together on reservations by whites later in their history, altering the various subdivisions. For example, the San Carlos and White Mountain groups, sometimes together called the Western Apache (along with the San Carlos subgroup, the Aravaipa, as well as the Cibecue and Tonto), came to include members from other more easterly groups, such as the Chiricahua and Mimbreno.

Lifeways

The Apache were primarily nomadic hunters and gatherers, seeking whatever game, especially deer and rabbits, and whatever wild plant foods, especially cactus and mesquite seeds, found within their territory. (The Mescalero band was named after a kind of cactus important in the Apache diet, mescal.) When they could not find enough food to eat in their rugged lands, much of which was desert country, Apache raided the farming villages of the PUEBLO INDIANS, as well as, in later years, Spanish, Mexican, and Anglo-American settlements.

The various Apache groups adopted lifeways from other Indians with whom they came into contact. For instance, some of the Western Apache, living close to the Indians of the Rio Grande pueblos, took up farming. The Jicarilla Apache borrowed cultural traits from the PLAINS INDIANS. On acquiring horses in the late 1600s through raids on the Spanish and on Pueblo Indians, mounted Jicarilla often rode in pursuit of the great buffalo herds (see PLAINS INDIANS). The Kiowa-Apache lived close to the KIOWA, a Plains tribe, and their culture was closer to that of the Kiowa than to their own Apache kin. Similarly, the Lipan shared some traits with Mexican tribes to their south, such as raising dogs to eat.

The most common type of dwelling for most Apache bands was the wickiup, a domed or cone-shaped hut with a pole framework covered with brush, grass, or reed mats.

Apache wickiup

Wickiups frequently had central fire pits and a smokehole. The Jicarilla and Kiowa-Apache used hide tipis.

The Apache originally wore deerskin clothing. They never grew or wove cotton as many Southwest peoples did, nor did they become sheepherders as the Navajo did, preferring to eat the sheep instead. But Apache acquired cotton and wool clothing through trade or raids.

The Apache made little pottery. Yet they were master basketmakers, crafting coiled baskets of many shapes and sizes and with intricate designs. After the coming of non-Indians, the Apache became known for an instrument called the Apache fiddle. The painted sound box was crafted from a yucca stalk and held a single string of sinew attached to a tuning peg. The instrument was played with a bow made of wood and sinew.

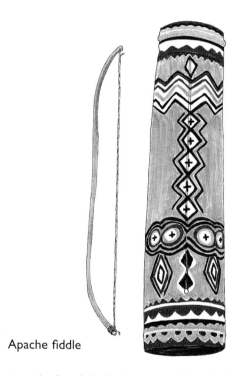

Apache fiddle

Apache bands had a loose social and political organization. Each band, which was made up of extended families, had a headman who was chosen informally for his leadership abilities and military prowess. But other warriors could launch raids without the headman's permission.

Shamans presided over religious rituals. The Apache believed in many supernatural beings. They considered Ussen (also spelled Yusn), the Giver of Life, the most powerful of the supernatural beings. The Gans, or Mountain Spirits, who supposedly brought agriculture to the people and who are the guardians of wildlife, were especially important in Apache ceremonies. Men dressed up in elaborate costumes to impersonate the Gans in dances, wearing kilts, black masks, tall wooden-slat headdresses, and body paint, and carrying wooden swords. The headdresses of the dancers show four colors symbolizing the Gans: the white of pollen, the black of eagle feathers, the yellow of deerskin, and the blue of turquoise.

Apache Wars

Early Apache contacts with non-Indians were friendly. The Spanish explorer Francisco de Coronado called Apache people he encountered in 1540 the Querechos. Yet by the late 1500s, Apache bands were sweeping southward in raids on Spanish settlements. During the 1600s, the Spanish established a line of presidios (forts) across northern Mexico to try to protect their settlements from Apache attacks. Yet the Apache continued their raids, disappearing into the wilderness before the soldiers could rally an effective defense. The Spanish tried to convert Apache to Christianity and move them into missions, but with little success. However, the Apache did not mount an organized rebellion as the Pueblo Indians did in their successful revolt of 1680. Instead, the Apache preferred to raid the Spanish settlers for plunder, especially horses and cattle. The Apache kept up their raids against the Spanish throughout the 1700s and into the 1800s. The COMANCHE, who advanced into Apache territory from the east starting about 1740, managed to hold their own against the much-feared Apache.

In 1821, Mexico and New Mexico gained independence from Spain. But the new government in Mexico City did no better than the old one had in stopping the relentless Apache attacks along Mexico's northern frontier. During this period, the Apache also proved hostile to early Anglo-American traders and trappers who traveled through or near their territory.

In 1848, with the Treaty of Guadalupe Hidalgo following the Mexican War, Mexico ceded its. northern holdings to the United States. Soon U.S. troops began arriving in Apache country in great numbers. At this same time, with the discovery of gold in California, the number of Anglo-Americans traveling westward dramatically increased. Although the U.S. government now claimed their land, the Apache considered the travelers as trespassers. The United States had defeated Mexico, the Apache leaders reasoned, but since Mexico had never defeated the Apache, their lands still rightfully belonged to them.

During the 1850s, the Apache still preyed mostly on ranchers in Mexico. Major hostilities with the Americans did not occur until the 1860s. The first significant outbreak involved the Chiricahua Apache. Their headman at the time was Cochise. A lieutenant in the U.S. Army, George Bascom, wrongly accused Cochise's band of kidnapping children and stealing cattle, and Bascom took some of Cochise's people as hostages. In retaliation, Cochise and his warriors began laying ambushes along Apache Pass on the Butterfield Southern Route (or the Southern Overland Trail) that ran through the Southwest from El Paso to Los Angeles.

Before long, the Mimbreno Apache, led by Cochise's father-in-law, Mangas Coloradas, joined the resistance. U.S. troops managed to drive the insurgents into Mexico for a while but then abandoned the region to head east to fight in the American Civil War. California volunteers under General James Carleton rode in to man the posts in Chiricahua country, but the Chiricahua and Mimbreno proved unconquerable to the new troops. The Apache lost one of their most important leaders, however. Mangas Coloradas was captured in 1862 through trickery and was later killed by angry guards.

Meanwhile, to the east, the Mescalero Apache carried out raids on travelers near the El Paso end of the Butterfield Southern Route. General Carleton appointed the former fur trader, scout, Indian agent, and Union soldier Christopher "Kit" Carson as his leader in the field against the Mescalero. Through relentless pursuit, Carson and his men wore down the Mescalero and forced their surrender. The Mescalero were relocated to the east at Bosque Redondo in the barren flatlands of the Pecos River valley near Fort Sumner. After this phase of the Apache Wars, Carson turned his attention to the Navajo militants, who also were relocated to Bosque Redondo.

In 1871, settlers from Tucson marched on Camp Grant and massacred more than 100 innocent Aravaipa Apache—most of them women and children—under Chief Eskiminzin. This incident convinced President Ulysses S. Grant that there was a need for a reservation system to separate Apache from white settlers.

After extensive negotiations, the formerly hostile Cochise of the Chiricahua signed a treaty, and from that time until his death in 1874, he helped keep peace along Apache Pass.

Another important episode occurred in 1872–73, when General George Crook led the successful Tonto Basin Campaign against the Apache militants from various western bands and against their YAVAPAI allies.

The final two episodes in the Apache Wars had much in common. Both involved warriors from earlier fighting. Victorio, a Mimbreno Apache, had fought alongside

An Apache warrior of the Apache Wars

Mangas Coloradas. Geronimo (or Goyathlay, "he who yawns"), a Chiricahua, had fought alongside Cochise. Both Victorio and Geronimo began uprisings on the San Carlos Reservation in Arizona. In both rebellions, the insurgents escaped from the reservation and hid out in the rugged country in much of the Southwest as well as in Mexico. In both cases, the army was forced to put many men in the field for long campaigns.

The first of the two conflicts, Victorio's Resistance, lasted from 1877 to 1880. After numerous skirmishes with both U.S. and Mexican armies, he was defeated by a Mexican force at the Battle of Tres Castillos. His death in that battle brought the Mimbreno resistance to a virtual end.

Some of the survivors of Victorio's Resistance joined Geronimo's Resistance of 1881–86, the last sustained Indian uprising in the United States.

The Apache, who had been wanderers throughout their history, had a hard time adapting to the confining reservation life. Geronimo spent some time on the Ojo Caliente Reservation (established for the Mescalero) in New Mexico. Then he joined his people, the Chiricahua, at the San Carlos Reservation in Arizona. At that time in history, Indians on reservations were not permitted to leave. But Geronimo and his followers managed to escape three times.

The first breakout resulted from the death of the White Mountain medicine man named Nakaidoklini, who preached a new religion claiming that dead warriors would return to drive the whites from Apache territory. Soldiers out of Fort Apache, Arizona, tried to arrest Nakaidoklini for his teachings, but when fighting broke out at Cibecue Creek in August 1881, they killed him instead. Chiricahua and Apache from other bands fled the San Carlos Reservation and began a new series of raids. After a prolonged campaign led by General George Crook and after many negotiations, Geronimo and his men agreed to return to San Carlos in 1884.

The second breakout resulted from the reservation ban on a ceremonial alcoholic drink of the Apache called *tiswin*. Again, the Apache resented interference in their religion by white officials. Crook's soldiers tracked the militants to Canyon de los Embudos in the rugged highlands of Mexico; after negotiations, Geronimo and his men surrendered a second time, in 1886. Yet on the return trip to San Carlos, Geronimo and some of his followers escaped.

Because of this incident, General Crook was relieved of his command, replaced by General Nelson Miles. Miles put some 5,000 men in the field. They rode through much of the Southwest, on both sides of the Mexican border, in pursuit of the Indian guerrillas.

Hunger and weariness brought in Geronimo and his followers the final time. They surrendered at Skeleton Canyon in 1886, not far from Apache Pass, where the Apache Wars had started 25 years before.

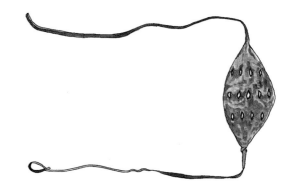

Apache sling for rock-throwing

Geronimo and the other men were put in chains and sent by train to Fort Pickens in Pensacola, Florida. They were also imprisoned for a time at Mount Vernon Barracks in Alabama. Confined under terrible conditions, many died from tuberculosis. Finally, survivors were allowed to return to the West. Because the citizens of Arizona opposed the return of the Chiricahua to San Carlos, Geronimo and his followers were taken to Fort Sill on Comanche and Kiowa lands in the Indian Territory. By that time, Geronimo was a legend all over the United States. People came from far away to get a glimpse of him and to take his picture.

U.S. officials never let Geronimo return to see his homeland. When he died many years later, in 1909, he was still a prisoner of war. The other Chiricahua were permitted to return home in 1914.

Contemporary Apache

The San Carlos Reservation still exists. It is located in Gila and Graham counties of Arizona. Apache also live on other reservations in Arizona: on the Camp Verde Reservation, which they share with the Yavapai, in Yavapai County; on the Fort McDowell Reservation, which they share with MOJAVE and Yavapai, in Maricopa County; and on the Fort Apache Reservation in Apache, Gila, and Navajo Counties. In New Mexico, there is the Jicarilla Reservation in Rio Arriba and Sandoval Counties; and the Mescalero Apache Reservation in Otero County. The Fort

Sill Apache have their business committee headquarters in Apache, Oklahoma. They are sometimes referred to as Chief Geronimo's Band of Apache.

Apache pottery ashtray (modern)

Apache support themselves through a number of tribal enterprises, including stock raising, sawmills, stores, gas stations, oil and gas leases, and more and more, tourist facilities. In recent years, tribally run casinos in New Mexico and Arizona have increased the number of visitors to Apache lands. Individual tribal members also farm and hire themselves out as laborers to earn a living. Some Apache supplement their income by making traditional arts and crafts, in particular, baskets, cradleboards, and beadwork.

APALACHEE

The Apalachee homeland was situated in what is now northwest Florida, near the capital of the state, Tallahassee. The nearby bay on the Gulf of Mexico is named after the tribe: Apalachee Bay. *Apalachee,* pronounced ap-uh-LATCH-ee, is a CHOCTAW word, meaning "people of the other side [of the Alabama River]."

The tribe no longer exists. The Apalachee once had at least 20 villages of pole-frame houses with palmetto-thatched roofs. Sometimes villagers packed the walls of their houses with mud, a technique called wattle and daub. Next to the villages were fields of corn, beans, squash, and other crops. Probable direct descendants of the MOUND BUILDERS, they built mounds with temples on top for religious ceremonies. The tribe is classified as part of the Southeast Culture Area (see SOUTHEAST INDIANS).

To the north of the Apalachee lived the CREEK. Although both peoples spoke dialects of the Muskogean language family, they were enemies. The less numerous Apalachee managed to hold their own against the larger tribe.

In 1528, the Apalachee attacked and drove off an early Spanish expedition led by the explorer Pánfilo de Narváez. But Hernando de Soto and his men lived among the tribe in the winter of 1539–40 during the first part of de Soto's expedition in the Southeast. Some of the more militant Apalachee resented the presence of the conquistadores and quarreled with them.

By 1633, Spanish missionaries had a foothold among the Apalachee. By the 1640s, the Spanish had built seven churches and had converted eight of the principal

Apalachee chiefs to Catholicism. In 1647, the Apalachee, angry because they were forced to work on the Spanish fort at St. Augustine, rebelled. But Spanish soldiers, having superior weapons, quickly put down the uprising. Then in 1656, some Apalachee joined their trading partners the TIMUCUA in their revolt. The faction that wanted the Spanish as allies, valuing European trade goods and protection against other Indians, prevented further violence in the ensuing years.

As allies of the Spanish, the Apalachee suffered attacks from other colonists, in 1703–4, Carolina militiamen and Creek warriors under Colonel James Moore. The force destroyed many villages and killed many inhabitants, and they took some Apalachee captives back to South Carolina. Some of these Apalachee later joined with the YAMASEE in the Yamasee War of 1715.

During the remainder of the 1700s, the Apalachee migrated often. Some joined their former enemies, the Creek. Others moved to new villages among the Spanish. After 1763, at the end of the French and Indian War, when Spain lost Florida to England, many Apalachee moved to Louisiana settling on the Red River. The Spanish regained control of Florida in 1783 after the American Revolution, holding it until 1819. By that time, however, most of their Apalachee allies had dispersed. The small bands that remained intermarried with other Indian peoples, as well as with African Americans and European Americans, and gradually lost their tribal identity.

ARAPAHO

The Arapaho originally called themselves *Inuna-ina,* meaning "our people." To their CHEYENNE allies, they were *hitanwo'iv* for "people of the sky" or "cloud people." Some tribes also called them "dog-eaters" in their various languages. *Arapaho,* pronounced uh-RAP-uh-ho, now the official name of the tribe, is probably derived from the PAWNEE word *tirapihu* or *carapihu,* meaning "trader." It is also close to the KIOWA name for the tribe: *Ahyato.*

It is thought that the Algonquian-speaking Arapaho once lived in the Red River region of what is now Minnesota and North Dakota, one people with other ALGONQUIANS, the GROS VENTRE. Other Algonquian tribes who eventually settled in the West, the BLACK-FEET and the Cheyenne, might also have been relatives of the Arapaho.

The Arapaho and the Gros Ventre are believed to have migrated westward to the headwaters of the Missouri River sometime in the 1700s, possibly as far west as territory now in Montana. At some point, a split occurred. The Gros Ventre migrated to the north to what is now northern Montana and southern Saskatchewan. The Arapaho headed southward.

At some point in the 1800s, the tribe again divided into the Northern Arapaho and the Southern Arapaho. The northern branch of the tribe settled in the vicinity of the North Platte River in what is now Wyoming. The southern branch settled along the Arkansas River in what is now Colorado. The two groups stayed in close contact with each other, however.

Lifeways

By the 1800s, the Arapaho had adopted lifeways into a typical tribe of the Great Plains Culture Area. They were master horse trainers and riders, using their horses to hunt buffalo and to carry out raids on other Indians and on white settlers. They lived in buffalo-skin tipis. They changed their campsites often, following the migrations of buffalo herds.

Three customs shared by many of the tribes that migrated onto the plains are secret societies, medicine bundles, and the Sun Dance.

The secret societies of the PLAINS INDIANS were clubs built around the act of warfare. The societies had different initiation rites, pre-battle and post-battle ceremonies, songs and dances, and costumes. In the case of Arapaho,

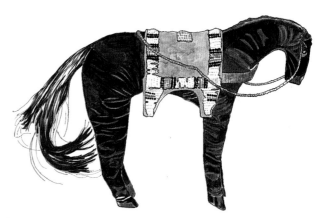

Arapaho leather and bead toy horse

Arapaho drumstick with head of green-painted hide and quillwork eagles on both sides

the eight secret societies were age-graded. That is to say, boys of a certain age joined one society, then graduated into others. Other tribes with age-graded military societies were the Gros Ventre, Blackfeet, MANDAN, and HIDATSA. Some tribes with nongraded military societies, often with membership determined by invitation only, were the Cheyenne, SIOUX (DAKOTA, LAKOTA, NAKOTA), CROW, ASSINIBOINE, and OMAHA.

Medicine bundles were containers of various shapes and sizes with objects inside thought to have magical powers. Some were owned by individual Indians, and the owner might have seen the objects in a dream or vision during his vision quest, the ceremony that marked the passage into adulthood. Medicine bundles belonging to the medicine men were used in healing ceremonies. Each secret society had its own medicine bundles. Other medicine bundles belonged to the whole tribe. The most important medicine bundle for the Cheyenne contained many objects, including a hat made from the hide of a buffalo, plus four arrows, two for warfare and two for hunting. The Sioux treasured a pipe supposedly given to the tribe by a white buffalo calf. The most sacred object of the Arapaho was the flat pipe. This was a long tobacco pipe with a stem about the length of a man's arm. It was wrapped in a bundle, to be opened and smoked only on special occasions and with elaborate rituals. Another secred relic of the tribe kept in a bundle was a wheel or hoop.

For the Arapaho many everyday acts had symbolic meaning. For instance, when Arapaho women crafted beadwork on clothing, bags, or tipis, or when they painted designs with vegetable coloring, they depicted tribal legends or spiritual beings.

An important ceremony for the Arapaho was the Sun Dance, also called the Offerings Lodge by the Arapaho, which they used to ask for the renewal of nature and future tribal prosperity. This event took place once a year, when berries were ripening. The Lodgemaker directed the construction of an enclosure of poles and greenery. A sacred tree trunk was erected at the center, and a rawhide doll was usually tied to the top. The various societies performed complex rituals around the tree, many of them involving medicine bundles, and gazed toward the Sun. The Offerings Lodge was a test of endurance for Arapaho participants. They went without food or sleep for days. But the Arapaho version of the ritual did not involve extreme self-torture. Among some Plains tribes, participants, attached to the sacred tree by ropes and wooden skewers in their chests, danced backward until their flesh actually ripped.

Wars for the Great Plains

The Arapaho made war at one time or another against the SHOSHONE, UTE, PAWNEE, Crow, Sioux, COMANCHE, and KIOWA. By 1840, the Arapaho had made peace with the Sioux, Comanche, and Kiowa. Other 19th-century allies of the Arapaho were the Cheyenne.

The Arapaho played a major role in the wars with whites for the Great Plains. The Northern Arapaho, along with the Northern Cheyenne, fought alongside the Sioux in most of their wars for the northern plains. The Southern Arapaho fought as allies of the Southern Cheyenne in the wars for the central plains, and as allies of the Comanche and Kiowa in some of their conflicts for the southern plains. A number of Southern Arapaho died alongside Southern Cheyenne of Black Kettle's band at the Sand Creek Massacre in Colorado on November 29, 1864.

Two of the most famous Indian leaders in the plains wars were Black Bear of the Northern Arapaho and Little Raven of the Southern Arapaho. At the start of the War for the Bozeman Trail, described in detail under the entry SIOUX, it was Black Bear's band that suffered the only major defeat at the hands of the whites, in 1865. Little Raven, famous for his grasp of legal issues and his oratorical abilities, proved a wily match for any negotiator the federal government could come up with.

By the Medicine Lodge Treaty of 1867, in which Little Raven served as a spokesman for his people, the Southern Arapaho were placed on a reservation in the Indian Territory along with the Southern Cheyenne. The Northern Arapaho resisted placement on a reservation longer than their southern kin. By the Fort Laramie Treaty of 1868, they were supposed to settle on the Pine Ridge Reservation in South Dakota with the Sioux, but they wanted their own hunting grounds. In 1876, they were supposed to settle in the Indian Territory with their southern kin, but they insisted on staying in Wyoming. In 1878, the federal government pressured the Northern Shoshone, traditional enemies of the Arapaho, into accepting them on their Wind River Reservation.

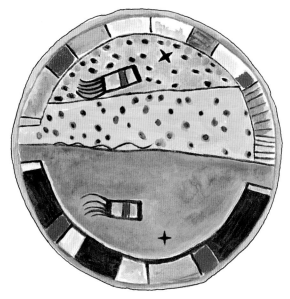

Arapaho painted hide shield

The Ghost Dance

As a very religious people who had lost their homeland and their traditional way of life, the Arapaho, especially those on the Wind River Reservation, became involved with the Ghost Dance Religion that spread among the Plains tribes in the late 1880s. The founder of the religion, Wovoka, was a PAIUTE. The brief uprising that resulted from the religion occurred among the Sioux. As a result, the Ghost Dance Religion is discussed in detail under the entries PAIUTE and SIOUX. But most of the Ghost Dance songs recorded by historians are from the Arapaho people. Here is an example:

Hey, my children, here is another pipe!
Now, I am going to holler on this earth.
Everything is in motion!

Contemporary Arapaho

Many descendants of the Southern Arapaho still live in Oklahoma and earn a living through farming. Many descendants of the Northern Arapaho still live on the Wind River Reservation in Wyoming and earn a living by raising cattle. The Arapaho recently have turned to gaming as a new source of revenue.

ARAWAK (Taino)

This book for the most part discusses Native Americans in the continental United States and Canada. Of course, there were and there still are many other Indian peoples throughout the Americas, each group with its own complex culture and history. One example is the people known as the Arawak (pronounced AH-ruh-wock or AH-ruh-wak) who lived south of the North American mainland on the islands of the Caribbean. The Arawak are important to the history of the rest of the Americas because of their contacts with Christopher Columbus.

Location

The Arawak lived throughout much of the West Indies, the archipelago, or chain of islands, stretching from the southern tip of Florida to the northern tip of South America. The West Indies, also called the Antilles, are now subdivided roughly north to south into: (1) the Bahama Islands; (2) the Greater Antilles, including Cuba, Jamaica, Hispaniola (Haiti and the Dominican Republic), and Puerto Rico; and (3) the Lesser Antilles, including the Leeward Islands, the Windward Islands, Barbados, and Trinidad-Tobago. These islands in the Caribbean Sea became known as the West Indies because Christopher Columbus, the first European to explore them, was seeking a route to India at the time. He thought he had landed in the East Indies. And this is the same reason he referred to the native peoples he encountered as *Indians*.

Christopher Columbus has been referred to as the "discoverer" of the Americas. Since there were already millions of people living in the Western Hemisphere, the term is misused. Moreover, it now is thought that the Vikings reached the Americas much earlier than Columbus did. Yet Christopher Columbus brought the Americas to the attention of the rest of the world and set in motion the European exploration and settlement of the "New World," thus changing the course of history for Europeans and Indians alike. He can thus be called the European discoverer of the Americas. Columbus never reached North America proper, but other European explorers soon did.

On this initial trip across the Atlantic Ocean from Spain, Columbus first landed on a small island in the Bahama Group. The exact location of the first landfall has never been proven. Until recently, it was thought that Columbus first reached Watling Island (now San Salvador). Now some scholars believe that he and his men first touched soil on Samana Cay, 65 miles southeast of Watling Island. After a stopover of a few days, Columbus and his men sailed farther west, sighting Cuba and landing on Hispaniola. He established a colony of men among the Arawak of Hispaniola before returning to Spain. He later led three more expeditions to the Caribbean Sea, among the islands and along the coastline of Central and South America. Island-dwelling Arawak, however, were the only Indians with whom he had extensive contact.

The Arawak lived on many different islands. They also had relatives—people of the same language family, Arawakan (part of the Andean-Equatorial language phylum)—living in Central and South America. Before European came to the Americas, the Arawak had migrated northward from South America onto the Caribbean islands. These Arawak on the islands called themselves Taino, or "good people."

Lifeways

The West Indies have a tropical climate, warm all year with abundant rain. The Arawak were farmers, as well as hunter-gatherers. Their most important crops were cassava, corn, potatoes, sweet potatoes, beans, peanuts, peppers, cotton, and tobacco. The cassava plant was grown for its roots, which were ground into a pulp to make a kind of bread (nowadays cassava is used to make tapioca pudding). The juice from grinding the roots was used as the stock for soup. The Arawak also collected edible wild plants to supplement their diet.

The Arawak hunted a variety of animals and birds. The main source of meat was the small furry mammal called the hutia. Hunters used clubs as well as spears, bows and arrows, and blowguns. Using torches and trained dogs, they also drove hutias into corrals. In addition to dogs, the Arawak kept parrots as pets.

The Arawak fished from dugout canoes, using spears, nets, and hooks and lines. They had an ingenious method of catching the large sea turtles. Remoras, a kind of fish with sticky patches on their heads, would swim under turtles and attach their heads to them; using a lines attached to the remoras, Arawak fishermen would then pull the giant turtles to the surface.

Each Arawak village had a chief usually referred to as a *cacique,* from the Arakan term *kasequa,* a supreme ruler who made decisions in times of both peace and war. The position was hereditary. The next in line to the chief was his oldest sister's oldest son. A class of nobility, made up of the chief's relatives, served as his counselors. Women rulers were called *cacicas.*

The Arawak needed little clothing in the mild Caribbean climate. Men and children usually went naked. Women wore aprons made from grass, leaves, or cotton. Both men and women wore necklaces, bracelets, earrings, and nose pendants, made from shell, bone, stone. or clay. They also twisted cotton into jewelry. Chiefs and nobles wore ornaments of gold and copper, hammered and beautifully shaped.

Arawak gold frog pendant

At ceremonies Arawak men wore wooden or shell masks with feathers in their hair. They also painted their bodies, usually red or white.

The chiefs lived in rectangular houses with slanted roofs forming a peak. The houses of the common people had circular walls with cone-shaped roofs. Both types of houses were made from the stems of palm trees and cane plants. Palm leaves were sometimes used as thatch for roofs. The Arawak slept in hammocks made from twisted cotton.

In general, the Arawak were a peaceful people. They took up arms to defend themselves only when necessary, as when attacked by the Carib Indians. (The Carib, in fact, advancing northward from the South American mainland, had driven the Arawak off most of the islands of the Lesser Antilles in the years before Columbus's arrival.)

Many Indians of the region had seaworthy dugouts of varying shapes and sizes, some of which could hold 100 people, leading to extensive trade contacts between the

Caribbean Indians and the South and Central American Indians. The Arawak also traded with North American peoples of the Florida coast, such as the TIMUCUA and CALUSA.

With the exchange of food, crafts, and raw materials, other cultural traits were passed. That is why, for instance, many of the people living in or around the Caribbean Sea and the Gulf of Mexico, such as the Arawak, AZTEC, and NATCHEZ, shared rigidly structured societies with supreme rulers and distinct social classes, unlike the more democratic societies of other Indians to the north.

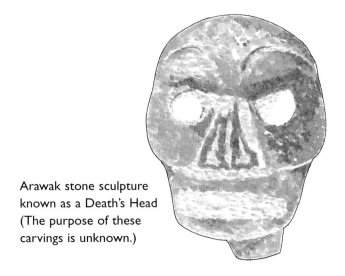

Arawak stone sculpture known as a Death's Head (The purpose of these carvings is unknown.)

Interaction with Europeans

The meeting between Columbus's men and the Arawak was momentous in more ways than one. Not only did it lead to the European exploration and settlement of the Americas, but it also led to the diffusion of various cultural traits all over the world. For example, this was the first time Europeans had seen or heard of the tobacco plant. In fact, the word *tobacco* comes from the Spanish word *tabaco,* derived from the Arawak word for "cigar." Moreover, the Europeans had never thought to use hammocks before encountering the Arawak. Afterward, they started using these comfortable beds on their ships. This also was the first time the Europeans saw most of the plants cultivated by the Arawak. Some of these, such as corn and potatoes, would eventually become food staples all over the world.

The peaceful Arawak treated the Spanish well, sharing food and knowledge with them. They also helped rescue some of Columbus's men during a shipwreck off Hispaniola. But Spanish mistreatment of the Arawak led to conflict. Columbus forced some Arawak from Watling Island to accompany him on the rest of his first journey, setting a precedent. Colonists left behind by Columbus on Hispaniola forced Arawak men to help look for gold. Some among them rose up in rebellion, killing all the outsiders.

On his second voyage, Columbus established another colony on the coast of Hispaniola. The Spaniards used the threat of violence to have the Arawak bring gold to them on a regular basis. But the hoped-for riches were not obtained. Instead, Columbus began taking Arawak as slaves for profit.

This pattern of cruelty continued in Spanish and Indian relations. Columbus eventually lost favor with the king and queen of Spain and never realized many of his ambitions. When he died in Europe, he was a forgotten man. But the Spanish who followed him to the Americas further exploited the Indians, forcing them to work in mines and on farms. They also made the native peoples give up their traditional religions to practice Catholicism. The Spanish pushed on into Mexico, Florida, and other parts of the Americas to expand their empire.

As for the native peoples of the Caribbean Islands, their numbers were depleted. Many were struck down by European diseases. Others died from starvation because the Spanish overworked them and underfed them. Some even committed suicide out of despair over the loss of their freedom. Mothers sometimes killed their newborn rather than see them grow up as slaves. Many survivors lost their tribal identity through intermarriage with the colonists.

Contemporary Arawak

A number of Arawak—the Indian peoples who were first called "Indians"—descendants of those who fled to the mountains to avoid Spanish rule, live in western Cuba. They live in *caserios,* traditional family groups, and hold *areitos,* round dances with storytelling. The Taino Nation of the Antilles, centered in Puerto Rico, was organized in the 1980s. They maintain a cultural center in Central Islip on New York's Long Island. Another group, the Jatibonuco Taino People, descendants of Arawak from Puerto Rico, have settled in Southern New Jersey. Other surviving people of Arawakan lineage, descended from South American ancestors, they live along the Amazon River in Brazil.

ARCHAIC INDIANS   *see* PREHISTORIC INDIANS

ARCTIC PEOPLES

The region known as the Arctic Culture Area extends more than 5,000 miles, from the Aleutian Islands in present-day Alaska to Labrador in Canada. Although most of it lies in northern Alaska and northern Canada, the culture area also includes territory in Siberia (part of Russia) to the west, as well as in Greenland (part of the Kingdom of Denmark) to the east. The Arctic Culture Area touches on three oceans—the Pacific, the Arctic, and the Atlantic.

The climate of the Arctic is fierce. Winters are long and bitterly cold, with few hours of sunlight. In the northernmost latitudes of the Arctic, beyond the Arctic Circle, the Sun never rises above the horizon for part of the winter. Likewise, for part of the summer, the Sun never sets below the horizon, resulting in the phenomenon known as midnight sun.

During the long winter, the land is covered by ice. The subsoil never thaws, remaining frozen all year round in a state known as permafrost. When the surface ice thaws during the short summer, the water does not drain, but forms numerous lakes and ponds along with mud and rising fog.

The Arctic Ocean freezes over in the winter, then breaks up into drift ice during the summer thaw. The Arctic is actually a frozen desert, having little precipitation. Arctic blizzards are not characterized by huge amounts of snowfall. Rather, gale-force winds stir up what surface snow already exists, forming snowdrifts.

The Arctic's land environment is called tundra. Because of the cold climate and permafrost, the tundra is treeless. Little vegetation grows other than mosses, lichens, and stunted shrubs. Most of the tundra consists

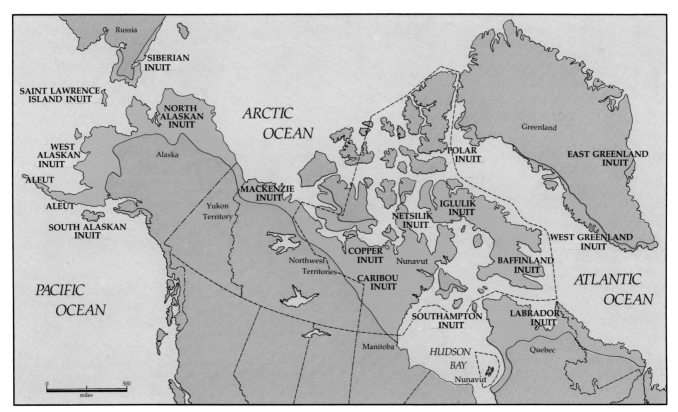

The Arctic Culture Area, showing the approximate locations of Inuit and Aleut bands—circa 1500, before displacement by non-Indians (with modern boundaries)

of rolling plains. In the western part, there are some mountains, the northern reaches of the Rockies.

Wildlife in the Arctic includes sea mammals, such as whales, walruses, seals, and sea lions; saltwater and freshwater fish; seagulls and other birds; polar bears; and caribou. These, along with other fauna appearing in certain locations on the tundra in summertime, such as rabbits, rodents, and owls, provided subsistence for Arctic peoples, who could not practice farming that far north. Arctic peoples migrated when necessary to obtain food.

The inhabitants of the Arctic came later to North America than did other native peoples. They came from Siberia in boats, starting about 2500 B.C., whereas the other native peoples traveled over the Bering Strait land bridge. Arctic peoples are generally shorter and broader than other Native North Americans, with rounder faces, lighter skin, and epicanthic eye folds, the small fold of skin covering the inner corner of the eyes that is typical of Asian peoples. As a result, Arctic peoples generally are not referred to as *Indians*. One sees instead phrases such as *native peoples* and *Arctic peoples.*

Arctic peoples include the Inuit and the Aleut. The Inuit formerly were called Eskimo, a name applied to them by ALGONQUIANS and meaning "eaters of raw meat." *Inuit* means "the people."

The Inuit and Aleut shared language (the Eskimaleut, or Eskaleut, language family) and many cultural traits. But there were differences too. For instance, the Aleut did not construct snow houses (igloos), as many Inuit peoples did.

The various subdivisions of the Inuit and Aleut, along with their respective cultures and histories, are discussed in detail under their respective entries.

ARIKARA

The Arikara are sometimes called the Arikaree, or simply the Ree. Their name, pronounced uh-RICK-uh-ruh, is thought to mean "horns," in reference to the ancient custom of wearing two upright bones in their hair, or possibly "elk people" or "corn eaters." The Arikara migrated farther north than all the other Caddoan-speaking tribes, splitting off from the PAWNEE. They settled along the banks of the upper Missouri River in what is now North Dakota near the South Dakota border, to the south of two Siouan-speaking tribes, the HIDATSA and MANDAN, with whom they have been associated throughout their history.

The Arikara, like the Hidatsa and Mandan, were villagers and farmers. It is thought that it was they who originally brought agricultural skills to other tribes of the upper Missouri River. They grew nine varieties of corn as well as beans, squash, pumpkins, and sunflowers. Unlike their Caddoan kin to the south, the Arikara did not live in grass huts. Rather, they built earthlodges on bluffs overlooking the river. They planted fields nearby.

The Arikara hunted buffalo to supplement their diet. After having acquired horses in the 1700s, they ranged even farther from their villages in pursuit of the great herds. They had hunting grounds in what is now eastern Montana as well as in the Dakotas. During their hunting trips, they lived in tipis. The Arikara are considered part of the Great Plains Culture Area (see PLAINS INDIANS). But they were not as nomadic as other Plains tribes (see PRAIRIE INDIANS).

The Arikara shared many cultural traits with the Mandan, a tribe more thoroughly documented than either the Arikara or the Hidatsa. Customs of all three tribes were passed from one to another. Sometimes customs were even bought and sold. For example, one tribe would trade horses, tools, and ornaments for the right to use a certain dance. One Arikara dance that spread to the other tribes was known as the Hot Dance.

An Arikara Indian

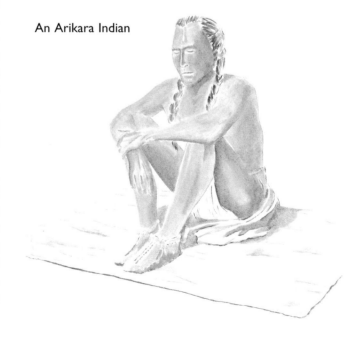

For the occasion, tribal members would build a large fire, place a kettle of meat cooking in water over it, and spread hot coals on the ground. Young men, naked and barefoot, with feet and hands painted red, would dance on the coals to prove their courage. Then they would dip their hands in the scalding water, grab the meat, and eat it.

Because of their location on the Missouri River, the villages of the Arikara, like those of the Mandan and Hidatsa, became important centers of commerce. Other Plains peoples often traveled to the villages to trade buffalo meat and robes, as well as horses, for farm products. French and English traders also stopped regularly at the river villages to exchange guns and other European trade goods for furs.

After the Louisiana Purchase by the United States in 1803, the federal government sponsored the Lewis and Clark Expedition up the Missouri River to explore the new American holdings. Meriwether Lewis and William Clark encountered the Arikara on the Missouri between the Grand and Cannonball Rivers and wrote about them in their journals.

In 1823, after Arikara warriors had attacked an American trading party and killed 13 people, most tribal members, fearing revenge by the whites, hid out for two years with the Pawnee in what is now Nebraska. On returning to the upper Missouri, the Arikara settled farther north. By 1851, they had villages as far north as the mouth of the Heart River. Disease, brought to them by white traders, greatly reduced their numbers. They suffered through the great smallpox epidemic of 1837, which practically wiped out the neighboring Mandan.

In 1862, the Arikara moved to Fort Berthold, North Dakota. The federal government established a permanent reservation there for the Arikara, Hidatsa, and Mandan in 1870 that the tribes still share today.

In 1950, the federal government constructed Garrison Dam, flooding the Arikara homeland and forcing them to relocate to the west side of the new Lake Sakakawae. The Three Affiliated Tribes have a museum at New Town, which gives visitors a glimpse of upper-Missouri Indian history and culture. Each of the tribal communities hosts a powwow every summer.

ARKANSAS   *see* QUAPAW

ASSINIBOINE

The Assiniboine speak a Siouan dialect. Their name, pronounced uh-SIN-uh-boin, is from the CHIPPEWA (OJIBWAY) dialect of the Algonquian language and means "those who cook with stones." This refers to stone-boiling, the practice of heating stones directly in a fire then placing them in water to make it boil for cooking. British explorers and traders also used the name *Stoney* for the tribe and it is still applied in Canada.

The Assiniboine lived as one people with the SIOUX (DAKOTA, LAKOTA, NAKOTA) in the Lake Superior region of what is now northern Minnesota and southwestern Ontario. The Assiniboine probably split off from the Sioux in the 1600s. They migrated westward onto the northern plains, first settling west of Lake Winnipeg in what is now the province of Manitoba. Some bands later moved farther west to the banks of the Assiniboine and Saskatchewan Rivers in what is now Saskatchewan. (The

southern part of Saskatchewan was once known as Assiniboia.) The Assiniboine also lived at times in territory that is now Montana and North Dakota.

By the time whites encountered them, the Assiniboine did not live in permanent villages. Rather, they were nomadic hunter-gatherers, moving their tipis when necessary to find more food. After they had acquired horses through trade with other Native Americans, they ranged over greater expanses in search of buffalo and wild plant foods. Some of the more northerly bands pursued moose, bear, beaver, and porcupine in the northern evergreen forests bordering the plains. The Assiniboine sometimes traded their meat and pelts with farming tribes for agricultural products. After white traders had entered their domain, the Assiniboine also bartered their furs with both the French and English in exchange for guns and other European trade goods.

Because of their typical Great Plains way of life, the Assiniboine are classified as PLAINS INDIANS. Like other tribes who became hunters on the plains, the Assiniboine gave up making pottery, which was too heavy and fragile on the trail. They instead began using buffalo-hide bags.

The Sun god and Thunder god were the most important manifestations of the Great Spirit for the Assiniboine. Like many Plains Indians, they participated in the Sun Dance. They also took guidance from personal visions, a practice known as the Vision Quest.

For part of their history, the Assiniboine were allied with the CREE (the Plains Cree) against the BLACKFEET and the Sioux. In a well-known incident, traditional tribal enemies became lifelong friends. In 1857, a group of Sioux warriors attacked a party of Assiniboine. Among the Sioux was Sitting Bull, who would later become one of the most famous of Indian leaders in the wars against the U.S. government for the plains. There was an 11-year-old boy among the Assiniboine named Jumping Bull. The young boy did not flee from the attacking Sioux but fought valiantly with his childsized bow. When Sioux warriors threatened to kill Jumping Bull, Sitting Bull ran in front of the youth and proclaimed, "This boy is too brave to die! I take him as my brother." Jumping Bull died along with Sitting Bull in 1890, trying to defend him.

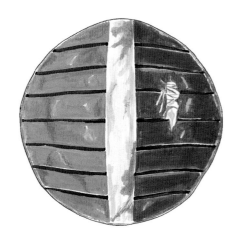

Assiniboine shield with attached medicine bundle

Some Assiniboine worked as scouts for the whites. In 1885, Assiniboine scouts helped the Canadian North West Field Force track down renegade Cree who were participating in the Second Riel Rebellion of MÉTIS.

In the 1870s, different bands of Assiniboine were settled on reservations on different sides of the border of the United States and Canada. In Montana, the Assiniboine now share the Fort Belknap Reservation with the GROS VENTRE, and the Fort Peck Reservation with the Sioux. In Canada, Assiniboine bands hold a number of tracts of land in Saskatchewan and Alberta, some of which they share with the Sioux, Cree, and Chippewa (Ojibway).

ATHAPASCANS

Athapascan, pronounced ath-uh-PAS-kun and sometimes spelled *Athapaskan* or *Athabascan,* refers to a family of Indian languages, one of the most widespread language families in western North America. (The Athapascan language family is part of the Na-Dene language phylum, which includes language isolates of the HAIDA and TLINGIT.)

As is the case with *Algonquian, Athapascan* is commonly used to refer to a particular tribe as well as a language family. And just as the name *Algonquian* is usually used to group together eastern ALGONQUIANS to the exclusion of western Algonquians, *Athapascan* is used to group together northern Athapascans as separate from southern Athapascans.

The southern Athapascans broke off from the other Athapascans and migrated southward before Europeans came to North America. Migrations may have first occured as early as A.D. 850 or as late as 1400. They came

to be known as APACHE and NAVAJO and played an important part in the history of the American Southwest.

Other Athapascans dispersed from the original group in the north and ended up in the midst of peoples speaking different languages. For example, the SARCEE lived among northern PLAINS INDIANS. The HUPA and other tribes migrated down the Pacific Coast and settled among CALIFORNIA INDIANS. And other Athapascans are classified as NORTHWEST COAST INDIANS.

The northern Athapascans, the Indians to whom the name is usually applied, are categorized as part of the Subarctic Culture Area (see SUBARCTIC INDIANS). Subarctic refers to the territory of the taiga, or the great northern forest of mainly spruce and fir trees, stretching all the way across North America. It lies to the south of the tundra of the Arctic Culture Area (see ARCTIC PEOPLES). The Athapascans lived in the western part of the subarctic.

The Subarctic Athapascans did not make up unified tribes. Rather, they lived and traveled for the most part in small bands of families or extended families, including in-laws. Yet by studying the various locations, languages, and lifeways of the various bands, scholars have been able to group the Athapascans into tribes. Because of limitations of space, most of the distinct Athapascan groups do not have separate entries in this book, although each deserves further in-depth study.

The northern Athapascans were nomadic hunter-gatherers who did not farm. For many of them, the caribou was a staple food and source of materials for clothing, dwellings, and babiche (leather thongs used as bindings). The quest for food in the cold northern environment was all-consuming. Many of the Athapascans lived in portable skin tents, smaller versions of the Plains tipis. Many domesticated dogs and depended on them for hunting and hauling. Many used snowshoes and toboggans in the winter. Many were important to French and British fur trading in the late 1700s and early 1800s.

But there were several cultural distinctions among the various tribes. The northern Athapascans can be further broken down into three general groups:

The **Canadian Rocky Athapascans** occupied ancestral territory in or near the northern part of the Rocky Mountains. They include the CARRIER (at the headwaters of the Fraser River); Chilcotin (Chilcotin River); Nahane (Liard and Nahani Rivers); Sekani (Finlay, Parsnip, and upper Peace Rivers); Tahltan (upper Stikine River); Tsetsaut (Iskut and White Rivers); and Tutchone (Yukon River east of Saint Elias Mountains).

The **Lake Athapascans** occupied ancestral territory near the Great Slave and Great Bear Lakes. They include the Beaver (Peace River); CHIPEWYAN (between Great Slave Lake and Churchill River); Dogrib (between Great Slave and Great Bear Lakes); Hare (northwest of Great Bear Lake along lower Mackenzie River); Slave (between Mackenzie River and Great Slave Lake); and Tatsanottine (between Coppermine River and Great Slave Lake).

The **Alaskan Athapascans** occupied ancestral territory now in Alaska, plus neighboring parts of Canada. They include the Ahtena (Copper River); Eyak (mouth of Copper River); Han (upper Yukon River); Ingalik (Anvik and Kuskokwim Rivers); Kolchan (upper Kuskokwim River); Koyukon (Yukon River); KUTCHIN (Yukon River to Mackenzie River); Nabesna (Nabesna and Chisana Rivers); Tanaina (Cook Inlet); and Tanana (Tanana River).

In this book, the culture and history of three northern Athapascan tribes, one from each group, are discussed in detail: Carrier, Chipewyan, and Kutchin.

ATSINA *see* GROS VENTRE

AZTEC

The Aztec (pronounced AZ-tec), unlike most Native American peoples discussed in this book, call up images of great cities, tall pyramids, golden objects, feathered priests, and human sacrifices. The culture of the Aztec is often compared to that of ancient Rome, as that of the MAYA is to ancient Greece. Like the Romans, the Aztec were a warlike people who founded a great empire and who drew on knowledge from other peoples to further their civilization.

The Aztec were influenced especially by the TOLTEC before them and by the MAYA. These various peoples owed much to the OLMEC, the founders of the first great Mesoamerican civilization. *Mesoamerica* is the name given by scholars to an Indian culture area in parts of Mexico and elsewhere in Central America where Native American society was centralized and highly organized.

The Olmec reached their cultural peak in what is called the Preclassic period in Mesoamerica, from about 1000 B.C. to A.D. 300. The Maya flourished during the so-called Classic period, from about A.D. 300 to 900. The Postclassic period is defined as from A.D. 900 to 1500. The Toltec were dominant from about 900 to about 1200. Aztec civilization was at its height from about 1200 to the time of the arrival of the Spanish, about 1500.

Like the Toltec, the Aztec, originally known as the Mexica, were an offshoot of the Chichimec people. They spoke the Nahuatl dialect of the Uto-Aztecan language family. Nomadic hunters, they migrated into the valley of Mexico from the highlands to the north, arriving in that region about 1168.

At the time of the Mexica arrival, the Toltec Empire was in a state of decay. Mexica warriors, armed with powerful bows and long arrows—weapons passed to Mesoamerican peoples by Indians to the north—found work as mercenaries in the armies of local cities. Finally in 1325, they founded two villages of their own on swampy islets in Lake Texcoco—Tenochtitlán and Tlatelolco.

The Aztec Empire

Eventually the inhabitants of Tenochtitlán, who called themselves Tenocha, conquered Tlatelolco. Tenochtitlán rapidly expanded. The Tenocha actually created new land to farm and build on by anchoring wicker baskets to Lake Texcoco's shallow bottom and piling silt and plant matter on top of them, thus making *chinampas,* artificial islands.

The Tenocha formed an alliance with a people called the Alcohua against other peoples of central Mexico. They took a new name too. They began to call themselves *Aztec* after Aztlan, their legendary homeland.

In the following years, Tenochtitlán grew on top of the *chinampas* to a city of thousands of stone buildings, interconnected by many canals, with about 200,000 inhabitants. This population center now is the site of Mexico City, one of the largest cities in the world.

The Aztec launched many military campaigns against surrounding peoples, from the Gulf of Mexico to the Pacific Ocean. Aztec armies were well organized and well armed. They used bows and arrows, darts and dart throwers, clubs, maces, and swords with blades of volcanic glass. Thick, quilted cotton was used to make shields as well as armor. Through conquest, the Aztec Empire came to comprise 5 million people.

The Aztec conquered their neighbors for economic purposes. They imposed taxes on their subjects, taking raw materials from them (such as gold, silver, copper, jade, turquoise, obsidian [or black volcanic glass], and pearls), as well as food products (such as corn, beans, squash, tomatoes, potatoes, chili peppers, mangoes, papayas, avocadoes, and cacao, or chocolate). They also demanded cotton for clothing and for armor, and domesticated animals, such as dogs and turkeys, for meat.

Religion

Through warfare the Aztec obtained captives for human sacrifice. In their religion, the letting of human blood was believed to appease the many different deities. An important god for the Aztec was Quetzalcoatl, the Great Plumed Serpent, who was central to the religions of the earlier Mesoamerican civilizations as well. But Quetzalcoatl was a benign figure who, according to tradition, showed mercy. It was the war god Huitzilopochtli who demanded the most blood. Priests sacrificed thousands of prisoners to Huitzilopochtli in the temples at the top of the massive stone pyramids. Earlier Mesoamerican civilizations had practiced human sacrifice, but the Aztec carried out their bloody rituals on the largest scale.

Aztec sacrificial knife

Social Structure

In Aztec society, the priests had a great deal of influence. They shared the power with nobles, who each ruled a sector of the city. An emperor, or Chief of Men, was the most powerful ruler of all. The nobles selected him from among the royalty. After the emperor, nobles, and priests, the next most influential social classes were the war chiefs—Eagle Warriors and Jaguar Warriors—and the wealthy merchants. Beneath them were common soldiers, craftspeople, and farmers. Still lower on the social scale were a group of unskilled laborers who owned no land. And below them were the slaves.

For the Aztecs, land ownership was communal, with the *calpulli* local groups consisting of several families, jointly owning parcels of land. The *calpulli* had to pay taxes in the form of crops grown on the land.

Clothing

Aztec clothing revealed social status. The Chief of Men wore tunics of coyote fur, white duck feathers and plumes from other birds, and dyed cotton. He also wore gold, silver, and jade jewelry, including a nose ornament made from turquoise. He was the only person in Aztec society who could wear turquoise jewelry or turquoise-colored clothing. The noblemen also wore brightly colored cloaks, plus a variety of jewelry, including necklaces, earrings, armbands, and nose and lip ornaments. The merchants wore white cotton cloaks, sometimes decorated with designs. Eagle Warriors wore feathered outfits and helmets in the shape of eagle heads. Jaguar Warriors dressed in jaguar skins, including the heads of the animals. Common soldiers wore breechcloths and knee-length shirts. They shaved their heads except for a scalplock in back, but they were allowed to grow their hair long and wear decorated tunics if they had taken prisoners in battle. For footwear, soldiers and the higher social classes wore sandals made of leather or woven from plant matter. Workers and farmers went barefoot and could not wear bright colors. These men wore only breechcloths of woven plant leaves, and the women wore plain white shirts and ankle-length skirts.

Aztec rhythm instrument made from a human bone

Houses

Housing also was determined by social class. The Chief of Men and the wealthiest nobles had two-story, multi-roomed palaces, with stone walls and log and plaster roofs. Less wealthy nobles and merchants had one-story houses. Some of the rich planted gardens on the flat roofs. Commoners lived in small huts, made from clay bricks or from pole frames and plant stems packed with clay, typically with one room.

Food

Much of the modern Mexican diet, including tortillas and tamales, came from the Aztec. Corn and beans provided the basic Aztec diet, as they still do in that part of the world. The Aztec upper classes had a much more varied diet, with other foods such as meat, fruits, tomatoes, chili peppers, and a beverage made from chocolate, vanilla, and honey. The Aztec also made beer and wine from different plants. Alcoholic beverages were used in rituals and in medication and prophecy, but public intoxication was frowned upon. In some instances, for both nobles and commoners, drunken behavior was punished by death.

Writing

The Aztec carried on the Mesoamerican tradition of a form of writing called hieroglyphics, although not to such a degree as the Maya. Most hieroglyphics were pictures of the objects they represented, but some represented sounds. The Aztec used their writing to record history, geography, religion, poetry, public events, and time.

The Coming of the Spanish

When the Spanish reached the mainland of the Americas, after having explored the Caribbean islands, the Aztec Empire was still intact. The Spanish explored the Panama region in Central America and the Yucatán Peninsula in the early 1500s. During these expeditions, they heard of the powerful Aztec Empire to the north, with a great city of towering pyramids, filled with gold and other riches, rising out of Lake Texcoco. In 1519, Hernán Cortés landed with about 400 soldiers and marched toward the city of Tenochtitlán.

Even with such a small army, Cortés managed to conquer the huge armies of the Aztec for a number of reasons. First of all, he managed to gain as allies other Mesoamerican peoples who wanted to be free of Aztec rule—peoples such as the Totonac, Tlaxcalan, and Cholulan (from the ancient city of Cholula, site of the largest structure in the Americas, the Great Pyramid, 180 feet high and covering 25 acres). In order to accomplish these alliances, Cortés played various factions against one another. He also had the help of a talented Maya woman, originally a slave, named Malinche, called Lady Marina by the Spanish, who served as a translator and arbitrator among the different peoples. Moreover, the conquistadores were armed with guns, which frightened the Indians. Nor had the Indians ever seen horses.

Still another factor played an important part in the Spanish conquest of the Aztec. Aztec legend told of the return of the god Quetzalcoatl. The Aztec thought that the white-skinned Cortés might be this god. The Aztec emperor Montezuma (also spelled Moctezuma) was indecisive in his actions when faced with this possibility. He lost his life during the period of political maneuvering, at the hands of either the Spanish or some Aztec who resented his indecisiveness. By the time the Aztec mounted a sizable defense against the invaders, the Spanish had thousands of Indian allies. The Spanish conquest, after fierce fighting in the streets of Tenochtitlán, was complete by 1521.

The Spanish worked to eradicate all traces of Aztec civilization. They destroyed temples and pyramids; they melted down sculptured objects into basic metals to be shipped back to Spain; they burned Aztec books. They also forced the Aztec to work for them as slaves. New

Spain (Mexico) became the base from which the Spanish sent conquistadores northward to explore what is now the American Southwest and California, as well as southward into South America.

Some Spanish eventually intermarried with Aztec survivors. As a result, there is some Aztec blood in modern-day Mexicans. The Aztec language, Nahuatl, has also survived among some of the peasants living in the small villages surrounding Mexico City.

BANNOCK

The Bannock (pronounced BAN-uck) are considered an offshoot of the northern branch of the PAIUTE. Both peoples are part of the Uto-Aztecan language family, as are the UTE and SHOSHONE. Scholars classify these tribes as GREAT BASIN INDIANS. Great Basin Indians foraged and dug for anything edible—wild plants, rodents, reptiles, insects—in their harsh mountain and desert environment. They also had a staple food in common with the PLATEAU INDIANS to their north—the roots of the camas plant.

The nomadic Bannock occupied ancestral territory that has since become southeastern Idaho and western Wyoming. After they had acquired horses in the early 1700s, they ranged over a wider area into parts of Colorado, Utah, Montana, and Oregon. Their way of life came to resemble that of the PLAINS INDIANS, including buffalo-hunting and the use of tipis.

A mountain man by the name of Jim Bridger opened up trade relations with the Bannock in 1829. Yet in the following years, Bannock warriors preyed on migrants and miners traveling through their territory on the Oregon Trail. In 1869, after the Civil War, when more federal troops could be sent west to build new forts and to pacify militant bands, the government established the Fort Hall Reservation in present-day Idaho for the Bannock and northern branch of Shoshone.

The Bannock resisted reservation life. Their food rations on the reservation were meager, and tribal members continued to wander over a wide expanse of territory in search of the foods they had hunted and gathered for generations. As more and more whites settled in the region, they disrupted these traditional food staples of the Bannock; non-Indian hunters were killing the buffalo wholesale on the plains to the east. In addition, hogs belonging to white ranchers were destroying the camas

Bannock parents with child

plants near Fort Boise, Idaho. The Bannock, along with their neighbors, the Northern Paiute, revolted.

The Bannock War occurred in 1878. A Bannock warrior wounded two whites, who reported the incident to the army. Meanwhile, about 200 Bannock and Northern Paiute warriors gathered under a Bannock chief named Buffalo Horn. This war party clashed with a volunteer patrol in June. When Buffalo Horn was killed, his followers headed westward into Oregon to regroup at Steens Mountain with Paiute from the Malheur Reservation. Two Paiute became the new leaders: a chief named Egan and a medicine man named Oytes.

Regular army troops rode out of Fort Boise in pursuit. They were under the command of General Oliver O. Howard, who had tracked down the NEZ PERCE during their uprising the year before. The soldiers caught up with the insurgents at Birch Creek on July 8 and dislodged them from steep bluffs. Warriors under Chief Egan tried to hide out on the Umatilla reservation. The Umatilla sided with the whites, however. They killed Egan and led soldiers to his men. Oytes managed to elude capture until August, but eventually turned himself in. A party of Bannock escaped eastward to Wyoming, but they were captured in September.

After the short-lived Bannock War, the Malheur Reservation was closed. The Paiute were settled among the YAKAMA on their reservation in the State of Washington. The Bannock were held prisoners at military posts for a time but were finally permitted to return to their reservation in Idaho.

That same year, 1878, another Indian war broke out in Idaho, known as the Sheepeater War. The Sheepeaters were Bannock and Shoshone who had migrated north-ward into the Salmon River Mountains of central Idaho and hunted mountain sheep as their main food. They too began raiding settlers crowding their homeland. There were not many of them, perhaps only 50, but they proved a stubborn enemy for the army in the rugged highlands. They routed one army patrol and eluded another. But the army wore them down with continuous tracking, and the Sheepeaters surrendered in October. They were placed on the Fort Hall Reservation in Idaho with their Bannock and Shoshone kin.

The Shoshone-Bannock tribes of the Fort Hall Reservation, also referred to as the Sho-Bans, hold many traditional festivals every year, including a week-long celebration in August, several Sun Dances, and an all-Indian rodeo. They also maintain the Trading Post complex and offer high-stakes bingo.

BEOTHUK

The ancient Beothuk language has some word roots in common with the Algonquian language. As a result, the Beothuk originally were classified as ALGONQUIANS. But the two languages differ in vocabulary to such a degree that now the Beothuk language is classified alone as Beothukan, and the Beothuk are considered a distinct people with different ancestors. Their name is pronounced BAY-uh-thuk.

The Beothuk, along with the INUIT, are therefore the only native people along the Atlantic coast of Canada and the northeastern United States who did not speak an Algonquian dialect. Perhaps one reason the Beothuk were a distinct group with their own language was that they lived on an island—the large island of Newfoundland.

Because of their location at the northeastern corner of North America, the Beothuk had early contacts with many explorers. It is theorized that either the Beothuk or the MICMAC were the peoples the Vikings supposedly encountered in A.D. 1000. In their writings, the Vikings referred to them as *Skraeling*. It is certain that John Cabot, sailing in the pay of England, encountered the Beothuk in 1497; Giovanni da Verrazano, sailing for France, met up with them in 1523; and Jacques Cartier, also sailing for France, made contact with them in 1534.

After these early contacts, the Beothuk continued to associate with European fishermen, especially the French, who frequented their shores. A problem arose between the two peoples when the Beothuk stole from the fishermen.

In Beothuk culture, ownership of possessions was a relative concept, and petty thievery was allowed. The French, however, incensed by the loss of equipment, turned on their former friends. Not only did they use their own guns in attacks on the Beothuk, but they also armed the Micmac and placed a bounty on Beothuk scalps.

By the early 1700s, the Beothuk were practically extinct. Those who survived did so by hiding out among other Indians, mostly the NASKAPI. A century later, the Beothic Society for the Civilization of the Native Savages combed the island for Beothuk descendants but did not find any. The last Beothuk on record, Shanawdithit or Nancy April, a captive at St. Johns, Newfoundland, died in 1829.

The Beothuk lived a lifestyle similar to both Algonquians and Inuit. Like the Algonquians, they slept in birch-bark wigwams and cooked in birch-bark containers. They also made birch-bark canoes, but with an original design. The gunwales, or sides, curved up, not just at the ends, but also in the middle, like two sets of crescent moons. In the winter, the Beothuk lived like subarctic Algonquians, staying in the inland forests and hunting land mammals, and are classified as SUBARCTIC INDIANS. In the summer, however, they traveled to the ocean to hunt sea mammals, using Inuit-style weapons and methods.

The Beothuk had other cultural traits unlike those of either the Algonquians or the Inuit. For example, in caves and rock shelters where the Beothuk buried their

Beothuk birch-bark canoe

dead long ago, archaeologists have found uniquely carved bone ornaments.

The Beothuk had a custom in which they painted their bodies and clothing with red ocher, a mineral found in the soil. They probably did this for practical as well as religious reasons, because the substance helped keep insects away. The Micmac called them *Macquajeet* for "red people." It has been theorized that the derivation of the term *redskin* for Native Americans results from the practice, and not because of the color of ther skin, as is commonly believed. The tribal name *Beothuk* is thought to mean "human body."

BLACKFEET

The powerful Blackfoot Confederacy once controlled a huge expanse of the northeastern High Plains, from the North Saskatchewan River in what is now Alberta all the way to the upper Missouri River in Montana, flanked on the west by the Rocky Mountains. Members of the Blackfoot Confederacy included three subtribes or bands, the Blackfoot proper (or *Siksika,* meaning "those with black-dyed moccasins" in Algonquian), the Blood (or *Kainah,* meaning "blood," so named because they painted their bodies with red clay), and the Piegan (or *Pigunni,* meaning "poorly dressed"), plus the GROS VEN- TRE and SARCEE. The first three appear in books together as the Blackfeet (the plural form common in the United States, pronounced as spelled) or the Blackfoot (the singular form common in Canada) because they all dyed their moccasins black. The three Blackfeet bands, plus the Gros Ventre and Sarcee, all are Algonquian-speaking peoples. The Blackfoot proper lived the farthest

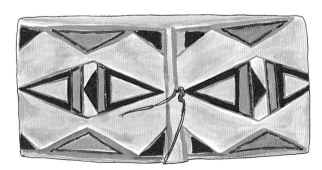

Blackfeet parfleche (rawhide storage bag)

north (and are sometimes called the North Blackfoot), then the Blood to their south, and the Piegan to their south. The Gros Ventre lived to the southeast of the three Blackfeet bands, and the Sarcee to the northwest.

Lifeways

The Blackfeet migrated to their homeland from the east, after having separated from other ALGONQUIANS. They became adapted to the nomadic life on the open grasslands, with buffalo meat as their "real food," as they called it. They hunted other game, including deer, elk, and mountain sheep, but ate little fowl or fish. They also gathered wild plants, such as berries and chokecherries. They moved their camps of hide-covered tipis to new hunting grounds when necessary, but during the cold northern winters, the various bands generally stayed in one place. The Blackfeet grew only one crop, tobacco. After the Blackfeet had obtained horses in the mid-1700s, their way of life came to resemble that of other PLAINS INDIANS.

The Blackfeet are known for their beautiful craftwork—tipis, riding equipment, clothes, tools, and weapons. They had unique headdresses, the feathers of which stood straight up. They practiced the Sun Dance, as did other Plains tribes, but unlike other tribes women participated in the Blackfeet version. The women also had a powerful society known as Motokik. It was thought that their blessing of a child would give that

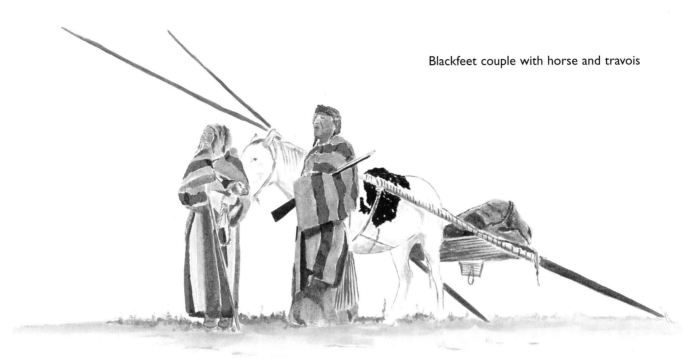

Blackfeet couple with horse and travois

child lifelong good fortune. The Vision Quest, another Plains Indian custom, was critical for the Blackfeet in the passage from childhood to adulthood. Blackfeet men were organized into warrior societies based on age, called the Ikunuhkats, or "All Comrades."

Warfare and Treaties

The Blackfeet were enemies of the CROW and SIOUX (DAKOTA, LAKOTA, NAKOTA) on the Great Plains; and the SHOSHONE, FLATHEAD, and KOOTENAI in the mountain country to their west. Blackfeet war parties would ride hundreds of miles on raids. A boy going on his first war party was given a silly or derogatory name. But after he had stolen his first horse or killed an enemy, he was given a name of which he could be proud.

Early contacts with non-Indians were friendly. David Thompson, who explored for the Hudson's Bay Company, wintered among the Blackfeet in 1787–88 and documented that they had had guns, metal tools, and horses for some 50 years. Blackfeet hostility toward whites apparently started when one of their warriors was killed in a horse-stealing raid on the Lewis and Clark Expedition in 1804. The Blackfeet henceforth preyed on American explorers, traders, miners, and settlers who traveled the Oregon and Bozeman Trails. The Blackfeet name, probably more than any other, aroused fear in the mountain men. In 1867, the Blackfeet killed the man after whom the Bozeman Trail, the cutoff from the Oregon Trail, is named—John Bozeman. The Blackfeet

stayed on better terms with the British than with the Americans. Canadian traders encouraged Blackfeet warriors to kill American traders to stop their northward advance.

Because they were so warlike, the Blackfeet slowed down the opening of both the Canadian West and the American West. Smallpox epidemics in 1836, 1845, 1857, and 1869–70, along with the decline of the buffalo herds, did more to weaken the Blackfoot Confederacy than Canadian or U.S. armies did. One incident, however, proved especially costly to the Blackfeet. In 1870, U.S. soldiers under the command of Colonel E. M. Baker, who were tracking several warriors for killing a white settler, attacked the Blackfeet winter camp of chiefs Heavy Runner and Red Horn on the Marias River in Montana. They killed 173 men, women, and children and took 140 more Blackfeet prisoner.

The Blackfeet signed the first treaty with the United States in 1855 and ceded additional lands in 1886 and 1895, and with Canada in 1877. Tribal members were settled on reservations on both sides of the U.S.-Canadian border in the 1880s. The parcels they managed to keep were part of their ancestral homeland.

Crowfoot (Isapo-Muxika) was the most famous principal chief and spokesperson for the Blackfoot Confederacy in the latter part of the 19th century. Although he had lost most of his children to diseases brought to the Blackfeet by whites, he strived to prevent further bloodshed and was instrumental in having his people sign the treaty with Canada in 1877. Just before his death in

Blackfeet headdress with upright feathers

Blackfeet eagle head, with brass button eyes (worn as a headdress for protection from bullets)

1890, he said: "What is life? It is the flash of a firefly in the night. It is the breath of a buffalo in the winter time. It is the little shadow which runs across the grass and loses itself on the sunset."

Contemporary Blackfeet

Three bands—the North Blackfoot, Blood, and North Piegan—have rights to lands in Alberta, Canada. Another group, made up mostly of South Piegan, has a reservation in Montana. Their tribal headquarters is located in the town of Browning, the gateway to Glacier National Park. The Museum of the Plains Indian also is located at Browning.

The Blackfeet have been attempting to protect a sacred site known as Badger Two-Medicine in the Lewis

and Clark National Forest in northwest Montana. Oil and gas companies are seeking to drill the site for oil and gas. Blackfeet and other peoples have held Sun Dances, Vision Quests, and sweats there since pre-horse times.

Blackfeet toy drum (modern)

BLOOD   *see* BLACKFEET

CADDO

The people who became known as the Caddo were really many different bands living in territory stretching from the Red River valley, in what is now Louisiana, to the Brazos River valley in Texas, including parts of Arkansas

and Oklahoma. They included bands of the Natchitoches Confederacy in Louisiana; the Hasinai Confederacy in Texas; and the Kadohadacho Confederacy in Texas and adjacent parts of Arkansas and Oklahoma. *Caddo,* pronounced CAD-o, is derived from the latter name *Kadohadacho,* meaning "real chiefs." There were other tribes of the same Caddoan language family who migrated farther to the north, the ARIKARA, PAWNEE, and WICHITA.

The Caddo are usually included as part of the Southeast Culture Area unlike their more nomadic Caddoan relatives in the Great Plains Culture Area. They were primarily villagers and farmers. They had a class system in their social organization, like other SOUTHEAST INDIANS. They lived in grass houses, about 15 feet high and 20 to 50 feet in diameter, framed with poles in a domed or conical shape and covered with grass thatch. The smoke from cooking fires did not exit through smokeholes but seeped out directly through the thatch. The Caddo also built temples in which they kept sacred fires burning. For travel on the rivers in their territory, they carved dugouts from single logs.

Caddo traditional dances include the Turkey Dance, a victory dance that must be completed before sunset; the Drum Dance, performed in the evening and telling in song and dance the Caddo creation story; and the Morning Dance, celebrating dawn.

Since the Caddo lived on the edge of the plains, they also possessed some cultural traits of PLAINS INDIANS. After they had acquired horses from the Spanish, the Caddo roamed over a wider area in search of buffalo.

The Caddo had early contacts with the Spanish. Some tribesmen met up with Hernando de Soto's expedition in 1541 soon after the conquistadores crossed the Mississippi. After René-Robert Cavelier de La Salle had claimed the Mississippi Valley for France

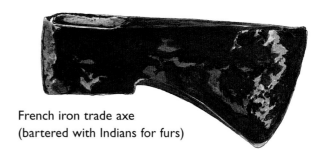

French iron trade axe
(bartered with Indians for furs)

in 1682, the Caddo established a lasting trade relationship with French fur traders.

Caddo and Wichita, called *Taovayas* by the French, acted as middlemen for French traders. The Indians grew crops to barter with other tribes for animal pelts, which they then traded with the French. The Taovayas and backwoods fur traders conducted most of their business from villages on the Red River—San Bernardo and San Teodoro (called the Twin Villages), and Natchitoches—which became centers of commerce. The Taovayas prospered during the mid-1700s. Although the French lost their claim to the Louisiana Territory in 1763 after the French and Indian War, the Taovayas remained active for some years to come. But Spanish restrictions on their trade eventually ended their prosperity.

The French regained the Louisiana Territory from Spain in 1801, but sold it to the United States in 1803. Soon afterward, the Louisiana Caddo ceded their lands and moved to Texas. Texas became a republic in 1835 and part of the United States in 1845. In 1859, the federal government settled the Caddo on a reservation along the Washita River in the Indian Territory in what is now Caddo County, Oklahoma, near Anadarko (named after one of the Caddoan bands). The Wichita, who were granted the reservation with the Caddo, lived in Kansas during the Civil War before joining their kin.

After 1865, the Caddo provided scouts for the U.S. Army. One of their chiefs, Guadalupe, considered the wars more a struggle between farmers and raiders than a war between whites and Indians. Since he was a farmer, he encouraged his warriors to assist whites against the nomadic tribes of the Great Plains.

With the General Allotment Act of 1887, much of the Caddo-Wichita reservation in Oklahoma was divided among tribal members. The Caddo tribe now jointly holds certain trust lands in the state with the Wichita and LENNI LENAPE (DELAWARE). Oil, gas, and ranchland leasing provides some income for tribal members.

Caddo wooden
figurine with
human hair

CALIFORNIA INDIANS

The phrase *California Indians* refers to people of many different tribes within the California Culture Area. This geographical region roughly corresponds to the state of California as it exists today, along with the Lower California Peninsula, which is part of Mexico. In the eastern part of this geographical region, the Sierra Nevada, a tall and rugged mountain range, provides a natural barrier. As a result, some of the tribes that once lived in territory now mapped as the eastern part of the state of California are categorized in the Great Basin and Southwest Culture Areas. And to the north, some of the tribes who lived on both sides of the California-Oregon border are included in the Northwest Coast and Plateau Culture Areas.

In addition to the Sierra Nevada, the smaller Coast Range runs north-south within the California Culture Area, extending into Mexico. Between the two mountain ranges, in the heart of the culture area, is the Great California Valley, formed by the San Joaquin and Sacramento Rivers and their tributaries.

The amount of rainfall in the culture area varies dramatically from north to south. The northern uplands receive the greatest amount of precipitation, mostly in winter. As a result, there are many tall forests in northern California. The south of the culture area is much drier. Near the California-Arizona border is the Mojave Desert. In Mexico, most of the coastal lowlands, especially along the Gulf of California, are also desert country.

For the most part, the culture area offers bountiful wild plant foods and game. California Indians prospered and grew to high population levels as hunter-gatherers without a need for farming. The only cultivated crop found was tobacco.

There were many different California peoples, speaking at least 100 distinct dialects. The main language groups identified are the Athapascan language family (part of the Na-Dene language phylum), the Hokan language phylum, the Penutian language phylum, and the Uto-Aztecan language family (part of the Aztec-Tanoan language phylum).

Among the ATHAPASCANS, mostly in the north, are the Bear River, Cahto, Chilula, HUPA, Lassik, Mattole, Nongatl, Sinkyone, Tolowa, Wailaki, and Whilkut.

Among the Hokan tribes, speaking dialects of a number of small language families or language isolates, are the Achomawi, Atsugewi, Chimariko, CHUMASH, Esselen, Karok, Konomihu, Okwanuchu, POMO, Salinas, Shasta, YAHI, and Yana. The larger Yuman language family is also part of the Hokan phylum. The Yuman-

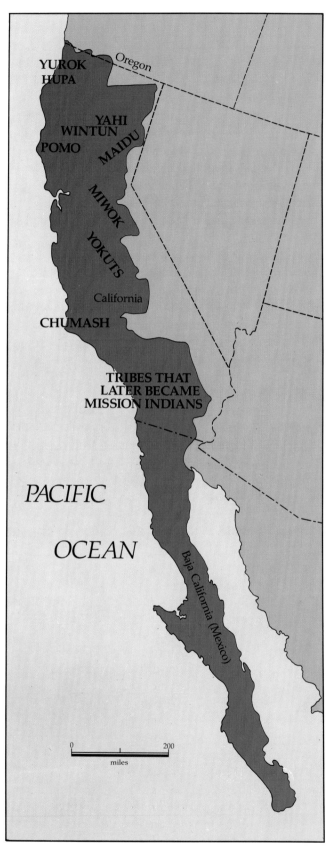

The California Culture Area, showing the approximate locations of Indian tribes listed in this book—circa 1500, before displacement by non-Indians (with modern boundaries)

speaking tribes in the culture area are Akwaala, Diegueño, Kamia, plus tribes to the south in Baja California, now part of Mexico.

Among the Penutian tribes, speaking dialects of a number of small language families, are Costanoan, MAIDU, MIWOK, WINTUN, and YOKUTS.

Among the Uto-Aztecan-speaking tribes, mostly in the south, are Alliklik, Cahuilla, Cupeño, Fernandeño, Gabrieliño, Juaneño, Kitanemuk, Luiseño, Nicoleño, Serrano, Tubatulabal, and Vanyume. Many of these Uto-Aztecan peoples came to be known historically as MISSION INDIANS.

Other languages are identified in the California Culture Area as well: dialects of Algonquian (Ritwan subgroup), spoken by the Wiyot and YUROK, making these peoples the westernmost ALGONQUIANS; and a language family known as Yukian (of undetermined phylum affiliation), spoken by the Huchnom, Wappo, and Yuki.

Food

The dietary staple of California Indians was the acorn, the fruit of the oak tree. Native peoples collected them in the fall. They removed the kernels from the shells, placed them in the sun to dry out, pounded them into a flour, then repeatedly poured hot water over the flour to remove the bitter-tasting tannic acid. Then they boiled the acorn meal into a soup or mush or baked it into a bread. Other wild plant foods included berries, nuts, seeds, greens, roots, bulbs, and tubers. Sun-dried berries, roots, and seeds also were used to make cakes.

California Indians also ate insects. They picked grubs and caterpillars off plants. They boiled the caterpillars with salt, considering them a delicacy. They drove grasshoppers into pits, then roasted them. And they collected honeydew as another delicacy, rolling it into pellets. (Insects called aphids suck the juices of plants and secrete sweet-tasting honeydew.)

Rabbits were common throughout the culture area. The Indians used snares and other kinds of traps to catch them, as well as bows and arrows and clubs. To catch deer, California Indians journeyed into the hill country, hunting with bows and arrows or herding them into corrals. Waterfowl also provided meat. Ducks, geese, swans, and other birds migrating from the north in the autumn descended on the marshes. The Indians shot at them from blinds with bows and arrows or bagged them from boats with nets.

California Indians had many different methods of fishing, including hooks and lines, spears, nets, and

weirs. Lakes, rivers, and the sea offered their catch. Along the seashore and in tidal basins, the Indians also gathered clams, oysters, mussels, abalones, and scallops. And they hunted seals and sea otters.

Houses

California Indians lived in many different kinds of houses. The most typical house throughout the culture area was cone-shaped, about eight feet in diameter at the base. It was constructed from poles covered with brush, grass, reeds, or mats of tule (a kind of bulrush). Other kinds of dwellings included domed earth-covered pithouses and lean-tos of bark slabs. In the northern part of the culture area, some Indians built wood plank houses more typical of the NORTHWEST COAST INDIANS. Most of the California houses served as single-family dwellings, but some were communal or ceremonial. Others served as sweathouses.

One type of California dwelling, tule (cattail) over a framework of poles

Clothing

Clothing in much of the region was minimal because of the warm climate. Men often went completely naked or wore simple animal-skin or bark breechcloths. Women always wore at least fringed aprons in the front and back, made from animal skins or shredded willow bark. After the coming of the whites, cotton came to replace bark in many instances. Headwear included basket hats, iris fiber hairnets, feather headbands, and feather crowns. Some California Indians went barefoot; others wore ankle-high leather moccasins or sandals made from the yucca plant. In cold weather, robes and blankets of rabbit skin, sea-otter fur, or feathers were draped over the shoulders. Shell jewelry was widespread, as was the practice of tattooing.

Transportation

With regard to transportation, California Indians usually traveled by foot. But they also had different kinds of craft for transporting supplies by water. Some peoples, such as the Yurok, made simple dugouts, carved from redwood logs. Rafts were more common in the culture area, made from logs or from tule. The tule rafts are known as balsas. The tule reeds were tied together into watertight bundles. The bundles would become waterlogged after repeated use, but would dry out in the sun. One tribe, the Chumash, made boats out of pine planks lashed together with fiber cordage and caulked with asphalt, the only plank boats made by Native Americans.

Arts and Crafts

California Indians are famous for their basketry. They used baskets for cooking, placing heated stones in them to boil water (stone-boiling), as well as for carrying, storing, winnowing, and other purposes. There were six to eight different kinds of baskets alone for processing acorns. Basketwork was also used to make hats, mats, traps, and baby carriers. The Pomo decorated their baskets with feathers.

Other California household items included wooden and ceramic bowls, soapstone (steatite) vessels, antler and shell spoons, tule mats, and wooden headrests. Ceremonial objects included stone and clay pipes; rattles made from gourds, rawhide, turtle-shell, deer hooves, and cocoons; plus various other instruments, including drums, flutes, whistles, bull-roarers, and stick-clappers. Strings of disk-shaped dentalium shells were used as a medium of exchange. Trading was widespread among California peoples.

Religion

Some California tribes had single shamans; others had secret societies made up of several members, such as the Kuksu cult of the Wintun and Maidu, and other tribes of the central California region. Initiation rites were important to most California peoples, especially rites involving passage from childhood into adulthood. Death rites were also important. Many California Indians, especially in the central and southern region, cremated their dead. As with all Native Americans, music and dancing played an important part in ceremonies. Some peoples used a tea made from parts of the poisonous jimsonweed plant to induce visions.

Social Structure

Concerning social and political organization, the California peoples were not made up of true tribes, but rather interrelated villages. The term *tribelet* is often applied to California Indians in reference to the relationship between the permanent central village and temporary satellite villages. A single chief, a fatherly figure, presided over each tribelet. Most clans, groups of related families within the tribelet, were traced through the father's line. California Indians did not have war chiefs, as did other Native Americans, nor systems of bestowing war honors. Warfare was usually carried out for the purpose of revenge rather than for acquiring food, slaves, or possessions.

Recreation

California Indians enjoyed many kinds of games. One favorite was hoop-and-pole, in which a pole was thrown or slid at a rolling hoop. Another game involved catching a ring on a stick or throwing the ring at a pin, as in quoits. Ball games were also popular, including a variety of both lacrosse and soccer. Shinny, in which participants used curved sticks to throw blocks of wood, was also widespread. Indoor games included dice and other counting and betting games. Cat's cradle, in which a string looped on one person's hands in the shape of a cradle is transferred to another person, was a favorite hand game.

As this book shows time and again, it is difficult to generalize about Indian tribes even in a region where the peoples had as many cultural traits in common as they did in the California Culture Area. In order to grasp the subtleties and distinctions among California Indians and what happened to them after contacts with non-Indians, see the entries for particular tribes: Hupa and Yurok, northern California tribes; Maidu, Miwok, Wintun, Yahi, and Yokuts, central California tribes; and Chumash, a southern California tribe. Other California Indians are discussed as Mission Indians.

CALUSA

The Calusa were cannibals, pirates, and master builders and carvers. Or were they? Were they a Muskogean-speaking people from the north or some unknown people, perhaps even migrants from the Caribbean or South America?

The Calusa (pronounced cuh-LOO-suh) lived along the Gulf Coast of the Florida peninsula from present-day Tampa Bay southward to the Florida Keys. One mystery surrounding these people is their origin. It is thought that they were related linguistically to other Muskogeans of the Southeast Culture Area, but this connection is not known for certain. Since the Calusa had as many cultural traits in common with native peoples across the Gulf of Mexico as with other SOUTHEAST INDIANS, for example the use of blowguns for hunting and fighting and the use of poison for fishing, it has even been theorized that they arrived in Florida from the sea. In any case, it is known that the Calusa had seaworthy dugout canoes and communicated with the ARAWAK (TAINO) of the Caribbean.

The Calusa perhaps had another trait typical of native peoples to their south—human sacrifice, along with cannibalism. Some North American tribes practiced cannibalism, but it was usually for ritualistic purposes, such as eating an enemy's heart to gain his strength. Eating human flesh for survival, as some South American tribes did, was rare. The exact extent of the Calusa cannibalism is unknown, however. Early explorers sometimes exaggerated the extent of the practice in their writings about Indians. (A captive among them in the mid-1500s, the Spaniard Hernando de Escalante Fontaneda, claimed their name means "fierce people," although others assert it was derived from the Spanish name *Carlos* after Charles V, King of Spain.)

It is known that the Calusa had a class system similar to that of both Caribbean and Southeast tribes, with nobles, commoners, and slaves. Slaves were for the most part captives from other tribes.

The Calusa have been referred to as pirates. By the time the Spanish had contact with them in the 1500s, the Calusa already had quantities of gold and silver. Some Calusa might have raided Spanish galleons on treasure runs from Mexico to Spain. Others might have attacked shipwrecked crews. In any case, it is known for certain that the Calusa were beachcombers who gathered the cargos of ships destroyed in the tricky waters off their coast.

One other tantalizing mystery surrounds the Calusa. Were they the Indians of Key Marco? In 1884, an archaeologist by the name of Frank Hamilton Cushing

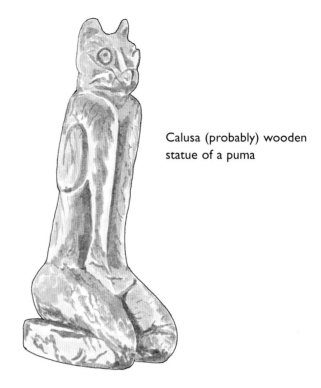

Calusa (probably) wooden statue of a puma

found on this small island the remains of a highly developed culture, including human-made seawalls, jetties, and drainage basins; shell, bone, and tooth tools; and exquisitely carved wooden masks and wooden animal figures with movable parts. These complex structures and beautifully crafted objects may have been the work of early Calusa.

What is known about the Calusa comes from the writings of early Spanish explorers as well as from those of later Euroamerican military men and settlers. Other tribes have also passed on information about the Calusa through their own oral traditions.

It is known that Juan Ponce de León, the man who claimed Florida for Spain and gave that part of North America its name (*florida* is the Spanish word for "flowers"), visited the Calusa Indians in 1513; Diego Miruelo made contact with them in 1516; and Hernandes de Córdoba did in 1517. Ponce de León again landed among them in 1521, with intentions of founding a settlement. But he offended his hosts, who attacked him and his men, fatally wounded him with an arrow, and forced the Spaniards back to Cuba. A Spaniard by the name of Hernando de Escalante Fontaneda was shipwrecked on Calusa shores and held captive from 1551 to 1569. He wrote about his experience, recording details of Calusa lifeways.

The Spanish again tried to establish a mission among the Calusa about this same period, but they abandoned the post before very long without having converted the tribal member to Catholicism. Because of their trade relations with the Spanish, the Calusa were later subject to attacks by the British and their Indian allies. By 1745, many Calusa, along with APALACHEE and TIMUCUA, had been taken to the Carolinas as slaves. Other Calusa emigrated to the West Indies to escape the raids.

Descendants of those Calusa who stayed behind later fought alongside the SEMINOLE in the Second Seminole War of 1835–42. In 1839, a band of Calusa, calling themselves Muspa after a village name, attacked the camp of Colonel William Harney, killing 18 of his men. What happened to the Calusa after this period is not known. Perhaps remaining tribal members traveled west with the Seminole or disappeared into the Everglades with them. Perhaps survivors followed their ancestors to Cuba. Their ultimate fate is a mystery, like so much else about this tribe.

CARRIER

The name of the Carrier (or Carriers), translated into English from the dialect of a neighboring tribe and pronounced as spelled, refers to a custom in which a widow had to carry the charred bones of her dead husband in a basket for three years. The French name for Carrier is *Porteur,* with the same meaning. The Carrier preferred to use their various band names or, starting in the 1900s, the shared name *Takulli,* meaning "people who go upon the water."

The Carrier ancestral homeland is located in the southwestern corner of the cultural region known as the Subarctic Culture Area (see SUBARCTIC INDIANS). Their territory included the headwaters of the Fraser River as well as the territory around Babine, Stuart, and François Lakes. This rugged terrain lies between the Coast Mountains and the Rocky Mountains in present-day British Columbia. Other ATHAPASCANS living near them in the foothills of the Rocky Mountains with similar ways of life were the Chilcotin, Nahane, Sekani, Tahltan, and Tsetsaut, and Tutchone (Mountain).

The Carrier, like other Subarctic peoples, were hunter-gatherers who did not farm at all. They hunted the caribou and other game in the forests; they fished the lakes and rivers; they foraged for roots and berries. They wore leather clothing—robe, leggings, and moccasins, with a cap and mittens for cold weather.

But the Carrier are an interesting cultural mix because they had lifeways in common with NORTHWEST COAST INDIANS west of them along the Pacific Coast as well as lifeways in common with PLATEAU INDIANS south of them along the Columbia River. For example, like Northwest Coast peoples, the Carrier lived in villages of plank houses much of the year; they had social classes of nobles, commoners, and slaves; tribal members could

Carrier moccasins (modern)

improve their social position through the potlatch, the custom of giving possessions away for prestige; warriors wore armor made from slats of wood; and they prized Chilkat blankets that they received in trade from coastal peoples, such as the TLINGIT. Like the Plateau Indians, the Carrier depended on fish as their primary food staple, pursuing salmon during the summer runs up the rivers. They also built pithouses like the Columbia Plateau peoples' for winter use. Nor were their summer houses the conical skin tents typical of the Subarctic peoples, but rather open shelters with spruce-bark roofs and no walls. Another way the Carrier differed from other Subarctic Indians: They did not use snowshoes or toboggans.

The Carrier, being an inland western people, avoided early contacts with whites. Alexander Mackenzie, the Scots explorer and fur trader who worked for the North West Company out of Montreal, visited the Carrier in 1793 during his journey across North America. Simon Fraser, another Canadian explorer for the North West

Company, established trading posts in Carrier territory in 1805–06. And in 1843, a Catholic missionary, Father Demers, began work among the Carrier. Many miners came to Carrier country, starting in the late 1850s. The building of the Canadian Pacific transcontinental railroad, completed in 1885, brought more white settlers to the Carrier homeland. Contacts with non-Indians brought epidemics to the Carrier and eroded their traditional way of life.

The Carrier have gradually rebuilt their lives. They work in a variety of fields, including farming and railroad work. Some tribal members earn a living through hunting and trapping as their ancestors did. The various Carrier bands hold about 100 small reserves in British Columbia.

CATAWBA

For a long time, scholars were unable to place the unusual Catawba dialect in any language family. Now it is thought that the dialect is Siouan. There were many other Siouan-speaking peoples in the Southeast, especially in the Carolinas and Virginia, but few exist as tribes today. The Waccamaw of South Carolina, like the Catawba, still have communities there.

Catawba pottery

The Catawba occupied ancestral territory in the present-day border region between North and South Carolina. Like most SOUTHEAST INDIANS, they were village dwellers depending heavily on agriculture for food. They typically located their villages along river valleys, especially along the Catawba River. Their native name, *Issa* or *Essa,* in fact means "people of the river." *Catawba,* pronounced cuh-TAW-buh, possibly is derived from the CHOCTAW *katapa* or *katapu,* for "divided" or "separated," or from the YUCHI *kotaha,* "robust men." The Catawba lived in pole-frame, bark-covered houses. They also constructed temples of worship, as did other Southeast tribes. They supplemented their diet with fish and game from river and forest. They were skilled potters.

The Catawba, once a very numerous and powerful tribe, were traditional enemies of the CHEROKEE. Catawba war parties traveled great distances to raid other Indians, sometimes even across the Appalachian Mountains to the Ohio Valley.

The Spanish were the first Europeans to have contact with the Catawba, in the latter part of the 1500s. The English explored, settled, and developed the region in the late 1600s and early 1700s. The Catawba wanted European trade goods, so when war broke out between the colonists and the TUSCARORA in 1711–13, they aided the colonists. In the Yamasee War of 1715, however, some Catawba war parties joined the YAMASEE in attacks on British settlements, rebelling against unfair trade practices, forced labor, and slave raids on Indians. After this brief period of unrest, the Catawba maintained peace with the colonists. But their numbers were steadily depleted. European diseases took their toll on them. Two outbreaks of the dreaded smallpox, in 1738 and 1758, reduced the tribe by more than half. The Catawba also suffered from attacks by other Indians who were not always on friendly terms with the colonists, such as the SHAWNEE and the IROQUOIS (HAUDENOSAUNEE). The Catawba sided with the rebels in the American Revolution against the British.

The Catawba had villages on both sides of the North and South Carolina border. Up until 1762, they lived mainly in North Carolina. Afterward, they lived mostly in South Carolina, where they came to hold reservation lands.

Many other Siouan peoples of the region merged with the Catawba, such as the Cheraw, Congaree, Eno, Pee Dee, and Wateree, as possibly did the Keyaunee, Santee, Sewee, Sissipahaw, and Sugeree. In the 1800s, some Catawba settled among the Cherokee and Choctaw.

The Catawba relationship with the federal government as a unified tribe ended in 1962 during the federal Indian policy of Termination. At that time, the tribe distributed its remaining lands to individuals, many of whom still hold the same tracts. In 1993, the Catawba received $50 million in compensation for a land claim against the state of South Carolina. The settlement bill passed by the U.S. Congress included the restoration of federal status.

The Catawba Indian Nation operates out of Rock Hill, South Carolina. The Catawba are the only eastern tribe to maintain pure pottery-making techniques going back to pre-contact times. The Catawba Pottery Association helps maintain this tradition through classes.

CAYUGA

The Cayuga (pronounced kah-YOO-guh), one of the five original tribes in the Iroquois League, had cultural traits in common with other IROQUOIS (HAUDENOSAUNEE). Yet the Cayuga were a distinct group of NORTHEAST INDIANS with their own villages, leaders, and traditions.

The Cayuga ancestral homeland is located in the Finger Lakes country of what now is New York State, especially along the longest of the lakes (38 miles), Cayuga Lake, named after them. Sandwiched between the SENECA to the west and the ONONDAGA to the east, the Cayuga controlled the smallest expanse of territory of all the tribes in the Iroquois Confederacy. They had at least 13 important villages. Since many of these villages were near wetlands, the Cayuga were known as the "people of the great swamp." The native version, *Guyohkohnyoh,* also has been translated as "people of the place where the boats were taken out," referring to a town Oioguen, or "people of the place where locusts were taken out." The Cayuga sent 10 sachems, or chiefs, as tribal representatives to the confederacy's Great Council. The Cayuga totem, or symbol, at the annual gathering was the Great Pipe.

Cayuga headdress. (Different Iroquois tribes used varying numbers of feathers.)

In 1774, the year before the American Revolution, Iroquois living on the Ohio and Scioto Rivers in Pennsylvania, known as the Mingo band, joined the SHAWNEE in their fight against the British in Lord Dunmore's War. The Mingo chief Logan was a Cayuga.

Yet during the American Revolution, when the various Haudenosaunee tribes chose sides, most Cayuga sided with the British, along with the MOHAWK, Onondaga, and Seneca, against the American rebels. Their former allies, the ONEIDA and TUSCARORA, opposed them. After American victory in the war, many Cayuga migrated to Ontario, Canada, where they were granted lands along with the Mohawk and other Iroquois who had sided with the British. Their shared reserve at Oshweken on the Grand River is called the Six Nations Reserve. Other

An Iroquois boy of the Six Nations

Cayuga settled with the Seneca and Onondaga in New York. The Seneca-Cayuga tribe of Oklahoma is a federally recognized group in Ottawa County, Oklahoma.

Cayuga representatives have been pursuing a land claim against the state of New York. As the Cayuga Peter Wilson (Wa-o-wo-wa-no-onk) communicated to the New-York Historical Society in 1847 about ancestral lands:

That land of Ganono-o—or "Empire State" as you love to call it—was once laced by our trails from Albany to Buffalo—trails that we had trod for centuries—trails worn so deep by the feet of the Iroquois that they became your own roads of travel. . . . Your roads still traverse those same lines of communication and bind one part of the Longhouse to another. The land of *Ganono-o,* the Empire State, then is our monument! We shall not long occupy much room in living. The single tree of the thousands which sheltered our forefathers— one old elm under which the representatives of the tribes were wont to meet—will cover us all. But we would have our bodies twined in death among its roots, on the very soil on whence it grew. . . . In your last war with England, your red brother—your elder brother—still came up to help you as of old on the Canada frontier. Have we, the first holders of this prosperous region, no longer a share in your history? Glad were your fathers to sit down upon the threshold of the Longhouse, rich did they then hold themselves in getting the mere sweeping from its door. Had our forefathers spurned you from it when the French were thundering at the opposite side to get a passage through and drive you into the sea, whatever has been the fate of other Indians, the Iroquois might still have been a nation, and I, instead of pleading here for the privilege of living within your borders—I—I might have had a country!

CAYUSE

The name of the Cayuse, pronounced ki-YOOS, has come to mean "pony" in the English language. The original meaning of their name is unknown. But since the Cayuse were such proficient horsebreeders and horsedealers, their tribal name has taken on the general meaning of a small, domesticated Indian horse. Their native name is *Waiilatpu.*

The Cayuse occupied ancestral territory along tributaries of the Columbia River, such as the Grande Ronde, Umatilla, and Wallawalla rivers, in what today is northeast Oregon and southeast Washington. They are classified as part of the Plateau Culture Area (see PLATEAU INDIANS). The Cayuse dialect of Penutian, called Waiilatpuan, was spoken only by one other people, the neighboring Molala. The Cayuse lived in oblong lodges as well as in cone-shaped tents, each type of structure covered with woven-reed mats or buffalo hides. The family made up the most important social unit, with several families organized into bands with chiefs. Salmon, deer, small game, roots, and berries were the main food sources.

The Cayuse were famous as traders, exchanging buffalo robes and reed mats with the coastal Indians for shells and other items. Horses, brought to North America by the Spanish, reached them in the early 1700s and became their most important product for trade with other Indians. In later years, once the fur trade with whites was under way, the Cayuse traded buffalo robes and other animal pelts for guns, tools, and blankets.

The Cayuse were involved in the first war between Indians and whites in the Columbia Plateau region, the Cayuse War of 1847–50. Earlier, in 1836, about 30 years after the Lewis and Clark Expedition had opened this part of North America to white settlement, Marcus Whitman founded a Presbyterian mission known as Waiilatpu among the Cayuse. His wife, Narcissa Whitman, came with him from the East. She and Eliza Spalding, the wife of Henry Spalding, another missionary to the region, were the first white women to cross North America.

Even though they worked among the Cayuse for 10 years, the Whitmans never developed a strong rapport with the Indians. They were intolerant of Indian culture and beliefs and demanded conversion to Presbyterian ways. Moreover, when increasing numbers of white emigrants arrived in Oregon Country, the Whitmans turned their attention to them and became rich from trade and land sales, keeping the money for themselves and not sharing it with the Indians who worked alongside them.

The particular incident that sparked the Cayuse War was an outbreak of measles. Cayuse children enrolled at

A Cayuse man with pony and dog

the mission school came down with the disease and started an epidemic among the Indians. Cayuse leaders blamed the missionaries. In 1847, two Cayuse, Chief Tilokaikt and Tomahas, came to the mission for medicine. Before leaving, however, they attacked Marcus Whitman and killed him with tomahawk blows. Soon afterward, other Cayuse raided the mission, killing 11 other whites, including Narcissa Whitman.

Oregon Country organized a volunteer army under clergyman Cornelius Gilliam. When the militiamen attacked an encampment of innocent Cayuse, killing as many as 30, other Indians, including warriors from the PALOUSE and WALLA WALLA, joined the Cayuse cause. Gilliam's continuing campaign enraged other Indians and threatened to unite even more Plateau tribes in a general uprising. When Gilliam was killed by his own gun in an accident, his troops abandoned the field.

Tilokaikt and Tomahas hid out for two more years. Growing tired of the fugitive life and hoping for mercy from white courts, they surrendered. But white jurors convicted them of murder and the judge sentenced them to hang. Before their execution, the two rejected Presbyterian rites and asked for Catholic ones instead.

The Cayuse War hastened the pace of change in Oregon Country. The federal government established new military posts in the region and organized a territorial government. Furthermore, many tribes of the Columbia Plateau now distrusted whites. Other wars eventually occurred. The Cayuse supported the YAKAMA and BANNOCK in the Yakama War of 1855–59 and the Bannock War of 1878. Some Cayuse also settled among the NEZ PERCE and fought alongside them in their uprising of 1877.

Most Cayuse were settled with the UMATILLA and the Walla Walla on a reservation, established in 1853. Their descendants live there today, with a tribal headquarters for Confederated Tribes of the Umatilla Indian Reservation in Pendleton, Oregon.

CHEROKEE

The Trail of Tears occupies a special place in Native American history. Many tribes have similar incidents from their history, as this book shows, such as the CHICKASAW, CHOCTAW, CREEK, and SEMINOLE. Yet this event, the name of which originally was applied to the Cherokee, has come to symbolize the land cessions and

Cherokee cane-stalk blowgun plus darts

relocations of all Indian peoples, just as the Wounded Knee Massacre of 1890, involving the SIOUX (DAKOTA, LAKOTA, NAKOTA), has come to represent the numerous massacres of Indian innocents.

When Europeans first arrived in North America, the Cherokee occupied a large expanse of territory in the Southeast. Their homeland included mountains and valleys in the southern part of the Appalachian chain. They had villages in the Great Smoky Mountains of what now is western North Carolina and the Blue Ridge of present-day western Virginia and West Virginia, as well as in the Great Valley of present-day eastern Tennessee. They also lived in the Appalachian high country of what now is South Carolina and Georgia, and as far south as present-day northern Alabama. Cherokee people also probably lived in territory now part of Kentucky. At one time, they had more than 60 villages.

In Native American studies, this region of North America is classified within the Southeast Culture Area (see SOUTHEAST INDIANS). The Cherokee were the southernmost Iroquoian-speaking people. Their ancestral relatives, the IROQUOIS (HAUDENOSAUNEE), as well as most other Iroquoians, lived in what is defined as the Northeast Culture Area.

The Cherokee native name is *Ani-Yun'wiya,* meaning "principal people." The name *Cherokee,* pronounced CHAIR-uh-kee, probably is derived from the Choctaw name for them, *Tsalagi,* meaning "people of the land of caves." The LENNI LENAPE (DELAWARE) version of the same name is *Tallageni.* Some linguists theorize, however, that *Cherokee* is derived from the Creek name for them, *Tisolki,* or *Tciloki,* meaning "people of a different speech."

Lifeways

The Cherokee placed their villages along rivers and streams, where they farmed the rich black soil. Their crops included corn, beans, squash, pumpkins, sunflowers, and tobacco. They grew three different kinds of corn, or maize—one to roast, one to boil, and a third to grind into flour for cornbread. They also took advantage of the wild plant foods in their homeland, including edible roots, crab apples, berries, persimmons, cherries, grapes, hickory nuts, walnuts, and chestnuts.

The rivers and streams also provided food for the Cherokee, who used spears, traps, and hooks and lines to catch different kinds of fish. Another method included poisoning an area of water to bring the unconscious fish to the surface.

The Cherokee were also skilled hunters. They hunted large animals, such as deer and bear, with bows and arrows. To get close to the deer, they wore entire deerskins, antlers and all, and used deer calls to lure the animals to them. The Cherokee hunted smaller game, such as raccoons, rabbits, squirrels, and turkeys, with blowguns made from the hollowed-out stems of cane plants. Through these long tubes, the hunters blew small wood-and-feather darts with deadly accuracy from as far away as 60 feet.

The products of the hunt were also used for clothing. In warm weather, Cherokee men dressed in buckskin breechcloths and women in buckskin skirts. In cold weather, men wore buckskin shirts, leggings, and moccasins; women wore buckskin capes. Other capes, made from turkey and eagle feathers along with strips of bark, were used by Cherokee headmen for ceremonial purposes. Their leaders also wore feather headdresses on special occasions.

Ceremonies took place inside circular and domed council houses or domed seven-sided temples. The temples were usually located at the summit of flat-topped mounds in the central village plaza, a custom inherited from the earlier MOUND BUILDERS of the Southeast.

Cherokee river cane basket

Cherokee families, as is the case with other people of the Southeast, typically had two houses—a large summer home and a smaller winter home. The summer houses, rectangular in shape with peaked roofs, had pole frameworks, cane and clay walls, and bark or thatch roofs. The winter houses, which doubled as sweathouses, were placed over a pit with a cone-shaped roof of poles and earth. Cherokee villages were usually surrounded with walls of vertical logs, or palisades, for protection from hostile tribes.

The Cherokee practiced a variety of crafts, including plaited basketwork and stamped pottery. They also carved, out of wood and gourds, Booger masks, representing evil spirits. And they shaped stone pipes into animal figures, attached to wooden stems.

Cherokee Booger mask (The term *booger,* from which *bogeyman* comes, is African in origin, taken by the Cherokee from the native language of black slaves.)

Among the many Cherokee agricultural, hunting, and healing rituals, the most important was the Green Corn Ceremony. This annual celebration, shared by other tribes of the Southeast, such as the Creek, took place at the time of the ripening of the last corn crop.

Another important event for the Cherokee, shared with other Southeast peoples, was the game of lacrosse. This game was played between clans from the same villages as well as between clans from different villages. Chunkey, or *chenco,* a game played by throwing sticks at rolling stones, also was popular.

With regard to political and social organization, the many Cherokee villages, about 100, were allied in a loose confederacy. Within each village, there were two chiefs. The White Chief, also called the Most Beloved Man, helped the villagers make decisions concerning farming,

lawmaking, and disputes between individuals, families, or clans. He also played an important part in religious ceremonies, along with the Cherokee shamans. The Red Chief gave advice concerning warfare. One such decision was choosing who would be the War Woman, an honored woman chosen to accompany warriors on their war parties. The War Woman did not fight but helped feed the men, offered them council, and decided which prisoners would live or die. The Red Chief also was in charge of the lacrosse games, which the Cherokee called the "little war."

From First Contacts through the Colonial Years

Early explorers to encounter the Cherokee were impressed by their highly advanced culture. Hernando de Soto, the Spanish explorer who traveled throughout much of the Southeast, was the first European to come into contact with the Cherokee, when he arrived in their territory from the south in 1540. In later years, occasional French traders worked their way into Cherokee territory from the north. But the most frequent Cherokee-white contacts were with English traders from the east. The traders began appearing regularly after England permanently settled Virginia, starting with the Jamestown colony of 1607 and then, before long, the Carolina colonies.

In the French and Indian wars, lasting from 1689 to 1763, the Cherokee generally sided with the English against the French, providing warriors for certain engagements. In these conflicts, they sometimes found themselves fighting side by side with other Indian tribes that had been their traditional enemies, such as the Iroquois.

In 1760, however, the Cherokee revolted against their English allies in the Cherokee War. The precipitating incident involved a dispute over wild horses in what is now West Virginia. A group of Cherokee on their journey home from the Ohio River, where they had helped the English take Fort Duquesne, captured some wild horses. Some Virginia frontiersmen claimed the horses as their own and attacked the Cherokee, killing 12. Then they sold the horses and collected bounties on the Cherokee scalps, which they claimed they had taken from Indians allied with the French.

On learning of this incident, various Cherokee bands, led by Chief Oconostota, began a series of raids on white settlements. The Cherokee warriors managed to capture Fort Loudon in the Great Valley of the Appalachians. The war lasted two years, before the British troops defeated the militant bands by burning their villages and crops. Even then, many insurgents continued to fight from their mountain hideouts for a period of time. Eventually, war-weary and half-starving, the holdouts surrendered. In the peace pact, the Cherokee were forced to give up a large portion of their eastern lands lying closest to British settlements.

In spite of the Cherokee War, the Cherokee supported the British against the rebels in the American Revolution of 1775–83. Most of their support consisted of sporadic attacks on outlying American settlements. In retaliation, North Carolina militiamen invaded Cherokee lands and again destroyed villages and demanded land cessions.

During the colonial years, the Cherokee also suffered from a number of epidemics. The worst outbreaks—from the dreaded smallpox that killed so many native peoples—occurred in 1738 and 1750.

Tribal Transformation

Despite these various setbacks, the Cherokee rebuilt their lives. They learned from the settlers around them, adopting new methods of farming and business. They now were faithful allies of the Americans, even fighting with them under Andrew Jackson in the Creek War of 1813. A Cherokee chief named Junaluska personally saved Jackson's life from a tomahawk-swinging Creek warrior at the Battle of Horseshoe Bend. In 1820, the Cherokee established among themselves a republican form of government, similar to that of the United States. In 1827, they founded the Cherokee Nation under a constitution with an elected principal chief, a senate, and a house of representatives.

Much of the progress among the Cherokee resulted from the work of Sequoyah, also known as George Gist. In 1809, he began working on a written version of the Cherokee language so that his people could have a written constitution, official records, books, and newspapers like the whites around them. Over a 12-year period, he devised a written system that reduced the Cherokee language to 85 characters representing all the different sounds. Sequoyah is the only person in history to invent singlehandedly an entire alphabet (or a syllabary, because the characters represent syllables). In 1821, he finished his vast project. In 1827, tribal leaders wrote down their constitution. And in 1828, the first Cherokee newspaper, the *Cherokee Phoenix,* was published in their language.

The Trail of Tears

Despite the new Cherokee way of life, the settlers wanted the Indians' lands. The discovery of gold near Dahlonega,

Georgia, helped influence white officials to call for the relocation of the Cherokee, along with other eastern Indians. In 1830, President Andrew Jackson signed the Indian Removal Act to relocate the eastern tribes to an Indian Territory west of the Mississippi River.

Despite the fact that the principal chief of the Cherokee, the great orator John Ross, passionately argued and won the Cherokee case before the Supreme Court of the United States; despite the fact that Junaluska, who had saved Jackson's life, personally pleaded with the president for his people's land; despite the fact that such great Americans as Daniel Webster, Henry Clay, and Davy Crockett supported the Cherokee claims; still, President Jackson ordered the eastern Indians' removal. And so began the Trail of Tears.

The state of Georgia began forcing the Cherokee to sell their lands for next to nothing. Cherokee homes and possessions were plundered. Whites destroyed the printing press of the *Cherokee Phoenix* because it published articles opposing Indian removal. Soldiers began rounding up Cherokee families and taking them to internment camps in preparation for the journey westward. With little food and unsanitary conditions at these hastily built stockades, many Cherokee died. In the meantime, some tribal members escaped to the mountains of North Carolina, where they successfully hid out from the troops.

The first forced trek westward began in the spring of 1838 and lasted into the summer. On the 800-mile trip, travelers suffered because of the intense heat. The second mass exodus took place in the fall and winter of 1838–39 during the rainy season; the wagons bogged down in the mud, and then came freezing temperatures and snow. On both journeys, many died from disease and inadequate food and blankets. The soldiers drove their prisoners on at a cruel pace, not even allowing them to bury their dead properly. Nor did they protect Cherokee families from attacks by bandits.

During the period of confinement, plus the two separate trips, about 4,000 Cherokee died, almost a quarter of their total. More Cherokee died after arrival in the Indian Territory because of epidemics and continuing shortages of food. During the 1830s, other Southeast tribes endured similar experiences, including the Chickasaw, Choctaw, Creek, and Seminole.

The Indian Territory

The Indian Territory was supposed to be a permanent homeland for various tribes. Originally, the promised region stretched from the state boundaries of Arkansas, Missouri, and Iowa to the 100th meridian, about 300 miles at the widest point. Nonetheless, with increasing white settlement west of the Mississippi in the mid-1800s, the Indian Territory was reduced again and again.

In 1854, by an act of Congress, the northern part of the Indian Territory became the territories of Kansas and Nebraska, which later became states. Starting in 1866 after the Civil War, tribes living in those regions were resettled on lands to the south, supposedly reserved for the Southeast tribes, now known as the "Five Civilized Tribes."

During the 1880s, the Boomers arrived—white home-seekers squatting on Indian reservations. Various white interests—railroad and bank executives, plus other developers—lobbied Congress for the opening of more Indian lands to white settlement.

Assimilation and Allotment

In 1887, Congress passed the General Allotment Act (or the Dawes Severalty Act). Under this law, certain Indian reservations held by tribes were to be divided and allotted to heads of Indian families. Some politicians believed that the law would help Indians by motivating individuals to develop the land. They also believed it would bring about the assimilation of Indians into the mainstream American culture. But others were just interested in obtaining Indian lands, since it was much easier to take advantage of individuals than of whole tribes. Many of the same people advocated stamping out Indian culture and religion and sending Indian children to white-run boarding schools. This period in United States Indian policy sometimes is referred to as the Assimilation and Allotment period.

By 1889, 2 million acres had been bought from the Indians, usually at ridiculously low prices, and thrown open to non-Indian settlement. The Oklahoma Land Run took place that year, with settlers lining up at a starting point to race for choice pieces. Those who cheated and entered the lands open for settlement were called "sooners." In 1890, Oklahoma Territory was formed from these lands.

Cherokee and Choctaw leaders refused allotment and took their case to federal courts, as John Ross had done years before. In reaction, Congress passed the Curtis Act of 1898, designed to dissolve their tribal governments and tribal courts and extended land Allotment policy to them against their wishes. Piece by piece, the Indian lands continued to be taken. Oklahoma, all of which had once been Indian land, became a state in 1907.

During this period, in 1924, the federal government passed the Citizenship Act, conferring citizenship on all Native Americans. Two states—Arizona and New Mexico—delayed giving Indians voting rights until much later.

Restoration and Reorganization

In 1934, with the Indian Reorganization Act (or the Wheeler-Howard Act), the policies of Assimilation and Allotment ended. This was the start of the Tribal Restoration and Reorganization period, sponsored by President Franklin D. Roosevelt and his commissioner of Indian affairs, John Collier. The Cherokee and other native peoples began to rediscover their cultural heritage, which the assimilationists had tried to take away, and to reorganize their tribal leadership into vital and effective governing bodies.

Yet those tribes who underwent allotment never regained the lands lost to whites. Remaining Indian lands in Oklahoma are not called reservations, as most tribally held pieces are in other states. In Oklahoma, they are called Indian trust areas. Some are tribally owned and some are allotted to families or individuals. Yet by an act of Congress in 1936, the lands are protected from outside speculators.

Termination and Urbanization

The federal government went through other phases in its policy toward Indians. In the 1950s, some politicians sought to end the special protective relationship between the government and Indian tribes (see MENOMINEE). Indians in Oklahoma and elsewhere were encouraged to move to cities in order to join the economic mainstream. This phase of federal Indian policy is referred to as the Termination period.

Self-Determination

Termination as a policy failed. The Cherokee and other tribes knew that their best hope for a good life in modern times was tribal unity and cultural renewal as called for in the earlier policy of Restoration and Reorganization. Since the 1960s, the federal Indian policy has been one of tribal Self-Determination, which means Indian self-government and strong tribal identity.

Two Homelands

Cherokee tribal headquarters in the West is in Tahlequah, Oklahoma. Some of the western Cherokee have made money from oil and other minerals found on their lands. A famous American humorist by the name of Will Rogers was a western Cherokee. He gained a wide audience in the 1920s and 1930s through radio, movies, books, and newspapers. He was called the "cowboy philosopher."

Cherokee still live in the East too, in North Carolina, descendants of those who hid out in the mountains during the relocation period. They presently hold rights to the picturesque Cherokee Reservation in the Great Smoky Mountains in the western part of the state. The eastern Cherokee have operate a cooperative artists' and craftspeoples' organization known as Qualla; its members make crafts sold in stores all over North America. The Cherokee also run a lumber business, and motels, and shops and programs for tourists. The Cherokee lease some of these businesses to whites.

In 1984, the Cherokee Nation of Oklahoma and the Eastern Band of Cherokees held a joint council for the first time in almost 150 years. The groups now meet in council every two years.

In 1985, after having served as deputy chief, Wilma Mankiller became the first modern-day woman to become principal chief of a major Native American tribe, the Cherokee Nation of Oklahoma, when Ross Swim-mer resigned. She completed the remaining two years of his term. Then Mankiller won reelection in 1987 and again in 1991. She since has become a spokesperson and author on both Native American and women's issues. She wrote *Mankiller: A Chief and Her People* (with Michael Wallis; 1993); and she coedited *The Reader's Companion to the History of Women in America* (1998). Because of health problems, Mankiller decided not to run for reelection in 1995.

Among other Cherokee groups maintaining tribal identity are the following: in North Carolina, the Cherokee Indian Tribe of Robeson and Adjoining Counties and the Cherokee Indians of Hoke City; in Alabama, the Cherokee of Jackson City, the Cherokee of Northeast Alabama, the Cherokee of Southeast Alabama, the Echota Cherokee Tribe of Alabama, and the United Cherokee Tribe of Alabama; in Georgia, the Cherokee Indians of Georgia, the Georgia Tribe of Eastern Cherokee, the Southeastern Cherokee Confederacy; in Tennessee, the Red Clay Inter-Tribal Indian Band of Southeastern Cherokee Confederacy; in Florida, the Tuscola United Cherokee Tribe of Florida and Alabama; in Missouri, the Northern Cherokee Nation of the Old Louisiana Territory; and in Oregon, the Northwest Cherokee Wolf Band of Southeastern Cherokee Confederacy.

CHEYENNE

The Cheyenne native name, *Tsetchestahase, Tsistsistas,* or *Dzitsistas,* means "beautiful people" or "our people." *Cheyenne,* pronounced shy-ANN or SHY-ann, was the SIOUX (DAKOTA, LAKOTA, NAKOTA) name for the tribe, meaning "red talkers" or "people of a different speech." To the Sioux, a Siouan-speaking people, the Algonquian language of the Cheyenne sounded foreign.

Migrations

The Cheyenne originally lived close to other ALGONQUIANS in territory that is now Minnesota. They lived in permanent villages and practiced farming in addition to hunting and gathering. The general location and time period is confirmed in the historical records of the French explorer René-Robert Cavelier de La Salle. In 1680, a group of Cheyenne came to visit La Salle's fort in Illinois, the first time Europeans came into contact with members of the tribe.

At some point soon after this date, the Cheyenne crossed the Minnesota River and migrated westward into what is now North and South Dakota. They were probably pushed westward by hostile bands of Sioux and CHIPPEWA (OJIBWAY). The Cheyenne settled along the Missouri River, still living as villagers and farmers.

Sometime in the late 1700s, the Cheyenne gained use of the horse. During that period, their way of life became that of nomadic buffalo hunters on the grasslands of the Great Plains. As their legend tells it, they "lost the corn," meaning they stopped planting crops. They also gave up making pottery because it broke too easily on the trail. And the Cheyenne began living in temporary skin tipis instead of permanent earthlodges. Yet at least some Cheyenne bands still lived along the Missouri River in 1805, when Lewis and Clark made their expedition up the Missouri.

Sometime in the early 1800s, the Cheyenne migrated westward along the Cheyenne River, a branch of the

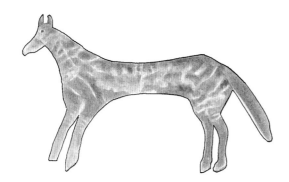

Cheyenne rawhide horse effigy

Missouri, into the Black Hills. During this period, another Algonquian people originally from east of the Missouri, known as the Sutaio tribe, merged with the Cheyenne and became one of the 10 bands of their camp circle.

The Sioux pushed the Cheyenne farther south to the vicinity of the North Platte River in what now is eastern Wyoming and western Nebraska. The Cheyennes in turn pushed the KIOWA southward.

About 1832, the Cheyenne separated into two groups. One branch stayed along the headwaters of the Platte River and became known to whites as the Northern Cheyenne. In time, they became allies of their former enemies, the Sioux. The other branch migrated farther south to the upper Arkansas River in what is now eastern Colorado and western Kansas. They became known as the Southern Cheyenne. In their new location, the Southern Cheyenne made war against the Kiowa and COMANCHE. But then in 1840, they formed a loose alliance with these two tribes against their enemies, the CROW, PAWNEE, SHOSHONE, UTE, and APACHE.

During this period too, the Northern Cheyenne became close allies of the Northern Arapaho, who lived near them in Wyoming. Likewise, the Southern Cheyenne became allies of the Southern Arapaho in Colorado. These various tribes—the Cheyenne, ARAPAHO, Sioux, Comanche, and Kiowa—were the most important players in the Native American struggle against whites for the Great Plains.

Lifeways

The Cheyenne are classified as part of the Great Plains Culture Area—that is, as PLAINS INDIANS—because of their nomadic lifestyle, their use of horses, their buffalo hunting, and their use of tipis.

As for their particular political organization, the Cheyenne were organized into the Council of Forty-four. Each of the 44 peace chiefs represented a band and

was the headman of an extended family. The responsibilities of the chiefs included such matters as settling disputes and deciding on when to move camp. The ideal character traits for these chiefs, and by extension all Cheyenne, were wisdom, calmness, kindliness, fairness, selflessness, generosity, energy, and bravery. The chiefs were concerned with the well-being of the tribe as a whole and also with the well-being of individuals. They readily made sacrifices to help others improve their life.

The Council of Forty-four also made decisions concerning tribal war policy and alliances with other tribes. But they involved themselves little in specific raids or military strategy. These decisions were left to the military societies. The chiefs on the Council of Forty-four had in all likelihood once been members of the soldier societies themselves. But after joining the council, they resigned from their military positions.

The military societies consisted of warriors from different bands, who carried out raids together and fought side by side. Members also met to review military campaigns in addition to discussing plans for future ones. Each society had its own rituals, sacred objects, symbols, and articles of clothing. In the case of the Cheyenne, the military societies were not grouped by age. Some tribes, such as the Arapaho, had societies based on age, with members graduating upward to different societies as the members got older.

Cheyenne societies included the Dog Soldiers, Fox, Elk (or Hoof Rattle), Shield, Bowstring (or Contrary), Wolf, and Northern Crazy Dogs societies. The last two came later in Cheyenne history than the others. The most famous of all of these was the *Hotamitanio,* or the Dog Soldiers, who played an important part in the wars against the United States for the Great Plains.

In Cheyenne social organization, the most important unit was the family, then the band, then the tribe as a whole. The Cheyenne had many rules governing behavior inside and outside these groups. For example, Cheyenne women were famous for their chastity. They were desired as wives only if they behaved properly before they were married.

Because of the taboo on relationships before marriage, courting was very complicated and prolonged. Sometimes it took a young man as long as four years to court his bride-to-be. He sometimes waited for hours day after day along a path she traveled daily—from her family's tipi to the stream where she went for water or the stand of trees where she went for firewood—hoping to have a word with her. He sometimes tugged on her robe as she walked by to get her attention, or whistled to her, or

Cheyenne backrest of willow rods, lashed together with sinew and supported by a wood tripod

called out to her. If she did not like him, she would never talk to him. But if she liked him, she eventually stopped to make small talk, but never about love. That came later after many meetings, when they finally met outside her tipi. Before the two could join in marriage, however, both families had to be consulted. And the man's family had to offer gifts to the woman's family to prove good intentions.

The most important ceremonies of the Cheyenne were the Arrow Renewal, the New Life Lodge, and the Animal Dance. The Arrow Renewal concerned the four Sacred Arrows of the tribe that were supposedly passed to the tribe by its legendary ancestral hero, Sweet Medicine. Sweet Medicine supposedly made a pilgrimage early in the tribe's history to the Sacred Mountains near the Black Hills where Maiyun, the Great Spirit, gave him four arrows—two for hunting and two for war. The Cheyenne kept the Sacred Arrows (Mahuts) in a medicine bundle with other tribal objects, including the Sacred Buffalo Hat (Isiwun), made from the hide of a female buffalo. The objects symbolized the collective existence of the tribe. After much planning, the 10 Cheyenne bands camped together once a year or every several years to renew the arrows. They placed their tipis in a circle. At the circle's center stood three special lodges—the Sacred Arrow Lodge, the Sacred Arrow Keeper's Lodge, and the Offering Lodge. During a four-day period, the male participants performed a series of rituals to renew the Sacred Arrows and in so doing renew the tribe.

The New Life Lodge, or Sun Dance, also was a renewal ceremony, performed yearly to make the world over again. Many Plains tribes practiced the Sun Dance with varying rituals. For all the tribes it was an eight-day ceremony, involving the building of a special lodge with a sacred pole in the center, rituals performed by medicine men, dancing before the pole, and self-torture. This last was usually carried out with ropes stretching from the center pole to skewers in the chests of men. When the participants danced or leaned backward, the skewers tore at their flesh, eventually ripping through it. This self-torture aspect of the ceremony led to the banning of the Sun Dance by the federal government in 1910.

The Animal Dance was a hunting ceremony supposedly taught to Sweet Medicine at the Sacred Mountain to help Cheyenne hunters provide enough food for their people. This five-day ceremony was held every year as long as there was an individual to organize the event. The first four days were given over to preparations, such as painting a wolf skin to be worn by the pledger and the building of a corral. Women helped in preparations for this event, unlike in the Arrow Renewal and Sun Dance. On the fifth day, the fun began for everyone. Men dressed up as animals. Members of the Bowstring Society pretended to hunt them and herd them into the corral. During the dance, these warriors did everything backwards. There was much clowning around, to the delight of all the spectators. Because of their silly backwards behavior, the Bowstring Society was also known as the Contrary Society, and the Animal Dance was also known as the Crazy Dance.

Wars for the Great Plains

Most of the Cheyenne bands wanted peace with the whites. Representatives signed a treaty with the federal government in 1825. Soon afterward, traders built Bent's Fort on the upper Arkansas River. The Southern Cheyenne settled nearby to trade with the newcomers. In 1849, the Cheyenne suffered from a devastating cholera epidemic, which killed as many as 2,000 of their people. In 1851, the Cheyenne participated in the first of two treaties signed at Fort Laramie in Wyoming, the purpose of which was to assure safe passage for white settlers along the Oregon Trail from Missouri to Oregon.

Yet white settlers violated the terms of the treaties. Prospectors entered the Cheyenne domain along the Smoky Hill Trail to the Rocky Mountains, and some of the Southern Cheyenne attacked them. Cavalrymen rode in to punish the militant bands in 1857, resulting in the Battle of Solomon Fork in western Kansas, where the cavalry mounted a saber charge to force the warriors to retreat.

The next year brought the start of the Pikes Peak gold rush, also known as the Colorado gold rush. Increasing numbers of miners and settlers came to Colorado to stay. In the following years, Colorado officials, especially Governor John Evans, sought to open up Cheyenne and Arapaho hunting grounds to white development. But the two tribes refused to sell their lands and move to reservations. Evans decided to force the issue through war and ordered volunteer state militiamen into the field under the Indian-hating territorial military commander Colonel John Chivington.

In the spring of 1864, Chivington launched a campaign of violence against the Cheyenne and Arapaho, his troops attacking any and all Indians, plundering their possessions and burning their villages. Indians began, raiding outlying settlements. This period of conflict is referred to as the Cheyenne-Arapaho War (or the Colorado War) of 1864–65.

The ongoing military campaign pressured the Indians into holding negotiations at Camp Weld outside Denver. At this meeting, tribal leaders were told that if they camped nearby and reported to army posts, they would be declaring peace and would be safe from attack. Black Kettle led his band of about 600 Southern Cheyenne, plus some Southern Arapaho, to Sand Creek near Fort Lyon. He informed the garrison of his people's peaceful intentions.

Shortly afterward, Chivington rode into the fort with the Third Cavalry. The post commander reported that Black Kettle's band had surrendered. But Chivington, believing in the policy of extermination of Indians, ignored him.

Sand Creek rates as one of the most cruel massacres in Indian history. Although it is not as famous as the incident involving the Sioux at Wounded Knee, it is just as horrible, with even more people dying. It is also important historically because it began the most intense period of warfare on the plains after the Civil War. It can be said that Wounded Knee ended those wars.

In the early morning of November 29, 1864, Chivington's men, many of them drunk, took up positions around the Indian camp. Black Kettle raised both a white flag of truce and a United States flag over his tipi. Yet Chivington ordered the attack. His men opened up with cannon and rifles. A few warriors, including Black Kettle, managed to take cover behind the high bank of Sand Creek and fight back briefly before escaping. When

A Cheyenne man with a sacred pipe

the shooting stopped, 200 Cheyenne were dead, more than half of them women and children.

Chivington was later denounced in a congressional investigation and forced to resign. Yet it was too late to prevent further warfare. The Indians who escaped the massacre spread word of it to other tribes. The incident confirmed the worst fears of tribal leaders about the behavior of the outsiders who had permanently invaded their homeland.

In the years after the Civil War, the army launched two campaigns against the Plains Indians—the Bozeman Campaign on the northern plains and the Hancock Campaign on the southern plains. In the War for the Bozeman Trail of 1866–68, some Northern Cheyenne under Dull Knife fought alongside Red Cloud's Sioux.

Cheyenne painted shield (taken by Custer on the Washita River in 1868)

To the south, after an unproductive parley with the Southern Cheyenne chiefs Tall Bull and White Horse, General Winfield Scott Hancock ordered troops to round up Cheyenne rebels. One of his leaders in the field was a young cavalry officer named George Armstrong Custer (who would later be killed in one of the greatest Indian victories in American history, at Little Bighorn). The war parties stayed one step ahead of the soldiers and continued their attacks on wagon trains, stagecoaches, mail stations, and railroad work sites.

The failure of the army in both the Bozeman and Hancock campaigns, plus the earlier massacre at Sand Creek, caused white officials to seek peace with the powerful plains tribes. In the Fort Laramie Treaty of 1868, the Sioux were granted a reservation on the northern plains. In the Medicine Lodge Treaty of 1867, the Southern Cheyenne and Southern Arapaho received lands in the Indian Territory, as did the Comanche and Kiowa.

Again whites violated the terms of the treaties, settling on Indian lands, and warriors continued their raids. Cheyenne Dog Soldiers attacked settlements along the Sabine and Solomon Rivers. General Philip Sheridan was given the new command. The first major conflict involving his troops was the Battle of Beecher Island in 1868, which ended in a stand-off. Lieutenant Frederick Beecher and a much-revered Dog Soldier named Roman Nose along with several others on both sides lost their lives in this battle.

The following winter, Sheridan launched a three-pronged attack, with three converging columns out of forts in Colorado, Kansas, and New Mexico, against Cheyenne, Arapaho, Comanche, and Kiowa. The Sheridan campaign broke the resistance of most Southern Cheyenne bands.

The first critical battle took place along the Washita River in the Indian Territory in November 1868. A column under Custer attacked Black Kettle's band. Even after Sand Creek, Black Kettle had never gone to war. He had led this group into the Indian Territory to avoid the fighting in Kansas and Colorado. But Custer, desperate for a victory, like Chivington four years before, attacked anyway. The Indians managed only a brief counterattack. Black Kettle and about 100 others died in this tragic repeat of history.

The army kept up its pressure. In March 1869, Southern Cheyenne bands under Little Robe and Medicine Arrows surrendered. Then soon after, the Dog Soldiers under Tall Bull were cut off by troops as they headed northward to join their northern relatives. Tall Bull and about 50 others died in the Battle of Summit Springs in Colorado.

Pockets of Southern Cheyenne resistance remained, however. Some Cheyenne warriors fought with the Comanche and Kiowa in the Red River War of 1874–75. Others reached the Northern Cheyenne and with them joined the War for the Black Hills of 1876–77, fighting at Little Bighorn in 1876 and getting their revenge on Custer by killing him and all his men. But the same year, a force under Colonel Wesley Merritt intercepted and defeated a force of about 1,000 Cheyenne at War Bonnet Creek in Nebraska before they could join up with Sitting Bull and Crazy Horse of the Sioux. Then troops under Ranald Mackenzie routed Northern Cheyenne under Dull Knife in the battle named after that famous Northern Cheyenne leader.

Cheyenne resistance had ended. Dull Knife's band was placed in the Indian Territory among the Southern Cheyenne. Spurred by scarce food rations, an outbreak of malaria, and a longing for their homeland in Wyoming and Montana, Dull Knife and his followers made an epic flight northward in September 1877. Crossing lands now developed by whites—having ranches, farms, roads, and railroads—the approximately 300 Cheyenne avoided a pursuing force of 13,000 for six weeks before they were finally caught. Many Cheyenne died in the bloody roundup, including Dull Knife's daughter. Dull Knife and others surrendered on the Sioux reservation at Pine Ridge in South Dakota. But other Cheyenne made it to the Tongue River in Montana. In 1884, after further negotiations, the Northern Cheyenne were finally granted reservation lands in Montana.

Contemporary Cheyenne

Most Northern Cheyenne still live on the Northern Cheyenne reservation. The tribal headquarters is located at Lame Deer, Montana. The Southern Cheyenne currently share federal trust lands with the Southern Arapaho in Oklahoma. Their tribal headquarters is located at Concho. Farming, ranching, and the leasing of mineral rights play an important part in the economies of both groups.

The Sacred Arrows and the Sacred Buffalo Hat, passed down from earlier generations, are still revered by Cheyenne traditionalists. Traditional Cheyenne arts still practiced include pipe carving, woodworking, feather-working, leather-working, and quillworking. Other Cheyenne artists have made a name for themselves in fine arts, drawing on traditional themes.

A prominent Northern Cheyenne who has succeeded in politics while also pursuing the craft of jewelry-making is Ben Nighthorse Campbell from Colorado. After having served in the U.S. House of Representatives in 1987–92, he was elected to the U.S. Senate in 1992, becoming the first Native American to serve as a senator in more than 60 years. As such, he was central to passage of the bills renaming Custer National Monument to Little Bighorn Battlefield National Monument and founding the National Museum of the American Indian as part of the Smithsonian Institution. Nighthouse Campbell was reelected in November 1998.

CHICKASAW

The heart of the Chickasaw ancestral homeland was located in what is now northern Mississippi, with some additional territory in present-day western Tennessee, western Kentucky, and eastern Arkansas. The Chickasaw were closely related in language and culture to the CHOCTAW of southern Mississippi. Both peoples had cultural ties to the CREEK living to the east in Alabama and Georgia. *Chickasaw* (pronounced CHICK-uh-saw) probably means "to leave."

In terms of political organization, the Chickasaw were somewhere between the Creek and the Choctaw; not as rigidly structured as the Creek, but not as informal as the Choctaw. None of these people had the elaborate social structure of the NATCHEZ, who also lived along the lower Mississippi River. The Chickasaw and these other Muskogean-speaking tribes are all classified as SOUTHEAST INDIANS.

Homeland and Lifeways

The land once inhabited by Chickasaw is a fertile floodplain formed by soil deposited when the Mississippi overflows its banks. The wild vegetation along the river is generally thick and low. Some trees, such as the bald cypress tree, grow in the lowland swamps of Mississippi and Louisiana. Drier parts of the floodplain have tall hardwood trees, such as oak, ash, and hickory. The black, moist soil of the floodplain makes for excellent farming. The forests are home to all sorts of wildlife, such as white-tailed deer and black bear. The Mississippi River and its several tributaries offer many kinds of fish, such as the huge Mississippi catfish, sometimes weighing as much as 200 pounds.

The Chickasaw typically built their villages on patches of high ground, safe from flooding. They placed them near stands of hardwood trees in order to have a source of wood for building houses and dugouts. They also sought fertile soil for planting corn, beans, squash, sunflowers, and melons. Chickasaw houses had the pole-frame construction found throughout much of the Southeast, with a variety of materials used as coverings—grass thatch, cane thatch, bark, or hide.

Contacts with Non-Indians

The Chickasaw, like other Indian peoples, practiced what some scholars have called the "law of hospitality." An English trader named James Adair, who lived among many tribes of the Southeast, including the Chickasaw, for almost 40 years in the 1700s, wrote:

> They are so hospitable, kind-hearted, and free, that they would share with those of their own tribe the last part of their own provisions, even to a single ear of corn; and to others, if they called when they were eating; for they have no stated meal time. An open, generous temper is

a standing virtue among them; to be narrow-hearted, especially to those in want, or to any of their own family, is accounted a great crime, and to reflect scandal on the rest of the tribe. Such wretched misers they brand with bad characters.

The Spanish had early contacts with the Chickasaw. Hernando de Soto led his expedition into their territory in 1541. True to the "law of hospitality," the Chickasaw let the outsiders live among them. But de Soto tried to force the tribal chiefs into providing 200 bearers to carry his supplies. He also had his men execute two Chickasaw for stealing pigs and cut off the hands of a third. In retaliation, the Chickasaw launched an attack on the conquistadores from three different directions, inflicting much damage before disappearing into the wilderness.

In the later colonial period, the Chickasaw became allies of the English. They were among the few tribes of the lower Mississippi not to join with the French in the French and Indian wars, and the Chickasaw support of the English created a balance of power in the region. English traders from the Carolinas, such as James Adair, helped keep this alliance with the Chickasaw intact.

In the 18th century the Chickasaw regularly attacked French travelers on the Mississippi River between New Orleans and Canada. The French ordered the Chickasaw to expel British traders. They also demanded the expulsion of Natchez refugees who had fled to Chickasaw villages after the Natchez Revolt of 1729. And the French armed their allies, the Choctaw, against the Chickasaw. But the Chickasaw refused to yield. They carried out raids against both the French and Choctaw. They even managed to halt all traffic on the Mississippi for a time. The French organized many armies against the Chicka-

saw—in 1736, 1741, and 1752—but they were all unsuccessful. The Chickasaw remained unconquered right up until 1763 and the ultimate English victory in the last of the French and Indian wars.

In the American Revolution of 1775–83, the Chickasaw attempted to remain neutral, although some warriors fought for both the British and the Americans. When the SHAWNEE chief Tecumseh tried to organize a united Indian stand against the United States in 1809–11, the Chickasaw again withheld total commitment.

Non-Indian settlement increased rapidly in the early 19th century. During the 1820s, many Chickasaw migrated west of the Mississippi by their own choice. But the majority remained in their ancestral homeland. In 1830, President Andrew Jackson signed the Indian Removal Act to relocate eastern Indians west of the Mississippi in a specified territory away from white settlements. The Chickasaw removal occurred mostly after 1837. This tribe did not suffer as much during the actual journey as the other relocated tribes—the CHEROKEE, Choctaw, Creek, and SEMINOLE—who later, with the Chickasaw, became known as the "Five Civilized Tribes." But many Chickasaw died of cholera and food poisoning after their arrival in the Indian Territory.

Within the Indian Territory (which became the state of Oklahoma in 1907), the Chickasaw have had political ties with the other relocated Southeast tribes from the 1830s until today. Like all Native Americans, they have experienced many different approaches by the federal government to the Indian issue: Allotment and Assimilation; Restoration and Reorganization; Termination and Urbanization; and Self-Determination. The Chickasaw have blended elements from both their traditional culture and non-Indian society to rebuild their lives in their new homeland.

CHINOOK

People living east of the Rocky Mountains in both the United States and Canada at times feel warm, dry Chinook winds blowing from the west. In the Swiss Alps and elsewhere, winds of this kind are called *foehn* winds. The Chinook name, pronounced shi-NOOK, was originally applied to moist sea breezes blowing from the coast in Oregon and Washington. There, early settlers referred to the winds by that name because they came from the general direction of the village of Chinook, or Tchinouk.

The Chinook ancestral homeland is situated at the mouth of the Columbia River where it opens up into the Pacific Ocean, mostly on the north side in territory now part of the state of Washington. On the south side of the Columbia River, in Oregon, and farther inland in both states lived other tribes who spoke similar Chinookian dialects of the Penutian language phylum. Some of the other Chinookian-speaking tribes are the following: Cathlamet, Cathlapotle, Chilluckittequaw, Clackamas, Clatsop,

Clowwewalla, Multomah, Skilloot, Wasco, Watlala (Cascade Indians), and Wishram. Some scholars divide them into the Lower and Upper Chinook depending on their location on the river, near the mouth (Lower) or more inland (Upper). Their location also determines in what culture group they are classified, either the Northwest Coast Culture Area or the Plateau Culture Area.

One way to think of the Chinook proper and all the other Chinookian-speaking tribes along the Columbia River is as those people who provided the link between NORTHWEST COAST INDIANS and PLATEAU INDIANS. The Columbia River was a main trading thoroughfare between coastal and inland peoples, and the Chinook met with Plateau tribes regularly at the Dalles, an area of rapids up the river. With the trading of food and objects, ideas and customs were also exchanged.

The Chinook, like their Northwest Coast neighbors, constructed rectangular houses of cedar planks, but they placed them partly underground over pits, an architectural style more common to the plateau. They also built temporary mat shelters when on the trail, again similar to those of the Plateau peoples. The Chinook carved large dugout boats, as did their coastal neighbors, but they did not make large totem poles. They were known instead for their horn carvings, made from the horns of bighorn sheep and other animals. They practiced the potlatch, a system of exchanging gifts, as did all Northwest Coast peoples, but they did not have the many secret societies common to the area. The Chinook depended on salmon as a food staple, as did both Northwest Coast and Plateau tribes. But they were less dependent on sea mammals as a food source than were their coastal neighbors.

The river was the primary domain of the Chinook as it was for the Plateau Indians along the upper Columbia. The Chinook even charged other Indians tolls to paddle through their territory.

Of all the tribes of the southern Northwest Coast, the Chinook were the most famous traders. Like the TLINGIT to the north, they acted as middlemen among many different tribes. They used tooth shells as a form of money and dealt in dried fish, fish oil, seal oil, furs, dugouts,

Chinook bowl made from the horn of a bighorn sheep

cedar boards, cedar bark, mountain sheep horns, jadeite, copper, baskets, other goods, and even slaves. In fact, the Chinook developed a special trade language, a mixture of local languages, to carry out their bartering.

The Chinook continued to work as middlemen after non-Indians reached the area. Early European explorers reached the Oregon coast as early as the 1500s. It wasn't until the late 1700s, however, that the area came to be developed for trade, especially after 1792 when the American Robert Gray and the Englishman William Broughton explored the Columbia River. Thereafter, both British and American trading ships anchored near Chinook territory, seeking to exchange European trade goods for pelts. Lewis and Clark, traveling overland rather than by sea, reached Chinook country in 1805. In 1811, John Jacob Astor, the owner of the American Fur Company and the Pacific Fur Company, founded a trading post called Astoria near Chinook lands. Before long, a trade language that came to be called Chinook Jargon (or the Oregon Trade Language), had incorporated English and French words as well as Indian ones and was utilized throughout the entire Northwest, from Alaska to California. An example of a word in Chinook Jargon is *hootchenoo* for homemade liquor, from which our slang word *hootch* is derived.

The traditional way of life of the Chinook began to change in the 1830s, when a Methodist minister named Jason Lee established a mission among Chinookian-

Chinook paddle

speaking tribes of the Willamette Valley. Lee encouraged white development of the rich farmland, and by the 1840s, settlers were arriving in great numbers. By 1859, Oregon had achieved statehood; Washington followed in 1889.

Many of the Chinook settled among the Chehalis, a Salishan-speaking tribe, for whom a reservation had been established near present-day Oakville, Washington,

in 1864. Others settled among other area peoples, such as the Quinault, also Salishan-speaking. The Chinook have since strived to maintain tribal government and identity as well as to establish land and fishing rights. As of yet, the Chinook have not received special federal status despite their efforts through the Federal Acknowledgment Program.

CHIPEWYAN

Chipewyan bands once ranged over much of western Canada between Great Slave Lake and the Churchill River. What was once Chipewyan ancestral homeland now falls within the southeastern part of the Northwest Territories and the northern parts of Alberta, Saskatchewan, and Manitoba Provinces. The Chipewyan also controlled a wedge of land on the west shore of Hudson Bay, between the INUIT to the north and the CREE to the south.

The Chipewyan name, pronounced chip-uh-WHY-an, given to them by the Cree, means "pointed skins," because of their shirts, which were pointed at the bottom. The name of a band of Chipewyan, *Athabasca,* has come to be used for all Indian peoples of the Athabascan or Athapascan language family. The Chipewyan were the most numerous ATHAPASCANS living in Canada and Alaska. Their lifeways are typical of their neighbors in the vicinity of Great Slave and Great Bear Lakes, such as the Beaver, Dogrib, Hare, Slave, and Tatsanottine, all of whom are classified as part of the Subarctic Culture Area. SUBARCTIC INDIANS were organized into small bands of extended families, all of whom were nomadic hunter-gatherers.

The Chipewyan lived along the northern edge of the subarctic where the northern forest, or taiga, gives way to the barren grounds, or tundra. Winters were long and bitterly cold; summers were all too short and plagued with blackflies and mosquitoes. The Chipewyan, frequently on the move in search of food, lived in portable

skin tents similar to the tipis of the PLAINS INDIANS. They constructed a framework of poles by setting them in a circle and leaning them against one another and tying them at the top; they then covered the framework with caribou hides sewn together; they left a hole at the top for smoke to escape; and they placed spruce boughs and caribou skins at the base to form a floor.

Life for the Chipewyan bands revolved around the seasonal migrations of the caribou herds. In the spring, many bands gathered at the edge of the forested taiga to intercept the animals as they migrated northward onto the treeless tundra. In the fall, the Chipewyan returned to hunt the caribou on the animals' southern migration. The hunters used a variety of tricks to catch the animals. They drove them into corrals made of brush, where they could kill them in great numbers. Or they snared animals with ropes strung between two trees. Or they attacked the caribou from canoes—made from either birchbark or spruce bark—as the animals swam across rivers or lakes. Another trick was to bang antlers together to make a caribou bull think two other bulls were fighting over a female. The chosen weapon was a birch bow with stone-tipped or bone-tipped arrows, but spears were also used for the kill.

The Chipewyan used every part of the caribou. Fresh meat was baked in birch-bark or caribou-skin containers, by adding heated stones. The head and the stomach with all its contents was eaten. Some of the meat was made

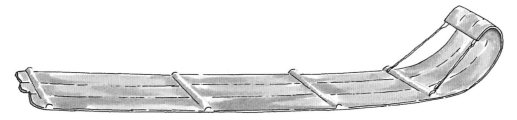

Chipewyan toboggan

into pemmican—dried and pounded meat mixed with fat—which was packed into the animal's intestines (like sausage) to be carried on the trail. The hide of the caribou was cured to make tents, clothing, and babiche for snowshoes, nets, and many other applications. The bones and antlers of the caribou were used to make tools.

The Chipewyan hunted other animals too, such as moose, musk-ox, buffalo, deer, bear, beaver, and waterfowl. In the winter, they stalked game on snowshoes and used toboggans to haul their catch. They also fished lakes and rivers, going after freshwater fish such as trout, bass, pike, and whitefish. They used many different techniques in fishing, including nets, hooks, barbed arrows, and spears. The Chipewyan also built weirs, wooden or stone pens, to trap fish. They fished from canoes too. Fish not eaten immediately were smoked or sun-dried for preservation.

The Chipewyan had few plants in their diet. But they did use some of the tundra plants for nourishment. They made moss into a soup and they ate lichens retrieved in a fermented state from the stomach of caribou.

In addition to their leatherwork, woodwork, stonework, and bonework, the Chipewyan also worked in metal. They found copper nuggets in the soil along the Coppermine River and used annealing techniques—alternate heating and hammering—to work the material into the desired shape. They made knives, axes, awls, drills, ice chisels, scrapers, arrowheads, spearheads, and other tools from copper. They also traded the raw material to neighboring tribes for food, shells, and other products.

The women did much of the hard work within the Chipewyan bands—making fires, preparing food, curing leather, and many other chores. They also did much of the hauling, carrying supplies on their backs as well as pulling toboggans. In fact, women ranked at least as low if not lower in Chipewyan society than among any other Native American peoples, and they were at the mercy of their husbands. When the food ran out, the women were the first to go hungry. Despite all their other hard work, Chipewyan women became known in post-contact times for their quillwork, beadwork, and silk embroidery.

The dog held a special place in Chipewyan mythology. In their creation myth, it was a dog that fathered the human race. Tribal members fed their dogs well whenever possible. But when faced with starvation in the worst of the winter months, they would eat their dogs to survive. When desperate enough, the Chipewyan also would eat their own dead to survive, although cannibalism was taboo and used as a last resort. Normally, the Chipewyan left their dead exposed, to be devoured by scavenging birds and animals.

The Chipewyan played an important role in the non-Indian exploration of western Canada. Fur-trading companies had early contacts with them. The Hudson's Bay Company founded the trading posts of York Factory, in 1682, and Churchill, in 1717, on Hudson Bay, establishing a trade relationship with the tribe. Samuel Hearne, who explored the Churchill, Coppermine, and Slave Rivers all the way to the Arctic Ocean for the Hudson's Bay Company from 1768 to 1776, had a Chipewyan guide named Matonabbee. Alexander Mackenzie, an explorer for the North West Company and the first non-Indian to cross the entire North American continent, from 1789 to 1793, also had the help of Chipewyan guides. His base of activity was Fort Chipewyan, founded on Lake Athabasca, in the heart of the tribe's territory, in 1788.

The arrival of the fur traders and the establishment of trading posts in their territory changed the life of the Chipewyan. For one thing, French traders armed the neighboring Cree with guns. The Cree, who had been longtime enemies of the Chipewyan, were then able to take over some Chipewyan land. The traders also carried disease to the Chipewyan. A smallpox epidemic ravaged the most of their bands in 1781, killing more than half their people.

The first missionary to the Chipewyan was the Catholic priest Henri Faraud, in 1858 at Fort Resolution. He wrote an abridged version of the New Testament in the Chipewyan dialect.

The tribe signed a series of treaties with the Canadian government in 1876, 1877, 1899, and 1906, in exchange for reserve lands, supplies, and annual payments. A number of Chipewyan bands presently hold a number of reserves in Alberta, Saskatchewan, Manitoba, and in the Northwest Territories. Many tribal members still hunt as a way of life.

Chipewyan birch-bark canoe

CHIPPEWA (Ojibway)

The Chippewa (pronounced CHIP-uh-wah) are also known as the Ojibway, Ojibwa, or Ojibwe (pronounced oh-JIB-wah). The former name is commonly used in the United States and the latter in Canada. Both names, different versions of an Algonquian phrase, refer to a puckered seam in their style of moccasins. The Chippewa native name *Anishinabe* (pronounced ah-nish-ih-NAH-bey), meaning "first people," is becoming widely used.

The Anishinabe were one of the largest and most powerful tribes in North America. They inhabited the country of the western Great Lakes, especially around Lake Superior. When they migrated to the region, before the arrival of non-Indians, the Anishinabe were supposedly one people with other ALGONQUIANS, the OTTAWA and POTAWATOMI. The three tribes remained allies through much of their history—the Council of Three Fires.

Lifeways

Anishinabe lifeways varied according to the environment. Southern bands can be classified in the Northeast Culture Area and northern bands in the Subarctic Culture Area (see NORTHEAST INDIANS and SUBARCTIC INDIANS). Or they can all be referred to as Great Lakes Algonquians. Other bands adopted the Plains Indian lifestyle in the southern part of what now is Manitoba and came to be known as Plains Ojibway (see PLAINS INDIANS).

Although they sometimes relocated if wildlife became scarce, the Anishinabe generally maintained year-round villages (other than the Plains Ojibway). They used birch bark for their wigwams, canoes, and containers. They usually dressed in buckskin. They were farmers who grew corn, beans, pumpkins, and squash in small patches. They also were hunter-gatherers who sought the mammals, fish, shellfish, fowl, and wild edible plants of the forest, lakes, and rivers.

A staple food of the Anishinabe was wild rice. This plant, found along the edges of lakes, streams, and swamps, is a tall grass with an edible seed resembling rice. The Anishinabe harvested it in the summer months. While the men hunted ducks and geese from their sleek and swift birch-bark canoes, the women, also in canoes, drifted beside the clumps of the lush plants and collected the seeds in the bottoms of the boats.

Like certain other Indian peoples of the Great Lakes and the prairies flanking the Mississippi River, the Anishinabe participated in the secret Midewiwin Society,

Anishinabe cone-shaped birch-bark wigwam

also sometimes called the Grand Medicine Society. In early times, entry into this club (or sodality) was very difficult to achieve. A man or woman normally had to have a special visitation by a spirit in a dream to even be considered for membership. A secret meeting to initiate those accepted was held only once a year in a specially constructed elongated lodge. One member recorded the events of the meeting on bark scrolls, using a bone implement for carving and red paint for coloring. The members might sing, "We are now to receive you into the Midewiwin, our Mide brother." And the initiate might reply, "I have the medicine in my heart and I am strong as a bear."

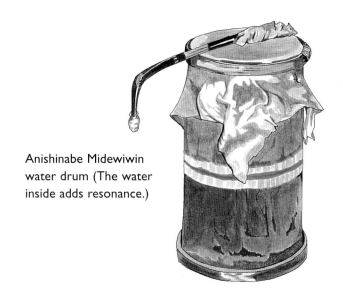

Anishinabe Midewiwin water drum (The water inside adds resonance.)

Members in the Midewiwin Society wore *mide,* or medicine bags, made from mink, weasel, rattlesnake, hawk, or owl skins, or from wildcat or bear paws around their necks. The Anishinabe believed that all living and nonliving things had spirits that could be tamed to help the sick or to harm one's enemies. And like other Algonquians, the Anishinabe believed in one all-pervasive spirit from which lesser spirits drew their power—the Manitou.

Manabozho, the central culture hero of the Anishinabe, a trickster figure, is considered the provider of medicine for the Midewiwin Society. Nowadays, the Midewiwin Society has incorporated elements of Christianity and is no longer so difficult to join.

History and Wars

The Anishinabe were early and consistent allies of the French. Because they were trusted friends and trading partners, they were among the first Indians to receive French firearms. With these guns, they drove the SIOUX (DAKOTA, LAKOTA, NAKOTA) westward onto the Great Plains, and the SAC, FOX (MESQUAKI), and KICKAPOO southward from what today is northern Wisconsin. Some of these engagement were naval battles, with warriors fighting from canoes. The Anishinabe even managed to repel the powerful IROQUOIS (HAUDENOSAUNEE), invading from the east.

During the late 1600s and early 1700s, various Anishinabe bands, such as the Missisauga and Salteaux, came to dominate parts of Wisconsin, Minnesota, Michigan, North Dakota, and southern Ontario, their empire stretching from Lake Huron to the Missouri River.

In the mid-1700s, the Anishinabe fought the British in the French and Indian wars (see entries on the ABENAKI and Iroquois) and in Pontiac's Rebellion (see OTTAWA entry). Then in 1769, the Anishinabe joined forces with the Ottawa, Potawatomi, Sac, Fox, and Kickapoos to defeat the ILLINOIS.

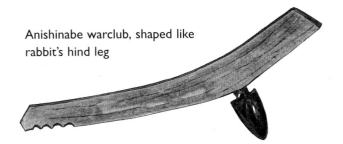

Anishinabe warclub, shaped like rabbit's hind leg

In the American Revolution, the Anishinabe became allies of the British against the American rebels. Then they fought the Americans again in the Indian wars for the Old Northwest, including Little Turtle's War, Tecumseh's Rebellion, and in the War of 1812 (see MIAMI and SHAWNEE). In 1815, when the British surrendered the Anishinabe were forced to cede much of their land to the expanding United States.

Modern-Day Activism

The fighting spirit has carried over to modern-day Anishinabe. In 1968, three Anishinabe—Dennis Banks, George Mitchell, and Clyde Bellecourt—founded AIM, the American Indian Movement, in Minneapolis, Minnesota. Many of its original members were urban Indians who had left the reservations to work in the cities. Of course, not all Native Americans live on reservations or on tribal trust lands. In fact, it is estimated by the United States Census Bureau that more than half of all Native Americans live elsewhere. AIM has been one of the most active and militant of all the Native American political groups fighting for Indian rights and improved social conditions on and off reservations.

Members of AIM participated in the 1969 takeover of Alcatraz Island in San Francisco, the 1972 occupation of the Federal Bureau of Indian Affairs in Washington, D.C., and the 1973 seizure of Wounded Knee in South Dakota, the site of the Wounded Knee Massacre of 1890. Like many of the conflicts of past centuries, each of these events is a dramatic story of moves and countermoves—and sometimes violence—between Indians and federal agents. At the 1973 Wounded Knee incident, two Native Americans—Frank Clearwater, a CHEROKEE, and Buddy Lamont, a Sioux—were killed and a federal marshall was wounded. One result of these protests was to help call public attention to the violation of treaty rights by the federal and state governments and to the resulting poverty of the Native American.

Songs and Writings

Like many Native Americans, the Anishinabe are known for their self-expression in songs and chants. The following is the traditional love song of an Anishinabe girl:

Oh, I am thinking
Oh, I am thinking
I have found my lover
Oh, I think it is so.

Anishinabe birch-bark transparency, made from a piece of inner bark, folded and bitten to form a design that shows clearly when held up to light

As a married woman and a mother, she might sing the following cradle song:

Who is this? Who is this?
Giving light on the top of my lodge?
It is I, the little owl, coming,
It is I, the little owl, coming,
Down! Down!

The modern writer Louise Erdrich, an Anishinabe of North Dakota, has continued this tradition of self-expression through novel-writing, including *Love Medicine* (1984), *The Beet Queen* (1986), *Tracks* (1988), *The*

Bingo Palace (1994), *Tales of Burning Love* (1995), and *The Antelope Wife* (1998). With her MODOC husband, Michael Dorris, she coauthored *The Crown of Columbus* (1991). Gerald Vizenor, another Anishinabe author, has written *The Heirs of Columbus* (1991), *Hotline Healers: An Almost Browne Novel* (1997), and numerous works about Native American literature.

Traditional and Modern Ways of Life

Nowadays, the still-populous Anishinabe live on reservations in Minnesota, Wisconsin, Michigan, North Dakota, Montana, Ontario, and Manitoba, as well as in cities in the Midwest and central Canada. Some tribal members maintain close to a traditional way of life, with hunting and fishing and/or the making of traditional arts and crafts providing primary income. Others have adapted to mainstream non-Indian culture. Some Anishinabe groups have increased tribal revenue through the operation of casinos.

Anishinabe container, made of porcupine quills, birch bark, and sweetgrass (modern)

CHITIMACHA

The Chitimacha occupied ancestral territory in what is now the lower part of the state of Louisiana, along the Mississippi Delta in the vicinity of Grand River, Grand Lake, and the lower course of Bayou La Teche. They actually consisted of three subtribes, the Chitimacha proper, the Chawasha, and the Washa, sharing a unique language, Chitimachan, which may be related to Tunican, spoken by neighboring tribes, such as the TUNICA and YAZOO.

The Chitimacha, classified as SOUTHEAST INDIANS, lived in pole-frame houses with walls and roofs of palmetto thatch. Sometimes the walls were plastered over with mud, a technique called wattle and daub. Alliga-

tors, turtles, fish, and shellfish were abundant in their territory, along with other game. The men used blowguns in addition to bows and arrows to shoot small game, and they could send the small darts flying up to 60 feet. The Chitimacha grew sweet potatoes and melons in addition to corn, beans, and squash. For food storage, the women made patterned cane baskets with fitted tops. They also made pottery. The name *Chitimacha,* pronounced chid-uh-MA-shuh, means "those who have pots."

In 1682, René-Robert Cavelier de La Salle claimed the Mississippi Valley for France, naming it Louisiana, after France's King Louis XIV. Then in 1699, Pierre Le Moyne, sieur d'Iberville, founded a settlement near present-day Biloxi. And in 1718, Iberville's brother, the sieur de Bienville, founded New Orleans. The Chitimacha therefore were under the French sphere of influence for most of the colonial period.

The relations between the two peoples were not always peaceful, however. In 1706, after some of their people had been enslaved by Indians living among the French, the Chitimacha killed a French missionary to the NATCHEZ, named St. Cosmé, and his three companions. For the next 12 years, the Chitimacha and the French engaged in a series of raids and counterraids. During that period, the majority of Indian slaves among the French colonists were from the Chitimacha tribe. Peace was made in 1718, when the Chitimacha agreed to settle at a site on the Mississippi River, near present-day Plaquemine.

By 1881, the only surviving Chitimacha lived at Charenton, Louisiana, where a small community exists today. The Chitimacha are still famous for their beautifully crafted baskets of narrow cane splints with black, red, and yellow designs. Other tribal members have become known for their silverwork.

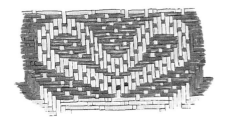

Detail of Chitimacha basket showing intricate weave and vegetable-dye colors

CHOCTAW

According to tribal legend, the Choctaw originated from Nanih Waiya, the Mother Mound, at a location near what is present-day Noxapater, Mississippi. This creation myth indicates that the Choctaw were descended from the earlier MOUND BUILDERS of the Southeast. At the time of early European contacts with them, the Choctaw were one of the largest tribes of the region, occupying territory in what is now southern and central Mississippi, with some bands in Alabama, Georgia, and Louisiana as well.

Lifeways

The Choctaw, a Muskogean-speaking people, are closely related in language and culture to other possible descendants of the Mound Builders—the CHICKASAW, living to their north, and the CREEK, living to their northeast. Yet the Choctaw had a more democratic system of government than other SOUTHEAST INDIANS. In this regard, they were more like NORTHEAST INDIANS, who did not have autocratic rulers.

The Choctaw, like most Southeast peoples, were primarily villagers. They used a variety of materials to build their dwellings—wood for the pole frames; grass or cane reeds for thatched roofs; clay and crushed shells for walls (or in some cases bark, hide, or woven mats). Tribal mem-

bers had both winter and summer houses. To keep the winter houses warm families built fires, and to keep them moist they poured water over heated rocks. For additional warmth, they twisted turkey feathers into thread to weave blankets.

The Choctaw were highly skilled farmers, having large fields in the fertile bottomlands of the lower Mississippi River. Their main crops were corn, beans, squash, sunflowers, and melons. For the Choctaw, hunting, fishing, and the gathering of edible wild plants were secondary in importance to their frequent plantings and harvestings.

The Choctaw carved dugout canoes for hunting, fishing, and trading trips. Choctaw traders developed a simple trade language that they could use in combination with sign language to communicate with other tribes.

Choctaw men let their hair grow long, unlike the males of most other Southeast tribes, who shaved their heads. The Chickasaw called them Pansh Falaia, meaning "long hairs." The Choctaw and Chickasaw both practiced head deformation for esthetic purposes, using a hinged piece of wood to apply pressure over a period of time to the foreheads of male infants. It is theorized that the name *Choctaw,* pronounced CHAHK-taw, is derived from the Spanish *chato* for "flat" (although it may come from the native name for the Pearl River, *Haccha*).

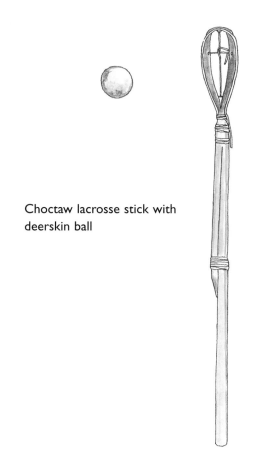

Choctaw lacrosse stick with deerskin ball

The Choctaw, like many eastern Indian peoples, play lacrosse, sometimes called Indian stickball. The purpose of the game was to toss a leather ball between posts with sticks having curved and webbed ends. Touching the ball with the hands and using the sticks to fight were forbidden, but just about everything else was fair play—tripping, bumping, stomping, and piling on top of other players. There were many injuries, even deaths, during lacrosse games, a kind of mock war. Sometimes great matches were held between villages with hundreds of participants. There would be pregame ceremonies with dancing and singing during the days preceding the big event. Villagers would place bets on their team, gambling many of their possessions. Medicine men would act as "coaches," but they would use incantations rather than strategy to get their team to score the 100 points that they needed to win. After the men played their marathon games, the women played their own rough version.

The Choctaw also held song competitions. Individuals from different villages would write songs for festivals, keeping their new melodies and words secret until performance time. Someone from another village or tribe who spied on a musical practice was called a "song thief." The following is a hunting song, sung by a hunter to his wife:

Go and grind some corn, we will go camping.
Go and sew, we will go camping.
I passed on and you were sitting there crying.
You were lazy and your hoe is rusty.

The following is a verse from a song written by a Choctaw girl whose father and brothers were killed in a raid:

All men must surely die,
Though no one knows how soon.
Yet when the time shall come
The event may be joyful.

After a death, the Choctaw placed the deceased on a scaffold. There was a "cry-time" for family members, during which they went into retreat, fasted, covered their heads, and mourned. When the corpse had dried out in the open air, tribesmen, officially appointed as bone-pickers, scraped the flesh away with their extra-long fingernails. Then the bones would be buried.

Contacts with Non-Indians

The Spanish were the first Europeans to come into contact with the Choctaw. Warriors harassed Hernando de Soto's expeditionary force near the Mississippi River in 1540. The conquistadores possessed firearms, but the Indians proved a stubborn menace.

The Choctaw later became important allies of the French, who established themselves along the lower Mississippi valley after René-Robert Cavelier de La Salle's expedition of 1682. Choctaw warriors helped crush the Natchez Revolt of 1729 (see NATCHEZ). The fact that the Choctaw generally sided with the French, and the Chickasaw with the English, created a balance of power in the region during the French and Indian wars from 1689 to 1763.

After 1763, the English controlled the part of the Southeast that included the Choctaw homeland. At the end of the American Revolution in 1783, when the British were defeated, the Spanish gained control of the Gulf of Mexico region as payment for helping the American rebels. In 1819, the United States gained Spanish holdings in the Southeast after General Andrew Jackson had invaded Florida.

The Choctaw generally sided with the Americans against the British. Choctaw warriors fought under American generals in the American Revolution, the War of 1812, and the Creek War of 1813–14. Moreover, it was a Choctaw chief named Pushmataha who was instrumental in keeping many Southeast bands from joining the SHAWNEE Tecumseh's Rebellion of 1809–11.

Relocation

In spite of all their contributions to U.S. causes and their acceptance of white ways of life, the Choctaw were mistreated. White settlers wanted their lands, and both state governments and the federal government sided with whites over Indians. In the Creek War, the Choctaw had fought under the man who later became president of the United States, Andrew Jackson. Even so, Jackson signed the Indian Removal Act of 1830, calling for the relocation of all eastern tribes to territory west of the Mississippi River. This was the start of the Trail of Tears, a phrase originally used to describe the CHEROKEE removal but which has come to stand for the forced march of all the relocated Southeast tribes.

The Choctaw were the first tribe to be relocated. In 1830, a few among them, who did not represent the majority, were bribed into signing the Treaty of Dancing Rabbit Creek, which ceded to the whites all Choctaw lands in the state of Mississippi. Some Choctaw refused to depart and hid out in the backwoods of Mississippi and Louisiana. But the vast majority were herded westward by U.S. Army bluecoats. Conditions on the many forced marches from 1831 to 1834 were horrific. There were shortages of food, blankets, horses, and wagons. The soldiers turned their backs when bandits ambushed the migrants. Disease also struck down the exhausted travelers. About a quarter of the Choctaw died on the trip, and many more died after their arrival in the Indian Territory, from disease, starvation, and attacks by hostile western Indians.

The Choctaw persisted, reorganizing as a tribe and making the most of their new home. Because they adopted a republican style of government modeled after that of the United States, as well as other Euroamerican customs, the Choctaw came to be referred to as one of the "Five Civilized Tribes" along with the Chickasaw, Creek, Cherokee, and SEMINOLE. Pressures caused by white expansion did not cease, however. The General Allotment Act of 1887, designed to force the breakup of tribal landholdings for increased white development, caused the eventual loss of much acreage. What was supposed to exist permanently for native peoples as the Indian Territory became the state of Oklahoma in 1907. (*Oklahoma* is a Muskogean word, coined by the Choctaw Allen Wright to mean "red people," and first applied to the western half of the Indian Territory in 1890.)

Contemporary Choctaw

The western Choctaw presently hold trust lands near Durant, Oklahoma. In the 1950s, they reestablished their traditional government. Descendants of those who stayed in the East have a reservation near Pearl River, Mississippi. The western Choctaw sponsor the Choctaw Nation Labor Day Festival. The eastern Choctaw hold an annual Choctaw Indian Fair. Games of stickball are part of both powwows.

CHUMASH

The Chumash (pronounced CHOO-mash) of the Pacific Coast are the only North American native peoples who built boats out of planks. Other Indians used planks to make houses but never applied this technology to boat-making, instead either carving dugouts from single logs or fashioning boats by stretching bark or skin over a wooden frame.

Chumash craftspeople split logs of cedar with antler wedges and smoothed the lumber with shell and stone rubbing tools. Then they lashed the planks together with animal sinew or plant bindings, and caulked them with asphalt to form 25-foot double-bowed hulls. A crew of four paddlers could handle these boats in ocean waters.

The Chumash—probably eight different bands—lived in the vicinity of present-day Santa Barbara in central California, on the mainland and on the three closest of the eight Channel Islands. It is thought that they used their boats for passage among the different Chumash villages, as well as for fishing and hunting sea mammals. The Chumash are sometimes referred to as the Santa Barbara Indians.

The Chumashan-speaking (part of the Hokan language phylum) Chumash are classified as part of the California Culture Area. They shared many traits with neighboring CALIFORNIA INDIANS. They were politically organized by villages rather than by tribe; they hunted small game and fished; they prepared various foods from acorns; they lived in domed houses covered with various plant materials; and they wore little clothing.

Detail of Chumash rock painting from the roof of a rock shelter

Yet the Chumash culture was more maritime than that of their inland neighbors. For that matter, the Chumash depended on the sea for food more than did the Salinas and Costanoan to their north, between them and San Francisco Bay. The Santa Barbara Channel's kelp beds drew many different species of fish, which in turn drew many sea mammals. To honor the marine life so essential to their existence, the Chumash carved exquisite animal figures in soapstone.

The Chumash supposedly were the first California coastal Indians in contact with explorers for Spain, namely Juan Rodríguez Cabrillo and Bartolomé Ferrelo, who reached the Santa Barbara Channel in 1542. For the next two centuries, the Spanish used the channel as a stopover for galleons making the Pacific crossing from Mexico to the Philippines, and the early impact on the Chumash was minimal. But then the Franciscan order of Catholic priests began building missions in the region in 1772 and began converting the Indians to a new religion and a new agricultural way of life (see MISSION INDIANS).

In 1834, 13 years after Mexican independence from Spain, the Mexican government secularized the missions and released the Indians from their servitude. But by that time, many native peoples had forgotten how to survive in the wilderness. With the Euroamerican population increasing, especially after the California gold rush of 1849 and California statehood in 1850, the Indians suffered from further losses of land and culture, as well as from white violence and diseases. The Chumash, although nearly driven to extinction, with only a few tribal members remaining by the early 1900s, have rallied. Descendants hold the Santa Ynez Reservation in Santa Barbara County, California. Business enterprises include high-stakes bingo and a campground. Tribal members have strived to revive traditional crafts, dances (one of them the Dolphin Dance), songs, and storytelling.

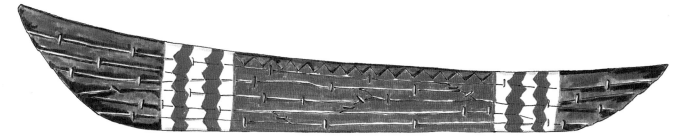

Chumash plank boat

COEUR D'ALENE

Coeur d'Alene, pronounced kur-duh-LANE, is a French name, meaning "heart of awl" or "pointed heart." The phrase was probably first used by a chief as an insult to a trader who then mistook it for the tribe's name. The tribe's native name is *Skitswish,* the meaning of which is unknown.

The Coeur d'Alene occupied ancestral territory that has since become northern Idaho and eastern Washington

State, especially along the Spokane River and Coeur d'Alene River and around Coeur d'Alene Lake. Like other Salishan-speaking tribes of the region, such as the FLATHEAD, KALISPEL, and SPOKAN, the Coeur d'Alene are classified as part of the Plateau Culture Area (see PLATEAU INDIANS). They depended heavily on salmon fishing and the gathering of wild plant foods in addition to the hunting of small game. They lived in cone-shaped dwellings placed over pits and built out of poles covered with bark or woven mats.

The Coeur d'Alene, like other Interior Salishan tribes, had extensive contacts with whites only after the Lewis and Clark Expedition in the early 1800s. They were generally peaceful toward whites and bartered their furs with them for guns, ammunition, and other trade goods. In the 1850s, however, because of white treaty violations, the Coeur d'Alene joined in an uprising against settlers. The Coeur d'Alene War of 1858 grew out of the Yakama War of 1855–56 (see YAKAMA). Other tribes participating in this second rebellion included the PALOUSE, PAIUTE, and Spokan.

In May 1858, a combined force of about 1,000 Coeur d'Alene, Spokan, and Palouse attacked and routed a column of 164 federal troops under Major Edward Steptoe at Pine Creek in the western part of Washington Territory. Next, about 600 troops under Colonel George Wright rode into the field to engage the rebels. In the first week of September, the two forces met at Spokane Plain and Four Lakes. The Indians, who were not as well armed as the soldiers, suffered heavy losses.

Afterward, Wright's force rounded up Indian dissidents, including Qualchin, one of the Yakama warriors who had started the Yakama War three years earlier with an attack on white miners. Qualchin was tried, sentenced to death, and hanged. Kamiakin, his uncle, the Yakama chief who had organized the alliance of tribes, escaped to Canada, but he returned in 1861 and lived out his life on the Spokan reservation. He died in 1877, the same year that the next outbreak of violence occurred in the region, this one among the NEZ PERCE.

In 1873, a reservation was established for the Coeur d'Alene. Tribal members living on Coeur d'Alene Reservation in Benewah County, Idaho, nowadays earn a living through timber sales and farming. Other Coeur d'Alene live off-reservation in the region and work as professionals. As a member of the Affiliated Tribes of Northwest Indians and the Upper Columbia United Tribes, the Coeur d'Alene are working to restore natural resources despoiled by mining operations in the late 19th and early 20th centuries.

Sherman Alexie, a writer of Coeur d'Alene/Spokan heritage, made news when he and CHEYENNE/ARAPAHO Chris Eyre made a full-length feature film about Indians, in which the Indian roles were all played by actual Indians. *Smoke Signals,* based on a story from Alexie's 1994 book, *The Lone Ranger and Tonto Fistfight in Heaven,* was released in 1998. Much of the movie was shot on location on Coeur d'Alene Reservation. Alexie has also written *The Business of Fancydancing: Stories and Poems* (1992), *First Indian on the Moon* (1993), *Water Flowing Home* (1995), *Reservation Blues* (1995), *The Summer of Black Widows* (1996), and *Indian Killer* (1996).

COMANCHE

The tribal name *Comanche,* pronounced cuh-MAN-chee, possibly is derived from the Spanish *camino ancho* for "main road," or from the UTE *komon'teia* or *kohmaths* for "one who wants to fight me." Their native name is *Nermurnuh* (*Nimenim, Ne-me-ne, Nuumu*) for "true human being." Comanche bands included the Kewatsana, Kotsai, Kwahadie, Motsai, Nokoni, Patgusa, Penateka, Pohoi, Tanima, Wasaih, and Yamparika.

Migrations

The Uto-Aztecan language of the Comanche is similar to that of the SHOSHONE. It is thought that sometime during the 1600s the Comanche separated from the Shoshone in territory that is now Wyoming and migrated southward along the eastern face of the Rocky Mountains. Sometime in the late 1600s, they gained use of the horse, perhaps through raids or in trade with PUEBLO INDIANS, who had acquired horses from the Spanish. By 1719, the Comanche were in present-day Kansas. During the 1700s and 1800s, as horse-mounted hunters and raiders, the Comanche roamed through territory that now includes Texas, eastern New Mexico, western Oklahoma, southwestern Kansas, southeastern Colorado, and northern Mexico. Even the warlike APACHE, whose territory in New Mexico the Comanche first invaded about 1740, could not contain them.

Lifeways

Because of their wide range, the Comanche helped spread horses through trade to more northern PLAINS INDIANS. Through much of their history, they raided white settlements and other tribes to steal horses. They also tracked wild mustangs. The Comanche became skilled horse breeders and trainers and maintained huge herds, more than any other tribe.

Comanche horse whip

Both boys and girls were given their first mounts when they were only four or five years old. Boys worked hard to become skillful riders; then, as teenagers and young men, they used these skills in warfare. A Comanche rider, galloping at full speed, could lean over to use his horse as a shield while he shot arrows from under its neck. He could also rescue a fallen friend by pulling him up onto his horse while in motion. Comanche horses were so well-trained, in fact, that they responded to spoken and touch commands. Girls also became accomplished riders. When they grew up, they went antelope hunting with the men.

As was the case with other tribes of the Great Plains Culture Area, horses enabled the Comanche to travel great distances in pursuit of the buffalo herds, which the Plains Indians relied on for food, clothing, bedding, and shelter. The Comanche lived in temporary villages of buffalo-hide tipis year-round, so they would be ready to follow the buffalo migrations when necessary.

Wars for the Southern Plains

It is estimated that, in proportion to their numbers, the Comanche killed more non-Indians than any other tribe. The Spanish were the first Europeans to try to contend with them, but without much success. Comanche riders rode hundreds of miles to launch surprise attacks on Spanish settlements for horses, slaves, and other booty. In fact, the Comanche presence helped prevent the Spanish from extensively developing the Texas region. During the 1700s, the Spanish managed to establish and maintain only a few missions there, such as the one at San Antonio in 1718.

About 1790, the Comanche allied themselves with the KIOWA, another tribe of the southern plains, who had settled directly to the north of them. About 1840, they also united in a loose confederacy with the southern branches of the CHEYENNE and ARAPAHO, who also lived to their north.

In 1821, Mexico achieved independence from Spain, and part of the territory falling under Mexican rule was Texas. In the following years, more and more Mexican-American and Anglo-American settlers arrived in Texas. Many died at the hands of the Comanche. The Comanche also attacked travelers heading to New Mexico from Missouri on the Santa Fe Trail. Comanche warriors even attacked soldiers who dared to enter their territory. For example, in 1829, a Comanche war party attacked an army wagon train that had been sent out under Major Bennett Riley to explore the Santa Fe Trail.

In 1835, the Texas Revolution against Mexican rule erupted. The next year, the famous battle of the Alamo occurred. It was during this revolution that the Texas Rangers were organized. Their principal function during the 10 years of the Texas Republic, and after the annexation of Texas by the United States in 1845, was to protect settlers from attacks by hostile Indians, in particular the Comanche.

During the 1830s, the Comanche had the upper hand, defeating the Texas Rangers in several battles. In the Council House Affair of 1838, the Rangers tried to seize a tribal delegation who had come to San Antonio for negotiations concerning the release of white captives. A fight broke out and 35 Comanche were killed. Other warriors under Chief Buffalo Hump took their revenge in raids on white settlements as far south as the Gulf of Mexico.

During the 1840s, the Rangers fared somewhat better in their encounters with the Comanche because John Coffee Hays, a strict disciplinarian, was in charge, and new guns, Walker Colt six-shooters, were used. The Battle of Bandera Pass in 1841 proved a standoff. Yet the Comanche lost few men in battle. White diseases,

Comanche metal-tipped arrow

especially a cholera epidemic in 1849–50, carried by travelers heading westward during the California gold rush, exacted a much heavier toll on the Comanche.

From 1849 to 1852, after Texas had become part of the United States, federal troops moved in to build a chain of seven forts from the Red River to the Rio Grande to help police the frontier. In 1853, officials in Kansas negotiated the Fort Atkinson Treaty with southern plains tribes to protect the Santa Fe Trail. Yet many Comanche bands kept up their raids.

In 1854, the federal government placed some Comanche and Kiowa on one of two reservations on the Brazos River. The Indians, however, did not take to the sedentary lifestyle forced upon them. In 1859, the Brazos River reservations were abandoned.

A new offensive was launched in 1858 by both Texas Rangers and army regulars, who engaged the Comanche north of the Red River in the Indian Territory and in Kansas. The Texas Rangers fought the Comanche in the Battle of Antelope Hills. Then the army's Wichita Expedition fought the Battle of Rush Springs against Buffalo Hump's band and next the Battle of Crooked Creek. Despite some losses in these battles, the powerful Comanche and Kiowa would continue their resistance to white settlement on the southern plains for almost 20 more years.

During the Civil War years, from 1861 to 1865, when federal troops went east to fight against the Confederacy, the Comanche took advantage of the situation to step up their campaign of raiding. The Confederates even supplied the Comanche with guns, trying to encourage their support against Union soldiers. The only offensive against the Comanche during this period was by troops under Colonel Christopher "Kit" Carson, who had previously fought Apache and NAVAJO in New Mexico. In 1864, Carson's men fought the Comanche at the first Battle of Adobe Walls on the Staked Plain of the Texas Panhandle, driving them off with howitzer cannon and burning their winter supply of food.

During the post–Civil War years, the army launched new campaigns to pacify the southern plains. One of these was the Sheridan Campaign. Most of the action was against Southern Cheyenne and Southern Arapaho, but General Philip Henry Sheridan's southern column fought Comanche and KIOWA at the Battle of Soldier Spring on Christmas Day in 1868. The soldiers drove the Indians away, burned their tipis, and destroyed their food supplies. By the Medicine Lodge Treaty of 1867, a new reservation had been established for the Comanche and Kiowa in the southern part of the Indian Territory

between the Washita and Red Rivers. But both peoples refused to be confined on reservations. They had been nomadic hunters and raiders for generations and resisted giving up their traditional way of life.

Yet time was running out for them. The 1870s saw the last uprising of the Comanche and Kiowa. It also saw the end of the great buffalo herds. During this last period of bitter fighting, a great Comanche chief, Quanah Parker, would become famous.

Quanah Parker was of mixed ancestry; his white mother, Cynthia Parker, had been kidnapped in 1836 as a nine-year-old by CADDO Indians, who then traded her to the Comanche. As a teenager, she had become the wife of the Comanche chief Peta Nocona of the Nocona band. She had become a dedicated Comanche, preferring their way of life to that of her blood relatives.

Quanah, the son of Cynthia and Peta, also grew up favoring the Comanche way of life. As a young boy, he proved himself by his horsemanship, bravery, and leadership. He later came to hate whites, who were responsible for destroying his family. First, his father died from a wound inflicted by whites. Then his mother was captured by soldiers and returned to the white world. She died soon afterward, reportedly of a broken heart at being separated from her adopted people. Next, Quanah's brother died of a white disease. On his own now, Quanah joined the powerful Kwahadie band of Comanche who lived in the Texas Panhandle. In 1867, only 15 years old, he became one of their chiefs.

The final phase of the combined Comanche and Kiowa wars began in 1871 with Kiowa attacks on travelers along the Butterfield Southern Route (or Southern Overland Trail), leading from St. Louis through the Southwest to California. In retaliation, General William Tecumseh Sherman sent the Fourth Cavalry under Colonel Ranald Mackenzie into Kiowa and Comanche country. They swept through the reservation, then invaded the Staked Plain of the Texas Panhandle.

It was here the army first became aware of Quanah Parker. The fearless young leader personally led two charges against the cavalry. In the first, he and his warriors rode right through the army camp at Rock Station, stampeding and capturing many of their horses. In the second, he led a rout of a scouting party. The teenager personally killed and scalped a soldier.

Although military expeditions against the Comanche and Kiowa had so far been unsuccessful, another activity by whites threatened the native way of life. Before 1870, white hunters had killed buffalo only during the winter when their furs were long. But then a new tanning process was developed that enabled furriers to make short-hair hides workable as well, leading to year-round hunting. Furthermore, by the 1870s, white hunters were armed with new kinds of guns, high-powered telescopic rifles effective at a range of 600 yards. The animals, essential to the Plains Indians economy, were now being slaughtered by whites at a furious pace.

When the hunters entered the Staked Plain and set up camp at the abandoned trading post of Adobe Walls, where Comanche and Kiowa had fought Kit Carson's men a decade before, Quanah Parker called a council of war. He even had his warriors hold a Sun Dance, which was not a traditional Comanche custom, so that Cheyenne and Arapaho from the neighboring reservation would come. Preparations were made for an attack.

In June 1874, Quanah Parker led his sizable force against the buffalo hunters at Adobe Walls. This was the start of the Red River War of 1874–75, sometimes also called the Buffalo War. Despite their overwhelming numbers, the allied Indians were repelled by the repeater rifles of the buffalo hunters.

In the following months, Comanche and Kiowa warriors, with some Cheyenne and Arapaho, carried out numerous raids on white settlements. But then General Philip Henry Sheridan launched a massive offensive with troops out of Texas, Kansas, and New Mexico under two experienced Indian fighters, Colonels Ranald Mackenzie and Nelson Miles. They kept up pressure on the militant bands, finally dealing a crushing blow to the Indians in September at their stronghold in Palo Duro Canyon. The soldiers managed to kill most of the Indians' horses and destroy most of their tipis.

With relentless pursuit by the soldiers, the freedom fighters, weary and half-starved, began trickling in to the army posts to surrender. The last of the Kiowa militants held out until February 1875. Quanah Parker and his Comanche warriors turned themselves in the following June.

The Peyote Road

Quanah Parker's influence on Indian history was not over, however. He quickly adapted to the reservation life. He taught himself the ways of the Euroamericans, such as the laws governing the leasing of lands and right of way, and he made deals with non-Indian investors for the benefit of his people.

Moreover, Quanah Parker played a major role in spreading a new religion to Native Americans of many tribes. This religion involved the use of the peyote cactus, which grows in northern Mexico, especially along the Rio

Grande valley. The Indians cut off the rounded top of the plant, dried it, and made it into a "peyote button." When eaten raw or brewed into a tea, the buttons create a heightening of the senses, a feeling of well-being, and visions. Earlier Comanche had probably helped spread the use of peyote northward when they brought back knowledge of the plant and its properties after raids in Mexico.

Quanah Parker discovered what is known as the Peyote Road, or the use of peyote for religious purposes, sometime after 1890, following the collapse of the Ghost Dance Religion associated with events at Wounded Knee that involved the SIOUX (DAKOTA, LAKOTA, NAKOTA). His work and that of other peyotists, such as Big Moon of the Kiowa, led to the spread of peyote use among Indians of the plains, Southwest, prairies, and Great Lakes and the eventual founding of a church. Quanah Parker died in 1911, revered by Indians of many tribes. In 1918, the Native American Church was chartered. This organized religion incorporated certain Christian beliefs and practices with the sacramental use of peyote. Oklahoma Territory tried to ban the use of peyote in 1899 as did some states in later years, but after 1934 and the new policy of Tribal Restoration and Reorganization, no more official attempts were made at suppression. By the 1930s, about half the Indian population in the United States belonged to the church. Today, the Native American Church still plays a central role in Indian religion and the fight for Indian rights.

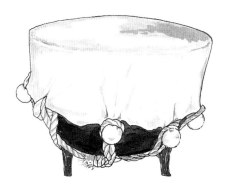

Comanche drum for peyote ceremonies

Contemporary Comanche

The Comanche Indian Tribe as well as individual tribal members have holdings in Caddo, Comanche, Cotton, Grady, Kiowa, Tillman, and Washita Counties in Oklahoma. Tribal members earn a living in a wide range of professions. Farming and the leasing of mineral rights provide income for some. Many Comanche strive to preserve traditions, including language, song, and dance.

The annual Comanche Homecoming Powwow is one of the largest in the area. Tribal members sponsor other events with neighboring Kiowa and Apache.

One Comanche woman who has made a difference in the ongoing struggle for Native American rights and economic opportunity is LaDonna Harris. In 1970, she founded Americans for Indian Opportunity (AIO), which operates out of Bernalillo, New Mexico, and of which she is president. She also founded INDIANnet, an organization dedicated to the establishment and development of communication systems and access to computerized information for Native Americans.

COUSHATTA

The Coushatta occupied ancestral territory in what is now the state of Alabama, especially where the Coosa and Tallapoosa Rivers merge to form the Alabama River. A Muskogean-speaking people, they were closely related to the CREEK and the ALABAMA in language, culture, and history. All three tribes were part of the Creek Confederacy. The Coushatta, village farmers, are classified, along with these other tribes as SOUTHEAST INDIANS. *Coushatta*, pronounced coo-SHAH-tuh, possibly means "white cane" in Muskogean. Alternate spellings are Koasati and Quassarte.

It is thought that the Coushatta had contact with the Spanish expedition of 1539–43 led by Hernando de Soto, and, following De Soto's death, Moscoso de Alvaro. Other Spanish explorers passed through their territory in the 1500s and 1600s.

After René-Robert Cavelier de La Salle's 1682 voyage of exploration along the lower Mississippi River, the French became established in the region. They founded the settlement of Mobile on the Gulf of Mexico in 1710 and became allies and trading partners with many of the Muskogean tribes of the area. Meanwhile, the English were pushing inland from the Atlantic Coast and developing relations with the Creek living to the east.

When the French were forced to give up their holdings in the Southeast in 1763, having lost the French and Indian War against the British, most of the Coushatta dispersed. Some moved to Louisiana. Others joined the SEMINOLE in Florida. Still others went to Texas.

Those who stayed in Alabama threw their lot in with the Creek and were relocated west of the Mississippi to the Indian Territory (now Oklahoma) at the time of the Trail of Tears in the 1830s; their descendants still live there today as part of the Alabama-Quassarte Tribe. Descendants of those Coushatta who moved to Louisiana presently have a nonreservation community near the town of Kinder, as well as a recently purchased 15-acre reservation. Those in Texas were granted reservation lands in Polk County along with the Alabama—the Alabama-Coushatta Tribe.

Coushatta alligator basket

CREE

When French traders, seeking furs, and French missionaries, spreading the Catholic faith, first learned of the existence of the Cree, these ALGONQUIANS were widespread. Bands of Cree hunted in territories extending all the way from the Ottawa River in the present-day province of Quebec to the Saskatchewan River of western Canada. The name *Cree*, pronounced the way it is spelled, is thought to be a shortened form of *Kristineaux* (or *Kiristino*), a French derivation of *Kenistenoag,* their native name.

Most Cree are classified as SUBARCTIC INDIANS. They made their homes in a part of North America where winters were long and summers were short, and the seasons dictated the rhythm of life. Lakes, rivers, and forests of spruce and fir trees were plentiful. Snowshoes and birch-bark canoes served as the main methods of transportation. The bark of the birch tree was also used to cover dwellings, small cone-shaped tents. Mammals, fowl, fish, and edible wild plants were the main source of food, since farming was so difficult in the cold climate and the rocky topsoil.

Different groups of Cree took on names based on their surroundings. There were the Swampy Cree (Maskegon) of the wet north country near Hudson Bay, and the Western Wood Cree of the forests north of Lake Winnipeg. Those who headed southward onto the Great Plains and began to hunt buffalo in addition to moose, caribou, deer, and elk, and began using true tipis of hide like other PLAINS INDIANS rather than the bark-covered tents common to their woodland relatives, and came to be called Plains Cree. Other important Cree groupings were the Tête de Boule Cree (Attikamek) and the Mistassini Cree in what is now Quebec, both of whom can be called the Eastern Wood Cree. With their wide range, the Cree Indians are historically one of the most important tribes of Canada.

The Fur Trade

In early Canadian history, the Cree are associated with the fur trade. The Cree trapped the animals of the northern forests, especially the beaver; then they exchanged the animal pelts for French trade goods, such as tools, cloth, beads, and, most valued of all, guns. With firearms, the Cree could hunt more efficiently. They could also gain the upper hand over other Indians who did not yet possess firearms, such as their traditional enemies to the west, the ATHAPASCANS.

Many of the French fur traders chose to live and raise families among the Cree. The French traders and canoemen who worked for fur companies were called *voyageurs* (the French word for "traveler") because they traveled through the network of rivers and lakes in search of furs. Their offspring—the Cree-French mixed-bloods, or MÉTIS—carried on this tradition. The unlicensed backwoods traders, who did not work for fur companies, were known as coureurs de bois, or "runners of the woods." Like the voyageurs, some of them were mixed-bloods.

Both the voyageurs and the coureurs de bois were a rugged breed. They usually dressed in buckskin shirts,

breechcloths, and leggings, like full-blooded Cree, and they knew native survival techniques. Yet they also practiced European customs such as the Catholic religion. Those who wanted to prove their courage might even undergo the Cree custom of tattooing, a painful process in which needles were run under the skin, followed by leather threads dipped in water and pigment.

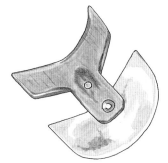

Cree knife for skinning animals

The most far-reaching fur companies in the 1700s and 1800s were the British-run Hudson's Bay Company, formed in 1670, and the North West Company, formed

Cree powderhorn with copper ornamentation and leather pouches, from the fur-trading period

in 1779. Fur-trading posts came to dot the Canadian wilderness, places where Indians, whites, and mixed-bloods would come together to barter their goods. The two big trading companies united in 1821 under the Hudson's Bay Company name. The Hudson's Bay Company helped bring about the exploration of Canada and at one time it claimed much of the Canadian West and Northwest as its own property.

The Indians and mixed-bloods were the most skilled scouts and made it possible for the white traders to find their way through the wilderness. Many of the later fur traders were Scots, and they too mixed with the Cree. As a result, some of the Métis were Cree-Scots. Like the Cree-French, the Cree-Scots knew how to live off the land Indian-style, but this group practiced Protestantism, not Catholicism.

Cree pipe bag of caribou hide with quillwork (modern)

The Second Riel Rebellion

The Cree were involved in one of the few Canadian Indian wars, which occurred in Saskatchewan late in the 1800s during the building of the Canadian Pacific Railway. Along with the railroad came more and more white settlers who wanted Indian lands. The western Cree joined up with their Métis relatives in the Second Riel Rebellion to protect their land rights.

The chiefs Poundmaker and Big Bear led warriors against two different forces: the North-West Mounted Police (also known as the Mounties), who patroled the western wilderness; and the North-West Field Force, an army sent from the East to put down the uprising. In an Indian council at Duck Lake in 1884, Big Bear said, "I have been trying to seize the promises the whites made to me; I have been grasping but I cannot find them. What they have promised me straight away, I have not yet seen the half of it."

Poundmaker and 200 warriors attacked the settlement of Battleford in March 1885, and Big Bear plus the same number of warriors took the settlement at Frog Lake the following April. Government troops pursued the two renegade bands. They caught up with Poundmaker's warriors at Cut Knife Creek in April, but the Indians counterattacked, then escaped. Big Bear's men outflanked their enemy at Frenchmen's Butte in May and again at Loon Lake in June. Neither Cree chief was captured in the field. But because the Métis had given up the fight, the Cree leaders also eventually surrendered. They were imprisoned for two years. Both Poundmaker and Big Bear died shortly after their release from prison, reportedly broken and bitter men.

Contemporary Cree

Although Cree numbers have decreased because of many epidemics from diseases introduced by whites over the years and a continuing low birthrate, tribal members are still widespread in Canada, having reserve lands in Alberta, Saskatchewan, Manitoba, Ontario, and Quebec. The Cree also share a reservation with the CHIPPEWA (OJIBWAY) in Montana, the Rocky Boy Chippewa-Cree Reservation.

The Cree struggle for land rights has continued to modern times. Cree people living on both sides of Hudson Bay—now known as East Main Cree and West Main Cree—lost a huge expanse of territory during the James Bay I hydroelectric project, first announced in 1971 and carried out over subsequent years. The building of La Grande Dam and Reservoir in northern Quebec in order to provide power to Canadian and U.S. communities to the south resulted in the flooding of some 7,500 square miles of traditional Cree and INUIT territory. The James Bay II project, the Great Whale Project, which would have flooded 2,000 square miles, was blocked in 1994 through the work of allied First Nations (as native groups in Canada are known) and environmental organizations, such as the Sierra Club and the Audubon Society. (The revelation that the flood waters resulting from the first project had released natural mercury from the soil and polluted the waters and made the eating of fish from the region dangerous, and the cancellation of the New York Power contract with Hydro-Quebec, spurred on by activists, helped in the process.) Yet there is renewed talk of a revised hydroelectric project along the Great Whale River. The Cree and their allies must be ever vigilant.

CREEK

The Native Americans known as the Creek received their tribal name, pronounced as spelled, from early English traders because they built most of their villages on woodland rivers and creeks. In reality, the Creek were not just one group but consisted of many different bands and villages with many names. The majority of Creek villages were situated along the banks of the Alabama, Coosa, Tallapoosa, Flint, Ocmulgee, and Chattahoochee rivers. Their ancestral territory included what now is most of Georgia and Alabama, as well as small parts of northern Florida, eastern Louisiana, and southern Tennessee. The various bands are discussed as two branches, the Upper Creek, mostly in Alabama, and the Lower Creek, mostly in Georgia.

The native name for the most powerful band of Creek, sometimes applied to other groups as well, is *Muskogee.* From *Muskogee* comes the name of one of the important language families: Muskogean. Other important Muskogean-speaking tribes were the ALABAMA, COUSHATTA, CHICKASAW, CHOCTAW, and SEMINOLE. In historic times, the Alabama and Coushatta, along with the Muskogee and many other Creek bands, were part of a loose organization referred to by scholars as the Creek Confederacy.

Lifeways

The Creek, along with the other tribes mentioned, are part of the Southeast Culture Area, and all of them shared many cultural traits (see SOUTHEAST INDIANS). Since the Creek were the most widespread and powerful of all these tribes, they are cited in many books as representing the typical Southeast Indian way of life. It is thought that the Creek were descendants of the MOUND BUILDERS who lived in the Southeast in prehistoric times.

As indicated, the Creek lived along the rivers and streams coursing through the piney woods of their extensive territory. The villages were the main political unit. Each had a chief called a *micco.* He was not an absolute ruler as in other Southeast tribes, such as the NATCHEZ and TIMUCUA. His functions were more like those of a modern-day mayor. A council of elders, the Beloved Men, helped him make decisions, and a town crier announced the decisions to the other villagers.

The villages were organized into "red towns" and "white towns." In the "red towns" lived the warriors who launched raids for purposes of honor and revenge; cere-monies such as war dances were held there. In the "white towns" lived the peacemakers who kept track of alliances and gave sanctuary to refugees; ceremonies such as the signing of treaties were held there.

Each village had a town square at its center with earthen banks where spectators could sit. The square was used for ceremonies and games. Each village also had a central circular house with clay walls and a cone-shaped bark roof about 25 feet high, the ceremonial lodge, as well as a shelter for the old and the homeless. Other houses were grouped in clusters of four small rectangular, pole-framed structures with bark-covered, slanted and peaked roofs. One of these clusters had tiers of benches and served as a meeting place for the Beloved Men.

Creek house

The other clusters of houses served as homes for individual families. Each family had a winter house, a summer house, a granary, and a warehouse. The winter house and summer house were built with closed mud-packed walls for insulation from the cold and heat. The summer house doubled as a guesthouse. The granary was half-open, and the warehouse was open on all four sides like a Seminole chickee.

The major form of social organization beyond the family was the clan, each of which had an animal name. In the case of the Creek, as with many other agricultural tribes, one's ancestral identification and clan membership was determined by the mother and not the father. Marriage with someone in one's own clan was forbidden.

The Creek were skilled farmers, growing corn, beans, squash, pumpkins, melons, and sweet potatoes. Each family planted and tended its own garden. But everyone helped with a communal field and contributed to communal stores that were used to feed warriors, the poor, and guests. They supplemented their diet through hunting and gathering.

The Green Corn Ceremony was the most important of the many Creek ceremonies. It is also called the Busk, from the Creek word *boskita,* meaning "to fast." Other tribes of the Southeast also practiced this renewal ritual, which took place near the end of the summer when the last corn crop ripened and which lasted four to eight days.

In preparation for the ritual, men made repairs to the communal buildings; women cleaned their houses and cooking utensils, even burning some possessions, then extinguished their hearth fires. The highest ranking villagers, including chiefs and shamans plus elders and warriors, all fasted. They then gathered at a feast where they ate corn and participated in the lighting of the Sacred Fire. They also drank the Black Drink, a ceremonial tea made from a poisonous shrub called *Ilex vomitoria,* tobacco, and other herbs, which induced vomiting and supposedly purified the body. Some participants danced the Green Corn Dance.

Then other villagers joined in the ceremony. They took coals from the Sacred Fire to rekindle the hearth fires and they cooked food for an even bigger feast, this time of deer meat. Games, such as lacrosse and archery contests, were held. There was more dancing. Villagers closed the ceremony with a communal bath in the river for purification. At the end, the entire village was ready for a fresh start of the New Year. All past wrongdoings were forgiven, except murder.

The Early Colonial Years

The first known European to make contact with the Creek was the Spanish explorer Hernando de Soto, who passed through their territory in 1540. In his journals, he wrote about their tall physique and their proud bearing, as well as their colorful dress. Because of their central location in the Southeast—between English, Spanish, and French settlements—the Creek played an important role in colonial affairs in later years.

For most of the colonial period, the Creek were allies of the British. Early British traders cultivated a relationship with them by giving them European tools and other goods. In the late 1600s and early 1700s, Creek warriors joined Carolina militiamen in attacks on Indians who

had been missionized by the Spanish, such as the APALACHEE and Timucua.

Creek warriors also launched attacks on the Choctaw, allies of the French. They also battled the CHEROKEE regularly.

Some Creek bands sided with the victorious British forces in the French and Indian War of 1754–63. Some bands later joined the losing British troops against the rebels in the American Revolution of 1775–83. Yet many village leaders hedged in choosing sides in these conflicts in order to play the white powers against each other to their own advantage.

The Creek War

In the early 1800s, the SHAWNEE Tecumseh traveled south to seek allies for his rebellion against the United States. Again many Creek leaders hedged. But during the years immediately following Tecumseh's Rebellion of 1809–11, many Creek joined forces in their own uprising, which became known as the Creek War of 1813–14.

The Red Stick faction of Creek wanted war with the whites; the White Stick faction wanted peace. Two mixed-bloods, Peter McQueen and William Weatherford, led the Red Sticks; Big Warrior, a full-blooded Creek, led the White Sticks.

The first incident concerned another full-blooded Creek by the name of Little Warrior, who had led a band of Creek against the Americans in the War of 1812. On the trip back from Canada after the engagement, his men killed some settlers along the Ohio River. The White Stick faction arrested and executed him for his deeds. Soon afterward, Peter McQueen led a force of Red Sticks to Pensacola on the Gulf of Mexico, where the Spanish gave them guns. This group then raided a party of settlers on Burnt Corn Creek in July 1813.

The most famous incident of the Creek War occurred the following month. William Weatherford, also known as Red Eagle, led a force of about 1,000 Red Sticks, as whites called the militants after the tall red poles elected as declarations of war (or from a method of time-keeping using sticks to record the number of days of a war expedition), against Fort Mims on the Alabama River. Black slaves reported to the commanding officer of the garrison, Major Daniel Beasley, that Indians were crawling toward the fort in the high grass. Yet Beasley failed to order the outer gates closed. The attack soon came, and Beasley himself was killed in the first onslaught. The settlers took cover behind the inner walls and held the warriors at bay for several hours. Eventually, flame-tipped arrows enabled the attackers to break through the defenses. Once inside Fort Mims, they killed about 400 settlers. Only 36 whites escaped. But the Red Sticks freed the black slaves.

Federal and state troops were mobilized to suppress the uprising. General Andrew Jackson, whom the Indians called "Sharp Knife," was given the command. Davy Crockett was one of his soldiers. There were many more battles. In November 1813, soldiers drew the Red Sticks into a trap at Tallasahatchee, then relieved the White Stick village of Talladega, which was under attack by a party of Red Sticks. In December, Red Eagle managed to escape troops closing in on his hometown of Econochaca by leaping off a bluff into a river while mounted on his horse. In January 1814, there were two indecisive battles at Emuckfaw and Enotachopco Creek.

The final battle took place at Horseshoe Bend in March 1814. There, Jackson's men moved into position around the Red Sticks' barricades, removed their canoes, and attacked. Fighting lasted all day until the Indians, with most of their warriors killed, retreated. Red Eagle survived, however, because he had departed before the attack to inspect other fortifications.

Red Eagle surrendered several days later. He walked into Jackson's camp and announced, "I am Bill Weatherford." To punish the Creek, Jackson forced them to sign the Treaty of Horseshoe Bend, which took away 23 million acres of land—from both the militant Red Sticks and the peaceful White Sticks.

Relocation

In 1830, Andrew Jackson, who was now president of the United States, signed the Indian Removal Act, beginning a period of relocation of eastern tribes to the Indian Territory west of the Mississippi River. Thus the Creek lost their remaining ancestral lands to whites. Many lost their lives too. During their forced march in 1836 and soon after their arrival in the Indian Territory, about 3,500 of the 15,000 who were forced to leave the Southeast died from exposure, hunger, disease, and bandit attacks. The Cherokee called their journey the Trail of Tears, a phrase now applied to the removal of the Creek, Chickasaw, Choctaw, and Seminole as well. After their relocation, these tribes came to be called the "Five Civilized Tribes" by whites because they adopted many of the customs of the white settlers around them.

The Indian Territory was supposed to have been a permanent homeland for Native Americans. Yet after many reductions in its size, in 1907, it became the state of Oklahoma. This event took place six years after a Creek by the name of Chitto Harjo (Crazy Snake) led a rebellion against the allotment, or the breaking up of tribal holdings to give them to individuals, which made it easier for unscrupulous non-Indians to take over the lands. In the Snake Uprising, as newspapers called it, the rebels harassed whites and destroyed their property until overwhelming government forces rode in to arrest them.

The following is a traditional song by a Creek woman:

> I have no more land
> I am driven away from home
> Driven up the red waters
> Let us all go
> Let us all go die together.

Chitto Harjo was an Upper Creek, the more traditional tribal faction. In 1917, the Upper Creek and more progressive Lower Creek became embroiled in a conflict referred to as the Green Corn War. The political struggle between the two groups lasted until tribal reorganization in the 1970s.

Contemporary Creek

The Creek have rebounded from the loss of their lands and traditional way of life. Early in the 20th century, tribal members recognized the need for education and began learning the skills necessary to cope in the culture that had displaced their own. As a result, many Creek have succeeded in a variety of well-paying fields, such as medicine and law.

Creek Indians, among other Oklahoma Indians, are part of the largest class-action suit ever filed by Indians, started in 1996. The plaintiffs claim that the Interior Department's Bureau of Indian Affairs has mismanaged billions in funds owed them from the federal government's leasing of trust lands for oil, gas, timber, and other resources.

Some Alabama-COUSHATTA are joined with the Creek Nation in the present-day Creek Confederacy, which has its seat of government at Okmulgee in eastern Oklahoma. Scattered pockets of Creek maintain tribal identity in Alabama, Georgia, and Florida.

CROW

The Crow native name is *Absaroka,* Siouan for "bird people." Their name among Europeans became that of the well-known bird and is pronounced the same way. Early in their history, they split off from another Siouan-speaking people, the HIDATSA, of the upper Missouri in what is now North Dakota because of a dispute over buffalo. The Crow then migrated farther upriver, to the Yellowstone River at the foot of the Rocky Mountains, territory now part of southern Montana and northern Wyoming.

The Crow who settled north of the Yellowstone toward the Musselshell River became known as the Mountain Crow because of the high terrain. Those who ranged to the south along the valleys of the Big Horn, Powder, and Wind Rivers came to be called the River Crow.

Lifeways

Both groups of Crow gave up the village life of their Hidatsa kinsmen. They stopped farming for food, growing only tobacco crops; they no longer constructed earthlodges; and they ceased making pottery. The Crow chose the life of the High Plains instead: They lived in hide tipis in camps which they moved often, following the herds of buffalo and other game, and they ate wild plant foods. Horses, when they acquired them in the 1700s, revolutionized hunting and warfare, allowing PLAINS INDIANS to travel faster and farther than before.

The Crow, like many Plains tribes, participated in the Sun Dance and the Vision Quest. They also had their own special societies, such as the Crow Tobacco Society, with rituals surrounding their one crop.

A Crow warrior

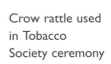 

Crow rattle used in Tobacco Society ceremony

The Crow had elaborate rules governing the behavior of adults toward children. For example, fathers sponsored feasts where they made speeches about their children's future success. Fathers also taught their sons survival skills, such as archery, lavishing praise on them whenever they showed improvement. On returning from his first war party, a boy would be surrounded by the *aassahke,* members of his father's clans, who would sing praise songs and offer prayers. One of these relatives, usually a cousin, would be the "joking relative," who offered ridicule in a friendly way if the boy's behavior called for it. Mothers would give great care to their daughters' upbringing, preparing them in the maternal and domestic skills essential to the survival of the tribe, such as preparing food and making clothing.

The Crow were also known for their striking appearance: hair sometimes reaching all the way to the ground with the help of added interwoven strands; their elegantly crafted clothes dyed in bright colors with intricate quillwork, and later beadwork, forming geometric and flower designs; plus their beautiful blankets, pouches, saddles, and bridles also with quillwork and beadwork. Some traders called the Crow the "Long-haired Indians." George Catlin, the frontier painter who lived among many different Plains peoples in the 1830s, painted many stunning portraits of tribal members.

The Crow were longtime enemies of the other powerful tribes on the northern plains—the SIOUX (DAKOTA, LAKOTA, NAKOTA) and the BLACKFEET—fighting for horses, hunting grounds, and fame. To achieve glory in battle, Crow and other Plains Indians used the coup stick to touch their enemies and prove bravery.

Wars

The Crow, like many other Plains peoples, launched raids for horses against other tribes and against white traders. In 1821, mountain men held a fur-trading rendezvous along the Arkansas River with CHEYENNE, ARAPAHO, COMANCHE, and KIOWA. A party of Crow camped within striking distance. Every night, no matter how many guards were posted, Crow warriors would sneak into the camp and silently make their way to the log pens where the horses were kept. Fighting would sometimes break out and men would be killed on both sides. But more often than not, the Crow would be too fast for the traders, escaping with the choice mounts.

In the wars for the West, the Crow earned a reputation as allies of the U.S. Army. They served as scouts and fought alongside the bluecoats, especially during the 1870s against the Sioux and the NEZ PERCE. Chief Plenty Coups encouraged his warriors to side with the army because, as he expressed it, "When the war is over, the soldier-chiefs will not forget that the Absaroka came to their aid."

With increasing numbers of miners and settlers in Indian country, the building of forts and railroads, and the depletion of the buffalo herds, the nomadic life of the Crow ended. The Crow were treated no differently than the resisting tribes. After a series of treaties through 1888, they were forced into ceding most of their land and settling on a reservation. The territory they were allowed to keep was part of their ancestral homeland.

The Crow were given a place of honor in a historic national ceremony. In 1921, after World War I, the now-aged Crow chief Plenty Coups was the Indian chosen to represent all other Indians at the dedication of the Tomb of the Unknown Soldier in Washington, D.C. To close the national ceremony, Plenty Coups placed his warbonnet and coup stick on the grave.

Contemporary Crow

In the 1950s, the Crow reservation in Montana was further reduced so that the Yellowtail Dam could be built in the Bighorn Canyon. Although remaining holdings are rich in natural resources—farming and grazing lands and coal reserves—many individual tribal members still have a difficult time earning a decent living because of earlier unfair leasing deals or lack of funds to develop mining.

The Little Bighorn Battlefield National Monument adjoins the Crow reservation. The Crow Tribe holds reenactments of the Battle of Little Bighorn (or the Battle of the Greasy Grass, as Native Americans refer to it), in which Lieutenant Colonel George Armstrong Custer and his Seventh Cavalry were wiped out by Sioux and Cheyenne warriors. (Two Crow, Curly, and White-Man-Runs-Him served as scouts for the army. Custer sent most of his Indian scouts to the rear before the battle, which enabled their survival. Curly and White-Man-Runs-Him became informants on the battle, providing valuable information to historians.) The Crow Tribe also sponsors the annual Crow Fair in August, with a rodeo and dance parades, and holds annual Sun Dances.

Crow bow

DAKOTA *see* SIOUX (DAKOTA, LAKOTA, NAKOTA)

DELAWARE *see* LENNI LENAPE (DELAWARE)

DINEH *see* NAVAJO

ESKIMO *see* INUIT

FLATHEAD

The Flathead Indians also are known by the name *Salish,* which means "people." The latter name can be confusing, however, since this tribe is just one of many different Salishan-speaking groups. As a result, the term *Flathead* is generally used; it is pronounced as spelled.

But the term *Flathead* can be misleading. Some other Salishans to the west along the Northwest Coast practiced a custom known as head-flattening, a gradual process of deformation by tying a padded board to the forehead of infants. With growth, their heads took on a tapered, pointed look. The NORTHWEST COAST INDI-ANS with the deformed heads thought that people with normal heads looked funny, and they called them "flat-heads." French fur trappers also started using this name for the Interior Salish instead of the Coast Salish, and the name has stuck until modern times.

The Flathead ancestral territory now is part of western Montana. But they ranged into present-day northern Idaho as well. Much of this territory is mountainous, part of the Rocky Mountain chain. The Flathead are classified as PLATEAU INDIANS and, like the other tribes of the region, they depended on fishing in the rivers that coursed through their lands, as well as on hunting. Early in their history, the Flathead, like other Plateau tribes, built pithouses, using pole frames and vegetable coverings, such as cedar bark or woven mats of Indian hemp. In later years, they lived mainly in conical tents, the poles of which were placed around the edges of an excavated pit and then covered with grass or bark, and finally earth.

After they had acquired horses in the early 1700s, the Flathead began venturing onto the northern plains to their east to hunt buffalo and adopted cultural traits similar to those of the PLAINS INDIANS. They continued to use veg-

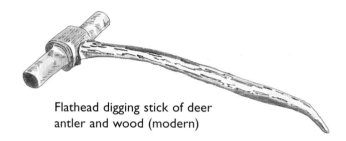

Flathead digging stick of deer antler and wood (modern)

etable coverings for their dwellings, however, rather than the typical buffalo-skin coverings of Plains Indian tipis.

The BLACKFEET were traditional enemies of the Flat-head and kept them from expanding their territory east-ward. The two tribes were in a deadly cycle of raid and retaliation when the Lewis and Clark Expedition first had contact with them in 1806. A Jesuit missionary by the name of Father Pierre Jean de Smet, who lived among the Flathead and other Plateau Indians from 1840 to 1846, finally established peace between the two peoples.

The Flathead signed a treaty in 1855 in which they ceded the majority of their lands in Montana and Idaho except for two pieces. In 1872, they lost one of these. The present-day Flathead Reservation is situated south of Flathead Lake near Dixon, Montana. The Flathead share the reservation with other Salishans—the KALISPEL and SPOKAN—as well as with the KOOTENAI. The Confeder-ated Salish and Kootenai Tribes of the Flathead Reserva-tion receive revenues from the Kerr Dam on the lower Flathead River. In the year 2015, the current lease agree-ment will run out and the tribes will assume the license to operate the dam, which will improve finances. They have constructed a large resort on Flathead Lake, know as KwaTaqNuk, and they sponsor two powwows every July.

FORMATIVE INDIANS *see* PREHISTORIC INDIANS

FOX (Mesquaki)

The Fox occupied ancestral territory in the western Great Lakes region. Like most other ALGONQUIANS, they are classified as a Woodland people of the Northeast Culture Area (see NORTHEAST INDIANS). They typically located their villages along river valleys where the soil was rich enough for crops. Their native name, *Mesquaki* (also spelled Mesquakie or Meskwaki), pronounced mes-KWAK-ee, means "red earth people," after the reddish soil in their homeland. (The name of their neighbors and allies, the SAC, is derived from an Algonquian word for "yellow earth people.") Their alternate, more widely known, name—after the animal and pronounced as spelled—possibly was the symbol of a particular clan and mistakenly applied to the entire tribe by Europeans.

Mesquaki courting flute

The Mesquaki are also sometimes classified as PRAIRIE INDIANS, because they lived near the prairies of the Mississippi valley, with its tall, coarse grasses and few trees and its herds of buffalo.

Being seminomadic, the Mesquaki could take advantage of both forests and prairies. During the summer, they lived in villages of bark-covered houses and raised corn, beans, squash, pumpkins, and tobacco; during the winter they tracked herds of game and lived in portable wigwams.

The Mesquaki and other tribes of the western Great Lakes region sometimes are referred to as the "people of the calumet" because they used calumets, or sacred pipes, in their ceremonies. The Indians placed tobacco, or *kinnikinnik,* a mixture of tobacco and willow bark, in the pipe bowls carved from pipestone (catlinite); then they inhaled the burning matter through long wooden or reed stems.

The Mesquaki had three kinds of leader: the peace chief, the war chief, and the ceremonial leader. The first position was the only one that was hereditary, passed on from father to son. The peace chief kept peace within the tribe and was in charge at councils when village matters were discussed. On these occasions, the calumets were decorated with white feathers and were truly "peace pipes," the popular name for the long Indian pipes.

A war chief was chosen for each military campaign by his peers on the basis of fighting skills and visions. He would be in charge at councils when matters of war were discussed. On these occasions, the calumets would be decorated with red feathers.

The ceremonial leader, or shaman, instructed others in religious rituals. These ceremonies had many purposes, such as making game plentiful, or helping crops grow, or curing the sick. On these occasions, participants would smoke the sacred pipe.

Historically, the Mesquaki are most closely associated with Wisconsin. The territory where they first had contact with whites in the 1600s—along the Fox River named after them is now part of that state. But the Mesquaki might have earlier lived east of Lake Michigan in what is now the state of Michigan.

The Mesquaki were the only sizable Algonquian tribe to make war on the French during the early part of the French and Indian wars, especially in the 1720s and 1730s. Most of the other Algonquians sided with the French against the British. The Mesquaki followed a different path, however, because they were traditional enemies of the CHIPPEWA (OJIBWAY), who maintained close ties with the French. The Mesquaki demanded tolls in the form of trade goods from any outsiders who passed along the Fox River, which angered the French. The French and Chippewa launched a campaign against the Mesquaki and drove them down the Wisconsin River to new homelands.

It was during this period, in 1734, that the Mesquaki joined in an alliance with the Sac, one that has lasted to present times. Starting in 1769, the two tribes plus others drove the ILLINOIS from their lands, and some Mesquaki moved further south into what has become

Mesquaki skirt (made in modern times using antique ribbon appliqué)

the state of Illinois. In 1780, Mesquaki also formed a temporary alliance with the SIOUX (DAKOTA, LAKOTA, NAKOTA) to attack the Chippewa at St. Croix Falls, but in this conflict they were defeated.

After the American Revolution and the birth of the United States, Mesquaki history closely follows that of their permanent allies, the Sac. The Mesquaki were active in Little Turtle's War of 1790–94 (see MIAMI) and Tecumseh's Rebellion of 1809–11 (see SHAWNEE). Mesquaki warriors also fought alongside the Sac under the Sac chief Black Hawk in the famous Black Hawk War of 1832, the final Indian war for the Old Northwest. Today, the two tribes share reservations and trust lands in Iowa, Kansas, and Oklahoma under the official name of the Sac and Fox. The Sac and Fox of the Mississippi in Iowa now use the name Mesquaki Nation since most of their people are Mesquaki.

GREAT BASIN INDIANS

Great Basin is a geographical term for an immense desert basin in the western part of North America. The Great Basin has the shape of a bowl: a central depression surrounded by highlands. To the east stand the Rocky Mountains; to the west, the Sierra Nevada; to the north, the Columbia Plateau; and to the south, the Colorado Plateau. The Great Basin Culture Area, where Indians shared a similar way of life, includes territory now comprising practically all of Nevada and Utah; parts of Idaho, Oregon, Wyoming, Colorado, and California; and small parts of Arizona, New Mexico, and Montana.

The Great Basin is a region of interior drainage. That is to say, rivers and streams drain from the flanking higher ground and flow into the central depression, disappearing into "sinks" in the sandy soil. The mountains block weather fronts from the ocean. Few rain clouds ever reach the Great Basin, resulting in little precipitation and high evaporation. In past ages, the region contained many large lakes; the largest lake remaining is the Great Salt Lake in what is now Utah. Because of the geological formation of the region, the Great Basin has many alkaline flats—soil with mineral salts from bodies of water that have since evaporated. Only occasional low

and long rocky uplands break up the long stretches of barren desert.

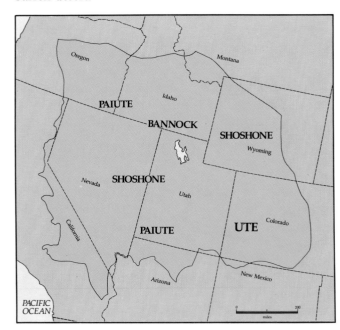

The Great Basin Culture Area, showing the approximate locations of Indian tribes listed in this book—circa 1500, before displacement by non-Indians (with modern boundaries)

Death Valley is part of the Great Basin. This depression in the desert is the lowest point in all the Americas—280 feet below sea level. It also has some of the most extreme temperatures, as high as 140 degrees Fahrenheit.

Because of the aridity, little vegetation grows in the Great Basin. The dominant flora on the desert floor are low grasses and sagebrush, a plant that sends its roots far down into the earth for moisture. The hills have some trees that are adapted to dryness, such as juniper and piñon trees. Also because of the dryness, there is little game. The most common large mammal is the antelope, which grazes on grass and brush and which can go a long time without water. Mountain goats subsist in the rocky highlands. Jackrabbits live in the desert, as do rodents, including field mice, kangaroo rats, muskrats, gophers, and ground squirrels. Certain birds and reptiles, particularly snakes and lizards, also are suited to desert life, as are insects, such as the grasshopper.

All these creatures provided food for Great Basin Indians. The Indians also foraged and dug for edible wild plants—roots, berries, seeds, and nuts. With a few exceptions, Great Basin inhabitants practiced no agriculture in the extreme environment. Because of their foraging practices, the hunter-gatherers of the region have been referred to collectively as "Digger Indians."

Having such meager food supplies, Great Basin Indians traveled for the most part in small bands of extended families. Most lived in small, simple cone-shaped structures, made of pole frames covered with brush or reeds.

Most peoples of the Great Basin are of the Uto-Aztecan language family, part of the Aztec-Tanoan phylum. Although band and clan identities in the region were more important historically than tribal identities, linguistic relationships have led scholars to define four Great Basin "tribes": Bannock, Paiute, Shoshone, and Ute. The Paiute are further divided into the Northern Paiute and the Southern Paiute, and the Shoshone into the Northern Shoshone, Western Shoshone, and Eastern Shoshone. Other small Uto-Aztecan groupings—the Chemehuevi, Kawaiisu, Koso, and Mono of what now is eastern California and western Nevada, with dialects similar to those of the Paiute, and the Goshute of what now is western Utah and eastern Nevada, with a dialect close to that of the Shoshone—are related ancestrally to the other Uto-Aztecans. The only linguistic exception are the Washoe of what now is western Nevada and eastern California, a Hokan-speaking people.

GROS VENTRE

Gros ventre, pronounced grow VAHN-truh, means "big belly" in French. Early French fur traders on the northern plains gave this name to two different tribes, the Atsina and the HIDATSA, because of the hand motions used to designate both tribes in the sign language of the PLAINS INDIANS. In this sign language, invented by the Indians so that they could communicate with each other despite their many different spoken languages, each tribe had a particular hand sign. In the case of the Atsina, the sign was a sweeping pass in front of the abdomen with both hands to show that they were big eaters. In the case of the Hidatsa, an early sign was a similar gesture in front of the abdomen, to indicate their custom of tattooing parallel stripes across the chest. Therefore, to the French the Atsina were the Gros Ventre of the Plains, and the Hidatsa were the Gros Ventre of the River. Yet in modern usage only the Atsina are called Gros Ventre; with the Hidatsa referred to by their actual name.

The Gros Ventre native name is *Ah-ah-nee-nin,* meaning "white clay people." In their creation myth, the Creator shaped them out of clay to keep himself company.

The Gros Ventre, or Atsina, lived for most of their history on the Milk River branch of the Missouri River in territory that is now northern Montana. They also ranged into southern Saskatchewan as far north as the Saskatchewan River. Language similarities indicate that the Gros Ventre split off from the ARAPAHO, another Algonquian-speaking people. For much of their history, the Gros Ventre were part of the Blackfoot Confederacy; the BLACKFEET, another Algonquian people, lived to their northwest.

On acquiring horses and guns, the Gros Ventre became a typical Plains tribe. They depended on buffalo more than any other game for sustenance and lived in camps of tipis. They also conducted raids on other tribes for horses.

In the mid-1800s, the Gros Ventre joined the CROW in a fight with their former Blackfeet allies. They suffered a major defeat in 1867. Disease brought to the northern plains by white traders also killed many of their people.

In 1888, the surviving Gros Ventre were placed on Fort Belknap Reservation in northern Montana, where their descendants live today. They share the reservation with the ASSINIBOINE. The economy of the reservation is agricultural-based with farming, ranching, and the leasing of lands.

The elders among the Gros Ventre are currently working to preserve the tribe's language and traditional culture for future generations. Their traditional religion involves rituals surrounding their sacred pipes, the Feathered Pipe and the Flat Pipe, given to the Ah-ah-nee-nin by the Creator. At their annual powwows traditional dances, such as the Clown Dance, are performed.

Gros Ventre pouch

HAIDA

The Pacific Northwest Coast was a region of master woodcarvers. NORTHWEST COAST INDIANS crafted giant totem poles as well as elaborate ceremonial masks, chests, headdresses, and other objects. Of the many skilled woodworkers along this heavily populated strip of coastal land, stretching from northern California to southern Alaska, the Haida crafts workers perhaps were the most highly skilled. Their seaworthy boats were especially prized by other tribes. Individuals of other tribes showed off their wealth by trading for a Haida dugout and displaying it at ceremonies, such as weddings.

The Haida occupied ancestral territory on the Queen Charlotte Islands off present-day British Columbia. In the early 1700s, a group of Haida migrated northward to the southern part of Prince of Wales Island, now part of Alaska, where they used the name *Kaigani*. The Haida, whose name pronounced HI-duh means "people," belong to the Na-Dene language phylum, distant relatives of the TLINGIT to their north and perhaps of the ATHAPASCANS to the east.

Lifeways

Since the Haida lived on an island whose streams were too small for salmon, they depended more on fish such as halibut and cod. The candlefish provided oil for cooking and lamps. The Haida also hunted sea mammals, such as seals, sea lions, and sea otters. Unlike the NOOTKA and MAKAH to the south, however, the Haida did not pursue whales. The forests in the interior of the Queen Charlotte Islands had little game, but the Haida did hunt black bears.

Haida dugout

Haida fishhook

Haida men constructed some of the largest gabled houses in the Pacific Northwest, some of them 60 feet by 100 feet. The structures were made from cedar planks, and their openings faced the sea, with one or more totem poles in the front.

Haida clothing was made from woven cedar bark or from the pelts of otters and other animals. The women tattooed their faces and bodies and the backs of their hands with family symbols.

Haida society was divided into two clans, the Bear Clan and the Raven Clan. The Haida practiced the potlatch, the ritualistic giving of gifts to guests. Shamans were organized into secret societies and held great power through their supposed contact with the Ocean Beings. The shamans used "soul-catchers," carved bone tubes, to capture the wandering souls of sick people and return them to their bodies. The dead were placed in carved grave-houses overlooking the ocean, and only the shamans could visit these open coffins.

The favorite wood of the Haida for making their famous dugouts was the giant redwood, although cedar was also used. A tall, straight tree would be felled and floated to the worksite. The log would be split along its center with wooden wedges. Then the remaining round side of one of the logs would be further split to flatten it. The wood would be charred with a torch to make it easier to scrape with a stone adz (later, the Haida used metal tools, acquired from whites). Both the inside and outside of the hull would be scraped, chiseled, and rubbed smooth, until the sides of the boat would be two fingers thick at the bottom, one inch at the top. The cockpit would be widened by putting water inside and adding hot rocks, by burning fires near the outside to further heat the wood, and by forcing the sides outward with oversize wooden braces. The bow and stern pieces, the former longer than the latter, would be carved separately and attached with either cedar pegs or spruce lashings. Strips of cedar would also be added to the tops of the sides. The hull would be sanded with stone and polished with sharkskin to prevent friction in the water. The bow and stern would be decorated with carvings, inlays, and paintings of totemic designs. The resulting boat could be as much as 60 feet long and seven feet wide at the center and could hold about 60 warriors or the same weight in cargo. At first the Indians propelled their boats with paddles, but added sails after contact with Europeans.

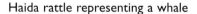

Haida rattle representing a whale

Haida paddle

Contacts with Non-Indians

Spanish, Russian, British, and French explorers reached the Haida homeland in the mid- to late 1700s. After the first trips of exploration, the fur traders came and established trading posts. (Hudson's Bay blankets bought from whites became the main gift at Indian potlatches.) Soon came the missionaries, both Episcopal and Methodist. Disease, liquor, and alien religions all contributed to the gradual decline of the Haida people and their traditional culture.

Haida whistle

Contemporary Haida

Only two organized Haida communities remain in Canada—Masset and Skidegate. Work in fishing and canning provides income for some tribe members. Others generate income through their rediscovered traditional artwork. A community of Haida lives at Hydaburg on the southern end of Prince of Wales Island in Alaska. This group has joined in a corporation with the Tlingit, called the Sealaska Corporation. Both Haida and Tlingit have a reputation as being among the best Alaskan fishermen. Other Haida have moved to urban centers in the region.

HAUDENOSAUNEE   *see* IROQUOIS (HAUDENOSAUNEE)

HAVASUPAI

The Havasupai ancestral homeland, from about A.D. 1100, was Cataract (or Havasu) Canyon and vicinity, part of the Grand Canyon complex. This territory, now part of northwestern Arizona, contains some of the most spectacular landforms in all of North America—high-walled canyons with colorful layers of sandstone, deep caves, and steep waterfalls.

The Havasupai are an offshoot of the HUALAPAI. Both peoples, along with the YAVAPAI, are discussed as Upland Yumans and lived north of the River Yuman tribes, such as the MOJAVE and YUMA (QUECHAN). Scholars classify all these Yuman-speaking peoples as SOUTHWEST INDIANS.

Although the Havasupai lived in dry country, the Colorado River and its tributaries defined their way of life and came to be associated with them. *Havasupai,* pronounced hah-vah-SOO-pie, means "people of the blue-green water." Cataract Canyon, formed by the Havasu tributary, is a fertile strip of land unlike any other in that arid and rocky region.

The Havasupai learned to irrigate their fields with water from the river and till the soil with planting sticks. They grew corn, beans, squash, melons, sunflowers, and tobacco. Tribal members thus were able to live most of the year in permanent villages. They lived in two different kinds of dwellings: pole-framed houses, circular or rectangular in shape and covered with brush and earth, and rock shelters, either naturally formed or dug by hand in canyon walls. The Havasupai also built small domed lodges that doubled as sweathouses and clubhouses. In their agricultural lifestyle, the Havasupai resembled the HOPI to the east more than they did their Yuman kin to the south. The Havasupai often traded with the Hopi, exchanging deerskins, salt, and red mineral paint for agricultural products, pottery, and cloth.

After the autumn harvest, the Havasupai left their villages. They climbed the canyon walls to the top of the plateau, where they lived in temporary camps in the midst of plentiful game for the winter. Individual hunters, carrying bows and arrows, stalked mountain lions and other wildcats, deer and antelope, and mountain sheep. Men, women, and children also participated in communal hunting drives. By stomping and beating the ground, they forced rabbits into the open, where they could be clubbed. The Havasupai also gathered piñon nuts, the edible seed from a small pine tree, on the canyon rims.

The Havasupai wore more clothing than most other Yumans, mostly buckskin. They painted and tattooed their faces. They made both baskets and pottery for use as containers and cooking vessels.

The main unit of social organization for the Havasupai was the family. The tribe as a whole was loosely structured under six hereditary chiefs. Their religion was dominated by shamans, but with few organized rituals other than the use of prayer sticks and dances for a particular purpose, such as to ask for rain. Tribal members participated in at least three ceremonies a year, with music, dancing, and speechmaking.

The Havasupai were peaceful; not one of their leaders was a war chief. Their seclusion behind canyon walls enabled them to avoid attacks by more warlike neighbors. The only early Spanish explorer thought to have visited them was Father Francisco Garcés, in 1776. The tribe managed to avoid further contact with outsiders well into the 1800s.

The Havasupai still live in Cataract (Havasu) Canyon, now on a reservation originally established in 1880; Supai, Arizona, is the site of the tribal population. In 1975, with the signing of the Grand Canyon National Park Enlargement Act, the tribe regained a portion of its ancestral homeland along the Grand Canyon's south rim. Because of their location, 3,000 feet below the rim of the Grand Canyon, the Havasupai earn a decent income from tourism. The Havasupai Tourist Enterprise provides facilities, guides, and mules for tourists.

HIDATSA

The Hidatsa, also known as the Minitaree, occupied ancestral territory along the upper Missouri River in what now is North Dakota. In early colonial history, they were called the Gros Ventre of the River by French traders, but the name *Gros Ventre* is more commonly applied to another tribe (see GROS VENTRE). *Hidatsa*, pronounced hee-DOT-suh, possibly means "rows of lodges"; the alternative name *Minitaree*, pronounced min-uh-TAR-ee, means "willows."

The Siouan-speaking Hidatsa are close relatives of another Siouan-speaking people who lived to their west in what is now Montana, the CROW. According to tribal tradition, the Hidatsa once lived near Devil's Lake, also in what is now North Dakota, but were pushed southwestward by the SIOUX (DAKOTA, LAKOTA, NAKOTA). The Hidatsa settled along the Missouri River and came to be associated with the tribes whose villages flanked their own—the MANDAN and ARIKARA.

All three peoples—the Hidatsa, Mandan, and Arikara—were primarily village farmers. They lived in earth lodges on bluffs overlooking the Missouri River. They made pottery, unlike other more nomadic tribes of the region, who used less fragile hide bags for cooking and storing food. The Hidatsa acquired some of their meat through trade with other tribes, exchanging corn for buffalo and deer meat and hides.

The Hidatsa shared many rituals with the Mandan. One custom the two tribes had in common was the Corn Dance Feast of the Women. They believed that the Old Woman Who Never Dies sent waterfowl to them in the spring as a symbol of the seeds the Indians planted. The geese represented corn; the ducks, beans; and the swans, gourds. To repay the Old Woman, the elderly women of the tribe would hang dried meat on poles as a sacrifice, then perform a dance. During the ceremony, young women of the tribe would feed the dancing

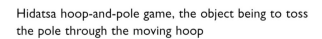
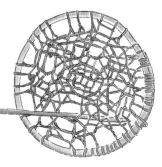

Hidatsa hoop-and-pole game, the object being to toss the pole through the moving hoop

women meat and receive grains of corn to eat in return. Some of the consecrated grain from the ceremony would be mixed with the tribe's planting seeds. The sacrificed meat would be left on the poles until harvest time.

The Hidatsa hunted as well as framed. They organized an annual buffalo hunt. Like the Mandan, the Hidatsa had a White Buffalo Society for women only. Women would dance in ceremonies to lure the buffalo to the hunters. After the Hidatsa had acquired horses from other tribes through trade, they tracked buffalo herds farther from their villages, onto territory that is now South Dakota and Montana. The Hidatsa also shared customs, such as the Sun Dance, with their more nomadic Siouan relatives. They are usually classified as PLAINS INDIANS but are also referred to as PRAIRIE INDIANS.

Early French and English traders plying the muddy waters of the Missouri River in their flatboats and pirogues (boats resembling canoes) made regular stops at Hidatsa villages to barter their trade goods—guns, liquor, tools, cloth, glass beads—for furs. Early explorers traveling the Missouri, such as Lewis and Clark during their expedition of 1804–6, also lived among the Hidatsa.

After the smallpox epidemic of 1837, which decimated the tribes of the upper Missouri, Hidatsa survivors regrouped into a single village. In 1845, the tribe moved this village to the vicinity of Fort Berthold, North Dakota. In 1870, by executive order of the federal government, a reservation was established for the Hidatsa, to be shared with the Arikara and Mandan.

A copy of a map, drawn by the Hidatsa Indian Little Wolf, about 1880. It shows the route he took along the Missouri River in a successful raid for horses on a Sioux encampment. The circles represent Hidatsa lodges, with dots showing the number of poles supporting each roof. The crosses represent Sioux tipis. Combined circles and crosses represent dwellings belonging to intermarried Hidatsa and Sioux. Squares represent dwellings of whites. The square with a cross represents the house of a white man and Sioux woman. Lean Wolf's original path is shown in footprints and his return with the stolen horses in hoofprints.

The Three Affiliated Tribes still share this reservation today, where they run a tourism complex. Each tribe sponsors an annual powwow. Traditional warbonnet dances are featured parts of the festivities. A casino, in operation since 1993, has increased tribal revenues.

HOHOKAM *see* SOUTHWEST CULTURES

HOPEWELL *see* MOUND BUILDERS

HOPI

Hopi legend tells how tribal ancestors climbed up through three cave worlds along with all the animals. They were helped by two Spirit Masters who were brothers. After time spent in each chamber of the underworld, the people and animals finally emerged from the Grand Canyon into a fourth world, which was the earth. But darkness blanketed all the land. And the land was wet. The people met with different animals to try to bring light to the world.

Spider spun a ball of pure white silk to make the Moon. The people bleached a deerskin and shaped it into a shield, which became the Sun. Coyote opened a jar he had found in one of the cave worlds. Sparks flew out of it, turned his face black, then flew into the sky and became stars. Then Vulture flapped his wings and made the water flow away, forming dry land. The Spirit Masters helped the water flow by forming grooves in the earth, which became the valleys. Different clans then formed with various animal names and traveled to many different locations before finally settling in their permanent homes.

The above is one of many different Native American creation myths. Although mythological, the story contains many elements relating to the history and culture of the Hopi. For example, as the legend indicates, Hopi ancestors migrated from various locations to form the tribe. They settled near the Grand Canyon. They lived in arid desert country, depending on natural springs to water their crops. Both guardian spirits and animals played an important part in their elaborate religion. Underground chambers, called kivas, were considered as the doorway to the underworld and were used for ceremonies. The legend also shows how the Hopi were a cooperative and peaceful people, willing to work with others to make their life better.

In fact, the Hopi name, pronounced HO-pee, is a shortening of their word *Hopituh,* meaning "peaceful ones." These people were formerly called the Moki (or Moqui) Indians, probably a name given to them by another tribe.

The Hopi were the westernmost of the PUEBLO INDIANS, classified with them in the Southwest Culture Area (see SOUTHWEST INDIANS). They are the only Pueblo peoples to speak a dialect of the Uto-Aztecan language family. Yet like other Pueblo Indians, they were probably descended from Anasazi peoples, earlier inhabitants of the Southwest (see SOUTHWEST CULTURES).

The Hopi occupied different village sites on what they called the First Mesa, Second Mesa, and Third Mesa, all part of a still-larger rocky formation called Black Mesa. These various tablelands, overlooking dry valleys, were carved by erosion out of the enormous Colorado Plateau situated between the Colorado River and the Rio Grande. The Hopi homeland has since become part of northeastern Arizona in the center of NAVAJO lands.

The Hopi are famous for their religious, intellectual, and peaceful worldview. They called their approach to life the Hopi Way. The Hopi Way refers to varying aspects of existence as a whole, including religious beliefs, the relationship to nature, behavior toward other people, craftsmanship, and survival.

Pueblos

The Hopi built the walls of their pueblos with stones set in mud, then plastered the surface with more mud. Trees were rare in their homeland, so tribal members traveled far to find pine and juniper trees for beams. The men provided the building materials, but the women shaped them into houses. They stretched the beams from one wall to another, forming a flat roof, which was filled in with poles, branches, leaves, and grass, then packed with plaster. The walls had no doors or windows. Family members entered through an opening in the roof, climbing down a notched log. Just as in an apartment building, the walls of one dwelling were connected to the walls of others. When a family wanted another room, they might have to build upward. Pueblos were sometimes four or five stories high.

The Hopi usually dug kivas, underground rooms with stone walls, in the village plazas. Hopi men used them for chapels as well as for clubhouses. In most kivas, a *sipapu,* a stone-lined hole in the floor, represented the entrance to the cave world from where the Hopi ancestors supposedly

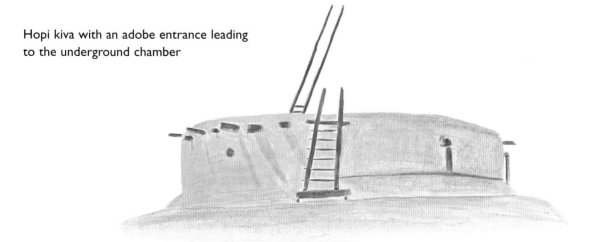

Hopi kiva with an adobe entrance leading to the underground chamber

came. Women were not permitted in kivas unless men invited them for a special purpose, such as taking part in a council. Yet Hopi women owned their houses.

Food

The Hopi were highly skilled farmers who supplemented their diet with some hunting and gathering. The men farmed and hunted; the women collected wild plant foods and did all the cooking. The women also owned crops. Because of the hot and dry climate, the men studied all the patches of soil for miles around their pueblos, looking for areas of moisture. They usually planted their crops in the sandy soil at the base of the mesas, where they could catch runoff from the tablelands after the rare rainstorms. They also looked for underground springs. They protected their plants from sandstorms by building windbreaks out of branches and brush. They grew corn, beans, squash, cotton, and tobacco. Corn by far was the most important food for the Hopi. They had more than 50 ways to prepare it, including a thin bread called *piki*. The Hopi also kept flocks of tame turkeys, which helped provide meat, since deer, antelope, rabbits, and other game were scarce in their homeland.

Arts and Crafts

Hopi women crafted clay bowls, decorating them with geometric designs. They also wove beautiful baskets out of plant matter. Hopi men wove cotton to make blankets and clothing. Women dyed the threads with orange, yellow, red, green, and black dyes made from plants. The Hopi used leather for moccasins and rabbit skins for robes. Young, unmarried Hopi women, in a style unique to their tribe, wore their hair protruding from both sides in the shape of a squash blossom.

Social Structure

Most Indian tribes had civil chiefs as well as medicine men, or shamans. In the case of the Hopi, the shamans were the chiefs. Different clans, groups of related fami-

Hopi sash made from cocoons

A Hopi woman with the squash-blossom hairdo, a symbol of maturity and readiness for marriage

lies, such as the Snake, Badger, and Antelope Clans, also helped direct the annual cycle of religious events and make village decisions.

Religion

The Hopi conducted religious ceremonies all year long. The purpose of most of these rituals was to affect the weather and bring enough rain to ensure bountiful harvests. Kachinas played a major role in the Hopi religion. These guardian spirits, re-created in masks and dolls by the tribesmen, were also important in the religion of the ZUNI, another Pueblo people on the southern Colorado Plateau.

The Hopi believed that the kachinas were supernatural beings dwelling in their own world high up in the mountains to the west. Every year, at the winter solstice, the shortest day of the year, the kachinas supposedly traveled to the world of humans, where they entered people's bodies and stayed in residence until the summer solstice, the longest day of the year. Hopi men impersonated the kachinas with elaborate painted masks of wood, feathers, and other materials.

The masked kachina dancers performed at many festivals, such as the 16-day summer festival called the Niman Kachina. One of the many rain dances was the Snake Dance, performed last of all. The kachina danced with live snakes wrapped around their necks and arms, and even in their mouths. At the end of the dance, they threw the snakes on a design made with corn meal. The snakes were released outside the pueblo, and the kachina dancers were sent off at the same time to bring cloudbursts of rain.

Scare-kachinas had faces with long teeth and bulging eyes. Hopi men wore scare-kachina masks to frighten children who had been bad.

Children could learn the names of the different kachinas, and what they stood for, through the dolls their fathers and grandfathers carved for them. These are known as kachina dolls, but a better description would be statues or god-figures. They are not for play, but to be treasured, studied, worshiped, and passed on to one's own children.

The fear caused by the scare-kachinas, as well as great love and attention from their parents, helped the Hopi children grow up to be friendly and sharing. This was the Hopi Way: to be in balance with both nature and other people. If a child or adult acted with cruelty, he was shunned by others until he changed. But the Hopi Way also taught forgiveness.

Contacts with Non-Indians

The fact that the *Hopituh,* the "peaceful ones," went to war with the Spanish shows what an impact the outsiders

Hopi kachina doll

had on them. The first explorers to reach the Hopi were two of Francisco de Coronado's men, Pedro de Tobar and Juan de Padilla, in 1540. The Hopi let these two Franciscan priests and their soldiers stay with them for several days. The Spanish learned of the existence of the Grand Canyon at this time.

Another Spanish explorer, Antonio de Espejo, visited the Hopi in 1583. Then Juan de Oñate followed with many more men in 1598. He made the Hopi swear allegiance to the Spanish Crown. The first missionaries settled in Hopiland in 1629, more were to follow.

Because of the Spanish soldiers, the Hopi were forced to tolerate the new religion among them. But they continued to practice their traditional beliefs. When the Spanish tried to eliminate all kachina worship, the normally peaceful Hopi rebelled. They joined the Rio Grande pueblos in the Pueblo Rebellion of 1680 and destroyed the missions in their midst. At that period in their history, the Hopi established new pueblos that were easier to defend. The Spanish reconquered the Rio Grande pueblos, starting in 1689, but they did not push westward to the Hopi pueblos. The Hopi remained free to practice their own religion. Some Tewa Indians from the Rio Grande pueblos fled to Hopiland at this time to start a new life.

Contemporary Hopi

None of the current Hopi pueblos are on the exact sites of the pueblos of the early 1500s. The names of present-day villages on the Hopi reservation are as follows: Walpi, Sichomovi, and Hano on First Mesa; Shungopovi, Mishongnovi, and Shipaulovi on Second Mesa; and Oraibi, New Oraibi (Kyakotsmovi or Kiakochomovi), Hotevilla, Bakabi, and Upper and Lower Moenkopi on Third Mesa. Modern pueblos have doorways and glass windows as well as other present-day conveniences, in some cases electricity. But the Hopi homes have much in common with those of their ancestors.

In fact, of all the Native North American peoples, the Hopi probably live closest to their traditional way. Many Hopi still farm their traditional crops, along with wheat. They have also learned to raise sheep. Many continue to produce traditional craftwork: pottery, basketry, weaving, and kachina dolls. The Hopi are also famed for their silverwork, a craft learned later in the mid-1800s from the Navajo, who learned it from the Mexicans. The Hopi are especially known for belt buckles, bracelets, and boxes with silver cutouts overlaid on a dark background of copper, oxidized silver, or a kind of coal called jet.

Hopi culture can be studied and appreciated at the Hopi Cultural Center on Second Mesa.

Many Hopi continue to shape their lives around their ancient religion. Many still perform traditional dances, some with kachina masks and some without. Certain of these colorful and complex dances are open to the public. The dances are a form of prayer for the Hopi, who use the rituals to ask the gods for rain, food, and the well-being of the human race.

Yet the Hopi Way has been in flux in the 20th century, with many outside pressures. Traditionalists have sought the return of sacred objects taken without consent and improperly displayed in museums. They also have striven to preserve sacred lands from strip mining and pollution. In the case of Big Mountain, considered a place of healing and energy to both the Hopi and Navajo, Hopi tradi-tionalists have been at odds with the federally recognized Hopi Tribal Council. The Hopi Tribal Council has called for the return of Big Mountain and the relocation of those Navajo living on what has been determined to be Hopi treaty lands in order to receive new leasing income from non-Indian mining companies seeking coal. The traditionalists, on the other hand, have backed the right of Navajo families, mostly fellow traditionalists, to stay. The federal government, ignoring the arguments of the traditionalists and succumbing to lobbyists of mining interests, passed the Navajo-Hopi Land Settlement Act of 1974 and the Navajo-Hopi Land Dispute Settlement Act of 1996. Although many Navajo families have since relo-cated, others have stayed on and, with Hopi allies, have continued the resistance to the destruction of sacred lands and culture.

HUALAPAI

The name of this tribe, pronounced WAH-lah-pie and sometimes spelled *Walapai,* means "pine tree people," after a kind of small pine—the piñon—growing in the Hualapai homeland.

The Hualapai, along with their kinsmen the HAVASU-PAI and YAVAPAI, are often described as Upland Yumans (or as the Pai) to distinguish them from the River Yumans living to their south, such as the MOJAVE and YUMA (QUECHAN). These various Yuman-speaking peo-ples lived along the Colorado River in territory now part of western Arizona and southeastern California. All the Yumans are classified by scholars as SOUTHWEST INDIANS.

The Hualapai occupied the middle course of the Col-orado River in northwestern Arizona between the Mojave and Havasupai territory. Most of their mountainous homeland, unlike that of their neighbors, was not farmable. As a result, other than occasional farming, the tribe depended on wild plant foods, such as piñon nuts, as well as various animals, such as deer, antelope, and rabbits, plus some fish. They often had to wander far from the river in small bands to find enough to eat. They lived in domed huts of poles, brush, thatch, and earth, as well as more temporary brush wickiups similar to those of the APACHE, who lived to their southeast.

Hualapai crafted simple clothing out of buckskin or bark. Men usually wore shorts and breechcloths; women wore skirts or aprons. In cold weather both men and women used blankets made from rabbit skins and wrap-around robes.

The Hualapai religion centered on an unseen world of gods and demons. Hualapai shamans supposedly took their power from dreams. Through a combination of singing, shaking a gourd rattle, pretending to suck out disease through a tube, and applying various herbs, they tried to cure the sick.

The Hualapai had extensive trade contacts with the Mojave and HOPI, but were traditional enemies of the Yavapai.

The Spanish, exploring out of Mexico, reached the Hualapai homeland in the 1500s—probably Hernando de Alarcón in 1540 and definitely Marcos Fárfan de los Godos in 1598. Then in 1776, Francisco Garcés made contact with the tribe. But the Spanish and subse-quently the Mexicans never settled Hualapai country to the extent they did other parts of the Southwest and California.

The pace of change quickened for the Hualapai after the Mexican Cession of 1848. A growing number of Euroamericans entered their domain, many to develop mining in the region. Hualapai found work in the mines, but cruel and exploitative treatment by the mine owners led to outbreaks of violence. In retaliation, non-Indian miners and troops sent into support them destroyed

Hualapai homes and crops. In 1874, the Hualapai were interned among the Mojave. After two years, they were allowed to return to their homelands, where, in 1883, they were granted their own reservation.

The Hualapai Reservation, a land of high plateaus and deep canyons, is located in northwestern Arizona, not far from the Grand Canyon, with tribal headquarters at Peach Springs. Tribal members support themselves through forestry, cattle ranching, farming, hunting, fishing, and Colorado River raft operations. There is some leasing of lands to non-Indians. The sale of Hualapai baskets also provides additional income to families.

HUPA

The Hupa, or Hoopa, occupied ancestral territory along the Trinity River in what now is northwestern California. Their villages were located especially on an eight-mile stretch, known as the Hoopa Valley, where the Trinity River flows northwestward from the Coast Range, merging with the Klamath River flowing out of Oregon. To the north of the Hupa, along the Klamath River, lived two tribes with whom the Hupa are closely related culturally, the Karok and YUROK. In fact, their tribal name, pronounced HOOP-uh, is taken from the Yurok name for the valley where the Hupa lived. The Hupa native name is *Natinook-wa* from the valley, *Natinook,* "where the trails return."

All three tribes shared lifeways with other CALIFORNIA INDIANS: hunting, fishing, and gathering; the making of bread and other foods from acorns; and the crafting of finely twined basketry for storage, cooking, hats, and cradles. The three tribes also shared cultural traits with NORTHWEST COAST INDIANS living directly north of them: cedar-planked houses using pole-and-beam construction and dugout canoes. Also, in their social organization, the Hupa, like Northwest Coast peoples, defined status by material possessions. Moreover, if there were a dispute or a crime between individuals, differences could be settled by paying a fine. A mediator would negotiate the amount between the opposing parties.

The Hupa, Karok, and Yurok all practiced annual World Renewal ceremonies. The season they were held and their length varied from group to group. For all three peoples, however, the event involved two parts: First, a shaman, who had purified himself with special rites, would lead his assistants to different locations where he performed secret rites to renew nature; then dancers performed for all the villagers. Sometimes tribe members would provide the dancers with their costumes in order to show off their wealth and their standing in the tribe.

The participants, whose numbers increased throughout the ceremonies, performed two main dances: the White Deerskin Dance and the Jumping Dance. In the former, the dancers wore animal-skin aprons, tooth-shell necklaces, and feather headdresses. They carried poles draped with deer hides, the heads of which were decorated with the red-feathered scalps of woodpeckers. Rare white deer-skins were thought to cast the greatest powers of renewal and provided the dancer and his sponsor with much prestige. In the latter ritual, the Jumping Dance, the dancers wore woodpecker scalps, fashioned into headdresses, on their own heads and carried tubular wands woven out of plant materials.

Interestingly, although all three peoples had so much in common in terms of culture, their languages differ. Different tribes in a given region typically spoke different dialects, but usually from the same language family. In this case, the Hupa are Athapascan-speaking (see ATHAPASCANS); the Karok, Hokan-speaking; and the Yurok, Algonquian-speaking. (This language discrepancy among neighboring tribes demonstrates that geography plays a more important role in determining a tribe's culture than language does.)

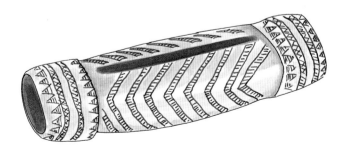

Hupa purse made from an elk's antler, the incised design rubbed with pigment

Because of the isolated location of the Hoopa Valley in California's highlands, the Hupa had few historical contacts with non-Indians. The Spanish and the Russians never colonized their domain. Occasional fur traders and trappers followed the Trinity River from the Klamath but never established permanent posts. Some Euroamericans and Chinese mined the river with pans during the California gold rush of 1849, but there were not enough gold strikes to cause prospectors to overrun Hupa territory. More and more settlers arrived in the region after California statehood in 1850, but the Hupa managed to hold on to their ancestral homeland. In 1876, the federal government made Hoopa Valley a reservation.

Hupa people live in Hoopa Valley today, with members from other area tribes. The Hoopa Valley Reservation is the largest and most populous in California. Inhabitants farm, raise livestock, cut lumber, and are generally self-sufficient. They still practice traditional customs, such as hunting, fishing, acorn-gathering, basketmaking, beadwork, and the White Deerskin and Jumping dances. The ancient village of Takimildin on the reservation remains a spiritual center. Because the Hupa live where their people have always lived and because they retain many of the ancient ways, they have a sense of continuity with their ancestors and a sense of tribal vitality.

A Hupa Indian using a fire-drill (based on a cigarette silk, distributed with cigarettes as souvenirs in the early 1900s)

HURON (Wyandot)

The Huron are important to both United States and Canadian history. One version of their tribal name, *Huron,* was given to them by the French and means something close to "rough" or "boorish" (although it is thought to refer to their bristly hairstyle, not their behavior). Their native Iroquoian name is *Wyandot* (or *Wendat* or *Guyandot*), meaning "peninsula dwellers" or "islanders." The Huron name, pronounced HYUR-on, generally is used when discussing early Canadian history. *Wyandot,* also spelled *Wyandotte* and pronounced WHY-un-dot, is used in reference to tribal members who relocated to the United States.

The Huron had lifeways in common with other Iroquoians classified as NORTHEAST INDIANS. Yet they are not referred to as IROQUOIS (HAUDENOSAUNEE), a name applied to the six tribes of the Iroquois League. The Huron originally lived north of these other tribes in the Lake Simcoe region of Ontario lying between Georgian Bay (part of Lake Huron) and Lake Ontario. In some historical accounts, the Huron homeland is called Huronia.

Lifeways

The Huron were divided into various clans, living in different parts of Huronia. These were the Rock Clan, the Cord Clan, the Bear Clan, the Deer Clan, and the One House Lodge.

Like their Iroquois neighbors, the Huron built elm-bark longhouses within walled villages. They typically located their villages on high ground near a navigable river and a clear spring. They cultivated the same crops as the Iroquois, mainly corn, beans, squash, and sunflowers for food, and tobacco for smoking. They supplemented their diet by hunting, fishing, and gathering wild plant foods.

Huron pottery pipe

The Huron sometimes drove deer into the rivers or into fenced-in areas, then used bows and arrows to kill them. They often snared beaver with nets. They also snared bears in traps, then fed and fattened them over a period of one or two years before eating them. Tribal members also fished the bay, lakes, and rivers. Unlike the Iroquois, they had birch-bark canoes similar to those of the ALGONQUIANS. They used bone hooks and bone harpoons. They also used huge nets—some 400 yards long—woven from plants called nettles and held in place by stone weights and wood floats. Every fall, they traveled to the islands of Georgian Bay to fish, especially for whitefish. A Preacher to the Fish cast spells to draw the fish to the nets. The Huron also made annual expeditions to the north to gather ripe blueberries.

The Huron kept fires burning constantly in fire-pits for cooking or warmth. One of their many ritualistic dances was the Dance of Fire. The dancers carried smoldering coals or heated stones in their mouths; they also plunged their arms into boiling water. This was thought to invoke a spirit, or *oki,* to cure the sick.

When the soil in one area became depleted, or the game became scarce, or wood for building, heating, and cooking ran out, the Huron moved their villages to new sites.

European-made tomahawk for trade with Indians

The Huron wore deerskin shirts, breechcloths, leggings, skirts, and moccasins, plus fur cloaks for extra warmth. They often decorated articles of clothing with fringed edges, painted designs, and strips of fur. Sometimes they painted their faces black, red, green, or violet with vegetable and mineral dyes mixed with sunflower oil or bear fat.

The Huron were very affectionate toward their children, praising them for good behavior but rarely scolding them for bad behavior. Mothers carried their babies in wooden cradleboards, cushioned with moss or cattail down. When babies were old enough to eat solid food, mothers would make digestion easier for them by partially chewing the food first.

Children had to start mastering adult skills when they were young. Boys learned how to shoot with bows and arrows and how to throw harpoons, plus other skills of hunting, fishing, and warfare. Girls learned how to plant crops, store food, cook, sew, make pottery, and weave baskets and nets.

When a Huron died, the village held a feast for relatives and friends. The corpse, wrapped in furs, was placed on top of a litter inside the village. Mourning went on for days. After a period of time, villagers carried the litter to a cemetery, where they built a small cabin over the body. They placed food, oil, and tools inside the cabin to help the dead person on his journey to the spirit world. Presents were also given to the relatives to comfort them.

Every 10 years or so, the Huron held the Feast of the Dead. At this celebration, families brought remains of their dead relatives from the cemetery back to the village, scraped the bones clean of any dried flesh, and rewrapped them in furs. The villagers also feasted, told stories about the dead, gave presents to children, and held sporting events.

The Fur Trade

The Huron became early trading partners of the French. Samuel de Champlain, who founded New France in the early 1600s, established a lasting trade relationship with them. Jesuit missionaries also settled among them. Quebec City on the St. Lawrence River was originally a Huron village called Stadacona. Montreal, farther south on the St. Lawrence, was the Huron village of Hochelaga. The Huron traded their furs to the French for European goods. But their most important role in the fur trade was as middlemen between the French traders and other Indian tribes.

From 1616 to 1649, the Huron were the central tribe in a great trade empire resulting from the European demand for beaver pelts to make hats and coats. The Huron had a regular river and portage route over hundreds of miles, plus a fixed yearly schedule. At specific places and times, they traded their own agricultural products to other tribes in exchange for pelts; carried the furs to the French in Quebec City and Montreal, where they bartered them for European goods, such as glass beads, cloth, paints, kettles, knives, and hatchets; then returned to the tribes with these goods to trade for more pelts. The Huron dealt with many different tribes all over the Northeast: fellow Iroquoians, known as the Tobacco, Neutral, and Erie (living between Lake Erie, Lake Ontario, and Lake Huron); Algonquians, such as OTTAWA, ALGONKIN, and CHIPPEWA (OJIBWAY) (living north of Lake Huron); and Siouan-speaking tribes, such as WINNEBAGO (living west of Lake Michigan).

But the days of the Great Huron Trade Circle came to a close with Iroquois invasions from the south in 1648–49. The tribes of the Iroquois League and the Huron had been traditional enemies for generations. The Iroquois also had become enemies of the French after several hostile encounters with Champlain and his forces, and had begun a trade relationship with the Dutch, who supplied them with firearms. When beaver became hard to find in their own country, the Iroquois looked to Huron country in the northern woods for a fresh supply so they could keep up their trade.

The well-armed and well-organized Iroquois launched many raids into Huron territory. The Huron burned their own villages as they scattered in retreat through the countryside. The Iroquois captured Jesuit missionaries who stayed behind, burning some at the stake. In the following years, the powerful Iroquois also attacked other tribes in the area, disrupting French fur trade and settlement.

Migrations

A small group of Huron managed to find safety among the French and were granted reserve lands at Lorette near Quebec City, where their descendants now live. Other Huron settled among other tribes for a time, such as the Tobacco, but eventually began a series of migrations in the 1600s and 1700s to territory that became the states of Michigan, Wisconsin, Illinois, and Ohio. They became known by their native name rather than the French one.

The Wyandot fought the British in OTTAWA Pontiac's Rebellion of 1763. Yet they sided with the British in both the American Revolution and the War of 1812. By 1842, the Wyandot had sold off all their lands east of the Mississippi River and moved to the part of the Indian Territory that became Wyandotte County, Kansas. In 1867, however, the Wyandot were relocated in the northeastern part of the new Indian Territory, which later became the state of Oklahoma. Their descendants still live there today as the Wyandotte Tribe of Oklahoma. Thus, like many Indian tribes, the Huron-Wyandot presently have members in both the United States and Canada.

ILLINOIS

The name *Illinois,* pronounced like the name of the state, is a French adaptation of *Ilaniawaki* or *Illinik,* the tribe's word for "people." It was taken for the name of a river, and then for the name of a territory—the Illinois Territory—which, in 1818, became a state. An alternative form of the tribal name is *Illini.*

The Illinois are classified as part of the extensive Northeast Culture Area, running from the Mississippi River to the Atlantic Coast and peopled mostly with ALGONQUIANS (see NORTHEAST INDIANS). The Illinois lived in the western reaches of this area. Their extensive territory was situated to the south of the Great Lakes and to the east of the Mississippi River. Important bands in the loose Illinois Confederacy were the Cahokia, Kaskaskia, Metchigamea (Michigamea), Moingwena, Peoria, and Tamaroa.

The Illinois located villages in the wooded river valleys where there was a good supply of fresh drinking water and shelter from the wind and sun, as well as plenty of wood for fuel and for shaping houses, boats, tools, and weapons. Birch trees did not grow that far south, so the Illinois did not have that pliable bark for coverings as did other Algonquians. They used elm bark instead, as well as mats made from woven cattails. They carved large dugout canoes—30 to 40 feet in length—from butternut trees. There was abundant game in the forests and fish in the rivers; along the riverbanks was rich soil for growing corn, beans, and squash.

But the Illinois also ventured out onto the windswept prairies along the wide Mississippi valley to hunt the

Illinois (Kaskaskia) wooden effigy bowl in the shape of a beaver

herds of buffalo that grazed in the tall grass (see PRAIRIE INDIANS). Before acquiring horses, Native Americans had to hunt on foot. These early buffalo hunters had the most success when they worked in groups. A proven method was to surround a herd with a ring of fire, then while the animals were trapped, pick them off with bows and arrows. To kill even one of these huge hoofed mammals meant a good supply of meat for one's family, plus a large shaggy fur for robes and blankets. Women went along on the hunts to pack in the meat and dry it and to tan the hides; children also helped with these chores. The elk—the second in size only to the moose in the deer family—also was a valuable catch.

When Europeans arrived in Illinois villages in the late 17th century, the center of their territory was situated along the Illinois River in what since has become the state of Illinois, as well as in present-day southern Wisconsin. Some bands also lived to the west of the Mississippi River in what now is eastern Iowa and Missouri and northeastern Arkansas.

The French Jesuit priests Louis Jolliet and Jacques Marquette had contacts with the Illinois in the 1670s. Father Claude Jean Allouez lived among them for several years. Henri Tonti, the lieutenant of René-Robert Cavelier de La Salle, established a trade relationship with them in 1680. La Salle himself visited them in 1682. The Illinois were important to the French because they controlled a stretch of the Mississippi River, the trading lane to Louisiana.

Also during the 1680s, the Illinois suffered attacks from the IROQUOIS (HAUDENOSAUNEE), who invaded from the east. But the failure of the Iroquois to take Fort St. Louis on the Illinois River marked the end of the Iroquois League's westward expansion.

Yet in the following century, the Illinois were defeated by an alliance of other tribes. For many years, the Illinois had been intermittent enemies of the Great Lakes Algonquians as well as of the SIOUX (DAKOTA, LAKOTA, NAKOTA). As allies of the French against the British in the struggle for colonial North America (the French and Indian wars, from 1689 to 1763), however, they maintained an uneasy truce with these other tribes, who also backed the French. Some Illinois warriors even fought under the Ottawa leader Pontiac in his rebellion against the British in 1763. Yet when an Illinois Indian, supposedly in the pay of the British, killed Pontiac in 1769, many tribes—OTTAWA, CHIPPEWA (OJIBWAY), POTAWATOMI, SAC, FOX (MESQUAKI), and KICKAPOO—united against the Illinois. Many bands from these tribes came to support the British in the American Revolution. The fact that the Illinois threw their support to the Americans further incensed other tribes.

Attacks against the Illinois were relentless, and the Illinois did not have the numbers to resist them. With the Illinois's defeat, many other Indians migrated south onto their lands. Supposedly, by the end of this conflict, the population of the Illinois had fallen from 1,800 to 150. The few survivors took refuge at the French settlement of Kaskaskia, where the Kaskaskia River meets the Mississippi in Illinois.

Then in 1833, with increased numbers of American settlers in the region, this group of Illinois—the Kaskaskia and Peoria bands—sold off their land and moved west of the Mississippi River to Kansas. There they joined MIAMI bands—the Wea and the Piankashaw—in the northeastern corner of the Indian Territory, which later became the state of Oklahoma. Illinois descendants still live there today as the Peoria Tribe of Oklahoma. Another group of Tamaroa and Metchigamea moved upriver to what they called Sisipiwe Shikiwe for "two rivers land" between the Illinois and the Mississippi River and broke off dealings with the federal government. Thus, a number of Illinois descendants still reside in the state bearing the tribal name.

The Illinois are currently undergoing a revival of traditional culture. In 1993, they held their first South-Wind (or Stomp) Dance in more than 100 years. They also are striving to protect archaeological sites—their ancestors' village and grave sites—from development and desecration.

INUIT

The Inuit have been known among non-Indians as *Eskimo* (*Esquimaux* in French), a name based on an Algonquian word and commonly translated as "eaters of raw meat," although it may refer to the making of snowshoes. *Inuit,* pronounced IN-yoo-it, meaning the "people," is now the accepted term, especially among Canadian bands. *Inuk* is the singular form; *Innuk* is a plural form referring to two Inuk. Variations in Alaska are Inupiat (or Inupiaq) and Yupik (or Yup'ik).

The Inuit language family is called Eskimaleut, or Eskaleut, with dialects of many different bands closely related. The similarity with dialects of the ALEUT people indicate an ancestral link between the two peoples.

The Inuit and Aleut generally are considered a separate group from other Native Americans. They usually are shorter and broader than Indians, with rounder faces and lighter skin. They look much more like Asians than Indians do. Based on archaeological evidence, it is thought that their ancestors arrived in North America from Siberia from about 2500 to 1000 B.C., whereas the ancestors of the Indians arrived much earlier by foot over the Bering Strait land bridge (see PREHISTORIC INDIANS).

There still are Inuit in Siberia; they are now citizens of Russia. There also are Inuit as far east as Greenland, now citizens of Denmark. This book primarily discusses Inuit located in what now is U.S. and Canadian territory, including Alaska, the Northwest Territories, Quebec, and Labrador.

The Inuit can be subdivided as follows: one, the Alaskan Inuit (including North Alaskan Inuit, West Alaskan Inuit, South Alaskan Inuit, and Saint Lawrence Island Inuit, plus the Mackenzie Inuit in Canada and the Siberian Inuit in Russia); two, the Central Inuit (including Iglulik Inuit, Netsilik Inuit, Copper Inuit, Caribou Inuit, Baffinland Inuit, Southampton Inuit, and Labrador Inuit); and three, the Greenland Inuit (including the East Greenland Inuit, West Greenland Inuit, and Polar Inuit). These general groups can be further divided into various bands and villages, much too numerous to list here. (These categories do not indicate individual band names.)

Inuit peoples had lifeways and language in common (with varying dialects). But there were differences among the various groups too. For example, not all Inuit lived in igloos as popularly believed.

The homeland of all the Inuit, as well as the Aleut, is classified as the Arctic Culture Area (see ARCTIC PEOPLES). The Arctic is a frozen landscape. So far north that trees are unable to grow there, it consists of plains called tundra, where only mosses, lichens, scrub brushes, and a few kinds of flowering plants can live. Winters are long and cold, with only a few hours of daylight each day. Summers are short. The ground never completely thaws, a condition called permafrost. Although there is less precipitation in the cold Arctic climate than there is farther south, the snow that does fall is whipped up by frigid winds into intense blizzards and huge drifts.

Most Inuit peoples lived along the sea—the Arctic Ocean, Pacific Ocean, Atlantic Ocean, or Hudson Bay. Some of these northern waters freeze over in winter, then break up into ice floes during the short summer thaw.

An Inuit man navigating Arctic waters in a kayak

Food

The Inuit adapted remarkably well to the harsh Arctic environment. To survive where there was so little edible vegetation, they had to become highly skilled and resourceful hunters and fishermen. They migrated often in quest of whatever game was available. Sea mammals provided a reliable source of food as well as a source of materials for clothing, bags, tools, and weapons, plus oil for lighting and cooking. The Inuit called them *puiji,* meaning "those who show their noses," because sea mammals surface to breathe, unlike fish.

Of all the sea mammals, the seal was the most important to the Inuit economy. In the summer, the Central Inuit hunted them with harpoons from their kayaks—light and maneuverable boats made by stretching seal or walrus hides over driftwood frames. Or crawling on their bellies over ice floes, hunters snuck up on the seals and harpooned or netted them. In the winter, when the Arctic Ocean freezes over, hunters had another way of capturing the creatures. The hunter's dog, a husky, would help him find one of the seals' breathing holes in the ice. Then the hunter would place a feather on the tiny patch of exposed water and wait until a seal returned. When the feather moved, the hunter would strike with a harpoon. To pull the heavy animal up onto the ice, the hunter would usually have to enlarge the hole. Some Inuit had a system of netting seals through the holes in the ice.

Inuit also hunted walruses and sea lions who swam around the ice floes during the summer or lay on top of them to bask in the sun. The tusks of the walrus provided ivory for tools, ornaments, and ceremonial objects. In the winter, these mammals left the ice-covered Arctic Ocean to head south for warmer waters, where they could still surface to breathe.

Some Inuit also pursued whales. Along the Arctic coast, they used their kayaks to frighten small species of whales close to or onto the shore. Along the Alaskan coast, hunters went after larger whales in another kind of boat, called an *umiak,* similar to a kayak but open and much bigger, up to 40 feet long. Like the MAKAH whalers, the Alaskan Inuit used harpoons attached to inflated buoys to wear down the animals before closing in with spears for the kill.

Most Inuit also depended on land mammals, especially the caribou, for meat and materials. When these animals made their summer migration to the coast to graze on the tundra and to escape the inland swarms of black flies and mosquitoes, hunters used a variety of techniques to get close enough to kill them with either bows and arrows or spears. Hunters snuck up on individual animals on foot or in kayaks; they hid in snow pits near where the caribou were known to travel; or they drove herds into corrals or into the water. The Central Inuit band known as the Caribou Inuit were an inland people who did not hunt sea mammals but followed the caribou herds on their migrations.

Other game for Inuit hunters in different parts of the Arctic included polar bears, musk oxen, mountain sheep, wolves, wolverines, and smaller mammals as well, such as foxes, hares, marmots, squirrels, and wildfowl. In addition to spears and bows and arrows, the Inuit used bolas, weighted ropes thrown at animals game to entangle them. They also used blinds to hide from game, as well as a variety of snares and traps. Still another method of hunting wolves and other meat-eating animals was to conceal dried and folded whalebones in pieces of fat; when the bait was swallowed, the fat would melt, and the bones would straighten to full size and slowly kill the animal.

Similarly, the Inuit had many ingenious techniques for fishing. They fished from kayaks; they fished through holes in the ice; and they fished in shallow waters were they built enclosures, called weirs, out of stones. They used hooks and lines, lures, harpoons, and leisters. (The Inuit-style leister is a spear with three bone prongs—one for penetrating and two for grasping the catch.)

Transportation

For transportation, in addition to the kayak and umiak, the Inuit had a kind of sled called a *komatik.* To make their sleds, Inuit craftsmen lashed together wooden frames with strips of rawhide and attached either slats of wood or a large piece of rawhide to form a raised platform. They shaped the runners out of wood or bone and covered them with a coating of ice to reduce friction. Sometimes they also put hide on the runners with a coating of frozen

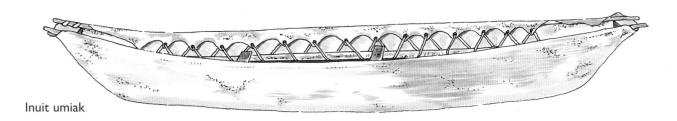

Inuit umiak

mud and moss. Teams of huskies pulled the sleds. Hunters traveling on ice floes sometimes pulled their own sleds, with upside-down kayaks on top. Then when they reached the water between the drift ice, they could turn the sleds over and use the kayaks without detaching them. Some Inuit used snowshoes, as did the Subarctic peoples to their south. Others used crampons, spikes attached to their boots, for walking on the ice, as well as test staffs, resembling ski poles, to judge the thickness and strength of the ice. The Inuit and other Native North Americans did not have skis, however.

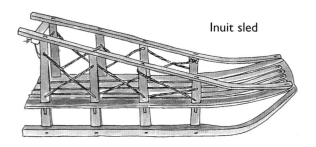

Inuit sled

Houses

The Inuit lived in all kinds of dwellings—igloos, hide tents, and huts. The igloo, or snow house, is the most recognizable of their dwellings. Nevertheless, this type of house was used only by the Central Inuit and only in the winter.

Inuit igloo (unfinished, showing positioning of blocks of ice)

To build an igloo, an Inuit man looked for an area of snow of the same consistency—preferably a layer that fell in a single storm, then hardened into ice all at once. He then drew a circle 9 to 15 feet wide that served as the floor plan. Then he cut the large blocks of ice—about 24 inches long, 20 inches wide, and 4 inches thick—from within the circle and started the first row of blocks along the circle's outline. Every row he added spiraled upward and leaned inward slightly, so that each one was smaller than the one before it. When he added the single top block, he had a nearly perfect dome. In the meantime, his wife covered the outer walls with soft snow. A hole in the dome provided ventilation and a block of clear ice served as a window. Igloos normally had a second, smaller domed porch for storage and a covered passageway as an entrance. Sometimes a third, sizable dome was joined to the two so that an Inuit family could have a separate bedroom and living room. A platform of ice covered with furs served as a bed. The igloos were warm—sometimes even too warm—when oil was burned in stone lamps for lighting and cooking.

In the summer, the Central Inuit used tents made from driftwood poles and caribou-hide coverings. But Inuit in Alaska and Greenland had more permanent houses made from either stones and sod or logs and sod, depending on what materials were available. These were sometimes built in a dome shape, like igloos, but more often they were rectangular. Whale ribs were also used in construction. And the intestines of sea mammals were stretched over the windows. The native name for these dwellings is *karmak*.

Clothing

Inuit clothing was as ingenious as other aspects of Inuit life. It offered protection from the cold but was comfortable to wear even for arduous tasks. The basic clothes, in a variety of materials and styles, were parkas, pants, mittens, stockings, and boots. The favored materials were seal and caribou skin. Sealskin was water-resistant, so it was good for summer when the rains came and when hunters went to sea. Caribou skin was better suited for winter since it was warmer and lighter in weight. Other animal skins were used as well in different parts of the Arctic: hides of dog, bird, squirrel, marmot, fox, wolf, wolverine, and polar bear. Sea mammal intestines were sometimes sewn together in place of hides. The fitted tunics known as parkas (*anorak* among eastern groups) were tailored to fit the contours of the body and fit snugly at the waist, neck, and wrists to keep cold air out. They were worn with the fur facing the body. Many of the winter parkas had two layers for added insulation—the sleeveless inner one with the fur facing in, and the outer one with the fur facing out. The parkas had hoods.

The Inuit used as many as four layers of caribou fur on their feet. They also insulated their mukluks (boots) and their mittens with down and moss.

The Inuit decorated their clothing with designs and borders of different colored furs, leather fringes, embroidery, and ivory buttons. Some of them, mostly women, wore jewelry, such as ear pendants, nose rings, and labrets (lip-plugs or chin-plugs, placed in slits cut in the flesh, and made of ivory, shell, wood, or sandstone). Tattoos also were common.

Recreation

The Inuit played a variety of games. A favorite outdoor sport was kickball, played with a soft leather ball stuffed with caribou hair. This was played much like modern-day soccer, but without goals. A player and his team simply tried to keep control of the ball longer than the other side. Men, women, and children played this game. The Inuit also enjoyed gymnastics in warm weather. A favorite indoor game was *nugluktag,* in which players tried to poke sticks through a twirling spool that dangled from above.

Another way to pass the cold and long winter days was by telling stories. To illustrate their tales, the storytellers used story knives—usually made of ivory with etched designs—to draw scenes in the snow.

Religion

The Inuit carved beautiful objects out of various materials—especially wood, bone, and ivory, with fur and feathers added—for their religious rituals. At ceremonial dances, men wore face masks while women wore tiny finger masks. The masks represented the spirits of animals and the forces in nature. The carving and the ceremonies themselves were directed by the *angagok,* or shamans.

One such ceremony, performed by Alaskan Inuit, was the Bladder Dance. This event lasted for days inside the large *kashim,* the men's ceremonial lodge. The Inuit thought that animals' souls resided in their bladders. They danced to music and performed rituals with inflated bladders of sea mammals, then returned them to the sea.

Social Structure

The extended family was the most important unit of social and political organization for the Inuit. Villages were loosely knit without headmen and lasted only as long as the food supply. Yet to allow for friends and allies in the difficult Arctic environment, the Inuit had special

Inuit mask representing the Soul of the Salmon

kinds of partnerships with non-family members. The men had "sharing partners," with whom they shared their food catch. They also had "song partners," with whom they performed religious rituals. Their friendship was so great that "song partners" sometimes even shared their wives. Men and women had "name partners," people of the same name with whom they exchanged gifts.

The Inuit were a peaceful people, but they would fight vigorously if attacked by other Inuit bands, which was very rare, or by Indian tribes, which was more common. Some Inuit wore ivory armor that was stitched together with rawhide. Within Inuit bands, an act of murder created blood feuds that might last for generations despite their forgiving nature in other matters.

Contacts with Non-Indians

Because of their locations in the remote northern wilderness, the Inuit had few early contacts with non-Indians. The Inuit of Greenland, however, were the first native peoples of the Western Hemisphere to encounter Europeans. In this case, their contacts were with the Vikings, who first arrived on Greenland about A.D. 984 under the Norseman called Eric the Red. Inuit in Labrador also might have had contacts with Vikings who reached North America from 986 to 1010.

The English explorer Martin Frobisher, who sought the Northwest Passage—a nonexistent water route through North America to the Far East—is the next European on record to have had contacts with Inuit (both Greenland and Central Inuit) during his three trips from 1576 to 1578. Frobisher kidnapped an Inuk and took him back to England.

Other explorers from various European nations visited the Arctic regions from the east, still in search of the Northwest Passage, from the late 1500s into the 1800s. Europeans came in contact with Alaskan Inuit from the west starting in 1741 with Vitus Bering's exploration for Russia. The ensuing presence of the Russian fur traders in Alaska had a much greater impact on the Aleut, however. In the late 1700s, Samuel Hearne, exploring for the Hudson's Bay Company, reached the Central Inuit by land. Some of the Central tribes had no contacts with whites, however, until the expeditions of Vilhjalmur Stefansson and Diamond Jenness in the early 1900s. In the meantime, starting in 1721, the Danes settled Greenland and had extensive contacts with Greenland Inuit. And during the 1800s, there were many missionaries, especially Moravians, among the Labrador Inuit. After 1848, commercial whaling ships began working Alaskan and Arctic waters.

It was during the early 1800s that many Inuit began using white trade goods, such as guns, knives, kettles, and cloth, which altered their traditional culture. Alcohol and European diseases also had a great impact on the Inuit as on other native peoples.

In the late 1800s, two developments led to further rapid change among the Inuit. In 1867, the United States purchased Alaska from Russia and began developing it economically. About this same time, the Hudson's Bay Company of Canada established many posts in the Arctic for the development of the fur trade.

Contemporary Inuit

Although the harsh Arctic conditions still determine much about Inuit lives, many of their customs have changed. Inuit now have rifles and shotguns instead of harpoons, spears, and bows and arrows; power-driven canvas canoes instead of kayaks; snowmobiles instead of dogsleds; frame houses instead of igloos, hide tents, and wood, stone, and sod huts; electricity, kerosene, or oil as fuel instead of animal fat; factory-made wool, cotton, and synthetic clothes instead of handmade sealskin and caribou ones; and so on.

Nonetheless, since the 1950s, there has been a renaissance in Inuit art, with traditional techniques, materials, and themes, as well as new ones. Inuit sculptures, drawings, and prints are valued the world over by art collectors.

Two other developments are helping to improve the quality of Inuit life in the modern world. In 1971, the Alaska Native Claims Settlement Act protected United States Inuit lands and granted the bands funds for economic growth. The numerous Inuit villages are now organized into six native corporations, some of which are united with either Aleut or ATHAPASCANS. Hunting and fishing are still central to the Alaskan Inuit economy. Some groups also still practice whaling.

In Canada, on April 1, 1999, the Inuit were granted their own territory—Nunavut—carved out of the eastern and northern parts of the present Northwest Territories, an area about the size of France. The idea to split the Northwest Territories into two new territories had been introduced as a bill in Canada's House of Commons in 1965. The inhabitants of the Northwest Territories had voted in favor of the division in a 1982 plebiscite. Boundaries had been determined in a second plebiscite in 1992. The final agreement had been ratified by the Canadian Parliament in the Inuit and the Nunavut Act of June 1993. Nunavut is the first territory to enter the federation of Canada since Newfoundland in 1949. All Nunavut citizens—Inuit and non-Inuit alike—are subject to the Canadian Constitution and the Charter of Rights and Freedoms and have the same rights. But the population in the new territory is about 85 percent Inuit, giving them the greatest political power. Nunavut's capital is Iqaluit, the territory's largest community. *Nunavut* means "our land."

IOWAY

The Ioway, or Iowa, usually pronounced I-oh-way, lived for most of recorded history in territory now part of the state bearing their name. (The tribal name is derived from the SIOUX [DAKOTA, LAKOTA, NAKOTA] name for them, *ayuhwa,* meaning "sleepy ones," or possibly from *ai'yuwe,* meaning "squash"; the Ioway native name is *Pahodja* or *Paxoje,* meaning "dusty noses.") Yet according to tribal legend, the Ioway migrated to the prairies between the Mississippi and Missouri Rivers from the Great Lakes region, where they once were a united people with other Siouan-speaking tribes, the WINNEBAGO, OTOE, and MISSOURIA. Supposedly, a group separated from the Winnebago and followed the buffalo to the mouth of the Iowa River, where it feeds the Mississippi. This group further divided, and the band that continued farther westward later became the Otoe and Missouria. The band that stayed closer to the Mississippi River became the Ioway.

It is not known for certain whether these locations and this sequence of events are historically accurate. But language similarities indicate that the four tribes share ancestry. Furthermore, the Ioway did retain some customs of the woodland tribes in the East, such as farming and living in villages. Sometimes the Ioway are referred to as PRAIRIE INDIANS because they lived in permanent wood-frame houses and hunted buffalo in the tall-grass prairies of the Mississippi and Missouri river valleys. When the Ioway began using horses and ranged farther, they became more like the western PLAINS INDIANS.

Because of pressure from other tribes and from white settlers, the Ioway moved their villages many times within the region now comprising the state of Iowa, as well as into territory now a part of other states. In 1700, they lived in what is now southwestern Minnesota, near the Red Pipestone Quarry where Indians collected catlinite to make pipes and other carvings. Some Ioway lived in Nebraska for a while before returning to lands in Iowa. The Ioway had numerous early contacts with French explorers and traders along the Mississippi River. In the early 1800s, some bands established villages near the Platte River in Missouri, where Lewis and Clark encountered them during the two explorers' survey of the American West.

One Ioway woman, Marie Dorion (or Dorion Woman), became, like the Shoshone woman Sacajawea of the Lewis and Clark Expedition of 1804–6, a renowned guide, interpreter, and peacemaker with western tribes. She was 20 years old and living along the Red River in present-day Arkansas when she met and married Pierre Dorion, Jr., a French Canadian–Sioux trader, working between St. Louis and the MANDAN villages. While on a trip to St. Louis, Pierre Dorion was hired to join the expedition to the Pacific Northwest backed by John Jacob Astor and headed by Wilson Price Hunt. It was agreed that his wife and two sons could go along. The expedition

set out from St. Louis in March 1811 and reached Astoria at the mouth of the Columbia in present-day Oregon in February 1812. The presence of Marie Dorion, who translated for Hunt, helped convince tribes of the Astorians' peaceful intentions. In December, Marie Dorion gave birth to a third boy, who died within eight days.

Because of the War of 1812, Astoria was sold to the North West Company out of Canada. The members of the Astor Expedition set out on the return trip in 1813. Another group including the Dorions set out for the Snake River country of what now is Idaho to find an earlier trapping party, collect pelts, then meet up with the Astorians returning to St. Louis. But all were killed in this group—most in attacks by local Indians—except Dorion Woman and her boys. In early 1814, she managed to cross the Snake River but could not pass through the Blue Mountains in winter. She killed her horses, drying their meat for food and using the hides for a tent. In the spring, she led her boys safely through the wilderness to WALLA WALLA country in eastern Washington. Her trip to safety was about 250 miles. Dorion Woman met up here with the other Astorians and reported the fate of her party. She did not return with them to St. Louis, however, staying in the Pacific Northwest and remarrying. Her oldest son Baptiste Dorion became an interpreter attached to the Hudson's Bay Company on the Columbia River.

In the 1820s and 1830s, with white settlement increasing, the Ioway signed a series of treaties ceding to the United States claims to lands in Iowa, Missouri, and Minnesota. In 1836, they were assigned a reservation on land that was later subdivided between the states of Kansas and Nebraska. In 1854 and again in 1861, this tract was reduced in size. The Northern Ioway still hold the remainder of this reservation in Brown County, Kansas, and Richardson County, Nebraska. Other Ioway were relocated to the Indian Territory in 1883. The Southern Ioway now has a federal trust area in Lincoln, Payne, and Logan counties of central Oklahoma. Both groups sponsor annual powwows. In modern usage the preferred name is Iowa for the legal tribal entities—that is, the Iowa Tribe of Kansas and Nebraska and the Iowa Tribe of Oklahoma—and Ioway for the people themselves.

IROQUOIS (Haudenosaunee)

The term *Iroquois,* pronounced IR-uh-koy or IR-uh-kwah, thought to be derived from the French rendering of the Algonquian word *ireohkwa* for "real adders"

(snakes), refers to the Iroquoian-speaking Six Nations: CAYUGA, MOHAWK, ONEIDA, ONONDAGA, SENECA, and TUSCARORA. When speaking of themselves collectively, the Iroquois now generally call themselves *Haudenosaunee,* pronounced ho-dee-no-SHOW-nee, for "people of the longhouse."

Iroquoian once was a widespread language family in eastern North America, with a number of tribes other than the Haudenosaunee. The HURON (WYANDOT) and SUSQUEHANNOCK also are classified as NORTHEAST INDIANS, as are a number of smaller tribes, the Erie, Honniasont, Meherrin, Neusiok (probably Iroquois), Neutral, Nottaway, Tobacco (Petun), and Wenro. The CHEROKEE, also Iroquoian-speaking, are classified as SOUTHEAST INDIANS.

It has been a mystery among scholars how Iroquoian-speaking peoples came to live in the midst of the more numerous ALGONQUIANS. The Haudenosaunee might have reached their homelands in what now is upstate New York and the Lake Ontario region of Canada from the St. Lawrence River to the north; or from west of the Mississippi River; or from the south. Or they might have been descendants of an earlier woodland culture, such as the Owasco culture found in various archaeological sites. This last theory, although still unproven, now is the most widely believed.

The Iroquois League

As for the Haudenosaunee after the arrival of whites, much is known from both historical writings and archaeological studies. The Haudenosaunee were organized into the Iroquois League, also known as the Iroquois Confederacy. At first, about 1570, the Haudenosaunee formed the League of Five Nations—that is, Cayuga, Mohawk, Oneida, Onondaga, and Seneca.

Two men brought the five tribes together to found the League: Deganawida, the Peacemaker, a Huron prophet from the north, who had had a vision of the tribes united under the sheltering branches of a Tree of Great Peace; and Hiawatha, a Mohawk medicine man, who paddled through Haudenosaunee country preaching the message of unity and carrying a wampum belt that symbolized the Great Law of Peace. Over a century later, in the early 1700s, when the Tuscarora migrated to New York from North Carolina, the alliance became the League of Six Nations.

The Founding Fathers of the United States who shaped the new democratic government after the American Revolution—people like George Washington, Thomas Jefferson, and Benjamin Franklin—are thought to have used the Iroquois Confederacy as a model for the new democracy. The various states were like the different tribes; the senators and congressmen, like the 50 sachems, or chiefs, chosen as representatives or spokesmen; the president and his cabinet, like the honorary Pine Tree Sachems; and Washington, D.C., like Onondaga, the main village of the Onondaga tribe, where the Grand Council Fire burned continually and the Grand Council was held every year.

Lifeways

For their villages, the Haudenosaunee made clearings in the woods, usually near streams or rivers, and surrounded them with palisades, tall walls made from sharpened logs stuck upright in the earth. They lived in longhouses made of elm bark. These structures, from 50 to 100 feet long, were communal with more than one family sharing the space. The longhouses, sometimes crowded with as many as 20 families, plus their dogs, were noisy and smelly. And because inhabitants used only holes in the roof to let out smoke from the fires escape, they were smoky.

The Haudenosaunee used the longhouse as a symbol for their confederacy. They thought of their league as one big longhouse extending across their territory, with the Mohawk guarding the Eastern Door and the Seneca guarding the Western Door.

Like the Algonquians, the Haudenosaunee often are referred to as Woodland peoples and were skilled in chasing and trapping the animals of the northern forests. They used their catch for both food and clothing. They made deerskin shirts, skirts, leggings, breechcloths, and moccasins. They made robes and mittens from beaver and bear furs. They used feathers and porcupine quills for decoration. They used seashells to make belts of wampum that served as public records of treaties, and after the arrival of Europeans, as a form of money. The Haudenosaunee considered animals their kindred spirits and took animal names to identify clans: for example, the Beaver Clan, the Deer Clan, the Wolf Clan, the Bear Clan, the Turtle Clan, the Hawk Clan, the Heron Clan, the Snipe Clan, and the Eel Clan.

The Haudenosaunee were also skilled farmers, using stone, bone, antler, and wooden implements to work the

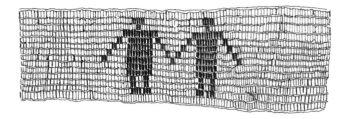

Detail of Haudenosaunee wampum belt

Haudenosaunee elm-bark longhouse

soil. Their three most important crops—corn, beans, and squash—were the Three Sisters in their religion. Three important festivals related to the growing of corn: the Corn-Planting Festival, the Green Corn Festival, and the Corn-Gathering Festival. Two of the other festivals involved wild plant foods: the Maple-Sugar Festival and the Strawberry Festival. The other most important festival was the New Year Festival, at the first new moon of the new year.

Haudenosaunee society is matrilineal, with descent and property passed through the female line. Women owned the crops and chose the sachems.

In healing ceremonies, Haudenosaunee shamans wore masks, known as False Faces, that were carved from a living tree. Wearing these sometimes fierce and sometimes comical faces, the shamans danced, waved turtle-shell rattles, and sprinkled tobacco. They invoked the good spirits to drive away the evil spirits that made people sick. The Iroquois believed that the most powerful spirit of all was Orenda, the Great Spirit and the Creator, from whom all other spirits were derived.

The Haudenosaunee version of lacrosse was much rougher than the modern game and many of the participants suffered injuries. Warriors from different villages competed and spectators placed bets on them. Another favorite Haudenosaunee sport was snowsnake, in which a player would see how far he could slide a javelin along a trench dug in the snow.

The Haudenosaunee traveled to hunt and to make war. They covered their canoes with elm or spruce bark. These boats were sturdy, but not as fast or nimble as the birch-bark canoes made by their Algonquian neighbors. But Haudenosaunee canoes possessed other advantages. Because of the thick, rough bark, they could be used as ladders to scale enemy walls or as shields to block enemy arrows.

Haudenosaunee boys began developing military skills when young, practicing with knives, warclubs, and bows and arrows. By the time they were teenagers, they were ready for their first raids against hostile bands of other Indians or against intruding whites. Through military exploits they could gain respect in their society. A man who gained great prestige in this way might become a war chief.

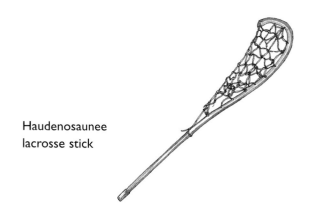

Haudenosaunee
lacrosse stick

Haudenosaunee toy elm-bark canoe

Although women and children captured in raids were sometimes adopted by the Haudenosaunee, male prisoners were usually forced to run the gauntlet. The prisoners had to move between two lines of men, women, and children, who lashed out at them with sticks or thorny branches. Those who made it all the way to the end might be accepted into the tribe. Those who did not might be given to the widows of Haudenosaunee warriors, who would avenge the death of their husbands by torturing the prisoners. In order to extend their influence, the Haudenosaunee also followed the practice of adopting whole tribes as allies.

Wars Involving the Iroquois

During the 1600s, the Haudenosaunee expanded their territories in every direction, helping one another when necessary. Their main purpose for invading the territory of other Indian peoples was to find a new source of furs. Their trading partners—first the Dutch, then the English—wanted especially the pelts of beavers. At the time, beaver hats were popular in Europe. Haudenosaunee tribes held the advantage over other Native Americans on the battlefield because they were united in a confederacy and because they obtained firearms from the Europeans. Indians also traded with whites to obtain tomahawks with metal heads.

In the mid-1600s, the Haudenosaunee decimated the Huron to the north as well as smaller Iroquoian-speaking tribes, such as the Tobacco, Neutral, and Erie. They also attacked the Susquehannock to the south. They made war on the Algonquian tribes of the Northeast too, including the ALGONKIN, OTTAWA, ILLINOIS, MIAMI, POTAWATOMI, LENNI LENAPE (DELAWARE), MAHICAN, and WAPPINGER. The Haudenosaunee eventually controlled a huge expanse of territory, east to west from the Hudson River to the Illinois River, and, north to south, from the Ottawa River to the Tennessee River.

The Haudenosaunee were so powerful in fact that they stopped the French from expanding southward from Canada. Iroquoia, the huge wedge of Hau-denosaunee homeland across upstate New York, served as a barrier to European travel and development. The British and their Iroquois allies suffered occasional setbacks but were the eventual victors against the French and their Algonquian allies in the French and Indian wars from 1689 to 1763. These long struggles were marked by: King William's War, 1689–97; Queen Anne's War, 1702–13; King George's War, 1744–48; and the French and Indian War, 1754–63.

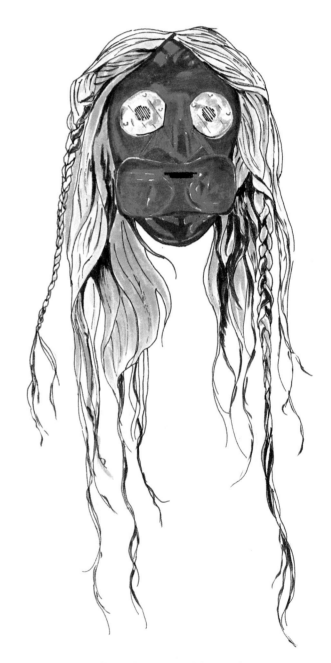

Haudenosaunee False Face carved from a living tree

New York trader and politician Sir William Johnson developed friendly relations with the Haudenosaunee, especially the Mohawk. He lived in Mohawk country along the Mohawk River, which branches off from the Hudson River. Johnson lived with a Mohawk woman named Molly Brant. With Mohawk warriors under Chief Hendrick, he defeated the French at Lake George in 1755, one of the critical British victories in the last of the French and Indian wars.

Haudenosaunee warriors participated in other wars after the French were defeated. Some Seneca joined the Ottawa leader Pontiac to fight the British in his rebellion of 1763. Some other Haudenosaunee, usually referred to as Mingo, under the Cayuga chief Logan, joined the SHAWNEE in Lord Dunmore's War of 1774. The Haudenosaunee fought their former allies, the British, in these conflicts because English-speaking settlers were appropriating their lands.

In the American Revolution from 1775 to 1783, however, many Haudenosaunee again sided with the British, this time against the American rebels. The Haudenosaunee thought that the Americans offered the greater threat to Indian lands. During this period, the Mohawk Thayendanegea, or Joseph Brant, Molly Brant's brother, rose to prominence. William Johnson had treated Joseph Brant like a son and had provided for his education. Joseph Brant had grown up as a close friend to John Johnson and Guy Johnson, Sir William's son and nephew. Brant drew on both his Indian and white experience, becoming an eloquent speaker in several different languages as well as a master tactician in warfare.

After having visited England with Guy Johnson to meet King George III, Joseph Brant traveled among all the six nations to encourage their support for the British. His people, the Mohawk, agreed with him, as did the Seneca, Onondaga, and Cayuga. Chiefs Cornplanter and Red Jacket, both Seneca, were other important leaders in the fight. But the Oneida and Tuscarora sided with the Americans, causing the first major split in the Iroquois League in 200 years. Samuel Kirkland, a Protestant missionary living among the Oneida, counteracted the influence of the Johnson family and won that tribe over to the American side.

The tribes who sided with the British launched many raids on American settlements near their territory. In one of the most famous incidents, Joseph Brant and his warriors, plus Walter Butler and his Tory troops, raided the Cherry Valley settlement, west of Albany, on November 11, 1778. Although the fort held, those settlers who did not make it from the outlying settlements or fields to the stockade in time were killed or taken prisoner—32 dead and 40 captured.

Because of the threat on the New York frontier, the American commander in chief, General George Washington, who would later become the first president of the United States, sent an invading army into Iroquoia in 1779 under generals John Sullivan and James Clinton. The Sullivan-Clinton Campaign defeated the Haudenosaunee, not so much through direct warfare, but by burning their houses and destroying crops. The Haudenosaunee called Washington "Town Destroyer."

In the years following the Revolution and the birth of the United States, the Haudenosaunee had to give up most of their vast land holdings. Some tribes were granted small tracts of state reservation lands. Other Haudenosaunee, like Joseph Brant, moved to Canada.

Contemporary Iroquois

Haudenosaunee live on reservations in New York, Ontario, and Quebec as well as in large cities of the Northeast, such as New York City, Buffalo, Albany, and Toronto. Others live in Wisconsin and Oklahoma.

Representatives of the Six Nations still meet in council and recite the Great Law. There currently are two Grand Councils with two Council Fires—one at the traditional site of Onondaga in central New York State and the other at Grand River in Ontario, the location of the Six Nations Reserve. The former council negotiates with the U.S. federal government and the New York state government concerning Haudenosaunee affairs; the latter negotiates with Canada's federal and provincial governments. The two councils meet to discuss matters affecting all Haudenosaunee.

Tribal members have intermarried, leading to familial ties among the Six Nations. Individuals of different nations also meet regularly at powwows, such as at the Iroquois Indian Museum in Howes Cave, New York,

Haudenosaunee soapstone turtle (modern)

where they sell their traditional and modern art—paintings; stone, wood, bone, and antler sculptures; baskets; leather goods; featherwork; beadwork; and lacrosse sticks. They give demonstrations of their work. They speak of their history, legends, and traditions. They perform songs and dances.

The Six Nations—Cayuga, Mohawk, Oneida, Onondaga, Seneca, and Tuscarora—have much in common: political unity through their confederacy, similar histories, and similar lifeways. But as contemporary Haudenosaunee will point out, although the ties among the nations are strong, each has a unique identity.

KALISPEL

The name *Kalispel,* pronounced KAL-uh-spell, means "camas" in the tribe's Salishan dialect, after the wild plant that many western Indians dug up for food. An alternate name, *Pend d'Oreille,* pronounced pon-duh-RAY, is French for "earrings"; when French traders first met the Kalispel, many of them wore shells dangling from their ears.

Different bands of Kalispel, discussed as two divisions—Upper Kalispel and Lower Kalispel—occupied ancestral territory in present-day northern Idaho, southern British Columbia, northwestern Montana, and northeastern Washington. A lake at the heart of their homeland bears their French name with an alternate spelling, Pend Oreille, as does a river flowing west of the lake. The Kalispel also lived along the Clark Fork to the east of the lake. The Bitterroot Range, part of the Rocky Mountain chain, rises up in Kalispel country.

The Kalispel depended heavily on fishing in the waterways that were part of the Columbia River network winding along the Columbia Plateau to the Pacific Ocean. They supplemented their diet by hunting small game and gathering wild plant foods. They lived in cone-shaped dwellings constructed over pits. (First they dug circular holes; they set poles around the edges of the holes, their tops leaning against one another; they covered the framework with branches, grass or cedar bark, and earth.) The Kalispel, like other Interior Salishan tribes, are classified as PLATEAU INDIANS. They eventually adopted some of the cultural traits of PLAINS INDIANS living to the east, in particular horse-mounted buffalo hunting.

The Lewis and Clark Expedition encountered the Kalispel in 1805. The North West Company established trading posts on Pend Oreille Lake and Clark Fork in 1809. In later years, the American Fur Company, founded by John Jacob Astor, also developed the fur trade with the Kalispel. A Jesuit priest by the name of Father Pierre Jean de Smet established a mission among them in 1844 and ensured the continuing tradition of friendly relations between the Kalispel and Euroamericans. He also worked among the FLATHEAD, neighboring Salishans.

After having signed a treaty in 1855 with the federal government, the Kalispel were settled on the Kalispel and Colville reservations in Washington and on the Flathead (or Jocko) Reservation in Montana.

In 1872, another agreement was signed with a band of Kalispel living in the Bitterroot Mountains of Idaho and Montana for their relocation to the Flathead Reservation in Montana. Their principal chief, known as Charlot, after a French trader, resisted passively through oratory, excuses, and delays. White officials declared Charlot's rival Arly the new chief. Arly took 71 members of the band to the reservation with him. The rest—several hundred—stayed with Charlot in their ancestral valley. In 1884, the Indian agent Peter Ronan took Charlot to Washington, D.C., in order to negotiate a compromise. Neither side budged. In the following years, with continuing white expansion, many in Charlot's band made the move to the reservation. Charlot and his most faithful held out until 1890, when troops were sent in to relocate them by force.

Present-day Kalispel are seeking to purchase additional land for redevelopment. The Kalispel Indian Development Enterprise has been looking into a variety of agricultural, industrial, and recreational possibilities.

KANSA *see KAW*

KAW

The Kaw (pronounced the way it is spelled) are also known as the Kansa (pronounced KON-za), a longer version of the same native word meaning "people of the south wind." A Siouan-speaking people, they are close relatives of the OSAGE and also related to the OMAHA, PONCA, and QUAPAW. It is thought that common ancestors of these tribes lived as one people along the Ohio valley in early times, then migrated west of the Mississippi onto the prairies before white explorers reached their domain. The Kaw, or Kansa, settled along the river that bears their name, the Kansas River, which is a tributary of the Missouri River. Their name has also been given to the state where their homeland was situated. Kaw territory stretched north of Kansas into southern Nebraska as well.

The Kaw are classified as part of the Great Plains Culture Area because they hunted buffalo, as did other PLAINS INDIANS. Yet the Kaw originally were villagers who farmed as well as hunted and sometimes are discussed as PRAIRIE INDIANS. After they had obtained horses in the early 1700s from other tribes, the Kaw adopted even more cultural traits of the nomadic Plains tribes, ranging over a wider area to hunt.

Since the Kaw occupied territory in the center of North America, many travelers passed through their homeland: the Spanish from the southeast; the French from the northeast; and the English, and later the Americans, from the east. In the early 1800s, an old Indian trail, running from the Missouri River to New Mexico through the heart of Kaw territory, assumed importance as a trade and migration route for white settlers: the Santa Fe Trail. All its travelers—traders, migrants, soldiers—were able to recognize the Kaw by their distinct hairstyle: Tribal members plucked or shaved their entire head, except for a single lock at the back.

From 1820 to 1846, the Kaw lost most of their territory in Kansas and Nebraska. William Clark, formerly of the Lewis and Clark Expedition of 1804–6, which had come into contact with the Kaw and other Missouri River tribes, negotiated many of the land cessions with them. Kaw holdings were originally the northern part of the Indian Territory. In order to make room for tribes relocated from east of the Mississippi, government officials forced local tribes to occupy smaller pieces of land. In 1846, the Kaw were assigned a reservation at Council Grove on the Neosho River.

Yet non-Indian settlers overran these lands. In 1852, by an Act of Congress, the northern part of the Indian Territory became the territories of Kansas and Nebraska. In 1861, Kansas became a state. In 1862, the Homestead Act opened up Indian lands in both territories to white homesteaders. In 1867, Nebraska became a state. In 1873, the Kaw were granted a new reservation near their kinsmen, the Osage, in the diminished Indian Territory, which came to be the state of Oklahoma. In 1887, tribal lands were allotted to individual tribal members. The Kaw Nation still holds a small trust area in Osage County, Oklahoma, not far from the Kansas border.

A part-Kaw Indian, Charles Curtis, served as vice president from 1929 to 1933, under President Herbert Hoover. He was a successful jockey when young, then became a lawyer. He was elected to Congress in 1892. He served 14 years in the House of Representatives and 20 in the Senate before being chosen by Hoover as his running mate on the Republican ticket. During his career, he helped pass some legislation helpful to Native Americans, including the Citizenship Act of 1924, giving the right of citizenship to them. His work in favor of the Allotment policy, designed to break up tribal lands and distribute them to individuals—the Curtis Act of 1898 and the Kaw Allotment Act of 1902—proved counterproductive, however.

KERES *see* PUEBLO INDIANS

KICKAPOO

The tribal name *Kickapoo,* pronounced KICK-a-poo, possibly is derived from *Kiikaapoa,* the meaning of which is unknown, or *Kiwegapaw,* meaning, "he moves about, standing now here, now there." The latter interpretation is appropriate because throughout history the Kickapoo have lived in a number of different locations.

The Kickapoo originally were a western Great Lakes people, closely related to the SAC and FOX (MESQUAKI), fellow ALGONQUIANS. When white missionaries and traders first made contact with them, all three tribes lived in what now is Wisconsin. The French Jesuit priest Claude Jean Allouez claimed that in the late 1600s, the Kickapoo lived between the Wisconsin and Fox Rivers. Yet all three tribes might have previously lived on the other side of Lake Michigan in present-day Michigan. But as is the case with most tribes, ancient locations and migration routes are uncertain. Tribal legends, passed on through the spoken word, provide only a certain amount of information. Explorers' written records sometimes are unreliable because early mapmaking techniques were inexact and because different explorers used different names for the same tribes.

In any case, the Kickapoo did not stay in Wisconsin. About a century after Allouez's visit, they joined with many of the neighboring tribes—Sac, Fox, CHIPPEWA (OJIBWAY), OTTAWA, and POTAWATOMI—to defeat the ILLINOIS to the south and divide their territory. This happened after the Kickapoo had joined Pontiac in his rebellion of 1763. During this period, most Kickapoo migrated to the Illinois River in present-day Illinois. The tribe eventually split in two. Some among them headed a little farther southward to the Sangamon River. This western group, the Prairie band, hunted buffalo. Other Kickapoo headed eastward toward the Vermilion branch of the Wabash River, now part of the border between Illinois and Indiana. The Vermilion band hunted the animals of the forest. Because of this split, Kickapoo can be referred to as either Prairie Algonquians or Woodland Algonquians (see PRAIRIE INDIANS and NORTHEAST INDIANS).

The Kickapoo lived in this part of the Old Northwest into the 1800s. When non-Indian settlers began arriving in increasing numbers, the Kickapoo made several stands against them, in Little Turtle's War of 1790–94 and Tecumseh's Rebellion of 1809–11, involving MIAMI, SHAWNEE, and other area tribes. However, these conflicts only delayed American expansionism. By 1819, the Kickapoo were being harassed by settlers and land agents working for the federal government, and some of their chiefs signed away all their lands in Illinois.

Two Kickapoo leaders, Mecina and Kennekuk, and their followers held out longer than other bands. Mecina's followers used sabotage, destroying and stealing white property, to resist forced relocation. Kennekuk (or Kanakuk)—also known as Kickapoo Prophet because he was a medicine man as well as a chief—used passive resistance to stall government officials for years. He came up with one excuse after another for not relocating: There was no food; his people were sick; he had seen evil omens. But finally, after more troops had entered the region because of the Black Hawk War of 1832, involving the Sac and Fox, the remaining Kickapoo departed for Missouri.

Missouri proved only a temporary home. The Kickapoo pushed westward across the Missouri River into Kansas, which at that time was the northern part of the Indian Territory. Some Kickapoo settled there permanently, and their descendants hold the rights to a reservation in the northeastern part of the state, incorporated as the Kickapoo Tribe of Indians.

But other Kickapoo moved on in search of a new homeland. One group moved to the Indian Territory in 1873, where they were granted a reservation along the North Canadian River. Their descendants are known as the Kickapoo Tribe of Oklahoma.

Kickapoo prayer stick with carved symbols representing prayers, myths, and historical events

Other Kickapoo, starting in 1839 with more joining them over the years, lived in both Texas and across the Rio Grande in Mexico, becoming known as the Mexican Kickapoo. This branch of the tribe staged an uprising during and after the American Civil War. The outbreak came when different groups of Kickapoo migrants from Kansas, traveling through Texas on their way to join their southern relatives, were attacked—at Little Concho River in 1862 by a Confederate battalion and at Dove Creek in 1865 by the Texas Rangers. The Mexican Kickapoo retaliated with attacks on Texas border settlements. In 1873, the federal government sent in Colonel Ranald Mackenzie and his Fourth Cavalry, veteran Indian fighters from a campaign against the COMANCHE. Government troops illegally crossed the international border and destroyed the main Kickapoo village at Nacimiento on the Remolino River. They also led women and children hostages back to the Indian Territory. During negotiations, many of the Mexican Kickapoo agreed to resettle in the Indian Territory to be with their families, more of whom joined them from Kansas. Their descendants still live in what now is the state of Oklahoma, federally recognized as the Texas Band of Kickapoo. Other Texas/Mexican Kickapoo maintain a village near Eagle Pass, Texas, and at Nacimiento, Mexico, holding dual citizenship.

KIOWA

The name *Kiowa,* pronounced KI-uh-wuh, comes from the word *Kaigwu,* meaning "main people" in the Kiowa language. It once was thought that the Kiowa language had a distant connection with the Uto-Aztecan languages of the AKIMEL O'ODHAM (PIMA), BANNOCK, COMANCHE, PAIUTE, TOHONO O'ODHAM (PAPAGO), SHOSHONE, UTE, and Mexican tribes. Now it is theorized that the Kiowa language is closely related to the Tanoan dialects of the Rio Grande PUEBLO INDIANS.

Migrations

Despite this linguistic connection with Indians of the Southwest, the first known homeland of the Kiowa, during the 1600s, was far to the north in what is now western Montana. From there, about 1700, the Kiowa migrated eastward across the Rocky Mountains to the Yellowstone River region in what is now eastern Montana. Soon afterward, the CROW gave the Kiowa permission to move to the Black Hills of what is now eastern Wyoming and western South Dakota.

While at this location, the Kiowa probably first acquired use of the horse through trade with the upper Missouri tribes, the MANDAN, HIDATSA, and ARIKARA. With increased mobility, the Kiowa became typical PLAINS INDIANS, following the huge buffalo herds and living in tipis. They also began to practice the Sun Dance, keep medicine bundles, and organize into secret societies, also typical of Plains tribes. One of the most renowned of all the warrior societies was the *Koitsenko,* the Principal Dogs (also called the Ten Bravest) of the Kiowa. This was an exclusive society, limited to 10 warriors who had proven their courage time and again. The leader of the Principal Dogs wore a long sash reaching from his shoulders to the ground. When the Kiowa were engaged in battle, he would dismount from his horse, fasten the sash to the earth with a spear, and fight from that spot or shout encouragement to the other warriors.

A Kiowa woman and child

Even if surrounded by enemy warriors or struck by enemy arrows, he could not leave the spot until another Principal Dog removed the spear.

Two unique cultural traits of the Kiowa, in addition to their language, suggest a possible ancient connection with Indians in Mexico. The Kiowa worshiped a stone image they called the *taimay* and drew tribal records in the form of a pictographic calendar. Both these customs are more typical of Mesoamerican peoples, such as the AZTEC, than of Plains Indians.

Toward the end of the 1700s, the Kiowa migrated again, because, it is thought, of pressure from the SIOUX (DAKOTA, LAKOTA, NAKOTA) and CHEYENNE. The Explorers Lewis and Clark, reported in 1805 that the Kiowa lived along the North Platte River of what is now Nebraska. Yet soon afterward, they settled south of the Arkansas River in territory that is now southern Kansas and northern Oklahoma. The tribe eventually established its council fire on the Cimarron River.

To the south of the Kiowa lived the Comanche, who at first proved hostile to the newcomers. About 1790, however, the two tribes formed an alliance that has lasted until modern times. An APACHE band settled near the Kiowa and came to be closely associated with them, their leaders part of the Kiowa camp circle. They became known as the Kiowa-Apache.

The Kiowa Wars

The Kiowa were among the most tenacious fighters among all the North American Indians. They launched raids for horses and other booty on many other Indian peoples—the CADDO, NAVAJO, Ute, and Apache bands other than the Kiowa-Apache. They also fought the ARA-PAHO, Cheyenne, and OSAGE until reaching peace accords with these tribes in the 1830s. They also proved a much-feared menace to Spaniards, Mexicans, and Euroamericans traveling the Santa Fe Trail and the Butterfield Southern Route (Southern Overland Trail). They raided settlements far and wide, even into Mexico.

The Kiowa wars of the 1800s closely parallel the Comanche wars. In most engagements, Comanche, Kiowa, and Kiowa-Apache fought side by side. (Most of these conflicts are described in this book under the COMANCHE entry.) Yet certain Kiowa leaders should be mentioned here because they were among the most important individuals in the history of the American West.

From the 1830s until the 1860s, Little Mountain was the principal Kiowa chief. It was his hand that recorded the tribal history with pictographs on buffalo hide. When the hide wore out, the entire chronicle was recreated on a new hide. And in later years, when the buffalo herds had been slaughtered, Little Mountain's nephew used heavy manila paper to redraw 60 years of Kiowa history.

By the 1870s and the final phase of the Comanche-Kiowa wars, the Kiowa had a number of chiefs whose names fill the history books. Sitting Bear (Satank) was the elderly leader of the Principal Dogs. White Bear (Satanta) led a faction of Kiowa who wanted war with the whites; he led many raids into Texas. Kicking Bird was the leader of the peace faction. When Little Mountain died in 1866, Lone Wolf was chosen as the principal chief; he was a compromise choice instead of White Bear or Kicking Bird. Yet Lone Wolf came to support White Bear and the militants. Big Tree was the youngest of the Kiowa war chiefs in the Kiowa wars of the 1860s and 1870s. Sky Walker (Mamanti) was a medicine man who was supposed to have prophetic powers.

Sitting Bear died in 1871. Held as a prisoner by whites, he preferred to die fighting for his freedom, with a knife against army carbines. Kicking Bird died mysteriously in 1875 right after the Red River War—probably from poison given to him by members of the militant faction, who resented his friendship with whites. Sky Walker died a prisoner at Fort Marion in Florida in 1875, supposedly right after learning about the death of Kicking Bird. Tribal legend has it that the medicine man willed himself to die because he had used his magical powers to kill a fellow Kiowa, Kicking Bird. White Bear

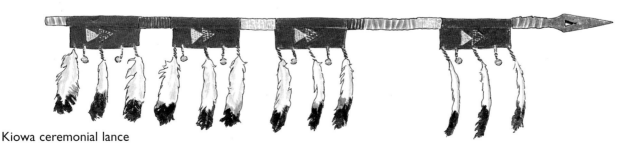

Kiowa ceremonial lance

died in 1878, while in a prison at Huntsville, Texas. Depressed at his fate, he jumped headfirst from the second-story balcony of a prison hospital. Lone Wolf had contracted malaria while imprisoned at Fort Marion in Florida and died in 1879, within a year after he was finally permitted to return to his homeland. Big Tree, the young warrior, outlasted the others. In 1875, he was released from the Fort Sill prison in the Indian Territory and in later years became a Sunday school teacher for the Rainy Mountain Baptist Church.

Many of these Kiowa leaders, including White Bear and Kicking Bird, along with other famous Indian leaders, including the Comanche Quanah Parker and the Apache Geronimo, are buried in a graveyard at Fort Sill. Since there are so many Native American warriors there, this cemetery is known as the Indian Arlington, after Arlington National Cemetery in Washington, D.C., where American soldiers are buried.

Kiowa pin of silver and turquoise, representing the Peyote Spirit Messenger Bird (modern)

Contemporary Kiowa

Modern-day Kiowa are still allied with the Comanche and the Apache of Oklahoma (descendants of both Kiowa-Apache and Geronimo's band). Most of the Kiowa lands, now protected as a federal trust area, are in Caddo County, Oklahoma, with tribal headquarters at Carnegie. Many Kiowa have become professionals. Other tribal members earn a living through farming, raising livestock, and leasing oil rights to their lands.

The Kiowa have maintained traditional culture in the form of stories, songs, and dances. The Kiowa Gourd Dance, as performed by the warrior society known as the Kiowa Gourd Clan, can be seen at intertribal powwows.

Kiowa artists have played an important part in the recent flowering of Native American art. In the late 1920s, the "Kiowa Five"—Spenser Asah, James Auchiah, Jack Hokeah, Stephen Mopope, and Monroe Tsatoke—became known internationally. T.C. Cannon picked up the tradition in the 1970s. Parker Boyiddle, Sherman Chaddleson, and Mirac Creepingbear painted 10 murals illustrating Kiowa history for the Kiowa Nation Culture Museum in Carnegie, Oklahoma, in the 1980s. Another Kiowa, N. Scott Momaday, a professor of comparative literature, won the 1969 Pulitzer Prize for his novel *House Made of Dawn*. Among his other works are *The Way to Rainy Mountain* (1969) and *The Ancient Child* (1990).

KLAMATH

The tribal name *Klamath,* pronounced KLAM-uth, is of uncertain derivation. A name formerly used by the Klamath for themselves is *Maklaks,* thought to mean "people" or "community." Their ancestral territory in the vicinity of Upper Klamath Lake and the Klamath River has since become part of Oregon, near the Oregon-California border.

Because of their dependence on fishing in inland waterways, the Klamath are usually categorized as PLATEAU INDIANS. The Klamath also depended heavily on small game and wild plant foods, especially roots and water lily seeds.

The Klamath dialect of Penutian sometimes is grouped with that of the MODOC, another southern Oregon and northern California tribe, as the Lutuamian language isolate.

The Klamath, unlike many of the California peoples to the south of them, were a warlike people. Kit

Carson, the mountain man and scout, and later Indian agent and brigadier general, called the Klamath arrows the truest and most beautiful he had ever seen. Supposedly, Klamath bowmen could shoot these arrows right through a horse. Their warriors carried out many raids on the northern California tribes, taking captives to keep as slaves or to sell to other tribes. Yet the Klamath were friendly toward whites. The Canadian Peter Skene Ogden, who explored for the Hudson's Bay Company, first established trade relations with them in 1829.

Upon signing a treaty with whites in 1864, the Klamath were settled on the Klamath Reservation in Oregon, northeast of Upper Klamath Lake. They also agreed to give up the practice of slavery, an issue over which the North and the South were fighting the Civil War.

Klamath wooden effigy with feathers

The Klamath later played an indirect part in the Modoc War of 1872–73. Because of tensions between the two tribes when the Modoc were forced to settle on the Klamath Reservation, a band of Modoc headed southward and began a chain of events leading up to the most violent Indian war in California history. Some PALUTE—from the Yahooskin band of Snake Indians—also were settled among the Klamath.

In 1954, the U.S. Congress terminated federal recognition of the Klamath tribe. Tribal assets were liquidated and passed out to individual tribal members. The experience proved to be a difficult one for the Klamath, who lost control of some of their lands and had to struggle to maintain tribal identity. Termination, as this policy of ending the special relationship between the federal government and Native American tribes is called, was phased out in the 1960s. It took until 1986 for the Klamath to regain federally recognized status. The Klamath still are struggling to reestablish a land base.

KOOTENAI

The meaning of the tribal name *Kootenai,* also spelled Kootenay and Kutenai (and all pronounced KOOT-uh-nay), is unknown. People of this name, discussed as the Upper Kootenai and Lower Kootenai divisions, lived in ancestral territory that is now northwestern Montana, northern Idaho, northeastern Washington State, and southeastern British Columbia. The Kootenai depended heavily on the waterways in their homeland for food, including Kootenay Lake, Kootenai River, and the upper course of the Columbia River. They used spears, basket traps, and wicker weirs to catch fish. They had both bark canoes and dugouts. They lived in cone-shaped dwellings, with pole frames and rush-mat coverings. They also made watertight baskets from split roots. The tribe is classified in the Plateau Culture Area (see PLATEAU INDIANS).

The Kootenai, especially the Upper Kootenai division in Montana, acquired horses through trade with other Indians in the 1700s and adopted many of the customs of PLAINS INDIANS, venturing east of the Rocky Mountains on seasonal buffalo hunts, during which they lived in buffalo-skin tipis.

The Kootenai language differs from that of the other Penutian-speaking or Salishan-speaking Plateau Indians and seems to be related to the Algonquian language family. There were Algonquian-speaking peoples living near the Kootenai—the BLACKFEET—traditional enemies of the Kootenai, who kept them from expanding their territory eastward.

The Kootenai were friendly toward whites. The Canadian explorer David Thompson, who established trade

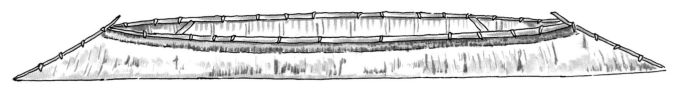

Kootenai birch-bark canoe in the "sturgeon-nose" style

relations with many tribes for the North West Company, entered their domain in the early 1800s. This fur-trading company, whose headquarters were in Montreal, built a trading post called Kootenai House in 1807. When the western international boundary between the United States and Canada was defined once and for all in 1846, the territory of the tribe was divided.

Today, some Kootenai live on the Kootenai Reservation in Idaho; others live among the FLATHEAD and other Salishans on the Flathead Reservation in Montana; still others live on tracts of land in British Columbia. They have retained many of their traditions, including ceremonials, and are active on regional Native American affairs.

KUTCHIN

The homeland of the Kutchin once stretched from the Yukon to the Mackenzie River. Their ancestral territory included parts of present-day Alaska, as well as part of Canada's Yukon Territory and Northwest Territories.

The Kutchin consisted of nine major bands: Dihai, Kutcha, Natsit, Tennuth, Tranjik, and Vunta in Alaska; and Nakotcho, Takkuth, and Tatlit in Canada. The general tribal name *Kutchin* (also spelled *Gwih'in*), pronounced kuch-IN, means "people." The various band names refer to locations. After whites made contact with the Kutchin, five eastern bands came to be known as the Loucheux, French for "squinty-eyed."

The Kutchin belong to the language family called Athapascan. The majority of ATHAPASCANS had their ancestral homelands in the taiga of the northern latitudes, a land of scrubby evergreen forest, plus numerous lakes, rivers, and swamps. This environment is also referred to as the Subarctic because it lies south of the Arctic tundra, leading to the term SUBARCTIC INDIANS.

In their lifeways, the Kutchin are typical of a number of tribes not listed in this book, including the Ahtena, Han, Ingalik, Koyukon, Nabesna, Tanaina, and Tanana. Most of these peoples had extensive contacts with INUIT and were influenced by them.

Food

The Kutchin generally spent the summer fishing and the winter hunting. For fishing gear they had dipnets, baskets, hooks, and harpoons. The harpoons resembled those of the Inuit, as did their hunting bows, formed by three pieces of wood joined together and backed with twisted sinew. The Kutchin also used snares of babiche (rawhide strips) to trap animals, as well as corrals to capture caribou. Moose and mountain sheep were other much sought after large game. Dogs were used to stalk game and keep it at bay. Waterfowl migrating through the Kutchin domain were hunted in great numbers.

Houses

The Kutchin built unique dwellings. Dried, curved poles were placed upright in the ground, meeting at the top. Caribou hides were then sewn together and placed over the pole framework. A smokehole was left at the top. Fir boughs were placed on the floor. And snow was piled and banked around the walls for insulation. The Kutchin also erected food caches, covered platforms high up on poles, to keep food safe from animals.

Kutchin caribou-skin dwelling

Transportation

The Kutchin used Inuit-type sleds, rather than the more common subarctic toboggans. They also used snowshoes, which were long and narrow, sometimes six feet long. Kutchin birch-bark canoes had a shape similar to Inuit umiaks, with flat bottoms and nearly straight sides.

Clothing

Kutchin clothing, mostly made from caribou hides, also showed some Inuit influences; mittens, outer garments with hoods, and shirts with long, pointed tails in the front and back were Inuit-like. Kutchin shirts, however, for both men and women, had long fringes decorated with seeds or with tooth shells, plus porcupine-quill or bead embroidery. Women sometimes enlarged their shirts at the back to make room for carrying a baby against their naked back, as Inuit women did, but the Kutchin more commonly used cradleboards. Leggings for men and women formed one piece with the moccasins, providing protection from cold and wetness. Headbands and bright feathers provided decoration, as did necklaces and nose pendants made from shells. Compared to other northern Athapascans, the Kutchin were exceptionally colorful in their dress. They also painted their faces with the minerals red ochre and black lead or tattooed their faces.

Social Structure

The Kutchin bands were loosely knit. Their chiefs were chosen for their wisdom and bravery, but they had little authority beyond their own families, other than to settle disputes and lead war parties. A man without any relatives might attach himself to a family as a servant. Otherwise, the women did most of the hard work around camp and most of the hauling. The men saved their energy for hunting, fishing, and warfare. When food became scarce, the Kutchin sometimes killed their female children to prevent overpopulation. The old and sick sometimes requested to be strangled to spare their families the task of providing for them.

Religion and Ritual

The Kutchin believed in supernatural beings haunting certain locations. They also thought that spirits lived in plants, animals, and natural phenomena such as the weather. Before important communal hunts, men fasted and burned pieces of caribou fat on a fire as a form of sacrifice to their moon god.

In Kutchin mythology, an important legend tells how one of the Kutchin ancestors invented the tricks of the hunt as a small boy—the corral for caribou and the snare for other game. As a reward for his ingenuity, he asked for the fattest caribou in the world. When the gods refused, he fled in anger to the Moon. If one looks closely, one can see the boy on the Moon, carrying a skin bag of caribou fat.

The Kutchin were horrified at the thought of burial in the ground. Instead, unlike most Native American peoples, they cremated their dead, along with the person's possessions. The ashes were hung in trees or on poles, painted and draped with streamers. When a chief died,

his body was placed in a coffin on a platform for a year before being burned. At the funeral feasts, Kutchin sang and danced and gave gifts in honor of the deceased.

Recreation

The Kutchin played many kinds of games, including gambling games, guessing games, and games of strength and skill with or without weapons. Chiefs sometimes organized wrestling matches to settle minor disputes between families.

The Kutchin had a reputation for great hospitality. They were known to entertain visitors for several weeks on end.

Contacts with Non-Indians

The Kutchin came into contact with whites when Alexander Mackenzie entered their territory in 1789 during his voyage of exploration along the river now named after him. Most subsequent encounters with whites in the early and mid-1800s were through the Hudson's Bay Company, especially after the original Hudson's Bay Company and the North West Company merged in 1821. Starting in 1862, the Catholic missionary Father Emile Petitot worked among northern Athapascan peoples, including the Kutchin, and wrote papers about their language and culture. That same year, the Episcopal missionary W. W. Kirby came to the region to preach to the Kutchin and to study their language. Many other missionaries followed.

In 1896, the discovery of gold deposits in the Klondike started a rush of prospectors to the area. As with other gold rushes in North America—the California of 1849, the Colorado of 1858–59, and the Black Hills of 1874—the Klondike gold rush led to much hardship among native peoples. The miners ignored the rights of the Kutchin and other Athapascans, appropriating their lands and carrying out acts of violence against them.

Contemporary Kutchin

There currently are eight Kutchin (or Loucheux) bands in Canada with reserve tracts of land. Kutchin also live in Athapascan villages in Alaska. The communities are organized into native corporations, some of them united with Inuit. The Kutchin have a blend of traditional and modern customs. Many still hunt and fish as their ancestors did. Yet snowmobiles, televisions, and other modern tools and conveniences have changed their way of life.

KUTENAI *see* KOOTENAI

KWAKIUTL

The Kwakiutl ancestral homeland was the northern corner of Vancouver Island in the Pacific Ocean, as well as smaller islands and a large portion of the adjacent mainland, including its many bays and inlets. This territory now lies in western British Columbia, Canada. The name of this tribe, pronounced KWAH-kee-oo-tel, probably means "beach at the north side of the river," perhaps referring to the Nimkish River. The native name is *Kwakwaka'wakw.*

The Kwakiutl dialect is part of the Wakashan language family known as Kwakwala. Neighbors on Vancouver Island to the south, the NOOTKA, also spoke a Wakashan dialect, as did the MAKAH, farther south on Cape Flattery in present-day Washington. Other NORTHWEST COAST INDIANS not listed separately in this book, the Haisla and Heiltsuk (or Heitsuk), are related dialectically and sometimes are discussed, along with the Kwakiutl proper, as subdivisions of Kwakiutl.

Lifeways

The Kwakiutl had a typical Pacific Northwest culture. They fished and hunted in the ocean and in rivers, especially for salmon, seals, and sea lions; they hunted in the tall forests, especially for elk and deer; they foraged for sea grass, shellfish, roots, and berries. They traded extensively with neighboring peoples. Tribal members carved beautiful functional and ceremonial objects out of wood. They had an elaborately structured society and religion and practiced the potlatch.

Kwakiutl wooden spoon

The Kwakiutl potlatch was the most extravagant of all versions of this ritualistic gift-giving. The Kwakiutl developed a system in which a recipient of a gift had to repay twice as much in the next potlatch. In other words, if he were given 50 goat's-hair blankets or sea otter furs, he had to repay the giver with 100 of the same item during the next ceremony. Or an arbitrator could decide that a certain number of cedar chests or copper plates had the proper value. Or perhaps a number of slaves would be given or even killed with a ceremonial club called a "slave killer" as a symbolic gift. In order to repay a debt, a man might be forced to give away all his possessions. The potlatch could therefore be used to humiliate and ruin enemies as well as to honor friends.

The Kwakiutl, along with the HAIDA, were considered the most skilled woodcarvers of the Northwest Coast. They built large wooden houses, as long as 60 feet. They made large seaworthy dugouts out of red cedar wood. They carved tall totem poles. They shaped wooden hats.

The most famous of all the Kwakiutl woodcarvings were their masks. These were beautifully shaped and painted objects, with feathers and hair added. Worn in special ceremonies and used as props for storytelling, the masks depicted various spirits in Kwakiutl mythology. Yet no two masks were exactly alike, even when representing the same spirit. Some masks even had removable parts, such as different mouths, that were changed during the course of a story.

Some of these masks were used in the Hamatsa, or Cannibal Dance. The Kwakiutl, like other Northwest Coast Indians, had secret societies with exclusive membership. The most powerful club was the Shamans' Society, and their most influential members were the Hamatsas. During a Hamatsa dance, one member acted out the Cannibal Spirit, who was like the Devil. Other members represented his army of creatures, most of them birdlike. There was the Crooked Beak of Heaven, who supposedly devoured human flesh; the Raven, who devoured human eyes; the Hoxhok, who had a taste for human brains; and the Grizzly Bear, who used his massive paws to tear humans apart (he was usually portrayed by a member of the Bear Society). The Hamatsas did not really practice

Kwakiutl totem pole

cannibalism. In fact, the ceremony showed the evil in eating fellow humans and helped discourage the practice. But the Hamatsas sometimes ended the ceremony with the ritualistic eating of dog meat. Then they held a potlatch to display further their power and wealth.

To be accepted as a Hamatsa, a candidate had to fast for several days in the woods until he acted hysterically, as if possessed by a cannibal spirit. Wearing hemlock boughs on his head and wrists, he would be lured into the Hamatsa lodge by a woman. Then he would dance a frenzied dance while the Hamatsas sang:

Now I am about to eat,
My face is ghastly pale.
I am about to eat
What was given me by Cannibal
At the North End of the World.

Contacts with Non-Indians

Russian, British, and American trading ships sailed along Kwakiutl territory in the 1700s. Yet these Indians did not have numerous contacts with whites until the establishment of the settlement of Victoria on Vancouver Island in 1843. White diseases, alcohol, and missionaries all contributed to the change in the Kwakiutl way of life. A Canadian law of 1884 abolishing the potlatch ceremony also altered Kwakiutl culture.

Cultural Preservation

In 1881–83, George Hunt, born a TLINGIT but raised Kwakiutl, was hired as a guide and interpreter by Johan Adrian Jacobsen to help in the acquisition of Indian artifacts for museum collections. In 1886, Hunt met the anthropologist Franz Boas and worked with him as a guide, interpreter, and informant. He again served as guide and interpreter for the Morris K. Jesup North Pacific Expedition in 1897, which sought to investigate the connections of the ALEUT, INUIT, and ATHAPASCANS of Alaska with the native inhabitants of Siberia.

In 1903, Hunt helped organize the Northwest Coast Indian exhibit of the American Museum of Natural History in New York City. He was Boas's informant and collaborator on *Kwakiutl Texts* (1905–6) and *The Ethnology of the Kwakiutl* (1921). Other projects included helping secure artifacts of the Northwest Coast tribes for the collection of George Heye, the founder of the Museum of the American Indian in New York City;

Kwakiutl painted wooden mask of Spirit of Sea with a killer whale on top

and, in 1912, helping the photographer Edward Curtis in the making of the motion picture *In the Land of the War Canoes.* Hunt was eventually selected as a chief of the Kwakiutl.

A Kwakiutl woman, the daughter of a chief

In the 1950s, another Kwakiutl helped in the preservation of his people's traditional culture. Naka'penkim, or Mungo Martin, was a hereditary chief and also a master carver. He called public attention to the fact that many totem poles had been destroyed by overzealous missionaries and that others were rotting in the humid weather of the Pacific Northwest. His efforts began a period of conservation of remaining totem poles and other artifacts.

Contemporary Kwakiutl

Many Kwakiutl of the existing bands in British Columbia earn a living in the salmon industry, either in fishing or canning. The Kwakwaka'wakw, as they prefer to be known, are undergoing cultural revitalization, once again practicing the potlatch on a regular basis. The Kwagiulth Museum at Quathiask, and the U'mista Cultural Centre both house potlatch items returned to the tribe by the Canadian Royal Ontario Museum and by the U.S. national Museum of the American Indian.

LAKOTA   *see* SIOUX (DAKOTA, LAKOTA, NAKOTA)

LENNI LENAPE (Delaware)

Lenni Lenape (or Leni-Lenape), pronounced len-ee len-AH-pay, means "real people" or "people of the standard." The tribe also is known simply as *Lenape,* the "people." An alternate tribal name, common in history books, is *Delaware.* The latter name, given by the English, comes from the name of the river where many of the Lenape originally lived. The river itself was named after Lord De La Warr, the second governor of Virginia, in whose honor the state of Delaware is named.

The Lenape, sometimes called the Delaware Confederacy, consisted of numerous Algonquian-speaking bands who maintained distinct identities. The northern bands spoke the dialects known as Munsee (or Munsi, Muncie, or Muncey); the southern bands spoke the Unami dialect. A third dialect of coastal groups later came to be called Unalachtigo. Other ALGONQUIANS called the Lenape "Grandfather" in their various dialects, because they considered Lenape territory the original homeland of all Algonquians.

The Lenape, classified as NORTHEAST INDIANS, placed their villages along river valleys. Lenape villages were dominated by one of three clans: *tukwsi-t,* the wolf; *pukuwanku,* the turtle; and *pele',* turkey. Each village was surrounded by sovereign hunting lands and fields of corn, beans, and squash. Houses were domed wigwams similar in style to IROQUOIS (HAUDENOSAUNEE) longhouses.

An important ceremony of the Lenape is known as the Big House (*Ga'mwi*), lasting 12 days and involving a log structure symbolizing the universe, the lighting of a new sacred fire, and offerings to Misinghalikun, the legendary Guardian of the Game, for the purpose of renewal, good fortune, and tribal unity.

Migrations

The Lenape were forced to cede their lands and migrate time and again on account of the increasing number of white settlers. At one time, different bands of these people held territory in what now is New York, New Jersey, Pennsylvania, and Delaware.

The Dutch first entered Lenape homelands in the 1600s from the Hudson River. The Dutch were interested in fur trade with the Indians. To the south, traders from Sweden lived in Lenape country along Delaware Bay, starting in 1638. During this early period, many Lenape moved inland and settled along the Susquehanna River.

In 1664, England took control of the entire region. English settlers, hungry for more and more land, pushed farther and farther westward. By the mid-1700s, Lenape were beginning to settle along the Ohio River in Ohio, then in Indiana, believing the whites would never settle as far west as Ohio.

But the whites kept coming: next the Americans, who pushed into the Old Northwest around the Great Lakes. In the late 1700s, some Lenape moved to Missouri for a time, then to Texas. By 1835, many from this group had resettled in Kansas in the northern part of the original Indian Territory. In 1867, when whites broke their promises and began to settle west of the Mississippi River in great numbers, most of the Lenape relocated to the southern part of the Indian Territory, which is now the state of Oklahoma. In the meantime, other Lenape had chosen to live in Canada.

Lenni Lenape centerpost for use in a longhouse

Early Relations with Colonists

In the course of this long and complicated story of migration, in which the Lenape lived in at least 10 different states and signed 45 different treaties with the whites, the tribe made its mark on American history. They were involved in many key events.

One famous early incident is the selling of Manhattan Island, now the central borough of New York City. First, the Canarsee band from Brooklyn tried to sell the island to the Dutch. But it was really the Manhattan band who controlled this territory. In 1626, they made the deal with Peter Minuit for 60 guilders' (24 dollars') worth of trade goods—that is, beads, trinkets, and tools.

Some scholars believe that the Manhattan Indians were part of the Wappinger Confederacy and should be classified as WAPPINGER rather than as Lenape. In any case, the Lenape and Wappinger both spoke the Algonquian language and were closely related. The Lenape generally lived west of the Hudson River and the Wappinger east of it.

The Manhattan did not really believe that they were selling the land forever. To them no one "owned" land; it belonged to all people. Rather, they thought they were selling the right to use the land, more like a lease. Lenape have a saying about the sale of Manhattan Island: "The great white man wanted only a little, little land, on which to raise greens for his soup, just as much as a bullock's hide would cover. Here we first might have observed his deceitful spirit."

Other important historical events involving the Lenape were the treaties of friendship signed in 1682–83 with William Penn, the Quaker founder of Pennsylvania, the first treaties Indians ever signed with Europeans. Of the early colonial leaders, William Penn was among the most fair in his dealings with Native Americans, protecting their rights to land as well as their freedom of religion. A famous Lenape chief at these meetings was Tamanend. Because he was so effective in his dealings with non-Indians, in 1786 his name was taken, in the form of Tammany, as the name of a political club important in New York history.

Penn's example and the respect whites held for Tamanend did not prevent other whites from massacring a band of Moravian Christian Lenape at Gnaddenhutten, Pennsylvania, in 1782, because of a stolen plate.

The Lenape are also famous as the first tribe to sign a treaty with the U.S. government—at Fort Pitt in 1778 during the American Revolution.

Wars Involving the Lenni Lenape

The Lenape fought in many wars. Some of their warriors first rebelled against the Dutch in 1641, when settlers' livestock destroyed some cornfields of the Raritan Indians, a band living on Staten Island at the mouth of the Hudson River. Willem Kieft, governor-general of New Netherland at the time, placed a bounty on Raritan heads and scalps, making it profitable for Dutch settlers to kill local Indians.

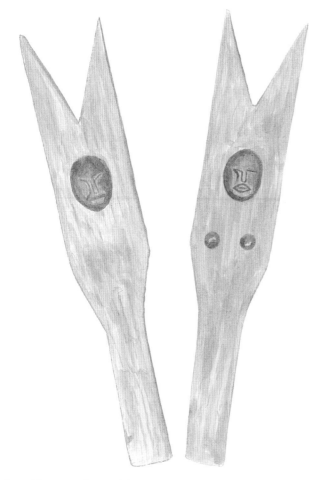

Lenni Lenape drumsticks

An incident called the Pavonia Massacre occurred two years later: Dutch soldiers tortured and murdered a band of Wappinger who sought protection among the Dutch from the MOHAWK. After the incident, many Algonquians of the region, Lenape and Wappinger alike, began raiding outlying settlements. By attacking and burning Indian villages, Kieft's armies crushed the uprising in a year.

The Lenape and Wappinger also battled the Dutch under Peter Stuyvesant, the next governor-general, in the so-called Peach Wars, starting in 1655, when an Indian woman was killed by a farmer for picking peaches from his orchard. After warriors have taken revenge against the farmer, Stuyvesant not only raided Lenape and Wappinger villages and burned their homes and crops, but also took children hostages, threatening to kill them so that their fathers would not fight.

In later conflicts, the western Lenape sided with the French in the French and Indian wars of 1689–1763. They again fought the British in Pontiac's Rebellion of 1763–64. A shaman known as Delaware Prophet played an important role in Pontiac's Rebellion. In 1762, he began preaching to the Indians of the Old Northwest, urging them to make peace among themselves, to give up alcohol, and to live pure lives according to traditional Indian ways. The message of this Lenape helped inspire and unite the tribes who fought together against the British under the OTTAWA Pontiac the following year. Some Lenape later sided with the British in the American Revolution of 1775–83. They also supported the MIAMI and SHAWNEE in Little Turtle's War of 1790–94 and Tecumseh's Rebellion of 1809–11.

Walam Olum

There is a traditional history of the Lenni Lenape in the form of pictographs (picture writing) supposedly engraved on reeds, called the *Walam Olum,* or "Red Score," which speaks of legends and early migrations. As the *Walam Olum* says, "Long ago the fathers of the Lenape were in the land of spruce pines . . . A great land and a wide land was the east land. A land without snakes, a rich land, a pleasant land." (Some scholars have questioned the authenticity of the *Walam Olum* because the originals have not survived beyond the 19th century for verification.)

Contemporary Lenni Lenape

The Delaware Tribe of Western Oklahoma presently holds trust lands in southeastern Oklahoma. The Lenni Lenape (or Eastern Delaware) live in northeastern Oklahoma. Munsee descendants share the Stockbridge-Munsee Reservation near Bowler, Wisconsin; others make up the Munsee Delaware Indian Tribe in Ohio; others live in Ontario, among the Iroquois of the Six Nations Reserve and part of the Moravian of the Thames and Muncey of the Thames bands. In New Jersey, two bands, the Native Delaware Indians and the Nanticoke–Lenni Lenape Tribe (with the Nanticoke), maintain tribal identity. A group known as the Delaware-Muncie Tribe are centered in Pomono, Kansas. The Delaware of

Idaho operate out of Boise. Lenni Lenape descendants also live in the Allentown, Pennsylvania, region, the location of the Lenni Lenape Historical Society and Museum of Indian Culture. In 1992, the Delaware Nation Grand Council of North America, was incorporated in Ohio to foster unity among all Lenni Lenape.

LUMBEE

Throughout American history, from colonial times to the present, one of the largest concentrations of Native Americans in the United States has been located in Robeson County and the surrounding counties of southeastern North Carolina. The exact Indian ancestry of these people never has been established. It is possible that the Lumbee have ancestors from tribes of all three major Indian language families of the region, including ALGONQUIANS, Iroquoians, and Siouans. The view held by most modern scholars is that the majority of Lumbee are descended from the Cheraw, a Siouan people living in what is now northwestern South Carolina at the time of contact with Spanish explorers. The fact that the Lumbee, following interaction with English and Scottish settlers who came to the region in the late 1700s, lost their native language and many of their traditional customs sometime in the 18th century has made it impossible to determine exact ancestry.

For much of their history, the Lumbee have sought tribal recognition, trying to change the attitude of those who referred to them in general terms, such as "people of the color." In 1885, the North Carolina General Assembly gave them the name "Croatan Indians," because at that time the prevalent theory was that they were primarily descended from a combination of coastal Algonquians and Raleigh's Lost Colonists from the 1587 British settlement on Roanoke Island (see ROANOKE). In 1911, the North Carolina legislature assigned to them the unwieldy name "Robeson County Indians." In 1913, the legislature used the name "Cherokee Indians of Robeson County," which was historically inaccurate since few CHEROKEE have been known to settle among them. But then in 1953, the General Assembly accepted a name the Indians themselves had chosen—the *Lumbee* (pronounced LUM-bee)—after the Lumber River running through their territory. And in 1956, the federal government followed suit, giving them recognition as the Lumbee Indians. Yet it did not grant them special tribal status, which would have guaranteed federal services. Finally in 1993, Congress voted to recognize the Lumbee.

Before the Civil War, the Lumbee were ill-treated by many southern whites as were other Native Americans and African Americans. During the Civil War years, Lumbee men were forced to work on Confederate fortifications under terrible conditions—with minimal sleep, prolonged exposure to the elements, and little food. Some Lumbee hid out to avoid this forced labor; others managed to escape. The Home Guard troops tracked them down, terrorizing the entire Lumbee community in the process. In 1864, a teenager named Henry Berry Lowrie (also spelled Lowerie), on the execution of his father and brother—they had been accused of aiding Union soldiers—began a campaign of resistance against this cruel treatment. He led a band of young men in raids on rich plantations and distributed the stolen food to poor Indians, blacks, and whites alike.

The Home Guard came after Lowrie and his fighters, but the insurgents escaped into the swamplands they knew so well. Lowrie's men kept up their resistance even after the Civil War, now eluding federal troops. Lowrie was tricked into capture on three occasions but managed to escape each time. He became a mythical figure among the Lumbee, some of whom claimed he could not be killed by bullets. Lowrie also stood up to the Ku Klux Klan, the racist group that preached white supremacy, protecting his people from the Klan's violence. In 1871, 18 militiamen ambushed Lowrie from a bank of the Lumber River as he paddled by in a canoe. He jumped into the water and, rather than trying to escape, he used the boat as a shield as he returned fire with his rifle. Slowly advancing toward the militiamen, he singlehandedly routed them. Yet the following year, Lowrie disappeared. His death was never proven and, as late as the 1930s, some among the Lumbee claimed he was still alive.

Lowrie seemed to be present in spirit almost a century after his disappearance, in 1958, when hundreds of tribal members, angered by the racism of Ku Klux Klansmen, marched on a rally held by the group and drove them out of Robeson County once and for all.

The town of Pembroke, North Carolina, presently is a center of Lumbee activity. Tribal members have held such political offices as mayor, chief of police, and city councilman. Pembroke State University, originally founded as a four-year state-supported school for Lumbee (formerly Pembroke State College for Indians), is now part of the University of North Carolina system and has students of all backgrounds. Other communities in the region, such as Harpers Ferry, Moss Neck, Prospect, Saddletree, and Union Chapel, also consist almost entirely of tribal members.

MAHICAN

The Mahican and MOHEGAN, with similar-sounding tribal names, often are confused. Both peoples are ALGONQUIANS and perhaps are descended from the same distant ancestors, but they have distinct identities and histories. The Mahican lived along the northern end of the Hudson valley, mainly in present-day New York, but also in southern Vermont, western Massachusetts, and the northwestern corner of Connecticut. Many Algonquian bands and villages near the Hudson River were united into the loosely knit Mahican Confederacy.

The Mohegan lived in Connecticut and were an offshoot of the PEQUOT. The name *Mahican,* pronounced muh-HEE-cun, is derived from their native name *Muh-he-con-ne-ok,* meaning "people of the waters that are never still." *Mohegan* is from *Maingan* for "wolf." Both tribes have been referred to as "Mohican." This alternate spelling became widespread with the publication of the book *The Last of the Mohicans* by James Fenimore Cooper in 1826, a fictionalized account involving Indian peoples, perhaps drawing on both the Mahican and Mohegan for inspiration.

The capital and largest Mahican village at the time white explorers became aware of them in the early 1600s was Schodac, near present-day Albany, New York. The Mahican were enemies of the IROQUOIS (HAUDENOSAUNEE) tribes, especially the MOHAWK immediately to their west, who often invaded their villages. The Mahican traded with Algonquian allies to their east and south. They were masters of spears and clubs, bows and arrows, nets and traps. They depended on hunting and fishing, gathering wild plants, especially maple syrup, as well as growing corn, beans, and squash. They built long bark lodges as well as domed wigwams that they covered with birch bark, elm bark, or mats woven from plant materials. They had light birch-bark canoes. They used porcupine quills to decorate their clothing and containers. They believed that Manitou, the Great Spirit, lived in all things.

Mahican life changed drastically with the arrival of Europeans. Trading with the whites for iron tools and other goods made life easier, but disease and alcohol took their toll. Moreover, Europeans aggravated traditional Indian rivalries by supplying some tribes with firearms to use against others. The *swanneken* (the Indian word for Dutch traders) provided the Mohawk with guns in order to gain dominance over the Mahican along the Hudson River, the primary trade route for Dutch boats.

In 1664, the same year that the British took control of the region from the Dutch, the Mohawk drove the Mahican away from Schodac to lands farther to the east. The Mahican Confederacy moved the council fire to Westenhuck, among the Housatonic Band of Mahican. But whites were settling in the Housatonic valley of Massachusetts. The settlers called the village Stockbridge and, in 1736, established a Calvinist mission there for the Mahican. The various Mahican bands came to be known as the Stockbridge Indians. In the meantime, other Mahican moved to Pennsylvania and Indiana and merged with other Indian peoples, especially their Algonquian kin the LENNI LENAPE (DELAWARE).

The Stockbridge band moved several more times in the 1700s and 1800s. In 1756, they founded a new settlement among the ONEIDA of central New York. In 1788, white officials forced many Algonquians of the region, including some Mahican bands, to settle in eastern New York, not far from Stockbridge, Massachusetts. This group became known as the Brotherton Indians. Then in 1822, both the Stockbridge and the Brotherton were relocated to Wisconsin. There, in 1856, they were granted reservation lands along with the Munsee band of Lenni Lenape. They still hold this reservation today and use the Stockbridge-Munsee name (as well as Mohican). Other Mahican descendants have chosen to live in Connecticut.

MAIDU

The name *Maidu,* pronounced MY-doo, is derived from a native word referring to all that is living. The people of this name occupied ancestral territory along the eastern tributaries of the Sacramento River, including the Feather, American, and Bear Rivers flowing out of the Sierra Nevada in present-day northern California, not far from the Nevada border. There were three main divisions of Maidu, speaking an estimated 20 dialects of the Penutian language family: the Maidu proper (Northeastern or Mountain); the Konkow (Northwestern or Foothills); and the Nisenan (Southern or Valley). The valley group had the most villages or tribelets—permanent main hamlets with a number of temporary satellite hamlets. The Maidu, although not a particularly warlike people, regularly posted sentries on the hills surrounding their villages to protect themselves and their hunting grounds from outsiders.

The Maidu had many cultural traits in common with other central California Penutian tribes, such as the MIWOK, YOKUTS, and WINTUN. All were hunter-gatherers who depended on acorns and other wild plant foods, small game, and fish. They wore minimal clothing. Some Maidu lived in pole-framed, brush-covered shelters, as did other central California tribes, but some built earth-covered, domed pithouses as large as 40 feet in diameter. The openings in the roofs of these dwellings served as both a door and a smokehole. The Maidu, like many of their neighbors, participated in the Kuksu Cult. And typical of CALIFORNIA INDIANS, they crafted beautiful baskets.

The Maidu, like all Native North Americans, enjoyed a variety of games. Some of their favorite pastimes were hoop-and-pole, tossing games, dice games, and hand games. In a popular hand game, one player would switch marked and unmarked bones back and forth in his hands, then stop to let other players bet on which hand held which. Sometimes the participants would wager away all their possessions—shell money, baskets, furs, tools, and weapons—over several days in a marathon game.

The Maidu and their neighbors maintained their traditional culture longer than the southern California tribes and the coastal peoples despite Spanish attempts to move them into missions during the late 1700s and early 1800s. But in 1849 the California gold rush had a significant impact on them, their numbers drastically decreased through violence and disease.

Contemporary Maidu live for the most part in Plumas County, California (especially of the Maidu branch); Butte County (especially of the Konkow branch); and El Dorado, Placer, and Yuba Counties (especially of the Nisenan branch). They hold a number of rancherias (small reservations). They have undergone a cultural revitalization and regularly perform traditional dances, such as the Acorn, Bear, Coyote, Deer, Flower, and Toto Dances.

MAKAH

The ancestral homeland of the Makah was situated along Cape Flattery, territory now in northwestern Washington. The Juan de Fuca Strait, merging with the Pacific Ocean, separates Cape Flattery from Vancouver Island and serves as the international boundary between the United States and Canada. The Makah were the southernmost Wakashan-speaking people. Their name, sometimes spelled Macaw and pronounced mah-KAW, means "cape people" in the Wakashan language.

Makah culture was similar to that of other NORTHWEST COAST INDIANS. They were master wood carvers. They lived in villages of large, multifamily cedar-plank houses. They carved large oceangoing dugout canoes, totem poles, chests, and other wood products. They wore cedar-bark raincoats and hats. They wove blankets on a loom out of dog hair. They practiced the potlatch, the custom of giving away possessions to prove one's wealth. They were active traders.

A Makah whaler, the harpooner. His harpoon has a razor-sharp shell tip, with protruding bone spurs. It is attached by a line of sinew to a sealskin float.

With regard to subsistence, the Makah ate food from the sea, especially salmon. They also ate deer, elk, and bear meat from the forests, plus wild greens, roots, and berries. They also were among the foremost whalers in North America, respected for their precise skill by Indians and whites alike. Most of the Pacific Northwest people waited for beached whales. The Makah, like the neighboring NOOTKA on Vancouver Island, actively hunted them.

Makah whalers hunted with 18-foot-long wooden harpoons, tipped with sharp mussel-shell blades and protruding bone spurs. The spurs would keep the weapon hooked inside the whale once the blade penetrated the tough skin. The whalers used ropes of sinew to tie the harpoon to a number of sealskin floats. When dragged, the floats would tire the whale out and then, after the animal died, keep it afloat.

The chief harpooner, an honored position in the tribe, stood in the front of the dugout, usually with six paddlers and a helmsman behind him. The harpooner sang to the whale during the pursuit, promising to sing and dance for the whale and give it gifts if it let itself be killed.

Whale-hunting of course was very dangerous. Whales might swim under a dugout and flip it. Or they might smash it with their enormous tails. It took many harpoons to kill the large sea mammals—the initial harpoon with floats to weaken it, then others carried by spearsmen in other dugouts to finish it off.

The catch was towed back to the village, where it was butchered by the men and women. The chief harpooner was presented the choicest piece of blubber, taken from the animal's back. The villagers used every part of the whale. They ate both the meat and skin; they shaped the intestines into containers; they braided the tendons into rope; and they extracted oil from the blubber.

Much is known about early Makah because of an archaeological find at Ozette at the tip of Cape Flattery. (A storm in 1970 exposed part of the village and prompted excavations.) At least five centuries ago, a mudslide from a steep cliff buried this prehistoric seaside village, preserving skeletons, houses, and artifacts. Some 55,000 artifacts found at the site include sculptures, harpoons, baskets, and various other household utensils.

Visitors can see some of these artifacts at the Makah Tribal Museum at Neah Bay, Washington, on the Makah Reservation. Since 1978, the Makah Cultural and Research Center, which runs the museum, also has operated a language-preservation program.

In 1998, the Makah took up their traditional practice of whaling for the first time in 70 years, despite protests by environmental groups protecting whales.

MALISEET

The Maliseet, or Malecite, an Algonquian people, once located their wigwams along the St. John River in what now is New Brunswick, Canada, as well as in territory that is now the northeastern corner of Maine (see NORTHEAST INDIANS). In some historical accounts, they are referred to as the Etchemin.

Maliseet beaverskin hood, used as protection from cold and as a hunter's disguise

The Maliseet are close relatives of the PASSAMAQUODDY, their allies with other ABENAKI in the Abenaki Confederacy. They helped the French fight the British in the French and Indian wars. Maliseet frequently intermarried with French settlers.

Maliseet culture resembled that of other ALGONQUIANS of the Maritime Provinces, the MICMAC of Nova Scotia. It is thought that the tribal name *Maliseet,* pronounced MAL-uh-seet, comes from the Micmac word for "broken talkers." The Maliseet were less dependent on hunting and fishing than the Micmac and more dependent on farming, with large fields of corn.

Both the Maliseet and Micmac preferred their version of football, a kicking game, over lacrosse. Like Indians in many parts of the continent, they also liked to gamble, using pieces of stone, wood, and metal as dice; they threw the dice up in the air and caught them in a dish of wood or bark. Both the Maliseet and Micmac wore caps to shield their heads from the cold winter winds, a rare custom among other Algonquians.

Seven Maliseet bands presently hold reserve lands in both New Brunswick and Quebec. Some descendants, the Houlton Band of Maliseet, live in Maine. The Jay Treaty of 1794 gives the Maliseet and other tribes with members living on both sides of the United States–Canada border, such as the MOHAWK, special crossing rights. The various bands are united as the Maliseet Nation. The Houlton Band, along with the Passamaquoddy and PENOBSCOT, were part of the 1980 Maine Indian Land Claims Settlement Act.

MANDAN

The Mandan (pronounced MAN-dun) were among the earliest Native Americans on the Great Plains. By 1400, they had migrated westward from the Ohio River or Great Lakes country, breaking off from other Siouan-speaking peoples. They settled along the Missouri River, first near the mouth of the White River, territory now part of South Dakota; then, following the Missouri northward, they eventually settled near the mouth of the Heart River, in present-day North Dakota. They lived in the latter location, near the Big Bend of the Missouri, when non-Indians first made contact with them in the 1700s.

The Mandan lived in permanent villages and farmed. Like their immediate neighbors along the Missouri—the HIDATSA to the north and ARIKARA to the south—the Mandan are sometimes referred to as PRAIRIE INDIANS. But since they ventured from their villages at least once a year to hunt buffalo on the open grasslands, the Mandan and other Missouri River tribes are usually classified as PLAINS INDIANS. On acquiring horses in the mid-1700s,

the Mandan traveled even farther in search of the huge buffalo herds.

Mandan rake with antler blade

Houses

The Mandan built walls of upright logs—sturdy palisades—around their villages. Each village had anywhere from a dozen to more than 100 earth lodges. They were usually grouped around a central plaza. Each round lodge held several families, sometimes as many as 60 people, plus their dogs and in some cases even their horses. Each family had its own bed or beds next to the outer wall. A fireplace stood in the center, under a smokehole in the ceiling that was covered with a twig screen. The lodges were built around a pit one to four feet deep. They had wooden frames, tied together with plant fibers, and were covered with layers of willow rods, coarse grass, and thick strips of sod overlapped like shingles. The lodges were so strong that many people could stand on the domed roofs at once. In fact, the Mandan often congregated on top of their houses to play games and to gossip, to do chores, or simply to doze in the sun. The roofs also served as places to store possessions.

Mandan earth lodge

Transportation

The Mandan are known for their use of bull boats, small, round, cup-shaped boats made from hide stretched over a wooden framework. (Similar craft in other parts of the world have been referred to as coracles.) The trick for the two paddlers was to keep the round boats from going in circles.

Mandan bull boat

The Mandan used the bull boats to haul their meat and hides across the Missouri after buffalo hunts, bringing their catch as far as the water's edge on travois pulled by dogs and later by horses. (A travois is a primitive sled made with poles in the shape of a V.) Some families stored their bull boats on top of their lodges. They also used the boats to cover the smokeholes when it rained.

Food

The staple foods of the Mandan were crops—corn, beans, squash, and sunflower—and buffalo meat. The buffalo hunt was an important event for the entire Mandan village. Scouts were posted on the grasslands to watch for a big herd. On spotting one, the scouts would report back to the village. Men, women, and children hurriedly made preparations, gathering up bows and arrows, food supplies, and tipis, which they placed on their travois.

Before acquiring horses, which allowed a solo hunter to catch a bison, the Mandan typically hunted in groups. First they would build a trap out of two rows of piled stones or with a fence made of poles and brush. At one end, the trap had a wide opening. At the other, it narrowed, leading to the edge of a cliff or to an enclosure. Everyone except the Buffalo Caller would hide behind the rockpiles or the fences with blankets in hand. The caller, who wore a buffalo skin on his back, would creep on all fours near the grazing herd. He would imitate the cry of a sick buffalo to lure the herd toward the mouth of the trap. When the herd was inside the rows of stones, the other hunters would jump up, shout, and wave their blankets to make the animals stampede. If events went as planned, the frightened buffalo would run toward the narrow end of the trap and over the cliff or into the corral. Then, standing at a safe distance, the Indians would kill the injured beasts with arrows.

After skinning their catch, the Mandan would hold a great feast on the spot, gorging on buffalo steak, liver, kidneys, and bone marrow. What they couldn't eat, they would preserve by smoking. They would pack up and take every part of the animal back to the village for future use—the meat for food; the hides for tipis, bull boats, shields, bindings, blankets, robes, and moccasins; and the bones and horns for spoons and cups to use with their pottery bowls.

The Mandan hunted other animals as well: deer, elk, antelope, bear, wolf, fox, beaver, rabbit, turtle, and various birds, in short, whatever hunters could track down in the wild. The Mandan also fished in the Missouri River.

Ceremonies

Mandan ceremonies reveal how important corn and buffalo were to their economy. Tribal members, usually women, performed corn dances, and the men's Bull Society performed buffalo dances.

An important event for the Mandan was the annual Okipa ceremony, held in the late spring or summer. Most of the ceremony centered around a sacred cedar post erected on the village plaza inside a small enclosure. The various rituals celebrated the creation of the Mandan and tried to ensure food supplies and bring about visions for youths passing into manhood. The ceremonies lasted four days. Unlike other Plains Indians, the Mandan did not practice the Sun Dance. But their Okipa ceremony was very similar. Youths fasted for days; had their chests, backs, and legs slashed; and were raised toward the roof of a ceremonial lodge on rawhide thongs and ropes. This torture proved their manhood and brought about trance-like states in which dreams seemed especially vivid and meaningful. This type of ritual is called a Vision Quest.

Medicine bundles were important in Mandan ceremonies, as they were in the rites of many Plains and Great Lakes tribes. These sacred objects served as portable shrines. Each one had its own special mythology. For example, the Lone Man medicine bundle, the post used in the Okipa ceremony, was supposedly given to the Mandan by the first human who triumphed over the hostile powers of nature. The Sacred Canoe medicine bundle was supposedly made from the planks on which tribal ancestors survived a great flood.

Games

Games played an important part in the upbringing of children. A good example is the sham battle in which boys were taught the art of war. All the boys in a village between the ages of seven and 15 would be divided into two groups, each headed by an experienced warrior. The two warriors would coach their charges in battle techniques, then stage a mock fight outside the village. The boys shot at one another with small bows and blunt arrows. After the pretend battle, the boys returned to the village and engaged in a sham victory dance, using imitation scalps as props. During the dance, girls pretended that the boys were true heroes and acted out their great admiration for them.

Contacts with Non-Indians

The first non-Indians to report the existence of the Mandan were a family of explorers—a father and three sons and a nephew—named La Vérendrye. Exploring out of Quebec and establishing fur-trading posts along the way, they cut over to the Missouri River from the Assiniboine River and reached the Mandan villages in 1738.

The upper Missouri Indian villages had always been important trading centers for many native peoples. Nomadic Plains tribes bartered products of the hunt for the crops of farming tribes. Then in the mid-1700s, the

Plains tribes began exchanging horses for farm products. The Mandan in turn bartered some of the horses to other tribes. In the meantime, French traders wanted pelts from the Indians and offered guns and European tools for them. As a result, the Mandan became middlemen, dealing in all sorts of products with various tribes and with Europeans.

Lewis and Clark wintered among the Mandan in 1804–5 and wrote about them extensively. Other explorers followed, frontier painters among them. George Catlin, who traveled among different native peoples from 1830 to 1836, painted portraits of and wrote about Mandan life. Another frontier painter, Karl Bodmer, a Swiss who traveled with the German prince Maximilian zu Wied, also painted portraits and scenes of the Mandan in 1833–34. And Prince Maximilian wrote about them in detailed journals.

Yet their friendly contacts with non-Indians proved deadly for the Mandan. In 1837, they suffered a devastating epidemic of smallpox. It is estimated that of about 1,600 Mandan, all but 125 died that terrible year. The words of Four Bears, a Mandan chief dying of smallpox, have become famous and symbolic of the great misery endured by Indians from white diseases: "Four Bears never saw a white man hungry, but when he gave him to eat . . . and how have they repaid it! . . . I do not fear death . . . but to die with my face rotten, that even the wolves will shrink . . . at seeing me, and say to themselves, that is Four Bears, the friend of the whites."

In 1845, when the neighboring Hidatsa moved to Fort Berthold, the surviving Mandan went with them. The Arikara followed in 1862. In 1870, the federal government established a permanent reservation at that location for the three tribes.

Contemporary Mandan

The Three Affiliated Tribes of the Fort Berthold Reservation in western North Dakota—the Arikara, Hidatsa, and Mandan—present a united front in dealing with state and federal officials and in the operation of a museum and casino. Yet they maintain separate tribal traditions.

In 1934, Mandan representatives undertook a cause relating to their identity, traveling to New York City to lobby for the return of the Water Buster clan bundle from the Heye Foundation's Museum of the American Indian (now the George Gustav Heye Center, National Museum of the American Indian, part of the Smithsonian Institution). After initial resistance, the museum finally complied. The Native American Graves Protection and Repatriation Act of 1990 has since made it easier for Indian nations to reacquire sacred objects.

MASSACHUSET

The tribal name of the Massachuset was first given to the bay, then to the colony, which later became a state. The name, pronounced like that of the state but often spelled with one *t* instead of two, means "at the range of hills," one of some 5,000 place-names in New England derived from native words.

The NORTHEAST INDIANS known as Massachuset lived along the coast about present-day Boston and as far inland as the Charles and Seekonk Rivers. They lived like other ALGONQUIANS of the coastal region: they built palisaded villages of wigwams; they cultivated lands next to their villages and planted corn, beans, and squash; they hunted deer and other game in the forests; they gathered wild plant foods; they fished the rivers; they also fished the ocean and collected shellfish.

At the time of first contacts with English settlers in the region, six sachems—Cato, Chickataubut, Cutshamequin, Manatahqua, Nahaton, and Nanepashemet—ruled the six main Massachuset bands. They directed their people to help the newcomers and establish trade contacts with them, and hostilities were rare.

But the early English traders carried diseases to the native population. Massachuset families were ravaged in a smallpox epidemic from 1616 to 1620. Settlement by the English—starting with the Pilgrims in 1620—led to another epidemic in 1633–35.

There were cultural pressures on the Massachuset as well as from Protestant missionaries. The Puritan John Eliot came to Boston in 1631 and, in the following years, preached to the Massachuset and other Algonquian peoples, such as the NIPMUC. Starting in the 1650s, Eliot established 17 villages—communities where the Indians practiced the Puritan religion and lived like Europeans. The first and most famous of these was Nat-

ick (now a town near Boston). Converts became known as Praying Indians. Although Eliot's work helped give some of the converted Indians a secure life for a time and helped preserve for posterity the Massachuset language, it also stripped them of tribal identity and led to confusion and depression among them. Caught between two worlds, some turned to alcohol.

The Masachuset also suffered because of the revolt of the WAMPANOAG and NARRAGANSETT in King Philip's War of 1675. Because they had such close ties with the English, the Praying Indians were attacked by other Indians in the area. They also were attacked by settlers who sought revenge against all Indians. Some were sold into slavery to British families in Bermuda.

Surviving Massachuset chose one way of life or the other, living among the colonists or among other Algonquians. They are considered extinct as a tribe, but some extended families—in Massachusetts as well as in Bermuda—have maintained a sense of their tribal ancestry.

Massachuset bowl, carved from the burl of a tree, with animal-like handles that represent mythical creatures

MAYA

The name *Maya* (pronounced MY-uh) is applied to a people and a series of related but evolving cultures that culminated in a complex civilization. They shaped the Mayan language.

The Maya lived in Mesoamerica, the name given by scholars to the Indian culture area including Mexico (except the northern part, which is included in the Southwest Culture Area); all of the present-day countries of Guatemala, Belize, and El Salvador; and parts of Hon-

duras, Nicaragua, and Costa Rica. Maya territory for the most part was situated in the Yucatán Peninsula of eastern Mexico and in Guatemala and Belize, with some population centers as well in western Honduras and El Salvador.

Lifeways

The Maya were influenced by the OLMEC culture before them. The Olmec are sometimes called the "mother

Maya jade statuette

civilization" of Mesoamerica. But the Maya carried the Olmec cultural traits to new heights of refinement.

The Maya world, like that of the Olmec, revolved around ceremonial and economic centers in the tropical forest. More than 100 such Maya centers are known. They are often referred to as city-states, because each population center had its own rulers.

The center consisted of many stone structures, including pyramids topped by temples, shrines, platforms that served as astronomical observatories, monasteries, palaces, baths, vaulted tombs, ball courts, paved roads, bridges, plazas, terraces, causeways reservoirs, and aqueducts.

Each city-state had distinct social classes. The priests were the keepers of knowledge. The Sun Children were in charge of commerce, taxation, justice, and other civic matters. There were craftsmen, including stoneworkers, jewelers, potters, clothiers, and others. In the countryside surrounding the central complex of buildings lived

farmers, in one-room pole-and-thatch houses. They cut down and burned trees to make fields and used irrigation to water their crops—corn, beans, squash, chili peppers, cassava, and many others.

In addition to their architecture, the Maya are famous for their jade carvings and masks; ceramic figures of deities and real people, and other colored pottery; wood carvings, often mounted on buildings over doors; cotton and feather clothing; jade, pearl, alabaster, and shell jewelry; among other objects.

The Maya also are known for their scientific knowledge. They developed intricate mathematical, astronomical, and calendrical systems. The number system used bars, dots, and drawings of shells as symbols; it included the concept of zero. Their writings about astronomy and their calendars were expressed in the form of painted hieroglyphics on the bulk paper, with pictures representing events and units of time. But in addition to pictographs the Maya had glyphs representing words and sounds.

These writings are now being deciphered by scholars, expanding or altering earlier notions of the Maya. For example, the Maya have had a reputation as the most peaceful of the Mesoamerican civilizations. They definitely were not as warlike as the later TOLTEC and AZTEC peoples, who founded their empires through far-reaching military campaigns. Yet it now appears that Maya city-states made war on one another and that captives were sacrificed to their deities. Their ball games were especially violent, with captives playing for their lives and with human heads sometimes used instead of rubber balls. Also, Maya aristocrats mutilated themselves to please their gods and to demonstrate their dedication to the commoners.

A great deal remains to be learned about Maya history. Who and what brought about the change from villages into city-states? How far-reaching was the influence of particular rulers? How extensive were Maya relations, economic or otherwise, with other peoples (such as the

The Castillo, a Maya pyramid temple at Chichén Itzá in the Yucatán, Mexico

inhabitants of the huge city of Teotihuacán to the west, which prospered at the same time as many of the Maya city-states)? Why did Maya civilization eventually decline?

History

What is known about Maya history is organized as follows: The period when Maya culture developed is called the Preclassic, which occurred in the centuries before A.D. 300, during the time of the Olmec civilization.

The period of Maya dominance and highest culture is called the Classic period. The approximate dates assigned to this stage are A.D. 300 to 900. City-states such as Tikal and Palenque in what is now Guatemala prospered during the Classic period. Their inhabitants are sometimes called Lowland Maya. Tikal alone had 3,000 structures, including six temple pyramids, located over one square mile. One structure there was a terraced, four-sided pyramid, 145 feet high, with a flight of steep stone steps leading to a three-room stone temple, topped by a roof comb (an ornamental stone carving). Another temple pyramid was 125 feet high.

The phase from about A.D. 900 to 1450 is known as the Postclassic period. During this time, Maya culture thrived in the Guatemalan mountains to the south. The Maya of such sites as Chama, Utatlán, and Kaminaljuya are referred to as Highland Maya. These peoples learned techniques of metallurgy, probably through trade with the Indians living to their south in Peru and Ecuador, and crafted beautiful objects out of gold, silver, tin, and zinc.

After about A.D. 1000, during the Postclassic period, still another strain of Maya culture flourished, on the Yucatán Peninsula in what is now eastern Mexico. An invasion of Toltec from the west spurred this new flowering of culture. The Toltec interbred with the Maya and adopted many of their cultural traits. City-states such as Chichén Itzá, Tulum, and Mayapán reached their peak with many of the same traits as the Classic Lowland Maya, such as elaborate stone architecture and carvings. Mayapán, the last great city-state, serving as a regional capital, suffered a revolt in 1450, leading to political fragmentation.

The exact chain of events leading to the decline of Postclassic Maya civilization, as with the decline of Classic Maya civilization, is not known. Civil wars between different cities, or between farmers and the ruling classes, are thought to have played a part, as are calamities, such as crop failure due to soil depletion or drought. Overpopulation may have contributed to the decline.

Contacts with Non-Indians

The first contact between the Maya and Europeans came about in 1502, when Christopher Columbus sailing for Spain met a Maya trading canoe in the Gulf of Honduras. Subsequent Spanish colonization of Maya territory was sporadic and incomplete because of the inaccessibility of Maya population centers and villages in the dense jungles. Yet disease and forced labor took their toll on the Maya over the centuries. The Spanish also persisted in the eradication of Maya culture, stealing or destroying their ceremonial objects and burning their writings (of the thousands once in existence, only a few remain today). With time, many Maya lost their language, native religion, and distinct identity.

Yet several million people, especially in the Guatemalan highlands and in the northern Yucatán, continue to speak Mayan dialects. Most of them are peasant farmers and own their crops collectively. Some supplement their earnings through arts and crafts, making copies of ancient artifacts. Some still worship the Maya gods and gather in the ruins of their ancestors' temples for renewal ceremonies.

Maya doll (modern)

MENOMINEE

Wild rice, also known as Indian rice, once had at least 60 different names in the many Indian dialects. One of the Algonquian versions, the CHIPPEWA (OJIBWAY).

name for the plant, is *manomin* for "good berry." A variation of *manomin* became the name of a tribe of ALGONQUIANS living along the western Great Lakes and who harvested large quantities of wild rice—the Menominee (also spelled *Menomini* and pronounced muh-NOM-uh-nee). The native version is *Omenomenew.* Explorers and historians have also referred to these Indians by the English translation—that is, "wild rice men," or Rice Indians.

The Menominee collected the wild rice (actually not rice at all but the seed of a kind of grass) from canoes in summertime. The women usually performed this task while the men used bows and arrows to hunt small game from other boats or fished for sturgeon with hooks, spears, traps, and nets. First, the women would bend the tops of the tall aquatic grass over the canoe's sides. Then they would hit the heads with a paddle, knocking the seeds into the boat's bottom. The seeds could then be dried in the sun or by fire to open the hulls; next they were stamped on or pounded; and finally they were winnowed with a birch-bark tray, in the wind, to separate the hulls from the grain. The grain was usually boiled and served with maple syrup or in a stew.

Wild rice is sometimes found in the shallows of small lakes and ponds. But the marshes bordering the western Great Lakes are especially lush. No wonder the Menominee and other Algonquians, such as the Chippewa, OTTAWA, and POTAWATOMI, plus the Siouan WINNEBAGO, vied with one another for this territory (see NORTHEAST INDIANS). No wonder, also, when there was peace among the tribes, it was an uneasy peace. A tribe that had access to wild rice did not have to depend on farming for food and had a trade commodity that could buy hard-to-get items, such as buffalo furs from the prairies to the west of the Great Lakes. No wonder wild rice captured the Indian imagination and pervaded Indian mythology.

When the first European explorer reached the region—the Frenchman Jean Nicolet in about 1634—the Menominee controlled the northwestern shore of Lake Michigan in what is now Wisconsin and Michigan. Because of wild rice, the menominee moved less often than other tribes of the region, having year-round villages with two kinds of structures. Their cold-weather houses were domed wigwams, framed with bent saplings and usually covered with mats of cattails and reeds rather than the more common birch or elm bark. Their much larger warm-weather houses were rectangular with peaked roofs. The largest Menominee village stood at the mouth of the Menominee River where it empties into Green Bay, near the site of present-day Green Bay, Wisconsin.

The Menominee were known for their colorful clothing. Men generally wore deerskin shirts, breechcloths, leggings, and moccasins; women wore shirts of woven nettles, along with deerskin tunics, leggings, and moccasins. Both men and women decorated their clothing with painted designs, porcupine quills, and in post-contact times, beadwork.

The Menominee also wore copper jewelry, pounded and shaped from the surface deposits of copper near their homelands. Menominee women also were famous for their woven pouches. They utilized plant fibers, especially those from basswood trees, plus buffalo hairs. They dyed, spun, and wove the materials into large, supple bags with intricate geometric designs. The bags served many purposes, such as carrying and storing food or protecting ceremonial objects. The women also wove durable nets of bark fiber for fishing.

Like other tribes of the region, the Menominee made frequent use of tobacco, smoking it in their long pipes, or calumets. Just about every important ritual—making peace, preparing for war, curing the sick, or initiating someone into the Midewiwin Society—was accompanied by the smoking of tobacco. The Menominee thought that tobacco not only made a good ritualistic offering to Manitou, the Great Spirit, but that it also increased an individual's intelligence for problem solving and decision making.

The Menominee avoided many of the wars that flared up in the Old Northwest in the 1700s and 1800s. Yet some Menominee warriors did fight against Americans in the American Revolution and the War of 1812. In 1854, the Menominee were pressured into giving up their lands except for a reservation on Wolf River in north-central Wisconsin.

Menominee warclub

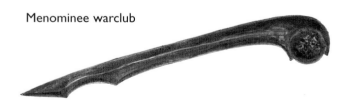

Then in 1961, the tribe suffered the effects of the Federal Indian policy of Termination, introduced in the 1950s. The idea was to terminate the special rela-

Menominee arrow with knobbed tip

A Menominee boy, mounted on his horse, at the turn of the century

tionship between the federal government and Indian tribes so that Native Americans could fit better into mainstream American culture. The Menominee were told by federal officials that they would be denied certain federal funds unless they agreed to Termination. The reservation became a county and the tribe became a corporation.

But the Menominee suffered a series of setbacks. They lacked enough money to get their lumber corporation going. Many individuals could not afford the new property taxes, from which they had previously been exempt. They were no longer protected from lumber companies seeking the rich stands of timber. And without federally sponsored programs in housing, education, and health, the tribe sank deeper and deeper into poverty.

Finally in 1972, after Termination as a policy was recognized as counterproductive to economic development, the federal government passed the Menominee Restoration Act to restore special trust status and to protect tribal lands and interests. The Menominee Ada Deer, who helped found DRUMS (Determination of Rights and Unity for Menominee Shareholders) in 1970 to lobby for restoration, became the assistant secretary for Indian Affairs in the U.S. Department of the Interior in 1993, the first woman to hold the position. The Menominee have continued to develop their timber resources. Gaming operations, including the successful Menominee Nation Casino, also have contributed to tribal revenues.

The Menominee Nation Powwow on the first weekend of August and the Veterans Powwow on Memorial Day weekend further tribal unity, as does the celebration of Menominee Restoration Day every December 22. Tribal members are working to preserve the Menominee language and traditional customs. Many practice the Big Drum religion, which began in the late 1880s among tribes of the western Great Lakes region as a revitalization movement and which involves the playing of sacred drums.

MESQUAKI *see* FOX (MESQUAKI)

MÉTIS

Métis means "mixed-blood" in French. When it is used with a lowercase *m*, the word refers to all peoples with mixed racial ancestry. When the word is used with a capital, it refers to a particular group of economically and politically unified people with a special place in Canadian history. It is pronounced may-TEE and usually appears with an accent.

Most of the Métis were of French and CREE descent. Some had a parent or grandparent from another Indian tribe, especially the CHIPPEWA (OJIBWAY), and from among Scottish and Irish settlers. The sizable population of mixed-bloods in Canada resulted primarily from the fur trade. In Europe during the 1700s and part of the 1800s, beaver hats, as well as other fur fashions, were very popular, and fortunes were made by shipping furs back to Europe. Traders depended on Native Americans as suppliers of the valuable pelts.

Lifeways

Many traders, especially among the French, adopted native customs. Some lived among the Indians, intermarried, and had children with them. The men who paddled the trading canoes through the western wilderness for the big fur companies came to be called *voyageurs,* the French word for "travelers." Those who were independent and unlicensed traders were the *coureurs de bois,* or "runners of the woods." The mixed-blood children of both voyageurs and coureurs de bois were the Métis, many of whom eventually took the same occupations as their parents did.

By the 1800s, the Métis had developed a unique lifestyle, with elements from both European and Indian cultures. They spoke both French and Indian languages, the latter mostly Algonquian, the language of the Cree and Chippewa (see ALGONQUIANS and SUBARCTIC INDIANS). Sometimes they practiced Catholic rites; at other times, Indian rituals. They farmed and lived in frame houses part of the year; they hunted and lived in hide tents the rest. Because of their uniqueness, the Métis came to consider themselves a separate group with their own special interests and destiny. Out of their common hopes came the Métis wars, usually called the Riel Rebellions. The Second Riel Rebellion came to involve their Cree kinsfolk as well.

The First Riel Rebellion

The First Riel Rebellion, also known as the Red River War, occurred in 1869, two years after the Canadian colonies became independent from Britain and united into a confederation with a centralized government at Ottawa. (Britain had taken control of Canada from the French in 1763.)

The Red River of the North runs from Lake Winnipeg in Canada to the Minnesota River in the United States. (It is not to be confused with Red River of the South, in Texas.) The Métis used to live along the Red River valley in great numbers. Every year, these Red Riverites would lead their ox-drawn carts laden with furs along the valley all the way to St. Paul, Minnesota, to trade with the Americans. It is estimated that 2,000 different Métis caravans made this long trek in some years. The Métis had had to become politically active for this right to cross the border to trade. A man named Louis Riel had led the Courthouse Rebellion of 1849, demonstrating at Winnipeg with a force of men for the release of a fellow Métis arrested by officials for smuggling goods across the border. Twenty years later his son, also named Louis, led the so-called First Riel Rebellion.

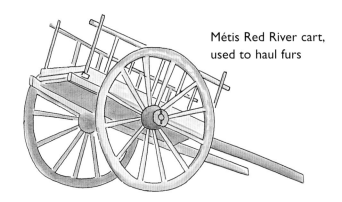

Métis Red River cart, used to haul furs

The reason for the revolt was not so much freedom of trade as land rights. After confederation, more and more non-Indians were streaming into the Red River region in search of homelands. In protest against land-grabbing by outsiders, Louis Riel, Jr., and the Métis took over Fort Garry at Winnipeg. They also formed the Comité National des Métis (National Committee of Métis) and issued a List of Rights, declaring themselves independent from the rest of Canada. Riel's right-hand man was Ambroise Lepine, a skilled hunter and tracker. The Métis were such good fighters that the central government decided to negotiate with them rather than fight. When the Métis agreed to peace, Ottawa passed the Manitoba Act, making the Red River area a province and guaranteeing most of the Métis' List of Rights.

The Second Riel Rebellion

Nevertheless, settlers broke the terms of the treaty and kept coming onto Métis lands. Little by little, the Métis lost much of what they had been fighting for. Many decided to move westward to the Saskatchewan River to start a new life hunting the buffalo on the Great Plains. But the fight for a homeland and autonomy was not over. The central government was sponsoring the construction of the Canadian Pacific Railway linking the east and west coasts. In the 1880s, white Protestant settlers sought lands along the Saskatchewan River. Métis rights were again ignored.

Louis Riel was now at a mission school in Montana, teaching Indian children. The Métis thought him the man to lead another fight for Métis land rights and freedom of religion. They sent the renowned buffalo hunter, horseman, and sharpshooter Gabriel Dumont to fetch him. Riel agreed to return to Canada to lead the resistance, but only on condition that the Métis try to avoid violence. Dumont, Riel's close friend and general, organized the Métis into an efficient force. Riel gave his approval for a campaign of sabotage—occupying government property, taking hostages, and cutting telegraph lines. The Métis also sent an ultimatum to the North-West Mounted Police (the Mounties) at Fort Carlton, demanding the surrender of the post. The year was 1885; the Second Riel Rebellion had begun.

In spite of Riel's wish for a nonviolent campaign, the situation escalated. The Canadian government used the new railway to send troops, called the North-West Field Force, from the East. Several battles resulted—at Duck Lake, Fish Creek, and Batoche. The Batoche battle in May 1885 was the turning point. Earlier that day, Dumont and his men had knocked out of commission the *Northcote,* a riverboat converted by the North-West Field Force into a gunboat. Dumont's men had damaged the boat by stringing a cable across the South Saskatchewan River to trap it, then fired on it. But at Batoche the Métis rebels were no match for the much more numerous government troops. After a three-day siege by their enemy, the Métis surrendered. Meanwhile, the Cree had been fighting their own battles. After several more encounters and a period of hiding out in the wilderness, they too surrendered.

Following the Second Riel Rebellion, the government dealt harshly with the rebels. Louis Riel was sentenced to death. French Catholics wanted to spare him, but the British controlled the government. He probably could have saved his life by pleading insanity, but he refused to denounce his actions. The execution of Louis Riel was carried out on November 16, 1885, just nine days after the railroad was finished. Gabriel Dumont managed to escape to the United States and gained some notoriety in later years by appearing in Buffalo Bill Cody's Wild West Show. Métis power and culture were broken. Saskatchewan became an English-dominated province, as Manitoba had earlier.

Métis knife with iron blade and black bone handle, iniaid with brass and white bone

Contemporary Métis

In addition to Métis individuals and families living throughout much of western Canada, there are Métis communities in both Canada and Montana. They have become increasingly organized in recent years, forming tribal councils and working together for common goals, such as the preservation of their unique culture and economic advancement.

MIAMI

Miami, pronounced my-AM-ee, is a common place-name in the United States. But in different parts of the country it has different origins. In Florida, for example, it probably comes from *Mayaimi,* the name of a CREEK village. In Oregon, it comes from the CHINOOK word *memie,* meaning "downstream." In the Midwest and Southwest, however, it comes from an Algonquian tribal name, probably meaning "people of the peninsula."

Lifeways

The tribe bearing this name, the Miami, occupied ancestral territory south of Lake Michigan in what is now Indiana, western Ohio, and eastern Illinois. They lived along timbered river valleys and shared many of the cultural traits of other ALGONQUIANS. Without birch trees growing that far south, the Miami used elm bark or mats of woven plant materials to cover their houses of various shapes. And they made dugout boats from single trees, usually butternuts.

The Miami, although classified as NORTHEAST INDIANS, sometimes are called PRAIRIE INDIANS because in addition to farming, like their neighbors to the west, the ILLINOIS, they hunted buffalo on the open prairies. Unlike the later PLAINS INDIANS, who chased the herds on horses, early hunters on the prairies typically trapped the animals in a ring of fire, then picked them off with arrows. Most villagers, except the old and weak and a handful of warriors as guards, would go on the buffalo hunts. The women and children would help prepare the meat and hides for travel back to the river valley.

Many of the cultural traits of the later Plains Indians evolved from those of the forest/prairie tribes. The calumet, or peace pipe, is one such example. The stone used to make the bowls—pipestone, or catlinite—comes from the Great Lakes country. Blood red in color, it was carved and fitted onto a long reed, then decorated with feathers, white in times of peace, red during war. So-called peace pipes might actually be used as "war pipes."

Another custom that spread westward from the forests and prairies was the Scalp Dance. After a battle, the warriors who had fought recounted their exploits by chanting and dancing while the calumet was passed around. In the dance, a warrior might show how he tracked an enemy, struck him dead, and then scalped him. It was important that he tell the truth. If he fabricated an incident or even just exaggerated what had happened, others would shout out the real events and disgrace him before all the village.

Little Turtle's War

The Miami must have danced furiously on the night of November 2, 1791, after one of the greatest Indian victories in American history—St. Clair's Defeat—during what is known as the Miami War (or Little Turtle's War) of 1790–94.

Before this first of the wars for the Old Northwest between the young United States and various Indian tribes, the Miami supported the French against the English and the IROQUOIS (HAUDENOSAUNEE), in the French and Indian wars from 1689 to 1763. They continued the fight against the English in Pontiac's Rebellion of 1763. In the American Revolution from 1775 to 1783, the Miami supported their old enemies, the British, against the American rebels.

And then in the 1790s, with one of their own tribesmen, Little Turtle (Michikinikwa), as general in chief of all the warriors—including CHIPPEWA (OJIBWAY), OTTAWA, POTAWATOMI, LENNI LENAPE (DELAWARE), SHAWNEE, and ILLINOIS—the Miami fought the Americans again.

Little Turtle was one of the great military geniuses of all time. Although a great orator, he was not as famous a personality as other great Indian leaders of his age, such as the Ottawa Pontiac, the MOHAWK Joseph Brant, and the Shawnee Tecumseh. Yet he rates with the great generals from all over the world, having help develop many methods of guerrilla warfare that modern armies now use, especially decoy techniques.

Little Turtle's War really started just after the American Revolution. With American victory in 1783, more and more settlers began arriving in the region and settling on Indian lands. The Indians responded with many raids. It is estimated that the Indians killed 1,500 settlers from 1783 to 1790. In 1790, President George Washington ordered an army into the field under General Josiah Harmar, with militiamen from Pennsylvania, Virginia, and Kentucky making up the large force.

The army organized at Fort Washington (present-day Cincinnati, Ohio). When they set out in the fall toward the many Indian villages along the Maumee River that feeds Lake Erie, the militiamen were cocky. Many of these same men had helped defeat the British in the Revolution.

The soldiers underestimated their enemy. Little Turtle used swift, small strikes to confuse the enemy. He told his warriors, after an ambush, even without any losses, to retreat into the wilderness. He also had them burn some of their own villages to make the retreat convincing. When the exhausted soldiers were far from a supply base, Little Turtle launched two big attacks and routed Harmar's army, inflicting more than 200 casualties.

General Arthur St. Clair's was given the new command. In the fall of 1791, under President Washington's orders, St. Clair mustered an even larger force at Fort Washington. And on the way toward the Maumee River, he built new bases for added security—Fort Hamilton and Fort Jefferson. But in the end he fared even worse against Little Turtle. Warriors surprised St. Clair and his men on the upper Wabash River, killing many, then retreated into the forest. The soldiers fell for the ploy and split up into groups. Those who chased the Indians were picked off. Then warriors surrounded the remaining force and pressed the attack. After three hours of fighting, when the count was taken, there were only a few Indian casualties. But St. Clair's force had 900 casualties—about 600 dead and 300 wounded. It was an enormous victory for the united tribes.

Washington ordered a third army out, this one 3,000 strong under General "Mad" Anthony Wayne, a Revolutionary War hero. Wayne took two years to organize and train this force before sending it into battle. His men built new, better-equipped forts—Fort Greenville and Fort Recovery. Little Turtle's warriors attacked Fort Recovery but were repelled.

Little Turtle recognized the inevitable. Wayne had built a huge, disciplined force. Whites would keep coming no matter how many armies the Indians defeated. Hoping to save Indian lives, Little Turtle counseled peace. But many of the still-angry warriors wanted war. They voted to have a new leader, Turkey Foot. It was their turn to be overconfident after the two earlier victories.

In 1794, Wayne's army advanced cautiously into Indian country. The Indians retreated. This time, without Little Turtle, they were disorganized, and Wayne used the element of surprise to his advantage. In the

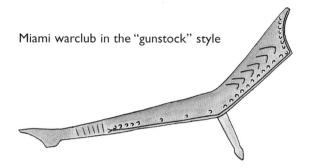

Miami warclub in the "gunstock" style

Battle of Fallen Timbers, the Indians lost hundreds of men, including Turkey Foot, and the whites lost only a few.

A year later, in August 1795, many of the chiefs of the allied tribes, including Little Turtle, signed the Treaty of Fort Greenville. The Indians ceded much of their territory to the whites—all of Ohio and most of Indiana. In exchange they were guaranteed other lands farther west, lands that they would, in time, have to fight for again.

Little Turtle never fought again. He became a celebrity among non-Indians. He traveled a great deal and met many famous people. But he died of a disease he developed as a result of living among whites—gout.

Land Cessions

The Miami were pressured into ceding more of their lands in a series of treaties from 1818 to 1840. About half the Miami—mostly of the Wea and Piankashaw bands—were relocated to Kansas in 1846 and united with the Peoria and Kaskaskia bands of Illinois. In the late 1860s, these lands were opened to non-Indian settlement as well, and the Miami and Illinois moved to the northeastern Indian Territory. The Miami Nation of Oklahoma is a federally recognized entity and still holds trust lands with tribal headquarters in Miami, Oklahoma.

The Miami who stayed in Indiana gradually lost most of their remaining lands too. As of 1897, they no longer were recognized by the federal government and lost the benefits of special status. Despite their inability to regain recognition, they have managed to maintain tribal identity as the Miami Nation of Indiana. In 1990, they established tribal offices in Peru, Indiana, and, in 1992, purchased a sacred site along the Mississinewa River.

MICCOSUKEE   *see* SEMINOLE

MICMAC

Micmac, pronounced MICK-mack, means "allies." The native term is *Mi'kmaq.* For much of their history, these NORTHEAST INDIANS of the Canadian Maritime Provinces were allies of other ALGONQUIANS to the south in the Abenaki Confederacy—the ABENAKI, MALISEET, PASSAMAQUODDY, PENOBSCOT, and PENNACOOK—as well as allies of the French. They were enemies of other neighbors: the INUIT and BEOTHUK to their north and the IROQUOIS (HAUDENOSAUNEE) to their south.

It is possible the Micmac were the first North American Indians ever encountered by Europeans. Their wigwams once dotted all of what now is Nova Scotia and Prince Edward Island, the Gaspé Peninsula of Quebec, the north shore of New Brunswick, and islands in Newfoundland. The Norseman who arrived along the shores of northeastern North America about A.D. 1000 possibly had some interaction with them, although the Skraeling of whom the visitors wrote might have been Beothuk or Inuit.

It is known for certain that as early as 1497, the Italian explorers John and Sebastian Cabot, who sailed under the English flag, kidnapped three Micmac warriors and took them to England. In 1534, the Micmac had peaceful contacts with the French explorer Jacques Cartier and, in 1603, Samuel de Champlain. The Micmac stayed faithful allies of the French after these early contacts, even serving as middlemen for them by gathering furs from other tribes, much as the HURON (WYANDOT) did for the French in later years. When the Beothuk stole from French fishermen, the Micmac, armed with French flintlocks, carried out attacks on behalf of their European allies.

The Micmac signed a series of treaties with new allies, the British, starting in 1725, guaranteeing them the right to hunt and fish in their ancestral territory. The rights were reaffirmed in another agreement in 1752 and again in 1763, following the defeat of the French by the British in the last of the French and Indian wars.

A Woodland people, the Micmac lived and tracked game in small bands in the winter. The Micmac hunted mainly moose, caribou, and porcupine in the winter

Micmac birch-bark moose call

with spears and arrows. They had spears with double-edged blades made from moose bone, plus arrows with stone points. They also used calls, such as birch-bark moose calls, to attract game, and snares and deadfalls as traps. The bands gathered and camped together in the summer. In the spring and summer, the Micmac fished the rivers with harpoons, hooks, and nets. They also collected shellfish along the ocean and harpooned seals. One method of food preparation was suspending fish from a tree and letting it begin to decay before eating it.

The Micmac were masters of quillwork, using porcupine quills dyed with vegetable colors to create intricate patterns on clothing and containers. Tribal members also mastered the use of birch bark, using it as a covering for their long canoes and conical wigwams.

The Micmac had a spiritual relationship with nature. In every person, animal, plant, and rock, they saw a manifestation of the Great Spirit.

Today, Micmac have integrated into Canadian society. Many of them are farmers and many are Catholics. But some tribal members still practice traditional crafts on their reserves in Nova Scotia, New Brunswick, and Prince Edward Island. Micmac descendants still live in the United States. In 1992, the Aroostook Band of Micmac in northern Maine gained federal recognition of its tribal status and are allied with the 28 Canadian bands as the Micmac Nation. Tribal members can cross the international border freely under the terms of the Jay Treaty of 1794.

MINITARI *see* HIDATSA

MISSION INDIANS

The phrase *Mission Indians* is applied to many different native peoples in North America converted by Christian missionaries and resettled on missions. Soon after the European discovery of North America, various churches sent out missionaries to seek converts among the native population. At every stage of development thereafter, missionaries carried their work to the edge of the frontier.

Much of what is known about early Indians comes from the writings of missionaries. Some of the most famous North American explorers were churchmen, such as Isaac Jogues, who explored the eastern Great Lakes and New York's Lake George; Claude Jean Allouez, who explored the western Great Lakes; Louis Jolliet and Jacques Marquette, who reached the Mississippi River. French Jesuit priests, members of the Roman Catholic Society of Jesus, were the most active of all the missionaries in colonial times, exploring Indian territory from bases in Quebec. Work by them and others like them among the ALGONQUIANS and Iroquoians—the IROQUOIS (HAUDENOSAUNEE) and the HURON (WYANDOT)—during the middle to late 1600s brought about settlements of Mission Indians, such as the MOHAWK at Kahnawake. Other Catholic orders had an impact on Indian history as well, such as the Franciscans and Dominicans, mostly based in Mexico.

Some of the Protestant denominations active in missionary work were the Puritans, the Society of Friends (the Quakers), Moravians, Presbyterians, Anglicans, Baptists, and Methodists. These missionaries advanced into Indian country mainly from the East Coast. Some of the better known mission settlements resulting from their efforts were Natick among the MASSACHUSET; Stockbridge among the MAHICAN; Conestoga among the SUSQUEHANNOCK; Gnaddenhutten among the LENNI LENAPE (DELAWARE); and Metlakatla among the TSIMSHIAN.

Many of these missionized peoples are referred to in history looks as *Mission Indians.* The phrase, however, is most often applied to CALIFORNIA INDIANS, many of whom lost their tribal identities under the influence of Spanish missionaries.

After the Spanish had explored and settled ARAWAK (TAINO) lands in the West Indies in the Caribbean, they pushed on into Central and South America. The colony of New Spain (now Mexico) was founded in 1521 after the conquest of the AZTEC city of Tenochtitlán. Spain then gradually spread its dominion northward. In 1565, Pedro Menéndez de Avilés founded St. Augustine in Florida, the first permanent European settlement in North America.

The territory that was to become the American Southwest also was soon developed by the Spanish. Explorers, the conquistadores, worked their way northward through Mexico. A military man and a priest often traveled together so that both state and church were represented. In 1598, Juan de Oñate founded the settlements of San Juan de Yunque and Santa Fe in New Mexico in 1609 among the PUEBLO INDIANS. In 1718, Martín de Alarcon founded San Antonio in Texas. By the mid-1700s, the Spanish were establishing missions, presidios (forts), and rancherias in Baja California, which is now part of Mexico. The first Spanish settlement in the part of California that is now U.S. territory was San Diego, founded in 1769 by Gaspar de Portolá and the Franciscan priest Junípero Serra.

Junípero Serra stayed on in California and along with other Franciscans founded many more missions—21 in the coastal region between San Diego and San Francisco. The Indians they missionized had been peaceful hunter-gatherers, and soldiers had little trouble rounding them up and forcing them to live at the missions. The friars taught them to speak Spanish and to practice the Catholic religion. They also taught them how to tend fields, vineyards, and livestock, as well as how to make adobe and soap. Then they forced them to work—to build churches and to produce food. If the Indians refused or if they ran away and were caught, they received whippings as punishment.

The Spanish brought Indians of different tribes to each mission, mostly from groups living near the Pacific coast. Before long, the Indians had lost their own language and religion as well as their tribal identity. Most came to be identified historically by the name of the mission. Thus the tribal names that have been passed down through history sound Spanish: Cahuilla; Cupeño; Diegueño; Fernandeño; Gabrieliño; Juaneño; Luiseño; Nicoleño; Serrano. All these peoples originally spoke a dialect of the Uto-Aztecan language family before being forced to speak Spanish, except the Diegueño who spoke Yuman dialect. Other tribes of different language families and living farther north— CHUMASH, Salinas, Esselen, and Costanoan—were also missionized. The Chumash, Salinan, and Esselen spoke Hokan dialects; the Costanoan spoke a Penutian one.

The missions robbed the Indians of their culture and broke their spirit. The Mexican government closed the missions in 1834, 13 years after Mexican independence from Spain. Mission Indians who had not already been killed by white diseases or poor working conditions, had a hard time coping without mission food. Their numbers continued to decline drastically. The United States took control of California after the Mexican Cession of 1848. The California gold rush further affected native peoples, even those who had avoided mission life during the Spanish occupation.

By the time the United States government finally began establishing reservation lands for the Mission Indians in the late 1800s, much of California had been settled by whites. The Indians received numerous small pieces, sometimes called rancherias. Today, there are many different bands of Mission Indians living on these parcels. Some have integrated into mainstream American culture, holding jobs in industry and agriculture. Some have rediscovered the traditional ceremonies and crafts of their ancient ancestors.

MISSISSIPPIAN *see* MOUND BUILDERS

MISSOURIA

According to tribal legend, the Siouan-speaking Missouria, or Missouri, once lived in the Great Lakes region as one people with the IOWAY, OTOE, and WINNEBAGO. Yet at some early point in their history, before whites reached the area, a group separated from the Winnebago in search of larger herds of buffalo to the southwest. On reaching the mouth of the Iowa River, where it enters the Mississippi River, another separation occurred. One group, who became the Ioway, stayed in this region. Another group continued westward to the Missouri River, where the group again divided.

Legend has it that this last division happened because of a quarrel. The son of one chief supposedly seduced the daughter of another. The one chief led his people north up the Missouri River. His people came to be known as the Otoe, or "lechers," because of his son's behavior. The group that stayed behind became the Missouria (pronounced miz-OAR-ee-uh).

A version of their name later was taken as the name of the Missouri River. It probably originally meant "people with the dugout canoes." But it has come to be translated as "big muddy" after the river, which carries a lot of silt. The name also was adopted by whites as the name of the state.

When they lived farther to the east, the Missouria were woodland Indians who farmed as well as hunted. They took their knowledge of woodworking and farming westward with them. They also continued to live in villages much of the year. Sometimes the Indians who once lived along the Mississippi River and its tributaries are discussed as PRAIRIE INDIANS because of the tall prairie grass there. But the Missouria usually are classified as PLAINS INDIANS, since, after having acquired horses, they began to wander over greater distances in search of buffalo and adopted cultural traits similar to those of the western Plains tribes.

In 1673, the French explorer Jacques Marquette visited Missouria villages on the Missouri River where it is joined by a tributary called the Grand River. The tribe lived in this part of what now is the state of Missouri for more than 100 years. In 1798, the SAC and FOX (MESQUAKI) swept down from the northeast to defeat the Missouria. Survivors lived among the Otoe, OSAGE, and KAW for several years, then established some villages south of the Platte River in present-day Nebraska. The Missouria lived there when the Lewis and Clark Expedition encountered them in 1805. Yet the Osage later attacked the Missouria, dispersing them. In 1829, the Missouria joined their ancestral relatives, the Otoe. By 1882, the majority of both tribes had moved to the north-central part of the Indian Territory. They now are united as the Otoe-Missouria Tribe.

MIWOK

The Miwok, or Mewuk, of central California can be divided into three main groups: Valley Miwok, Coast Miwok, and Lake Miwok. The main group, the Valley, or Eastern, Miwok occupied ancestral territory on the western slope of the Sierra Nevada along the San Joaquin and Sacramento Rivers and their tributaries. (The Valley Miwok are further divided into the Bay Miwok, Plains Miwok, Northern Miwok, and Southern Sierra Miwok.) The Coast Miwok lived to their west along the Pacific coast north of San Francisco Bay. And the Lake Miwok lived near Clear Lake north of San Francisco Bay. *Miwok,* pronounced MEE-wuk, means "people" in the Penutian dialect of the tribe.

The lifeways of the three Miwok groups varied with the food sources available near their more than 100 village sites. Like other CALIFORNIA INDIANS, they gathered wild plant foods, especially acorns, hunted small game, and fished in rivers, ocean, and lakes. Miwok houses had frameworks of wooden poles covered with swamp plants, brush, grass, or palm fronds. Their coiled baskets had flared-out sides and black designs.

The Miwok generally maintained peaceful relations with the Spanish, who did not missionize peoples of this region to the degree they did the southern California tribes. The Mexican government pretty much left the Miwok alone after Mexico had gained its independence from Spain in 1821 and had taken control of California. The presence of Russian fur traders, who maintained Fort Ross on Bodega Bay from 1812 to 1841, had some impact on Miwok groups because of acts of violence and the spread of disease. Yet the majority of Miwok people were spared non-Indian settlement in their midst until the mid-1800s. In 1848, by the Treaty of Guadalupe Hidalgo, Mexico ceded California to the United States. At the end of that same year, gold was discovered in the region, starting the California gold rush.

Anglo-American settlers began coming in great numbers to California over the next years in search of the mother lode, the miners' name for a big strike of gold. The Indians suffered greatly. White diseases killed many of them. The presence of mining camps disrupted their hunting. And some miners shot Indians on sight.

The Valley Miwok and a powerful neighboring tribe, the YOKUTS, fought back. In 1850, the same year that California became the 31st state of the Union, warriors under the Miwok chief Tenaya bagan attacking prospecting parties and trading posts. The owner of the trading posts, James Savage, organized a state militia, called the Mariposa Battalion, which he led into the Sierra Nevada highlands in pursuit of the Indians. The two forces met in a number of indecisive skirmishes. By 1851, however, with continuing white patrols, the Miwok and Yokuts gave up their campaign of violence.

The Miwok presently hold a number of *rancherias* (small reservations) in their ancestral homeland. Since many tribal members intermarried over the years with neighboring peoples, such as the POMO, MAIDU, WINTUN, Wailaki, and Yuki, there are Miwok descendants living among at least 17 other federally recognized tribes or bands as well on their rancherias. The Miwok preserve their traditional culture in the form of songs, dances, hand games, weaving, and beadwork. The Tuolumne Band of Me-Wuk Indians of the Tuolumne Rancheria holds an Acorn Festival every September.

MODOC

The Modoc (pronounced MO-dock) occupied ancestral territory along what is now the southern Oregon and northern California border, in the vicinity of Modoc Lake, Little Klamath Lake, Clear Lake, Goose Lake, Tule Lake, and Lost River. Their homeland was just south of that of the KLAMATH, who spoke a similar dialect of the Penutian language, sometimes referred to as the Lutuamian language isolate. The Klamath called them Mo-adok for "southerners." Both the Modoc and Klamath are thought of as tribes of the Plateau Culture Area, like their more northern Penutian kin, with whom they often traded.

PLATEAU INDIANS were seminomadic hunter-gatherers. Their migrations revolved around the seasonal availability of food. Salmon runs were an important time of year. When these ocean fish swim upriver to lay their eggs, they make for an easy catch. So the houses of the migratory peoples of the Columbia Plateau included not only permanent, semi-underground earth lodges, but also temporary mat-covered tents.

Although their way of life was similar to that of peoples to their north, the Modoc are often discussed historically with CALIFORNIA INDIANS living south of them because of the Modoc War, one of the few Indian wars to occur within the boundaries of the state of California. Because California Indians generally tolerated mistreatment by whites without resorting to violence, and because the federal government under the post–Civil War administration of President Ulysses Grant had a Peace Policy toward Native Americans at the time, the Modoc uprising of 1872 proved shocking to much of the nation.

The Modoc War

The causes of the Modoc War dated back to 1864. At that time, the Modoc and Klamath signed away most of their territory and retired to the Klamath Reservation in Oregon, northeast of Upper Klamath Lake. But the Modoc never felt content among the Klamath. There was not enough food for both tribes. Many people became sick. Tensions mounted among respective tribal members over petty issues. The Modoc longed for a separate home and asked for their own reservation across the California border, along the Lost River north of Tule Lake. The federal and California governments turned down the tribe's request.

A group of Indians under a young leader named Kintpuash, nicknamed Captain Jack by whites, took matters into their own hands. In 1870, they set out for their longed-for homeland and reestablished a village in the Lost Valley. For a time, officials ignored their move. But as white settlement in northern California increased, so did complaints about the Modoc presence. The federal government ordered out troops.

In November 1872, Captain James Jackson set out from Fort Klamath with instructions to bring back the renegades. When Jackson announced his intentions to the Modoc, a fight broke out in the village. One Modoc and one soldier died in the shooting. Captain Jack and his followers escaped to Tule Lake, then worked their way farther south to what the Indians called the "Land of Burnt Out Fires." This was a volcanic highland formed by hardened lava, a rugged and desolate place that made for natural fortifications. Meanwhile, a party of Modoc under Hooker Jim, who had been away from the village, eluded a posse of civilians trying to round them up. This group carried out several attacks on ranchers in the region, killing 15. Then they too fled to the lava beds.

Captain Jack had hoped that perhaps peace negotiations might be possible. On learning of Hooker Jim's actions, however, he knew that war was inevitable. California and Oregon regulars and volunteers under Lieutenant Colonel Frank Wheaton massed near the lava beds. The attack came in January 1873. While the bluecoat infantry advanced, the artillery fired rounds into the dense fog enveloping the "Land of Burnt Out Fires." But the shells fell closer to the advancing infantry than to the Indians. And the Modoc warriors, moving along lava trenches with sagebrush in their hair as camouflage, successfully, counterattacked. The soldiers, suffering many casualties at the hands of Modoc sharpshooters, retreated.

The third phase of the war began. General Edward Canby, the military commander of the entire Northwest District, decided to personally lead the campaign. He built up a force of about 1,000 men. To his credit, he also set a peace plan in motion. With the help of Captain Jack's cousin Winema, who was married to a white man, he arranged for negotiations with the Indians. President Grant's peace commissioners, Alfred Meachem and Reverend Eleasar Thomas, represented the government along with General Canby.

Captain Jack thought that peace might still be possible. But he refused to turn over Hooker Jim and the militants who had killed the ranchers. A medicine man named Curly Headed Doctor convinced Captain Jack that if he killed the leaders of the army, the troops would be powerless to act. Captain Jack and his best friends among the warriors agreed to a plan of treachery.

At a parley on April 11, Captain Jack drew a hidden revolver and shot and killed General Canby. Boston Charley killed Reverend Eleasar Thomas. Then the warriors escaped.

Now there would be no mercy for the Modoc. Any hope for their own reservation had ended. Some outraged whites even called for their complete extermination. The new commander in the field, Colonel Alvan Gillem, launched an attack that was again repulsed. The Modoc managed to sneak away to another lava formation farther south. A war party under Scarfaced Charley led an ambush on one army patrol in a hollow. Twenty-five soldiers, including all five officers, died in that one-sided fight.

Yet the Modoc rebellion was winding down. The Modoc lacked food and water and were arguing among themselves. A new commander, General Jeff Davis, organized a relentless pursuit of the now-scattered small bands. Hooker Jim turned himself in and, bargaining for his own life, betrayed Captain Jack, who had faithfully protected him. He led the troops to Captain Jack's hideout. Cornered in a cave, Captain Jack and his friends—Boston Charley, Black Jim, and Schonchin John—surrendered.

At the court-martial, Hooker Jim served as a witness against the others. Captain Jack and his friends were sentenced to hang. The execution took place on October 3, 1873. On the night after the hanging, grave robbers dug up Captain Jack's body, embalmed it, and displayed it in a carnival that toured eastern cities.

Surviving Modoc were sent to live among the QUAPAW in the Indian Territory. In 1909, 51 Modoc were allowed to return to the Klamath Reservation. Today, Modoc descendants live in both places. The Modoc Tribe of Oklahoma gained federal recognition in 1978 and approval of their constitution in 1991. Tribal members are working to recover and preserve language, oral traditions, and ceremonies.

MOGOLLON *see* SOUTHWEST CULTURES

MOHAVE *see* MOJAVE

MOHAWK

The Mohawk thought of themselves as Kanienkahagen, or the "people of the place of flint." Of the Six Nations of the Iroquois League, they occupied the easternmost ancestral territory, with the ONEIDA, ONONDAGA, CAYUGA, SENECA, and, in later years, the TUSCARORA to their west. To the IROQUOIS (HAUDENOSAUNEE), the confederacy resembled a longhouse extending across upstate New York, making the Mohawk the Keepers of the Eastern Door. The Mohawk also used the symbol of the shield for themselves at the Iroquois League's annual Great Council. The Mohawk sent nine sachems, or chiefs, to the meeting as their representatives.

The name *Mohawk,* pronounced MO-hawk, originally *Mohowawog,* is Algonquian, not Iroquoian, and means "eaters of men." The ALGONQUIANS used this name because the Iroquoian-speaking Mohawk were known to practice ceremonial cannibalism to absorb the strength of their enemies.

The Mohawk built most of their longhouses in villages along the northern valley of the river now named after them, the Mohawk, which flows into the Hudson River. Tribal members could travel on it in their elm-bark canoes when they headed eastward to trade, hunt, or go to war.

The Mohawk shared history and culture with their allies, as summarized under the IROQUOIS (HAUDENOSAUNEE) entry. Yet, as is the case with all the Six Nations, they retain a distinct identity.

Trade Contacts

As the easternmost of the Haudenosaunee, the Mohawk had the earliest regular trade contacts with Europeans. The Dutch became early trade partners and allies, exchanging firearms and other European manufactured goods for furs. Following their takeover of the Dutch colony of New Netherland in 1664, the English became allies of the Mohawk. Through the French and Indian wars of 1689–1763, the Mohawk were for the most part allies of the English and enemies of the French in the struggle for colonial in North America.

Joseph Brant

The most prominent Mohawk in American and Canadian history is Theyendanegea, better known by his English name, Joseph Brant. What makes Joseph Brant so interesting historically is that he was successful in both the Indian and white worlds. He was born in the Ohio Valley in 1742, while his Mohawk parents were on a hunting trip there. But he grew up in the Mohawk valley of New York State.

An Englishman of Irish descent named William Johnson, a land speculator and trader who built Fort Johnson and later Johnson Hall in Mohawk territory, was a good friend to the Haudenosaunee and was fair in his dealings with them. He admired their character, participated in their ceremonies, and married a Mohawk woman by the name of Molly Brant. Her brother, Joseph Brant, played with William Johnson's son, John, and his nephew, Guy. Because of William Johnson's close relationship to the Indians, the king of England made him the superintendent of Indian affairs for the northern colonial region.

When fighting broke out between the British and French in the last of the French and Indian wars, starting in 1754, William Johnson asked for the help of his Mohawk friends in an expedition to Lake George. Chief Hendrick led a Mohawk contingent. One of the Mohawk participants was Thayendanegea, also known as Joseph Brant, a boy of only 13. Johnson and his British and Mohawk troops won the Battle of Lake George in 1755. He received a knighthood from the king in recognition of his victory. He later led an expedition against Fort Niagara on Lake Ontario. Again, many Mohawk, including the young Joseph Brant, fought with him.

William Johnson recognized Joseph Brant's exceptional talents. After the war, which ended in 1763, he sent the 19-year-old youth to Moor's Indian Charity School in Connecticut (which later was moved to New Hampshire and became Dartmouth College). Brant proved himself an excellent student, mastering spoken and written English.

Joseph Brant later acted as interpreter for Sir William Johnson. When Sir William died in 1774, Guy Johnson became the new superintendent of Indian affairs, and Brant became his interpreter and personal secretary. This was the period just before the outbreak of the American Revolution. When violence erupted in 1775 at Lexington, Massachusetts, with "the shot heard round the world," the Haudenosaunee tribes were pressured to choose sides—their traditional allies, the British, or the American rebels.

At this time, Joseph Brant traveled to England with Guy Johnson. He made quite an impression abroad as an Indian ambassador. He met many famous Englishmen, such as the writer James Boswell and the painter George Romney, who painted his portrait. Brant also met King George III. At the time, most people, when presented to kings, knelt and kissed their hands, but, as legend has it, not Brant, who considered himself the king's equal. Instead, he ceremoniously kissed the queen's hand.

When Joseph Brant returned to North America, he worked hard to win over all the Haudenosaunee tribes to the British cause against the rebelling Americans. His natural leadership abilities and statesmanship now revealed themselves. His fellow Mohawk, plus Seneca, Onondaga, and Cayuga bands accepted his leadership, but not the Oneida and Tuscarora, who had many friends among the American settlers.

Joseph Brant, who had already demonstrated himself as a fighter, student, translator, secretary, ambassador, orator, and statesman, now proved himself as a general in the field. He led his warriors and Tory troops in many successful raids on settlements and forts in both New York and Pennsylvania.

One of the most famous battles took place in Cherry Valley, New York, on November 11, 1778. The small settlement was located about 50 miles west of Albany, near Otsego Lake. Joseph Brant and Ranger Captain Walter Butler led approximately 700 troops out of the southwest along an old winding Indian trail. They first attacked outlying settlements, picking off stranded settlers who could not make it back to the fort in time. Then they attacked the stockade, defended by the Seventh Massachusetts Regiment. The American troops repelled the Indian and Tory attack. Yet by the end of the fighting, 32 settlers were dead. Forty more had been captured and led off to Fort Niagara. It is said that Brant personally saved the lives of many settlers, restraining his warriors from further attack. Time and again, he proved himself merciful in combat, urging his men to spare the innocent—not only women and children, but also men who didn't take up arms.

The Cherry Valley raid and others convinced General George Washington to send an invading army into Iroquoia, as the land of the Haudenosaunee sometimes is called. The Sullivan-Clinton Campaign, named after the generals in charge, succeeded in its goal of conquering the Iroquois by destroying their villages and crops. The Iroquois surrendered and in the coming years ceded vast holdings of land and retained only small state reservations. Most Mohawk left the United States for Canada.

Joseph Brant and his followers were granted a parcel of land by the Canadian government at Oshweken on the Grand River in Ontario. There he helped found the town of Brantford. He also founded a Mohawk chapel and translated the Book of Common Prayer and Gospel of Mark into the Mohawk dialect. He died in 1807.

The Eight Mohawk Territories

Haudenosaunee descendants of all six tribes still live on the Six Nations Reserve at Oshweken, Ontario, where Joseph Brant made his new home. Other Mohawk fled to Montreal at the end of the American Revolution and were granted reserve lands at Tyendinaga on the north shore of Lake Ontario.

Not all Mohawk followed this same order of migration or this exact pattern of alliance. Some had moved to Canada much earlier, as allies of the French. From 1667 to 1676, a group of Mohawk migrated from the Fonda, New York, region to La Prairie, a Jesuit mission, on the St. Lawrence River in Quebec. After having lived in several different locations in the area, they finally settled just south of Montreal at a site they called Caughnawaga, after their original village in New York State. The spelling *Kahnawake* now is used.

The Kahnawake Mohawk practiced Catholicism, like the French. They also sometimes worked for the French as scouts and fur traders and sometimes fought with them as allies against the English. But they remained part of the Iroquois Confederacy and, at various times during the French and Indian Wars, supported the English, along with other Haudenosaunee, against the French. They were a proud and independent people whom neither the French nor English could take for granted.

One celebrated Kahnawake Mohawk was Kateri Tekakwitha, called "Lily of the Mohawks." She was born and baptized a Christian in the Mohawk valley but later moved to Kahnawake in Canada to escape persecution by non-Christian Indians. Her parents and brother died in a smallpox epidemic. She caught the disease too and her skin was severely scarred. But, it is said, because of her great faith in Catholicism and her dedication to helping others, when she died at the age of 24 in 1680 a miracle occurred—her pockmarks disappeared. In 1943, the Roman Catholic Church declared Kateri "venerable." Then in 1980, the church declared her "blessed," the second step toward canonization.

In 1755, at the urging of Jesuits who wanted to establish a French presence farther westward, a group of Mohawk from Kahnawake moved to a site on the St. Lawrence, south of present-day Cornwall, Ontario, and east of Massena, New York. What was known as the St. Regis Mission, the oldest permanent settlement in northern New York, became the St. Regis Reservation on the U.S. side of the St. Lawrence and the Akwesasne Reserve on the Canadian side, the preferred name among the Mohawk. Akwesasne Mohawk, who negotiate with four different governmental bodies—the U.S. and Canadian federal governments as well as New York and Ontario state and provincial governments—have had to struggle for sovereign rights. In 1968, they staged a protest by blocking the St. Lawrence Seaway International Bridge. They claimed that the Canadian government was not honoring the Jay Treaty of 1794, guaranteeing them the right to travel unrestricted back and forth between Canada and the United States. Border officials changed the policy, making crossings easier for tribal members. Moreover, until recent changes in the Indian Act of Canada, a Canadian Mohawk woman who married an American Mohawk man lost her Indian status and benefits. Akwesasne Mohawk also have had to struggle against big business threatening to pollute their homeland. In 1984, it was discovered that toxic wastes, especially deadly PCBs, from ˀ neighboring off-reservation General Motors factory were endangering inhabitants.

Kahnawake and Awkwesasne Mohawk have become especially renowned as high-steel workers. Tribal members have traveled all over North America, and to other continents as well, to work on tall buildings and bridges, a tradition that began in 1886 when the Mohawk proved sure-footed and fearless in the construction of a bridge across the St. Lawrence River. The degree of risk in the profession was indicated in 1907, with the collapse of a portion of another bridge across the St. Lawrence, due to a faulty design, killing 33 ironworkers. A community of Mohawk ironworkers and relatives developed in Brooklyn, New York.

In the 19th century, Mohawk also settled the Lake of Two Mountains Reserve (now called Kanesatake) near Oka, Quebec, and the Gibson Reserve (Wahta) on Georgian Bay in Ontario.

In 1974, some 200 Akwesasne Mohawk and others occupied New York State–held land at Eagle Bay on Moss Lake in the Adirondacks, claiming original title to it. They called this 612-acre parcel of land Ganienkeh (or Kanienkah). In 1977, after negotiations with the state, the Mohawk activists were granted reservation lands at Schuyler and Altona Lakes in Clinton County.

In 1990, after a dispute between Canadian Mohawk and Quebec police over the construction of a golf course on land considered sacred to the Mohawk at Kanesetake—which led to barricades being erected and a standoff with police at Kahnawake as well—a group of Mohawk left Canada, purchasing 200 acres near Akwesasne on the United States side of the border in New York State.

In 1993, following a conflict between traditionalists who opposed casino gaming at Akwesasne and a pro-gambling faction, a group of traditionalists purchased a piece of property in their ancestral homeland—on the north shore of the Mohawk River west of Fonda, New York—and established a community known as Kanat-

Mohawk ash-splint and sweetgrass basket (modern)

siohareke. The residents speak the Mohawk language, hold traditional ceremonies, and practice traditional farming. For additional income, Kanatsiohareke Mohawk maintain a bed-and-breakfast and a crafts store.

The Mohawk Nation Council of Chiefs is responsible for political, social, and cultural affairs of the eight current Mohawk territories—Akwesasne, Ganienkeh, Kahnawake, Kanesatake, Kanatsiohareke, Six Nations, Tyendinega, and Wahta—and tribal members who choose to live elsewhere.

A Mohawk girl and her bike

MOHEGAN

The Mohegan actually were a subgroup of the PEQUOT. When English settlers arrived in their territory soon after the Pilgrims landed at Plymouth Rock in 1620, the sachem Sassacus headed the Pequot. Their main village was on the Thames River in Connecticut. But a subordinate chief named Uncas rebelled and led a group to another village on the Thames near Long Island Sound. They became known as the Mohegan, pronounced mo-HEE-gun, derived from *maingan* for "wolf."

The Mohegan had lifeways similar to other NORTHEAST INDIANS in New England and Long Island. Forests, oceans, bays, rivers, and lakes provided their food, their raw materials, and inspiration for their myths and legends. They lived in both domed wigwams and rectangular houses, usually covered with birch bark. They used framed birch-bark canoes as well as dugouts made from a single tree.

Because of the similarity of their tribal names, the Mohegan often are confused with other ALGONQUIANS, the MAHICAN, living along the northern Hudson valley. Although both people might be descended from the same distant ancestors, along with the Pequot, they are distinct groups. Another point of confusion is that both have been referred to as "Mohican," a spelling popularized by the writer James Fenimore Cooper in his 1826 novel *The Last of the Mohicans*. It seems likely that in his writings about events in upstate New York during the French and Indian wars in the 1700s, Cooper was more likely drawing on what he knew of the Mohegan because the character Chingachgook, an Algonquian chief and best friend of the hero Natty Bumppo, mentions a "Mohican land by the sea," which would apply to the Mohegan but not the Mahican. Moreover, Cooper used the name Uncas for the son of Chingachgook. In any case, the work is fictional. For their part, despite some difficult times in the course of their history, the Mohegan have endured.

Following the defeat of the Pequot by the colonists in the Pequot War of 1637, Uncas, who had befriended the whites, became chief of the remaining Pequot as well as the Mohegan. As allies of the English against the French, Uncas's group preserved their autonomy longer than their neighbors, the WAMPANOAG and NARRAGANSETT, who were defeated in King Philip's War of 1675–76. But British settlers eventually turned against the Mohegan too and appropriated most of their lands. Some Mohegan were sold into slavery along with captives from other tribes. The Mohegan also suffered from a series of smallpox outbreaks in New England, ravaging New England's Algonquians.

The Mohegan Tribe gained federal recognition in 1994, at which time it settled its land claims with the state of Connecticut dating back to the time of Uncas. Many Mohegan live on ancestral lands in the area of Uncasville. The Mohegan Sun Resort in Uncasville, the third largest casino in the United States, opened in 1996. Along with the equally highly successful Foxwoods Resort, operated by the Mashantucket Pequot Tribe, the Mohegan Sun has revitalized the economy of the region and has provided new income and opportunity for tribal members. Another group known as the Golden Hill Pequot and Mohegan Tribes operates out of Trumbull, Connecticut.

Mohegan wooden doll

MOJAVE

Mojave, or *Mohave*, both pronounced mo-HAH-vee, is a derivation of *Ahamecav*, meaning "people who live along the river." The Mojave occupied ancestral territory near other Yuman-speaking peoples along both sides of the Colorado River, the present border between the states of Arizona, California, and Nevada. They are grouped together with the YUMA (QUECHAN) in a category called the River Yumans. The Upland Yumans, such as the HAVASUPAI, HUALAPAI, and YAVAPAI, lived to the north and east of the Mojave. All the Yumans are considered part of the Southwest Culture Area, although they lived on the edge of the Great Basin and California culture areas (see SOUTHWEST INDIANS).

The Mojave Desert, named after the Mojave people, is one of the most extreme environments in North America. Temperatures often climb above 100 degrees Fahrenheit in the hot sun, then drop drastically at night. But the Mojave coped with these extremes by settling along the bottomlands of the lower Colorado River. Every year, with the melting of snows in the mountains to the northeast, the lower Colorado floods and provides suitable conditions for farming. In this strip of silty soil cutting through the desert, the Mojave planted corn, beans, pumpkins, melons, and, after they had received seeds brought from Europe by whites, wheat. They also fished the Colorado River, hunted small desert game, especially rabbits, and gathered wild plant foods, such as piñon nuts and mesquite beans.

The Mojave lived in dwellings made of brush and earth. For the warm weather, they built flat-roofed, open-sided structures; for the cold periods, they made low, rectangular structures. Mojave clothing consisted of sandals and breechcloths for men, and sandals and aprons for women. In cold weather, both men and women wore rabbit-skin blankets and robes. Both men and women decorated their skin with tattoos and body paint.

The Mojave had a reputation as fierce fighters. A special society of warriors, called the *Kwanamis,* led the other men in battle. Mojave war parties were organized into three different fighting groups: archers, clubbers, and stickmen.

The Mojave made war with certain neighboring peoples, such as the AKIMEL O'ODHAM (PIMA) and TOHONO O'ODHAM (PAPAGO), but they traded with others. Mojave traders traveled all the way to the Gulf of California or to the Pacific Ocean to barter agricultural products with coastal tribes for shells and feathers. To cross the Colorado and other rivers, the Mojave made rafts from bundles of reeds.

The Mojave had early contacts with Spaniards, who entered their domain out of Mexico. Hernando de Alarcón may have encountered them as early as 1540 during his trip along the Gulf of California. Juan de Oñate, who explored much of the Southwest, reached them in 1604.

Mojave effigy jar

Francisco Garcés visited them in 1775–76. Mojave worked for Garcés as scouts in his expedition to the Grand Canyon.

Despite Spanish attempts to move them to missions, the Mojave kept their independence. The Spanish called them "wild Indians." When Anglo-Americans began entering their domain, the Mojave often raided their caravans. Mojave warriors attacked the trapping expedition of the mountain man Jedediah Smith in 1827.

With the Mexican Cession of 1848, which granted most of the Southwest to the United States, and the discovery of gold in California late that same year, more and more whites began crossing Mojave lands along the Southern Overland Trail. Mojave warriors harassed many of the travelers. The establishment of Fort Yuma at the Yuma Crossing of the Colorado just south of the Mojave territory decreased the number of raids.

Today, the Mojave live on three different reservations: (1) the Colorado River Reservation (in Yuma County, Arizona, and San Bernardino and Riverside Counties, California), which they share with the Chemehuevi, a River Yuman tribe not listed separately in this book; (2) the Fort Mojave Reservation (in Clark County, Nevada, San Bernardino County, California, and Mohave County, Arizona); and (3) the Fort McDowell Reservation (in Maricopa County, Arizona), which they share with APACHE and Yavapai. The Mojave have developed 4,000 acres of their Nevada lands into a new community known as Ana Macau with new homes, casinos, a golf course, an RV park, and a shopping center.

MONTAGNAIS

The Montagnais of what now is northeastern Canada traditionally had much in common with the Naskapi living even farther to the north. The two peoples spoke nearly identical dialects of the Algonquian language family and, living in small nomadic bands, had similar lifeways in the rugged subarctic environment of present-day Labrador and northern Quebec (see SUBARCTIC INDIANS). The Montagnais also were close neighbors to the Mistassini band of CREE, also ALGONQUIANS, but their respective dialects differed.

Montagnais, pronounced mon-tun-YAY, means "mountaineers" in French. The Laurentian Mountains loom up in Montagnais territory, which extended from James Bay to the Gulf of St. Lawrence. Samuel de Champlain, the explorer and founder of New France (now the eastern part of Canada), encountered the Montagnais at the mouth of the Saguenay River in 1603. The Montagnais stayed allied to the French during French rule in North America, trading furs with them and helping them fight the IROQUOIS (HAUDENOSAUNEE) and English to the south. For one campaign southward, the Montagnais sent some 1,000 warriors along with the French.

The Montagnais did not try to farm their land of rocky soil and short growing season. Rather, they hunted and fished and gathered what wild plant foods they could. In order to eke out enough food in the harsh wilderness, they had to stay on the move. When snow covered the landscape, the Montagnais used snowshoes and toboggans.

The moose, common to the northern forests, was the chosen game in winter and early spring. Moose hunting necessitated long hours of tracking, usually on snowshoes. Because the animals weighed almost 1,000 pounds and had sharp horns and hoofs, they were difficult and dangerous to hunt with spears or arrows. But the heavy animal would sink into the deep snow while the hunters on snowshoes could stay on top. Another way to kill a moose was to sneak up on one while it was feeding along a lake or river and drive it out into deep water. Then in canoes the hunters could overtake the animal and spear it from behind. The moose could not defend itself as well in water.

At the rivers in spring and summer, the Montagnais speared salmon and eels. Sometimes they traveled all the way to the St. Lawrence River to harpoon seals. Occasionally on these trips the small nomadic bands would join up to form much larger groups. The mood after the long, isolated winter months was festive. However, spring and summer were the seasons when insects were abundant, especially black flies and mosquitoes. The Indians had to smear their bodies with seal oil to repel them.

Like most Algonquians, the Montagnais covered their cone-shaped wigwams with birch bark, a prized material in forests that had many more spruce and fir trees than birch trees. When the Montagnais could not find enough birch bark or elm bark, their second choice, they would do what their Naskapi friends and relatives to the north did—stretch animal hides over the wigwam frameworks. But the Montagnais would use moose hides instead of the caribou hides the Naskapis utilized.

One custom of the Montagnais demonstrates just how hard their existence was in the subarctic. When old people could no longer keep up on the constant journeys in search of food, their families would not let them die of hunger and exposure. Instead, they would kill them as an act of mercy.

Many Algonquians of the eastern subarctic, including the Montagnais, believed in the legend of the windigos. (The Naskapis had a different name for these creatures—Atsan.) The windigos supposedly were monsters, from 20 to 30 feet high, who terrorized the northern forest. They had mouths with no lips but with long jagged teeth. They hissed when they breathed. They had claws for hands. They would eat animals if they had to, or other windigos, but most of all they craved human flesh. Their mouths, eyes, and feet were steeped in blood. Every hunter lost in the woods, every child who disappeared, was thought to have been devoured by windigos. Sometimes the windigos took possession of human bodies and lived inside them. These people with windigo souls would start desiring human flesh and would become cannibals. The legend probably originated when humans resorted to cannibalism in the face of starvation. Having such fearful creatures as windigos in Algonquian mythology served to discourage the practice in a land of little food and much hardship.

Montagnais bone knife

In spite of the extreme environment, the Montagnais survived year after year, century after century. Their numbers were stable until diseases brought to North America by Europeans caused their population to decline.

Today, the remaining Montagnais live on reserves in northern Quebec, Canada. Most of them are still hunters and trappers, living a rugged existence and coping much as their ancestors did. The Montagnais have joined the Naskapi in the formation of the Innu Nation. Presenting a united front under the Innu name, they have been protesting since 1987 the use of air space over their hunting grounds for practice flights by supersonic military jets.

MONTAUK

Long Island, which extends eastward from New York City about 118 miles into the Atlantic Ocean, is the largest island in the United States, not counting islands in either Alaska or Hawaii. There were once many Algonquian-speaking peoples living on Long Island, governed by as many as 13 chieftains. Many of their band names, or village names, are familiar-sounding because they exist today as place-names, such as Manhasset, Massapequa, Poospatuck, and Shinnecock.

Some of the bands in the western part of Long Island, such as the Canarsee and Rockaway, spoke dialects similar to those spoken by the Algonquians on Manhattan Island. For that reason, these bands generally are classified among the LENNI LENAPE (DELAWARE) or WAPPINGER. But the bands in the central and eastern part of Long Island are classified in their own group. They were united in an alliance named after one of the most powerful bands, the Montauk Confederacy and are referred to in history books collectively as Montauk (pronounced MON-tawk), possibly derived from *meuntauket* for "at the fort."

The Montauk lived along the flat Atlantic Coast Plain that stretches southward from Long Island. As a result, their way of life was most similar to that of ALGONQUIANS living to the south, along the New Jersey, Delaware, and Virginia shoreline (see NORTHEAST INDIANS).

The Montauk planted their crops in the sandy lowlands. They speared fish and collected clams in the many bays and lagoons. They also hunted small mammals and gathered wild plant foods in the piney inland forests. Here too they could find the materials they needed for dugout canoes and wigwams.

The Montauk hunted whales on the open sea in their large dugouts. They also took advantage of "drift whales." The Montauk believed in a legendary figure named Moshup who stranded whales on beaches or in shallow waters in order to feed the people.

The Montauk also used dugouts to cross the arm of the Atlantic Ocean that separates Long Island from Connecti-

Montauk wigwam (unfinished, showing the sapling framework beneath a cattail covering)

cut—the Long Island Sound. Here they could trade with other Algonquians, such as the PEQUOT and NARRAGANSETT, who lived along the opposite shore. But contacts with the different groups were not always friendly. In the years just before white settlement, the Pequot attacked and conquered the Montauk. Then in later years, after the Pequot were defeated in the Pequot War, the Narragansett also made forays into Montauk territory.

The Montauk were generally on friendly terms with whites. Because of their location on the Atlantic, they had many early contacts with explorers from many European nations. They also traded with white settlers, first the Dutch in the early 1600s, then the English after 1664. The Long Island Indians were among the most productive manufacturers of wampum (called *sewan* or *siwan* by the Dutch), beads of polished shells strung together and used for ceremonial purposes, ornaments, and, after Europeans arrived, money. In fact, Long Island was known to its native inhabitants as *seawanhacky,* since it was such a good place to collect the seashells that were ground into the purple and white wampum beads. In later years, the Indians began using glass beads imported from Europe to make wampum. The European settlers also made wampum from glass beads to trade with the Indians for furs.

The population of the Indians on Long Island steadily declined after the arrival of whites. Part of the reason was intertribal warfare. In 1759, some of the Montauk took refuge from other Indians with the whites at East Hampton, Long Island. Others joined the Brotherton Indians up the Hudson River in 1788 (see MAHICAN). Still others lost their lives on whaling expeditions or in other maritime activities. One famous incident occurred in the winter of 1876, when Shinnecock Indians, who were part of the rescue team trying to save the grounded English cargo ship *Circassian,* lost their lives in a violent storm. Yet all in all, white diseases took the greatest toll on the Long Island Indians.

The Shinnecock and Poospatuck (Unkechaug Nation) each held a small reservation on Long Island. Like many of the reservations in the East, these are state reservations, not federal, with rights guaranteed by the State of New York rather than by the federal government. People of Matinnecock descent also still live on Long Island and maintain tribal identity.

The Shinnecock, who have 400 acres near Southampton, Long Island, sponsor a large annual powwow on Labor Day Weekend that draws Native American participants from all over North America. The Shinnecock National Museum helps further awareness of the tribe's history and culture. In 1984, the tribe created a business enterprise, the Oyster Project, which is the first solar-assisted oyster hatchery ever developed.

MOUND BUILDERS

In the eastern part of North America, especially along the Ohio and Mississippi river valleys, there are thousands of mounds, not formed by geological processes. Although it was realized long ago that these earthworks, many of them enormous and some in the shape of animals, were human-made, it was not known who the makers were. Archaeologists of this century and the last have since provided the answers. It is now known that the Mound Builders were PREHISTORIC INDIANS whose cultures lasted many centuries. The Mound Builders have been classified as four different cultural groups: Poverty Point, Adena, Hopewell, and Mississippian.

The various Mound Builders lived during the phase of North American prehistory known as the Formative period, which followed the Paleolithic and Archaic periods. The Formative period lasted from about 1000 B.C. until A.D. 1500 and was characterized by farming, house building, village life, pottery, weaving, plus other advances in technology. Along with the SOUTHWEST INDIANS, the Mound Builders had the most complex and organized way of life of all the Indians north of Mexico during this period. Some of their villages expanded into actual cities.

Poverty Point Culture

The Poverty Point site near present-day Floyd in northern Louisiana represents the earliest evidence of mound building. Flourishing at an early stage—the various

mounds constructed between 1800 to 500 B.C., and apparently by a nonagricultural people (although some scholars theorize a certain amount of farming among them)—Poverty Point can be called a transitional culture between Archaic Indians and Formative Indians.

The largest mound at Poverty Point—70 feet high and 710 by 640 feet wide—resembles a bird with outspread wings and was probably built for a ceremonial purpose. The site has five smaller conical mounds, four to 21 feet high, plus six concentric earthen ridges, the outermost with a diameter of two-thirds of a mile. Unlike later Mound Builders, Poverty Point Indians did not use any of their mounds for burials. The ridges are known to have held structures.

Poverty Point artifacts include finely crafted stone beads and pendants, clay figurines, and flint tools. The presence of copper, lead, and soapstone artifacts indicate widespread trade contacts.

More than 100 Poverty Point sites have been located in Louisiana, Arkansas, and Mississippi, with other sites in Tennessee, Missouri, and Florida also showing Poverty Point influences. Whether Poverty Point peoples migrated northward and helped create the next great mound building culture, the Adena culture, is not known.

Adena Culture

The Adena culture lasted from approximately 1000 B.C. to A.D. 200. The name *Adena,* pronounced uh-DEE-nuh, comes from an estate near Chillicothe, Ohio, where a large mound stands. The peoples of the Adena culture also built mounds in territory that is now Kentucky, West Virginia, Indiana, Pennsylvania, and New York, primarily along the Ohio valley.

Most of the Adena earthworks were burial mounds. Earthen hillocks were built up over burial pits or log-lined tombs. To make these imposing mounds in honor of their deceased leaders, the Indians dug up earth with sticks, bones, and shells and carried it to the burial site in woven baskets or animal-skin bags. With each new burial, another layer of dirt was dumped on a mound, making it even higher.

The Adena Indians buried objects along with their leaders, just as the ancient Egyptians buried objects with their pharaohs under the great pyramids. At Adena sites, archaeologists have found beautifully crafted tools and ceremonial objects, including a wide range of stone, wood, bone, and copper tools; pottery; cloth woven from plant fibers; bone masks; stone pipes; stone tablets, often with bird designs; ornaments made from a mineral called mica; pearl beads; and stone and copper gorgets (worn over the throat).

The Adena Pipe, made from catlinite

In addition to burial mounds, the Adena Indians constructed mounds with symbolic shapes. A famous example is the present-day Serpent Mound near Peebles, Ohio. This earthwork is a rounded mound about 2 to 6 feet high, 4 to 20 feet across, and 1,348 feet long. When viewed from above, it has the shape of a snake, with head and jaws seeming to close on another mound (possibly representing an egg) and a coiled tail. (It is assumed the Serpent Mound is of the Adena culture rather than Hopewell because a nearby burial mound has yielded Adena artifacts, but no artifacts have been found in the serpent itself.) Other Adena earthworks have geometric shapes, ridges of earth laid out in circles and usually surrounding the burial mounds.

The Adena Indians were primarily hunter-gatherers. They found enough game and wild plant foods in their homelands to be able to live in permanent villages of pole-framed houses covered with mud and thatch. Some among them might have grown sunflowers and pumpkins for food. Many of them eventually cultivated tobacco for smoking rituals.

It is not known for certain what became of the Adena Indians. Some of them might have been the ancestors of the Hopewell Indians whose culture came to displace them. Or perhaps the Hopewell Indians were outsiders who invaded Adena territory and killed off remaining Adena peoples.

Hopewell Culture

The Hopewell (or Hopewellian) culture lasted from about 200 B.C. to A.D. 700. Like the Adena culture, it was centered along the Ohio Valley. Yet archaeologists have found Hopewell mounds and objects over a much wider area composed of the Illinois river valley, the Mississippi river valley, plus many other river valleys of the Midwest and East.

The Hopewell Indians established a wide trading network. At Hopewell sites, archaeologists have found objects made of raw materials from distant locations, including obsidian (black volcanic glass) from as far away as the Rocky Mountains, copper from the Great Lakes, shells from the Atlantic Ocean, mica from the Appalachian Mountains, and alligator skulls and teeth from Florida. Hopewell peoples were highly skilled craftsmen. They shaped raw materials into exquisite objects, such as stone pipes with human and animal carvings; pottery with designs; ceramic figurines; obsidian spear points and knife blades; mica mirrors; shell drinking cups; pearl jewelry; gold and mica silhouettes (delicately carved in flat profiles); and copper headdresses and breast ornaments.

Like Adena peoples, the Hopewell Indians placed these objects in tombs and under mounds. The Hopewell burial mounds were generally larger than Adena mounds. Many of them covered multiple burials and stood 30 to 40 feet high. Other Hopewell earthworks represented creatures. Still others served as walls, as much as 50 feet high and 200 feet wide at the base. These are often laid out in geometric shapes. At a Hopewell site in Newark, Ohio, over an area of four square miles, are found walls or enclosures in different shapes, including circles, parallel lines, a square, and an octagon.

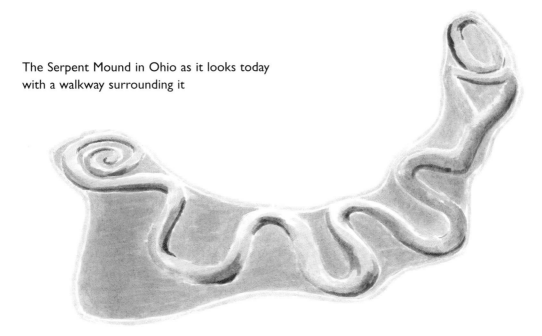

The Serpent Mound in Ohio as it looks today with a walkway surrounding it

The existence of these mounds indicates that the Hopewell Indians had a highly organized society. Villagers had to work in unison to build the giant earthworks, with their leaders and priests directing them. The trading expeditions required cooperation among the different villages.

The development of farming allowed villages to expand. Enough corn, beans, squash, and other crops could be cultivated to support growing populations. Hopewell villagers lived in domed structures, framed with poles and covered with sheets of bark, woven mats, or animal skins. The Hopewell dwellings were much like the wigwams of ALGONQUIANS.

Perhaps the Hopewell Indians were direct ancestors of the later Indian tribes of eastern North America. Yet there is no proof of what happened to them and why their great culture fell into a state of decay. Changes in

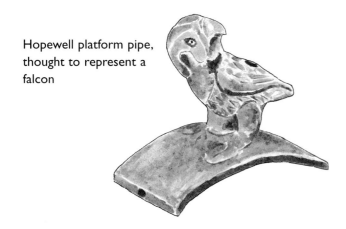

Hopewell platform pipe, thought to represent a falcon

the climate, with prolonged periods of drought as well as crop failures, might have brought about the cultural decline. Warfare and epidemics could have also depleted their numbers and disrupted their way of life.

Mississippian Culture

The age of mound building was not over, however. Starting about A.D. 700, around the time of the demise of the Hopewell culture, a new culture evolved throughout much of eastern North America. It was centered along the Mississippi River and is therefore referred to as the Mississippian culture. Mississippian sites can be found from Florida to Oklahoma and as far north as Wisconsin. Mississippian Indians constructed mounds for a new purpose. They placed their places of worship on top of them. As a result, Mississippian Indians are also known as Temple Mound Builders.

One of the most intriguing aspects in the study of prehistory is the question of contacts and influences between different cultures. Without hard evidence, such as an object from one culture found at the archaeological site of another, scholars have to guess about cultural connections, based on similarities in arts and crafts and other customs. A connection between the great Mesoamerican civilizations—OLMEC, MAYA, TOLTEC, and AZTEC—with early Indian cultures north of Mexico has long been theorized. For example, the Mississippian practice of placing temples on top of mounds is similar to the Mesoamerican practice of placing temples on top of stone pyramids. At various times in prehistory, Indians most likely crossed the Gulf of Mexico in boats, perhaps even venturing up the Mississippi River to trade or to resettle.

A typical Mississippian mound had sloping sides and a flat top where the temple stood. Log steps ran up one side to a pole-and-thatch structure. Some of the mounds had terraced sides where other, smaller structures stood. These were homes of priests and nobles. The higher the rank of an individual, the higher he lived on the mound. The chieftain or king of a particular village often lived on top of his own mound. Other villagers—merchants, craftsmen, soldiers, hunters, farmers, and laborers—lived in pole-and-thatch huts surrounding the mounds. Some Mississippian dwellings were pithouses, with vertical logs extending from rectangular pits. Villagers conducted their business in the village's central open plaza.

The temple mounds could be enormous. For example, Monk's Mound at the Cahokia site near present-day East St. Louis, Illinois, covered 16 acres and stood 100 feet high. Archaeologists have guessed that it was built in 14 different stages, from about A.D. 900 to about 1150. Cahokia, once a great village—more properly called a city because it housed more than 30,000 Indians—contained 85 mounds in all, both temple and burial mounds. In one burial mound, archaeologists have found remains of 110 young women, probably a sacrifice to the gods. The Native American city, covering about 4,000 acres near the Mississippi River where the Illinois River flows into it, had a central urban area and five suburbs.

Cahokia was the largest Mississippian population center. Other large villages are known as Moundville in

Mississippian cedar mask with shell eyes and mouth

Alabama; Etowah and Ocmulgee in Georgia; Hiwassee Island in Tennessee; Spiro in Oklahoma; Belcher in Louisiana; Aztalan in Wisconsin; and Mount Royal in Florida. (Many Temple Mound sites are state parks that welcome visitors. At some of them, there are ongoing archaeological excavations.)

In order to support such large, centralized populations, Mississippian Indians had to practice farming on a large scale. They grew corn, beans, squash, pumpkins, and tobacco in the rich silt of riverbeds.

In addition to being master farmers, the Temple Mound Builders were skilled craftsmen, working in a

Mississippian temple mound (hypothetical)

variety of materials—clay, shells, marble, mica, a mineral called chert, copper, and feathers. They made highly refined tools, pottery, masks, gorgets, pipes, headdresses, and carvings.

Many of the ceremonial objects found at the Mississippian sites reveal symbols of death and human sacrifice—skulls, bones, buzzards, and weeping eyes. It is thought that the Temple Mound religion, called the Death Cult (or Buzzard Cult or Southern Cult), and its powerful priests served to unify the various villages. Trade between villages also helped to keep the peace.

For some reason—warfare, overpopulation, drought, famine—the great Mississippian villages were abandoned. Cahokia ceased to be a thriving center about

1250. One theory has it that before European explorers reached the Temple Mound Indians, their diseases did. Coastal Indians might have unknowingly spread the European diseases inland through trade, starting deadly epidemics.

In any case, by about 1550, the period of mound building had ended. Many eastern Indians, especially the tribes of the Southeast, continued to use the ancient mounds. Some of them, such as the CHOCTAW and CREEK, might have been direct descendants of the Temple Mound Builders. Some tribes continued to practice many of the customs of the Mound Builders. The NATCHEZ in particular had a society that scholars consider to be typical of their Mound Builder ancestors.

MUSKOGEE see CREEK

NAKOTA see SIOUX (DAKOTA, LAKOTA, NAKOTA)

NARRAGANSETT

The Narragansett, the "people of the small point," occupied ancestral territory in the part of the Northeast that is now Rhode Island, especially between the Providence and Pawcatuck Rivers (see NORTHEAST INDIANS). They lived like other New England ALGONQUIANS. They stayed most of the year in stockaded villages of dome-shaped wigwams. They combined farming with hunting, fishing, and gathering, making use of resources from forest, river, and ocean. Narragansett Bay is named after them. Their name, spelled with either one or two *t*s, is pronounced nah-ruh-GAN-sit.

The Narragansett played an important part in early colonial history and suffered many of the same consequences as the other tribes of the region. When the English began settling the area in the 1620s, the Narragansett had six main divisions, with six sagamores (subordinate chiefs) under one principal chief, or grand sachem. The Narragansett managed to avoid the first smallpox epidemic of 1616–20 that ravaged many of the native peoples after contacts with Europeans.

But in 1633, about 700 tribal members died in a second outbreak.

The Narragansett were early allies of the English colonists, and some of their warriors fought against the PEQUOT in the Pequot War of 1636–37. In 1636, Canonicus, the grand sachem, sold tribal lands to Roger Williams, a renegade Puritan who broke away from the Massachusetts Bay Colony and founded Rhode Island Colony. Williams urged his fellow colonists to treat Indians humanely and to pay them fairly for their lands. In 1643, his dictionary of the Algonquian language was published, which helped further communication with tribal members.

Because of continuing appropriation of their lands, however, the Narragansett joined the WAMPANOAG and NIPMUC in King Philip's War of 1675–76 against the colonists. Canonchet, a later grand sachem of the Narragansett, became the Indian chief King Philip's most important general in battle, with 3,500 warriors under him.

The Narragansett suffered the most devastating defeat, which virtually ended the war—the Great Swamp Fight of December 1675. On a snowy day, a force of almost 1,000 Massachusetts, Connecticut, and Plymouth colonists under Josiah Winslow, plus about 150 MOHEGAN warriors, attacked the Narragansett village near Kingston, Rhode Island. It was a bitter standoff for many hours, with the colonial militia unable to breach the Indian village's thick log walls standing on high ground in the middle of a swamp. But the attackers finally broke through the rear entrance and drove the Narragansett into the swamp by setting most of their 600 wigwams on fire.

The Narragansett lost more than 600 men, women, and children, with 400 others captured and sold into slavery. Canonchet, the grand sachem, was brave to the end. When taken prisoner and sentenced to death, he said that, "It is well. I shall die before my heart is soft, before I have said anything unworthy of Canonchet."

When a Narragansett warrior died, he was wrapped in skins or woven mats, along with his tools and weapons, so that he would be equipped for the journey to the Creator, who the Narragansett believed lived to their southwest.

After King Philip's War, some of the surviving Narragansett settled among ABENAKI, MAHICAN, and Niantic. Those who lived with the Niantic continued to use the Narragansett name. Some of their descendants joined the Brotherton Indians, a band of Mahican and other Algonquians, in 1788. Other descendants still live in Rhode Island, near Charlestown.

In 1978, after a lengthy lawsuit the state of Rhode Island returned to the Narragansett tribe two pieces of land of 900 acres each in the Charlestown area, land that had been taken away from them in 1880. At the time of the official transfer, the tribal secretary, Lawrence Ollivierre, expressed his feelings: "It's pretty difficult to be an Indian and not have your own land. It's like being a people without a country."

NASKAPI

Because of language similarities, the Naskapi (pronounced NAS-kuh-pee) of northern Quebec and Labrador are often grouped with the MONTAGNAIS, fellow ALGONQUIANS living to their south. But they had different ways of finding food.

In the winter months, the Montagnais depended primarily on the moose common to the forests of their own territory. The Naskapi, however, tracked the caribou herds that grazed on the grasses and lichens of the open plateau of the Labrador Peninsula, in present-day Canada. In their reliance on caribou, the Naskapi were like many of the western SUBARCTIC INDIANS and certain Arctic INUIT. Nomads, they followed the seasonal migration of the herds, using snowshoes and toboggans. They covered their cone-shaped wigwams with caribou hides and bound their snowshoes with caribou thongs.

Like the Montagnais, the Naskapi hunted small game, such as beaver, porcupine, otter, and a kind of bird called a grouse. They also fished the rivers that ran high with melted snow in the springtime, using stone, bone, and antler gear. Their favorite catch was trout. They used birch-bark canoes to travel in the spring and summer, one way to find some relief from the abundant black flies and mosquitoes in their area.

Since the Naskapi lived so far north, where a layer of clothing could mean the difference between life and death in subzero weather, they adopted certain Inuit methods of retaining body warmth. They often wore hoods attached to their snug caribou shirts, plus fur trousers and stockings rather than breechcloths and leggings. And in the coldest months, they wore double layers of clothing, with the fur on the inner layer facing their bodies and the fur on the outer layer facing outward.

The Naskapi had a special fondness for bright colors, perhaps because their environment was so harsh and

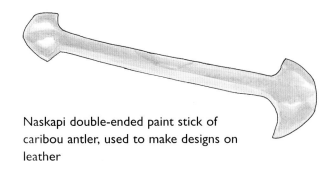

Naskapi double-ended paint stick of caribou antler, used to make designs on leather

bleak. They decorated their shirts with bright geometric patterns in red, yellow, or blue. They also tattooed their bodies, as did their CREE neighbors. The Cree pushed a needle through their skin, then ran a wet thread dipped in charcoal through the hole. The Naskapi, however, made cuts on the surface, then used a piece of stone to rub the charcoal or soot into the skin. Both methods were painful and served as a test of courage as well as decoration.

The Naskapi also proved their bravery in warfare, usually against their traditional enemies, the Inuit, who bordered their territory to the north. But they were not as efficient in battle as the Montagnais, who adopted some of the IROQUOIS (HAUDENOSAUNEE) fighting techniques.

Murder was uncommon in Naskapi society, as was the case among most Indian peoples. A killing in self-defense would go unpunished. But in an unprovoked murder, the slain person's relatives could take revenge. If they failed to do so, a band chief might call a council of elders. If they decided the killing was not in self-defense, the guilty man would be told to walk away. Then warriors chosen by the chief as executioners would shoot the condemned man in the back. No one would even bury his corpse.

Although hunger was often a problem, the Naskapi abhorred cannibalism even if survival depended on it. They believed in the existence of legendary beings called Atsan—evil creatures of the north country that kid-

Naskapi painted leather mask

napped children and ate them, much like the windigos in the legends of other Subarctic Algonquians.

For a long time after the arrival of Europeans—first the French, who became their allies and trading partners, and then the English—the Naskapi were able to maintain their traditional ways since they lived so far from most non-Indian settlements. But white diseases eventually depleted their numbers and devastated their culture. Many remaining Naskapi live by hunting in the north country as their ancestors once did. Naskapi bands have united with their Montagnais relatives as a tribal entity known as the Innu Nation.

NATCHEZ

When one envisions Native North Americans, one usually thinks about PLAINS INDIANS galloping after buffalo on horseback, or chiefs in eagle-feather warbonnets sitting in front of tipis and passing a peace pipe among them. Or one imagines woodland peoples prowling through forests with tomahawks in hand or paddling over rivers and lakes in birch-bark canoes.

One rarely thinks about a king, called the Great Sun, with absolute powers over all his subjects. One rarely calls to mind an image of this monarch, with a crown of red-tasseled swan feathers, seated on a throne of goose feathers and furs, high on a mound above the rest of his village; or a temple located atop another nearby mound, occupied by priests with shaved heads; or dwellings—four-sided and constructed of straw and sun-baked mud

Natchez house

with arched thatch roofs—placed in precise rows around a central plaza; or members of the warrior class, tattooed from head to foot, strolling about, fanning themselves and watching commoners at their work.

These images remind one of Indian civilizations of Middle America, (such as the OLMEC, MAYA, TOLTEC, and AZTEC). In fact, it is thought that Mesoamerican cultures did influence the ancient MOUND BUILDERS of North America. And it is thought that some among the native peoples whom Europeans contacted as late as the early 1700s were the last remnants of the once wide-spread Temple Mound civilization. These were the Natchez. Their name, pronounced NATCH-is, possibly means "warriors of the high bluff." They lived along the lower Mississippi River in territory that is now part of the states of Mississippi and Louisiana. They spoke a language isolate referred to as Natchez or Natchesan. They are considered part of the Southeast Culture Area.

Social Structure

Other SOUTHEAST INDIANS shared some of the Natchez cultural traits, having chiefs with great authority as well as an agriculture-based economy and organized village life. Yet when whites arrived and began recording information about the native peoples, the Natchez had by far the most elaborate caste system, that is, a division of society into social classes, with strict rules governing behavior.

In addition to the king, known as the Great Sun, there was a royal family at the top of the pecking order. The king's mother, referred to as White Woman, lived on top of her own mound and served as the king's adviser. From among his brothers or uncles, called Little Suns, were chosen a war chief and a head priest. His sisters were called Women Suns and also had influence and power among all the other Natchez.

Below the Suns were the Nobles, an aristocratic class decided by heredity. Nobles had positions of rank in war parties and village functions. Below them were the Honored Men and Honored Women, who were lesser nobles. One could achieve this social status through deeds, such as bravery in warfare or piety in religious matters.

Below the royalty and aristocracy was a class of commoners, called Stinkards (although not in their presence, because the name offended them). They performed all the menial tasks, such as farming and building mounds.

But there was a bizarre twist to this rigid social structure. All grades of royalty and nobility, even the Great Sun himself, could not marry among their own class. They had to marry Stinkards. Stinkards could marry among themselves, and their children would naturally be Stinkards too. But when a male from the upper classes had children, they were always a grade below him. For instance, children of male Suns and Stinkards were automatically nobles. The children of Nobles or Honored Men and Stinkards were automatically Stinkards.

On the other hand, the children of Women Suns and Stinkards were Suns; the children of female Nobles and Stinkards were Nobles; and the children of Honored Women were Honored People. In other words, although the men had the greater decision-making power in Natchez society, social rank was decided through the female line. And Stinkards had the opportunity to better their lives through marriage.

There was another strict rule governing the behavior of the nobility. When a Noble died, his or her Stinkard mate and servants would have to give up their lives to accompany the deceased to the next world.

This complex social system of the Natchez endured long after the arrival of Europeans in the Natchez homeland—first the Spanish in the 1500s (Hernando de Soto and his companions probably made contact in 1541–43), then the French in the 1600s (René-Robert Cavelier de La Salle was the first to use the Natchez name in writings about his travels along the Mississippi River in 1682). The caste system continued into the following century, when the French established a mission among the Natchez in 1706 and then, after 1713, a trading post and fort. Yet in 1729, Natchez culture was disrupted because of a war with the French. Soon afterward, the tribe faded to extinction.

The Natchez Revolt

The cause of the Natchez Revolt was a land dispute. In order to keep the peace between Indians and whites and to encourage settlement by whites, the French had constructed Fort Rosalie overlooking the Mississippi River and the main Natchez village. The Natchez, many of whom were sympathetic to the French, accepted the fort and the garrison of French soldiers in their midst. Tattooed Serpent and Tattooed Arm, the brother and mother of the Great Sun, were especially devoted allies of the French. When Tattooed Serpent died, however, his brother began listening more to the tribe's anti-French faction.

Sieur Chepart, recently appointed the new governor of Louisiana, was oblivious to the factions within the tribe. Moreover, he was arrogant. He decided he wanted the site of the Natchez Great Village for his plantation and ordered immediate evacuation by the villagers. Rather than submit to this insult, the Great Sun, his priests, and his warriors plotted a rebellion.

At the time of the first autumn frost of 1729, Natchez war parties attacked Fort Rosalie and other French settlements along the Mississippi River, killing about 250 and capturing about 300 more. One of those captured was Sieur Chépart. The Natchez warrior-nobles wanted their revenge, but they did not want to soil their weapons with the blood of this French scoundrel. So they had a Stinkard club him to death.

The YAZOO, a people living along the Mississippi north of the Natchez, joined them in the uprising and killed a missionary and French soldiers stationed in their territory. But the CHOCTAW to the east, who had promised the Natchez support, sided with the French instead, as did the TUNICA to the north.

The French sent two invading armies against the Natchez and succeeded in defeating and dispersing the tribe. Natchez captives were sold into slavery in the Caribbean. Other Natchez managed to hide out for a time and keep up their resistance, but without much effect. Some survivors settled with other tribes of the region, especially the CHICKASAW and CREEK. They were relocated to the Indian Territory with others in the 1830s where some settled also among the CHEROKEE. The last fluent speaker of the Natchez language, Watt Sam, died in 1965. Yet a number of individuals having Natchez ancestry continue to sing Natchez songs and tell Natchez stories in Oklahoma and other tribes have adopted their rituals.

NAVAJO

The Navajo occupied ancestral territory in what is now northern Arizona and New Mexico, plus a much smaller part of southern Utah and Colorado. The heart of their territory was situated on the lower part of the Colorado Plateau between the San Juan and Little Colorado Rivers. In Native American studies, this region is considered part of the Southwest Culture Area (see SOUTHWEST INDIANS).

The Navajo, like other ATHAPASCANS in the region, the APACHE, came to the Southwest later than other Indians, sometime before 1400.

The name *Navajo* or *Navaho* (pronounced NAH-vuh-ho), is not Athapascan, however. The PUEBLO INDIANS applied it to an area of land in the Southwest. The Spanish started calling the Navajo by the name *Apaches de Navajo* to distinguish them from the Apache, and this name has stuck through history. In their own language, the Navajo are the *Dineh* or *Diné,* meaning "the people," and pronounced dee-NAY. They call their homeland Dinetah.

Food and Shelter

When the Dineh first came to the Southwest, they survived in the rugged, dry environment as nomadic bands of hunter-gatherers. Along with their kinsmen, the Apache, they launched many raids on the agricultural Pueblo Indians for food, property, women, and slaves. Throughout most of their history, the Navajo were feared by Indian, Spanish, Mexican, and American inhabitants of the Southwest. Although they continued their raiding activity, the Dineh, through contacts with Pueblo Indians, gradually adopted new cultural traits. From the other Indians, they learned farming, in addition to some of the skills already mentioned above, such as weaving and sandpainting. They probably also learned how to make pottery, as well as new basketmaking techniques, from the Pueblo Indians. The Navajo acquired sheep and goats from the Spanish. But they did not use up their supply for food, as the Apache did. Instead, they raised them to increase their herds, which they kept for meat, milk, and wool. Livestock, especially sheepherding, soon became essential to Dineh economy. The Dineh first acquired horses at about the same time

Dineh hogan (facing east)

they acquired sheep and goats—the mid- to late 1600s. Horses gave them greater mobility on their raids.

The Dineh lived in shelters called hogans. These were generally cone-shaped, but later they were built with six or eight sides. Logs and poles were used for the framework, which was covered with bark and earth and, in later years, with stone or adobe. The doorways of the hogans always faced east.

Art and Religion

For the Dineh, as for all Native Americans, art and religion were intertwined. Art served a ceremonial purpose, as a way to relate to spiritual beings that the Dineh believed existed in both the natural and supernatural worlds. It was also a way to be closer to one's ancestors and a way to influence the spiritual beings to affect the weather or cure the sick. The Dineh had highly developed art and rituals for these purposes.

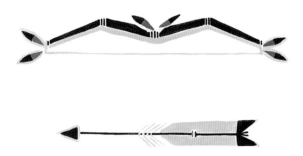

Detail of a Dineh sandpainting

One Dineh art form was oral chants. The Dineh and most other Indians did not use the written word to record their legends. Rather, they recited their myths in songs and poetry, usually to musical accompaniment. In the case of the Dineh, the chants were especially long. For example, their *Mountain Chant* has 13 different episodes, containing 161 songs. These tell of the mythological origins of the Dineh peoples—creation myths, as they are called, or emergence myths. The *Night Chant* has 24 episodes with 324 songs. Dineh shamans used these in healing ceremonies.

There were many more chants, passed on from one generation to the next through the spoken word without the help of writings. Legendary beings—many of them a combination of animals and people—come to life in Dineh oral tradition. Here is part of a creation song:

I am frivolous Coyote; I wander around.
I have seen the Black God's Fire; I wander around.

I stole his fire from him; I wander around.
I have it! I have it!
I am changing Coyote; I wander around.
I have seen the bumble-bee's fire; I wander around.
I stole his fire from him; I wander around.
I have it! I have it!

The coyote plays an important role in the mythology of tribes all over North America. Native Americans respected the animal for its cunning and its ability to survive in forest, mountain, prairie, and desert country. In some Indian stories, the mythical culture hero Coyote helps people. But usually he is a trickster who plays practical jokes on people, or a meddler who ruins people's plans. He is often regarded as greedy. Whether good or bad, however, Coyote is always clever.

Coyote was one of the Holy People in Dineh religion. Changing Woman, or the Earth Mother, was another. Unlike Coyote, she was always kind to the Dineh and gave their ancestors corn. Spider Woman, who, according to legend, taught the people weaving, and Spider Man, who warned the people of coming danger, could be mean like Coyote. The Hero Twins, who killed the monsters to make the world safe, could also turn nasty. There were many more Holy People in Dineh mythology. There were also the *chinde,* who the Dineh believed were malevolent ghosts of dead people inhabiting the earth. Ghosts caused sickness and accidents, they thought. The Dineh also believed in witches, real people who practiced black magic to harm others for revenge or for their own personal gain.

In addition to the mythology, poetry, songs, and music of their oral tradition, the Dineh developed an art form known as sandpainting. Other Native Americans painted permanent designs on pottery, clothing, and tipis. Yet Southwest peoples also created temporary drawings on the ground. The Dineh probably adopted this cultural trait from the Pueblo Indians, who might have learned it from the YAQUI.

The sandpaintings were actually altars used in healing ceremonies. The animals and designs had symbolic meanings. The Indians created these intricate and colorful dry paintings by trickling powders of minerals such as ocher, ground sandstone, gypsum, and charcoal into patterns on clean sand. At the end of the rituals, the paintings were destroyed. Participants took some of the powder away with them for its magical properties.

A distinction is usually made between arts and crafts. When an object is made for a practical purpose, its manufacture is usually thought of as a craft. Yet many Native American crafts were so highly developed that they can

A Dineh woman weaving a blanket on her loom

be thought of as true art. An example of this is Navajo weaving. The Dineh learned weaving from the Pueblo Indians. The Southwest Indians did not have domesticated sheep for wool until the Spanish introduced the animals, along with goats, to the region. Dineh women learned to spin the wool from sheep, dye the threads, and then weave them on a loom. The finished blankets and rugs had bright geometric designs, or in some cases, pictures of animals. They are now treasured all over the world as wall hangings.

Another Dineh craft considered a fine art is jewelry making. The Dineh learned the art of silversmithing from the Mexicans in the mid-1800s and passed this skill on to Pueblo Indians. The Dineh became famous for their silverwork, especially necklaces, bracelets, and belt buckles.

Dineh silver-and-turquoise bracelet (modern)

Warfare

The Spanish first became aware of the Dineh in the early 1600s. They sent missionaries to the tribe's homeland in the mid-1700s, but they had little success in converting the Dineh to Catholicism.

In the late 1700s and early 1800s, the Dineh became involved in a cycle of raids and counterraids with the Spanish and Mexicans, who rode northward for slaves, kidnapping Indian children. In response, Dineh warriors traveled south to prey on Mexican settlements, taking food, livestock, and slaves. The Dineh also made frequent attacks on early travelers of the Santa Fe Trail, the route connecting Missouri to New Mexico.

The Americans occupied New Mexico in 1846 during the Mexican War. Mexico did not formally cede the Southwest to the United States until the Treaty of Guadalupe Hidalgo two years later. Yet it was during the Mexican War that U.S. troops established American policy toward the Dineh. On taking control of the region, Colonel Stephen Kearny informed the Anglo Americans and Mexican Americans that they would henceforth be protected from Indian attacks. He did not inform the Indians, however, that they would be protected from Mexican slave raids.

During the winter of that same year, Colonel Alexander Doniphan led his Missouri volunteers into Dinetah to punish the Indians for stealing livestock. In their rugged highlands, the Dineh managed to avoid any major engagements. Most of the winter, they hid out in the deep and jagged Canyon de Chelly, their sacred stronghold. In 1846 and 1849, the Dineh signed treaties with the United States government, but they remained militant until the 1860s.

A point of contention between the Dineh and the soldiers during the 1850s was the grazing land at the mouth of Canyon Bonito near Fort Defiance. The soldiers wanted the pastureland for their horses. Yet the Dineh had led their horses there to graze for generations and continued to do so. When soldiers shot the horses, the Dineh raided army herds to make up for their losses.

The issue reached a climax in 1860 when the famous Dineh chief Manuelito and his ally Barboncito led warriors in an attack on the fort. They nearly captured it but were driven back. Colonel Edward Canby led troops into the Chuska Mountains in pursuit of the warriors. Once again, the warriors disappeared in the craggy terrain, appearing only for sudden attacks on the army before vanishing again into the wilderness.

Another fight broke out in 1861, during the Civil War. The incident that sparked this conflict was a horse race at Fort Lyon between Dineh and army mounts. The Dineh claimed that a soldier had cheated by cutting one of their mount's reins. When the judges refused to hold the race again, the angry Indians rioted. The soldiers fired artillery into the Indian crowd, killing 10.

The troubles continued. By 1862, Union troops had driven the Confederate troops out of New Mexico. They then turned their attention to the Apache and Dineh. General James Carleton, the new commander of the Department of New Mexico, chose Colonel Christopher "Kit" Carson as his leader in the field. Carson, a former fur trader, scout, and Indian agent, knew Indian ways well. He moved first against the Mescalero Apache. Then he began his campaign against the Dineh.

Rather than try to defeat the elusive Dineh in battle in their mesa and canyon country, Carson first began a scorched-earth offensive. During a six-month period in 1863, his men destroyed Dineh fields, orchards, and hogans and confiscated their livestock. Then in January 1864, as a final blow against the Dineh, his troops advanced on Canyon de Chelly. They blocked the steep-walled canyon at both ends, then flushed out the pockets of resistance.

The will of the Dineh had been broken. By March, about 6,000 half-starving tribal members had trickled into army posts, and by the end of the year, another 2,000, making the Dineh surrender the largest in all the Indian wars. Manuelito and many of his remaining 4,000 followers surrendered in 1866. In the meantime, the army carried out its plan to relocate the Dineh, along with Apache prisoners, to the eastern part of New Mexico, at Bosque Redondo near Fort Sumner on the barren flats of the Pecos River valley. About 200 Dineh died on the 300-mile trek eastward—the Long Walk, as they call it.

The Dineh were miserable at Bosque Redondo, suffering from outbreaks of disease, shortages of supplies, infer-

Detail of a Dineh blanket

tile soil for planting, and quarrels with the Apache. It is estimated that 2,000 Dineh died during their stay there. A delegation of chiefs, including Manuelito, traveled to Washington to plead their case for a return to their homeland. Finally in 1868, the federal government granted the Dineh 3.5 million acres of reservation lands in their ancestral homeland. The Dineh returned westward over the trail of the Long Walk and began rebuilding their lives.

The Navajo Reservation

The Dineh currently are the largest tribe in North America and have the most reservation lands, 28,803 square miles on the Colorado Plateau, mostly in northeastern Arizona, with additional holdings in western New Mexico and southern Utah. Reservation lands encompass a large part of Dineh ancestral territory, which they view as defined by four sacred mountains—on the north, Mount Hesperus in Colorado; on the east, Sierra Blanca Peak in Colorado; on the west, San Francisco Peaks in Arizona; and on the south, Mount Taylor in New Mexico.

Navajo Code Talkers

The term *code talker* is applied to Native Americans who used their native languages as combat communication codes in 20th-century wars. In World War I, CHOCTAW became the first to do so. In World War II, Choctaw again participated on the European front, as did COMANCHE for the army's Signal Corps. Dineh Code Talkers became renowned as marines on the Pacific front, serving against the Japanese, who had managed to decipher previous American military codes. It is said that without Dineh participation, the marines would never have taken Iwo Jima; during the first 48 hours of that battle, while the marines were establishing a beachhead, the Code Talkers sent and received more than 800 messages without error.

Varying Ways of Life

Many Dineh earn a modest living from raising sheep, goats, and cattle, herding their animals in the isolated areas of their reservation lands. The traditional Dineh religion is still practiced—the Dineh Ways—for purposes of purification, healing, and renewal. Many Dineh still speak their native language. Tribal members work in traditional arts and crafts, especially weaving and silverwork, as a supplement to their income. With modern irrigation methods, some Dineh have been able to farm the previously infertile soil of their homelands. Some among the Dineh have profited from oil, gas, coal, and uranium on their lands. Some leave the reservation to seek work elsewhere, often as migrant agricultural workers or to urban areas, especially in California. A number of Dineh have excelled in the fine arts.

Big Mountain

Dineh families recently have had to endure a modern "Long Walk." Since the Navajo Reservation surrounds HOPI holdings, Navajo sheepherders had come to live for several generations on lands reserved for the Hopi in the late 1800s—on and around Big Mountain, considered a place of healing by traditionalists of both tribes. The Hopi Tribal Council, with the support of the Navajo Tribal Council, has called for the return of Big Mountain in order to receive new leasing income from non-Indian mining companies seeking coal. The federal government decided in favor of the tribal councils and mining interests, plus Arizona politicians supporting them, in the Navajo-Hopi Land Settlement Act of 1974, establishing permanent boundaries. The subsequent Navajo-Hopi Land Dispute Settlement Act of 1996 allows for a longer period of time in the Dineh relocation, but further paves the way for the destruction of sacred lands and a traditional way of life. Although many Dineh families since have relocated, others have stayed on and, with Hopi allies, have vowed to continue their resistance to desecration of Big Mountain.

NEZ PERCE

"I will fight no more forever." These are among the most famous words ever spoken by an Indian. In 1877, at the time Chief Joseph of the Nez Perce spoke them, many Indians of the West had come to the conclusion that continuing war with the much more numerous whites was hopeless and that their Indian way of life would never be the same.

Nez Perce is a French-derived name, given to the tribe by fur traders, meaning "pierced noses." It can be pronounced the English way, nes PURSE, or the French way, nay per-SAY. Some tribal members did wear nose pendants, but not the majority. The Nez Perce native name is *Nimiipu* or *Nee-mee-poo,* meaning "the people." To Salishan-speaking peoples living near they were the Sahaptian (or Shahaptin). Lewis and Clark referred to them as Chopunnish. The name *Sahaptin* or *Sahaptian* has come to identify the Nez Perce language, which was related to Penutian languages.

The ancestral homeland of the Nez Perce is territory now comprising central Idaho, southeastern Washington State, and northeastern Oregon. The heart of their homeland was in the vicinity of the Snake and Salmon Rivers. These rivers merge with the Columbia River, which drains the high plateau country between the Rocky Mountains to the east and the Cascade Mountains to the west toward the Pacific Ocean. As a result, Indians of this region are classified as part of the Plateau Culture Area.

Lifeways

The Nez Perce and other PLATEAU INDIANS did not farm but wandered the dry, rugged high country in search of a variety of foods, moving their village sites with the changing seasons. Important foods were fish, especially salmon, which swam upriver from the ocean to spawn and lay their eggs; mammals, especially elk, deer, mountain sheep, and rabbits; and wild plant foods, especially camas (lily) bulb and roots, and berries.

The Nez Perce were inventive in their fishing gear, using a number of techniques. They stood on the bank or on platforms they built and thrust at fish with long-handled spears. They also used nets, both hand-held nets on long poles and large weighted one attached to floats, small traps made from poles and brush, and large enclosures called weirs. They normally did not fish with hooks and lines during the salmon spawning runs.

Tribal members had different houses for warm and cold weather. The warm-weather houses were easy to assemble and disassemble for moving from one place to another, such as to a streambed in late spring during the first salmon run. These temporary shelters consisted of poles in the shape of a ridged tent or a slanted lean-to, covered with mats of woven plant matter.

Earth-covered pithouses served as winter houses. A pole framework was made into a conical shape by erecting a large post in the center of a round pit and extending numerous other poles from its top to the edge of the pit. Then the roof poles were covered with mats of cedar bark, sagebrush, and other plants, as well as packed grass and earth.

A Nez Perce village usually consisted of five or six of these dwellings, with several families living in each pithouse. But the Nez Perce and other Plateau peoples were not organized into groups of families called clans, as many other Indian peoples were. They had shamans, but they did not have secret societies. Their chiefs were not as powerful as some other tribes' chiefs were. Their social, political, and religious organization was much looser than that of the NORTHWEST COAST INDIANS, their neighbors west of the Cascade Mountains.

The Nez Perce did not make pottery. The women did, however, weave exquisite baskets, which they used for cooking by placing heated stones in them, and for gathering wild plants. They also wove soft bags of marsh plants with intricate designs.

To make their clothes, the Nez Perce used cedar bark, deerskin, and rabbit skin. The women were famous for their basket hats, which they wove out of dried leaves.

In the early 1700s, the Nez Perce acquired the horse through trade with other tribes. They rapidly became skilled horse breeders and horse trainers, as did other tribes of the region, such as the CAYUSE and PALOUSE. With horses, the Nez Perce could range farther for food, even venturing onto the plains east of the Rocky Mountains to hunt buffalo. Instead of the small mat tents and lean-tos, they began using large hide tipis, like those of the PLAINS INDIANS, when on hunting and fishing trips.

Contacts with Non-Indians

Non-Indian America was unaware of the Nez Perce until Meriwether Lewis and William Clark returned home in 1806 after their expedition, and later published their journals. The explorers reported how friendly Nez Perce had provided them with food and shelter in the fall of 1805 and had even sent guides along to help them on part of their trip.

In the years following the Lewis and Clark Expedition, fur traders arrived in Nez Perce country: first the French Canadians, then the British Canadians, and then the Americans. Missionaries soon began arriving there. The Nez Perce proved reliable friends to these outsiders.

In 1855, at the Walla Walla Council, tribal leaders readily agreed to the terms offered by whites. In exchange for some of their territory for white settlement, the various Nez Perce bands were guaranteed the rest of their lands, along with schools, money, livestock, and tools.

Yet the whites broke their promises. In the early 1860s, many miners came to Nez Perce country seeking gold. Some decided to build their homes on Indian lands. In 1863, white officials, supporting the settlers over the Indians, convinced some Nez Perce bands to sign an agreement giving up more lands. But other bands refused. Old Joseph (Tuekakas) was the chief of a band living in the Wallowa valley of northeastern Oregon. Missionaries had earlier converted him to Christianity, but on learning that the whites were trying to take his beloved homeland, he tore up his Bible.

Still, in spite of the threat to their lands, which were the center of their existence and the source of their well-being, the Nez Perce kept the peace. Nez Perce even bragged that in all their history, they had never killed a white man.

The Nez Perce War

This situation changed, however. Old Joseph died in 1871. Two of his sons, Joseph and Ollikut, became the leaders of the Wallowa band. In 1877, the band still lived in their ancestral valley. By this time, even more settlers wanted their valley for its good grazing land. White officials gave the band 30 days to relocate to the Nez Perce Reservation at Lapwai, Idaho Territory.

It was during this period that violence erupted. Young warriors attacked and killed a group of whites who had earlier mistreated Indians. The tradition of peace had ended. Joseph, who had always been a friend to whites, now gave his support to the rebels. He joined them at their hiding place at White Bird Canyon on the Salmon River in Idaho.

A detachment of cavalry was sent out to locate the Indians in June 1877. A party of six Nez Perce approached under a flag of truce to negotiate with the army. Soldiers, ignoring the white flag, fired at them. Warriors fired back, killing two soldiers. In the ensuing Battle of White Bird Creek, the Nez Perce killed 34 whites and suffered no fatalities themselves.

Thus began the Nez Perce War. This war, often referred to as the Flight of the Nez Perce, is one of the most remarkable stories of pursuit and escape in military history. The winding flight through the wilderness took the Indians 1,700 miles, through parts of three territories (soon to be states): Idaho, Wyoming, and Montana. The refugees climbed through mountains: the Bitterroot,

Absaroka, and Bear Paw ranges in the Rocky Mountain chain. They descended canyons. They walked over many stretches of rocky and barren plains. They crossed many rivers: the Bitterroot, Yellowstone, Musselshell, and Missouri to name a few.

During this epic journey, the renegade band was chased by three armies. They fought numerous battles: Clearwater Creek in Idaho in July; Big Hole Valley (Montana) in August; Camas Creek (Idaho) in August; Canyon Creek and Cow Island (Montana) in September; and Bear Paw (Montana) in October. The Nez Perce, until the final battle, consistently outsmarted, outflanked, and outfought the larger white forces.

There were other adventures as well. In one incident, the soldiers went to a lot of trouble to build a barricade blocking the Lolo Pass through the Bitterroot Mountains out of Idaho into Montana. The Nez Perce managed to avoid a fight by leading their horses along the face of a cliff. Because the barricade served no purpose for the troops, they called it Fort Fizzle. In another incident, the Nez Perce entered the recently formed Yellowstone National Park in the northwest corner of Wyoming. The tourists were startled to see Indians marching through their midst. But the Nez Perce treated them well.

Many fascinating personalities participated in the conflict. In addition to Chief Joseph and his younger brother Ollikut, there were Looking Glass, Toohoolhoolzote, Red Echo, Five Wounds, Rainbow, and White Bird. There was also the mixed-blood Lean Elk, who was called Poker Joe by the whites. All of them played a part in the decision making and military strategy.

Leading the whites was a one-armed general named Oliver Howard. A humane man who had founded Howard University to provide an education for newly freed slaves, in the Nez Perce campaign he found himself in pursuit of a group of formerly peaceful Indians who had originally wanted only their homeland and now wanted only their freedom in Canada. Many died along the way. With every additional mile of the long trek, the survivors were increasingly weary, hungry, and desperate for survival.

The refugees never reached Canada. Their valiant march fell only 30 miles short. The troops overtook them once and for all at Snake Creek in the Bear Paw

Mountains. It was at Bear Paw, after six days of fighting, that Chief Joseph gave his famous surrender speech:

> Tell General Howard I know his heart. What he told me before, I have in my heart. I am tired of fighting. Our chiefs are killed. Looking Glass is dead. Toohoolhoolzote is dead. It is the young men who say yes or no. He who led the young men is dead [Ollikut]. It is cold and we have no blankets. The little children are freezing to death. My people, some of them, have run away to the hills, and have no blankets, no food. No one knows where they are—perhaps freezing to death. I want to have time to look for my children and see how many I can find. Maybe I shall find them among the dead. Hear me, my chiefs, I am tired. My heart is sick and sad. From where the sun now stands, I will fight no more forever.

Chief Joseph was never allowed to return to his ancestral Wallowa valley. Officials sent him and others of his people to Kansas, then to the Indian Territory, and finally to the Colville Reservation in Washington State where he died in 1904. The reservation doctor reported that "Joseph died of a broken heart."

Contemporary Nez Perce

Descendants of the Nez Perce live on the Nez Perce Reservation near Lapwai, Idaho, as well as on the Colville Reservation among other Sahaptian as well as Salishan tribes near Nespelem, Washington. Others have made their homes in the urban areas of the Pacific Northwest. Some have moved to British Columbia.

The Nez Perce are active in native causes in the region, in particular fishing rights through participation in the Columbia River Inter-Tribal Fish Commission. The tribe sponsors a number of powwows and ceremonies each year and is working to preserve its language among young people. The Nez Perce National Historic Trail, the route followed by the Nez Perce in their epic flight, was established in 1986. In 1992, after a 15-year struggle, the Nez Perce were successful in having Bear Paw Mountain Battleground, where Chief Joseph surrendered, declared a national historical site.

NIPMUC

In the state of Massachusetts, the low coastal plains rise up to an inland plateau. The plateau is separated from even higher country to the west, the Berkshire Hills, by the Connecticut River. This plateau, covered

with rich topsoil and dense woods and coursed by swift-flowing rivers, was the heart of the ancestral homeland of Algonquian bands, who came to be known together as the Nipmuc. Their territory, called

Nipnet, extended as far north as the present-day Vermont and New Hampshire borders and south into northwestern Rhode Island and northeastern Connecticut. (See NORTHEAST INDIANS.)

Their name, pronounced NIP-muck, is derived from the Algonquian word *nipmaug,* for "freshwater people." The fact that the Nipmuc primarily used inland freshwater lakes and rivers for their fishing rather than the Atlantic Ocean marks their major difference from many other New England ALGONQUIANS living closer to the coast. In other ways—such as their hunting and farming methods, their tools, and their beliefs—they were much like their other Algonquian neighbors. The Nipmuc were noted in particular for their basketmaking, weaving, and leatherwork.

Historically too, their story linked to other area tribes. The Nipmuc were associated in early colonial years with the MASSACHUSET tribe to the east, and many of them also became Praying Indians. But then in 1675, many Nipmuc men joined the WAMPANOAG and NARRAGANSETT in King Philip's War. At the end of the war, some Nipmuc survivors settled among Algonquian kinsmen, such as the MAHICAN on the Hudson River. Others joined Algonquians in Canada.

The Nipmuc Tribe is recognized by the state of Massachusetts with two active groups—the Hassanamisco Band in Grafton and the Chaubunagungamaug Band in Webster. Each has a small landholding and is seeking to acquire more. The Nipmuc celebrate their heritage through annual powwows and educational and cultural programs. Some 200 Nipmuc living in Connecticut hope to create a tribal entity and are seeking recognition by that state.

NOOTKA

Vancouver Island lies off the coast of the Pacific Northwest in Canadian waters, separated from the rest of the province of British Columbia by narrow straits. It is the largest island off western North America, approximately 285 miles long and 80 miles wide at its widest point. The island is made up of exposed parts of mountains in the Coast Range, their bases submerged in water. The tallest peak on the island, Golden Hinde Mountain, is 7,219 feet above sea level. Flat lands extend inland for a distance from the shore on the eastern side of the island before the foothills begin. The more rugged and rocky western side is indented with fjords and inlets. There is more rainfall on the island than in any other place in North America. The island is forested with many lakes and streams.

The rugged western part of Vancouver Island was the ancestral homeland of the Nootka Indians. The tribal name *Nootka,* pronounced NOOT-kuh, meaning "circling about," was originally applied to a group of people on Nootka Sound. But it has since come to be used for more than 20 tribes of the Aht Confederacy. These tribes all spoke related dialects of the Wakashan language family.

The Nootka are classified as part of the Northwest Coast Culture Area. Like other NORTHWEST COAST INDIANS, they hunted seal and sea otters; fished for salmon, halibut, cod, and herring; hunted game in the forest; foraged for roots and berries; lived in long cedar-plank houses; and carved giant totem poles.

The Nootka also shaped six different types of large dugout canoe. They made hats of woven fiber that have come to be called Nootka hats. They determined wealth by the number of possessions and practiced the custom of giving away possessions—known as the potlatch. (The name comes from the Nootka word *patshatl* for "sharing.") The principal gods of the Nootka were the Sky-god, the Thunder-god, and the Wolf Spirits. All Nootka boys had to undergo an ordeal in which they

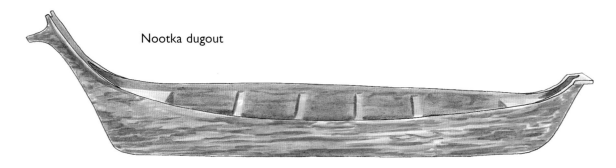

Nootka dugout

were kidnapped for days by men dressed up as wolves and taught Wolf songs and dances. Then they were rescued in a pretend battle and exorcised of the Wolf Spirits through more dancing.

The Nootka, unlike most other Northwest Coast tribes, hunted the largest sea mammals—whales. Their whaling techniques resembled those of their kinsmen across the Juan de Fuca Strait, the MAKAH. Here is a part of a Nootka whaling song:

> Whale, you must not run out to sea when I spear you.
> Whale, if I spear you, I want my spear to strike your heart.
> Harpoon, when I use you, I want you to go to the heart of the whale.

Because of their location along the Pacific Ocean, the Nootka had early contacts with explorers. Juan de Fuca, exploring for Spain, was the first white to visit them, in 1592. Both Spain and England claimed Vancouver Island—Juan Pérez for Spain in 1774 and Captain James Cook for England in 1778. Cook wrote extensively about the Indians. John Meares established a British trading post on Nootka Sound in 1788. The Spanish seized this post the following year, leading to a dispute between the two countries. Spain signed the Nootka Convention in 1790, ceding the Pacific Northwest to England. Captain George Vancouver further explored Nootka country for Britain in 1792 and 1794, opening up the region to white settlement.

The Nootka, who had always been great traders among Indian peoples, continued this tradition with the British and supplied them with furs. As a result, they were generally friendly toward whites. Nevertheless,

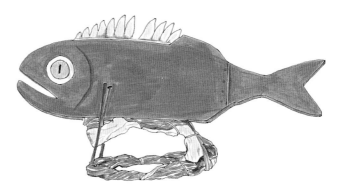

Nootka salmon headdress

when cheated by traders, they rose up against them. In 1803, Nootka attacked and killed all except two people on board the *Boston.* Then in 1811, Nootka seized another trading ship, the *Tonquin.* In this second incident, one of the ship's crew managed to reach the powder magazine and blow up the whole vessel and everyone on board, the attackers included.

With the founding of the settlement of Victoria in 1843, which later became the capital of British Columbia, the pressures on the Nootka increased. Missionaries tried to erase their culture, and white diseases killed many of them.

The Nootka have since rebounded from a population low in the early 1900s. They presently live in 18 small village reserves on Vancouver Island. Many tribal members fish as their main source of income or operate salmon canneries. Some Nootka have rediscovered traditional basketmaking skills. The Nootka have sought to restore tribal sovereignty and traditional customs, such as basketmaking. They have taken the new tribal name *Nuu-Chah Nulth,* which means "all along the mountains."

NORTHEAST INDIANS

The Northeast Culture Area is defined as covering the following territory: east-to-west, from the Atlantic Ocean to the Mississippi River; north-to-south, from the Great Lakes to the Ohio Valley, including the Chesapeake Bay and Tidewater region. The following present-day states are included in this huge expanse of land: Maine, Vermont, New Hampshire, Massachusetts, Rhode Island, Connecticut, New York, New Jersey, Pennsylvania, Delaware, Ohio, Indiana, Illinois, and Michigan; plus most of Maryland, West Virginia, Ken-

tucky, and Wisconsin; and smaller parts of Virginia, North Carolina, Missouri, Iowa, and Minnesota. The following present-day provinces of Canada are also included: Nova Scotia, New Brunswick, and Prince Edward Island, plus parts of Quebec and Ontario, as well as a tiny piece of Manitoba.

Most of this land is woodland. That is why the culture area is sometimes called the Northeast Woodland Culture Area and the Indians of this region sometimes are referred to as "Woodland Indians." Yet since there were

The Northeast Culture Area, showing the approximate locations of Indian tribes listed in this book—circa 1500, before displacement by non-Indians (with modern boundaries)

many other Indians living in the forests of North America—for example, in the northern forest of the subarctic and in the Pacific Northwest—the term *Woodland* can be confusing when used for just eastern Indians.

The forest is the one constant in the Northeast Culture Area. The terrain is otherwise varied, including sea coasts, hills, mountains, lakes, and river valleys. The Appalachian Mountains run in a general north-south direction through the culture area. Enormous inland bodies of water—the five Great Lakes—are located in the north-central region. Some of the big rivers flowing through the culture area are the St. Lawrence, Ottawa, Connecticut, Hudson, Delaware, Susquehanna, Allegheny, Ohio, Wabash, and Illinois.

The forests of the Northeast provided a great natural resource for the native peoples: wood for houses, boats, tools, and fuel (plus bark for clothing, roofing, and bedding). Moreover, the forests were the home of abundant game that provided the Indians with meat for food,

hides for clothing, and bones for tools. Of the many kinds of mammals living in the forests, deer were the most important resource for Native Americans. The oceans, lakes, and rivers were a plentiful source of fish and shellfish.

In addition to being hunter-gatherers, Northeast Indians were also farmers. Many of their villages, where they had their cultivated fields, were permanent. But Northeast Indians generally left the villages to hunt in certain seasons, living on the trail. Many Northeast Indians can be called "seminomadic."

The Indians of the Northeast Culture Area spoke dialects of two language families: Algonquian, part of the Macro-Algonquian language phylum, and Iroquoian, part of the Macro-Siouan language phylum. ALGONQUIANS and Iroquoians shared many cultural traits. Yet there were differences too. For example, most Algonquians lived in wigwams, and most Iroquoian peoples lived in longhouses.

The various Northeast Algonquians included in this book are listed under the entry ALGONQUIAN. The different Northeast Iroquoians included are the IROQUOIS (HAUDENOSAUNEE)—that is, the CAYUGA, MOHAWK, ONEIDA, ONONDAGA, SENECA, and TUSCARORA—as well as the HURON (WYANDOT), and SUSQUEHANNOCK.

See those entries to learn more about the two language families in general, but also see the various entries under particular tribal **nam**es. Only one tribe of the Northeast Culture Area spoke a language other than Algonquian or Iroquoian: the WINNEBAGO, who spoke a dialect of the Siouan language family.

NORTHWEST COAST INDIANS

The region defined as the Northwest Coast Culture Area is elongated, extending from north to south about 2,000 miles, but from east to west only about 150 miles at its widest. At its northern limits, it touches on territory that now is southern Alaska. At its southern limits, it touches on northern California. In between, it includes the western parts of British Columbia, Washington, and Oregon. A large part of the Northwest Coast Culture Area consists of islands, including Vancouver Island, the Queen Charlotte Islands, and the Alexander Archipelago, plus numerous smaller chains.

The many islands are actually the tips of submerged mountains, part of the Coast Range. These rugged mountains form a spine running north-south along the culture area. Many of the mountains extend right down to the ocean, forming rocky cliffs. There are numerous inlets and sounds along the shoreline, as well as numerous straits between the islands. Farther inland, in Washington and Oregon, another mountain range, the Cascade Range, also runs north-south.

The climate of the Northwest Coast is surprisingly warm for the northern latitudes because an ocean current, known as the Japan (Kuroshio) Current, warms the ocean as well as winds blowing inland. But the westerly winds also carry abundant moisture. The mountains block the moisture, which turns to rainfall, as much as 100 inches or more a year, more than in any other part of North America. Abundant springs and streams run from the mountains to the ocean.

These climatic conditions led to the growth of vast forests. Giant evergreen trees, among the tallest in the world, cover most of the land, except mountaintops and rock faces too steep to have soil. The branches of tall trees form a dense canopy, blocking out sunlight. The forest floor is therefore dark and wet, with little undergrowth other than ferns and mosses.

Northwest Coast peoples usually lived right at the ocean's edge on narrow sand and gravel beaches. Mountains rise up to the east. The island chains to the west offered protection from stormy seas.

The Indians situated their houses facing the sea. They built them entirely of wood taken from the giant forests. Cedar was the wood of choice. The master architects of the Northwest Coast used giant timbers for framing their rectangular houses. For their walls, they lashed hand-split planks to the framework, which ran either vertically or horizontally. They hung mats on the inside for additional insulation. The roofs were also plank-covered. Planks were used for flooring, sometimes on two different levels. There was usually a central firepit. Platforms ran along the walls for sleeping and storage. In size, the houses varied from about 20 by 30 feet, to 50 by 60 feet, to even 60 by 100 feet and provided shelter for several families.

Northwest Coast Indians often erected giant totem poles outside their houses. Powerful shamans and members of secret societies dictated the significance of the faces on the totem poles. Woodwork in the region included large, seaworthy dugouts and carved chests, boxes, masks, and other objects. Northwest Coast peoples were among the premier Native American woodworkers. They also made exquisite baskets, textiles, and other goods. Villagers demonstrated their wealth and social status by the number of possessions they gave away in a custom unique to this culture area—the potlatch.

Since travel over the mountainous land was so difficult, Northwest Coast Indians moved about by sea. They traveled up and down the coast for purposes of trade, slave-raiding, and hunting. The sea provided their primary game, sea mammals, including whales, seals, and sea lions. The sea also offered up plentiful fish, including salmon, halibut, herring, cod, and flounder. Northwest Coast Indians also fished the rivers when salmon left the ocean waters to lay their eggs. Their land game included deer, elk, bear, and mountain goat. The Indians in this part of North America had plenty of food and could support large

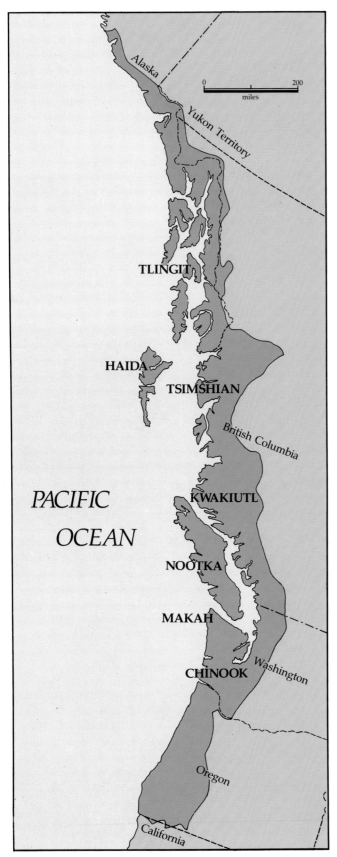

The Northwest Coast Culture Area, showing the approximate locations of Indian tribes listed in this book—circa 1500, before displacement by non-Indians (with modern boundaries)

Northwest Coast Indian house with totem poles

populations in their seaside villages without farming. Some Northwest Coast peoples did grow tobacco, however.

The language families of the Northwest Coast Culture Area are the following: Athapascan (of the Na-Dene language phylum); Chimakuan (of undetermined phylum affiliation); Chinookian (of the Penutian phylum); Kalapuyan (of the Penutian phylum); Kusan (of the Penutian phylum); Salishan (of undetermined phylum affiliation); Wakashan (of undetermined phylum affiliation); and Yakonan (of the Penutian phylum). Other Northwest Coast peoples spoke language isolates of both the Na-Dene and Penutian phyla. These various language groups were not segregated geographically but were interspersed. Sorting out and memorizing tribal locations and language connections is extremely difficult in the densely populated Northwest Coast Culture Area.

Athapascan-speaking tribes classified as Northwest Coast Indians include Chastacosta, Chetco, Clatskanie, Coquille, Dakubetede, Kwalhioqua, Taltushtuntude, Tututni, and Umpqua. Chimakuan-speaking tribes include Chimakum and Quileute. Chinookian-speaking tribes include Cathlamet, Cathlapotle, Chilluckittequaw, CHINOOK, Clackamas, Clatsop, Clowwewalla, Multomah, Skilloot, Wasco, and Watlala. Kalapuyan-speaking

Northwest Coast Indian shaman's wooden spirit helper

tribes include Ahantchuyuk, Atfalati, Chelamela, Chepenafa, Kalapuya, Luckiamute, Santiam, Yamel, and Yoncalla. Kusan-speaking tribes include Coos and Miluk. Salishan-speaking tribes include Bella Coola, Chehalis, Clallam, Comox, Cowichan, Cowlitz, Duwamish, Lumni, Muckleshoot, Nanaimo, Nisqually, Nooksack, Puntlatch, Puyallup, Quaitso, Quinault, Sahehwamish, Samish, Seechelt, Semiahmoo, Siletz, Skagit, Skykomish, Snohomish, Snoqualmie, Songish, Squamish, Squaxon, Stalo, Suquamish, Swallah, Swinomish, Tillamook, and Twana. Wakashan-speaking tribes include KWAKIUTL, MAKAH, and NOOTKA. Yakonan-speaking tribes include Alsea, Kuitsh, Siuslaw, and Yaquina. Tribes speaking isolates of the Na-Dene phylum include HAIDA and TLINGIT.

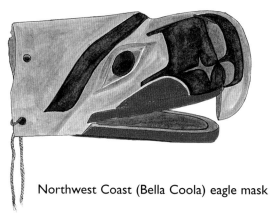

Northwest Coast (Bella Coola) eagle mask

Tribes speaking isolates of the Penutian phylum include Latgawa, Takelma, and TSIMSHIAN.

OJIBWAY   *see* CHIPPEWA (OJIBWAY)

OLMEC

The Olmec lived in Mesoamerica. The Mesoamerican Culture Area, or Middle America, comprises much of present-day Mexico as well as the northern part of Central America. In the centuries before Europeans reached the Americas, Mesoamerica was the most densely populated region, with many different Indian cultures. *Olmec* (pronounced OL-mek), also written as *Olmeca*, is a term derived from the rubber trees growing in the area and applied by scholars to the cultures.

Scholars believe the Olmec established the "mother civilization" of Mesoamerica. That is to say, their culture influenced other cultures that followed. From about 1200 B.C. to A.D. 300, Olmec culture dominated the region.

Sometimes the period when the Olmec dominated Mesoamerica is referred to as the Preclassic period. Then came the Classic period, when the MAYA flourished. Then followed the Postclassic period, when the TOLTEC and AZTEC flourished. (In the study of PREHISTORIC INDIANS north of Mesoamerica, however, these three periods together are usually called the Formative period.)

The Olmec homeland was situated mainly along the Gulf coast to the east of present-day Mexico City. Yet the Olmec had extensive trade contacts all over Mesoamerica. On finding Olmec objects at sites far from the Gulf coast, archaeologists are sometimes uncertain if the ancient inhabitants were actually Olmec or were other Indians who obtained Olmec objects in trade.

The Olmec carved giant heads from basalt, a type of volcanic rock. Some of these were as heavy as 20 tons, with helmet-like headdresses. The Olmec traveled far to obtain the basalt to make these mammoth sculptures. To transport the rock, they dragged it overland and floated it on rafts. The Olmec also traveled great distances to get jade to make statues, the mineral magnetite to make

Olmec mammoth basalt head-statue

mirrors, and an ore called serpentine to make pavement. Their statues, both large and small, were often representations of jaguars, which played an important part in Olmec religion. Another religious symbol frequently depicted, the Great Plumed Serpent (Quetzalcoatl), persisted as a deity among many other later peoples in Mesoamerica, indicating Olmec influence far and wide.

Olmec jade Kunz Axe, depicting a man-jaguar

The Olmec also influenced later Mesoamerican peoples with their system of social organization. Unlike most Indian tribes, Olmec society had classes of priests, merchants, and craftsmen, with the priests having the most power. The social classes were fixed; members were born into them and could not change occupations.

The Olmec upper classes lived in finely built stone structures. The buildings, some of them temples on top of pyramids, were situated along paved streets. Aqueducts carried water to them. The Olmec population centers are not thought of as true cities, but rather as ceremonial, civic, and economic centers. True cities with large populations, some of them on the very same sites, would evolve among later Mesoamerican peoples.

In the countryside, surrounding the Olmec centers, lived a population of farmers who supported the upper classes through agriculture. They practiced a method of farming called slash-and-burn in which trees are cut down and burned to make fields. The main crop was corn.

Farming in Mesoamerica dates back as early as 7000 B.C. Cultivated beans, peppers, pumpkins, and gourds have been discovered in a dry cave. The earliest cultivated strain of corn ever found, also in Mesoamerica, dates back to 4000 B.C. These early Indians were perhaps the ancient ancestors of the Olmec. It was agriculture that allowed the development of cities, because, with farming, a large number of people could live in a small area and still have plenty to eat.

Another Olmec cultural development passed to later Mesoamericans was a ball game that was played with a ball made from rubber on a paved court. The Olmec also were the first Indians known to have number and calendar systems as well as hieroglyphic writing, with symbols representing words and ideas.

The most important Olmec population centers were San Lorenzo, dominant from about 1200 to 900 B.C.; La Venta, dominant from about 900 to 400 B.C.; and Tres Zapotes, dominant from about 100 B.C. to A.D. 300. La Venta was the location of the largest Olmec pyramid. At Copalillo, an Olmec site situated to the west of these sites, have been found the oldest stone buildings in North America, dating back as early as 600 B.C.

It is not known why the Olmec culture declined. Invading tribes could have been responsible, or drought and failing crops, or disease. Because the Olmec culture has much in common with the later Maya culture, some scholars have theorized that the Olmec migrated eastward and became the direct ancestors of the Maya. Whatever happened to them, the Olmec, with their remarkable cultural developments and their great influence, changed the course of Native American history.

OMAHA

The Omaha belonged to a group of Siouan-speaking peoples who once lived along the Ohio River before migrating westward early in their history. In addition to the Omaha, these people became the various tribes known as KAW, OSAGE, PONCA, and QUAPAW. They settled at different locations on the eastern plains. The Omaha and Ponca settled farther north than the other tribes of this group. These two tribes probably separated

where the Niobrara River flows into the Missouri River. The Omaha eventually settled to the southeast of the mouth of the Niobrara River, downriver from the Ponca, in what is now northeastern Nebraska.

The Omaha are the tribe most closely associated with the state of Nebraska, where most tribal descendants live and whose largest city, Omaha, was named after them. But they occupied other territory as well. Before settling in Nebraska, the Omaha stayed for a time near the Pipestone Quarry, in what is now southern Minnesota, where Indians found catlinite (or pipestone) for carving into pipes. Bands of Omaha also had villages in South Dakota and Iowa in the course of their history. The Omaha can be thought of as one of the many Missouri River tribes. Rivers more than any other physical feature

Omaha mirror board with iron upholstery tacks and brass pins

helped them delineate their homelands. Their name pronounced O-muh-haw, means "those going against the current." The native spelling is *Umon'hon.*

Sometimes the tribes of the eastern plains, who lived along the Mississippi and Missouri Rivers, are referred to as PRAIRIE INDIANS. The Omaha were villagers and farmers. They lived in earth lodges most of the year and depended on their crops for food. They also fished the rivers in their territory. But they left their villages in search of buffalo, deer, and smaller game. When the Spanish brought horses to North America and the horses spread to Indian peoples, the Omaha adopted many of the traits of the western PLAINS INDIANS, ranging over a wider area in search of the buffalo and living in hide tipis when on the trail. As a result, they are classified as part of the Great Plains Culture Area.

Here is an Omaha dance song about the buffalo hunt:

One I have wounded, yonder, he moves,
Yonder he moves, bleeding at the mouth.
One I have wounded, yonder he moves,
Yonder he moves, with staggering steps.
One I have wounded, yonder he moves,
Yonder he falls, yonder he falls.

The Omaha had a complex social structure with many rules governing behavior. They also had many societies, some of them secret with exclusive membership, and others open to everyone. The Thunder Society served as custodians of the tribe's most sacred relics, two pipes that had mallard duck heads attached to the stems. Another society, the Buffalo Dreamers, cared for the sick. Still another, the Bear Dreamers, used sleight-of-hand tricks in their rituals. One trick was swallowing long sticks.

The Omaha fought often with the SIOUX (DAKOTA, LAKOTA, NAKOTA) living to their north and west. Yet a smallpox epidemic in 1802, brought to the Omaha by white traders, had a greater impact on them than intertribal warfare, greatly reducing their population.

In 1854, at the time the original Indian Territory was reorganized, the Omaha ceded all their lands east of the Missouri River to the United States and were granted a reservation in Thurston County, Nebraska. In 1865, the Omaha sold the northern part of the reservation to the federal government for the use of the WINNEBAGO.

The La Flesche family has had an impact on the history of the Omaha in the late 19th and early 20th century. Joseph La Flesche (Inshtamaza) was the head of the tribe's Progressive Party and principal chief as of 1853. Believing that his people should learn the ways of the Euroamerican culture, he encouraged the building of roads on the reservation and the division of lands into lots for individual farming. But he also advocated the preservation of traditional customs and pride in "Indianness." He had his children educated in white-run schools. Three of his 10 children became famous. Susette La Flesche, also known as Bright Eyes, became a well-known reformer, lecturer, and writer on Indian issues. She married non-Indian journalist and lecturer Thomas Henry Tibbles, who also worked on behalf of Indian peoples. Susette's sister Susan La Flesche became the first female Native American physician. Their brother Francis La Flesche became renowned as an anthropologist and writer on the Omaha and Osage.

In the late 19th century, Francis La Flesche gave Harvard University's Peabody Museum the tribe's Sacred Pole, known as Umon'hon'ti, the "Real Omaha" or "Venerable Man," believing the museum was best equipped to preserve it. A personification of a human being, it consists of a cottonwood pole, resting on a wooden "leg," with a scalp on its "head." In 1989, the Omaha, who have helped draft legislation for the return of sacred objects and human remains to Indian nations from museums, negotiated the return of the Sacred Pole, one of their revered objects.

Many Omaha still speak their native language, which is taught in their schools on the Omaha Reservation, and participate in traditional events, such as the He'dewachi, an annual tribal powwow, where the Hedushka is performed. The Hedushka, originally a war dance, probably evolved out of the Pawnee Irushka. Formerly called the Omaha Dance by a number of other Plains tribes after the people who taught it to them, the dance became more widely known as the Grass Dance because of the Omaha custom of tucking prairie grass in belts to symbolize scalps taken in warfare.

ONEIDA

The Oneida were one of the five original tribes of the Iroquois League. They controlled the wedge of territory in what now is central New York State between the MOHAWK to the east and the ONONDAGA to the west, especially between Oneida Lake and the upper Mohawk River. Their culture and history are summarized along with the other NORTHEAST INDIANS of the Iroquois Confederacy under IROQUOIS (HAUDENOSAUNEE). Yet as is the case with all six nations, the Oneida have a distinct tribal identity.

Their name, pronounced oh-NI-duh, is derived from the Iroquoian word *Onayotekaona,* or the "people of the upright stone," referring to a large rock within their territory. At the confederacy's annual Great Council in neighboring Onondaga territory, to which they sent nine sachems, or chiefs, as representatives of their tribe, the Oneida symbol was the Great Tree. At the Great Council the Oneida sachems also served as spokesmen for the TUSCARORA, the Iroquoian-speaking tribe from North Carolina that became the Sixth Nation of the Iroquois League in 1722.

The Oneida were loyal to the confederacy throughout the French and Indian wars of 1689–1763, valuable allies of the British against the French and the Algonquian tribes. Yet in the American Revolution of 1775–83, the Oneida, along with the Tuscarora, broke with the CAYUGA, Mohawk, Onondaga, and SENECA and sided with the American rebels against the British. At first they tried to remain neutral during the conflict, not wanting to take up arms against fellow Haudenosaunee or against Tory settlers near their homelands. But by 1777, two years into the war, Oneida warriors participated.

A Presbyterian missionary by the name of Samuel Kirkland won the Oneida over to the American side. He originally had settled among the Oneida in 1766 and preached to them and counseled them throughout this eventful period of American history. In 1793, with the help of Alexander Hamilton, Kirkland founded the Hamilton Oneida Academy near Utica, New York, for the education of both Indian and non-Indian youth. Few Indians attended the school, and it became chartered as Hamilton College in 1812.

Despite the fact that the Oneida had offered their support to the victorious Americans in the Revolutionary War, the state of New York made a concerted effort to open their lands to white settlers. With their shrinking land base, many Oneida departed. Some moved to Ontario to join Joseph Brant's Mohawk and other Haudenosaunee on the Six Nations Reserve on the Grand River. In 1822, a part-Mohawk missionary, Eleazar Williams, made an agreement with the MENOMINEE for lands near Green Bay, Wisconsin. He hoped to create a Protestant Iroquois empire in the West. Over the next 10 years, many Oneida and MAHICAN who had been living among them in New York relocated. In the 1840s, another group of Oneida purchased land on the Thames River in Ontario. Others stayed in New York on state reservation lands.

All three Oneida groups—the Oneida Nation of New York, the Oneida Tribe of Indians of Wisconsin, and the Oneida of the Thames—have land claims against the state of New York dating back to the 18th and 19th centuries. The federal government has joined the Oneida Indians in a lawsuit against state and local governments contending that lands were taken away unfairly from the tribal groups. The Oneida maintain they have no intention of forcing the eviction of non-Indian individuals, but want the state to reach a settlement.

Oneida soapstone sculpture

Both Oneida communities in the United States have improved their economic situation in recent years with gaming facilities—the Turning Stone Casino west of Utica, New York, and Oneida Bingo and Casino in Green Bay, Wisconsin. Profits have gone to administrative, social, and cultural programs. The highly successful Turning Stone, which opened in 1993, since has expanded into a resort with golf course and has helped revitalize the economy of Oneida County.

ONONDAGA

The Onondaga located their ancestral villages in the vicinity of Onondaga Lake and Oswego River just to the south of Lake Ontario, in what is now upstate New York not far from present-day Syracuse, New York. As the central tribe in the Iroquois League, the Onondaga played the role of Keepers of the Council Fire, the flame kept burning for two centuries—from about the 1570s to the 1770s. Their main village, Onondaga, was the meeting place of the IROQUOIS (HAUDENOSAUNEE) Great Council, held every year. (Since the Onondaga shared culture and history with the other NORTHEAST INDIANS of the Iroquois Confederacy, they also are discussed under IROQUOIS [HAUDENOSAUNEE].)

Onondaga is pronounced au-nun-DAG-uh and means the "people of the hills" in Iroquoian, after the hilly land surrounding their villages. At the Great Council, the Onondaga also bore the epithet Name-Bearer because they had the responsibility of keeping the wampum belt that served as a record of the meeting and of who was present. The Onondaga had the greatest number of sachems, or chiefs, as tribal representatives, 14 of the 50.

In Iroquois legend, an Onondaga chief known as Atotarhoh was the most stubborn in opposition to the formation of the league when the MOHAWK called Hiawatha traveled from tribe to tribe preaching the message of Haudenosaunee unity. Atotarhoh was so fierce and hostile to other tribes that he supposedly had serpents growing out of his head. To pacify Atotarhoh and

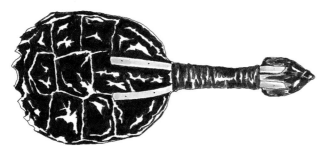

Onondaga turtle rattle

seal the alliance, Hiawatha combed the snakes from the chief's head. Atotarhoh had one condition, however, for the participation of the Onondaga: They must always serve as chairmen at the Great Council.

The Iroquois League split up during the American Revolution when the member tribes chose opposing sides. The Onondaga, along with the Mohawk, SENECA, and CAYUGA, supported the British, whom they had supported in the earlier French and Indian wars. The fact that the ONEIDA and TUSCARORA sided with the American rebels meant that the Great Peace had ended and that unity was no more. The Onondaga let the Council Fire, which had burned continuously for 200 years, die out.

It took some time after the Revolution to heal the wounds among the opposing factions of the Iroquois Confederacy. Most Onondaga took refuge for a time in western New York; they were finally granted a reservation on part of their original homelands near Nedrow, New York. Other Onondaga settled in Canada as part of the Six Nation Reserve at Oshweken on the Grand River. The Iroquois tribes have since rediscovered their unity, and today the Onondaga again play a central role in the confederacy. The Onondaga reservation is the capital of the confederacy. The spiritual leader of the allied Iroquois, the Tadodaho, is always of the Onondaga tribe. Only he can summon the Six Nation Council.

The Constitution of the Iroquois League reads as follows:

> The Onondaga lords shall open each council by expressing their gratitude to their cousin lords, and greeting them, and they shall make an address and offer thanks to the earth where men dwell, to the streams of water, the pool, the springs, the lakes, to the maize and the fruits, to the medicinal herbs and the trees, to the forest trees for their usefulness, to the animals that serve as food and who offer their pelts as clothing, to the great

winds and the lesser winds, to the Thunderers, and the Sun, the mighty warrior, to the moon, to the messengers of the Great Spirit who dwells in the skies above, who gives all things useful to men, who is the source and the ruler of health and life. Then shall the Onondaga lords declare the council open.

As one of their many fronts promoting Haudenosaunee unity, the Onondaga in recent years have successfully recovered wampum belts of the Iroquois League, held by museums.

Many Onondaga, who are considered the most traditional of the Haudenosaunee, participate in the Longhouse Religion founded by the Seneca Handsome Lake in 1799. He is buried next to the Onondaga Longhouse near Nedrow, New York.

OSAGE

The Siouan-speaking Osage once lived along the Ohio River valley, then later migrated onto the eastern plains. They were originally one people with the KAW, OMAHA, PONCA, and QUAPAW. The group who became the Osage settled along the Osage River tributary of the Missouri in what is now the state of Missouri. They also claimed territory as far south as the Arkansas River in what is now northern Arkansas, southeastern Kansas, and northeastern Oklahoma.

The Osage native name is *Ni-U-Ko'n-Ska,* meaning "people of the middle waters." *Osage,* pronounced OH-saje, is the French version of *Wazhazhe,* the largest Osage band. There were two main early bands: the Great Osage on the Osage River, and the Little Osage on the Missouri River. Another band broke off in the early 1800s from the Great Osage and migrated to the Arkansas River, becoming known as the Arkansas Osage.

Scholars classify the Osage among the prairie division of the PLAINS INDIANS (see PRAIRIE INDIANS). That is to say, they were seminomadic. Most of the year, they lived in villages along wooded river valleys and farmed the rich soil. While at home, they stayed in oval or rectangular pole-frame houses covered with woven mats or hides. But they also depended on the buffalo for food. They went on several buffalo hunts every year during which time they lived in tipis. Before acquiring horses, they often killed the large animals by waving fur robes to stampede the herd and lighting prairie fires to direct the animals toward the edge of a cliff.

Each Osage village had two chiefs, a peace chief and a war chief. One clan, the Sky People, under the peace chief, lived to the north; another clan, the Earth People, under the war chief, lived to the south. A council of elderly men, called the Little Old Men, made tribal laws and settled tribal disputes.

The French explorers Jacques Marquette and Louis Jolliet visited the Osage along the Osage River in 1673. During the 1700s, tribal members conducted much trade

Osage bear claw necklace with otter fur

with French traders, bartering furs for guns, horses, and European manufactured goods, giving them power and influence among the tribes of the region. They called all whites I'n-Shta-Heh, meaning "heavy eyebrows," because the Europeans seemed hairy to them. Osage warriors helped the French defeat the British under General Edward Braddock near present-day Pittsburgh in 1755 in the latter part of the French and Indian wars. After England and Spain had gained control of France's holdings in 1763, the Osage developed new trade contacts.

In 1801, France regained control of the huge Louisiana Territory, which then included the Mississippi and Missouri River valleys. Two years later, President Thomas Jefferson bought the land from Napoleon Bonaparte of France for $15 million. After the Lewis and Clark Expedition of 1804–6, American traders and settlers began arriving in great numbers on Osage lands.

At first, the Osage were hostile to the new intruders. But in 1808, they agreed to a treaty giving up huge tracts of their territory. They agreed to other land cessions in treaties of 1818, 1825, 1839, and 1865. The Osage served as scouts for the U.S. Army in Sheridan's Campaign of 1868–69 (see CHEYENNE). Another treaty in 1870 established the Osage reservation in the northeastern part of the Indian Territory (now near the town of Pawhuska, Oklahoma), which had formerly been Osage hunting grounds.

In 1896, oil was discovered on the Osage reservation. The fact that some lands were allotted to individuals in the 1906 Osage Allotment Act led to attempts by non-Indians to gain control of mineral rights. By the 1920s, however, many Osage had become wealthy from oil and natural gas leases. Others continued to earn a living from farming and ranching.

A famous Osage of recent times is the dancer Maria Tallchief, born in 1925. She was a prima ballerina who danced all over the world and gained respect for American ballet at a time when most great dancers came from other countries. Her younger sister Marjorie Tallchief, born in 1927, also became a well-known dancer.

OTOE

According to tribal legend, the Siouan-speaking Otoe or Oto were formerly one people with the WINNEBAGO, IOWAY, and MISSOURIA and lived in Winnebago country in the Great Lakes region. Then the ancestors of the Otoe, Ioway, and Missouria split off from the Winnebago and migrated soutwestward. Another separation took place at the mouth of the Iowa River, on the Mississippi River. The group that stayed in this location became the Ioway. The group that pushed westward divided into two other tribes on the Missouri. This final split supposedly occurred because two chiefs quarreled when the son of one seduced the daughter of another. Those who stayed where they were, the band of the girl's father, became the Missouria. The band of the boy's father traveled northward, farther up the Missouri River. They became known by the name Otoe, meaning "lechers," in reference to the boy's behavior. The name is pronounced oh-tow-EH or OH-tow.

The Otoe eventually settled south of the Platte River in what is now Southeastern Nebraska. They also roamed and had temporary villages in parts of neighboring states—Iowa, Kansas, and Missouri. The Otoe retained some cultural traits of the eastern woodlands, including farming and permanent villages. Scholars sometimes describe them as PRAIRIE INDIANS. But they eventually adopted lifeways typical of PLAINS INDIANS, including hunting buffalo and using horses and tipis. As a result, the Otoe are usually grouped in the Great Plains Culture Area.

The Otoe had contacts with early French explorers, such as Jacques Marquette and Louis Jolliet in 1673. The Lewis and Clark Expedition encountered them in 1804 on the banks of the Missouri River near their main villages on the lower course of the Platte River.

With increased white settlement west of the Mississippi, starting in the 1830s, the Otoe were pressured by U.S. officials into giving up their lands. Along with the Missouria, who joined them permanently in 1829, the Otoe signed away lands in Nebraska, Missouri, and Iowa in the 1830s. Then in 1854, the Otoe signed away all remaining lands in Nebraska except for a strip along the Big Blue River. When it was found out that there was no timber on this piece, they received instead a tract in Kansas. In 1876 and 1879, they sold off the western part of this reservation. In 1881, they sold the rest and moved to a reservation in the Indian Territory.

The Otoe and Missouria are presently known as the Otoe-Missouria Tribe and hold trust lands together in the Red Rock region of Oklahoma. Every July the joint tribe sponsors the Otoe-Missouria Powwow.

OTTAWA

With the CHIPPEWA (OJIBWAY) and the POTAWATOMI, the Ottawa formed the Council of Three Fires. All three Algonquian tribes supposedly migrated to the Great Lakes country from the north as one people, then separated. In the early 1600s, when French explorers and missionaries arrived in the area, the Ottawa controlled the northern reaches of Lake Huron—especially Manitoulin Island and the shores of Georgian Bay.

The Ottawa lived like other Great Lakes ALGONQUIANS—surviving through a combination of hunting in the forests, fishing in the lakes and rivers, gathering wild rice in the marshes, and, when conditions allowed, planting crops in cultivated fields (see NORTHEAST INDIANS). They shared many typical Algonquian beliefs—for example, in Manitou, the Great Spirit—but they had their own unique legends and traditions too. Their creation myth tells the story of their descent from three different creatures—Michabou, the Great Hare; Namepich, the Carp; and the Bear's Paw.

After the arrival of Europeans, the Ottawa became noted in two connections: first as traders, then as the tribe that produced one of the great Indian leaders, Pontiac. Their fame as traders came about while the French controlled much of North America, up until 1763. Their name, pronounced AHT-uh-wuh, means "to trade" or "at-home-anywhere people." (An alternate spelling, preferred by most tribal members, is *Odawa*, singular, or *Odawak*, plural.) The name was given to the river that runs through what was once their territory and which now separates Quebec from Ontario in Canada. (The name also was given to the capital city of Canada.) The Ottawa River was a main trade route for Indians and Frenchmen alike. It probably had more canoes going up and down it than any other river in history.

The Ottawa were part of the Great Huron Trade Circle. They supplied furs to HURON (WYANDOT) middlemen, who took them to the French in Quebec and Montreal and then returned to pay off the Indians with European trade goods. After 1649, when the IROQUOIS (HAUDENOSAUNEE) defeated the Huron, the Ottawa took over as middlemen. Now it was their turn to deal directly with the French, bartering furs for European-made knives, hatchets, tomahawks, pipes, cloth, beads, kettles, and paints.

But in 1660, the Iroquois (Haudenosaunee) defeated and dispersed the Ottawa too, breaking up

Ottawa birch-bark dish

their trade monopoly. The Ottawa took refuge in the west, fleeing in their boats to the islands off Green Bay. Some eventually went farther west to Keweenaw Bay in Lake Superior. Others passed overland as far as the Mississippi River, carrying their light birch-bark canoes between streams. This group migrated again because of attacks by SIOUX (DAKOTA, LAKOTA, NAKOTA). They ended up on Chequamegon Bay in northern Wisconsin. Ten years later in 1670, when the French promised to protect them from the Iroquois, many Ottawa returned to Manitoulin Island. Many also joined their old trading partners, the Huron, who were now at Mackinac in present-day Michigan. Michigan's northern lower peninsula became an adopted Ottawa homeland.

Yet these were just some of many migrations for Ottawa people. In the years to follow, most lives and homelands would be disrupted with increasing non-Indian settlement.

Pontiac's Rebellion

The French and Indian wars, from 1689 to 1763, pitted for the most part French and Algonquians against English and Iroquois. The Ottawa were loyal allies of the French. But both Quebec and Montreal fell to British forces, and French forces in Europe lost important battles. By the time the French signed the Treaty of Paris in 1763, which officially gave their North American territory (called New France) to Britain, British troops had marched in and taken control of the French forts in the Great Lakes country.

In the spring, summer, and fall of that year, an Ottawa chief by the name of Pontiac led an uprising of many Old Northwest tribes that came to be known as Pontiac's Rebellion. Pontiac, an energetic and dynamic man, resented having new landlords. He had a solid trade relationship with the French. In his experience, French fur traders generally treated Indians as equals whereas British settlers acted superior. Lord Jeffrey Amherst, the British commander in chief for America, was especially arrogant toward Indians. He was also stingy with supplies. Pontiac, who had previously fought alongside the French against the British, believed that if the Indians could unite, they could win French support and have enough forces to drive the British from the Great Lakes once and for all. Pontiac traveled among and sent messages to the tribes of the region to urge Indian unity.

A LENNI LENAPE (DELAWARE) Indian known as the Delaware Prophet helped Pontiac in his cause. A spell-binding orator like Pontiac, he claimed that Manitou, or the Great Spirit, had communicated with him to bring about a united Indian country where Indians could practice traditional ways. But whereas Delaware Prophet preached against guns, Pontiac considered force necessary to defeat the British.

After much planning, Pontiac and his warriors began a siege of Fort Detroit. He also sent messages—wampum belts calling for war—to chiefs of other tribes. Fighting broke out all over the region. Many tribes participated. In addition to Pontiac's Ottawa, Chippewa, KICKAPOO, ILLINOIS, MIAMI, Potawatomi, SENECA, and SHAWNEE made attacks on outlying settlements as well as on forts. About 2,000 settlers died during the rebellion. Many British posts surrendered to the Indian forces: Fort Sandusky, Fort St. Joseph (now Niles, Michigan), Fort Miami (Fort Wayne, Indiana), Fort Ouiatenon (Lafayette, Indiana), Fort Michilimackinac (Mackinac, Michigan), Fort Edward Augustus (Green Bay, Wisconsin), Fort Venango (Franklin, Pennsylvania), Fort Le Boeuf (Waterford, Pennsylvania), and Fort Presqu' Isle (Erie, Pennsylvania).

The allied Indians also were victorious at Point Pelee on Lake Erie, stopping supply boats on their way to Detroit and killing 56 whites, and at Bloody Run, just outside the fort, killing 54 British troops. The only major British victory was at Bushy Run, south of Lake Erie outside Fort Pitt (Pittsburgh, Pennsylvania). Nevertheless, despite these Indian victories, the British ultimately won the war.

Part of the reason Pontiac's Rebellion failed is that the two most important British forts did not surrender: Fort Detroit and Fort Pitt. The defenders at Fort Pitt used an early form of biological warfare to hold out against the siege. At Amherst's suggestion, the defending garrison sent out smallpox-infected blankets and handkerchiefs, starting an epidemic among the Indians that summer. Meanwhile, at Detroit, the schooner *Huron* broke through Indian lines with fresh men and supplies.

To Pontiac's dismay, the Indians began to lose interest in the siege of Detroit. The French never delivered the help they had led the Indians to expect. And with winter coming, men became worried about providing food for their families. The warriors dispersed.

Pontiac clung to his cause for some time to come. He traveled farther west, where there were fewer forts and fewer settlers. He continued to preach Indian unity. Then in 1766, he negotiated a peace accord with Sir William Johnson, friend to the MOHAWK, and was pardoned by British officials. He returned to his village on the Maumee River. During a trip west to Illinois in 1769, he was killed by an Illinois Indian, who, it is thought, was in the pay of the British. Although Pontiac had been counseling peace to younger, hot-blooded members of his band, the British had continued to distrust him and to fear his great leadership abilities. Pontiac would also be remembered by many great Indian leaders to follow. Men such as Joseph Brant (see MOHAWK), Little Turtle (see MIAMI), Tecumseh (see SHAWNEE), and Black Hawk (see SAC) would also call for unity among the tribes of the Old Northwest, but not against the British. The new enemy would be the Americans.

Three Homelands

The Ottawa living in Michigan had to struggle against non-Indian encroachment to hold on to their ever-shrinking land base. One group agreed to land cessions in exchange for reservation lands in Kansas, where they lived from 1831 to 1867, after which they were relocated to a small tract in the northeastern Indian Territory. They now are federally recognized as the Ottawa Tribe of Oklahoma. Of those Ottawa bands still on Michigan's lower peninsula, only the Grand Traverse band of Ottawa and Chippewa has federal trust status and resulting benefits. Other bands are seeking federal recognition. The Ottawa in Ontario have a number of small reserves on Manitoulin Island and Cockburn Island. In recent years, there has been renewed tribal unity among the various groups and a resurgence in traditional Ottawa culture.

PAIUTE

The Paiute, or Piute, included many different bands, spread out over a vast region. Based on varying dialects, they are usually organized into two distinct groups: the Northern Paiute (also called Numu or Paviotso) and the Southern Paiute. The northern branch occupied territory that is now northwestern Nevada, southeastern Oregon, southwestern Idaho, and northeastern California. The southern branch lived in territory now part of western Utah, southern Nevada, northwestern Arizona, and southeastern California. The Owens Valley Paiute, living along the eastern slope of the Sierra Nevada in southeastern California, sometimes are discussed as a third branch.

The varying dialects of the Northern and Southern Paiute belong to the Uto-Aztecan language family, related to the SHOSHONE dialect. The name *Paiute,* pronounced PIE-oot, is thought to mean "true Ute" or "water Ute," also indicating an ancestral relationship with the UTE.

Lifeways

The Paiute as a whole are considered part of the Great Basin Culture Area (see GREAT BASIN INDIANS). Nomadic Paiute bands wandered the rugged and arid Great Basin in search of whatever small game and wild plant life they could find, sometimes venturing into the highlands surrounding the desert lowlands—roughly the Rocky Mountains to the east, the Sierra Nevada to the west, the Columbia Plateau to the north, and the Colorado Plateau to the south.

For the Paiute bands, their activities and whereabouts in the course of a year were dictated by the availability of food. They traveled a great deal, constructing temporary huts of brush and reeds strewn over willow poles, known as wickiups, which were similar to APACHE dwellings. The first plant food available in the springtime was the cattail, growing in marsh ponds. The shoots were eaten raw. Other wild plant foods—roots and greens—soon followed. Spring was also a good time to hunt ducks in ponds on the birds' migration northward, and, in the highlands to the north of the Great Basin, to fish the rivers and streams during annual spawning runs.

In summertime, many more wild plant foods ripened, such as berries and rice grass. The Paiute ground the seeds of the latter into meal. In the autumn, the primary food was pine nuts. The Paiute collected them from piñon trees growing on the hills and plateaus rising above the Great Basin. In the late fall, the Paiute

Paiute wickiup

returned to the desert lowlands to hunt game throughout the winter, especially rabbits. Year-round, they ate whatever else they could forage, such as lizards, grubs, and insects. The Paiute, along with other Great Basin tribes, have been called "Digger Indians" by whites because they dug for many of their foods.

Wars Involving the Northern Paiute

The Northern Paiute are generally considered to have been more warlike than the Southern Paiute and fought in a number of conflicts with non-Indians. At first, in contacts with fur trappers and traders, such as Jedediah Smith in 1825, Peter Skene Ogden in 1827, and Joseph Walker in 1833, the Northern Paiute were friendly. But after gold was discovered in California late in 1848, and miners and migrants began streaming across Indian lands in great numbers, the Northern Paiute turned hostile.

The Northern Paiute played a prominent role as allies of the COEUR D'ALENE in the Coeur d'Alene War of 1858–59. Then the following decade, during the Civil War, while federal troops were busy fighting in the East, the Northern Paiute carried out numerous raids on miners and mining camps; stagecoaches and stage stations; wagon trains and freight caravans; and ranches and farms. Nevada and Oregon volunteers had little success in tracking down the hostile bands. In 1865, after the Civil War, army troops were assigned to forts in the region in an effort to bring peace to the area.

The conflict that followed during 1866–67 is usually called the Snake War. Two Northern Paiute bands, the Walpapi and the Yahooskin, were known collectively to whites as the Snake Indians. Two chiefs, Paulina and Old Weawea, led Snake warriors against troops in lightning-quick raids, after which the Indians would disappear into the highlands. But a rancher and stage driver named James Clark, who fought in many different campaigns, divided his troops into many small tracking patrols that kept constant pressure on the insurgents for a year and a half, forcing about 40 different skirmishes. In one of them, in April 1867, Chief Paulina was killed. Old Weawea eventually surrendered with 800 warriors. Most of them were settled on the Malheur Reservation in Oregon.

Some of these same warriors were caught up in the Bannock War of 1878. When the BANNOCK leader Chief Buffalo Horn was killed in that conflict, two Northern Paiute took over the leadership of the rebels, Chief Egan and the medicine man Oytes.

Other Northern Paiute bands fought in an uprising referred to as the Paiute War (or the Pyramid Lake War). This conflict started just before the Civil War, in 1860, when traders at the Williams Station, a Central Overland Mail and Pony Express station on the California Trial just east of the present-day Nevada-California border, kidnapped and raped two Northern Paiute girls. Warriors attacked and burned the station, killed five whites, and rescued the girls.

Miners in the region organized a volunteer force under Major William Ormsby. But a Northern Paiute chief named Numaga outmaneuvered them at the Big Bend of the Truckee River by having his men hide in sagebrush along the pass and attack from both sides. After this defeat, control of the military operation was given to a former Texas Ranger, Colonel Jack Hays. He organized a force of 800 Nevada and California volunteers plus some army regulars and tracked the insurgents to Pinnacle Mountain, where he defeated them. He then established Fort Churchill to guard the valley and keep the California Trail open.

The Ghost Dance Religion

The Paiute were indirectly involved in the last significant Indian violence to erupt in the West. In 1888–89, a Northern Paiute from Nevada by the name of Wovoka (also known as Jack Wilson) founded a religion called the Ghost Dance. He was the son of another mystic, Tavibo (or Numu-tibo'o), and was influenced by his father's teachings, as well as those of a prophet on the nearby Walker River Reservation named Wodziwob. Wovoka experienced a vision during an eclipse of the Sun and afterward began preaching that the earth would soon perish, then come alive again in a natural state, with lush prairie grass and huge herds of buffalo. There would be no more whites. American Indians, as well as their dead ancestors, would inherit this new world.

Wovoka believed that in order to bring about this new existence, Indians had to purge themselves of the white's ways, especially alcohol, and live together harmoniously. He also called for meditation, prayer, chanting, and, most of all, dancing. He claimed that Indians could catch a glimpse of this future paradise by performing the Ghost Dance.

The Ghost Dance Religion spread to tribes all over the West, especially Shoshone, ARAPAHO, and SIOUX (DAKOTA, LAKOTA, NAKOTA). Some of the Sioux Ghost Dance leaders called for violence against the whites, claiming that magical Ghost Dance Shirts could protect the Indians from bullets. This new found faith and militancy indirectly led up to the massacre of a Sioux band by soldiers at Wounded Knee in 1890.

The Winnemuccas

The name *Winnemucca* supposedly is derived from an incident in which the Northern Paiute Truckee, who served as a scout for John C. Frémont in his 1845–46 explorations of California, was seen wearing one moccasin, or "one *muck*," in his dialect. Truckee, or Winnemucca, who knew both English and Spanish, regularly acted as interpreter between non-Indians and Paiute bands. His son also became known as Winnemucca (later Old Winnemucca). During the Paiute War of 1860, in which militants were led by his nephew Numaga, the son Winnemucca kept his band at peace, leading them from Nevada to Yakima, Washington. In 1879–80, he traveled to Washington, D.C., with his daughter Sarah Winnemucca in an unsuccessful attempt to allow his band to live on the Malheur Reservation in Oregon rather than in Washington. Sarah Winnemucca went on to become a well-known lecturer on Indian issues, as well as an author of the book *Life Among the Paiutes, Their Wrongs and Claims* (1883). She also became known as an educator of Indian children.

Contemporary Paiute

Contemporary Northern Paiute have reservation lands in Nevada, California, and Oregon. Southern Paiute presently have reservations in Nevada, Utah, and Arizona. Some of these holdings they share with other tribes, especially the Shoshone. Many Paiute also live off-reservation in these states.

A Nevada Paiute by the name of Melvin Thom helped found the National Indian Youth Council (NIYC) in 1961, along with Clyde Warrior, a PONCA, and other young Native Americans. Operating out of Albuquerque, New Mexico, the NIYC works on behalf of Native American Youth and Indian nations.

PALEO-INDIANS *see* PREHISTORIC INDIANS

PALOUSE

The Appaloosa breed of horse, with its distinctive spotted coat and its renowned intelligence, speed, and stamina, is named after one of the tribes that developed the breed—the Palouse. Members of this tribe occupied ancestral territory along the Palouse River on lands that now include parts of eastern Washington State and northern Idaho. Horses, brought to North America by the Spanish, reached this part of North America by the early 1700s, after which the Palouse, NEZ PERCE, CAYUSE, and other tribes of the region became famous as horse breeders and horse traders.

The Palouse, or Palus (both pronounced puh-LOOS), are thought to have once been one people with the YAKAMA, another tribe speaking a dialect of the Sahaptian language family, part of the Penutian phylum. They also had close ties with the Nez Perce. It was among the Nez Perce that the Lewis and Clark Expedition first saw Appaloosa horses in 1805. These tribes and others on the Columbia Plateau depended heavily on fishing in the many rivers draining toward the Pacific Ocean, and they are considered part of the Plateau Culture Area (see PLATEAU INDIANS).

The Palouse played an important part in the heavy fur trade among whites and the tribes of the American Northwest during the first half of the 1800s. But with increased non-Indian settlement by the mid-1800s, the Palouse joined other tribes in their stand for ancestral lands. Palouse warriors fought as allies to the Cayuse and COEUR D'ALENE in the Cayuse War of 1847–50 and the Coeur d'Alene War of 1858.

The Palouse as a tribe declined to lead the reservation life forced on many tribes of the region. Some individuals did, however, join their Penutian kinsmen on reservations, such as the Colville Reservation in northeastern Washington, with both Sahaptian and Salishan peoples.

PAPAGO *see* TOHONO O'ODHAM (PAPAGO)

PASSAMAQUODDY

The Passamaquoddy, like the PENOBSCOT, are often discussed under the more general heading of ABENAKI Indians. These Algonquian-speaking people of present-day northern Maine were part of the Abenaki Confederacy. Their history, especially their participation in the Abenaki Wars (the New England phase of the French and Indian wars), is similar to that of other Abenaki, and their culture resembles that of other New England ALGONQUIANS. Their closest ancestral relatives, based on dialects, were the MALISEET.

Passamaquoddy, pronounced pah-suh-muh-KWOD-ee, means "those who pursue the pollock," in reference to their fishing. Although the Passamaquoddy were hunter-gatherers as well as farmers, they depended more on fishing than many other NORTHEAST INDIANS, taking advantage of the numerous lakes, rivers, and bays in their territory. The Passamaquoddy Bay in Maine, a major source of their food, bears their name.

The two existing Passamaquoddy reservations—Pleasant Point and Indian Township—are near the town of Calais, Maine. This is the easternmost land in the United States held by Native Americans. As stated in the ABENAKI entry, the name *Abenaki* means "those living at the sunrise" or "easterners."

Passamaquoddy knife for basketmaking

In 1980, the Passamaquoddy and the Penobscot won a judgment against the state of Maine in the Maine Indian Claims Settlement Act. The federal and state governments granted them $81.5 million as repayment for lands unfairly taken away from them by early settlers. With their share, the Passamaquoddy Tribe have purchased land and invested in tribal businesses, such as the Waponahki Resource Center and Sipayik Museum on the Pleasant Point Reservation.

PAWNEE

The Pawnee name, pronounced PAW-nee or paw-NEE, probably comes from the Caddoan word *pariki,* meaning "horn," after the upright and curved scalplock hairstyle particular to the tribe. Or their name might be derived from the word *parisu,* meaning "hunter."

The Pawnee split off from other Caddoan-speaking peoples and migrated northward from what is now Texas, first to the Red River region of southern Oklahoma, and then to the Arkansas River region of northern Oklahoma and southern Kansas. They may have been the first Native American on the Great Plains since much earlier PREHISTORIC INDIANS. The Pawnee lived there when early Spanish explorers pushing northeastward out of Mexico—such as Francisco de Coronado in 1541 and Juan de Oñate in 1601—encountered them.

By the early 1700s, the Pawnee had divided into four major bands: The Skidi (or Skiri or Wolf); the Chaui (or Grand); the Kitkahahki (or Republican); and the Pitahawirata (or Tapage or Noisy). The latter three, speaking a similar dialect, came to be called Southern Pawnee (or Black Pawnee). They stayed along the Arkansas River for much of their history. The Skidi Pawnee migrated farther north to the Platte River, the Loup River, and the Republican Fork of the Kansas River in what is now Nebraska. They sometimes are referred to as Northern Pawnee.

Relations with Non-Indians

During the 1700s, French traders made regular stops at Southern Pawnee villages to trade guns, tools, and other European trade items for buffalo robes and other animal pelts. Caddoan relatives of the Pawnee—the CADDO and WICHITA—were central to French trade west of the Mississippi River. Other Caddoan relatives, the ARIKARA, also had important trading villages on the upper Missouri.

When France lost its holdings in North America in 1763 after the French and Indian wars, the fur trade declined for the Missouri River Indians. In 1770, the Southern Pawnee migrated northward to join the Skidi Pawnee.

The opening of the American frontier after the Louisiana Purchase of 1803 brought more and more settlers to the lands of the Pawnee. From the very outset, the Pawnee were peaceful in their relations with the newcomers. In addition to trade advantages from this friendship, the Pawnee wanted allies against their traditional enemies—the SIOUX (DAKOTA, LAKOTA, NAKOTA), CHEYENNE, ARAPAHO, KIOWA, and COMANCHE—who often raided Pawnee villages and vice versa. (One Sioux warrior bore the name "Pawnee Killer," because of his deeds in battle against the Pawnee.)

The fact that the Pawnee were allies and friends of the settlers did not stop whites from taking their lands. By the mid-1800s, tribal representatives had signed a number of treaties giving all their territory to the United States, except for a reservation along the banks of the Loup River near present-day Fullerton, Nebraska.

Even so, the Pawnee continued to support the whites against other Indians in the wars for the plains. They

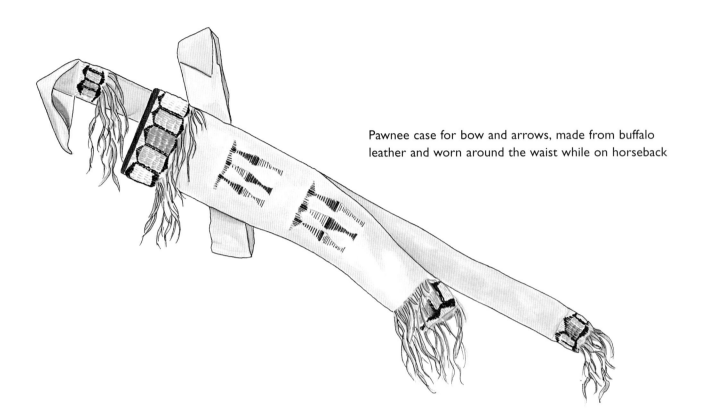

Pawnee case for bow and arrows, made from buffalo leather and worn around the waist while on horseback

became the most famous of all Indian scouts for the U.S. Army under Frank and Luther North, who organized a battalion of Pawnee scouts active from 1865 to 1885. Other Pawnee under Sky Chief worked as guards for railroad construction crews.

The tribe's assistance to whites angered other Native Americans. In 1873, a Sioux war party ambushed a Pawnee hunting party in southern Nebraska and killed 150, including Sky Chief, before an army detachment came to the rescue. The site of this incident became known as Massacre Canyon.

Despite their great contribution and sacrifice on behalf of the United States, the Pawnee were pressured into giving up their Nebraska reservation in 1876. They were relocated to the Indian Territory (Oklahoma), where their descendants live today near the city of Pawnee.

Lifeways

The Pawnee are an intriguing cultural mix. Since they lived in permanent villages much of the year and farmed, they are classified as part of the Prairie group of the Great Plains Culture Area (see PRAIRIE INDIANS and PLAINS INDIANS). They were such skillful farmers that some varieties of their seeds are still used by modern farmers. When in their villages, the Pawnee lived in earth lodges, unlike their kinsmen the Caddo and Wichita, who lived in grass houses. While on the trail in pursuit of buffalo, however, the Pawnee lived in tipis. After they had acquired horses, they roamed far from their homeland to hunting grounds in Wyoming and New Mexico. They shared many other customs of the Prairie and Plains tribes, such as several rituals surrounding the growing of corn and the buffalo hunt.

Pawnee skull representing the First Man

But the Pawnee also possessed cultural traits similar to the early MOUND BUILDERS of the Southeast and by extension to Mesoamerican cultures. They even kept these traits longer than their relatives the Caddo, who are classified among SOUTHEAST INDIANS.

Pawnee religion had a strict and complex structure. Their medicine men constituted a whole class of people, like a priesthood. These priests were responsible for many elaborate ceremonies, made up of songs, poetry, and dances, all rich in symbolism concerning the heavenly bodies. Like the AZTEC and the Mound Builders, the Pawnee can be called Sun-worshipers and Moon-worshipers.

There was one Skidi Pawnee custom that was especially unusual for Indians north of Mexico in the historic period—the practice of human sacrifice. As late as the early 1800s, the Pawnee still performed what they called the Morning Star Ceremony. The Skidi Pawnee believed that the supreme god was Tirawa, the Sun. Tirawa and Mother Earth conceived Morning Star, the God of Vegetation. Once a year, the Skidi Pawnee would raid another tribe with the purpose of capturing a young girl about 13 years old. They would let this girl live among them for months, treating her with kindness and keeping secret from her their plans. Early in the morning at the time of the summer solstice, the longest day of the year, the priests would paint half the maiden's body red, for day, and the other half black, for night. Then they would tie her to a rectangular frame in the fields outside the village. As the morning star rose, three priests would perform the sacrificial murder with a torch, an arrow, and a knife. Then every male who could handle a bow would shoot arrows into the body. The corpse was left behind to fertilize the earth. The tribe then held a festival of dancing and singing.

Not all Pawnee approved of this terrible act passed down among priests over the centuries. Finally, one

Pawnee chief was brave enough to stop it. His name was Petalesharo ("Man-Chief"). In 1816, when he was only 19, he rescued a Comanche girl from the scaffold at the last minute and commanded the priests to stop their barbarism and cruelty. Other warriors backed him up despite the priests' threats of placing curses on them. Petalesharo became a hero of future generations of Pawnee for standing up to the powerful priesthood.

Contemporary Pawnee

The Pawnee hold trust lands in Pawnee County, Oklahoma. Others live in and around Fullerton, Nebraska. In recent times, there has been a resurgence of traditional customs, with many tribal members participating in dances passed down from earlier generations.

It is thought that the dancing at modern-day pow-wows evolved out of a 19th-century ceremony of the Pawnee, the Irushka (or Iruska, "they are inside the fire"), sponsored by a medicine society, the members of which specialized in healing burns. Irushka dancers wore a special roach, or hairlock, symbolizing fire, and a belt supposedly given to humans by the Crow People to help overcome the fire. The dance was passed to the OMAHA, who called it the Hedushka and used braided grass tails to symbolize scalps taken in warfare. Other Plains tribes developed their own variations and symbolism, but always with the roach and belt. In modern times, the variations evolved into competitive and athletic fancy dancing, with elaborate headdresses and bustles.

In 1973, the Pawnee John Echohawk became the first Indian director of the Native American Rights Fund (NARF), an Indian rights organization providing legal representation for individuals and tribes. NARF, founded in 1970, operates out of Boulder, Colorado, with branch offices in Washington, D.C., and Anchorage, Alaska.

PEND D'OREILLE   see KALISPEL

PENNACOOK

The ancestral homeland of the Pennacook has since become the state of New Hampshire. The Pennacook also had hunting grounds in what now is western Maine, northern Massachusetts, and estern Vermont. Many different ALGONQUIANS, with different band names, living in the region have been grouped together under the general name of Pennacook, which was the name of a band and village at the site of present-day Concord, now the capital of the state. *Pennacook,* pronounced PEN-uh-cook, means "at the bottom of the hill." The various Pennacook bands are sometimes classified with the ABENAKI of Maine, with whom they were allied in a confederacy for part of their history. The Abenaki and Pennacook are classified as part of the Northeast Culture Area (see NORTHEAST INDIANS).

If one travels through New Hampshire, and all New England, one notices many towns and geographical features bearing Algonquian-derived names. Each place-name has a story that can shed light on Native American history, legend, and custom. For example, there is a town of Penacook and a lake called Penacook.

There are hundreds more Indian names across the granite-and-birch landscape of New Hampshire. A road through the Sandwich Range along the state's southern border, connecting Conway and Lincoln, is called the Kancamagus Highway. This name honors the last sachem, or chief, of the Pennacook; one of the mountains in the Sandwich Range also bears his name. Other mountains nearby in the same range bear the name of Paugus and Passaconaway.

In 1675, at the time of King Philip's War, led by King Philip of the WAMPANOAG, Kancamagus decided to keep the peace with the British colonists. His cousin Paugus, however, favored the path of war. Both men were grandsons of Passaconaway, the first Pennacook sachem to establish relations and trade with the British settlers.

The British tricked some of the peaceful bands into coming to a sporting meet at Dover. Then the whites attacked, killed, and captured many of their guests and sold many into slavery. At that time, Kancamagus became an enemy of the British. Years later in 1689, at the beginning of the French and Indian wars between England and France, Kancamagus found his revenge, with an attack on the settlement of Dover. A Pennacook woman tricked the settlers into leaving the gates of their stockade open. Many settlers died in the ensuing fight.

In retaliation, the British convinced their allies the MOHAWK to attack the Pennacook. They swept in from the west and destroyed many Pennacook villages. Kancamagus and his warriors took up positions behind log walls at Lake Winnisquam (an Algonquian name referring to the salmon there). The Pennacook repelled the attackers, then snuck away at night. This place of battle today has an Indian name—Mohawk Point. Then Kancamagus led his people through the mountains, following much of the route the Kancamagus highway now takes, to the Connecticut Valley and on to Quebec, in Canada, where they joined up with the Abenaki at St. Francis. (*Connecticut* is also an Indian name, meaning "the long river.")

Other place-names speak of Indian legends. One such location is Squaw Cove in Big Squam Lake (meaning "big salmon lake"). A granite boulder that once stood along the shore resembled a crouching woman. Legend has it that an old Indian sachem wanted a young bride and chose a girl named Suneta. But Suneta loved a young warrior by the name of Anonis. Anonis, far away at the time, could not make it back in time to prevent the wedding. After the wedding feast, the old sachem fell asleep. A storm arose on the lake. Suneta, alone in her wigwam, wept quietly. Anonis suddenly appeared out of the rain and darkness. He beckoned Suneta to flight. They would start a new life elsewhere. But as they hurried off, the sachem awoke. He strung his bow and shot Anonis in the back. Suneta, heartbroken, ran to the shore, crouched down, and prayed to Manitou, the Great Spirit, asking to be saved from her fate. At daybreak, when the storm had passed, the figure of Suneta still crouched on the shore. But she had been turned to granite. The rock became known as Squaw Rock.

Still other place-names tell of Indian customs. Those with animal or fish names, like Lake Winnisquam and Big Squam Lake, indicate that the Pennacook once came there in search of salmon for food. Another example is the place called Indian Leap along the Lost River Highway near Franconia Notch. Over the centuries, a stream has worn large potholes in the granite boulders, forming deep pools and high ledges. It is reported that Indians brought young boys to this spot to test their courage. They would have to jump from boulder to boulder, along the jagged points jutting out over the dark, cold pools 20 feet below. A slip would mean death or injury. Supposedly, those who hesitated were not ready for warfare. But those who leaped fearlessly would one day be great warriors.

Pennacook descendants live among the Abenaki at Odanak (St. Francis) and Wollinak (Bécancour) in Quebec. A band known as the Pennacook New Hampshire Tribe operates out of Manchester, New Hampshire, in their ancestral homeland.

PENOBSCOT

The Penobscot also are known as ABENAKI. They belonged to the Abenaki Confederacy and had language, culture, and history in common with other bands classified as Eastern Abenaki. But their descendants use their more specific band name, *Penobscot,* pronounced puh-NOB-scot, from *Panawahpskek,* meaning "rocky place" or "where the rocks spread out," and refers to rocky falls in the river where their ancestors lived and where they still live today. Like many towns and geographical features in the United States and Canada, the river bears an Indian name—their own name, Penobscot—as does the bay it feeds.

The following is a typical year on the life of Penobscot families and by extension other ALGONQUIANS of northern New England (see NORTHEAST INDIANS).

Winter

Winter, of course, was the hardest time. Food was scarce. Families had to leave the central Penobscot village of square houses with pyramid roofs plus cone-shaped wigwams and follow game animals into the snow-laden forests. Since no one area could support too many people, each family had its own hunting grounds. With everyone dressed warmly in furs and sometimes wearing foxskin hats, a father and mother would paddle their children and possessions in a birch-bark canoe, then carry the canoe the rest of the way over land. Sometimes they even carried fire in a shell inside a deerskin bag since fires were so hard to start with only the friction method of rubbing sticks.

Once established in their camp, having constructed their temporary wigwams and lean-tos, the father set out to track or trap whatever game, large or small, he could. Boys who were old enough to take care of themselves on the trail might accompany him, wearing snowshoes like their father's. Deer or elk was a favorite catch. Hunters wore deerskins, with the horns on their heads, in order to trick the swift animals. Sometimes a deadfall—a trap designed to drop a heavy weight on an animal—would prove more successful than an arrow or spear. The Penobscot did not shun dangerous game either, like bears. One method of catching the eastern brown bears was to throw a piece of wood at the animals when they reared up to attack. When the bears went to catch the wood with their deadly front claws, hunters could strike them on the head with a club. If lucky enough to capture game too big to carry, they could drag it back to camp on toboggans.

In the meantime, the women were working hard—keeping the fire going, cooking and storing food, curing leather, sewing furs, and making containers. Little girls had to learn these crafts at a young age. Survival depended on everyone doing his or her job. And when the game ran out in one area, the family had to move on, but not so far as to encroach on some other family's territory.

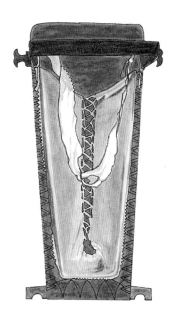

Penobscot cradleboard

Spring and Summer

The various families returned to their permanent villages along the river in the spring and summer. After the cramped quarters of the winter camps, the larger village lodges and wigwams seemed roomy and comfortable. The villages were surrounded by upright log walls, or palisades, as protection from raiding enemies, such as the MOHAWK to the west.

In early spring, the Penobscot harvested the sap from the maple trees and boiled it to make maple syrup. Then, when the ground thawed and early morning freezes stopped, they cultivated the rocky northern soil to plant their gardens. Corn was the staple crop. The first harvest came as early as July. But even during the mild months, when plant foods were available, the Penobscot men left the village to hunt. And they fished the river, using harpoons and nets. In the difficult Penobscot existence, there was never too much food. Any excess could be preserved by various means—drying in the sun, or smoking, to help endure the long winter months. Now that the weather was milder, children had more time to play games and make toys. Quite often their games, such as throwing a spear at a hoop, served to develop later survival skills.

One of the favorite times of year was the summer trip down the Penobscot River to the Atlantic Ocean. Here, the Penobscot had a change of diet—clams, lobsters, crabs, and possibly even seals. And the children rode the surf as children today do on summer trips to the beach. There was time for socializing and for rituals—song and dance and communication with the spirits of nature that the Penobscot believed provided their food.

Fall

Work was continuous. In the fall, families, back in their villages, made final preparations for the winter journey—preserving food, making and repairing weapons, utensils, and clothing. This was also a good time for moose hunting, because the animals began to travel farther in search of food.

Contemporary Penobscot

Penobscot families still live on their ancestral homeland—at Indian Island, the Penobscot reservation on the Penobscot River, next to Old Town, Maine. In 1980, the Penobscot and Passamaquoddy were granted a settlement of $81.5 million from the state and federal government because of lands unfairly appropriated by non-Indian settlers. The Penobscot have used part of the

Penobscot basket (modern)

settlement to purchase additional land and invest in tribally run businesses. Another portion is in a trust fund, from which tribal members receive quarterly dividends. They now operate the Penobscot Nation Museum at Indian Island.

PEQUOT

For early Indians southern New England was choice territory. First, this part of North America has good topsoil for growing corn, beans, and squash. The soil of the lower Connecticut River valley and along Narragansett Bay is especially fertile. Second, the forests, with all kinds of hardwood and evergreen trees, are a good environment for all sorts of game. And third, unlike the east shore in northern New England that faces the Atlantic, the south shore is sheltered from the elements. Long Island, which extends eastward into the Atlantic Ocean, protects much of the coast from the heavy winds and large waves of the open ocean. Block Island, Fishers Island, Martha's Vineyard, and Nantucket also break the path of storms, as do numerous smaller islands. As a result, in the southern part of all three states touching the south shore—Connecticut, Rhode Island, and Massachusetts—there are many quiet bays and inlets, with fish and shellfish for the taking.

Various groups of ALGONQUIANS competed for this rich territory (see NORTHEAST INDIANS). One of the most powerful and warlike tribes was the Pequot. Their ancestors supposedly had migrated from the Hudson River valley in present-day New York State, perhaps breaking off from the MAHICAN. They fought with other Algonquians, both the NARRAGANSETT and Niantic, for land. At the time of contact with the Puritans and other English colonists in the early 1600s, the Pequot con-

trolled most of the coastal area from the Connecticut River to Rhode Island. They had even attacked and defeated many of the MONTAUK bands on Long Island. No wonder they were known as the Pequot, pronounced PEE-kwot, meaning "destroyers."

At the time of Pequot dominance, Sassacus was the grand sachem, or great chief. His village was situated on the Thames River. He had 26 subordinate chiefs, each with his own palisaded village of wigwams. One of these lesser chiefs, Uncas, was dissatisfied with Sassacus's rule and broke off to form his own tribe, who came to be known as the MOHEGAN. The Mohegan became allies of the colonists. But Sassacus and his followers resented the growing presence of the British settlers, leading to disputes over land and trade goods.

The Pequot War

War broke out in 1636, the first major Indian-white conflict in New England. The death of a coastal trader, John Oldham, in July of that year caused the outbreak of violence. Another coastal trader, John Gallup, discovered Oldham's hijacked boat off Block Island, skirmished with the Pequot on board, then reported the incident to colonial officials.

Massachusetts Bay Colony ordered out an expedition under John Endecott. His force attacked Indians on

Block Island and burned their villages. But many of those killed were Narragansett, not Pequot. The soldiers did not bother to distinguish among the various Algonquian peoples.

Endecott's army then sailed to the Connecticut mainland in search of Pequot. The settlers at Fort Saybrook tried to talk Endecott out of further attacks because they feared Indian reprisals. But Endecott was intent on revenge and burned several Pequot villages, killing one man.

Sassacus now sought revenge. During the winter of 1636–37, his warriors laid siege to Fort Saybrook and raided isolated settlements. In the spring, they killed nine colonists at Wethersfield, up the Connecticut River.

The colonies mounted a large army under Captains John Mason and John Underhill. The force sailed westward along the Connecticut coast, then circled back, overland, from Narragansett Bay. Despite the attack on their people on Block Island, Narragansett joined the colonial force against their enemies the Pequot, as did Mohegan and Niantic.

At dawn on May 25, 1637, the invading army attacked Sassacus's village. Fighting from behind their palisades, the Pequot repelled the first attack. But the colonists managed to set the wigwams on fire. Those who fled the flames were cut down in the surrounding countryside. Those who stayed behind, mostly women and children, burned to death. From 600 to 1,000 Pequot died that morning. Sassacus and others escaped. His group was attacked in a swamp west of New Haven the following July, but he managed to escape again, seeking refuge in MOHAWK territory. To prove that they had no part in the Pequot uprising, the Mohawk beheaded the Pequot grand sachem.

Pequot captives were sold into slavery in the Caribbean or given as slaves to the Mohegan, Narragansett, and Niantic as payment for their help in the war. The colonists no longer permitted the use of the Pequot tribal name or the use of Pequot place-names. Some Pequot escaped to Long Island and Massachusetts, where they settled with other Algonquians. In 1655, the colonists freed Pequot slaves in New England and resettled them on the Mystic River.

The Pequot Bands

In 1651, the Mashantucket (Mushantuxet), also known as the Western Pequot, received a land grant of 500 acres at Noank (New London). In 1666, they received an additional parcel on the northwest side of Long Pond at present-day Ledyard. By 1720, they had relocated to the more productive Long Pond piece. In 1683, the Paucatuck, or Eastern Pequot, also were given land, their parcel along the eastern shore of Long Pond in North Stonington, Connecticut. For a time, the Mashantucket were known as the Groton band, and the Paucatuck as the Stonington band. Over the next years, with ongoing pressures from non-Indian settlers around them, both bands lost much of their acreage. Some tribal members also resettled elsewhere, some at Schaghticoke (Scaticook), founded by the Pequot Mahwee in the early 18th century, becoming known as the Schaghticoke Indian Tribe. Others settled among a community of Mohegan at Trumbull, Connecticut, becoming known as the Golden Hill Pequot and Mohegan Tribes.

By the late 1800s, the Mashantucket and Paucatuck each held less than 250 acres. In the 1970s, the Mashantucket began seeking federal recognition and made land claims against the state of Connecticut. In 1983, the Mashantucket became federally recognized and won a cash settlement for their land losses. The Paucatuck have been unsuccessful in their attempts for recognition, largely due to the unwillingness of factions within the band to work together.

Indian Gaming

Games of chance have been played for centuries by Native Americans. In guessing games like hidden-ball game, stick game, moccasin game, and handgame participants tried to guess the location of hidden objects, often betting prized possessions. Moreover, there were many different varieties of dice among Indian peoples. Pieces of wood, stone, bone, shell, reed, or fruit seeds were marked or numbered. Guessing games and dice games were often a part of harvest and renewal ceremonies. Indians also bet on footraces and horse races.

Modern Indian gaming for profit, because of laws promoting Indian sovereignty on reservations, has become one of the major areas of tribal economic development. The earliest form of public gaming on many reservations was bingo. In 1976, the U.S. Supreme Court ruled that states have criminal and civil jurisdiction over Indian tribes but do not have regulatory powers over them. In 1987, the Supreme Court upheld a Florida ruling regarding the SEMINOLE, holding that because states lack regulatory authority on Indian lands, state laws against gambling cannot be enforced against tribes. Then in 1988, Congress passed the Indian

Gambling Regulatory Act, granting tribes the right to pursue compacts with states for high-stakes gaming if the activity is not prohibited by federal or state laws. The National Indian Gaming Commission was established to ensure that the tribes and not individuals would profit from the gambling. Indian tribes thus had the right to purchase additional lands and start business on them that also become exempt from federal taxes. Many tribes have pursued the new potential for revenue. In some instances, tribal traditionalists have opposed the building of casinos on Indian lands because of the resulting cultural and environmental impact. They make the case that Native Americans are stewards of the land and should not develop it for the leisure industry.

After having reached a compact with the state of Connecticut—which included a provision that slot machines would be permitted if $1 million a year was donated from gambling profits to a state fund for helping troubled communities—the Mashantucket Pequot, with funds from international investors, constructed the Foxwoods Resort and Casino. It opened in 1992 and soon became more profitable than any one casino in Las Vegas or Atlantic City. The tribe has managed its revenues well, providing solid income for individual tribal members and reinvesting in a cultural center, museum, and other projects furthering the Pequot identity.

PIEGAN   *see* BLACKFEET

PIMA   *see* AKIMEL O'ODHAM (PIMA)

PLAINS INDIANS

Even those people who know little about Native Americans, their numerous tribes, and many different ways of life, are familiar with the Plains Indians. Their horsemanship buffalo hunting, tipis, and warbonnets are the most commonly represented symbols from Indian history.

Some people think that all Native Americans looked and lived like the Plains Indians. Some people even think that modern Indians still dress and act like the Plains Indians. As this book shows, there was and is a great variety to Native American culture, and it is difficult to generalize about the many different nations.

But why are the Plains Indians, of all the Native Americans, so famous? One reason is that many of the Plains tribes retained their original way of life longer than most other native peoples, through most of the 19th century. Most of the final wave of Indian wars involved the Plains tribes. This is a period of American history re-created time and again in books, movies, and television shows. The Indian fighters of that period captured the national imagination then, as they still do today, for their bravery, skill, and resourcefulness. More-

over, there is something especially romantic about the Plains way of life—freedom of movement and independence on the open range, plus colorful clothing and homes—that still strikes a chord in us.

Who exactly were the Plains Indians? What and where are the plains? The phrase *Plains Indians* is one way to refer to the many tribes of the Great Plains Culture Area. This region, as defined by scholars, extends over a vast area: east to west, from the Mississippi River valley to the Rocky Mountains; north to south, from territory in the present-day Canadian provinces of Manitoba, Saskatchewan, and Alberta all the way to what now is central Texas.

Most of the country in this region is treeless grassland. There are two types of grasslands: that of the Mississippi Valley region, where there is significant rainfall—about 20 to 40 inches—and tall grass; sometimes called the Prairie Plains, or simply the prairies; and that of the west, where there is less rain—about 10 to 20 inches—and short grass; known as the Great Plains, the High Plains, or simply the plains.

The Great Plains Culture Area, showing the approximate locations of Indian tribes listed in this book—circa 1820, after the acquisition of horses and migration onto the Plains, and before displacement by non-Indians (with modern boundaries)

The flat or rolling grasslands are interrupted in places by stands of trees, especially willows and cottonwoods along the numerous rivers flowing eastward into the Missouri and the Mississippi. In some locations, highlands rise up from the plains: the Ozarks of Missouri and Arkansas; the Black Hills of South Dakota and Wyoming; and the Badlands of South Dakota. These mountains, hills, plateaus, and buttes are often dotted by pine trees. Yet what is remarkable about the plains is the sameness—an enormous ocean of grass stretching over thousands of miles.

Many different kinds of animals, both large and small, lived on these grasslands, including antelope, deer, elk, bears, wolves, coyotes, and rabbits. The environment was especially suitable to one grazing animal: the shaggy-maned, short-horned, fleshy-humped, hoofed creature known as the American bison, or the buffalo. The buffalo was central to the Plains Indian economy, providing meat for food, as well as hides, bones, and horns for shelter, clothing, and tools.

The Great Plains Culture Area is different from other Native American culture areas in that the typical Indian way of life evolved only after the arrival of Europeans. What made the nomadic buffalo-hunting life possible was the horse, which was first brought to North America by the Spanish in the 1500s. (Native North American horses had died out in prehistoric times [see PREHISTORIC INDIANS].) SOUTHWEST INDIANS gained widespread use of horses by the late 1600s. And Plains tribes acquired use of the animal in the early to mid-1700s.

Tribes with horses were no longer dependent on farming along the fertile river valleys to supply enough food for their people. Hunters could now range over a wide area in search of the great buffalo herds, carrying their possessions with them. Portable tipis of poles and buffalo hide proved practical for life on the trail. Not all tribes completely abandoned their permanent villages of earth or grass lodges and their farming. But with horses, hunters could leave the villages for longer periods on wide-ranging expeditions.

Many different peoples adopted the new nomadic way of life, migrating onto the plains from different directions. Entire families traveled together. Many of these peoples were being pushed from their ancestral homelands by white settlers or by eastern tribes armed with guns acquired from whites.

Once on the plains, the varying tribes began sharing other customs besides horses, buffalo-hunting, and tipis. They passed on religious rituals and methods of warfare. In order to communicate with one another for purposes of council or trade, Plains Indians also devised a language of the hands. In this shared sign language, each tribe had its own gesture for identification.

Ancient Indians once had lived on the Great Plains. But it is thought they left the region in the 13th century, probably because of drought. The earliest inhabitants in the region after that time might have been the early agricultural tribes of the Missouri River valley: Caddoan-speaking ARIKARA, PAWNEE, and WICHITA (along with the smaller Caddoan groupings, the Kichai, Tawakoni, Tawehash, Waco, and Yscani, who eventually became part of the Wichita Confederacy), and Siouan-speaking HIDATSA and MANDAN. It is thought that there were only two nonfarming tribes on the Great Plains before 1500: the Algonquian-speaking BLACKFEET and the

Uto-Aztecan-speaking COMANCHE. But during the 1600s and 1700s, other tribes came to the region: Algonquian-speaking ARAPAHO, CHEYENNE, GROS VENTRE, and bands of CREE and CHIPPEWA (OJIBWAY)—the latter two tribes referred to as Plains Cree and Plains Ojibway; Kiowa-Tanoan-speaking KIOWA; Athapascan-speaking SARCEE and a band of APACHE, referred to as Kiowa-Apache; Tonkawan-speaking TONKAWA; and the Siouan-speaking ASSINIBOINE, CROW, IOWAY, KAW, MISSOURIA, OMAHA, OSAGE, OTOE, PONCA, QUAPAW, and SIOUX (DAKOTA, LAKOTA, NAKOTA).

Plains tribes actually consisted of bands of related families. Each band had a few hundred members. The bands lived apart most of the year, but gathered in the summer for communal buffalo hunts and religious rituals.

Some books make a distinction between the tribes of the tall-grass prairies and those of the short-grass high plains, since many of the former had permanent villages and continued farming part of the year, while the more western peoples set up only temporary camps and gave up farming altogether. This book groups them together, however, and the so-called PRAIRIE INDIANS are depicted on the accompanying map as part of the Great Plains Culture Area along with the western tribes. (See the entry under PRAIRIE INDIANS to learn which tribes sometimes are classified differently.)

The Horse

It has already been mentioned how the horse revolutionized the mode of transportation and the economy of many Indian peoples and led to the typical way of life found in the Great Plains Culture Area. With horses the Indians could travel great distances. They could also carry heavy loads with them on the trail. And they could hunt and do battle while mounted on them.

Many of the Plains Indians had originally used dogs to carry possessions. (Interestingly, some peoples called the horse terms that translate as "sacred dog," "spirit dog," and "medicine dog.") The dogs pulled two poles tied together in the shape of a V; the closed end rested on their shoulders, and the open end on the ground, with hide stretched between the poles. These primitive sleds are called *travois*. Women sometimes also pulled travois. But with horses, Indians could utilize much larger travois and place many more supplies on them. Horse travois could even support the sick or elderly or children if need be. And the wooden framework doubled as tipi poles.

In addition to travois, Plains Indians crafted other gear for horses. They generally rode bareback, with only a

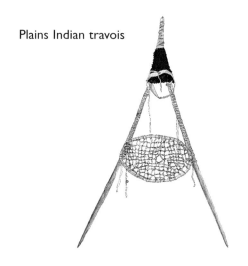

Plains Indian travois

rawhide thong noosed around the horse's lower jaw as a bridle. But some Indians used blankets or small hide saddles stuffed with buffalo hair or grass. Others used more elaborate wood saddles covered with deerskin and decorated with beadwork, plus decorated stirrups and bridles. Leather and beadwork ornaments were sometimes attached to bridles or draped over the horse's shoulders. Parfleches (leather bags) were also hung from saddles. And some Indians painted their war mounts with symbols, or trimmed and dyed their mounts' manes and tails, or placed eagle feathers or ribbons in their manes.

However they chose to ride, Plains Indians proved the best horsemen in the world. Their prowess on the hunt or in battle was legendary. With only ropes tied around their horses' neck, in which they hooked their elbows, some warriors could suspend themselves along the flanks, using the animals as shields, and shoot arrows under their necks. Grasping their mount firmly with their legs, some warriors could also bend over far enough while moving to pick up wounded comrades.

Horses became a sign of wealth for Plains Indians. Some war chiefs were known to own 1,000 animals personally. A man commonly gave horses to the family of his wife-to-be. Indians acquired horses that had gone wild and tamed them, but also carried out raids to take other tribes' horses. Plains Indians became skilled breeders as well as riders. They chose the fastest and most responsive stallions for breeding. Indian ponies consistently outperformed the larger U.S. Army mounts in battle during the plains wars of the 1800s.

The Buffalo

Before acquiring horses, Indians used various means to hunt buffalo, such as sneaking up on them in an animal disguise or stampeding them over cliffs or into corrals. On horseback, they could ride with the galloping herds, picking off game with bows and arrows, lances, or rifles. The early muzzle-loading rifles brought to the plains by European traders were less effective than traditional hunting weapons. They were difficult and slow to reload on horseback. The Indians readily took to the new breech-loading rifles in the mid-1800s, however.

Buffalo meat was the staple food of Plains Indians. It was eaten raw in small pieces or roasted. The flesh from the buffalo's hump was favored. Buffalo meat could also be prepared for use on the trail. Indians made jerky by drying meat in the Sun, and pemmican by pounding meat with fat and berries. Native Americans also ate the tongue, liver, kidneys, bone marrow, and intestines of buffalo.

Buffalo provided materials for numerous other applications. At least 86 nonfood uses have been counted. Some of them are: tipi coverings, shields, travois platforms, parfleches, blankets, and clothing from the skins, either in rawhide form or softened into leather; thread and rope for various purposes from sinews or buffalo hair; various tools from bones, including sled runners from ribs; rattles and other ceremonial objects from hooves, horns, and skulls; and buffalo chips as fuel.

Women mastered the art of preparing hides. They stretched the skins on frames or on pegs in the ground, then scraped away the flesh. They then worked the hide to an even thickness. If they stopped at this stage, they had rawhide. To soften the hide into leather, they worked a mixture of ashes, fat, brains, liver, and various plants into it, then soaked it in water. Sometimes the hair was left for warmth. In other instances, it too was scraped off.

Tipis

As few as six or as many as 28 buffalo skins were sewn together to make a tipi covering, depending on the size of the pelts and the size of the structure. Although men provided the materials for tipis, cutting the pine trees for poles as well as hunting the buffalos, women usually erected them.

According to tribal custom, either three or four poles were used as the basic framework. They were tied together near the top and raised with the bottoms at equal distances, forming a cone shape. Then other poles were propped against them. The final pole set in place served to hoist the sewn buffalo skins. This covering was stretched around the framework and held in place around the bottom edge with wooden pegs or stones,

Plains Indian tipi

and along the front seam with wooden lodge pins. Part of the front seam was left unfastened to serve as an entrance with closable flaps. An opening was left at the top to serve as a smokehole.

Tipis were practical in that the various openings could be adjusted for ventilation, as the bottom edge could be rolled up to allow for increased air flow. When completely sealed, with extra pelts added to the walls for insulation and a fire inside, the tipis were warm in wintry weather. Native Americans situated them in such a way as to reduce the wind factor. Because of prevailing westerly winds on the wide-open plains, the entrance faced eastward. And the tipis leaned slightly to the east so air could more easily flow over the top, thus decreasing wind pressure on the structure.

Plains Indians thought of tipis as more than just homes. They considered them sacred places, with the floor symbolizing the earth and the walls the sky. Moreover, the base of the tipi was in the shape of a circle, a sacred symbol for Plains Indians, indicating how all aspects of existence were interconnected. Every tipi had a small altar of stone or earth where incense was burned during prayers. Both the outside walls and inner linings were commonly painted with symbolic designs. Brightly colored figures and shapes referred to spirit beings, ancestors, family histories, and honors gained in battle. Others were for decoration.

Clothing

Similarly, the designs on Plains Indian clothing, such as honors insignia on robes, in some instances had specific meanings but in other cases simply provided decoration. Dyed quillwork was originally used to decorate buffalo-skin or deerskin shirts, vests, leggings, dresses, boots, and moccasins. It was later replaced by beadwork. Fringes added another decoration element to clothing. Other articles of clothing commonly seen on the plains included leather breechcloths in warm weather, and fur robes, caps, and headbands in cold weather. Native Americans also wore various types of headdresses.

Plains Indian eagle-feather headdress

The eagle-feather headdress, sometimes referred to as a warbonnet, is the most recognizable of all Native American clothing. At modern-day festivals and pow-wows, one sees warbonnets on Indians of tribes from other parts of North America. But this particular type of headdress originated among the Plains tribes.

Only a few men wore warbonnets, those who earned the privilege to do so in warfare. War chiefs usually had the longest headdresses. The number of black-tipped tailfeathers of the male golden eagle represented the wearer's exploits. The feathers were attached to a skullcap of buffalo or deerskin, with a brow band that was decorated with quillwork or beadwork and dangling strips of fur or ribbons. Additional downy feathers were tied to the base of the eagle feathers and tufts of dyed horsehair to their tips.

Counting Coup

In warfare on the plains, bravery was not measured simply by the number of enemy killed or wounded. Plains Indians had a custom known as "counting coup" in which the object was simply to touch an enemy in battle without hurting him. A special coup stick was sometimes used for this purpose, although a war club or lance or bow or even the hand itself would do. An eagle feather was awarded to the warrior for each coup. If after counting coup on an armed enemy, he managed to kill him, then scalp him, a warrior received three coup feathers. Capturing an enemy's possessions, especially eagle feathers, brought great honor.

Plains Indian coup stick

The Sacred Pipe

Another important possession of Plains Indians was the sacred pipe. Some pipes were owned by the entire tribe. These beautifully crafted pipes, with long wooden stems (sometimes as long as five feet) and stone bowls, are usually called peace pipes, although they were used in other ceremonies besides peace councils. Ash and sumac were the favorite woods for the stems because they were soft enough to be hollowed out easily. The chosen stone for carving the bowl was catlinite, also called pipestone. A pipestone quarry is located in Minnesota. Many different tribes came from far and wide to acquire the red-colored stone that was soft enough to carve with a knife until it dried in the air. Another workable stone was steatite, or soapstone. Sacred pipes were decorated with feathers, quills (later beads), fur, and horsehair. The most common smoking substance was tobacco, although other plants alone or in combination were used too.

Medicine Bundles and Sacred Shields

Pipes were kept in medicine bundles with other sacred objects. Skin pouches or wrappings generally were used as medicine bundles. The objects inside were thought to have magical powers. In addition to pipes, medicine bundles contained such objects as a stone or arrow or parts of an animal. Quite often these were objects seen in a dream or vision. Individuals kept their own personal medicine bundles for good fortune, but tribal chiefs or shamans kept bundles for the entire tribe. The talismans inside had special meanings with regard to tribal legends.

Plains Indian personal medicine bundle

Plains Indian shields also had religious meanings, intended to offer magical protection to the bearer. The paintings on sacred shields served as a link between the natural and spiritual worlds, pointing to mystical places.

Secret Societies

Some of the paintings also identified the warrior as belonging to a particular military society or soldier society. Each society or club, some of them intertribal, had its own insignia, costumes, medicine bundles, songs, dances, and code of behavior. Some societies were age-graded and open. That is to say, a member automatically entered a society depending on his age. Others were exclusive, and a warrior could join only when invited to, based on his deeds in battle. The most famous of the soldier societies were respected and feared all over the plains. Tribes had other types of societies as well, such as medicine societies for healing. Some societies were exclusive of women.

The Vision Quest

Visions, both those in dreams and those experienced in a semiwakeful state, played an important role in the religious and spiritual life of Indians all over North America. Visions were thought to have significance for individuals and for the entire tribe. Native peoples thought that through them, people could come in contact with the spirit world and receive power, or "medicine." The quest for visions usually occurred around some important event, such as passage from boyhood into manhood or preparation for war. There were various

ceremonies and means to induce them. Some involved the use of hallucinogenic plants, such as peyote or jimsonweed. The striving for visions among Plains peoples is usually referred to as the Vision Quest.

In order to achieve visions, a Plains Indian normally first purified himself with a sweat bath in a sweat lodge, stripped himself naked, painted himself with white clay, went off to a isolated place, and fasted for days. If hunger, thirst, and exposure to the elements alone failed to bring on a trancelike experience and resulting visions, the individual sometimes further tortured himself by cutting off a finger or by some other self-mutilation.

The vision usually came in the form of an animal. But it could relate to a plant, place, object, ancestor, or some natural phenomenon, such as a storm. After the experience, a shaman would help the individual interpret the vision. What was seen in the vision would henceforth symbolize the individual's guardian spirit. The individual would prepare a medicine bundle with sacred objects somehow relating to his vision.

The Sun Dance

The quest for visions also played a part in the ceremony common to many Plains tribes and known to most people as the Sun Dance. The name *Sun Dance* comes from the Sioux tribe. Other tribes had different names. The Cheyenne called it the New Life Lodge. The Ponca called it the Mystery Dance. Moreover, different tribes had different rituals. But for all those tribes who held the ceremony, the overall purposes were the same: to come into contact with the spirit world; to renew nature, including the Sun, the sky, and the earth; to keep buffalo plentiful, thereby assuring future prosperity; to bring victory in battle; to make marriages successful; to settle old quarrels; and to heal the sick.

Tribes held their annual Sun Dance in summertime. Summer was the season when the various bands of a tribe gathered for communal buffalo hunting. The bands set up their tipis in a great circle. Men and women of different bands socialized together and courted one another. They held horse races and other games. Tribal leaders smoked tobacco together and reestablished tribal unity. The Sun Dance, the most important of summer ceremonies, usually occurred during a full moon in the latter part of summer when berries were ripe. The entire ceremony lasted from eight to 12 days.

The various Sun Dance rituals were numerous and complex. Every act had a special significance. Many of

Plains Indian sacred pipe

the rituals involved drumming, singing, and dancing. In the course of the Sun Dance, the Indians found and erected a sacred tree trunk, usually a cottonwood, sometimes as much as 30 feet high, in the center of a sacred lodge of poles and branches. On top of the tree, they placed a figure, usually made of rawhide.

One particular ritual, coming near the end of the Sun Dance, has come to be associated with the entire ceremony above all others. Some men had skewers implanted in their chests which were tied to the sacred pole with ropes. Blowing eagle-bone whistles and dancing to the drumbeat, they danced backwards until the skewers ripped through their flesh. Other men dragged buffalo skulls about the camp, the skulls attached to their flesh with similar skewers. Their self-mutilation supposedly brought visions for their own well-being, and their self-sacrifice brought good fortune for the entire tribe.

There is much more to Plains Indian culture than what has been discussed here. For a view of differing tribal customs as well as a view of distinct tribal histories, see the entries for the tribes cross-referenced earlier in this section.

PLATEAU INDIANS

The term *Plateau Indians* is taken from the name of the Columbia Plateau. The Columbia Plateau is a region of highlands through which the Columbia River flows. Some 1,200 miles long, situated in both the United States and Canada, the Columbia River is one of the largest rivers in North America. It starts in the southeastern part of British Columbia, then flows a meandering route to the Pacific Ocean, forming much of the border between Washington and Oregon. It has many tributaries, including the Snake, Thompson, Okanagan, Deschutes, Umatilla, Willamette, and Kootenai Rivers. This system receives water from three mountain ranges—the Rocky Mountains, the Cascade Mountains, and the Coast Range. Another large river, the Fraser—also starting in the Rocky Mountains in British Columbia—is not part of the Columbia watershed.

What scholars define as the Plateau Culture Area is situated between the Cascades to the west and the Rockies to the east, the Fraser River to the north and the Great Basin to the south. It includes territory now mapped as southeastern British Columbia, eastern Washington, northeast and central Oregon, northern Idaho, western Montana, and a small part of northern California.

The mountains flanking the Plateau region—the Cascades and the Rockies—catch a great deal of rain and snowfall, making for the great number of rivers and streams. The mountains and river valleys have enough precipitation to support some of the tallest trees in the

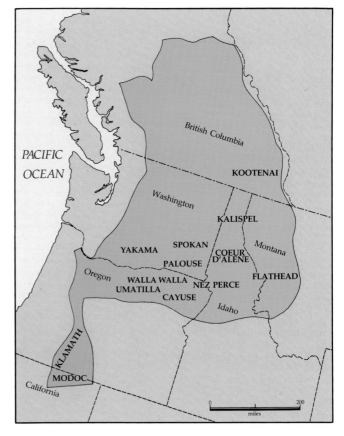

The Plateau Culture Area, showing the approximate locations of Indian tribes listed in this book—circa 1500, before displacement by non-Indians (with modern boundaries)

world. These are evergreen forests of needle-bearing conifers, including pine, hemlock, spruce, fir, and cedar. The giant forests are too dense and shady for much smaller vegetation to grow beneath them.

The Columbia Plateau has little rainfall, since the Cascades block the rain clouds blowing in from the ocean. The land consists mainly of flatlands and rolling hills. Grasses and sagebrush are the dominant vegetation in this part of the culture area.

The sparse ground vegetation of both mountain and plateau meant little game for the native peoples living there. Some elk, deer, and bear could be found at the edge of the forest. Some antelope and jackrabbits lived out on the dry plains of the plateau. Yet the abundant rivers and streams offered up plentiful food. Among the many different kinds of fish were the salmon that swam upriver from the ocean to lay their eggs. The river valleys also provided plentiful berries, including blackberries and huckleberries. On the grasslands of the plateau, the Indians found other wild plant foods—roots and bulbs, especially from the camas plant, a kind of lily; bitterroot; wild carrots; and wild onions.

Through fishing, hunting, and gathering, Plateau Indians could subsist without farming. In cold weather, most Plateau Indians lived along rivers in villages of semiunderground earth-covered pithouses, which provided natural insulation. In warm weather, most peoples lived in temporary lodges with basswood frames and bullrush-mat coverings, either along the rivers at salmon-spawning time or on the open plains at camas-digging time. Plateau Indians also used the rivers as avenues of trade, with many contacts among different tribes.

The varying dialects of the Plateau tribes are part of two main language families: Sahaptian (of the Penutian language phylum) and Salishan (of undetermined phy-

lum affiliation). The Plateau Sahaptian-speaking tribes with their own entries in this book are the NEZ PERCE, PALOUSE, UMATILLA, WALLA WALLA, and YAKAMA. The Salishan-speaking tribes with their own entries include the COEUR D'ALENE, FLATHEAD, KALISPEL, and SPOKAN. The related dialects of the KLAMATH and MODOC, two other Plateau tribes with entries, are an isolate of the Penutian phylum, referred to by some scholars as the Lutuamian language. The language of the KOOTENAI, another tribe with its own entry, is an isolate with undetermined phylum affiliation, although it has some similarities to Algonquian.

These are only a few of the tribes making their homes on the Columbia Plateau. Other Sahaptians include the Klickitat, Pshwanwapam, Skin, Taidnapam, Tenino, Tyigh, Wanapam, and Wauyukma. The Molalla language isolate is of the Penutian phylum, related to Sahaptian. Other Plateau Salishans include the Chelan, Columbia, Colville, Entiat, Lake, Lillooet, Methow, Ntlakyapamuk, Okanagan, Sanpoil, Shuswap, Sinkaieth, Sinkakaius, and Wenatchee. The Wishram are considered the only Plateau Chinookians (of the Penutian phylum). Many Salishans and Chinookians who occupied ancestral territory to the west of the Columbia Plateau are classified as NORTHWEST COAST INDIANS. The Stuwihamuk are Athapascan-speaking.

Plateau Indian (Colville) warclub

POMO

In a part of North America where native basketry reached an exquisite level of development, territory known to whites as California, the Pomo are considered the foremost basketmakers of all. They created their beautiful baskets for functional purposes, but collectors now value them as works of fine art. In some Pomo baskets, the weaving is so tight that a microscope is needed to count the stitches.

The Pomo crafted many different kinds of objects with their basketmaking skills, such as cooking pots,

containers, trays, cradles, hats, mats, ceremonial objects, games, fish traps, and boats. Unlike men of most other Indian tribes, Pomo men participated in this craft. Moreover, the Pomo, using grasses, reeds, barks, and roots as basic materials, had two distinct methods of weaving baskets: twining and coiling. In twining, two or more horizontal strands (called wefts) are twined around each other as they are woven in and out of a set of vertical strands (called warps). In coiling, thin strips of plant matter are wrapped in a bundle and coiled into a continuous spiral. The Pomo had variations of these basic techniques and created designs and decorations with dyes, shells, and feathers.

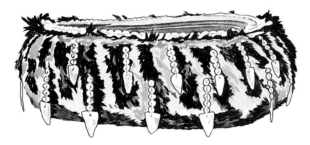

Pomo basket decorated with feathers and shells

The Pomo occupied ancestral territory along the Pacific Coast and some distance inland, starting about 50 miles north of San Francisco Bay. Their small villages were located as far as Clear Lake, with a concentration of communities around that lake and along the Russian River. There were actually at least 72 bands with distinct identities grouped together as Pomo. Linguists have established seven different dialects in the Pomoan language family of Hokan and speak of seven divisions: Northern, Central, Eastern, Northeastern, Southeastern, Southwestern, and Southern. The name applied to all groups, pronounced PO-mo, is taken from the sound *pomo* or *poma,* which was placed by them after village names and probably means "village."

The Pomo were hunter-gatherers like other CALIFORNIA INDIANS, relying on acorns, small mammals, fowl, and fish. The coast Pomo, separated from the inland Pomo by a redwood forest, piled slabs of redwood bark against a center pole to make cone-shaped dwellings, large enough for only one family. The Clear Lake and Russian River Pomo built pole-framed and thatch-covered rectangular structures that housed several families. The men shared partially underground, earth-covered buildings called singing lodges for councils and ceremonies. Many of their rituals surrounded the secret Kuksu Cult (see WINTUN). Smaller pithouses served as sweat lodges.

The Pomo were great traders. At times, they dealt in finished products, such as their baskets, but they also traded raw materials. The Clear Lake Pomo, for instance, had a salt deposit. They bartered the mineral for tools, weapons, shells, and furs. The Pomo also manufactured a kind of money. Many California tribes used tooth shells as a kind of currency. The Pomo, however, rejected this currency in favor of baked and polished magnesite and strings of beads made from ground, rounded, and polished clamshells. They became accomplished mathematicians. They did not learn multiplication or division, but by using units of strings, they added beads as high as the number 40,000.

The Pomo had contact with both the Russians and the Spanish. The Russians began developing the fur trade in North America along the Pacific coast, starting after Vitus Bering's exploration of the Bering Strait in 1741 (see ALEUT and TLINGIT). The Russians worked their way southward from Alaska. In 1811, they established a trading post, Fort Ross, on Bodega Bay in Pomo country. The heavily armed Russian traders forced the Pomo to hunt animals and clean hides for them. The Pomo resisted this oppression, carrying out acts of vandalism on Russian property. The traders punished individuals with death or torture in order to set an example for other Indians. Murder, disease, and forced labor reduced the Pomo population, but they kept up their resistance until the Russians abandoned the post in 1841.

A Pomo chief named Marin led an uprising against the Spanish during the early 1800s as well. In 1815 (or 1816), after his warriors had been defeated in battle by Spanish soldiers, Marin was captured and taken to San Francisco. He escaped, however, and crossed San Francisco Bay on a balsa (a raft made from reeds). Regrouping his warriors, Marin launched more raids against the Spanish, keeping them out of Pomo territory. In 1824, after the Republic of Mexico had taken over rule of California from Spain, Mexican troops under Lieutenant Ignacio Martínez plus Indian allies moved on Marin. He and his men, including the subchief Quintin, took refuge on two islands near the mouth of San Rafael Inlet and held off the soldiers for days before surrendering. Many of the warriors then looked to Pomponio for leadership, but he too was captured. After a year-long imprisonment, Marin became missionized, living at the San Rafael Mission in his homeland. He died there in 1834 or as late as 1848. Marin County, California, is named after him.

In the following years, especially starting in 1849, during the California gold rush, the Pomo suffered from other non-Indians entering their domain, this time Anglo-Americans. Despite encroachment by settlers, the Pomo managed to hold onto a number of parcels in their ancestral homeland. The largest of these is the Hopland Rancheria in Mendocino County.

In recent years, the various Pomo communities have succeeded in having federal trust status restored, having lost it in the Termination period of the 1950s to 1960s.

PONCA

The Ponca, a Siouan people, share ancestry with the KAW, OMAHA, OSAGE, and QUAPAW. Formerly living along the Ohio Valley, their ancestors eventually migrated westward across the Mississippi River onto the eastern plains. Various groups then separated under different chiefs. The ancestors of Ponca and Omaha lived together in what now is southern Minnesota near Pipestone Quarry, a site famous for the catlinite stone used to make pipes. But they too eventually separated. The Omaha ended up settling on the Missouri River in what is now northeastern Nebraska. But the Ponca built their villages farther to the northwest at the mouth of the Niobrara River, on both sides of what has become the boundary line between Nebraska and South Dakota.

The name *Ponca,* pronounced PONG-kuh, is thought to mean "sacred head." The tribe is classified as part of the Great Plains Culture Area because they hunted buffalo on the plains, especially after many gained use of the horse (see PLAINS INDIANS). But they also retained many of the traits of more eastern Indians, including permanent villages and agriculture (see PRAIRIE INDIANS).

In the 19th century, the Ponca were involved in an incident that had a positive, long-term effect on the rights of Native Americans. In 1876, Congress passed an act to relocate the Ponca from their homeland in Nebraska to the Indian Territory. Tribal members were forced to move the following year. They suffered greatly during the first years after removal. Their new land was difficult to farm. There was little grass to feed livestock. Winters were fierce. Hunger and disease took their toll, killing about a quarter of the tribe.

One of those sick was the son of Chief Standing Bear. Before dying, the youth made his father promise to bury him with his sister by the Swift Running Water of their homeland—along the Niobrara River in Nebraska. When the boy died, Standing Bear loaded the body in a box on a wagon drawn by two feeble horses, then headed north. Sixty-five members of his clan went with him on the long funeral procession.

Settlers living in Kansas and Nebraska were alarmed to see the Ponca crossing through lands that by now are supposed to be cleared of all Indians. They notified the army of a potential Indian uprising. Standing Bear and his people reached their earlier homeland but were soon arrested by a cavalry detachment and taken to Omaha as prisoners.

The Ponca had always been peaceful in their relations with whites. On learning of their real purpose in returning to Nebraska, some whites reacted with sympathy. General George Crook, who had led campaigns against many other tribes, expressed his support. Two lawyers, John Webster and Andrew Poppleton, offered their free services to the prisoners.

At the trial in 1879, Judge Elmer Dundy ruled in favor of the Indians, saying that they had inalienable rights under the law like all people, and that the government could not forcibly restrain them from returning to their original homeland. In 1879–80, Standing Bear accompanied the Omaha reformer Susette La Flesche on a tour of eastern cities to lecture on behalf of the Ponca cause. Because of public sympathy for Standing Bear's band, the federal government granted them a reservation along the Niobrara in 1880.

A precedent was established. In this case, Native Americans were shown to be equal under the law. Nevertheless, it would take many more years for all Native Americans to be treated fairly by government officials. For example, other Ponca in the Indian Territory—Standing Bear's brother Big Snake being one of them—were not allowed to join their relatives in the north for many years. But at least Judge Dundy's decision was a step in the right direction on the long road to equality for Native Americans.

Today, Ponca live in both locations, in Oklahoma and in Nebraska. Lands in both states have been allotted to individual tribe members during the Allotment period. Lands in Oklahoma now are designated as a federal trust area.

Modern Ponca have worked peacefully for Indian rights, as Chief Standing Bear did during the last

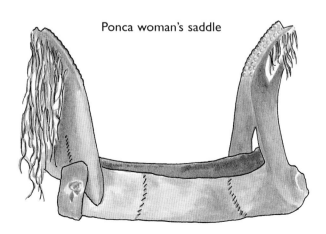

Ponca woman's saddle

century. In 1961, Indian leaders from 67 tribes gathered in Chicago for the American Indian Chicago Conference (also called the American Indian Charter Convention). The leaders issued a Declaration of Indian Purpose, calling for greater Indian involvement in the decision-making process in all federal and state programs affecting Indians.

Yet some of the younger tribal delegates did not think their tribal elders had gone far enough in making a stand for Indian rights. Soon afterward, this group, led by a Ponca named Clyde Warrior and a PAIUTE named Melvin Thom, founded the National Indian Youth Council (NIYC) in New Mexico. The NIYC has since been involved in many Native American causes. For example, in 1964, the NIYC sponsored a number of "fish-ins" along rivers in the state of Washington to make a case for Indian fishing rights. The NIYC also publishes a periodical called *ABC: Americans Before Columbus,* which covers issues concerning native peoples in both North and South America.

POTAWATOMI

The Potawatomi are also known as the Fire Nation because their name in Algonquian means "people of the place of fire." Different spellings are preserved in place-names as well as historical records. One sees *Potawatami, Pottawatami,* or *Pottawatomie.* But modern tribal members have designated the official spelling as *Potawatomi,* so this is the version most commonly used today. The name is pronounced pot-uh-WOT-uh-mee.

The ancestral homeland of the Potawatomi is usually given as the lower peninsula of present-day Michigan (see NORTHEAST INDIANS). It is reported that they lived between Lake Huron and Lake Michigan just before the arrival of French explorers. According to their tradition, they were originally one people with other ALGONQUIANS, the CHIPPEWA (OJIBWAY) and OTTAWA, at the time of their arrival in western Great Lakes country. By 1670, when the Frenchman Nicholas Perrot explored the region, the Potawatomi were living west of Lake Michigan near present-day Green Bay, Wisconsin, probably pushed westward by IROQUOIS (HAUDENOSAUNEE) invasions from the east. Then from there, over the years, they migrated south toward the present-day Chicago area.

The Potawatomi were military allies and trading partners of the French until the French were defeated by the English in 1763 to end the French and Indian War. The Potawatomi continued the fight against the English as allies of the Ottawa and other tribes in Pontiac's Rebellion of 1763. In 1769, the Potawatomi and other Algonquians joined to fight the ILLINOIS and push them southward. At that time, the Potawatomi expanded their territory around the southern end of Lake Michigan back toward their original homeland, almost a full circle.

While holding these lands, the Potawatomi joined their former enemies, the British, in the fight against the rebels in the American Revolution of 1775–83. Then in the late 1700s and early 1800s, the Potawatomi fought in a series of wars in a vain attempt to stop the American settlers from overrunning their lands—Little Turtle's War of 1790–94 (see MIAMI); Tecumseh's Rebellion of 1809–11 (see SHAWNEE); and the Black Hawk War of 1832 (see SAC). With each passing conflict, the situation became more hopeless for the Potawatomi and for the other tribes of the Old Northwest. Most of the Potawatomi relocated west of the Mississippi.

Potawatomi doll, used as a totem of love

Some Potawatomi moved from Illinois, Indiana, and Michigan to Missouri, then to Iowa, and from there to Kansas. Others went straight to Kansas from the Great Lakes region. Some of these Kansas Potawatomi then moved to the Indian Territory. Some Potawatomi stayed in both Wisconsin and Michigan. Others managed to return there from the west. During the 1800s, other Potawatomi accompanied the KICKAPOO to Mexico. Still others went to Canada.

The history of Potawatomi migration is very complex. Their many moves resulted from poverty and hardship. The Potawatomi struggled to find suitable lands and ways to earn a living after having been dislodged from their homeland and their way of life. The migration from Indiana that began in 1838 is called the Trail of Death because of the many lives lost to disease and hunger. It is not as famous as the CHEROKEE Trail of Tears, but just as tragic.

Today, the Prairie Band of Potawatomi has a reservation in Kansas; the Citizen Band of Potawatomi holds trust lands in Oklahoma; in Michigan are the Hannahville Indian Community of Wisconsin Potawatomi Indians of Michigan; the Huron Potawatomi Band; and Pokagon Band of Potawatomi Indians. In Wisconsin is the Forest County Potawatomi Community of Wisconsin and the Caldwell Band has a reserve in Ontario. Like most Native Americans, the Potawatomi are for the most part not a wealthy people. but they have raised their standard of living recently through sound business investments and they are reviving traditional crafts.

When speaking of traditional Potawatomi culture, one usually compares them to their kinspeople, the Chippewa and the Ottawa. Like those tribes and other Algonquians of the Great Lakes, the Potawatomi hunted in the forests, fished and gathered wild rice on the lakes, and grew corn and other crops in the fields. One of their bands, the Mascouten, also hunted buffalo on the prairies along the Mississippi valley.

As for their religious customs, the Potawatomi were like other Great Lakes Algonquians in that they smoked tobacco in calumets (sacred pipes) and participated in the Midewiwin Society, also known as the Grand Medicine Society, an exclusive club with elaborate rituals and important in religious and tribal matters. In the 1880s, long after their displacement by whites, the Potawatomi also helped develop the Big Drum Religion (also called the Drum Dance and Dream Dance), which some Native Americans still practice today. This is not a war dance, but one of good will, even toward whites. In this ritual, Indians dance for hours to the beat of a sacred drum, working themselves into a reverie. To seal the spirit of fellowship, gifts are exchanged.

POWHATAN

Much is known about the Powhatan from the writings of Captain John Smith and other Englishmen. The various Tidewater ALGONQUIANS, along with some Iroquoian-speaking peoples of the area, are usually classified as part of the Northeast Culture Area (see NORTHEAST INDIANS). This is because they shared most cultural traits with other Atlantic Coast Algonquians farther north. Other Virginia and North Carolina tribes farther inland, many of them Siouan-speaking, are classified in the Southeast Culture Area.

Lifeways

In some ways the Powhatan were more like the SOUTHEAST INDIANS. For example, they had a more autocratic system of government than the northern tribes. That is to say, their leaders had absolute authority, with power of life and death over their subjects. To the north, the Indian tribes were more democratic, with a council of leaders often making decisions.

The combination of hunting, fishing, gathering, and farming in and around Chesapeake Bay determines the Northeast classification for the Powhatan, ROANOKE, and other coastal Algonquians. The writings of Captain Smith describe in great detail how the Powhatan collected and prepared food. He speaks of how they hunted deer, beaver, opossums, otters, squirrels, and turkeys with various weapons, including bows and arrows, spears, clubs, snares, and rings of fire; how they dried acorns plus other nuts and fruits to keep for winter; how they made a milky drink from ground walnuts; how they fished in giant dugout canoes as much as 40 and 50 feet long, using spears and nets; how they planted their crops, making holes four feet apart with a digging stick and placing four grains of corn and two of beans in each; and how they roasted or boiled green corn to eat on the spot or soaked and pounded ripe corn to make cornmeal cakes.

Powhatan digging stick for planting corn

Captain Smith also wrote about how the Powhatan usually located their villages along a river, near a spring of water. Their houses, anywhere from two to a hundred per village, would be in the middle of their fields of 20, 40, 100, or even 200 acres. The houses were made of saplings, bent and tied and covered with bark or woven mats. The structures had rounded roofs but were elongated, much like Iroquoian longhouses.

As with Indians all over the continent, there was a division of labor between men and women. For the most part, the men were the hunters, fishermen, gatherers, and warriors. They built the houses and boats and most of the tools and weapons. The women were the farmers and food-preparers and made clothing, pottery, baskets, mats, and wooden vessels called mortars that were used for grinding foods.

The Powhatan and other area Algonquians practiced the *huskanaw,* a rite of passage in which boys underwent solitary confinement and fasting in preparation for manhood.

Pocahontas

Pocahontas is probably the most famous of all Indian women. She was the daughter of Wahunsonakok, a powerful chief of about 30 different bands and 200 villages in the part of North America that now is Virginia. The various bands under his rule have come to be called the Powhatan Confederacy after his band, although it was not a true confederacy in that power was centralized under a single leader. *Powhatan,* pronounced pow-uh-TAN or pow-HAT-un, means "at the falls." The English colonists who established the colony of Jamestown in Virginia in 1607, the first permanent English settlement in North America, had trouble pronouncing and remembering Wahunsonakok's real name. They started calling him by the name of his village—he became known as Chief Powhatan.

According to legend, Pocahontas saved the life of Captain John Smith, the leader of the Jamestown colonists. Supposedly, she intervened just before her father was about to behead Smith, who was his prisoner. Whether or not Smith's capture or Pocahontas's intercession actually happened is uncertain. But it is known for sure that the English angered Wahunsonakok because they took the best land for themselves, and he retaliated by having his warriors take prisoners, Captain Smith among them. The English appeased him by crowning him a king in an English-style ceremony. Wahunsonakok released Smith unharmed.

Then in 1613, Pocahontas was captured by the English and held as a hostage to bargain with Wahunsonakok for

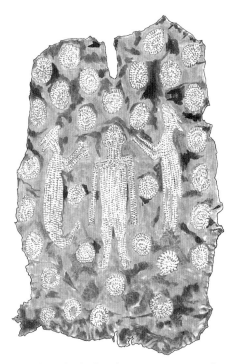

Hide decorated with shells, showing a man and two deer (It is thought to have belonged to Chief Powhatan and is known as Powhatan's Mantle.)

the freedom of other prisoners. While at Jamestown, she was converted to Christianity and baptized. Then she was courted by a settler by the name of John Rolfe. After having gained her father's permission, she married the Englishman in 1613. Their marriage brought about a period of peace between Indians and whites.

Pocahontas sailed across the Atlantic to visit England with her husband. There she was received as royalty herself and met the king and queen. Yet like so many Indians who came into contact with whites, she died from a European disease, in 1617. Wahunsonakok died the following year.

Wahunsonakok's earlier words of peace to Captain Smith were recorded for posterity:

Why will you take by force what you may quietly have by love? Why will you destroy us who provide you with food? . . . We are unarmed, and willing to give you what you ask, if you come in a friendly manner, and not with swords and guns, as if to make war upon an enemy.

Opechancanough's Wars

The peace that Wahunsonakok shaped lasted another five years. His brother Opechancanough was now the leader of the Powhatan Confederacy. He recognized a disturbing pattern in Indian-white relations.

Tobacco, now popular in Europe, was a lucrative cash crop. Boatload after boatload of settlers arrived along the ports of the Chesapeake Bay to cultivate it. Tobacco depleted the soil, necessitating new fields every several years. As a result, the English needed more and more land. But they usually ignored the rights of the native peoples, tricking them into signing away huge tracts. The settlers would then move in and carve the land into plantations, cutting down trees and killing or driving away the game. In the process, Indian hunting grounds were ruined, and a centuries-old way of life was disrupted.

Opechancanough wanted to break this pattern. He plotted a strike against the settlers to drive them from Powhatan country. Remembering the peace established by his brother and niece, he wavered in his purpose. He wondered if his warriors could really defeat the now-numerous colonists. The arrest and execution of a warrior by the name of Nematanou for the alleged murder of a white trader made up his mind once and for all. Opechancanough ordered a surprise attack.

On the morning of March 22, 1622, hundreds of warriors swept out of the forest and through the colony's tobacco fields, killing every colonist in sight—all in all, 347 men, women, and children. In response, the English organized a militia. The troops began a campaign of regular patrols against the Indians, burning houses and crops and pushing the Indians farther inland. Opechancanough agreed to a peace council. When he and his warriors arrived, they were poisoned and attacked by the colonists. Opechancanough escaped, however.

Both sides continued their raids for 10 years. Finally in 1632, they agreed on a peace treaty. But Opechancanough never forgave the English. Twelve years later in 1644, when he was supposedly more than 100 years old, he ordered another attack. This time, almost 500 colonists lost their lives. Again, the colonists responded with a stepped-up campaign. In 1646, Governor William Berkeley of Virginia and his militiamen captured the wily but weary leader and carried him on his royal litter back to Jamestown. He was jeered at by an angry crowd and later shot by a vengeful guard.

Before dying, Opechancanough reportedly said, "If it had been my fortune to take Sir William Berkeley prisoner, I would not have meanly exposed him as a show to my people."

His people received the same harsh treatment and were forced out of Virginia or placed on small reservations where their numbers dwindled over the centuries.

Contemporary Powhatan

Some Powhatan remain in Virginia today, members of the Accomac, Chickahominy, Mattaponi, Nansemond, Pamunkey, Potomac, Rappahannock, Werowocomoco, and Wicocomoco bands. Of these, only the Mattaponi and Pamunkey hold state reservation lands. A group known as the Powhatan-Renápe in the Delaware valley of Pennsylvania and New Jersey has Powhatan as well as LENNI LENAPE (DELAWARE) and Nanticoke descendants.

PRAIRIE INDIANS

Native American cultural studies are especially difficult because of the great number of tribes and their many different ways of life. In order to have some basis for making distinctions and comparisons among the many peoples, scholars have invented different cultural groupings based on geography. That way, the lifeways of more than one tribe can be discussed together. These cultural and geographic categories are called Indian culture areas.

Yet scholars differ on the number of culture areas. This book summarizes the most common groupings, showing them on maps. For the area now comprising the United States and Canada, the most common breakdown is as follows: Arctic, California, Great Basin, Great Plains, Northeast, Northwest Coast, Plateau, Southeast, Southwest, and Subarctic. But some books break down these culture areas

even further. For instance, they add a separate culture area for the prairies which includes territory most scholars represent as the western part of the Northeast Culture Area and the eastern part of the Great Plains Culture Area.

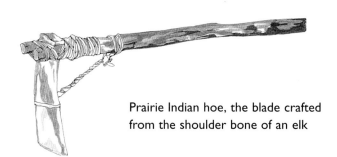

Prairie Indian hoe, the blade crafted from the shoulder bone of an elk

The grasslands flanking the Mississippi and Missouri Rivers are referred to as the prairies or Prairie Plains. The difference between the Great Plains and the Prairie Plains is the amount of rainfall and the resulting type of vegetation. The Great Plains are drier than the Prairie Plains. As a result, there are more ponds and swamps on the prairies. And with the more frequent rains, the Prairie Plains' grasses grow taller than those on the Great Plains. The Great Plains are located to the west of the Prairie Plains. To the east, the Prairie Plains give way to woodlands.

The Prairie Plains are located in the central part of the United States. Iowa and Illinois are mostly prairie country. North Dakota, South Dakota, Nebraska, Kansas, Oklahoma, and Texas all have prairies in their eastern parts. Minnesota has prairies in its southern and western parts. Missouri has prairies in its northern and western parts. Indiana has prairies in its northern part. Ohio has prairies in its western part. Some of these states, especially Illinois and Iowa, are referred to as Prairie States.

The Native Americans sometimes cited as Prairie Indians shared cultural traits with both the NORTHEAST INDIANS and the PLAINS INDIANS. Many of them lived in semipermanent villages along wooded river valleys. They lived for the most part in sizable earth lodges or in grass-covered dome-shaped houses. They had extensive cultivated fields where they grew corn, beans, squash, tobacco, and other crops. They made use of pottery for cooking, carrying, and storage.

Yet many of the Prairie peoples left their homes to hunt part of the year. While on the trail, they lived in temporary lean-tos or portable tents—tipis—and used unbreakable containers made of animal skins. Their chosen game was buffalo. Late in their history, after the arrival of Europeans, they acquired use of the horse for hunting and raiding.

The Prairie Indians east of the Mississippi are generally classified in the Northeast Culture Area. These include the tribes of the western Great Lakes: FOX (MESQUAKI), KICKAPOO, MENOMINEE, POTAWATOMI, SAC, and WINNEBAGO, as well as tribes to their south, the ILLINOIS, MIAMI, and SHAWNEE.

The Prairie Indians west of the Mississippi are generally classified as part of the Great Plains Culture Area. Most of them occupied territory in the stretch of land from the Missouri to the Mississippi Rivers. These include the following tribes: ARIKARA, HIDATSA, IOWAY, KAW, MANDAN, MISSOURIA, OMAHA, OSAGE, OTOE, PAWNEE, PONCA, QUAPAW, WICHITA, and some of the eastern bands of SIOUX (DAKOTA, LAKOTA, NAKOTA).

PREHISTORIC INDIANS

Most peoples listed in this book existed as tribal entities when Europeans first came into contact with Native North Americans. A few formed into tribal groups in postcontact times. Some tribes have since become extinct. These various tribes are central to the study of Indian peoples.

Yet Native American studies also involve the story of the ancestors of these tribal Indians—Prehistoric Indians. The term *prehistoric* means whatever occurred before there were written records. Another term, *precontact* refers to those peoples who had no contact with non-Indians. Another label applied is *pre-Columbian,* referring to Indians and cultures before the arrival of Christopher Columbus in the Americas in 1492.

Who were the early Indians? Did Indians always live in the Americas? If not, where did they come from? How did they live? What kind of tools did they make?

Scholars have not always known the answers to these questions. Archaeologists, who search for and analyze ancient material remains, and anthropologists, who study physical and cultural characteristics of humankind, have attempted to piece together information concerning ancient inhabitants of the Americas. Other scientists have helped them decipher these clues: paleontologists, who study fossils and ancient life forms; geologists, who study rock formations; and chemists, who study the composition of matter.

Knowledge of ancient Indians, as well as that of prehistoric peoples in all parts of the world, remains to a large degree hypothetical. Most human remains have disappeared, other than scattered bones; most ancient artifacts have decayed, other than stone articles and potsherds (pottery fragments). Moreover, scientific techniques for dating ancient matter, such as dendrochronology, the study of annual growth of tree rings preserved in wood samples, and radiocarbon dating, measuring the amount of C-14 (the radioactive isotope of carbon) present in materials with organic content, must allow for a margin of error.

As a result, the study of ancient Indians can be confusing. One scholar might have a theory about the migrations of a people, with which other scholars disagree. Another might use one term to label a period of prehistory or a cultural group or an artifact, while others apply different terms. Or a scholar might assign a set of dates for the existence of an ancient people that are different from those given by others. In any case, the following categories provide a general structure for organizing knowledge surrounding the evolving lifeways of prehistoric American peoples.

Paleo-Indians

In the geologic time scale devised by scholars, the Age of Mammals is called the Cenozoic era. The period in the Cenozoic era in which humankind came into existence is called the Pleistocene epoch. During the Pleistocene epoch, which is thought to be at least a million years long, the world experienced a series of four ice ages. In each of these ice ages, much of the world was covered with glaciers. Between the ice ages were periods of warmer weather and melting ice. During the last of the four ice ages, humans first arrived in the Americas.

It is theorized that during the last ice age, so much of the earth's water was locked up in glaciers that the oceans were lower than today and more land was thus exposed. Where there is now water between Alaska and Siberia (eastern Russia)—known as the Bering Strait—there was once a wide strip of land on four different occasions, each about 5,000 to 10,000 years long, during the last 60,000 years. Scholars refer to this once-exposed landmass as the Bering Strait land bridge, or Beringia.

Animals could have migrated across this land bridge—now-extinct creatures such as mammoths, mastodons, bighorn bison, and saber-toothed tigers. And the ancient ancestors of the Indians—the big-game hunters who depended on these animals for food—could have followed them out of Asia to North America.

The exact time that the first bands of hunters and their families arrived in North America is not known. The estimated time cited by scholars for years, based on early archaeological evidence, was sometime before 11,200 years ago. More recent finds have pushed the date back to sometime before 12,500 years ago. Growing evidence at a site in Chile known as Monte Verde is pushing the estimated date as far back as sometime before 33,000 years ago. Moreover, linguistic studies using computer projections have indicated that too

many native language families (as many as 150) exist in the Americas today to have evolved in 10,000 or so years. According to these results, 40,000 years ago is a more likely approximation for the arrival of the first Americans.

In any case, the migration of humans from Asia to North America did not happen all at once, but in many waves of small bands along the same route. Over the following thousands of years, their descendants worked their way southward, probably first during a temporary melt, following an ice-free passage along the Rocky Mountains, before dispersing throughout much of the Americas.

The first Indians, the true discoverers of the Americas, had only wooden and stone tools and no metal. The period in human evolution before the invention of metal tools is known as the Stone Age, or the Paleolithic Age. The earliest Indians are called Paleo-Indians, or Lithic Indians.

The Paleo-Indians lived for the most part in caves, under overhangs, and in brushwood lean-tos. They wore hide and fur clothing. They used fire to keep warm, to cook, to protect themselves from animals while sleeping, and to hunt. By lighting fires on the grasslands, the hunters could drive herds of animals over cliffs and into swamps and bogs, where they could be killed. The early Indians had different methods for lighting fires: striking a spark with certain stones, such as flint, or by rubbing wood together. Fire drills, made from two sticks and a strip of rawhide, enabled the rapid spinning of wood against wood to generate enough friction to ignite wood powder or other vegetable material.

In addition to woolly mammoths, mastodons, bighorn bison, and saber-toothed tigers, the Paleo-Indians hunted other extinct species: American lions, camels, short-faced bears, dire wolves, giant beavers, giant sloths, giant armadillos, curve-snouted tapirs, musk oxen, peccaries, native horses, plus smaller game. The first Indians were also gatherers of wild plant foods: greens, seeds, berries, roots, and bulbs.

The craftsmanship of the Paleo-Indians was essential to their big-game hunting way of life. The early Indians had techniques for making spearheads razor-sharp. The first Paleo-Indians did not have stone-pointed spears. They probably used fire to harden the tips of wooden spears, but this theory is unproven because the wooden spears decayed long ago. The earliest Indians did, however, have roughly shaped stone and bone tools for scraping and chopping. Later Paleo-Indians developed methods of shaping certain types of stone—especially flint, chert, and obsidian—into sharp points and edges. In percussion flaking, they removed chips and sharpened the point by striking it with a stone. In pressure flaking, they pressed antler or bone tools against the point to shape and sharpen it.

Scholars use the different types of points found at campsites, hunting sites, and quarry sites to determine different technological phases, traditions, or cultures among the Paleo-Indians. For example, the Clovis culture is named after the Clovis site in New Mexico, but Clovis-style points have been found all over North America, usually with mammoth and mastodon bones. They were one and a half to five inches long, with fluting (lengthwise channels) along both sides of the base, where they were attached to wooden shafts. The Clovis points have been dated from about 9200 to 8000 B.C.

Clovis point

The Sandia culture, named after a cave site in the Sandia Mountains of New Mexico, was characterized by stone points two to four inches long with rounded bases and a bulge on one side where they were attached to wooden shafts. The Sandia points have been dated from

Sandia point

about 9100 to 8000 B.C. The culture was located in the Southeast.

The Folsom culture is named after the Folsom site in New Mexico. Evidence of Folsom hunters has been found mostly in the Southwest and Far West, but also on the Great Plains along with the remains of bighorn bison. The Folsom tradition lasted from about 9100 to 8000 B.C. The Folsom points, three-quarters of an inch to three inches long, were unique in that they had fluting on both sides running almost the entire length of the point. It is theorized that these long channels, which are very difficult to make in stone, served an additional purpose besides helping to attach the point to the spear shaft. Per-

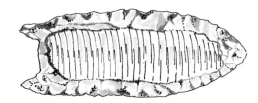

Folsom point

haps they increased the flow of blood from an animal or increased the spear's velocity when it was thrown.

Some time during the Paleolithic Age, Folsom Native Americans began first using spear-throwing devices called atlatls. These were wooden sticks about two feet long with animal-hide hoops to provide a firm grasp, a stone weight for balance, and a hook to hold the spear shaft. With an atlatl, a hunter had increased leverage that allowed him to fling his spear harder and faster. (Bows and arrows were not invented until much later.)

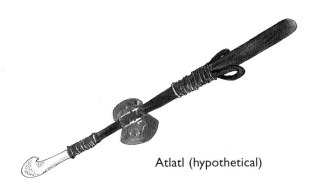

Atlatl (hypothetical)

The Plano, or Plainview, culture, named after the Plainview site in Texas, is also associated primarily with the Great Plains and the bighorn bison. Plano craftsmen did not flute their points, however. The Plano Indians also demonstrated a more varied culture than the Indians before them. For example, they built corrals to trap animals. They also developed a method of preserving meat by mixing it with animal fat and berries and packing it in hide or gut containers. The Plano period lasted from about 8000 to 4500 B.C.

The late Pleistocene epoch was a time of great transition. During the years from about 10,000 to 8000 B.C., the climate warmed and the great glaciers retreated northward once and for all. The Ice Age became what is referred to as the Watershed Age. The melting ice created numerous lakes and swamplands, many of which would eventually evaporate. North America gradually evolved to its present form by about 5000 B.C.

The changing climate probably contributed to the extinction of the big-game animals. The Paleo-Indians might also have played a part in this phenomenon. They became such skilled hunters—using atlatls and communal drives of huge herds—that they killed more game than they needed. Archaeologists hold this theory because they have found at kill sites the bones of many large animals with stone points in them. This killing of more animals than necessary is sometimes referred to as the Pleistocene Overkill.

Archaic Indians

The end of the Pleistocene epoch marked the beginning of the current geologic period called the Holocene epoch. The Paleo-Indian period also evolved into the Archaic Indian period at this time. The Paleo-Indian period lasted from about 50,000 to 8000 B.C. The transitional period (the Watershed Age) between the Paleo-Indian period and the Archaic Indian period lasted from about 8000 to 5000 B.C. The Archaic Indian period lasted from about 5000 to 1000 B.C. It should be kept in mind that these dates are general. The lifeways described for each period were the dominant ones. That is to say, while most Indians lived a certain way, there were other cultures in different parts of the Americas that were exceptions to the rule. For example, the Indians of the Plano culture, normally considered Paleo-Indians, continued their same way of life into the Archaic.

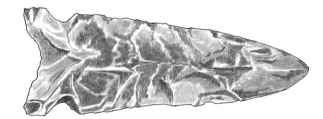

Archaic Indian point

In any case, what distinguished those who are labeled Archaic Indians from Paleo-Indians was a more varied diet. The big game were now extinct, and Archaic Indians hunted and trapped the species of mammals we know today. They fished in rivers and lakes. They gathered many different kinds of edible wild plants and planned their migrations around the ripening of berries as well as the movements of animal herds. Like the Paleo-Indians, the Archaic Indians generally led a nomadic way of life, but it was more localized since they no longer tracked the huge herds such great distances. Archaic Indians are sometimes referred to as Foraging Indians.

In addition to a more varied diet, the Archaic Indians had a wider variety of tools and utensils than their predecessors. Archaic craftsmen shaped spears, atlatls, bolas, harpoons, knives, axes, adzes, wedges, chisels, scrapers, celts, hammers, mauls, anvils, awls, drills, fishhooks and lines, traps, mortars and pestles, and pipes. They used many different kinds of material, including stone, wood, bone, antler, shell, and ivory.

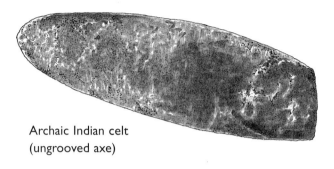

Archaic Indian celt
(ungrooved axe)

Archaic Indians made a number of key inventions. They learned to weave plant materials into clothing and baskets. They also learned new methods of food preparation and food preservation. For cooking, they placed heated stones into stone pots to boil water. They used their baskets and hide containers to store food. They constructed boats and domesticated the dog.

Archaic Indians also shaped materials into an assortment of ornaments and sacred objects. They had elaborate rituals surrounding the burial of the dead. Their religions were more highly ceremonialized than those of their predecessors.

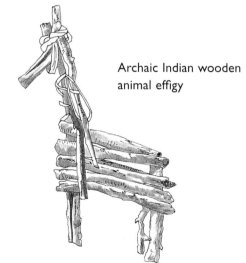

Archaic Indian wooden
animal effigy

Five cultures, each in a different region of North America, show the diversity of Archaic Indian life. The Old Cordilleran (or Cascade) culture, which actually began about 9000 B.C., during the Paleolithic period, existed in the Pacific Northwest along the Columbia River until

5000 B.C. or afterward. Cascade spear points, in the shape of willow leaves, were used to hunt small game.

Another culture that began early in the Paleo-Indian period but evolved to a more typically Archaic way of life was the Desert culture in the Great Basin region of what is now Utah, Nevada, and Arizona. It lasted from about 9000 to 1000 B.C. At Danger Cave in Utah, archaeologists have found woven containers, the first example of basketry in North America. They also have found grinding stones used to prepare seeds, and traps made of twine used to capture small game.

The Cochise culture in what is now Arizona and New Mexico evolved out of the Desert culture and lasted from about 7000 to 500 B.C. Cochise Indians hunted many different kinds of small mammals, such as deer, antelope, and rabbits. They also foraged for snakes, lizards, insects, and edible wild plants. Archaeologists have found many Cochise millstones, called manos and metates (like mortars and pestles), that the Indians used to grind seeds, nuts, and grains. The abundance of these utensils shows the growing importance of plant foods in the Archaic Indian diet.

Among Cochise remains have also been found the first evidence of farming north of Mexico. In Bat Cave, New Mexico, archaeologists discovered dried-up cobs of corn from a cultivated species of the plant, probably dating from about 3500 B.C.

Another Archaic culture is the Old Copper culture of the Great Lakes region, lasting from about 4000 to 1500 B.C. This grouping takes its name from the copper objects discovered among the culture's remains, the earliest use of metal known among Indians north of Mexico. Old Copper Indians used natural deposits of copper—sheets in rock fissures or nuggets in the soil—to make tools and ornaments. They shaped it by heating it then hammering it, again and again.

Still another eastern Archaic people were the Red Paint people of present-day New England and eastern Canada. The Red Paint culture takes its name from the use of ground-up red iron ore to line its graves. This culture lasted from about 3000 to 500 B.C.

Archaeologists have found objects of many other Archaic Indians in different parts of North America. Those mentioned above are among the most famous. Far to the north, another remarkable development occurred during this period. Ancestors of the INUIT and ALEUT migrated to North America across the Bering Sea in small boats, from about 2500 to 1000 B.C. The Inuit and Aleut are therefore not descended from the Paleo-Indians that migrated across the Bering Strait land bridge, as are other Indians probably are.

Formative Indians

As stated before, the end of the Archaic Indian period is given as about 1000 B.C. The next period of prehistoric Indians is usually called the Formative period, which lasted right-up until the time of Native American contact with Europeans, about A.D. 1500. Broadly speaking, the Formative period is defined by the following cultural traits: farming, domesticated animals, village life, houses, trade, pottery, weaving, basketry, the bow and arrow, refined craftsmanship, and elaborate religious ceremonies. Many of the cultural traits typical of Formative Indians were developed during the Archaic period or even before. For example, Indians in what is now Mexico cultivated plants as early as 7000 B.C.; Indians north of Mexico farmed as early as 3500 B.C.; but agriculture and other typical Formative lifeways became widespread among Native North Americans only after 1000 B.C.

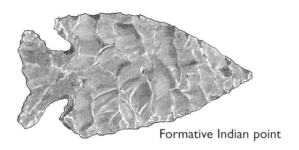

Formative Indian point

After 1000 B.C., highly developed civilizations came into existence, especially in territory that is now Mexico. When speaking of this region with regard to Native Americans, the term *Mesoamerica,* or Middle America, is used. Because a number of peoples—the OLMEC, MAYA, TOLTEC, and AZTEC—had such highly organized societies, with cities even, what is usually called the Formative period in North America is referred to as the Classic period in Middle America. (Before the Classic period was the Preclassic period; after the Classic was the Postclassic.)

Formative Indian pipe

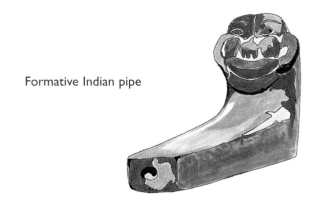

The Inca of the Andes Mountains in what is now Peru in South America also had a highly organized civilization, with farming, cities, classes of society, highly refined architecture and art forms, and hieroglyphic writing systems. Yet since this book deals only with North American Indians (with Mexico and the Caribbean area considered part of North America), the Inca are not included. The civilizations of both the Inca of South America and the Aztec of Mesoamerica existed at the time of contact with whites, and their downfall was brought about by the Spanish, as recorded in written records from the time. Moreover, Maya hieroglyphics have been discovered that give us a recorded history of these people.

There were also highly developed farming civilizations north of Mexico. These civilizations were influenced by the cultures of Mesoamerica. They occurred in the Southwest and are known as the Anasazi culture, the Hohokam culture, and the Mogollon culture (see SOUTHWEST CULTURES). Other highly advanced cultures occurred east of the Mississippi River and are known as the Adena culture, the Hopewell culture, and the Mississippian culture (see MOUND BUILDERS).

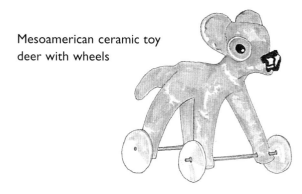

Mesoamerican ceramic toy deer with wheels

Once again, the terms used by scholars—such as *Prehistoric Indians, Paleo-Indians, Archaic Indians*, and *Formative Indians*—are designed to help in Native American studies. They are not absolute. Exact dates cannot be applied to them. Knowledge about early Indians keeps growing with continuing archaeological excavations. And different terms are applied in different parts of the continent, depending on how Indians evolved in that particular area. Yet these general terms help give an overview of the intriguing ancestry of Native American peoples and tribes.

PUEBLO INDIANS

Pueblo, pronounced PWEB-lo, means "village" or "town" in Spanish. The word has come to stand for a certain kind of Indian village with a certain type of architecture, as well as for the Indians themselves who occupied them. As a result, the word sometimes appears without a capital first letter to denote a village or building, or with a capital to denote the people.

The name, when used for people, is a general term. There were many different Pueblo peoples in the American Southwest, which is referred to as the Southwest Culture Area by scholars (see SOUTHWEST INDIANS). Some of these Indians lived on the Colorado Plateau. These were the HOPI and ZUNI. The Hopi were the westernmost Pueblo peoples, living in what is now northeastern Arizona. The Zuni lived to their east in what is now western New Mexico.

Other Pueblo Indians lived along a 130-mile stretch of the Rio Grande, the long river flowing through much of the Southwest all the way to the Gulf of Mexico. There were four tribal groups, speaking different languages: Tewa, Tiwa, Towa (or Jemez), and Keres. The first three spoke varying dialects of the Kiowa-Tanoan language family. The Keres spoke a different language, called Keresan.

All four groups had different pueblos, or villages, often situated on the tops of mesas (small plateaus). The different pueblos had names. These names are sometimes used as distinct tribal names because each village was a separate unit with its own leaders and traditions.

The Pueblo Indians are thought to be descendants of Anasazi and Mogollon peoples of the early Southwest cultures and inherited many cultural traits from them, including architecture, farming, pottery, and basketry.

Lifeways

Pueblo-style houses are unique among Indian dwellings because of their apartment-building design. They had as many as five different levels. The flat roof of one level served as the floor and front yard of another. The different stories were interconnected by ladders. For much of history, the walls, especially on the ground level, had no doors or windows, making the villages easier to defend from attacks. The Indians entered their rooms through holes in the roofs.

Two different types of building material were used for the walls: the Hopi and Zuni used stones that were mortared and surfaced with plaster; in addition to some stone, the Rio Grande Indians used adobe bricks, made from sundried earth and straw. The Pueblo Indians stretched log beams across the roofs, covering them with poles, brush, and more plaster. Sometimes the beams projected beyond the walls and were used to hang food for drying.

The Pueblo Indians also dug pithouses as ceremonial chambers or clubhouses. The Hopi name for these underground chambers, *kiva,* is a term now applied to all such Pueblo Indian structures. Kivas typically were located at a central plaza of the pueblo.

The Pueblo Indians cultivated a variety of crops, including corn of many varieties, squash, beans, sunflowers, cotton, and tobacco. They also kept domesticated turkeys. Pueblo hunters also pursued wild deer, antelope, and rabbits.

Pueblo men wore kilts of cotton plus leather sandals. The women wore cotton dresses and sandals or high moccasin boots. They also used deerskin and rabbit-skin for clothing. The women made coiled pottery, which they polished and painted with exquisite designs. They also made baskets, both coiled and wicker types.

Pueblo men carved wooden masks to wear in elaborate ceremonies. Many of these were for the purpose of bringing rain, essential to their farming. In the Hopi religion, these masks and the beings they were supposed to represent were called kachinas. The Indians also carved

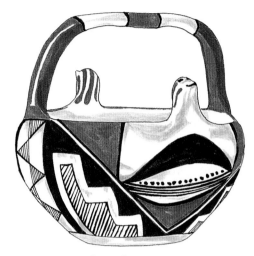

Pueblo Indian pottery from Acoma

kachina dolls to teach their children about their religion. Other peoples had different names for similar legendary beings, but the term *kachina* is now widespread.

Early Contacts with the Spanish

The early history of the Pueblo Indians in postcontact times is interwoven with that of the Spanish, who first claimed the region and gave it the name New Mexico. A Spanish explorer named Marcos de Niza reached Zuni country as early as 1539, only 18 years after the colony of New Spain was founded in North America. Then Francisco de Coronado explored the region in 1540, and Antonio de Espejo in 1582.

Yet these expeditions did not alter the Pueblo Indian way of life. In 1598, however, Juan de Oñate arrived with

Pueblo Indian adobe architecture

129 colonists—entire families—to establish the colony of New Mexico. He brought horses, goats, and sheep with him. In 1610, he founded the capital of this colony, Santa Fe. He also forced his will on the Indians through his soldiers. He made them pay taxes in cotton crops, cloth, and work. The Spanish taught the Indians to grow new crops, such as wheat, peppers, and peaches; to tend flocks; and to spin and weave wool. Catholic missionaries also tried to eradicate native religions and spread their own.

During his first year in New Mexico, Oñate sent word to the various Indians that they were henceforth subjects of the Spanish monarch. When the Keres Indians of the Acoma Pueblo rose up and killed the soldiers who brought this command, he sent others to punish the Indians. The soldiers, after scaling the steep cliffs of the mesa and capturing the pueblo, massacred hundreds of inhabitants. Oñate sentenced the survivors in a public trial. He ordered his soldiers to cut off one foot of all the males over 25. All females plus boys over 12 were to serve as slaves for 20 years. Children under 12 were to be placed in missions. Oñate's action against the Acoma Indians made it easier for the Spanish to subjugate the other pueblos because the Indians now feared Spanish reprisals.

The Pueblo Rebellion

The Pueblo Indians finally did rise up again in a revolt called the Pueblo Rebellion, in 1680. The uprising was led by a Tewa shaman named Popé. The issue of religion was central to the Pueblo Rebellion. The generally peaceful Pueblo Indians had tolerated the Spanish for years. They were willing to do the bidding of the Spanish if allowed to practice their traditional religion in the kivas. But when Spanish officials consistently punished practitioners through floggings, the Indians took up arms.

Popé prepared for war by sending runners to other villages from his pueblo at San Juan after word that the rebellion would soon come. They carried cords of maguey fibers indicating a certain number of days until the general uprising. On the given day, August 11, 1680, warriors from numerous pueblos, along the Rio Grande and to the west, moved against soldiers and priests stationed in the pueblos as well as ranchers living on outlying haciendas, killing many.

The Pueblo Indians actually drove the Spanish out of New Mexico. The Spanish did put up a fight at Santa Fe, holding out for days against Popé's men by firing brass cannon from behind the palace walls. But when the Indians grew tired of the siege and withdrew to their pueblos, the Spanish headed south to El Paso.

The Pueblo Indians had regained control of their homeland. They now were free to practice their tradi-tional culture and religion. Unfortunately, Popé's new-found power corrupted him and he became an exacting leader himself, not even permitting his people to use Spanish tools left behind.

Later History

Spanish troops marched north out of El Paso in 1689 and recaptured Santa Fe in 1692. The Pueblo Indians again became wards of the Spanish state. The Spanish treated the Indians less harshly, however, allowing them to practice their traditional religions to a greater degree.

A lasting cultural trait grew out of the Pueblo Rebellion and came to influence Indians far and wide. It was during the revolt that the Indians first acquired their own horses, left behind by the fleeing Spanish. The Pueblo Indians traded these with northern tribes or lost them in raids. The more northern Indians, such as the UTE, traded the horses with other PLAINS INDIANS. By the mid-1700s, horses had spread to many tribes and a whole new way of life was emerging on the Great Plains.

The Pueblo Indians remained under Spanish rule until 1821, the year of the Mexican Revolution. In 1848, following the Mexican War and the Mexican Cession of territory to the United States as defined by the Treaty of Guadalupe Hidalgo, the Pueblo Indians came under the authority of the U.S. government.

The Pueblo Indians remained peaceful through this period. The one exception occurred during the Mexican War of 1845–48, when the Tiwa of the Taos pueblo, angry because American troops stole their crops and livestock and even kidnapped their women, launched a series of raids against settlers. U.S. forces responded with a heavy artillery attack on the pueblo. The thick adobe walls repelled the shells, however. But the overwhelming firepower of the soldiers eventually routed the Indians.

Not all historic pueblos survived to modern times. Attacks by raiding tribes, such as the APACHE, NAVAJO and COMANCHE, took their toll as did diseases carried by Europeans and Euroamericans.

Pueblo Indian black pottery from San Ildefonso (modern)

Contemporary Pueblo Indians

The following is a list of current pueblos in the upper Rio Grande region of New Mexico, near Albuquerque and Santa Fe, with the tribal group in parentheses (Hopi and Zuni pueblos are discussed separately in this book): Acoma (Keres), Cochiti (Keres), Isleta (Tiwa), Jemez (Towa), Laguna (Keres), Nambe (Tewa), Picuris (Tiwa), Pojoaque (Tewa), Sandia (Tiwa), San Felipe (Keres), San Ildefonso (Tewa), San Juan (Tewa), Santa Ana (Keres), Santa Clara (Tewa), Santo Domingo (Keres), Taos (Tiwa), Tesuque (Tewa), and Zia (Keres).

The Ysleta del Sur Pueblo within the city limits of El Paso, Texas, has peoples of Tigua (an alternate spelling of Tiwa) ancestry as well as descendants of Apache and other peoples.

The various pueblos are a good place to experience traditional native America. Some pueblos have buildings dating back centuries. Some tribes encourage tourism and welcome visitors to their seasonal festivals and masked dances. Traditional arts and crafts are practiced, and, from their own homes, tribal members sell pottery, jewelry, drums, kachina dolls, and other artifacts. The way of life varies from pueblo to pueblo of course. Most Pueblo Indians have accepted modern technology in their homes. Others have kept much of their traditional architecture in their ancestral villages—such as at Acoma and Taos, the oldest continually inhabited villages in North America—building modern homes on surrounding reservation lands. Most pueblos also have centuries-old mission churches with active congregations; many Pueblo Indians leave room in their life for Catholicism as well as their traditional religions. Some pueblos have modern stores, restaurants, and casinos to generate income on reservation lands. The landscape surrounding many of the pueblos is spectacular, with the exposed multicolored rock of mountain, mesa, and canyon. Near some of the pueblos are Anasazi ruins, revealing a continuum of Pueblo culture through the ages.

Pueblo Indian jewelry from Santo Domingo (modern)

QUAPAW

Quapaw pronounced KWAW-paw, comes from the Siouan word *ugakhpa,* meaning "downstream people." This translation helps place the tribe geographically: the Quapaw lived most of their history along the west side of the lower Mississippi, south of other Siouan-speaking Indians.

The Quapaw also were called the Arkansas by ALGONQUIANS and the French. It is from this latter version of their name that the name of the river and state is taken. The *ansas* part of the word is Siouan for "people of the south wind," as found in the tribal name *Kansa* (see KAW). The *ark* part is taken from the French word *arc* for "bow." The territory of the Quapaw (and OSAGE) is famous for the wood of a kind of mulberry tree, called Osage orange, prized for making bows. The name of the Ozark Mountains is an Americanization of the French phrase *aux arcs,* meaning "at the place of bows."

The Quapaw are thought to have once lived in the Ohio Valley with their Siouan kinsmen, the Kaw, OMAHA, Osage, and PONCA. But they eventually migrated westward, descending the Mississippi to the mouth of the Arkansas River, territory now in southeastern Arkansas. Their kinspeople settled to the north of them.

The Quapaw lived in palisaded villages of bark-covered, rectangular houses with domed roofs. The Quapaw also covered their houses with woven mats, hides, and grass. They were skillful farmers. They built mounds to hold both temples and graves and they made exquisite pottery.

Sometimes Indians living along the Mississippi and possessing cultural elements of tribes from both the woodlands to the east and the Great Plains to the west are referred to as PRAIRIE INDIANS, after the tall grass prairies of the region. The Quapaw usually are classified as part of the Great Plains Culture Area, however. The horse, brought to North America by the Spanish, reached them in the early 1700s. From that time on, the Quapaw lived much like other PLAINS INDIANS, hunting herds of buffalo on horseback. The Quapaw lived just across the Mississippi River from tribes considered part of the Southeast Culture Area, such as the CHICKASAW and TUNICA, with whom they traded and exchanged ideas (see SOUTHEAST INDIANS).

The Quapaw had early contacts with French explorers, including Jacques Marquette in 1673, René-Robert Cavelier de La Salle in 1682, and Henri Tonti in 1686. They became allies of the French, who, in the 1700s, traveled the Mississippi between Quebec and Louisiana in order to trade.

The Quapaw, despite trade contacts with the French, avoided taking up arms in most of the clashes among the three European powers in North America—France, England, and Spain—over the Mississippi region. Yet starting in the mid-1700s, intertribal conflict over the fur trade plus the hardship resulting from contact with non-Indians from disease and alcohol, led Quapaw families to leave the Mississippi River valley and move closer to the Arkansas River on the south side.

In 1818 and 1824, with the great influx of American settlers from the east, the Quapaw were pressured into signing away all their lands.

In 1824, they agreed to live in Texas on the south side of the Red River among the Caddo. But because the Red River overflowed, destroying their crops, and because there was much illness among them, the Quapaw were unhappy in their new homeland and drifted back to the Arkansas River region.

In 1833, when white settlers complained about their presence in Arkansas, the federal government forced the Quapaw to relocate within the Indian Territory among the Osage. Then in 1867, soon after the northern part of the Indian Territory became the state of Kansas, the tribe again had to sign away their land in southeastern Kansas. They were allowed to keep only a small portion in what is now the northeastern portion of Oklahoma, where they still hold lands in trust.

Fortunately, the tribe has been able to make the most of its limited land holdings. In 1905, lead and zinc deposits were discovered on parcels of Quapaw land, which, despite early attempts by mining interests to defraud individuals with allotted pieces, have provided decent incomes for tribal members.

The tribe sponsors an annual intertribal powwow near Miami, Oklahoma.

QUASSARTE *see* COUSHATTA

QUECHAN *see* YUMA (QUECHAN)

ROANOKE

What now is the state of North Carolina once was the homeland of native peoples of many different language families. In the tidewater region of seacoast and sounds and along the rivers emptying into the sounds lived various Algonquian-speaking tribes. Along the coastal plain lived the Iroquoian-speaking TUSCARORA. Farther inland, on the Piedmont plateau—a region of rolling hills—were a number of Siouan-speaking tribes, such as the Cheraw, Eno, Keyauwee, Shakori, Sissipahaw, and Woccon. In the Blue Ridge Mountains to the west lived the Iroquoian-speaking CHEROKEE. Similarly, to the north in what now is the state of Virginia, Algonquian peoples, such as the POWHATAN, lived along the coast, and Iroquoians and Siouans lived inland. This pattern breaks down to the south in present-day South Carolina, where Siouans and Muskogeans occupied coastal regions.

The coastal ALGONQUIANS are classified as NORTHEAST INDIANS, because their way of life was similar to that of coastal Algonquians to the north, whereas the inland Iroquoians and Siouans in present-day North Carolina and Virginia are classified as SOUTHEAST INDIANS.

The Algonquians formerly living in present-day coastal North Carolina included the Chowanoc on the Chowan River; the Coree on the peninsula south of the Neuse River; the Hatteras on the Outer Banks; the Moratok at the head of the Roanoke River; the Machapunga at Lake Mattsmuskeet; the Neusiok (probably Algonquian) on the Neuse River; the Pomeiok (later called the Pamlico) on the Pamlico River; the Roanoke on Roanoke Island at the mouth of Albermarle Sound and on the opposite coastal mainland; the Secotan on Pamlico Sound; and the Weapemeoc on the north side of Albermarle Sound. With regard to densely populated regions such as this, where the tribes are extinct and the variations in dialect are not known, it is difficult to determine tribal versus band groupings. Certain villages had autonomy; others were allied under sachems. In fact, the Roanoke (or Roanoak or Roanoac), despite their political autonomy, often are discussed as a subtribe of the Secotan. *Roanoke,* pronounced RO-uh-noke, originally was a village name; it possibly means "white-shell place."

Yet a certain amount is known about North Carolina's Algonquians because it was among them that the English first attempted to establish colonies in the Americas. The two attempts at colonies failed—the second Roanoke Colony has become known as the Lost Colony because the fate of the colonists never has been determined—and the historical and cultural record about these early Algonquians covers only a brief period. Two decades later, in 1607, the English founded Jamestown to the north, in the Chesapeake Bay region, which became the first permanent English settlement in the Americas, leading to extensive contacts with and a much more detailed record of the Powhatan peoples. In 1620, the English reached Plymouth Rock, resulting in other permanent settlements and extensive contacts with New England Algonquians.

Because of their permanence, Jamestown and Plymouth are given much more attention in American history books than the Roanoke colonies, and the names of Powhatan, Pocahontas, and Opechancanough of the Powhatan and Squanto and Massasoit of the WAMPANOAG are more likely to be known than Manteo of the Hatteras; Ensenore, Granganimeo, Wingina, and Wanchese of the Roanoke; and Menatonon and Skyco of the Chowanoc. But the stories of North Carolina's coastal peoples and their relations with Europeans are just as relevant to North American history—and just as poignant, with native peoples experiencing death from disease and warfare, as well as shattered friendships. A pattern was established that would repeat itself time and again throughout history: early friendly relations between Native Americans and the first visitors to their lands; gradual deterioration of those relations through misunderstanding and treachery; and the eventual displacement of native peoples.

Exploratory Expedition

In July 1584, an exploratory expedition under Captains Philip Amadas and Arthur Barlowe, the first of the three Roanoke voyages sponsored by Sir Walter Raleigh with the support of Queen Elizabeth I, reached the Outer Banks, or Barrier Islands, of present-day North Carolina and explored Roanoke Island as well as parts of the neighboring mainland. Amadas and Barlowe and their men had friendly contacts with native peoples, meeting the Roanoke Indian Granganimeo, brother of Wingina, the current *werowance,* or sachem, who had inherited the position from Ensenore, their father.

Because of its secure situation, protected by the outer islands, and the welcome offered by native peoples in the village of Roanoke, Roanoke Island seemed a favorable site to establish a presence in the Americas from where privateering against Spanish ships could be conducted. It was decided that two Indians would return to England with the expedition—Manteo, a Hatteras of the village of Croatoan on the Outer Banks, and Wanchese of the Roanoke, cousin to Granganimeo and Wingina. They departed the Americas in August, reaching England in mid-September.

In London, Manteo and Wanchese met Raleigh and Queen Elizabeth. Their presence helped Raleigh raise funds for a permanent colony.

The First Roanoke Colony

The following April, 1585, Raleigh's fleet of seven ships, commanded by his cousin Sir Richard Grenville, set forth with as many as 600 men—among them the colonists planning to stay in the Americas. The ships reached Pamlico and Albermarle Sounds by June after a stopover in Puerto Rico. The colonists under Governor Ralph Lane built Fort Raleigh on Roanoke Island and explored the region, having contacts with many of the area tribes.

The scientist Thomas Harriot was one of the members of Raleigh's first colony. He studied the native peoples and cataloged the wildlife and resources. His work was published on his return to England as *A briefe and true report of the new found land of Virginia* (part of North Carolina originally was part of the "Virginia" patent). Also among the colonists was John White, who, in addition to serving as the cartographer, made watercolor drawings of peoples, animals, and plants that also were published in Europe. Their work informed Europeans of Native American customs, showing, for example, villages of rectangular wigwams with rounded roofs, some surrounded by palisades; fields of corn within or next to the villages; the burning and scraping out of the interior of logs to make dugout canoes; people fishing with nets and spears from dugouts or by trapping fish in weirs; food preparation, such as cooking in earthen pots or on wooden grills; communally eating from large dishes while sitting on mats of reeds; deerskin clothing, including apronlike skirts and full-length capes; ceremonial dancing around posts with carved faces; and funeral practices, such as placing the bodies of dead leaders on covered raised platforms.

Yet English relations with the Roanoke and other tribes deteriorated for a variety of reasons, especially over the provision of food. In one incident in the summer of 1585, the English burned a village on the mainland because a Secotan had stolen a silver cup. To assure the cooperation of the upriver tribes in offering supplies to his men during their search for gold and pearls, in spring of 1586, Lane had Skyco, son of the powerful Chowanoc sachem Menatonon, taken hostage. The deaths of Granganimeo and Ensenore, very likely from disease carried to the native population, probably further hurt relations because the former are thought to have headed the pro-English faction. In any case, Wingina, taking a new name, Pemisapan, turned militant and attempted to starve out the English. Wanchese, his cousin, turned against the English as well. Manteo, the Hatteras, remained pro-English. Why these two former friends, who both were honored in England, chose these separate paths is not known. The historical record also is incomplete about the fate of Skyco.

Using rumors of a planned Indian attack as his excuse and pretending to seek a council with Wingina, on June 1, 1586, Lane led an attack on the mainland village of Dasamonquepeuc. Wingina was shot and beheaded. Less than three weeks later, the colonists, "weak and unfit men," departed Roanoke Island with the visiting fleet of Sir Francis Drake. Manteo again accompanied them with another Indian by the name of Towaye.

The Lost Colony

In May 1587, another fleet set sail from England. The 150 colonists in Raleigh's second attempt at a colony, with John White as governor, included women and children. Manteo returned with them. (Towaye's fate is not known; he may have died in England.) The intended place of settlement was Chesapeake Bay, but on reaching the Roanoke Island region in July, Simon Fernandes, the pilot of the fleet, refused to take the colonists any further. They were forced to rehabilitate the former settlement and reestablish tenuous relations with area tribes. An attack by the Roanoke, now led by Wanchese, on a colonist while he was fishing away from the fort, showed that the Roanoke had not forgiven the outsiders for the death of Wingina.

That August, White christened Manteo and made him lord of Roanoke and Dasamonquepeuc, thus attempting to usurp Wanchese's power. Also, the first English child was born in the Americas—Virginia Dare—to John White's daughter Eleanor White Dare and son-in-law Ananias Dare.

At the end of August, with supplies dwindling and winter approaching, the colonists persuaded White to return to England for supplies. The following spring, March 1588, a relief expedition under Grenville was ordered not to sail because of warfare with Spain. White lined up two small ships for a crossing, but his ship was intercepted and looted by French pirates, ending the expedition. The invasion of England by the Spanish Armada in July–August 1588 further delayed his return. When he finally reached Roanoke Island in August 1590, the colonists had disappeared. To this day, it is not certain what became of them. The only clue White found was the word *Croatoan* carved on the stockade post, probably indicating that at least some among the vanished settlers had relocated to Manteo's village. Others may have built a boat in an attempt to reach Chesapeake Bay. There of course is the possibility that all were killed in attacks by Roanoke, Powhatan, or other area tribes. Some may have intermarried with native peoples. Theories on the fate of the Lost Colonists had led to an entire literature. One theory purports that the LUMBEE have Lost Colonists among their ancestors.

The Lost Algonquians

Development of the region by the English in the 17th century led to the displacement and attrition of the coastal Algonquians. By the early 18th century, only scattered individuals remained, and they tended to settle among inland peoples. Their legacy endures in books. It also endures in place-names, as in the case of Roanoke Island and two of its municipalities, Manteo and Wanchese.

Travel to present or former homelands of native peoples helps one get a sense of their culture and history. Roanoke Island and the surrounding region offer a view of the past: Fort Raleigh National Historic Site and Roanoke Island Festival Park have displays concerning the Roanoke and other coastal Algonquians. A docudrama shown in the Festival Park theater, *The Legend of Two Path,* recreates the story of Skyco, Manteo, and Wanchese.

SAC

This tribe has two common versions of its name, *Sac,* pronounced SACK, and *Sauk,* pronounced SAWK. The name is derived from the Algonquian word *Asakiwaki,* meaning the "yellow earth people." For much of their history, the Sac were allied with the FOX (MESQUAKI), the "red earth people." The two tribes were also closely related to the KICKAPOO. In their distant past, perhaps all three peoples were one.

Lifeways

The Sac are considered western Great Lakes ALGON-QUIANS because of their locations and their languages. They are also called Northeast Woodland Algonquians because they usually situated their villages in stands of trees along river valleys (see NORTHEAST INDIANS). They are also referred to as Prairie Algonquians because they hunted buffalo in the tall grass prairies of the Mississippi Valley (see PRAIRIE INDIANS).

The Sac year, as was the case with many other Northeast tribes, revolved around a farming village existence in warm seasons, then a hunting and nomadic existence in cold seasons. In the villages, their houses were relatively large—bark-covered wigwams that were either rectangular or domed. When Sac were out on the trail, the shelter had to be portable. Most favored the oval wigwam with a reed covering.

Migrations

Like many of the tribes of the region, the Sac migrated often, especially when non-Indian settlers started coming in great numbers into their original territory.

It is thought that the Sac once lived on Michigan's southern peninsula. Then they moved west of Lake Michigan to present-day Wisconsin sometime before European explorers came in the 1600s. At that time the biggest Sac villages were on the Wisconsin River. But in the late 1700s, they united with other tribes to defeat the ILLINOIS, after which most Sac resettled southward in what used to be Illinois land. Many Fox, allies of the Sac since 1734, lived near or among them. The Rock River in Illinois became the summer homeland of many bands.

The Black Hawk War

The Rock River bands played the biggest part in the Black Hawk War of 1832, the last of the wars for the

Old Northwest. The central issue, as with the majority of Indian wars, was land.

In 1804, some Sac and Fox bands were tricked into signing away all their tribal lands in Illinois by William Henry Harrison (who later became president of the United States). But the Sac and Fox of the Rock River claimed that those who had signed the treaty at St. Louis did not represent all the Sac. One such leader was Ma-ka-tai-me-she-kia-kiak, or Black Sparrow Hawk, or simply Black Hawk. He and his band from the village of Saukenuk (now Rock Island), at the junction of the Mississippi and Rock Rivers, refused to depart from their homeland.

As Black Hawk later wrote in his biography, "My reason teaches me that land cannot be sold. The Great Spirit gave it to his children to live on. So long as they occupy it and cultivate it they have the right to the soil. Nothing can be sold but such things as can be taken away."

The forces of history proved otherwise. White settlers kept coming and white officials kept favoring their land claims over Indian claims. In 1818, Illinois Territory became the 21st state of the Union. In 1829, when Black Hawk and his band left the village for the winter hunt, white squatters moved onto their land. They even took over some of the Indian lodges. On returning the following spring, some of the Sac and Fox under a Sac chief named Keokuk agreed to relocate across the Mississippi in Iowa. Yet Black Hawk and his followers stayed on in lodges that the squatters had not occupied. Despite some quarreling, the Indians and whites survived a planting season together. And Black Hawk vowed to return again the following spring.

Troops were called in to keep the Indians out of Saukenuk once and for all. There were some young men in this army who later became famous in American history, such as Abraham Lincoln, Zachary Taylor, and Jefferson Davis. Daniel Boone's son Nat was also among them. Despite warnings to stay away, Black Hawk's band of 300 warriors plus their families returned the next spring, in 1830. But when the combined force of state militia and federal regulars reached the village, they found that the Indians had slipped back across the Mississippi during the night. War had been avoided for the time being.

The clash finally came in 1832. By that time, Black Hawk's followers had grown in number. White Cloud, a Winnebago shaman, also known as Winnebago Prophet, preached against the whites and rallied WINNEBAGO, POTAWATOMI, and Kickapoo to the Sac and Fox cause.

His message of living according to traditional Indian ways resembled the teachings of other prophets before him, such as Delaware Prophet (see LENNI LENAPE [DELAWARE]) and Shawnee Prophet (see SHAWNEE).

The first fighting occurred in May. It broke out when jittery and inexperienced militiamen fired on tribal representatives sent to parley under a white flag of truce. Black Hawk had been prepared to surrender, but now his warriors attacked and routed the enemy, who fled in panic. The Indian victory is named Stillman's Run after Major Isaiah Stillman, who had been in charge of the unit.

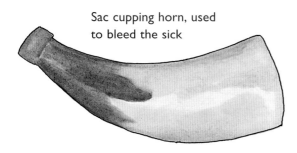

Sac cupping horn, used to bleed the sick

The allied Indians headed northward up the Rock River into Wisconsin. The army organized a pursuit. The next clash occurred in June along the Wisconsin River. Black Hawk had hoped to descend the Wisconsin to the Mississippi, from where his followers could reach the safety of Keokuk's village in Iowa. Many Indians died in the battle. The rest managed to escape across the river in makeshift rafts. Black Hawk decide to push on for the Bad Axe River, which also joined up with the Mississippi. By now, his people were exhausted and starving.

Troops caught up with them once more in July. Again Black Hawk tried to parley a surrender under a flag of truce. Again soldiers fired on his men. While the Indians were making rafts and canoes to cross the river, soldiers attacked them along the bank. Other soldiers fired on them from the steamship *Warrior,* which was outfitted with cannon. Many women and children were killed. Warriors trying desperately to swim across the swift waters were picked off by sharpshooters. As many as 300 Native Americans died in the massacre.

Black Hawk and Winnebago Prophet were among the few Indians to escape. They headed north into Winnebago country. But weary of hiding out, they turned themselves in the following July. Black Hawk closed his surrender speech with these words: "Farewell my nation! Black Hawk tried to save you, and avenge your wrongs. He drank the blood of some of the whites. He has been taken prisoner, and his plans are stopped. He can do no more. He is near his end. His sun is setting, and he will rise no more. Farewell to Black Hawk."

Black Hawk dictated his autobiography in 1833. He was eventually released under the condition that he no longer act as a chief among his people. He met President Andrew Jackson, the man who had shaped the policy of relocating eastern Indians westward, in Washington, D.C., and toured other eastern cities. But stripped of his homeland and his authority, Black Hawk died a bitter man in 1838. In a final insult to this great leader, grave robbers raided his tomb and displayed his head in a traveling carnival.

In 1842, the other Sac and Fox chief, Keokuk, was pressured into selling tribal lands in Iowa. The Sac and Fox moved to the part of the original Indian Territory that is now Kansas. Then in the 1850s, when whites were rapidly settling Kansas, some Sac and Fox relocated to the new, smaller Indian Territory that is now Oklahoma. Some later returned and bought back part of the Iowa land.

Present-Day Tribal Entities

The combined Sac and Fox now consist of three federally recognized tribal entities: the Sac and Fox Tribe of Missouri in Kansas and Nebraska, the Sac and Fox Tribe of Oklahoma, and the Sac and Fox of the Mississippi in Iowa. The Iowa group, mostly Fox, also call themselves the Mesquaki Nation.

Jim Thorpe

One of the most famous of all 20th-century Native Americans and thought by some to be the greatest all-around athlete who ever lived was a Sac (with mixed Fox, Kickapoo, Potawatomi, MENOMINEE, French, and Irish ancestry as well), Jim Thorpe or Bright Path. He was born in Oklahoma in 1888. He attended the Carlisle Indian School in Pennsylvania. Founded by Richard Henry Pratt in 1879, the Carlisle school was the first Indian school off a reservation to be funded by the federal government. Jim Thorpe was the halfback on the football team, which beat many big football powers.

In 1912, Thorpe participated in the Stockholm Olympics in Sweden, where he won gold medals in two events, the pentathlon and the decathlon. The following year, when it was discovered that he had played a season of semiprofessional baseball, which supposedly made him a professional athlete instead of an amateur, he was stripped of his awards. Thorpe did receive other recognition for his greatness, however, playing briefly for the New York Giants baseball team plus various professional football teams. And Jim Thorpe, Pennsylvania, is named after him. His Olympic gold medals were reinstated in 1983, 30 years after his death.

SALISH *see* FLATHEAD

SARCEE

Sarcee knife with steel blade

The Athapascan-speaking Sarcee occupied ancestral territory along the North Saskatchewan River in what is now the Canadian province of Alberta. They are thought to have branched off from the Beaver (Tsattine) living to the north along and around the Peace River. Since Sarcee territory was part of the northern plains, their lifeways came to differ from those of other ATHAPASCANS of the Subarctic (see SUBARCTIC INDIANS).

The use of the horse spread from the Spanish to the tribes of the West, starting in the 1600s. The Sarcee probably did not acquire horses until the early 1800s. On doing so, they lived a nomadic existence like other PLAINS INDIANS, depending on buffalo as their main food. They are the only Athapascan people classified as part of the Great Plains Culture Area. The name *Sarcee,* or *Sarsi,* both pronounced SAR-see, is thought to mean "not good." Since the Sarcee were traditional enemies of the Plains CREE, they became part of the Blackfoot Confederacy (see BLACKFEET) for mutual protection. The biggest killer of the Sarcee, however, was not intertribal warfare but disease brought to their people through regular contacts with Hudson's Bay Company traders. Many Sarcee died in the smallpox epidemics of 1836 and 1870 and the scarlet fever epidemic of 1856.

In 1877, the Sarcee signed away most of their lands to the Canadian government. In 1880, they were placed on a reserve near present-day Calgary, Alberta, where their descendants live today. The tribe operates a cultural center, Tsut'ina Kosa, on the reserve and sponsors an annual powwow.

SEMINOLE

Seminole, pronounced SEM-in-ole, is a derivation of the Spanish word *cimarron,* meaning "wild" or "runaway." The Seminole bear this name because their ancestors broke off from other Native Americans living to the north in what now are the states of Georgia and Alabama—mainly the CREEK—and migrated southward during the 1700s.

Lifeways

The Seminole are considered part of the Southeast Culture Area. Like other SOUTHEAST INDIANS, they were farmers as well as hunter-gatherers. They build their villages near rivers in swamplands. Their houses, known as chickees and made from palmetto trees, had pole foundations, thatched roofs, raised platforms, and open walls. They were perfectly suited to the warm, wet climate: open to stay cool and high enough to stay dry. A small attic was used for storage, as were outdoor poles from which utensils could be hung. The Seminole also built cooking huts that were shared by different families.

By throwing embers from a fire onto logs and removing the charred wood with stone and bone scrapers, the Seminole made sleek and graceful dugout canoes. Sometimes the hull walls were only an inch thick. These dugouts had platforms in the rear where a man could stand and use a long pole to push through swamps. Meanwhile, passengers could spear fish or alligators. Hunters also attacked alligators on land by pushing logs down their throats, flipping them over, and spearing and clubbing them.

Seminole children as young as four years old had to help with chores, such as gathering wood for fires, stirring soup, and kneading dough. Older boys went hunting and fishing with their fathers while the girls learned domestic skills such as cooking and sewing.

The Seminole developed a unique style of clothing. Using patchwork and rickrack techniques, they pieced together shirts and dresses with bright, stunning colors.

A Seminole man in a dugout

The Seminole Wars

In the early 1800s, the Seminole were friends of other runaways—escaped black slaves. They hid the slaves and welcomed them into their families.

Seminole chickee

General Andrew Jackson used the runaway slaves as an excuse to lead an army out of Georgia against the Seminole, starting the First Seminole War of 1817–18. Sharp Knife, as he was known to various tribes, had his troops loot and burn Seminole villages before returning north to Georgia. His invasion started a war with Spain, which at the time claimed Florida as its own. Afterward, Florida became part of the United States.

When Jackson became president, he wanted to send the Seminole to the Indian Territory west of the Mississippi River. About 3,000 Seminole were forced to relocate in the 1830s, along with Indians from other Southeast tribes, namely the CHEROKEE, CHICKASAW, CHOCTAW, and Creek.

The Indian families were herded westward like cattle by U.S. soldiers without enough food or blankets; many died of starvation, exposure, and disease. Others were killed by bandits. Survivors were not even permitted to stop and bury their dead. The Trail of Tears, a phrase originally applied to the Cherokee experience, is used to refer to the forced journey of all the "Five Civilized Tribes" as they came to be called after relocation.

Some Seminole refused to leave Florida and waged a guerrilla war from their native swamps, successfully using hit-and-run tactics. Their resistance is known as the Second Seminole War of 1835–42. Osceola was the most important Seminole leader in this struggle. He was not a hereditary chief, but rose to prominence because of his militant stand against whites. When officials tried to make him sign a treaty agreeing to leave Florida, he slashed it with a knife. Then he led his men into the wilderness to resist the forced removal. He and his warriors won a great victory at the Withlacoochee River against a much larger force of soldiers under General Duncan Clinch.

Osceola was captured through deceit. General Thomas Jesup tricked him to coming to a peace council, then had his men seize the fighter. Osceola lasted only three months in captivity, wasting away from malaria and a throat disease. The frontier painter George Catlin painted a famous portrait of the Seminole leader just before his death. Catlin reported that Osceola was ready to die, bitter at the whites for their treachery.

The Second Seminole War had not ended, however. Other Seminole continued to fight and never surrendered. The war wound down after the federal government had lost 1,500 men and spent at least $30 million, making it the most costly Indian war ever. For every two Seminole relocated, one soldier died.

The Third Seminole War took place in 1855–58. Billy Bowlegs's band attacked settlers, surveyors, trappers, and traders from their headquarters in the Florida Everglades. Once again, the army couldn't contain the Seminole. Some tribal members agreed to move to the Indian Territory when relatives from the Indian Territory were brought in to meet with them. Yet the tribe never signed a treaty and many Seminole stayed in Florida.

Contemporary Seminole

Descendants of those Seminole who never relocated incorporated as the Seminole Tribe of Florida in 1957. They presently have five reservation tracts in southern Florida. Tourism, especially on the Hollywood Reservation (Dania) near Miami—where high-stakes bingo is offered and events such as alligator wrestling are held—provides income for tribal members. Farming and cattle raising also provide livelihoods. A branch tribe, the Miccosukee (pronounced mick-uh-SOO-kee) incorporated as the Miccosukee Tribe of Florida in 1962. They have a reservation farther south along the Tamiami Trail. Although a traditional people, they too have developed a tourism industry—with a cultural center, bingo, airboat

Seminole palmetto doll with rickrack dress (modern)

rides, and gift shops. Several other Florida groups are seeking federal recognition as Seminole. Those who went west are organized as the Seminole Nation of Oklahoma and hold trust lands in Seminole County. Many earn a living in agriculture, the oil industry, construction, retailing, and small manufacturing.

SENECA

The ancestral homeland of the Seneca extended from Seneca Lake to the Allegheny River in what now is western New York. Their native name is *Onondowagah,* or *Nundawaono,* or the "people of the great hill." Another tribal name applied to them was *Osininka* for "people of the stone"; to non-Indians they became known by the familiar-sounding Latin name *Seneca,* pronounced SEN-uh-kuh. To the other members of the Iroquois League— the CAYUGA, MOHAWK, ONEIDA, ONONDAGA, and TUSCARORA—the Seneca were the Keepers of the Western Door, or simply Door-Keepers. The IROQUOIS (HAUDENOSAUNEE) thought of their combined territory as one large longhouse with the Seneca guarding the western entrance and the Mohawk guarding the eastern entrance. At the annual Great Council, held in Onondaga territory, the Seneca sent eight sachems, or chiefs, as representatives.

The Seneca, like the other Haudenosaunee nations, are classified as NORTHEAST INDIANS. Shared cultural traits and history are discussed under the IROQUOIS (HAUDENOSAUNEE) entry.

Cornplanter

Cornplanter (Gayentwahga, John O'Bail) was a Seneca who rose to prominence during the American Revolution as an ally of the British, leading war parties against American settlers. After the war, Cornplanter, unlike the Mohawk chief Joseph Brant (Thayendanegea) and his followers who resettled in Canada, recognized the sovereignty of the new American nation and negotiated for Seneca lands. Cornplanter became a trusted friend of the Americans.

Some of Cornplanter's most famous words were addressed to President George Washington:

> When your army entered the country of the Six Nations, we called you Caunotaucarius, the Town Destroyer; and to this day when that name is heard, our women look behind them and turn pale, and our children cling to the knees of their mothers . . . When you gave us peace, we called you father, because you promised to secure us in possession of our lands.

Red Jacket

Red Jacket (Sagoyewatha), another prominent Seneca leader during and after the American Revolution, received his English name from the British military coat he wore. Red Jacket held out against white influences, urging his people to live in their traditional manner. An eloquent man with an excellent memory for detail, he is remembered for many different speeches and letters.

When protesting Seneca land sales, he said:

> We stand as a small island in the bosom of the great waters . . . They rise, they press upon us and the waves will settle over us and we shall disappear forever. Who then lives to mourn us, white man? None.

When complaining about missionaries among the Seneca, Red Jacket said:

> The black coats tell us to work and raise corn; they do nothing themselves and would starve to death if someone did not feed them. All they do is pray to the Great Spirit; but that will not make corn and potatoes grow; if it will why do they beg from us and from the white peo-

ple. The red men knew nothing of trouble until it came from the white men; as soon as they crossed the great waters they wanted our country, and in return have always been ready to teach us to quarrel about their religion . . . We are few and weak, but may for a long time be happy if we hold fast to our country, and the religion of our fathers.

Handsome Lake

Another famous Seneca was Cornplanter's half-brother, Handsome Lake (Skaniadariio), who founded the Longhouse Religion in 1799 to help the Haudenosaunee adapt to their new life after they had lost most of their lands and had been surrounded by American settlers. The Longhouse Religion combines elements of both Christianity and the Haudenosaunee religion. Handsome Lake was raised traditionally, but he later studied the Quaker religion. Like Quakerism, his Longhouse Religion—which is still practiced by many Haudenosaunee—emphasizes good deeds and silent prayer. Followers worship one god, as Christians do, known to them as the Great Spirit. Their churches are longhouses.

Ely Parker

In 1869, Seneca Ely Samuel Parker (Donehogawa) became the first Native American commissioner of the Bureau of Indian Affairs. Parker had earlier fought under General Ulysses S. Grant in the Civil War as an assistant adjutant general and had served as Grant's secretary. At Appomattox in April 1865, because of his penmanship, Parker was asked to write out the terms by which General Robert E. Lee surrendered the Confederate army. When Grant became president, he appointed Parker commissioner. Parker helped shape Grant's peace policy toward the tribes of the Great Plains and Far West.

Contemporary Seneca

The Seneca Nation presently holds three state reservations in western New York near the city of Buffalo: the Allegany Reservation, the Cattaraugus Reservation, and the Oil Springs Reservation. Another group in western New York, the Tonawanda Band of Seneca, has a reservation near Akron, New York. Seneca also live on the Six Nations Reserve along with other Haudenosaunee near Brantford, Ontario. Other Haudenosaunee had settled on the Little Sandusky River in 1817–18; they later ceded their lands for a reservation in the Indian Territory in 1831. They now are the Seneca-Cayuga Tribe and hold trust lands in Ottawa County, Oklahoma.

The Seneca have been in the news in recent years because of questions concerning their lands in western New York. In the late 1950s and early 1960s, many tribal members opposed the flooding of lands on their Allegany Reservation for a dam. They lost their case, however, and the Army Corps of Engineers completed the Kinzua Dam in 1965, flooding approximately 10,500 acres. Some of these lands were sacred to tribal members; cornplanter's original gravesite was flooded.

In 1985, some Seneca tried to block construction of a part of Route 17, called the Southern Tier Expressway, crossing the Allegany Reservation. They claimed that tribal leaders had no right to sell the land to the state in 1976. But a New York State Supreme Court justice issued an order barring the group from further interference with construction, and the road was completed.

There also has been the issue of the Salamanca lease. The city of Salamanca is built on Indian reservation land. In 1892, white citizens signed lease agreements lasting 99 years with the Seneca Nation. Some of the leases cost only $1.00 a year for a piece of property. In 1991, the leases finally expired. They have been renegotiated for the next 40 years with much fairer terms for the Seneca people.

A still unresolved issue is that of a land claim to 18 Niagara River islands, the largest of which is Grand Island, by the Tonawanda Band of Seneca. Their lawsuit, originally filed in 1993, alleges that New York State illegally obtained the land in 1815, purchasing it without federal consent. (A 1790 federate statute prohibits the purchase of land from Indian nations without the consent of Congress.) The case will probably be settled in federal court or through negotiation between the Seneca, New York State, and the federal government, as similar land claims have been resolved.

The Seneca now operate a museum and tribal library on the Allegany Reservation.

Seneca ash-splint basket (modern)

SHAWNEE

Shawnee, pronounced shaw-NEE or SHAW-nee, is derived from the Algonquian word *chawunagi,* meaning "southerners" in the Algonquian language, a name resulting from the fact that for most of their history the Shawnee lived south of other ALGONQUIANS. The Shawnee split up into different groups and migrated often. The Cumberland River in what now is Tennessee is given as their original homeland, but perhaps it is more accurate to think of their territory as lying to the west of the Cumberland Mountains of the Appalachian chain, with the Cumberland River at the center. At one time or another, the Shawnee had villages along many other rivers of that region, including the Ohio and the Tennessee, an area now comprising parts of the states of Tennessee, Kentucky, West Virginia, and Ohio.

When whites first crossed the Appalachians, they found very few Indian villages in Kentucky and West Virginia. It is known that early Native Americans spent time there because there is much archaeological evidence of Indians in those states: Farmers still plow up spear points and arrowheads, and both amateur and professional archaeologists have found grave sites. Scholars theorize that perhaps this territory of forested mountains, hills, and valleys, plus rolling bluegrass prairies, served not so much as a homeland for the Shawnee and other tribes of the region, such as the CHEROKEE, but as sacred hunting grounds.

But the Shawnee also ranged far to the north, south, and east of this core area, on both sides of the great Appalachian Divide—especially as whites started entering the Indians' domain. In the course of their history, in addition to the states mentioned above, the Shawnee had temporary villages in northern parts of present-day South Carolina, Georgia, and Alabama; western parts of present-day Maryland, Virginia, Pennsylvania, and New York; and southern parts of present-day Indiana and Illinois. And then in the 1800s, Shawnee bands also lived in present-day Kansas, Missouri, Arkansas, and Texas, most of them ending up in Oklahoma.

As wanderers, the Shawnee had a unique place in Indian history and culture, introducing cultural traits of the northern tribes to the southern tribes and vice versa. They might be called intermediaries between different cultures. The Shawnee are generally classified as NORTH-EAST INDIANS, since they hunted, fished, gathered, and farmed in ways similar to the more northern Algonquians. But they picked up lifeways of SOUTHEAST INDIANS too. They are sometimes referred to as PRAIRIE INDIANS because they ranged as far west as the prairies of the Mississippi River valley.

The Shawnee not only shifted territory but also shifted allegiances among different colonial powers. Like most other Algonquians, they usually sided with the French against the English during the many conflicts from 1689 to 1763 known as the French and Indian wars. But some Shawnee bands considered English trade goods better than French goods. Pickawillany, in Shawnee territory in Ohio, became a major British trading post. Moreover, some Shawnee groups were conquered by the IROQUOIS (HAUDENOSAUNEE), and, as their subjects, fought alongside them and the English against the French.

Yet the majority of Shawnee joined the OTTAWA and other tribes in Pontiac's Rebellion of 1763 against the English. Then in 1774, one year before the start of the American Revolution, the Shawnee fought Virginians in Lord Dunmore's War.

Lord Dunmore's War

The Shawnee rebelled when the governor of Virginia, the earl of Dunmore, ignored the Proclamation of 1763, signed by the king of England, promising an Indian Country west of the Appalachians. Dunmore gave veterans of the French and Indian War who had fought under him land that belonged to the Shawnee. When the settlers came to stake their claims, the Shawnee, led by Chief Cornstalk, attacked them. Dunmore sent in a force of volunteers, but it was routed by a Shawnee ambush on the Kentucky River.

Next Dunmore organized a much larger army of 1,500 militia. Cornstalk asked the Iroquois for help. Most refused to fight their former allies, the British. But Logan, the Mingo (an Iroquois subtribe) chief, and some of his warriors joined the Shawnee cause.

The decisive battle occurred on October 6, 1774, at Point Pleasant, West Virginia. The Indians suffered many casualties in the bitter fighting. Cornstalk signed a peace treaty with Dunmore in which the Shawnee agreed to give up some lands.

The American Revolution and Little Turtle's War

The peace did not last long. The American Revolution erupted the following year, in 1775. Now the Shawnee sided with the British against the American rebels. It was after all the British government that had originally proclaimed an Indian country; and it was the American settlers who had ignored the proclamation.

During the Revolutionary War, the Shawnee fought the famous frontiersman Daniel Boone, the man who had cut a path through the Cumberland Gap. They even captured him in 1778 and held him prisoner at the village of Chillicothe in Ohio, but he managed to escape.

After having won the Revolutionary War, the new U.S. government turned its attention to clearing the path for white settlement. The Shawnee, many of whom were now living north of the Ohio River in the Old Northwest, joined other tribes of the region under the MIAMI Little Turtle to resist the incoming settlers. When army after army came at them, the Indians finally yielded in 1794. Another war was lost and more territory signed away.

Tecumseh's Rebellion

In the late 1700s and early 1800s, when the young United States was just beginning to flex its muscles and expand to its present shape, two Shawnee rose to prominence. They were twins, among the most remarkable set of twins in all of history. One was the medicine man Tenskwatawa, but called Shawnee Prophet by whites. Like Delaware Prophet before him of the LENNI LENAPE (DELAWARE), he preached to Indians of many tribes, telling them to return to traditional ways and abandon all customs that came from whites, such as the Christian religion and liquor. He claimed to have special "magic" in the fight against whites.

His twin brother, Tecumseh, was a great orator and a man of energy and action. Also a visionary, he dreamed of a great Indian country from Canada to the Gulf of Mexico, made up of allied tribes. He believed that no single Indian or tribe had the right to give up lands to whites because the lands belonged to all Indians and all tribes. For that reason, he refused to sign the Treaty of Fort Greenville in 1795 after Little Turtle's War. Tecumseh considered himself an Indian first and a Shawnee second. To carry out his dream, he believed a united military stand would be necessary.

Tecumseh did not hate whites, even though they had killed his father and brother in previous wars. He is said to have admired whites for their many accomplishments. He studied world history and literature in order to better understand them. He might have had a romance with a white schoolteacher, Rebecca Galloway. And he believed that one should treat prisoners fairly, whatever their nature or nationality, without degradation and torture.

For his wisdom, compassion, and, as he later proved, his military genius, many consider him the greatest man of his age, a man who would have made the perfect leader for the Indian country that might have been, a man to rival in capabilities any president the United States has ever produced.

Tecumseh worked hard to accomplish his goal. He traveled from the Old Northwest to the Deep South to urge unity among the Indians. He spoke to many tribes. Some resisted the idea of allying with former enemies. But Tecumseh persisted. Unity was everything, he claimed. If the tribes didn't unite, they would go the way of the tribes of the Atlantic seaboard who were now extinct or dispersed.

"Where today are the Pequots?" he asked his fellow Indians. "Where are the Narragansetts, the Mohawks, the Pocanets, and many other once-powerful tribes of our people? They have vanished before the avarice and oppression of the white man, as snow before the summer sun. . . . Will we let ourselves be destroyed in our turn without making an effort worthy of our race?"

Tecumseh was such a persuasive speaker and a magnetic personality that even stubborn chiefs started to come around to his way of thinking. With trip after trip, speech after speech, council after council, Tecumseh's dream was becoming a reality.

Yet all his work became unraveled by bad luck and by his brother's misjudgment. While Tecumseh was in the South, William Henry Harrison, then the governor of Indiana Territory, ordered an attack on Tenskwatawa's village of Prophetstown on the Tippecanoe River. Harrison's excuse for the expedition was that Indians had stolen army horses. Rather than avoid fighting at all costs and wait until the Indian military alliance was in place, Tenskwatawa followed the advice of some young militants and ordered an ambush. The Indians were repelled. Harrison's army marched on Prophetstown and burned the village to the ground. Most of the warriors escaped, however.

It was not a major victory in a military sense, although Harrison later claimed so in his presidential campaign.

But it broke the momentum of Tecumseh's Rebellion. Tenskwatawa's magic had been proven ineffective. Many of the tribes decided to make raids prematurely in their own territories, rather than wait for a united stand under Tecumseh.

The War of 1812 soon broke out between the United States and Great Britain, at that time in firm control of Canada. Tecumseh, hoping for British help in organizing an Indian homeland, joined the fight against the Americans. The British recognized his leadership abilities and made him a brigadier general in their army. Because of his participation, some Indians joined the British cause. But others held off their support, waiting to see the outcome.

Tecumseh proved himself a great general. His skill often made up for the incompetency of the other British generals. He helped take Detroit. He slowed the victorious advance of an American force under William Henry Harrison. When most of the British fled in panic back to Canada, Tecumseh and his men covered the white force's retreat. Unlike other generals, he stayed on the front lines, urging his men on. But on October 5, 1813, at the Battle of the Thames, Tecumseh took bullet after bullet from soldiers in the larger American force and finally fell dead.

Although a group of Kentuckians skinned a body they thought to be Tecumseh's for souvenirs, they never found his actual corpse. Fellow warriors must have hidden it from the enemy. Rumors persisted among the tribes that Tecum-

A modern-day Shawnee girl

seh would one day return. But of course he never did. His twin brother lived about another 20 years and continued to preach to the tribes of the region. Other Indian rebellions would occur, such as that of the SAC and FOX (MESQUAKI) in the Black Hawk War of 1832. But without Tecumseh's organizational abilities, there was no hope for an Indian rebellion on the huge scale he had envisioned. Eventually, most of the Indians of the Old Northwest and the Southeast were pushed west of the Mississippi.

Final Homelands

Three Shawnee entities maintain tribal identity in Oklahoma: the Loyal Shawnee (the main body of the tribe who lived in Indiana for a time, then Kansas, and then, after having supported the Union in the Civil War, moved to the part of the Indian Territory that later became Oklahoma, settling near the Cherokee); the Absentee Shawnee (who broke off from the main body of the tribe in Kansas, then lived in Arkansas and Texas for a time before being relocated to the Indian Territory); and the Eastern Shawnee (who were associated historically with the Seneca, moving with them from Ohio to the Indian Territory). The Shawnee Nation United Remnant Band, made up of descendants who managed to stay in the Ohio Valley in Ohio and Indiana following Tecumseh's defeat, received recognition from the state of Ohio in 1980.

SHINNECOCK *see* MONTAUK

SHOSHONE

The derivation of the Shoshone name, also spelled *Shoshoni,* both pronounced sho-SHO-nee, is unknown. The name is applied to a number of bands, spread over a vast area between the Rocky Mountains and the Sierra Nevada. Based on dialect, lifeways, and history, the Shoshone are divided into three groups: the Western Shoshone in present-day central and eastern Nevada, eastern California, and northwestern Utah; the Northern Shoshone in present-day southeastern Idaho and northern Utah; and the Eastern Shoshone (who branched off from the Northern Shoshone) in present-day western Wyoming. Some Shoshone groups also ranged into present-day western Montana.

Lifeways

It is difficult to place the Shoshone groups culturally. As a whole, the Shoshone are placed by scholars in the Great Basin Culture Area (see GREAT BASIN INDIANS). The Great Basin is the vast, cupped desert area lying west of the Rocky Mountains and east of the Sierra Nevada, broken up by intermittent highlands. Native Americans living in this arid and barren environment foraged for scarce food, such as roots, nuts, seeds, lizards, insects, squirrels, and rabbits.

This foraging way of life was especially true of the Western Shoshone, who lived in primitive brush shelters, open at one end. The Goshute, or Gosiute, a band of Shoshone living along the desolate shores of the Great Salt Lake in Utah, were typical of this group. Their name indicates the ancestral relationship among the Shoshone, UTE, and PAIUTE. The Panamint (or Koso) Shoshone band in eastern California, which lived in one of the most extreme environments in all of North America—the Panamint Mountains and Death Valley—also were typical foragers.

The Northern Shoshone shared cultural traits with the Plateau Indians to their north, fishing in the Snake and other rivers for salmon and collecting wild roots.

The Eastern Shoshone hunted game on the forested slopes of the Grand Teton and Wind River Mountains, part of the Rocky Mountain chain in present-day Wyoming. And with the acquisition of the horse in the late 1600s, the Eastern Shoshone gained greater mobility in their hunting. The pronghorn antelope was a favorite game for meat and hides, as was the buffalo. The Eastern Shoshone came to live in tipis like the PLAINS INDIANS east of the Rocky Mountains. They were traditional enemies of the ARAPAHO and BLACK-FEET, living to their east.

Sacajawea

Although early Spanish explorers might have had previous contacts with the Shoshone, particularly the Western group, it was the Lewis and Clark Expedition that made non-Indian America aware of them. This voyage of exploration is mentioned in connection with many Native American peoples, since Lewis and Clark covered so much territory and encountered as many as 50 tribes. Thomas Jefferson, the president at the time, conceived of a scientific expedition west of the Mississippi River. The United States was a young country seeking out its boundaries. In 1803, Jefferson signed the Louisiana Purchase with France, which had recently been ceded the land by Spain. A vast expanse of mostly wilderness terri-

tory, about 828,000 square miles, from the Gulf of Mexico to Canada, came under United States domain. Jefferson chose his private secretary, Captain Meriwether Lewis, to explore the northern part of this enormous tract. Lewis chose his friend, Captain William Clark, as his associate in command.

In the winter of 1803–04, Lewis and Clark organized a team of 29 additional men in Illinois, across the Missouri River from the settlement of St. Louis. One of these was a male African American known simply as York in historical writings. He would generate much interest among the Indians, who had never seen a person of his ancestry before. The explorers set out up the Missouri River in May 1804. They spent the next winter in MANDAN villages. It was during this period that a Montrealer named

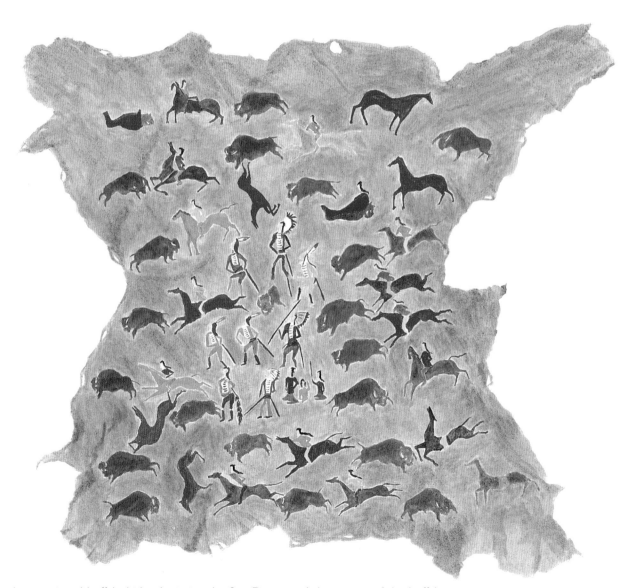

Shoshone painted buffalo hide, depicting the Sun Dance and the return of the buffalo

Toussaint Charbonneau and his Shoshone wife, Sacajawea (or Sacagawea, translated as "Bird Woman"), joined the expedition. Charbonneau had just purchased Sacajawea from the neighboring HIDATSA. She had been brought to their villages by GROS VENTRE, who had captured her four years earlier in a raid on a Shoshone band.

This was a remarkably fortunate turn of events for the explorers. Sacajawea's presence reassured Indians whom they later encountered. She was able to communicate with the different tribes through sign language. She obtained horses for the expedition from her own Northern Shoshone people to cross the Great Divide. She showed the way through the Lemhi Pass in the Rockies that led from the Missouri to the Columbia River. With her help, the expedition successfully reached the Pacific Ocean and made its way back again, with only one fatality. Charbonneau and Sacajawea left the expedition where they had joined it, at the Mandan villages. Lewis and Clark returned triumphantly to St. Louis in 1806.

It is not known for certain when or where Sacajawea died. Some historians believe she passed away about 1812. But others have claimed that she died in Wyoming many years later, in 1855. Next to Pocahontas (see POWHATAN), Sacajawea probably is the most famous Native American woman in history. Her involvement as guide, translator, and diplomat makes her as responsible for the success of the Lewis and Clark Expedition as anyone.

Later Contacts

After the opening of the American West by the Lewis and Clark Expedition, the Shoshone way of life would never be the same. Trappers and traders, mountain men such as Jedediah Smith in 1825, crisscrossed their territory. (Traders referred to Northern Shoshone, Northern Paiute, and Bannock collectively as Snake Indians). In 1847, the Mormons founded their settlement on Great Salt Lake. In 1849, during the California gold rush, prospectors and settlers also passed through Shoshone lands. Then in 1857, the discovery of the Comstock Lode, a rich strike of silver, led to mining settlements in Nevada.

Wars Involving the Shoshone

During the early 1860s, while federal troops were engaged in the Civil War in the East, Great Basin Indian bands resisted white expansion. They raided wagon trains and stagecoaches along the Central Overland Route to California; they waylaid Pony Express riders carrying mail along the route from Salt Lake City to Cal-

ifornia; they also attacked the crews stringing new telegraph lines and destroyed the wires.

To keep communication lines open, California officials sent the volunteer Third California Infantry eastward under Colonel Patrick Connor. In 1862, Connor founded Fort Douglas in the foothills of the Wasatch Mountains overlooking Salt Lake City.

Meanwhile, Chief Bear Hunter's band of Western Shoshone were raiding miners and Mormons alike. In January 1863, Connor led 300 troops out of Fort Douglas in the Bear River Campaign. In the bitter cold and over deep snowbanks, his men marched 140 miles north along the eastern side of the Great Salt Lake to Bear Hunter's village.

The Bear River Indians had time to prepare barricades of rocks and earth, further reinforcing their village, which was in a steep-walled ravine. But still they were no match for the superior firepower of the California volunteers, who poured round after round of ammunition into the village. With 224 of their people killed, the Shoshone retreated. Only 22 soldiers died.

That same year, the United States government laid claim to much of the Great Basin. In the so-called treaty, the Indians received no payment. By 1865, practically all native resistance had ended. In 1869, the Union Pacific and Central Pacific Railroads met at Promontory Point, Utah, in Shoshone country, completing the transcontinental railway and further encouraging white settlement in the West. In the 1860s and 1870s, all the Shoshone bands were assigned reservations.

In 1878, a band of Indians called the Sheepeaters, made up of both Bannock and Shoshone, launched a short-lived uprising in the Salmon River Mountains of central Idaho.

In the meantime, the Wind River band of Eastern Shoshone in Wyoming proved themselves valuable allies of the whites. Under Washakie, they helped the army fight the SIOUX (DAKOTA, LAKOTA, NAKOTA) in several battles, including the Battle of the Rosebud in 1876. The tradition of friendly relations between these easternmost Shoshone and whites dated back to Sacajawea. Yet the Wind River band felt betrayed when white officials placed their traditional enemies, the Arapaho, on their reservation in 1878.

Contemporary Shoshone

Western Shoshone currently hold a number of reservations in Nevada and California, some of which they share with the Paiute. The Goshute have one tract in Utah and another tract with land on both sides of the Nevada and Utah border. Northern Shoshone share the Fort Hall Reservation with Bannock in Idaho. Eastern Shoshone share the Wind River Reservation with Arapaho in Wyoming. The Northwestern Band of Shoshoni Indians of Utah is also federally recognized. Some of these reservations have generated income from grazing or mining leases. The harsh environment and lack of capital has made economic development difficult for many of the bands, but some have created their own businesses in agriculture and ranching and other ventures. Some groups, such as the Wind River Shoshone, have experienced a new interest in traditional culture: Arts and crafts are encouraged at a new tribal cultural center, and the Shoshone language is being taught to youth in tribal schools.

SIOUX (Dakota, Lakota, Nakota)

Horse-mounted Indians, wearing long eagle-feathered warbonnets and fringed leather clothing with colorful beadwork, ride across the grasslands of the Great Plains. They hunt buffalo. They fight the cavalry. They sit in council inside painted tipis, wearing buffalo robes and smoking long-stemmed peace pipes. These images of Indians have been shown to us again and again, in books, movies and television shows about the West. These images, more likely than not, depict the Sioux, more properly referred to as Dakota, Lakota, or Nakota.

Two of the most famous incidents in Indian and American history—Custer's Last Stand (also called the Battle of Little Bighorn) and Wounded Knee—involved the Sioux. The numerous Sioux fought many other battles against the U.S. army on the northern plains. Some of the most famous Indian fighters in history, such as Red Cloud, Sitting Bull, and Crazy Horse, were Sioux. And one of the most famous incidents in recent Indian history occurred on a Sioux reservation, again at Wounded Knee.

Branches of Sioux

The Sioux are really made up of different groups with varying histories and customs. In studying the Sioux, the first challenge is to learn the various names and locations of the different bands.

Siouan was a widespread Indian language family. Tribes in many parts of North America spoke Siouan dialects. The tribal name *Sioux,* pronounced SUE, is applied only to a specific group of Siouan-speaking people, however. The name is derived from the French version of a CHIPPEWA (OJIBWAY) word in the Algonquian language. The Chippewa tribe called their enemies *Nadouessioux* for "adders," a kind of snake. The Sioux also are known collectively (especially in Canada) as the Dakota (pronounced da-KO-tah), from which has come the names of two U.S. states, North and South Dakota.

In the Siouan language, *Dakota* (or *Lakota* or *Nakota*) means "allies."

There were four ancestral branches of Sioux, with different bands in each. The largest branch was the Teton (or Titonwan), with the following bands: (1) Oglala; (2) Brulé (Sicangu); (3) Hunkpapa; (4) Miniconjou; (5) Oohenonpa (Two Kettle); (6) Itazipco (Sans Arcs); and (7) Sihasapa.

A second branch was the Santee, with the following bands: (1) Sisseton; (2) Wahpeton: (3) Wahpekute; and

A Sioux war chief, a familiar image of the Plains Indian (as represented on a cigarette silk, distributed in metal tins of cigarettes in the early 1900s)

(4) Mdewakanton. (The term *Santee* used historically more accurately applies to just the Wahpekute and Mdewakanton groups, not Sisseton and Wahpeton as well. In any case, all four are considered distinct groups.)

A third branch was the Yankton (or Ihanktonwan), with only one band, the Yankton.

A fourth branch was the Yanktonai (or Ihanktonwanna), with the following bands: (1) Yanktonai; (2) Hunkpatina; and (3) Assiniboine. The ASSINIBOINE separated from their relatives and are discussed under their own entry.

Of all four branches, the Teton in their dialect use the *Lakota* version of the tribal name; the Santee say *Dakota;* and the Yankton and Yanktonai use *Nakota.*

The Teton, Yankton, Yanktonai, and four Santee groups also called themselves the *Oceti Sakowin,* or "Seven Council Fixes."

The Sioux originally lived as Woodland Indians along the upper Mississippi River. It is known from early records of Jesuit explorers of the 1600s that the Sioux once dominated territory that now comprises the southern two-thirds of Minnesota, as well as nearby parts of Wisconsin, Iowa, and North and South Dakota. By the mid-1700s, some Sioux were migrating westward toward and across the Missouri River. The reason: Their traditional enemies, the Chippewa, were now armed with French guns, making warfare with them much more dangerous. Moreover, with the European demand for furs, game in the Sioux's prairie country was becoming scarcer.

The Teton Lakota migrated the farthest west to the Black Hills region of what is now western South Dakota, eastern Wyoming, and eastern Montana. They sometimes also are called the Western Sioux. The Yankton Nakota settled along the Missouri River in what is now southeastern South Dakota, southwestern Minnesota, and southwestern Iowa. The Yanktonai Nakota settled to their north along the Missouri in what is now eastern North and South Dakota. The Yankton and Yanktonai are sometimes referred to together as the Middle Sioux. The Santee Dakota stayed along the Minnesota River in what is now Minnesota. They therefore are referred to as the Eastern Sioux.

Lifeways

The Sioux as a whole are classified as PLAINS INDIANS, part of the Great Plains Culture Area. But because of their different locations, the lifeways of the four branches varied. The Teton acquired horses, followed the great buffalo herds, and lived in tipis.

Sioux ceremonial buffalo skull with a design representing the sky, Sun, and rain

The way of life of the Yankton and Yanktonai became like that of other Missouri River tribes, such as the MANDAN and HIDATSA, other Siouan-speaking peoples. The Yankton and Yanktonai began using horses in the 1700s and also hunted buffalo like the Teton, but they lived most of the time in permanent villages of earth lodges. They also continued to cultivate crops. The Yankton and Yanktonai can be described as PRAIRIE INDIANS.

The Santee retained many of the cultural traits of the western Great Lakes Indians. Their culture was something like that of the WINNEBAGO, another Siouan-speaking people. They lived in wooded river valleys and made bark-covered houses. They hunted buffalo in the tall grassland country of the Mississippi River. They eventually began to use the horse, but they did not keep as many mounts as their more westerly relatives did. The Santee can be thought of as a cross between Woodland and Prairie Indians.

It should be remembered that the typical way of life on the Great Plains did not evolve until long after contact with whites, when Native Americans acquired the horse. Although most tribes on the plains became equestrian nomads who lived in tipis year-round, not all the tribes gave up their villages, their farming, and their pottery after having acquired horses.

As indicated, of the branches of Sioux, the Teton are the closest to the Native Americans so prevalent in the popular imagination. Teton lifeways—tipis, warbonnets, buffalo robes, medicine bundles, sacred shields, horsemanship,

Sioux wooden horse effigy with real horsehair

horse gear, military societies, buffalo-hunting, sign language, coup-counting, Sun Dances, and Vision Quests—are summarized under the entry PLAINS INDIANS. See also PRAIRIE INDIANS to help understand the more sedentary way of life of the Yankton, Yanktonai, and Santee branches of the Sioux people.

The Sioux Wars

The Sioux, because of their stubborn resistance to white expansion, were the most famous of Plains warriors. The various conflicts involving the Sioux have been given names by historians (sometimes more than one name). Nevertheless, the conflicts did not always have distinct beginnings and endings, but were part of an ongoing pattern of raids and counterraids lasting from about 1850 to 1890 and collectively known as the Sioux Wars.

The different phases of the Sioux Wars are: the Grattan Affair in 1854–55; the Minnesota Uprising (or Little Crow's War) in 1862–64; the War for the Bozeman Trail (or Red Cloud's War) in 1866–68; the War for the Black Hills (or Sitting Bull's and Crazy Horse's War) in 1876–77; and the Massacre at Wounded Knee in 1890.

The Grattan Affair

In 1851, white officials negotiated a treaty at Fort Laramie in Wyoming with the Sioux and their allies, the northern branches of CHEYENNE and ARAPAHO, in order to assure safe passage for whites along the Oregon Trail, running from Missouri to Oregon. It only took three years after the signing of the treaty for violence to erupt, however.

A party of Mormons traveling west lost one of their cows, which wandered into a camp of the Brulé band of Teton Lakota. The Mormons reported to troops at Fort Laramie that Indians had stolen the cow. In the meantime, a Sioux named High Forehead killed the cow for food.

Although the Brulé offered to pay for the cow, an over-eager lieutenant from the fort, named John Grattan, insisted on the arrest of High Forehead and rode to

the Indian camp with a force of about 30 men. When High Forehead refused to turn himself in, Grattan ordered an attack. A Brulé chief named Conquering Bear was killed in the first volley. The Sioux counterattacked and wiped out the detachment. The army sent in more troops to punish the Sioux. In 1855, at Blue Water in Nebraska, a force under General William Harney attacked another Brulé camp and killed 85.

War had been brought to the Sioux. They would not forget this treatment at the hands of the whites. In fact, a young warrior of the Oglala band of Teton Lakota—Crazy Horse—personally witnessed the killing of Conquering Bear. He would later become one of the most effective guerrilla fighters in history.

Sioux beads made from human finger and arm bones and traded as an early form of money

The Minnesota Uprising

Another outbreak of violence involving the Sioux occurred far to the east, in Minnesota, among the Santee Dakota bands. The central issue that caused the Minnesota Uprising (or Little Crow's War) was land, as more and more whites settled along the rich farmlands of the Minnesota River. Some of the young Santee braves wanted war against the people who were appropriating their land. The Santee chief Little Crow argued for peace. But young militants forced the issue by killing five settlers. Little Crow then helped the other Santee chiefs organize a rebellion.

In August 1862, Santee war parties carried out surprise raids on white settlements and trading posts, killing as many as 400 people. Little Crow himself led assaults on Fort Ridgely. The fort's cannon repelled the Indians, killing many. Another group of Santee stormed the village of New Ulm. The settlers drove the attackers away, but then evacuated the village.

General Henry Sibley led a large force into the field to combat the Indians. At Birch Coulee in September, the warriors attacked an army burial party, killing 23. But Sibley engaged the Santee at Wood Lake later that month and routed them with heavy artillery. Many warriors fled northwestward into the wilderness, Little Crow among them. Many others surrendered, claiming innocence in the slaying of the settlers.

Of those who stayed behind, 303 were sentenced to be hanged. President Abraham Lincoln took time out from his concerns with the Civil War to review the trial records, and he pardoned the large majority. Still, 33 Santee, proclaiming their innocence to the end, were hanged the day after Christmas in 1862, the largest mass execution in American history.

Of those Santee Dakota that fled, many settled among Teton Lakota and Yanktonai Nakota in Dakota Territory (the part that was soon to become North Dakota). General Henry Sibley and General Alfred Sully engaged Sioux from various bands at Big Mound, Dead Buffalo Lake, and Stoney Lake in 1863, and at Whitestone Hill and Killdeer Mountain in 1864. The Santee and the other Sioux who helped them paid a high price in suffering for their Minnesota Uprising. Little Crow himself died in 1863 on a horse-stealing expedition out of Canada into Minnesota. Settlers shot him and turned in his scalp for the bounty.

The War for the Bozeman Trail

The War for the Bozeman Trail (or Red Cloud's War) began soon after the Minnesota Uprising ended. Land was again the central issue of this conflict, but it was the mining fever that brought increased traffic to the lands of the Teton Lakota in what is now Montana and Wyoming.

In 1862, after having traveled to Montana's goldfields, the explorer John Bozeman followed a direct route through Teton lands back to the Oregon Trail in Wyoming rather than travel a longer way around to the east or west. Other migrants and miners followed along this new route. The various Teton bands—the Oglala under Red Cloud, the Hunkpapa under Sitting Bull, and the Brulé under Spotted Tail—resented the trespassing. So did their allies, the Northern Cheyenne under Dull Knife and the Northern Arapaho under Black Bear.

In 1865, the Indians began attacking military patrols and wagon trains as well as other travelers along both the Bozeman and the Oregon Trails. General Patrick Connor sent in three different columns that year to punish the militant bands. Their only success against the elusive warriors, who attacked swiftly and then disappeared into the wilderness, was the destruction of a camp of Northern Arapaho under Black Bear.

Sioux warclub

Some of the chiefs rode into Fort Laramie in 1866 to sign a treaty. Red Cloud insisted that no forts be built along the Bozeman, however. When the army refused to comply, the chief rode off with his warriors to make preparations for war.

Troops under Colonel Henry Carrington reinforced Fort Reno and built two new posts in northern Wyoming and southern Montana to keep the Bozeman Trail open. The Indian guerrillas used hit-and-run tactics to harass the soldiers. Crazy Horse, the young Oglala, began establishing his reputation as a fearless fighter and master strategist at this time. In 1866, he used a decoy tactic to trap an entire cavalry outfit: Several warriors attacked a woodcutting party and fled; then Captain William Fetterman led an 80-man cavalry unit after them and to their death at the hands of 1,500 concealed warriors.

After the Fetterman Fight, the army sent in fresh troops with new breech-loading rifles. In two battles in 1866, the Hayfield Fight and the Wagon Box Fight, the Teton lost many warriors to these modern weapons, but they succeeded in driving the whites back to their posts.

The insurgents kept up their raids. The federal government, realizing the high cost of maintaining the

Bozeman forts, yielded to Red Cloud's demands. In the Fort Laramie Treaty of 1868, the government agreed to abandon the posts if the Indians would cease their raids. When the army evacuated the region, the Indians celebrated by burning down the Bozeman forts. The Sioux and their allies had won this round of warfare on the Great Plains. But the whites would keep entering their domain. In the meantime, the southern and central Plains tribes—the COMANCHE, KIOWA, Southern Cheyenne, and Southern Arapaho—had forced concessions out of the whites in the Medicine Lodge Treaty of 1867.

The War for the Black Hills

The discovery of gold in the Black Hills of Wyoming and South Dakota in the year 1874 led to the next phase of the Sioux Wars: the War for the Black Hills (or Sitting Bull and Crazy Horse's War) of 1876–77. By now, Red Cloud and Spotted Tail had settled on reservations. Sitting Bull and Crazy Horse now led the allied hunting bands that refused to give up the traditional nomadic way of life. Opposing them were two generals who had become famous as Union commanders in the Civil War, General William Tecumseh Sherman, overall commander of the army, and General Philip Henry Sheridan, commander of the Division of the Missouri. In the field, the generals had various officers, including General George Crook, who had previously fought APACHE and PAIUTE, and Lieutenant Colonel George Armstrong Custer, who had earlier campaigned against the Cheyenne.

War broke out when the military ordered the hunting bands onto the reservation. When the bands failed to report, the army went after them in the winter of 1876. During that year, some of the most famous battles on the Great Plains took place. The first three were great Indian victories. The final five were victories for the army and brought the resistance of the Sioux, Northern Cheyenne, and Northern Arapaho to a virtual close.

At Powder River in Montana in March 1876, Oglala and Northern Cheyenne warriors under Crazy Horse repelled a cavalry attack led by Colonel Joseph Reynolds. At Rosebud Creek in June, Crazy Horse's warriors routed General George Crook's huge force of soldiers and their CROW and SHOSHONE allies. Then also in June, along the Little Bighorn River, Oglala under Crazy Horse and Hunkpapa under Sitting Bull and Gall, plus their Cheyenne allies, wiped out Custer's Seventh Cavalry.

The Battle of Little Bighorn is the most famous battle in all the Indian wars. It is also called Custer's Last Stand or the Battle of Greasy Grass. George Armstrong Custer was a vain, ambitious, and impulsive young cavalry officer, called "Long Hair" by the Indians because of his long blond locks. He was trying to use the Indian wars as a means to further his own career. Although he had had success as a Union officer in the Civil War, his only victory to date in the Indian wars had been against Black Kettle's peaceful band of Southern Cheyenne in the Indian Territory in 1868. He brashly underestimated his opponents.

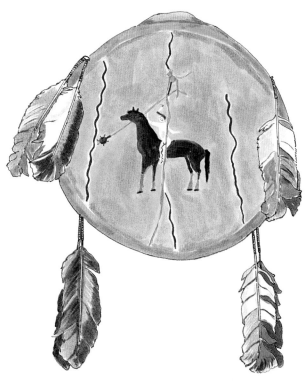

Sioux painted hide shield, representing a dream in which a warrior rides Thunder Horse in a contest with Turtle

When his scouts spotted the Indian camp along the Little Bighorn, rather than wait for reinforcements under General Alfred Terry and Colonel John Gibbon, Custer divided his men into four groups and ordered an attack. In a series of separate actions against the divided force, the Indians managed to kill at least 250 soldiers, including Custer's entire detachment and the lieutenant colonel himself.

This was the last great Indian victory on the plains. The following battles proved disastrous for the Sioux and their allies. In July 1876, at War Bonnet Creek in Nebraska, a force under Colonel Wesley Merritt intercepted and defeated about 1,000 Northern Cheyenne who were on their way to join up with Sitting Bull and Crazy Horse. In September 1876, at Slim Buttes in South Dakota, General Crook's advance guard captured American Horse's combined Oglala and Miniconjou band. In November 1876, in the Battle of Dull Knife in

Sioux Ghost Dance shirt

Wyoming, Colonel Ranald Mackenzie's troops routed Dull Knife's band of Northern Cheyenne. In January 1877, at Wolf Mountain in Montana, General Nelson Miles's soldiers defeated Crazy Horse's warriors. Then in May 1877, in the Battle of Lame Deer, General Miles's men defeated Lame Deer's Miniconjou band.

Crazy Horse died in 1877, stabbed with a bayonet while trying to escape from prison. Although photographs exist of other Native American from this period of history, there are none of Crazy Horse. He refused to pose for photographers, saying, "Why would you wish to shorten my life by taking my shadow from me." Sitting Bull and some of his followers hid out in Canada until 1881, when he returned to the United States to surrender. He went on to play a role in events leading up to the famous Wounded Knee incident.

The power of the northern plains tribes had been broken. The southern and central Plains Indians—the Comanche, Kiowa, Southern Cheyenne, and Southern Arapaho—had previously yielded. Other Indian tribes to the west of the Rocky Mountains—such as the Apache, NEZ PERCE, UTE, and BANNOCK—would continue their resistance for some years, but the Indian wars were winding down. The final Apache rebellion, under Geronimo, ended in 1886.

Wounded Knee

Yet the Indian wars of the previous four centuries were not quite over. One more incident shook the plains as late as 1890. Because it was so unnecessary, the Wounded Knee Massacre has come to symbolize the many massacres of Indians throughout American history.

The events of Wounded Knee sprung out of a new religion. In 1888, a Paiute Indian by the name of Wovoka started the Ghost Dance Religion. He claimed that the world would soon end, then come to be again. All Native Americans, including the dead from past ages, would inherit the new earth, which would be filled with lush prairie grasses and huge herds of buffalo. To earn this new life, Indians had to live in harmony and avoid the ways of whites, especially alcohol. Rituals in the Ghost Dance Religion included meditation, prayers, chanting, and especially dancing. While dancing the Ghost Dance, participants could supposedly catch a glimpse of this world-to-be.

Many western Indians began practicing the Ghost Dance Religion. Its teachings offered hope to once free and proud peoples now living in poverty and depression on reservations in the midst of their conquerors. But Sioux medicine men—Kicking Bear and Short Bull of the Miniconjou band of Teton Lakota—gave the religion their own interpretation. They claimed that special Ghost Shirts could stop the white man's bullets.

White officials became alarmed at the size of Indian gatherings and the renewed Indian militancy. As a result, they banned the Ghost Dance on Sioux reservations. But the Indians continued to hold the forbidden ceremonies. Troops rode into the Pine Ridge and Rosebud Reservations in South Dakota to enforce the new rule. In defiance, Ghost Dancers planned a huge gathering on a cliff in the northwest corner of the Pine Ridge Reservation known as the Stronghold. They even sent word to Sitting Bull, now on the Standing Rock Reservation in North Dakota, to join them. The general in charge, Nelson Miles, who feared Sitting Bull's influence, ordered the chief's arrest. In the fight that resulted, Sitting Bull and seven of his warriors were slain, similar to the way that Crazy Horse had lost his life 13 years before.

General Miles also ordered the arrest of a Miniconjou chief named Big Foot who had formerly advocated the Ghost Dance. But Big Foot, ill with pneumonia, only wanted peace now. He supported Red Cloud and other proponents of peace with the whites. He led his band of about 350—230 of them women and children—to Pine Ridge to join up with Red Cloud, not with the Ghost Dancers Kicking Bear and Short Bull. Nevertheless, a detachment of the army under Major S. M. Whitside intercepted Big Foot's band and ordered them to set up camp at Wounded Knee Creek. Then Colonel James Forsyth arrived to take command of the prisoners. He ordered his men to place four Hotchkiss cannon in position around the camp.

The next morning, Forsyth sent in troops to collect all Indian firearms. A medicine man named Yellow Bird called for resistance, saying that the Ghost Shirts would protect the warriors. Big Foot advocated peace. When the soldiers tried to disarm a deaf Indian named Black Coyote, his rifle discharged in the air. The soldiers shot back in response. At first the fighting was at close quarters. But then the heavy artillery opened fire, cutting down men, women, and children alike. Others were killed as they tried to flee.

At least 150—possibly as many as 300—Indians died at Wounded Knee, with others injured. Once again the spirit of the Sioux had been crushed. The Ghost Dancers soon gave up their dancing. Wounded Knee marked the end of the Indian wars. That same year, 1890, the Census Bureau of the federal government announced that there was no longer a line of frontier on the census maps.

That is to say, other than scattered Indian reservations, no large Indian wilderness area remained free of white settlements.

Sioux in the Twentieth Century

Starting in 1927, the federal government sponsored the 14-year carving of four of the presidents' faces on Mount Rushmore in the Black Hills of South Dakota, which insulted the Sioux. To the Indians, the act was like carving up a church, since the hills were sacred in their religion. In 1998, 15 miles away from Mt. Rushmore, near Crazy Horse, South Dakota, another carving in the Black Hills was unveiled. Begun in 1939, the one head covers an area greater than the four heads of Mt. Rushmore. The image is of Crazy Horse.

During the 20th century, the Sioux have rebuilt their lives. Many are still poor, but they have a great power of spirit. Many Native American writers and philosophers have been Sioux, such as Vine Deloria, Jr., who wrote *Custer Died for Your Sins* and many other books. A Sioux writer, educator, and physician by the name of Charles Eastman (Ohiyesa) helped found the Boy Scouts of America. The shaman Black Elk helped communicate Sioux religious believes in *Black Elk Speaks: The Life Story of a Holy Man of the Oglala Sioux.*

Some Sioux have devoted themselves to pan-Indian (intertribal) causes, joining organizations such as AIM, the American Indian Movement, formed in 1968. In honor of their ancestors and in protest of the treaties broken by the federal government and the lack of opportunity for Native Americans, members of AIM staged an occupation at Wounded Knee on the Pine Ridge Reservation in South Dakota in 1973. The incident ended in violence with two Indians, Frank Clearwater, a CHEROKEE, and Buddy Lamont, a Sioux, killed by federal agents.

Today, there are Sioux reservations in many different states: in South Dakota, North Dakota, Minnesota, Nebraska, and Montana. In Wyoming, some of which also was part of the vast Sioux homeland, no lands are held in trust for the tribe. There also are Sioux bands in Canada with reserves in Alberta, Saskatchewan, and Manitoba. Leasing of lands to outside interests provides income for some tribes. Others, especially those groups in Minnesota, have turned to gaming, with newly built casinos, for revenue. Many Sioux now live in urban areas, such as Minneapolis-St. Paul and Denver. Many Sioux Indians practice traditional ceremonies and traditional arts and crafts.

SKITSWISH   *see* COEUR D'ALENE

SOUTHEAST INDIANS

The Southeast Culture Area, showing the approximate locations of Indian tribes listed in this book—circa 1500, before displacement by non-Indians (with modern boundaries)

The Southeast Culture Area, as defined by scholars, is bordered on the east by the Atlantic Ocean; on the south by the Gulf of Mexico; on the west by the Trinity, Arkansas, and Mississippi Rivers (approximately); and on the north by the Tennessee and Potomac Rivers (approximately). It includes all of present-day Florida, Georgia, Alabama, Louisiana, and South Carolina; most of Mississippi, Tennessee, North Carolina, and Virginia; and parts of Texas, Oklahoma, Arkansas, Illinois, Kentucky, West Virginia, and Maryland.

This part of North America is mostly forested, much of it with yellow pine. As a result, the culture area is sometimes called the Southeast Woodland Culture Area. Yet there are many variations in terrain and vegetation in the Southeast. These include the coastal plains with saltwater marshes, grasses, and stands of cypress trees; the subtropical Everglades with jungle and swampland; the sandy soil of river valleys, plus the Mississippi floodplain; the fertile soil of the Black Belt; and the forested highlands of the Piedmont Plateau, Blue Ridge, Smoky

Mountains, and Cumberland Mountains, all part of the southern Appalachian chain.

Southeast Indians hunted and fished for many species of fauna, and they gathered wild plant foods. But they were also highly skilled farmers, growing corn, beans, squash, melon, sweet potatoes, and other crops. Because they could grow enough food to support a sizable population, Southeast Indians for the most part lived in permanent villages, usually located in river valleys. The main type of architecture was wattle and daub. Branches and vines were tied over pole frameworks, then covered with a

Southeast Indian (Seminole) headdress in the postcontact turban style

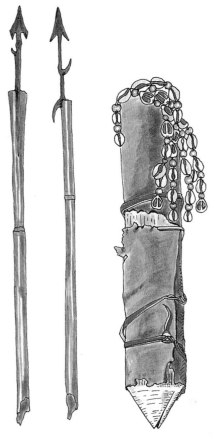

Postcontact Southeast Indian metal and leather quiver with shell beads, plus metal and bamboo harpoon

mixture of mud plaster. But plant materials were also used to cover the both rectangular and circular structures, including thatch, grass, bamboo stalks, palm fronds, bark, woven mats. Animal hides were utilized too.

Southeast tribes of the Muskogean language family (part of the Macro-Algonquian language phylum) having entries in this book are the ALABAMA, APALACHEE, CHICKASAW, CHOCTAW, COUSHATTA, CREEK, SEMINOLE, and YAMASEE. The CALUSA, also represented, probably were Muskogean-speaking as well.

The one Southeast tribe of the Iroquoian language family (part of the Macro-Siouan language phylum) with an entry is the CHEROKEE. The one Southeast tribe of the Siouan language family (part of the Macro-Siouan

language phylum) with an entry is the CATAWBA. The one Southeast tribe of the Caddoan language family (part of the Macro-Siouan language phylum) with an entry is the CADDO.

The LUMBEE, having an entry, are thought to be descended from peoples speaking mostly Siouan, but they perhaps have ALGONQUIANS and IROQUOIANS among their ancestors too.

Southeast tribes with unique languages, that is, speaking language isolates, with separate entries are CHITIMACHA (Chitimachan language isolate of the Macro-Algonquian phylum), NATCHEZ (Natchesan isolate of the Macro-Algonquian phylum), TIMUCUA (Timucuan isolate of undetermined phylum affiliation), and YUCHI (Yuchian isolate of the Macro-Siouan phylum). The Tunican language of the Macro-Algonquian phylum, spoken by the TUNICA and YAZOO, is discussed as a language isolate by some linguists and as a family by others.

There are many other tribes of the Southeast Culture Area, which, because of limited space, do not have separate entries. Most of them now are extinct.

Muskogeans without entries include Acolapissa, Ais, Apalachicola, Avoyel, Bayogoula, Chakchiuma, Chatot, Chiaha, Cusabo, Guale, Hitchiti, Houma, Kaskinampo, Mobile, Muklasa, Napochi, Oconee, Okelousa, Okmulgee, Pawokti, Pensacola, Quinipissa, Sawokli, Tamathli, Tangipahoa, Taposa, Tawasa, Tohome, and Tuskegee. (The following tribes also are thought to be Muskogean: Amacano, Caparaz, Chine, Choula, Guacata, Ibitoupa, Jeaga, Osochi, Pascagoula, and Tekesta.)

Siouans without entries include Biloxi, Cheraw, Manahoac, Monacan, Moneton, Nahyssan, Occaneechi, Ofo, Pee Dee, Santee (Issati), Saponi, Sewee, Shakori, Sissipahaw, Sugeree, Tutelo, Waccamaw, Wateree, Waxhaw, Winyaw, and Woccon. The Cape Fear, Congaree, Eno, Keyauwee, and Yadkin tribes of the region also are also assumed to be Siouan.

Caddoans without entries include Adai and Eyeish. Southeast tribes speaking language isolates without entries include Akokissa, Atakapa, Bidai, Deadose, and Patiri, speaking Atakapan; Griga, Koroa, and Tiou, speaking Tunican; and Taensa, speaking Natchesan.

SOUTHWEST CULTURES

Most of the tribes listed in this book existed when Europeans first reached the shores of the Americas, about 1500, or in the course of the following centuries, when whites explored inland. But what about

the ancestors of these tribal peoples? How did they live?

PREHISTORIC INDIANS are discussed as a whole under another entry. As seen in that section, Indian prehistory usually is divided into three periods, called Paleolithic, Archaic, and Formative. During the last of these three periods, the Formative, from about 1000 B.C. to A.D. 1500, Indian life north of Mexico reached a high degree of organization and artistic expression among farming peoples. Those east of the Mississippi River built mounds and sometimes are grouped together as MOUND BUILDERS as well as by different culture names. Those west of the Mississippi, in the Southwest, are known by a variety of culture names: Mogollon, Hohokam, and Anasazi. There were other cultures in the Southwest during the Formative period, such as Patayan, Sinagua, and Salado, but the Mogollon, Hohokam, and Anasazi cultures were the most organized and most widespread.

It was farming that shaped these three cultures and made them different from the hunting and gathering cultures of the same period. The cultivation of plants for food meant that people no longer had to travel to find wild foods. Village life led to the further development of tools, arts, and crafts, especially basketry and pottery. The earliest evidence of agriculture north of Mexico comes from Bat Cave, New Mexico, where archaeologists have found several cobs of corn from a primitive cultivated species, dating back to about 3500 B.C. The Indians who planted this corn are considered Archaic Indians, part of a culture known as Cochise. Yet farming did not become common in the region until centuries later—about A.D. 100, during the Formative period.

Why did farming flourish in this rugged and arid part of North America? Scholars suggest two reasons for this phenomenon. First of all, the peoples of the Southwest were close to the Mesoamerican civilizations of what is now Mexico and Central America. It was in Mesoamerica that farming originated in the Americas and reached a high level of development (see OLMEC); these skills could have been passed on to peoples to the north. Second, since the Southwest had scarce game and few edible wild plants, farming was a practical alternative for the Indians who lived there.

Mogollon Culture

The name *Mogollon,* pronounced mo-goi-YONE, is derived from the mountain range along the southern Arizona–New Mexico border, this cultural group's core area. The Indians of the Mogollon culture, probably direct descendants of Indians of the earlier Cochise culture, are considered the first Southwest people to farm, build houses, and make pottery. Their culture thrived from about 300 B.C. to A.D. 1300.

The Mogollon Indians farmed the high valleys in the rugged mountains, cultivating corn, beans, squash, tobacco, and cotton. They prepared the soil with primitive digging sticks. They also gathered wild food plants and hunted the small game living in the high country. The adoption of the bow and arrow about A.D. 500 made hunting easier for them.

Farming enabled the Mogollon Indians to live at one location all year long. For their villages, they chose sites near mountain streams or along ridges that were easy to defend from raiding peoples. They designed houses especially suitable to the extreme temperatures of the region—pithouses, with the ground providing natural insulation. The frameworks of these pithouses were made from logs, walls, from reeds, saplings, and mud. The largest of these structures served as social and ceremonial centers called kivas.

The earliest Mogollon pottery was brown. The Indians shaped it by rolling the clay into thin strips and then making coils in the shape of pots. They smoothed it over, then covered it with a slip (coat) of clay, and finally baked the pot in an oven. Late in their history, the Mogollon Indians painted their pottery with intricate designs. A subgroup of the Mogollon culture, the Mimbres culture, is famous for their black-on-white pottery from about A.D. 900.

Mogollon pottery dish in black-on-white Mimbres style

Mogollon Indians also wove plant matter into baskets. They used their cultivated cotton or animal fur to make yarn for weaving clothing and blankets. Feathers were added as decoration. The Mogollon Indians also had many tools and ornamental objects made from wood, stone, bone, and shell.

Hohokam Culture

The name *Hohokam,* pronounced ho-HO-kum, means "vanished ones" in the AKIMEL O'ODHAM (PIMA) language. The core area of Hohokam culture was along the Gila and

Salt River valleys in what now is southern Arizona. Their culture thrived from about 100 B.C. to A.D. 1500.

What once was the homeland of the Hohokam Indians is torrid desert country today, broken only by the slow-flowing rivers and rugged volcanic hills. In order to make use of the sandy soil, the Hohokam Indians developed a remarkable irrigation system. They dug wide, shallow canals as long as 10 miles, and they made dams using woven mats to redirect the water from the rivers to fields of corn, beans, squash, tobacco, and cotton.

Because of advanced farming techniques, the Hohokam Indians grew enough food to support a sizable population. The principal Hohokam village—Snaketown (near present-day Phoenix)—had about 100 pithouses. East of Snaketown was Point of Pines, another large settlement. The Hohokam houses resembled the Mogollon pithouses in construction but were larger and shallower. At Snaketown, archaeologists have also found the remains of two sunken ball courts and some rubber balls.

The evidence of an ancient ball game indicates a connection between the Hohokam culture and Mesoamerican cultures (see MAYA; TOLTEC; and AZTEC). Other artifacts and customs also indicate influence from the south: coiled pottery colored red and pale yellow, colorful textiles, mirrors made by inlaying small pieces of shiny minerals in stone disks, copper bells, stone palettes incised with designs and probably used in rituals, earthen pyramids, and the keeping of macaws as house pets.

The Hohokam Indians are thought to be the first people in the world to practice etching, starting about A.D. 1000. They covered shells with acid-resistant pitch from trees, carved designs on the pitch, then soaked the shells in an acid solution made from fermented saguaro cactus fruit. When they removed the pitch coating, the designs were etched in the shell's surface.

Anasazi Culture

Over the same period, from about 100 B.C. to A.D. 1300, a third culture, known as Anasazi, thrived in the

Hohokam acid-etched shell

Southwest. The generally accepted name for this culture, *Anasazi,* pronounced ah-nuh-SAH-zee, means "ancient ones who are not among us" or "enemy ancestors" in the NAVAJO language, depending on pronunciation. The Anasazi core area was the Four Corners region, where present-day Colorado, Utah, Arizona, and New Mexico meet. The Four Corners region is a dry, rugged country of high mesas and deep canyons. Anasazi was the most widespread of the three cultures described in this section and had considerable influence on the other two.

Anasazi development can be divided into distinct phases. The first of these is called the Basket Maker period, from about 100 B.C. to A.D. 700. During this phase, the Anasazi mastered the technology of weaving containers and sandals from plant matter, such as straw, vines, and rushes. They also refined their skills in farming and pottery. Like Mogollon and Hohokam peoples, the Anasazi of the Basket Maker period lived in pithouses. These semiunderground structures took a variety of shapes—circular, square, rectangular, or D-shaped—and were made from poles, brush, grass, or bark matting, with an earthen covering.

The second Anasazi phase is known as the Pueblo period. After about A.D. 700, the Anasazi developed a new kind of architecture. They kept the underground dwellings as kivas—ceremonial and social structures—but they also built aboveground structures called pueblos. Using either stone and adobe mortar, or adobe bricks, plus roofs of logs covered with sticks, grass, and mud, Anasazi peoples at first made single-room dwellings. Then they began grouping the rooms together and on top of one another, interconnecting the different levels with ladders. The later PUEBLO INDIANS built similar terraced, apartmentlike dwellings.

The Anasazi Indians usually built their pueblos on top of mesas or in canyons up against mesas. Chaco Canyon in what is now New Mexico—first occupied about A.D. 900—contains examples of Anasazi aboveground pueblos. Pueblo Bonito is the largest most famous of the Chaco ruins, a pueblo in the shape of a huge semicircle, with five stories and 800 rooms (although at any one time only 600 rooms probably were usable since others were trash-filled and served as footings for rooms above), and housing perhaps a thousand people. Among the many rooms have been identified 37 kivas, most of them bordering the central plazas (actually two plazas separated by a single row of rooms). The largest kiva—referred to as a great kiva—was 45 feet in diameter.

By about 1150, the Anasazi had evacuated Chaco Canyon and most of their other aboveground pueblos. In the latter part of the Pueblo phase until about 1300,

Remains of an Anasazi yucca fiber sandal

they built most of their homes on cliff ledges, which offered better protection against invaders. Examples of sizable villages built in recesses of canyon walls—or cliff dwellings—are Cliff Place at Mesa Verde in Colorado and Mummy Cave at Canyon de Chelly in Arizona.

During the Pueblo phase of Anasazi culture—both the aboveground and cliff-dwelling periods—sometimes referred to as the Anasazi Golden Age, Anasazi people used irrigation to increase their farm yields and to support large village populations. In addition to skilled builders and farmers, the Anasazi were master craftspeople, designing elaborately painted pottery, brightly col-

Montezuma National Monument in Arizona, a cliff dwelling of the Sinagua culture (about A.D. 1100), an offshoot of Anasazi culture

ored cotton-and-feather clothing, exquisite turquoise jewelry, and intricate mosaic designs.

During the Anasazi Golden Age, their culture influenced other Indians of the region. Charo Canyon in fact was the hub of an area of outlying towns interconnected by an extensive network of stone roads. With time, the Mogollon culture came to include many Anasazi traits and lost its distinct identity.

Cultural Decline

But what happened to the great Hohokam and Anasazi centers of civilization? Why did the Indians of the region abandon their homes, starting about 1300, and move to smaller settlements? It is not known for certain. Scientists do know that starting in 1276, a prolonged drought struck the entire Southwest. With no rain whatsoever, the Indians had to leave their villages and farmlands and track game in small hunting bands. Another contributing factor might have been invasions by other nomadic Indian peoples, such as the ATHAPASCANS who arrived from the north and became known as the Navajo and APACHE. Or perhaps the various pueblos began fighting among themselves for food. Growing archaeological evidence indicates that some among the Anasazi, perhaps descendants of the Toltec or other peoples who entered the region, practiced cannibalism as a means of social control of neighboring communities. The depletion of the wood supply might have been an additional reason to move.

Even though the great villages died out, the ancient Southwest peoples passed on much of their knowledge to later generations. Many SOUTHWEST INDIANS remained farmers, and many continued to live in pueblos. They also sustained their high level of craftsmanship. It is thought that Mogollon Indians were some of the ancestors of the ZUNI; the Hohokam Indians, the ancestors of the present-day Akimel O'odham (Pima) and TOHONO O'ODHAM (PAPAGO); and the Anasazi Indians, the ancestors of the Rio Grande Pueblo Indians, the HOPI, and some among the ZUNI.

Wondrous Ruins

As tourbooks to the region will show, there are many different archaeological sites to visit in the American Southwest. Visitors can stand in the wondrous ruins of great Indian cultures. Some are near cities and easily accessible; others are in remote regions. Imagining the daily life of ancient Native Americans is a powerful experience.

SOUTHWEST INDIANS

The Southwest Culture Area is defined as a geographical region in what is now the American Southwest, including most of Arizona and New Mexico and small parts of California, Utah, Colorado, and Texas, plus much of northern Mexico.

The accompanying map shows both United States and Mexican territory. But most of the Southwest tribes listed in this book under separate entries lived in what became part of the United States.

The Southwest Culture Area has varied topography. There is the rugged high country of the Colorado Plateau in the northern part, with its tablelands of flat-topped mesas separated by steep-walled canyons. The enormous Grand Canyon, cut by the long and winding Colorado River, is the most famous of all the world's canyons. There is mountain country as well, such as the Mogollon Mountains in New Mexico. Inland Mexico also has highlands of plateau and sierra. Much of the Southwest is desert. The Painted Desert lies along the Little Colorado River in Arizona. There are also desert lands along the Gulf of Mexico and Gulf of California.

All these different landscapes have aridity in common. The average annual rainfall for the region ranges from less than four inches a year to less than 20 inches. Most precipitation occurs within a six-week period of summer. Because of the extreme aridity, plants are sparse. There are three patterns of dominant tree growth in the Southwest, depending on altitude and rainfall: western evergreen trees; piñon and juniper trees; and mesquite trees, plus varying species of cacti and desert shrubs. Animals are also scarce: mostly small mammals and reptiles, such as deer, rabbits, squirrels, mice, and lizards; and some large birds, such as eagles, hawks, and vultures.

Two main ways of life evolved among Southwest Indians: farming, and nomadic hunting and raiding. Those peoples who practiced agriculture were such

The Southwest Culture Area, showing the approximate locations of Indian tribes listed in this book—circa 1500, before displacement by non-Indians (with modern boundaries)

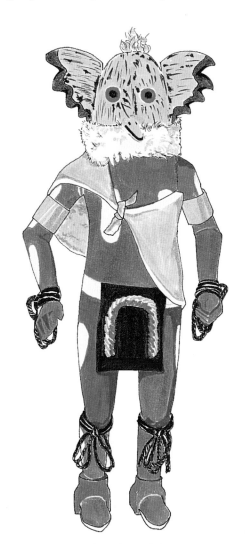

Southwest Indian (Hopi) kachina doll

skilled farmers that, even in the dry country, they could support sizable populations in permanent villages. Most Indian villages in the Southwest had what is known as pueblo architecture. The pueblos, made from adobe brick or stone and with different apartment-like levels connected by ladders, were generally located on mesa tops. Some villages were located in the desert lowlands, however, or along rivers, where the Indians lived in other types of houses, small pole-framed huts covered with plant matter or earth. Those who did not farm, the nomadic hunters and gatherers, supplemented their diet by raiding village peoples for their crops. The two main kinds of house among these people were wickiups (which were brush-covered) and hogans (which were earth-covered).

The tribes of the region can be grouped as follows, according to their different lifeways: agricultural Pueblo peoples, among them Rio Grande PUEBLO INDIANS, HOPI, and ZUNI; agricultural desert and river peoples, among them AKIMEL O'ODHAM (PIMA), HAVASUPAI, HUALAPAI, MOJAVE, TOHONO O'ODHAM (PAPAGO), YAQUI, YAVAPAI, YUMA (QUECHAN); and the nomadic hunting-and-raiding peoples, APACHE and NAVAJO. The ancestors of some of these peoples belonged to the Anasazi, Hohokam, and Mogollon cultures (see SOUTH-WEST CULTURES).

The Southwest Culture Area includes tribes of many languages. Of the above tribes, peoples of the Athapascan language family (or ATHAPASCANS, part of the Na-Dene language phylum) include Apache and Navajo. Peoples of the Kiowa-Tanoan language family (part of the Aztec-Tanoan language phylum) include some among the Rio Grande Pueblo Indians, the Piro, Tewa, Tiwa, and Towa (Jemez). Peoples of the Uto-Aztecan language family (part of the Aztec-Tanoan language phylum) include Akimel O'odham (Pima), Hopi, Tohono O'odham (Papago), and Yaqui. Peoples of the Yuman language family (part of the Hokan language phylum) include Havasupai, Hualapai, Mojave, Yavapai, and Yuma (Quechan). Peoples speaking language isolates include the Rio Grande Pueblo Indians known as Keres (Keresan language isolate of undetermined language affiliation); and Zuni (Zunian language isolate of the Penutian language phylum).

Other Southwest peoples without entries in this book include: Coahuiltec (speaking the Coahuiltecan isolate of the Hokan language phylum); Cocopah, Halchidhoma, Halyikwamai, Kohuana, and Maricopa (all Yuman-speaking); Jumano (probably Uto-Aztecan speaking); and Sobaipuri (Uto-Aztecan-speaking). There are many northern Mexican agricultural and desert and river peoples as well, considered part of the Southwest Culture Area, who are not discussed in this book.

SPOKAN

The Spokan, or Spokane, Indians occupied ancestral territory along the Spokane River, a tributary of the Columbia River, in what now is the eastern part of the state of Washington as well as northern Idaho. Their name, pronounced spo-KAN, probably means "people of the Sun." The Spokan are among those Salishan-speaking peoples classified as PLATEAU INDIANS. Other Salishans to the west are considered NORTHWEST COAST INDIANS. For Plateau peoples, fishing the Columbia River and its tributaries—especially for salmon during their freshwater spawning runs—provided a staple food, as did gathering wild roots, such as camas. Like other area tribes, the Spokan lived in dwellings placed over shallow pits and constructed out of pole frames with grass or woven-mat coverings.

Lewis and Clark had contact with the Spokan in 1805 during their expedition to the American Northwest. Fur trade in the region was developed in the fol-

lowing years by the North West Company and the Hudson's Bay Company of Canada, as well as by John Jacob Astor's American Fur Company. Astor, through the fur trade with western tribes became the richest man in America.

The Spokan had peaceful relations with whites until the late 1850s. They suffered the impact of smallpox epidemics in 1846 and 1852–53. They witnessed the Cayuse War of 1847–50, resulting in part from an outbreak of measles among the CAYUSE, and the Yakama War of 1855–56, resulting from the killing by whites of YAKAMA women and children. They saw the whites break the terms of the Walla Walla Council of 1855. When miners and settlers unfairly took their lands, they too revolted. They joined the COEUR D'ALENE, Yakama, PALOUSE, and PAIUTE in a general uprising in 1858. This conflict is known as both the Coeur d'Alene War and the Spokan War.

After the war, the Spokan settled on various reservations, including the Spokane Reservation near present-day Wellpinit, Washington, and the Colville Reservation near present-day Nespelem, Washington. Others joined the FLATHEAD, another Salishan-speaking people, on their reservation near present-day Dixon, Montana.

The completion of the Grande Coulee Dam on the Columbia River in 1941, blocking miles of fish runs, hurt the Spokan economy. The discovery of uranium oxide on the Spokane Reservation in 1954 led to a new source of income for tribal members. Recent reservation projects are a lumber mill and a fish hatchery.

STONEY *see* ASSINIBOINE

SUBARCTIC INDIANS

Scholars have defined the Subarctic Culture Area as territory stretching across northern latitudes from the Pacific to the Atlantic Ocean. It covers a vast region, including most of present-day Alaska's and Canada's interior.

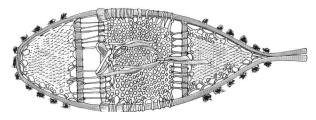

Subarctic Indian snowshoe

What is termed the Northern Forest, filled mostly with evergreen trees—pine, spruce, and fir, with some birch, aspen, and willow as well—grows in the subarctic. This kind of northern forest is called taiga. Since there is relatively little topsoil for deep root systems, the trees of the taiga are generally scraggy and short. The northern edge of the taiga borders the treeless tundra of the Arctic (see ARCTIC PEOPLES).

The Northern Forest is broken up by a network of inland waterways. Some of the largest lakes are the Great Bear Lake, Great Slave Lake, and Lake Winnipeg. Some of the largest rivers are the Yukon, Mackenzie, Peace, Saskatchewan, Red River of the North, and La Grande. There are thousands of smaller lakes and rivers, plus many ponds, streams, and swamps. In the western part of the subarctic, the rolling taiga and swamplands give way to highlands—the northern part of the Rocky Mountain chain, the Yukon Plateau, and the British Columbia Plateau.

The climate of the subarctic is fierce. Winters are long and severe. During the seemingly endless stretch of cold weather, deep snow covers the woodlands, and thick ice covers the lakes. The summers are short. During warm weather, mosquitoes and black flies breed in the swamplands.

The subarctic is home to abundant wildlife. Large mammals include caribou, moose, musk oxen, bear, and deer. Small mammals include beaver, mink, otter, porcupine, rabbits, and squirrels. Moreover, there are many species of birds, especially waterfowl, and fish.

Subarctic Indians were nomadic hunter-gatherers who traveled in small bands. The most common type of house was a small cone-shaped tent covered with animal hides. Lean-tos of brush and leaves were also fairly common, especially in the western part. Subarctic Indians did not farm.

Two main groups of native peoples made up the Subarctic Culture Area: the ATHAPASCANS to the west and the ALGONQUIANS to the east (see those entries for complete tribal listings). The Churchill River, flowing northeastward into Hudson Bay, divided the peoples of these two different language families. The particular subarctic tribes of each language family discussed in detail in this book are the following: Among the Athapascans are the CARRIER, CHIPEWYAN, and KUTCHIN; among the Algonquians are the CREE, MONTAGNAIS, and NASKAPI. Some of the Algonquian-speaking CHIPPEWA (OJIBWAY) bands are considered as part of the Subarctic Culture Area; most are classified within the Northeast Culture Area. The only people of the Subarctic Culture Area who did not speak either Athapascan or Algonquian dialects were the BEOTHUK of Newfoundland. They spoke a unique language called Beothukan.

The Subarctic Culture Area, showing the approximate locations of Indian tribes listed in this book—circa 1500, before displacement by non-Indians (modern boundaries)

SUSQUEHANNOCK

The Susquehannock lived along the river named after them, the Susquehanna River, flowing from the Catskill Mountains in New York, through central Pennsylvania, and emptying into the Chesapeake Bay in Maryland. Although the Susquehannock ranged up and down the entire length of the river in the course of their history, they lived mostly within the present-day boundaries of Pennsylvania. Their name, pronounced sus-kwuh-HAN-ock, and possibly meaning "roily river," also appears with the same spelling and pronunciation as the river—that is, *Susquehanna.* Or they are sometimes referred to as the Conestoga, or Andaste, both from the Iroquoian word *kanastoge,* meaning "at the place of the immersed pole."

The Susquehannock spoke an Iroquoian dialect, but they separated from other Iroquoians long before Europeans arrived in North America. They lived like other Woodland Indians, combining hunting, fishing, and gathering with farming, and they shared many other cul-

tural traits with fellow Iroquoians, such as the use of longhouses. But they are not referred to as IROQUOIS (HAUDENOSAUNEE), a name applied to the tribes of the Iroquois League living to their north.

In fact, for much of their history, the Susquehannock were bitter enemies of the Iroquois. During the 1600s, both tribes made frequent raids on each other. Small war parties, armed with bows and arrows, tomahawks, and scalping knives, would set out on foot through the virgin forests or in elm-bark canoes along the twisty Susquehanna River and travel into enemy territory for quick forays on stockaded villages. This was the period of Dutch activity in North America, and the colonists of New Netherland traded for furs with the Susquehannock.

In 1675, a decade after the British had taken control of Dutch lands in North America, the Susquehannock suffered a major defeat at the hands of their Iroquois enemies. It is thought that epidemics brought to the

Susquehannock by European traders helped weaken them prior to their defeat in battle. At this time, most Susquehannock bands left their original homelands.

Some of the Susquehannock who resettled in Maryland were involved in the conflict known as Bacon's Rebellion that rocked Virginia and neighboring Maryland in 1676. Nathaniel Bacon was a younger cousin to the governor of Virginia, William Berkeley. Bacon and his followers—mainly farmers and frontiersmen—rebelled against colonial authority for several reasons, including high taxes, low prices for tobacco, special privileges granted to the Jamestown aristocracy, and the failure of colonial officials to defend the frontier against Indian attacks.

Bacon and his vigilante army did not distinguish one group of Indians from another. Fighting originally broke out because of a dispute between Nanticoke Indians and settlers over stolen hogs. But Bacon led attacks on other Indians in the region, including Susquehannock. The Susquehannock responded with frequent raids on settlers.

Bacon, before his death from disease, marched on Jamestown with his army and forced Berkeley and other colonial officials to grant much-needed farm reforms. But there was no justice for the Susquehannock, who were reduced in numbers and dispersed from the area because of repeated attacks.

The Susquehannock found themselves in the middle of a similar situation of the OTTAWA and other tribes almost a century later, in 1763, during Pontiac's Rebel-lion. Colonists on the Pennsylvania frontier, angered because of attacks on their settlements by the rebelling tribes, sought revenge on all Indians. A mob out of Paxton, Pennsylvania, who came to be known as the Paxton Boys, descended upon the Christianized Indians of the Conestoga Moravian Mission and murdered three men, two women, and a boy, scalping all of them. For their attack, the Paxton Boys used the excuse that an Indian had stolen and melted down a pewter spoon. Some sympathetic whites gave the surviving Conestoga refuge in the Lancaster jailhouse. But the Paxton Boys broke in and massacred 14 more men, women, and children.

The governor of Pennsylvania at the time was John Penn, a descendant of the Quaker William Penn, who had founded the colony. Governor Penn issued a proclamation condemning the massacres. In response, the Paxton Boys marched on the capital of Philadelphia and threatened to kill all the Indians in the city. The city mobilized an army to defend itself, but Benjamin Franklin negotiated a treaty with the rebels. The Paxton Boys agreed not to attack peaceful Indians on the condition that the whites received bounties for scalps from the tribes participating in Pontiac's Rebellion.

It was already too late for the people known as Susquehannock. They had suffered too much disease and warfare. The survivors settled among other Indian peoples and lost their tribal identity. Some Susquehannock descendants live among the SENECA and CAYUGA in Oklahoma.

TAINO *see* ARAWAK (TAINO)

TEWA *see* PUEBLO INDIANS

TIMUCUA

The Timucua lived in the part of the Southeast that is now northern and central Florida. Their territory extended from the Suwannee River to the St. Johns River. The Timucua were really a confederacy of as many as 150 different villages with culture and language in common. *Timucua,* pronounced tim-uh-KOO-uh or tim-MOO-koo-uh, means "earth." The Timucua proper also are referred to as Utina. Both names generally are applied to all the Timucuan-speaking peoples. (Timucuan is a language isolate of undetermined phylum affiliation, that is, not associated with any other language families.) Other Timucuan-speaking peoples, classified by some scholars as distinct tribes, are Acuera, Fresh Water, Icafui, Mococo, Mosquito, Ocale, Pohoy, Potano, Saturiwa, Surruque, Tacatacura, Tocobaga, and Yui.

The Timucua had early contacts with the Spanish. Juan Ponce de León, who claimed Florida for Spain, encountered the Timucua in 1513. Pánfilo de Narváez passed through their territory in 1528 as did Hernando de Soto in 1539.

The French lived among the Timucua for a short time. Jean Ribault visited them in 1562. Then in 1564, the French under René de Laudonnière built Fort Caroline on the St. Johns River in their homeland.

After having driven the French out of Florida in 1565, the Spanish established missions among the Timucua. The Timucua suffered from several epidemics of European diseases in 1613–17, 1649–50, and 1672. In 1656, many of the Timucua villages, as well as APALACHEE villages, joined forces in an attempt to drive away the missionaries. Well-armed Spanish soldiers defeated the rebels, killing many.

During the French and Indian wars of the 1700s, when the English fought the French and Spanish for control of North America, the Timucua population declined further. The English and their Indian allies, the CREEK, raided Timucua settlements in the vicinity of the Spanish fort at St. Augustine. The Spanish surrendered Florida to the English in 1763. They gained it back in 1783 and held it until 1819. By then, however, the Timucua had died out or joined other tribes, making them extinct as a tribe.

Fortunately, much is known about the culture of the Timucua. The Spanish missionaries recorded their language. And a Frenchman by the name of Jacques Le Moyne who traveled among them in 1564 made many paintings with written commentaries depicting their lifeways. A Flemish artisan, Theodore de Bry, later converted Le Moyne's paintings into engravings for publication in 1591.

The Timucua villages were surrounded by walls of thick, upright logs about twice the height of a man. The log walls overlapped at one point to form a narrow entranceway with a gatehouse at each end, one just outside the palisades and one just inside. The village consisted of many round houses with pole frames and roofs of palmetto branches. The chief lived in the only rectangular building, at the center of all the other houses.

Each village had its own chief. But the chief of one particular village was the principal ruler and had king-like authority over all the other chiefs in the Timucua confederacy of villages. Each village had certain men, the notables, who participated in councils. At councils participants drank huge amounts of strong herbal tea.

The principal chief chose the most beautiful young woman among all the notable families as his wife. She was carried to the wedding ceremony on a litter covered with the fur of an animal. She was shielded from the sun by a canopy of boughs, as well as by two round screens on staffs carried by men walking next to her. Women, wearing skirts of moss and necklaces and bracelets of pearls, followed behind the litter bearers. Then came the bodyguards. The procession's arrival was signaled by trumpeters blowing on horns of bark. During the ceremony the principal chief and wife-to-be sat on a raised platform of logs with the notables seated nearby. The principal chief made a speech to the bride about why he had selected her. And she publicly expressed her thanks. Then the women performed. Holding hands, they formed a circle, chanted the praises of the couple, and, raising and lowering their hands in unison, danced.

The Timucua planted and harvested crops twice a year, including corn, beans, pumpkins, and squash. To prepare the soil, men used hoes made from fish bones attached to wooden handles. Then one woman made holes with a digging stick and another followed behind to place the seeds. Villagers also regularly harvested wild fruits. They made bread from a plant called arrowroot. Any excess food collected was placed in storage to be shared by all the villagers in hard times. This sharing impressed Le Moyne, who wrote: "Indeed, it would be good if among Christians there was as little greed to torment men's minds and hearts."

The Timucua hunted many kinds of animals, including alligators, deer, brown bears, wildcats, lizards, and turkeys. They also fished for trout, flounder, turbot, and mullet and collected clams, oysters, crayfish, and crabs. Methods of hunting and fishing included bows and arrows, clubs, spears, harpoons, and traps. The Timucua carved dugout canoes from single trees for travel on lakes, rivers, and the ocean. They traveled along the Atlantic coast of Florida to trade with other tribes, sometimes even crossing the open sea as far as Cuba. To catch alligators, the Timucua rammed logs into the animals' open jaws, flipped them on their backs, then killed them with arrows and clubs. Extra meat and fish were preserved for the winter months by smoking on a log rack over an open fire.

The Timucua prepared for war with special rituals. In one ceremony, a chief used a wooden platter to spill water on his warriors, saying: "As I have done with this water, so I pray that you may do with the blood of your enemies." Warriors carried tea in gourds with them for energy on military expeditions.

Timucua weapons included bows and arrows and heavy clubs. The warriors filed their fingernails to sharp points, which they used in close combat to gouge their enemies' foreheads and blind them with their own blood. Men also tied their long hair into a knot to hold arrows. Archers shot arrows tipped with flaming moss to set fire to the houses of the enemy. If the warriors were successful on a raid, they brought back trophies—severed arms, legs, and scalps—which they hung on poles at the victory celebrations. Timucua made war for both personal glory and to protect their hunting territory from intruders.

The Timucua tattooed their bodies with elaborate designs in black, red, and blue. The tattoos were a statement of individuality, status, and personal power. To make the designs, which in some instances covered their whole bodies, the Indians pricked their skin with needles

Timucua mask, used as a disguise while hunting

dipped in soot or vegetable dyes made from plants such as cinnebar.

TIWA *see* PUEBLO INDIANS

TLINGIT

The Tlingit, or Tlinkit, are unique among American Indian peoples in that they had much to do with ending the Russian colonial period in North America, proving a stubborn menace to the Russian fur-trading empire. The Russians called them *Kolush.* The name *Tlingit,* pronounced TLING-kit, means "people."

The Tlingit occupied ancestral territory along the Pacific Coast and nearby islands in what is now southern Alaska and northern British Columbia. To their north lived INUIT and ALEUT, and to their south lived the HAIDA and TSIMSHIAN. The Tlingit actually consisted of various independent bands: Auk, Chilkat, Gohaho, Hehl, Henya, Huna, Hutsnuwn (Killisnoo), Kake, Kuiu, Sanya, Sitka, Stikine, Sumdum, Taku, Tongass, and Yakutat. The various bands divided the Tlingit territory into different regions, or *kwans.* Many of the band names survive today as place-names. The Tlingit bands spoke various related dialects of the Tlingit language, part of the Na-Dene language family and related to that of the Haida. The Tlingit also are thought to have been distant relatives of the ATHAPASCAN living to their east.

Lifeways

The Tlingit are classified as part of the Northwest Coast Culture Area. Typical customs of the NORTHWEST COAST INDIANS include salmon fishing; sea mammal as well as land mammal hunting; large houses made from beams and planks of wood; totem poles; wooden ceremonial masks; dugout canoes; cedar chests and boxes; the potlatch (a ceremony for giving gifts) and other elaborate rituals; a society based on wealth and rank; powerful shamans and secret societies; the practice of keeping slaves; extensive trade contacts with other tribes. All are true of the Tlingit.

Tlingit totem poles were constructed as part of or separate from their houses. Each delicately sculpted and brightly painted figure on the poles, representing both people and animals, had a special meaning to a clan's history. When the pole was erected, a speaker would relate stories about the clan's ancestors and about animal spirits.

Of the southern Northwest Coast tribes, the CHINOOK were the most famous traders. But of the more northern tribes, the Tlingit had the most extensive trade contacts. They were middlemen among many different peoples: their coastal neighbors, the Athapascans of the interior, and the Inuit. They dealt in all kinds of goods, some their own and some made by other tribes: boats, blankets, baskets, boxes, raw copper, copper plaques, cedar boards and bark, seal and fish oils, whale oil and bones, ivory, mountain goat and mountain sheep horns and hides, elk meat, caribou meat, sinews, lichens, beads made from tooth shells, abalone and other seashells, the mineral jadeite, slaves, and more.

The most-sought-after Tlingit product was the Chilkat blanket (named after one of the Tlingit bands but made by other Tlingit bands and Tsimshian Indians as well). Tlingit women made these blankets from cedar-bark fiber and mountain goat or mountain sheep wool. They worked on them as long as half a year. Some of the yarn spun from these materials was left white; the rest was dyed black, blue-green, or yellow. Then the women wove them with their fingers into intricate abstract designs and animal forms. The completed blankets had an unusual shape. They were about six feet long with a straight edge at the top. But the bottom

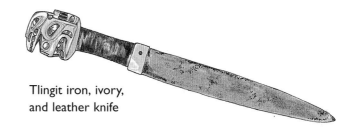

Tlingit iron, ivory, and leather knife

edge was uneven—about two feet at the ends and three feet in the middle. There were long fringes on the sides and bottom but none along the top edge. The women also made Chilkat shirts. The designs had special meanings for families or clans. And it was said that, if one knew how to listen, the Chilkat blankets and shirts could actually talk.

The Tlingit were also famous for their armor. They placed wood slats over two or three layers of hide to repel enemy weapons. They also wore helmets of solid wood for protection and masks to frighten their enemies. They used spears, bows and arrows, and different-shaped clubs in their fighting. They also made daggers of stone with ivory handles. After the arrival of Europeans, the Tlingit used steel for the blades.

Chilkat (Tlingit) blanket with designs that supposedly can talk

Wars Against the Russian Fur Traders

During Vitus Bering's voyage of exploration in 1741, in which he claimed Alaska for Russia, Tlingit warriors killed several of his men, the first incident in what might be called the century-long Tlingit resistance. The *promyshlenniki* (the Russian word for fur traders) followed soon afterward to exploit the huge supply of fur-bearing mammals. The Russians first developed the fur trade on the Aleutian Islands among the Aleut. The Russian traders, led by Alexander Baranov, and their Aleut hunters did not reach Tlingit territory until the 1790s.

After some early skirmishes with the Tlingit, the Russians built a fort at Sitka on Baranov Island in 1799. That same year, the Russian American Fur Company was founded. This huge monopoly competed with the British Hudson's Bay Company to supply the world with furs.

In 1802, Tlingit warriors under Katlian attacked and destroyed the fort, killed many Russians and Aleut, and stole thousands of pelts. They felt the furs belonged to them since they had been taken on tribal lands or in tribal waters. Two years later, Alexander Baranov returned with an armada. Russian ships bombarded the Tlingit with cannonfire, and Russian soldiers stormed and recaptured the post.

The Tlingit kept up their attacks, however. In 1805, they moved on a post at Yakutat. The Russians dreaded the Tlingit raids and used whatever means they could to calm the insurgents—violence and cruelty, or negotiations and gifts. But the Tlingit were not to be conquered or won over and kept up their resistance to Russian encroachment.

The Russians eventually gave up their foothold in North America, selling Alaska to the United States in 1867. The militant Tlingit presence helped influence their decision to abandon their posts in North America.

Yet the increasing number of Americans in the region—developing the fishing industry, searching for gold, or seeking new homes—during the 19th century led to hardship among the Tlingit. Prospectors and squatters violated their land rights. U.S. officials ignored Tlingit land claims and used the navy to prevent a new rebellion among the native population. Meanwhile, disease and alcohol were taking their toll. With the loss of their lands and depleted numbers, the Tlingit lost much of their traditional way of life too.

Economic and Cultural Revitalization

The Tlingit struggled to preserve their identity. To do so, they reached out to other Alaska Natives. In 1912, they helped found the Alaska Native Brotherhood, one of the earliest of the modern-day intertribal organizations.

A land and cash settlement to Alaska's Natives in 1971 as compensation for lost lands—the Alaska Native Claims Settlement Act—has helped the Tlingit and other tribes in the region rebuild their lives. The Tlingit and Haida are united in the Sealaska Corporation, which develops tribal resources. Both peoples are considered some of the best Alaskan fishermen.

More and more Tlingit practice traditional crafts, too, such as the making of Chilkat blankets and woodcarving. Some tribal members are building reputations as fine artists as well.

TOHONO O'ODHAM (Papago)

The Tohono O'odham have been popularly known as Papago. Tohono O'odham, their native name, pronounced TO-ho-no oh-OH-tum, means "desert people." Papago, pronounced PAH-puh-go, from *Papahvio O'odham,* given to them by the neighboring AKIMEL O'OD-HAM (PIMA), means "bean people." The Tohono O'odham occupied ancestral territory in the Sonoran Desert near the Gulf of California in territory now along the international border between southwest Arizona and northwest Sonora, a state of Mexico.

The Tohono O'odham speak a dialect of the Uto-Aztecan language family, similar to that of the Akimel O'odham. Anthropologists classify both the Tohono O'odham and Akimel O'odham in the Southwest Culture Area (see SOUTHWEST INDIANS). They theorize that the two tribes were descended from the ancient Hohokam culture (see SOUTHWEST CULTURES).

Lifeways

The peoples of the Hohokam culture irrigated their farmlands by channeling water from rivers. The Akimel O'odham also practiced desert irrigation and were able to live in permanent village sites year-round. The

Tohono O'odham, however, were seminomadic, with two different village locations. They passed the warm weather months—from spring until the fall harvest—in the desert, usually at the mouth of an arroyo where flash floods from rainstorms provided water for their fields of corn, beans, squash, tobacco, and cotton. They called these sites their "field villages." Tribal members spent the winter in the sierra, near mountain springs. These were the "well villages." Here they hunted deer and other game for food. In times of famine, Tohono O'odham families sometimes moved to the Akimel O'odham villages along the Gila River and worked under the supervision of the host tribe to earn their keep. While working with their kinsmen, the Tohono O'odham might sing the following corn song:

> Here on the field, corn comes forth.
> My child takes it and runs happy.
> Here on the field, squash comes forth.
> My wife takes it and runs singing.

Since farming in the Southwest was so dependent on scarce rainfall, native peoples also made extensive use of wild plant foods. They ate the heart of the mescal plant, which took them at least 24 hours to cook in a pit-oven. They also collected the bean-like seeds of the mesquite tree. The sweet and fleshy fruit of the giant saguaro cactus was a delicacy for them. Women used a long pole called a *kuibit,* made from the ribs of the plant, to knock the fruit down. It was eaten fresh or dried. The fresh fruit was also boiled into jam or syrup; the dried fruit was ground into powder and mixed with water for a drink. The Tohono O'odham also made saguaro syrup into wine. They believed that the drinking of saguaro wine ceremonially helped bring rain for their crops.

Other than their ways of getting food, the lifeways of the Tohono O'odham and Akimel O'odham were very similar. They both lived in houses covered with brush and mud. They also built open areas called ramadas for socializing. They both wore cotton and leather clothing and favored sandals over moccasins. Both peoples made beautiful coiled baskets out of a variety of materials, including willow, devil's claw, bear grass, and yucca. They both had village chiefs (although the Tohono O'odham had no overall tribal chief as the Akimel O'odham did). Each village had a ceremonial leader called the Keeper of the Smoke. The villages of both tribes were divided into two clans or family groups. The names of the Tohono O'odham clans were the Buzzard and the Coyote. Every four years, both peoples celebrated the Viikita, a ceremony with costumed and masked dancers and clowns in order

to bring about tribal good fortune. Both tribes worshiped the gods Earthmaker and Elder Brother.

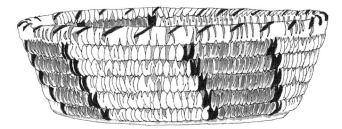

Tohono O'odham coiled basket

The Tohono O'odham, unlike the Akimel O'odham, made annual pilgrimages over the hot desert sands to salt flats near the Gulf of California. They believed that rain spirits lived there and prayed to them for more of the valuable water. Salt they collected became a trade product with other tribes.

The Tohono O'odham are also famous for their calendar sticks. These were sticks with carved markings to help tribal members remember their history over a number of years. Dots and circles indicated important ceremonies. Notches usually represented other events such as earthquakes or the building of waterworks or an attack by their longtime enemies, the APACHE.

Contacts with Non-Indians

Although the Tohono O'odham might have met up with Spanish explorers in the 1500s, they did not have extensive outside contacts until the late 1600s. Father Eusebio Kino reached what the Spanish called Papagueria in 1687 and, in the following years, established missions among the Tohono O'odham.

Because of their extreme desert environment, the Tohono O'odham managed to avoid much of the forced labor and agricultural taxes the Akimel O'odham endured under the Spanish. However, some tribal members participated in the Pima Uprising of 1751. The tribe came under Mexican rule in 1821, with Mexican independence from Spain. Then in 1853, with the Gadsden Purchase, Tohono O'odham territory was divided with most falling under United States domain. In the 1860s, for mutual protection from Apache raiders, the Tohono O'odham allied themselves with the Akimel O'odham and Maricopa (Pee-Posh) and the Anglo-Americans. That did not stop the white ranchers from taking Indian waterholes and grazing land for their cattle, resulting in some violence between Indians and ranchers.

Contemporary Tohono O'odham

The Tohono O'odham presently hold four reservations in Arizona: Maricopa (with the Akimel O'odham), Gila Bend, San Xavier, and Sells. Others are part of the Ak Chin Indian Community with Akimel O'odham near Maricopa, Arizona. There are also Tohono O'odham living in Mexico. Indians of both countries have come and gone across the international boundary through a gap in the barbed-wire fence known as "The Gate." Tribal members earn some income from farming, cattle raising, and arts and crafts. Tohono O'odham baskets are famous worldwide. Tribal members also make pottery, wooden bowls, horsehair miniatures, and horsehair lariats.

There are deposits of copper and other minerals on tribal lands. Powerful Arizona mining concerns origi-

Tohono O'odham awl of mesquite wood and pin (modern)

nally owned the rights to these resources. But this situation has been rectified, and the Tohono O'odham now earn income from mining leases. The Tohono O'odham Nation also recently opened the Desert Diamond Casino for tribal income. Some individuals earn a living through cattle ranching. About half of the tribal members live off-reservation, many in area cities such as Phoenix, Arizona.

TOLTEC

The Toltec (pronounced TOLL-tec or TALL-tec) migrated from the north into the Valley of Mexico about A.D. 900. Over the following centuries to about A.D. 1200, they created one of the four great Mesoamerican civilizations. (Mesoamerica is the name given by scholars to the culture area in what is now Mexico and parts of Central America, where Indians created highly organized agricultural societies with cities or city-states.)

When they first arrived in the Valley of Mexico, a broad valley on the Mexican Plateau, the Toltec were one of the many nomadic hunting tribes called Chichimec, meaning "sons of the dog." The local inhabitants feared them. After a prolonged power struggle, the Toltec became the dominant tribe under their leader Mixcoatl.

At that time in densely populated Mesoamerica, there were many different peoples and tribes. Some of them lived in population center with stone architecture. Some developed hieroglyphic writing. The OLMEC had developed the first great civilization in the Preclassic period before A.D. 300. The MAYA had followed in the so-called Classic period from about A.D. 300 to 900. Another great city during the Classic period was Teotihuacán. There were other centers of religion, learning, and commerce, many of these in the Valley of Mexico. Mixcoatl, the Toltec leader, encouraged his followers to learn from these other cultures. The Toltec built their own city, calling it Tula.

The Toltec and other peoples after them, such as the AZTEC, rose to power in a period labeled the Postclassic era, from about A.D. 900 to the arrival of Europeans in about 1500. This label is applied because many of the cultural traits of the Postclassic civilizations were adopted from the earlier Classic peoples, who made great strides forward in knowledge.

The Toltec adapted that earlier knowledge into new forms. Mixcoatl's son Topiltzín, who came to power in 968, encouraged learning and art among his people. Much of what is known about the Toltec comes from the later Aztec. In Aztec legends, the Toltec stood for what is civilized. Also in Aztec mythology, both Mixcoatl and Topiltzín were considered gods—the father, a hunting god, and the son, the Great Plumed Serpent, a deity among many different Mesoamerican peoples. The Aztec might have revered the Toltec leaders as gods because Topiltzín took the name Plumed Serpent, or Quetzalcoatl.

Under Topiltzín-Quetzalcoatl, the Toltec erected tall pyramids, beautiful palaces with columns and murals, ball courts, and other elegant stone structures; they developed new kinds of corn, squash, and cotton; they crafted exquisite objects in gold and silver; they shaped new designs in pottery; they made beautiful clothing from textiles, decorated with feathers; and they used hieroglyphic writing. They also conquered other Indian peoples around them and influenced

Toltec clay figurine
made from a mold

their architecture and art forms. At its peak, the Toltec Empire stretched from the Gulf of Mexico to the Pacific Ocean.

Yet Topiltzín-Quetzalcoatl fell from power. What led to his downfall is not known for certain. Aztec tradition says that the Plumed Serpent was overthrown when he tried to ban human sacrifice, which the Toltec practiced on a large scale. Legend has it that the followers of the Plumed Serpent were defeated by the devotees of Tezcatlipoca, the deity of the night, and that they then fled from Tula.

Perhaps Topiltzín-Quetzalcoatl and his followers were the Toltec who invaded the Yucatán Peninsula to the east, interbred with the Maya, and brought about the Maya Postclassic era. Whether the great king survived his downfall or not, the legend of Quetzalcoatl was so strong in the later Aztec culture that they awaited his return and thought that Cortés, the Spanish conquistador, might be he.

The Toltec who overthrew Topiltzín-Quetzalcoatl and stayed in power in Tula and the Valley of Mexico gradually fell into a state of decline. They were plagued by a series of droughts, famines, fires, and invasions of tribes who, as they themselves once had, came from the north. Tula was destroyed in 1160. After a period of tribal rivalries and power struggles, the Aztec, the founders of the last great Mesoamerican civilization, rose to dominance.

TONKAWA

The Tonkawa originally lived in territory that is now central Texas. They had a reputation as fierce raiders and skilled hunters who roamed the southern plains throughout most of present-day Texas and into eastern New Mexico and southern Oklahoma (see PLAINS INDIANS).

Tonkawa, pronounced TAHN-kuh-wuh, is thought to mean "they all stay together." The language of the Tonkawa, referred to as Tonkawan, is unique. As a result, Tonkawa ancestry and place of origin are uncertain. They might be distant relatives of people known as the Karankawa and the Coahuiltec, who once inhabited southern Texas and northern Mexico.

The Tonkawa had early contacts with Spanish explorers, probably both Alvar Núñez Cabeza de Vaca in the 1530s and Francisco Vásquez de Coronado in the 1540s. Other than occasional expeditions and a few missions, Spain did little to establish its claim to Texas until France gained a foothold along the lower Mississippi valley after René-Robert Cavelier de La Salle's expedition of 1682. Spain then competed with the French for the support of Texas tribes until France lost its territory to England in 1763 after the French and Indian wars. It was during the late 17th and early 18th century that the Tonkawa acquired horses from the Spanish or from other Indians, which increased their effectiveness as warriors and buffalo hunters.

The Tonkawa were traditional enemies of the APACHE, who lived to their west in New Mexico and Arizona. The two peoples often launched raids against each other. However, an Apache taken as a prisoner by the Tonkawa became a powerful chief among his new people. He was called by the Spanish name El Mocho, meaning "the cropped one," because he had lost his right ear while fighting the OSAGE. El Mocho's dream was to unite the Apache and Tonkawa. In 1782, he organized a great council that was attended by more than 4,000 people of both tribes. He argued for a unified stand against the Spanish. But the two peoples were unable to put aside old grudges, and El Mocho's dream of alliance was never realized. The Spanish later captured and executed him.

In 1845, Texas became part of the United States. In 1855, the Tonkawa, along with other Texas tribes, were assigned two small reservations on the Brazos River. During that period, the Tonkawa served as scouts with the Texas Rangers against the COMANCHE.

In 1859, because of increased settlement in the area by Anglo-Americans, the Tonkawa were relocated to the Washita River in the Indian Territory. During the Civil

War, some of the Tonkawa served as scouts for the Confederate Army. In 1862, other tribes used the Tonkawa involvement in the Civil War as an excuse to settle old scores. CADDO, LENNI LENAPE (DELAWARE), and SHAWNEE warriors raided the Tonkawa camps and killed many. The survivors fled to Texas, where they remained until 1884. At that time, government officials arranged a new home for them in the Indian Territory, farther north, near the PONCA. Their descendants live there today in Kay County, Oklahoma, organized as the Tonkawa Tribe of Indians of Oklahoma. Although no tribal members speak Tonkawan, they have revived traditional ceremonies and sponsor a powwow every June at the town of Tonkawa.

TOWA *see* PUEBLO INDIANS

TSIMSHIAN

Tsimshian, pronounced CHIM-shee-un or TSIM-shee-un, sometimes spelled *Tsimpshean,* means "people of the Skeena River." The lower courses on the Skeena and Nass Rivers flowing to the Pacific Ocean formed the heart of ancestral Tsimshian territory in what is now northern British Columbia and southern Alaska. Yet most of their villages of roomy beam-and-plank houses were located along the ocean shore.

The Tsimshian language isolate is classified by some scholars as part of the Penutian phylum, which would make them the northernmost Penutian-speaking people. Most other tribes who spoke Penutian dialects lived to the south in present-day Washington, Oregon, and California. Tsimshian-speaking peoples actually consist of three independent groups: the Tsimshian proper, on the lower Skeena River and coastal areas; the Nisga (Niska), on the Nass River and coastal areas; and the Gitskan (Kitskan), on the upper Skeena River.

The Tsimshian, like all NORTHWEST COAST INDIANS, depended on fishing for food. In the rivers, they caught salmon and candlefish, which left the ocean every spring to lay their eggs. Off the mainland and the Queen Charlotte Islands opposite their territory, they caught halibut, cod, flounder, and other fish from their long, sleek dugout canoes. Like modern fishermen, they used whatever means was best suited to the place and species: hooks and lines, harpoons, nets, traps, or weirs. The Tsimshian also dug up shellfish and seaweed offshore. And they went after the sea mammals that offered plentiful food and materials for tools, clothing, and blankets: seals, sea lions, and sea otters. But they did not hunt whales, as certain other Northwest Coast peoples did.

The Tsimshian were also hunter-gatherers. They entered the tall, dense forests of the interior highlands, part of the Coast Range, to track deer, bear, and mountain goats. They used snares, corrals, spears, and bows and arrows to kill their prey. Seeking a varied diet, they foraged for edible wild plant foods as well—roots, berries, and greens.

Like most Northwest Coast peoples, the Tsimshian made exquisite woodwork and basketry. Also typically, they frequently traded for other tribes' products. Tsimshian spiritual culture—with powerful shamans and secret societies—resembled that of other Northwest Coast tribes too. The potlatch ritual, where people gave away possessions, played a central part in their society.

Among the most valuable gifts that could be given away in the potlatches were copper plaques. The Tsimshian

Tsimshian bow

Tsimshian soul-catcher, supposedly containing the soul of a dead shaman (The charm was placed in a sick person's mouth from which point the soul was thought to enter the body and expel the demon that caused the sickness.)

hammered the ore into engraved metal sculptures. Copper tools were also highly valued.

The Tsimshian were famous for their Chilkat blankets. Their trading partners the TLINGIT, who lived to the north, also made these blankets, named after one of the Tlingit bands. The fringed blankets, and similar shirts, were woven from goat's hair and cedar bark into intricate animal and abstract designs. The mystical representations supposedly had the power to talk to people. On acquiring European materials, the Tsimshian and other Northwest Coast peoples became known for button blankets, a type of blanket, typically blue with a red border, on which animal shapes representing clans are formed by attaching mother-of-pearl buttons.

The postcontact history of the Tsimshian was more peaceful than that of the Tlingit, since the Tsimshian were not as close to Russian trading posts. Their experience paralleled that of the more southern peoples: in the late 1700s, frequent sailing expeditions along the coast sponsored by the world's colonial powers, including the Spanish, English, French, and Russians; in the early 1800s, fur-trading posts including the Hudson's Bay Company's Fort Simpson in 1831 and Fort Essington in 1835; in the mid-1800s, missionaries, including the Episcopalian William Duncan in 1857; and in the late 1800s, with the completion of the Canadian Pacific Railway, white settlements. The Klondike gold rush of 1896 led to an influx of prospectors.

Unlike some missionaries, who tried to eliminate native peoples' traditional culture, William Duncan proved a valuable friend to the Tsimshian. When he came to live among them, the Tsimshian way of life had been corrupted by liquor brought in by white traders. Tsimshian bands carried out acts of murder, rape, and thievery. Some even practiced ritualistic cannibalism. Duncan studied their language and mythology and preached to them about the Bible in terms of their own legends. By 1862, after five years among them, he had converted four of the nine principal chiefs to Christian nonviolence. That same year, he built a mission at Metlakatla. In 1887, he moved with his followers to New Metlakatla on Annette Island. There tribal members learned carpentry, blacksmithing, spinning, and soapmaking, as well as baseball and music. Duncan also helped the people develop a fishing and canning operation, plus a sawmill. Duncan stayed with the Tsimshian until his death in 1918, at the age of 85.

Today, those Tsimshian who moved to Annette Island are United States citizens, since the island is now part of Alaska. Fish processing and logging still provide ample incomes for the residents of the reservation. Many members of the Canadian Tsimshian (and Nisga and Gitskan) bands earn a living in the same occupations.

TUNICA

A number of Tunican-speaking tribes once lived along the lower Mississippi River valley: the Griga, Koroa, Tiou, Tunica, and YAZOO. The name of the Tunica, pronounced TYOON-uh-cuh and meaning "those who are the people," has been applied to the shared language. The Tunica lived in what is now the state of Mississippi near the confluence of the Mississippi River and the Yazoo River. Some Tunica also might have located their villages on the opposite bank of the Mississippi in territory that is now eastern Arkansas and eastern Louisiana.

The Tunica had lifeways in common with other SOUTHEAST INDIANS. Their societies were hierarchical, with autocratic rulers. Villagers farmed the black, moist soil of the Mississippi floodplain, formed by the river overflowing its banks, cultivating corn, beans, squash, sunflowers, and melons. They hunted, fished, and gathered wild foods to supplement these staples. They built thatched houses and temples of worship, carved dugout canoes, shaped pottery, and made a cloth fabric from the mulberry plant. They also mined salt to trade with other tribes.

The Spanish expedition of Hernando de Soto encountered Tunican-speaking peoples in 1541. Two centuries later, in the early 1700s, after René-Robert Cavelier de La Salle had claimed the region for France, a Jesuit missionary by the name of Father Davion lived among them. From that time on, the Tunica remained faithful allies of the French. In fact, some of their warriors helped the French suppress the Natchez Revolt of 1729. Their kinsmen, the Yazoo, supported the NATCHEZ, however. When the English gained control of the Tunica territory in 1763 at the end of the French and Indian wars, the Tunica began attacking their boats on the Mississippi River.

After the American Revolution, the Tunica gradually departed from their homeland. Some resettled in Louisiana, where there are still Indians of mixed descent with Tunican blood. In 1981, the federal government granted recognition to the Tunica-Biloxi tribe. (The Biloxi, a Siouan-speaking people, once had lived near Biloxi, Mississippi.) Other Tunica joined the CHOCTAW, with whom they migrated to Oklahoma.

TUSCARORA

The Tuscarora are an Iroquoian-speaking people, part of the Iroquois League of Six Nations along with the CAYUGA, MOHAWK, ONEIDA, ONONDAGA, and SENECA, known collectively as the IROQUOIS (HAUDENOSAUNEE). Their name, pronounced tusk-uh-ROAR-uh, or *Ska-Ruh-Reh* in its native form, identifies them as the "shirt-wearing people."

The Tuscarora originally lived in villages in the part of North America that was to become northeastern North Carolina and southeastern Virginia, especially along the Pamlico, Neuse, and Trent Rivers on the Atlantic coastal plain and the rolling hills of the Piedmont. Their way of life in this location included farming, woodland hunting and gathering, river fishing, and fishing and collecting shellfish in the ocean.

In the early 1700s, the Tuscarora migrated to New York among the Haudenosaunee. In 1722, they were formally recognized as the sixth nation of the Iroquois League. Their culture became closer to that of their new allies as they adjusted to the northern inland location and began participating in Haudenosaunee rituals. Their Iroquoian dialect also evolved.

The hostilities that caused their departure from North Carolina—the Tuscarora War—were especially unnecessary because the Tuscarora had been friendly to the English colonists. They not only had provided them with knowledge about wilderness survival and with food, but also had helped them in their conflicts with other tribes. In return for their friendship and generosity, the Tuscarora were taken advantage of by whites. Settlers took their best farmlands; traders cheated them; and slavers kidnapped them to ship them to the Caribbean or to Europe.

Because of the continuing abuses, Tuscarora warriors under Chief Hancock raided settlements between the Trent and Neuse Rivers in 1711, killing perhaps as many

Tuscarora silver belt buckle (modern)

as 200 men, women, and children. Angry settlers sought revenge. They managed to capture a Tuscarora man, whom they roasted alive. Area tribes, such as the Coree, joined the Tuscarora cause. The colonies of North and South Carolina raised a militia under Colonel John Barnwell. Many of his soldiers were YAMASEE. They marched into Tuscarora territory, moving on Hancock's village of Cotechney. After a standoff, peace was made. But Barnwell violated it by seizing other Tuscarora as slaves. The Indians commenced raiding once again.

Another colonial army was organized under Colonel James Moore. Many Yamasee joined this force too. This army marched on the Tuscarora village of Neoheroka in 1713 and killed or captured almost 1,000 Tuscarora. Captives were sold into slavery at 10 pounds sterling each to finance Moore's military campaign. It was at this time that many of the surviving Tuscarora migrated north. Some lived on the Susquehanna River in Pennsylvania for a time before moving to Haudenosaunee country in New York near the Oneida. Some members of those villages not part of the uprising were permitted to stay unmolested in North Carolina, but in years to come they too joined their relatives in the north. By 1804, only a few scattered Tuscarora families remained in the South.

The Tuscarora did not have direct votes at the Iroquois League's Great Council. The Oneida, among whom they originally settled, represented them. Otherwise, the Tuscarora were treated as equals.

In the American Revolution, most Tuscarora and Oneida sided with the Americans against the British. This caused a rift in the Iroquois League, since the other Haudenosaunee tribes supported the British. After the Revolution, despite their assistance in the American cause, settlers turned against the Tuscarora too and burned their longhouses along with those of the pro-British tribes. The Tuscarora eventually were granted state reservation lands in the northwestern corner of New York in Seneca country near Niagara Falls, where their descendants live today. They later purchased additional adjoining lands. Those Tuscarora who had sided with the British settled on the Grand River near Brantford, Ontario, as part of the Six Nations Reserve.

In 1957, the Tuscarora Nation of New York refused to sell off part of their lands for a proposed reservoir to be built by the New York State Power Authority. When state officials went forward with the plan, the Tuscarora protested. The case went to the U.S. Supreme Court, which decided against the Tuscarora. But their political and legal resistance, which received international attention, helped shape pan-Indian activism of the 1960s and 1970s.

Tuscarora, many of whom hold industrial jobs in Buffalo and Niagara Falls, continue to participate in the shared activities of the Haudenosaunee.

UMATILLA

The Umatilla (pronounced um-uh-TIL-uh) occupied ancestral territory in what today is northern Oregon and southern Washington State, along the banks of the river named after them, as well as along the Columbia River. They are considered part of the Plateau Culture Area. Like other Sahaptian-speaking PLATEAU INDIANS, the Umatilla fished the rivers of the region, especially for salmon during the spawning season; hunted small game; and gathered wild plant foods, especially the roots and bulbs of the camas plant.

After the Lewis and Clark Expedition of the early 1800s, the Umatilla and other Plateau tribes became important to the fur trade, developed in the region by both the North West Company and the Hudson's Bay

A Umatilla family in front of their rush-mat house

Company, both of Canada, and the American Fur Company. Their relations with whites were peaceful until the mid-1800s when they resisted white expansion in the Cayuse War of 1847–50 and the Yakama War of 1855–56 (see CAYUSE and YAKAMA). In the Bannock War two decades later, they aided the whites by alerting soldiers to the whereabouts of the rebels and by killing the PAIUTE chief Egan (see BANNOCK).

The Umatilla Reservation was established in 1853. Umatilla share this tract of land near Pendleton, Oregon, with Cayuse and Walla Walla. The Confederated Tribes of the Umatilla Reservation sponsor an annual powwow and rodeo called the Pendleton Roundup. Tribal members also participate in traditional ceremonies surrounding salmon fishing and root gathering.

UTE

The state of Utah takes its name from the Ute, pronounced YOOT, meaning "high up" or the "land of the sun." The tribe is also associated historically with the state of Colorado. Their territory once extended from the southern Rocky Mountains in present-day Colorado as far west as the Sevier River in present-day Utah. The Ute also ranged as far south as the upper San Juan River in what is now northern New Mexico and as far north as southern Wyoming.

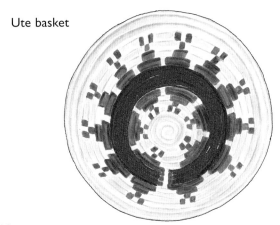

Ute basket

Lifeways

The Ute are classified as part of the Great Basin Culture Area, with lifeways similar to their neighbors the PAIUTE and the SHOSHONE, all speaking dialects of the Uto-Aztecan language family (see GREAT BASIN INDIANS). Peoples of the huge cupped desert area between the Rocky Mountains and the Sierra Nevada consisted of nomadic bands, the members of which dug for foods such as roots, seeds, rodents, lizards, and insects in this arid environment where little vegetation grew and where big game was scarce.

But the Ute, especially the bands to the east, can be thought of as mountain-dwellers as much as desert peo-

ples. The forested slopes of the Rockies offered much more wildlife than the desert. And the rivers flowing westward from the Great Divide provided plentiful fish for food.

The typical shelter of the Ute was a cone-shaped pole framework covered with brush, reeds, and grasses. The Ute were loosely knit into small bands that sometimes spent the winter together or joined one another for communal rabbit drives. Arrow and spearhead makers held a special place of honor in their society, along with the band leaders and shamans.

The Ute, who had frequent contacts with the PUEBLO INDIANS in northern New Mexico, acquired horses from them in the late 1600s. The Ute homeland had enough pasture to graze horses. Henceforth, the Ute way of life became somewhat similar to the PLAINS INDIANS east of the Rocky Mountains. With increased mobility, the Ute became wide-ranging raiders and traders. Yet they rarely hunted buffalo, and their new hide-covered tipis remained small, like their earlier brush shelters. They painted these lodges with bright colors.

Early Contact and Conflict

The Ute were reputed to be warlike. The first writings about them come from the journal of Fray Francisco de Escalante, a Franciscan priest who explored the Great Basin with Francisco Domínguez in 1776. By that time, mounted on horses, the Ute carried out regular raids on Indians and Spanish alike. They captured slaves to trade with other tribes for horses and other goods. They also warred intermittently with the ARAPAHO living on the other side of the Rocky Mountain Great Divide.

Nonetheless, because the Ute lived west of the Rockies in a rugged environment where few whites other than the mountain men traveled, they avoided early clashes with the Anglo-Americans who came from the east. Isolated early incidents of violence did happen when whites entered the Ute domain. For example, Ute warriors killed the famous mountain man William Sherley Williams, nicknamed Old Bill Williams, who had previously acted as John Frémont's guide during one of Frémont's voyages of western exploration.

Starting in 1847 and during the years to follow, waves of Mormon settlers arrived on Ute and Shoshone lands in Utah. The Ute resisted increasing encroachment in two uprisings: the Walker War of 1853 under Chief Wakara (or Walkara or Walter) and the Black Hawk War of the 1860s under Chief Black Hawk (not to be confused with the Black Hawk War of the 1830s involving SAC and FOX (MESQUAKI).

The Ute War

With the growth of mining in western Colorado and eastern Utah because of the Colorado gold rush of 1858–59, the Ute were pressured by whites into signing away most of their land in exchange for a reservation. When Colorado achieved statehood in 1876, mining companies tried to expel the Ute from a remaining tract along the White River. The phrase "The Utes must go" became a political slogan, even though Ute had served as guides and fighters for the federal regulars and state militiamen in campaigns against other Indians, such as the NAVAJO in the 1860s.

An important Ute leader at this time was Chief Ouray. He spoke English and Spanish in addition to several different Indian languages and understood U.S. law. He had for many years protected the rights of his people through complex negotiations with the whites. Kit Carson considered him one of the greatest men he knew.

Yet even such a respected statesman and peacemaker as Ouray could not prevent violence. Unrest was growing among his people, who felt betrayed by land-grabbing whites. Moreover, some of the Ute resented their treatment by the uncompromising Indian agent Nathan Meeker, who forced a new way of life on them at White River. He taught the White River Indians agriculture and the Christian religion. But most of the Indians preferred their ancient ways. When the Indians refused to farm, Meeker wanted federal troops to help him impose his will. The federal government ignored his requests until a fight broke out. A medicine man named Canella (also known as Johnson) grew angry at having to plow lands that had always been Ute grazing land for horses. He physically attacked Meeker in September 1879. On learning of this incident through correspondence from Meeker, federal officials sent in a detachment of 150 troops under Major Thomas Thornburgh.

Warriors under Chief Nicaagat (Jack) and Chief Quinkent (Douglas) threw their support behind Canella. Warriors rode out to block the army column at Milk Creek. Before a parley could be arranged, shots were fired. A bullet struck down Major Thornburgh. Captain J. Scott Payne organized a defense behind wagons on the opposite side of Milk Creek from the militants. The Ute lay siege for a week. On the third day, a regiment of African-American cavalrymen rode in as reinforcements. An even larger relief force arrived on the seventh day. The Ute withdrew, but they left behind 13 whites dead and 48 wounded.

The army advanced the rest of the way to the agency. On arriving there, they found the bodies of Meeker and nine other whites. Meeker's wife and daughter, plus another woman and two children, had been taken hostage. The ex–Civil War generals Philip Henry Sheridan and William Tecumseh Sherman wanted to launch major offensives against the Ute. But Secretary of the Interior Carl Schurz sent in a peace mission under Charles Adams.

Adams met with the one man whom he knew could defuse the situation—Chief Ouray. Demonstrating his skill at diplomacy, Ouray negotiated the release of the hostages and guaranteed the freedom of the rebellious Indians. The following year, however, the same year that Ouray died at the age of 46, the White River Ute were forced to move.

Ute children and cradleboard

Contemporary Ute

The Ute presently hold three reservations in Colorado and Utah. The Southern Ute Reservation near Ignacio, Colorado, includes the Mouache and Capote bands. The Ute Mountain Reservation near Towaoc, Colorado, with adjoining parcels of land in Colorado, Utah, and New Mexico, is the home of the Winimuche band. The Northern (Uintah and Ouray) Ute Reservation near Fort Duchesne, Utah, is the home of mainly White River descendants. Income for the Ute comes largely from oil, gas, and mineral leases; farming and raising livestock; gaming; and arts and crafts. The Ute of the Ute Mountain Reservation also run Ute Mountain Tribal Park and offer tours to Anasazi ruins and rock art on their reservation lands adjacent to Mesa Verde National Park. The bands hold annual Bear Dances and Sun Dances in the summer.

UTINA *see* TIMUCUA

WALAPAI *see* HUALAPAI

WALLA WALLA

The Walla Walla occupied ancestral territory along the lower Walla Walla River and along the junction of the Snake and Columbia Rivers in territory that is now part of northern Oregon and southern Washington State. Their name, pronounced WOL-uh WOL-uh, means "little river" in their Sahaptian dialect of the Penutian language phylum. The tribe shared cultural traits with other PLATEAU INDIANS, subsisting primarily through salmon fishing and root gathering with some hunting of small game.

The Walla Walla became known to whites after the Lewis and Clark Expedition in the early 1800s. Afterward, white fur traders had many contacts with them. Like other tribes of the region, they were peaceful toward whites until the 1850s, when several wars erupted. The Walla Walla participated in the Yakama War of 1855–56 with the YAKAMA and other tribes. An important chief of the Walla Walla during this period was Peopeomoxmox. Colonel James Kelly, who led a volunteer force into Indian country, called a parley with the chief. When the chief came, he was murdered by Kelly's men. Then they displayed his scalp and ears to the white settlers to show that they had taken revenge for earlier Indian attacks. Peopeomoxmox's murder rallied other tribes to rebellion and led to continued violence through 1858, involving the COEUR D'ALENE and other tribes.

The Walla Walla were settled on the Umatilla Reservation in Oregon with the UMATILLA and the CAYUSE, where their descendants live today as part of the Confederated Tribes of the Umatilla Reservation.

WAMPANOAG

The ALGONQUIANS known as the Wampanoag went from being the foremost friends of the New England colonists in the early 1620s—the Indian peoples whose friendship led to the holiday of Thanksgiving—to being among their worst enemies by the 1670s. How did this reversal come about?

Territory

The ancestral territory of the Wampanoag included what now is eastern Rhode Island, southeastern Massachusetts, Martha's Vineyard, Nantucket, and the Elizabeth Islands. Their tribal name, pronounced wam-puh-NO-ag, means "people of the east," since they lived along the Atlantic Ocean, and is similar in meaning to the tribal name ABENAKI in another Algonquian dialect. An alternative name for the Wampanoag, *Pokanoket,* "place of the clear land," is derived from a village name on the Bristol Peninsula on the east side of Narragansett Bay in present-day Rhode Island, one of some 30 villages or bands.

The Wampanoag had lifeways in common with other NORTHEAST INDIANS of the region. They lived in palisaded villages of domed wigwams, cultivated a number of crops in adjoining fields, hunted and gathered in the forests, and fished in the ocean, bays, and rivers.

Because of their coastal location, the Wampanoag had early contacts with European trading and fishing expeditions, as well as with English settlers who came to establish permanent homes. Early relations generally were friendly, and the friendship would endure through much of the 17th century.

Squanto and Massasoit

Tisquantum, or Squanto for short, was of the Pawtuxet band of Wampanoag, located at present-day Plymouth, Massachusetts. In 1615, he was kidnapped by Captain Thomas Hunt, an English trader, and taken to Spain and sold into slavery. But a sympathetic Englishman ransomed him and took him to England. In 1619, Squanto managed an ocean crossing under Captain Thomas Dermer, returning to his people.

When the Pilgrims arrived in North America and founded Plymouth in 1620, Squanto used his knowledge of English to instruct them in the ways of the wilderness, particularly in planting corn and fishing. Squanto interpreted for and acted on behalf of Massasoit of the Pokanoket band and grand sachem of all the Wampanoag bands, who signed an early peace treaty with the Pilgrims. Without the help of the Wampanoag, the Pilgrims probably would have perished during their first winter. It might be said that Squanto and Massasoit are the figures in history most responsible for the holiday of Thanksgiving, proclaimed in 1621 by the Plymouth governor, William Bradford, after a successful harvest.

Squanto died in 1622 from "Indian fever," or smallpox carried to the Indians by the settlers. Massasoit, who had signed an early peace treaty with the Pilgrims, remained an ally of the colonists for 40 years until his death in 1660. His friendship helped keep the Wampanoag neutral in the Pequot War of 1636–37 (see PEQUOT). It also enabled the Pilgrims and other colonists to maintain their foothold in the New World. If the Wampanoag had been hostile in these early years, they certainly could have slowed the pace of British expansion in North America.

Yet the colonists abused their friendship with the Indians time and again. They wanted land for farming and tried to trick the Indians into signing it away for little payment or no payment at all. One method they used was to get tribal representatives drunk before negotiating with them. Another was to bribe one Indian and make him an honorary chief, then have him sign away tribal lands.

King Philip's War

Massasoit had two sons, Metacomet and Wamsutta. The colonists came to call them Philip and Alexander, after Philip of Macedon and Alexander the Great. The boys grew up at a time when the number of settlers was rising dramatically—along with the number of abuses against Indians. Unlike their father, Massasoit, they became militant, believing it was necessary to make a stand to protect their way of life.

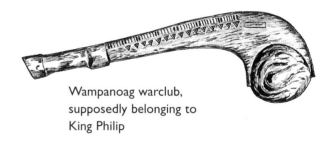

Wampanoag warclub, supposedly belonging to King Philip

The new generation of Wampanoag resented the fact that when an Indian committed a crime under English law, he was taken before a colonial court to be tried rather than before his own people. After one such incident, Wamsutta, who had succeeded Massasoit as grand sachem, died during the trip home. Metacomet, now grand sachem, believed that the colonial officials had poisoned his brother and wanted revenge. He also wanted the Wampanoag to regain their former greatness.

Yet Metacomet bid his time, sending runners to other tribes to ask their help. His goal was to organize an alliance of tribes that would be strong enough to oust all colonists from New England. He was the first great Native American leader to envision and work toward such an alliance of tribes. NARRAGANSETT and NIPMUC bands offered their support.

Colonial officials sensed the growing militancy and tried to harass Metacomet, calling him before a court and ordering the Wampanoag to turn in their flintlocks. Metacomet yielded to their demands in order to buy more time, relinquishing some but not all of the Wampanoag guns. Even so, fighting came prematurely. In June 1675, the colonists arrested and hanged three Wampanoag accused of killing a Christianized Indian. In the increased state of tension, fighting broke out near the Wampanoag village of Mount Hope. A settler fired at and wounded a tribal member in an argument over cattle. The Wampanoag retaliated, killing 11 colonists. King Philip's War had begun.

After these opening hostilities, the allied tribes—Wampanoag, Narragansett, and Nipmuc—began a campaign of violence against the settlers. Small war parties attacked outlying settlements all over New England, from the Connecticut River to the Atlantic Coast.

The New England Confederation of Colonies, including Massachusetts Bay, Plymouth, Rhode Island, and Connecticut, mustered armies. They engaged the Indians in several major battles. The first occurred in July at Pocasset Swamp, in Wampanoag territory. The next two occurred the following autumn along the northern Connecticut River valley in Nipmuc country—at Bloody Brook and Hopewell Swamp. Then the deciding battle took place in Narragansett territory—the

Great Swamp Fight of December 1675. The Narragansett lost more than 600 men, women, and children.

There were two more major encounters and colonial victories, one near Deerfield, Massachusetts, and the other near Plymouth, the latter known as the Bridgewater Swamp Fight. Soon afterward, Metacomet was betrayed by an Indian informer and killed at Mount Hope. His killers cut up his body and kept the parts as trophies.

In the aftermath of King Philip's War, Metacomet's wife and son were shipped to the Caribbean to be sold as slaves for 30 shillings apiece. The colonists took their revenge on peaceful tribes as well, seizing more and more Indian territory. Some Wampanoag did manage to retain their lands, in particular those on the islands of Martha's Vineyard and Nantucket, who stayed out of the conflict. White diseases continued to take their toll over the years, further reducing the Wampanoag population. But even as the number of non-Indians grew exponentially around them, the Wampanoag endured.

Contemporary Wampanoag

There currently are five Wampanoag bands in southern Massachusetts: the Gay Head, Mashpee, Assonet, Herring Pond, and Nemasket. Only the Wampanoag Tribe of Wampanoag on Martha's Vineyard have federal recognition, since 1987, but the Mashpee of Cape Cod have petitioned for it. Tribal events include the Gay Head Cranberry Day, the Mashpee July Fourth Powwow, and the Assonet Strawberry Festival.

WAPPINGER

The Wappinger once lived along the Hudson River between Manhattan Island and Poughkeepsie, especially on the east bank, now the southern part of New York State. Their name, pronounced WOP-in-jer, possibly means "easterners." Some of the Wappinger territory also extended into Connecticut. An Algonquian people, they consisted of numerous bands. They were flanked by the MAHICAN to the north and the LENNI LENAPE (DELAWARE) to the west and south. In fact, there is some confusion among scholars as to which bands belonged to which tribe.

Some scholars, for example, consider the Manhattan of Manhattan Island, the island now at the center of

New York City, to have been a Lenni Lenape tribe. Others write about them as Wappinger. And some scholars group the Paugussett, four bands living on the lower Housatonic River in Connecticut, with the Wappinger. Others classify them as a distinct tribe.

In any case, the bands of all three groups of NORTHEAST INDIANS living along the Hudson River—Wappinger, Lenni Lenape, and Mahican—were ALGONQUIANS and had typical Algonquian technologies and beliefs. Moreover, the histories of the various Hudson River Indians were similar, since they were all affected by the arrival of Dutch traders and settlers.

Henry Hudson, an Englishman sailing under a Dutch flag, explored the territory along the river that bears his name and claimed it for the Netherlands in 1609–10. In the following years, many Dutch trading ships plied the waters of the Hudson River, exchanging European trade goods for furs. The Algonquians called the Dutch traders *swanneken.*

In 1621, the Dutch West India Company received the charter to develop New Netherland. Dutch settlers started arriving in great numbers for the purposes of both fur trading and farming. They bartered with the Indians for land. The Manhattan sold Manhattan Island for 60 guilders' (24 dollars') worth of trade goods. The Mahican sold property near the northern end of the Hudson River. Soon both New Amsterdam (now New York) and Fort Orange (now Albany) were thriving Dutch communities. And with the expanding Dutch presence, there was a need for additional land on both sides of the Hudson River.

Pressures on the Indians along the Hudson River mounted. In the 1640s, violence erupted. The first incident involved the Raritan Indians on Staten Island, generally considered a subtribe of the Lenni Lenape. They rebelled in 1641 when Dutch livestock destroyed their crops.

The second incident, in 1643, called the Pavonia Massacre, or the Slaughter of Innocents, involved Wappinger bands living farther north on the Hudson. The governor-general of New Netherland at that time, Willem Kieft, believed in a policy of harassment and extermination of Hudson River Indians to make room for Dutch settlers. He paid the MOHAWK, traditional enemies of the Hudson River Algonquians, to attack

them. The Wappinger fled to the Dutch settlement at Pavonia for protection. Yet Dutch soldiers attacked the unsuspecting Indians while they slept, killing and beheading 80, many of them women and children, and taking 30 more as prisoners. The soldiers brought the 80 heads back to New Amsterdam, where they played kickball with them. They also publicly tortured many of the Indian prisoners. Governor-General Kieft is said to have "laughed right heartily" at the sight.

Algonquians from the Delaware Bay to the Connecticut River valley began raiding Dutch settlements in retaliation for the massacre. It was during this period that the Dutch built a defensive wall in lower Manhattan, where Wall Street is today. Dutch and English soldiers raided and burned Indian villages. By 1644, resistance had been crushed.

Still another outbreak of violence, usually called the Peach Wars, occurred in the 1650s. A Dutch farmer killed a Lenni Lenape woman for stealing peaches from his orchard, which sparked another Indian rebellion of Lenni Lenape and Wappinger. Peter Stuyvesant, the new governor-general, also was harsh in his treatment of Indians. He finally squelched this uprising in 1664 by taking Indian women and children hostages and threatening to harm them in order to make the men negotiate.

That same year, British troops invaded New Netherland and took control of the region, which became New York. But it was too late for the Wappinger. Their once-great power had been broken. In the years to follow, Wappinger survivors joined the Lenni Lenape and Nanticoke to the south or the Mahican and PEQUOT to the north and east.

WICHITA

The Wichita separated from other Caddoan peoples—the CADDO, ARIKARA, and PAWNEE—early in their history and migrated onto the southern plains. They came to occupy territory in what now is part of Kansas, Oklahoma, and Texas. Other Caddoans—Kichai, Tawakoni, Tawehash, Waco, and Yscani—merged with the Wichita in the 19th century and sometimes are referred to collectively as the Wichita Confederacy.

The Wichita are classified as part of the Great Plains Culture Area. They acquired horses about 1700 and

used them to hunt buffalo. While on the trail, they lived in skin tipis like other PLAINS INDIANS. Yet the Wichita had a mixed economy of hunting and farming and sometimes are grouped among the so-called PRAIRIE INDIANS. Much of the year, they lived in permanent villages and grew corn and other crops. Their village homes were conical grass houses, resembling something like haystacks. To construct their type of dwelling, the Wichita erected long poles in a circle, with the tops meeting in a dome shape. The framework was tied together with slender branches or reeds, then covered with thatch.

Because of these houses, the name *Wichita,* pronounced WITCH-uh-taw, in fact is thought to be derived from the CHOCTAW word *wia-chitoh,* meaning "big arbor." The Wichita native name is *Kitikiti'sh* for "racoon-eyed," derived from their practice of tattooing and face-painting. They also were known historically as Pict, from the French word *piqué* for "pricked," because tribal members used sharp implements in tattooing.

The Wichita were among those tribes who encountered the Spanish expedition of Francisco Vásquez de Coronado in 1541. At that time, the Wichita lived along the Arkansas River in what is now central Kansas. Coronado sought but never found great riches in Wichita country, which he called the Kingdom of Quivira. A Franciscan missionary named Juan de Padilla stayed behind with the Indians to try to convert them to Catholicism. But the Wichita killed him three years later when he began working with another tribe as well.

Over a century later in 1662, the Spaniard Diego Dionisio de Peñalosa led an army against the Wichita and defeated them in battle. Soon afterward, the tribe migrated southward to the Canadian River in what is now Oklahoma. The French explorer, Bernard de la Harpe, met up with them there in 1719 and established trade relations.

Wichita and Caddo traders were called Taovayas by the French. The Taovayas established a profitable business as middlemen between the French and the more westerly Plains tribes, who brought buffalo robes and other furs to trade for crops and French tools. The French traders, many of whom had Indian families, carried the furs on pack trains of horses from the Indian villages to river landings. From there, flatboats and canoe-like boats called pirogues carried the pelts downriver to the Mississippi and on the New Orleans. Then seaworthy ships transported the goods to Europe.

OSAGE war parties attacking from the north drove the Wichita farther south during the mid-1700s. They settled on the upper Red River in what is now southern Oklahoma and northern Texas. There the Taovayas and French traders kept up their trade out of San Bernardo and San Teodoro (called the Twin Villages), and out of Natchitoches. An alliance with the powerful COMANCHE helped protect the Taovayas from Osage, APACHE and the Spanish.

Wichita grass house

In 1763, at the end of the French and Indian wars, France lost its North American possessions to England and Spain. In the years to follow, Spanish traders managed to drive most of the French out of business, and the Taovayas no longer had a trade monopoly. In 1801, France regained the Louisiana Territory from Spain, but sold it to the United States two years later. American exploration and settlement west of the Mississippi followed.

In 1835, the Wichita signed their first treaty with the United States. By 1850, the Wichita had moved again into the Wichita Mountains near Fort Sill of the Indian Territory. The Wichita and Caddo were assigned a reservation north of the Washita River in 1859. During the Civil War in the 1860s, most Wichita returned to Kansas to a site that became the city of Wichita. They returned to the Indian Territory after the hostilities. In 1872, they officially gave up all their other lands to the United States.

The Wichita Indian Tribe presently holds the rights to one small tract in Oklahoma; with the Caddo and LENNI LENAPE (DELAWARE), however, the Wichita jointly hold a much larger trust area. The Wichita are also in close contact with their PAWNEE relatives. The two tribes entertain each other every year at a powwow. One year, the celebration is held at the Wichita center near Anadarko; the next, the events is held at Pawnee, Oklahoma.

WINNEBAGO

The Winnebago are the only Siouan-speaking tribe classified as NORTHEAST INDIANS, part of the Northeast Culture Area. Their language is close to the Siouan dialects of the IOWAY, OTOE, and MISSOURIA tribes, who split off from them and resettled farther west, and who are classified as PLAINS INDIANS. The name of the Winnebago, pronounced win-uh-BAY-go, is Algonquian, given to them by SAC and FOX (MESQUAKI). It means "people of the dirty waters." As a result, early Frenchmen among them sometimes called them *Puants,* and some Englishmen used the translation of the French "Stinkards." The Winnebago native name is *Ho-Chunk, Hochungra,* or *Hotcangara,* for "people of the parent speech" or "people of the first voice." But even this has been misrepresented, some outsiders believing it meant "fish-eaters." Another native name is *Wonkshiek,* for "first people of the old island [North America]."

The Winnebago had villages along the Door Peninsula, the eastern arm of Green Bay, on Lake Michigan, in what is now Wisconsin, when the French explorer Jean Nicolet encountered them in 1634. A large lake nearby in Wisconsin, feeding the Fox River which drains into Lake Michigan, is named after the tribe—Winnebago Lake.

Many Algonquian tribes also lived in the country just to the west of Lake Michigan along the Fox and Wisconsin Rivers, and they all eventually came to be allies of the Winnebago. The MENOMINEE on the opposite side of Green Bay were early trading partners of the Winnebago; in later years, the Sac, Fox, and KICKAPOO also became their allies.

But the Winnebago could also make dangerous enemies. Some of them fought against the British in the French and Indian wars of 1689–1763. Then they sided with the British against the rebels in the American Revolution of 1775–83, and in the SHAWNEE Tecumseh's Rebellion of 1809–11.

The Winnebago mounted further resistance to American settlers in 1826–27. The trouble began when tribal members started to take part in the lead mining that whites were developing around Galena, near the Wisconsin-Illinois border. Whites wanted all the profits for themselves, so government officials forbade Indian mining. As a result, the Winnebago raided a number of settlements. Then an incident occurred when two Mississippi keelboats stopped at a Winnebago village north of Prairie du Chien. The boatmen, who had been drinking, kidnapped some Winnebago women. Warriors followed the boat downriver, attacked it, managed to kill some of the whites, and liberated their women.

The Winnebago also took part in the Black Hawk War, involving Sac and Fox, which occurred soon afterward, in 1832. White Cloud, also known as Winnebago Prophet, fostered support among various tribes of the area for Black Hawk's fighters. Like Delaware Prophet of the LENNI LENAPE (DELAWARE) and Shawnee Prophet before him, Winnebago Prophet preached against white culture and called for a return to traditional Indian ways.

Winnebago bone tube, used to suck disease from the sick

The traditional Winnebago way meant living in villages in rectangular bark lodges; farming corn, beans, squash, and tobacco; cooking corn in a deep pit by piling up layers of husks, fresh corn, more husks, and a layer of dirt on top of heated stones, then pouring water on top to trickle down and make steam; tracking and trapping small game in the dense virgin forests; living in tents and lean-tos on the trail; buffalo hunting on the prairies of tall, coarse grass along the Mississippi Valley; paddling across Green Bay in birch-bark canoes to trade buffalo robes with the Menominee for wild rice; spearing fish on Lake Michigan or on the Fox and Wisconsin rivers; shaping artistic work with dyed porcupine quills, bright feathers, and supple leather; and carving sophisticated hickory calendar sticks that accurately marked lunar and solar years.

The traditional Winnebago way also meant social organization into two groups, or moieties—the Air (or Sky) and the Earth. Each moiety was further divided into clans with animal names symbolizing the air or earth, such as the Thunderbird and the Bear. It meant that one could only marry someone in the opposite moiety; that children would belong to the clan of one's father, not one's mother (patrilineal, not matrilineal); participation in the secret Midewiwin, or Grand Medicine Society; and belief in mythological beings or culture heroes such as Trickster, who supposedly played practical jokes on the Winnebago. The Winnebago way meant reverence for nature. As a Winnebago saying goes, "Holy Mother Earth, the trees and all nature, are witnesses of your thoughts and deeds."

In the years after the Black Hawk War, the Winnebago were forced to relocate west of the Mississippi, first to Iowa, then to Minnesota, then to South Dakota, and finally to Nebraska. During this period of forced relocation between 1840 and 1863, some 700 Winnebago died. The Winnebago Tribe of Nebraska presently has reservation lands adjoining those of the OMAHA. Other Winnebago managed to stay in or return to Wisconsin, where they were finally granted reservation lands and now are known as the Winnebago Nation of Wisconsin. Some tribal members also live in Minnesota.

WINTUN

The ancestral homeland of the Wintun was situated on the west side of the Sacramento River, extending from the valley to the Coast Range in territory now part of California. The Wintun, along with other Penutian-speaking CALIFORNIA INDIANS to their west, such as the MAIDU and MIWOK, as well as Hokan-speaking peoples living nearby, such as the POMO, although in territory now considered northern California, sometimes are designated central California Indians to distinguish them from tribes to the north, which drew some elements from NORTHWEST COAST INDIANS, and tribes to the south, which were heavily missionized by the Spanish, becoming known as MISSION INDIANS.

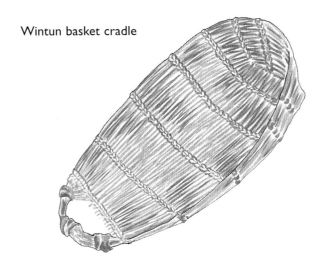

Wintun basket cradle

Their name, pronounced WIN-tun, means "people" in Penutian. The Wintun consisted of three divisions, the Wintu (Northern), the Nomlaki (Wintun proper or central), and the Patwin (Southern). All three branches are further categorized as hill, plains, and river valley subgroups. As is the case with other California Indians, the Wintun can best be described as being organized in a number of tribelets, made up of a main permanent village and several temporary satellite villages.

The Wintun were hunter-gatherers who did not farm. Their staple foods included deer, rabbits, grubs, grasshoppers, fish, acorns, seeds, nuts, and greens. They wore little clothing, mainly breechcloths, aprons, blankets, and robes. They lived in a variety of simple types of shelters—brush, grass, rush and bark-covered houses, sometimes partly underground. They made tightly woven baskets for cooking, storing, and carrying.

The Wintun had a system for passing from father to son such specialized skills as hunting, fishing, the making of ceremonial objects, bow and arrow making, pipe making, fire building, or salt making. In other words, a family had a monopoly on a certain activity and would perform this service for other members of the tribe in exchange for payment. This type of social organization was unusual among native peoples.

The Wintun, like most other central California Indians, participated in the secret society known now as the Kuksu Cult. Members impersonated spirit beings in order to get closer to them and acquire some of their power. Kuksus wore long feather or grass headdresses that disguised them from fellow villagers. Kuksu was a principal god, shared by several tribes. Different tribes had different names for their gods. To the Wintun, Moki was the most powerful god-figure. To disguise oneself as Moki was a major responsibility. The Wintun believed that to make a mistake in the ritual meant death. Other powerful spirits in the Wintun religion were Tuya the Big-Headed and Chelitu the Unmasked. The Kuksus held ceremonies in the cold months to bring about an abundance of wild plant foods and game the following spring and summer. The Wintun Kuksus called the first of their rituals Hesi. Hesi was a four-day dance, with one Kuksu acting out Moki, and others, in pairs, representing different versions of Tuya and Chelitu. While villagers looked on, drummers provided a beat for the dancers, usually by stomping on a foot drum, and singers chanted sacred songs.

The central California tribes managed to endure the first stages of white expansion: the period of exploration, when Spanish, Portuguese, and English navigators sailed the coast, starting in the 1500s; the Spanish mission period, from 1769 to 1834; and the Mexican occupation, from 1821 to 1848. But with the United States takeover of California in 1848, the gold rush that began in that year, and California statehood in 1850, pressures on the Indians increased and led to their rapid decline. Pollution from copper-processing plants at the turn of the century caused further hardship.

Of the three divisions, the northernmost, the Wintu, have fared the best, then the Nomlaki. Few pure Patwin remain. The Wintun presently hold several small rancherias and share the Round Valley Reservation with many other California tribes. Current issues affecting the Wintun people are the protection of Mt. Shasta as a sacred site and preventing waste disposal dumping on or near tribal lands.

WYANDOT *see* HURON (WYANDOT)

YAHI

For students of Native American history and culture the Yahi (pronounced YAH-hee) will always be thought of as Ishi's people. He was the last Yahi Indian, a people of the California Culture Area (see CALIFORNIA INDIANS). He was also the last known Indian in the United States to be pure of all non-Indian influences.

In August 1911, a gaunt and weary man walked out of the foothills of Mount Lassen in Northern California to a town called Oroville, about 70 miles northeast of Sacramento. Townspeople found him leaning in exhaustion against a fence. He wore little clothing, only a tattered poncho. He had apparently cropped his hair by singeing it with fire. His eyes showed his great fear. When questioned, his words were unintelligible. He was recognized as an Indian, but the sheriff who took him into custody had never seen an Indian with such light skin in the area. And none of the Native Americans brought to talk with him recognized his dialect.

Word spread about the mystery man. Two anthropologists in San Francisco, Alfred Kroeber and Thomas Waterman, read about him in a newspaper. They knew that the Yana Indians once lived in the Oroville region. They also knew that a neighboring, related band of Indians, who spoke a different dialect of the Hokan language phylum, had once lived to the south of the Yana. These were the Yahi. It occurred to them that the Indian at Oroville just might be a member of this supposedly extinct tribe. They hurriedly made arrangements to meet with him.

Waterman tried using a dictionary of the Yana language to communicate with him. The withdrawn, still frightened man, who had refused all food out of fear of being poisoned, did not recognize any of the words. Finally, the anthropologist read the Yana word for wood while pointing to the frame of a prison cot, *siwini*. The Indian became excited, smiling broadly. A word in common! He asked the scholar if he were of the same tribe, the Yahi. To gain his trust, Waterman replied that he was. With the Indian's help, he also learned how to modify the Yana language enough to fit the sounds of the related Yahi dialect.

The Anthropological Museum of the University of California took full responsibility for the Yahi. Kroeber and Waterman gave him the name Ishi, which was the word for "man" in the Yahi language. Ishi eventually managed to communicate his story to them.

He was born about 1862. During his youth, he witnessed the period in American history when California was growing at a rapid pace. In 1849 alone, during the California gold rush, about 80,000 prospectors came to California to seek their fortune. Then during the 1850s and 1860s, whites continued to enter the Yahi and Yana domain along the eastern tributaries of the Sacramento River, following Indian trails in search of goldfields and farmlands. They took the best lands for themselves and forced Native Americans to the rugged, parched highlands. When faced with resistance, miners and ranchers acted with swift violence against them. A pattern developed of small Indian raids, then white retaliation, culminating in an attack on a Yahi village in 1865 in which men, women, and children were massacred. In the ensuing years, whites launched further attacks on the Yahi in an effort to exterminate them. They thought they had accomplished this by 1868, when they killed 38 Yahi hiding in a cave.

Yet a dozen or so Yahi had escaped into the wilderness, including a boy about six years old. Over the next decades, the remaining Yahi hid out from whites and lived off the land, occasionally pilfering from white camps. There were some reports of sightings of mysterious Indians. But the Yahi were careful to camouflage their shelters, leave no footprints, make no noise, and light only small campfires. They assumed, even after so much time had passed since the conflict between Yahi and whites, that if they were discovered, they would be killed.

By 1908, only four Yahi remained—Ishi himself, now 40 years old; his sister; an old man; and an old woman. They lived at *wowunupo mu tetnu,* or "the grizzly bear's hiding place," a narrow ledge about 500 feet above Mill Creek. In that year, a party of whites discovered their hiding place. The Yahi fled, all except the old woman who was too sick to travel. She died soon after her discovery. The old man and Ishi's sister drowned while in flight.

Ishi lived in the wilderness for three more years, hunting small game and gathering wild foods. He burned his hair off in mourning for his lost friends and relatives. But the game ran out. Hungry and desperate, he opted for a quick death at the hands of whites rather than the slow death of starvation. At that time, August 1911, he made the walk to Oroville.

As it turned out, Ishi was treated well. The whites gave him work at the museum, which he performed with dedication. He demonstrated to museum visitors how his people used to make arrowheads and spearheads. He also helped clean the grounds. Ishi learned about 600 English words and became accustomed to non-Indian ways—clothes, table manners, urban transportation—but he never got used to crowds. He had spent most of his life with only a few family and friends and was continually amazed at the great number of people he encountered. When he went to a movie for the first time, he watched the audience instead of the film. When he visited the shore for the first time, he was in awe of the people on the beach rather than the water itself.

The gentle and kind-hearted Ishi met with many people who were interested in native ways. He proved an invaluable source of information concerning native culture. Kroeber and Waterman accompanied Ishi on a camping trip to Yahi territory, where he shared his earlier experiences and his wilderness skills with them.

Yahi glass arrowhead made by Ishi

Ishi demonstrated how to make arrow and spear points out of obsidian, and bows out of juniper wood for hunting; how to make two-pronged bone harpoons and how to weave nets out of milkweed fibers or animal sinew for catching salmon and other fish; and how to make a brush hut. He demonstrated how to start a fire with a wooden drill and softwood kindling; how to move noiselessly through the underbrush; how to swing on ropes over canyon cliffs; how to snare a deer or lure it into arrow-range by wearing the stuffed head of a buck; how to make animal and bird calls to attract game. Ishi also identified about 200 plants and their uses as food or medicine. He showed how to make acorn meal. He sang many songs and narrated many stories about his ancestors, about the spirit world, about wildlife, and about love and other emotions. He also demonstrated to the whites around him the qualities of bravery, stoicism, patience, kindness, enthusiasm, and humor. And all this from a man who had lost his friends and family, and his homeland.

Ishi became ill with tuberculosis in 1915 and died the following year. Those who knew him, and those who empathized with the plight of all native peoples in the Americas, mourned his passing. The last of the Yahi, the final holdout for an earlier way of life, had, through his knowledge and character, made an enduring impression on the culture that displaced him.

YAKAMA

The Yakama occupied ancestral territory along the river named after them, the Yakima, a tributary of the Columbia River, in what now is southern Washington State. A Sahaptian Penutian-speaking people, they are classified as part of the Plateau Culture Area. Their name, pronounced YAK-uh-muh and usually spelled *Yakima* until officially changed by the tribe in 1994, possibly means "a growing family" in the Salishan language of neighboring tribes or "the pregnant ones" in their own Sahaptian dialect. Another native name of the Yakama, or Lower Yakama, is *Waptailmin,* meaning "narrow river people," referring to a narrows in the Yakima River where their principal village was located. The related Pshwanwapam, the "stony rock people," sometimes are discussed as the Upper Yakama. Like other PLATEAU INDIANS, the Yakama primarily subsisted on salmon during their annual spawning runs, small game, roots, berries, and nuts.

Early Contacts with Non-Indians

In 1805, the Lewis and Clark Expedition met up with Yakama near the junction of the Columbia and Yakima Rivers. In the following years, both American and British traders did business with the tribe, trading manufactured goods for furs. The Yakama stayed on friendly terms with visitors to their homelands until the 1950s, staying out of the first major regional conflict, the Cayuse War of 1847–50, involving the CAYUSE living to the south. In the following years, what was known as Oregon Country was organized into the Oregon and Washington Territories, and new military posts were built. More and more non-Indian settlers and miners migrated westward along the Oregon Trail.

The Yakama War

In 1855, the governor of Washington Territory, Isaac Stevens, organized the Walla Walla Council, where he encouraged Indians of the region—the Yakama, Cayuse, UMATILLA, WALLA WALLA, and NEZ PERCE—to give up most of their land for reservations, homes, schools, horses, cattle, and regular payments. He also promised the various band a period of two to three years to relocate. Most tribal representatives signed. Others distrusted whites because of earlier broken promises.

Those with suspicions were proven right. Twelve days after the signing, rather than the promised two years, Governor Stevens declared Indian lands open to white settlement. Kamiakin, a Yakama chief, called for an alliance of tribes to resist intruders but not before they were ready to face the military. His nephew, Qualchin, forced events, however. He and five other young Yakama attacked and killed five prospectors. When an Indian

Yakama corn husk bag

agent tried to investigate the incident, he too was killed by angry young warriors.

A reconnaissance force rode out of Fort Dalles to learn the extent of the uprising. Five hundred warriors routed them and drove them back to the fort. Other expeditions also failed against the Indian rebels. Volunteers under Colonel James Kelly tricked a chief of the Walla Walla, Peopeomoxmox, into coming to a parley, where they killed him. This rash act caused Walla Walla, Cayuse, and Umatilla warriors to join the Yakama cause and to attack while settlements. Owhi, Kamiakin's brothers and Qualchin's father, also participated in the uprising.

A deadly pattern of raid and retaliation followed. The army built new forts. A few indecisive battles were fought, such as the engagement at Grande Ronde Valley in July 1856. But when troops were sent out to fight, the hostile warriors usually hid among tribes to the east. In some instances, the army had to protect innocent Indians from revenge-seeking whites.

Other people to the west along the Northwest Coast carried out raids on white settlements. Nisqually Indians under Leschi attacked the town of Seattle on Puget Sound, but were driven off by a naval force in the harbor in January 1856. Two tribes in what is now southern Oregon near the California border—the Penutian-speaking Takelma and the Athapascan-speaking Tututni—rose up against·settlers in their midst. The Takelma and Tututni were known to the whites as Rogue Indians because they frequently attacked travelers along the Siskiyou Trail. The river in their territory was also called the Rogue. And their conflict, although related to the Yakama War, is usually referred to by its own name, the Rogue River War. The three most important Rogue chiefs at the time were Old John, Limpy, and George. Because of a massacre of 23 of their people—men, women, and children—these chiefs led their warriors in raids on a white settlement, killing 27. In May 1856, at Big Meadows, a force of regular soldiers routed the rebels, who soon surrendered.

Meanwhile, the Yakama War to the east of the Cascade Mountains was in a period of inactivity. Another outbreak of violence involving more tribes, the COEUR D'ALENE and the SPOKAN, occurred in 1858. Since Kamiakin, Qualchin, and Owhi played a part in this conflict as well, the Coeur d'Alene War or Spokan War can be thought of as the second phase of the Yakama War. The execution of Owhi and Qualchin in effect put an end to the uprising. Kamiakin managed to escape to British Columbia, returning to the region in 1860 and living out his life among the PALOUSE.

Fishing Rights

After their defeat, most Yakama settled on the Yakama Reservation. Other Sahaptian peoples—Klickitat, Palouse, and Wanapam, plus the Chinookian-speaking Wishram—also were settled there. Tribes of the region have fished area rivers as their ancestors did. The construction of dams on the Columbia—the Bonneville Dam in 1938, the Grand Coulee Dam in 1941, and the Dalles Dam in 1951—altered the Yakama way of life and led to legal activism by the Confederated Tribes of the Yakama Indian Nation concerning fishing rights. The Yakama-Klickitat Fish Production Project, begun in the 1990s, is an attempt to rebuild endangered fish runs.

Religious Movements

The Yakama have maintained many traditional beliefs. Many involve rituals and festivals surrounding salmon, roots, and berries. Others are religious revitalization movements that were developed in postcontact times.

Some Yakama participate in the Waashat Religion (also called the Washani Religion, Longhouse Religion, Seven Drum Religion, Sunday Dance Religion, or Prophet Dance). The origin of this religious movement is uncertain, but it probably is associated with the arrival of whites or an epidemic in the early 19th century and the teachings of a prophet or "dreamer-prophet" who had experienced an apocalyptic vision. One of the rituals is the Waashat (or Washat) Dance with seven drummers, a feast of salmon, the ritual use of eagle and swan feathers, and a sacred song to be sung every seventh day. It is not known at what point Christianity came to influence its aboriginal form.

In the 1850s, the Wanapam Indian Smohalla used the earlier Waashat rituals as the basis for what has become known as the Dreamer Religion. He claimed he had visited the Spirit World and had been sent back to teach his people. His message was one of a resurgence of the aboriginal way of life, free from white influences, such as alcohol and agriculture. He established ceremonial music and dancing to induce meditations of a pure, primitive state. He also predicted the resurrection of all Indians to rid the world of white oppressors. Smohalla claimed that the truth came to him and his priests through dreams, thus the name Dreamer Religion. His oratory was known as Yuyunipitqana for "Shouting Mountain."

The Waashat Religion spread to other tribes of the region as well and influenced other religious revitalization movements. One that drew on it is the Indian Shaker Religion, or Tschadam, founded in 1881 by John Slocum (Squ-sacht-un), a Squaxon (a Salishan people of the Northwest Coast), still practiced among the Yakama. The name was derived from the shaking or twitching motion participants experienced while brushing off their sins in a meditative state, a ritual introduced to the religion by Slocum's wife, Mary Thompson Slocum. The religion combined Christian beliefs in God, heaven, and hell with traditional Indian teachings, especially the Waashat Religion. Slocum and his followers were imprisoned regularly by white officials for inciting resistance to governmental programs that attempted to eradicate Indian customs.

In 1904, the Klickitat shaman Jake Hunt founded the Feather Religion or Feather Dance, also called the Spinning Religion. This revitalization movement drew on elements of both the earlier Waashat Religion and the Indian Shaker Religion. Sacred eagle feathers were used in ceremonies, one of which involved ritual spinning, hence the name *Waskliki* for "Spinning Religion." The Feather Religion, although still active among other tribes of the region, is no longer practiced by the Yakama.

YAMASEE

Many SOUTHEAST INDIANS, especially of the Musko-gean language family, no longer exist as tribal entities. Some among them died out from the effects of disease and warfare. Some scattered and merged with other tribes, usually of the same language family. The Yamasee, as a result of both Spanish and British colonization, are considered an extinct tribe. Their name, pronounced YAM-uh-see, is thought to mean "gentle."

When Europeans first settled among them—Spanish missionaries in the late 1500s—the Yamasee lived along the Ocmulgee River above the junction with the Oconee in territory that was to become the southeastern part of Georgia. In 1687, the Yamasee became discontented with Spanish regulations and headed northward to British territory in the colony of South Carolina, settling on the north side of the Savannah River.

In South Carolina the Yamasee became valuable allies of the British, trading with and working for them. They even fought alongside them against the TUSCARORA in the Tuscarora War of 1711–13. Yet as it turned out, the British mistreated them as the Spanish had earlier.

British settlers cheated them by taking land without payment. British traders forced the Yamasee at gunpoint to help carry trade goods through the wilderness. And British slavers took them into captivity. Their method was to give Yamasee men all the rum they wanted plus trade goods. Then they demanded immediate payment. When the men could not pay off their debts, the slavers seized their wives and children for the slave market.

The Yamasee organized a surprise attacks. They asked the help of some neighboring tribes, including CATAWBA, APALACHEE, CREEK, CHOCTAW, and CHERO-KEE, who were also victims of the colonists' methods of trickery. On Good Friday, April 15, 1715, warriors raided many outlying settlements, killing more than 100 whites. Other settlers fled to the port city of Charleston.

The governor of South Carolina, Charles Craven, orga-nized a militia that, during a summer campaign and then a second fall campaign, attacked Yamasee villages and tracked bands of warriors through the wilderness. Surviv-ing Yamasee fled back southward to Georgia and Florida. One group settled near St. Augustine in Florida, once again becoming allies of the Spanish. Their village was destroyed by the British in 1727. Other Yamasee settled among the Apalachee, Creeks, and SEMINOLE, and eventually lost their tribal identity. A community of Native Americans in Burke County, Georgia—the Altamaha-Cherokee—per-haps include some people of Yamasee ancestry.

YAQUI

The name of the Yaqui, pronounced YAH-kee, is taken from the river along which these people originally lived, the Río Yaqui, and probably translates as "chief river" in a dialect of the Uto-Aztecan language family. The Río Yaqui flows from the highlands of present day Sonora, a state in Mexico, to the Gulf of California. Alternative Yaqui names are Cahita, Yoeme, or Yueme.

The Yaqui farmed, hunted, fished, and foraged to support themselves. They lived much like other Indians to the north, who are classified with them in the South-west Culture Area (see SOUTHWEST INDIANS). They made two plantings a year in the fertile soil along the river and its tributaries, which overflowed regularly. They cultivated corn and cotton, using the latter to make clothing. They lived in rectangular structures of poles, reeds, grass, and mud (or sometimes adobe bricks), with flat or gently sloping roofs. They cooked and performed other chores in connected shelters.

The Yaqui remained fiercely independent throughout Spanish and Mexican rule. Spaniards first had contact with them as early as 1533 when an expedition under Nuño de Guzmán entered their domain. In 1609–10, a force of 50 mounted soldiers and 4,000 Indian allies launched three successive attacks on the Yaqui, only to be repelled each time. Nevertheless, in 1610, the Yaqui signed a peace treaty with Spain. Before long, the Jesuits established missions among them, creating the "Eight Towns." Although they pretended to convert to Catholicism, the Yaqui never aban-doned their tribal customs and they considered themselves independent of Spanish authority.

Spanish settlers kept up the pressure for Yaqui land, and in 1740, the Yaqui revolted. Another rebellion fol-lowed in 1764. But the tenuous peace held for the remaining period of Spanish rule.

After having gained independence from Spain in 1821, the Mexican government declared the Indians full citizens and began taxing them. Once again, the Yaqui resisted interference in their affairs. They staged many guerrilla uprisings over the next century. In their rugged homeland they proved unconquerable, even when under attack by large Mexican armies.

Starting in the 1880s, the Mexican government began to deport Yaqui to work on plantations in the Yucatán, more than 2,000 miles away. But the Yaqui spirit remained unbroken. Some managed to escape and make the difficult return trek to their homeland. In the Mexican Revolution of 1910–11, some Yaqui joined the forces of the bandit general Pancho Villa. Then in 1927, another Yaqui uprising flared. A lasting peace was finally achieved, and the Yaqui were granted permanent landholdings along the Yaqui River. Descendants of these Yaqui currently live much as their ancestors did, still farming the rich soil along their ancestral river.

Yet during this period of forced labor, many Yaqui fled across the international border to the state of Arizona. Their descendants, the American Yaqui, now occupy six communities in southern Arizona, located at Eloy, Marana, Pascua, Scottsdale, Tempe, and Tucson. In 1964, the Pascua Yaqui Association received 202 acres from the federal government, and in 1978, the Pascua Yaqui Tribe of Arizona achieved federal recognition. All American Yaqui were allowed to enroll in the tribe.

Most American Yaqui earn a living as farm or construction workers. The tribe also has generated income through bingo and, in the 1990s, through high-stakes gambling.

The Mexican and American Yaqui maintain strong cultural ties. They often celebrate together the week-long Pascola ceremony at Eastertime, a blending of Catholic and native rituals. Musicians play drums, rattles, and rasping sticks while dancers in masks and deer costumes perform before a doll representing the infant Jesus.

Yaqui Pascola mask

YAVAPAI

The Yavapai, the "people of the sun," occupied ancestral territory now located in western Arizona, from the Pinal and Mazatzal Mountains in the east to the neighborhood of the Colorado River in the West, and from the Williams and Santa Maria Rivers in the north to the Gila River in the south.

Linguistically, the Yuman-speaking Yavapai are closely related to the Upland Yumans, such as the HAVASUPAI and HUALAPAI, who lived to their north, as well as the River Yumans, such as the MOJAVE and YUMA (QUECHAN), who lived to their west. Nevertheless, culturally and historically, the Yavapai had more in common with the Tonto band of APACHE living to their east, with whom they sometimes intermarried. In fact, at times the Yavapai (pronounced yah-vuh-PIE) have been referred to as Mojave Apache and Yuma Apache.

The Yavapai consisted of three major divisions: the Kawevikopaya, or southeastern Yavapai; the Yawepe, or northeastern Yavapai; and the Tolkepaya, or Western Yavapai. Their native name is *Ba'ja*.

The Yavapai were a nomadic people, traveling in families or in small bands. Their movements corresponded to the ripening of wild plant crops, such as mescal and saguaro cactus fruit. Some of the Yavapai, particularly those living near the Mojave and Yuma, grew corn, sunflowers, tobacco, and other crops in small plots. They hunted deer, antelope, rabbits, and other game and lived in either caves or dome-shaped huts framed with poles and covered with brush or thatch, much like Apache wickiups. Their crafts included pottery and basketry. Shamans presided over healing rituals.

The Yavapai first had contact with whites in 1582, when a Spanish expedition under Antonio de Espejo visited them. Other explorers from out of Mexico reached their domain. Juan de Oñate met with them in 1604. Father Francisco Garcés lived among them in 1776, after which contacts with white traders and trappers became common.

The Yavapai were ruggedly independent, resisting white missionary work and settlement. Some bands, especially the Kawevikopaya, joined with the Apache in raids on whites and on other Indians. Following the Mexican Cession in 1848 and the United States takeover of the region, the territory of the Yavapai came to be traveled and mined by increasing numbers of white prospectors, causing sporadic violence by Yavapai bands.

Their resistance reached a climax in 1872 during General George Crook's Tonto Basin Campaign against Tonto Apache and Yavapai. Crook's scouts located a war party in Salt River Canyon of the Mazatzal Mountains. In the ensuing Battle of Skull Cave, his soldiers pumped bullets into a cave high on the canyon wall. Some fired from below on the canyon floor, others from above on the rim of the canyon. Bullets ricocheted inside the cave, striking many of the Yavapai warriors. Some managed to escape from the cave and fight back from behind rocks. But soldiers on the escarpment rolled boulders down on top of them. About 75 Yavapai lost their lives at Skull Cave.

U.S. officials settled the Yavapai with Apache at Camp Verde and on the San Carlos Reservation. By 1900 most of the Yavapai had left San Carlos to settle at the former army posts of Fort McDowell, Camp Verde, and Fort Whipple. The Fort McDowell Reservation, shared by Mojave, Apache, and Yavapai, was established in 1903. The Camp Verde Reservation was established in 1910. In 1935, the Yavapai Reservation was created north of Prescott at the former Fort Whipple. The present Yavapai economy consists of raising stock, subsistence farming, and wage work. Some tribal members generate additional income by selling coiled baskets. Yavapai from the three reservations take turn hosting Ba'ja days, which celebrate traditional tribal culture.

A well-known Yavapai named Carlos Montezuma, or Wassaja, furthered the cause of Native Americans in the late 19th and early 20th century. Wassaja was born in 1867 in the Superstition Mountains of Arizona. When four years old, he was captured by the AKIMEL O'ODHAM (PIMA), who eventually sold him to a photographer-prospector by the name of Carlos Gentile. Meanwhile, his mother, who had left the reservation to search for her son, was shot by an Indian scout. Gentile took the boy—whom he renamed Carlos after himself, and Montezuma after ruins in the region—to Santa Fe, New Mexico, then east to Illinois and New York. On Gentile's death in 1877, a family by the name of Baldwin cared for Wassaja for a short period until George W. Ingalls, a Baptist missionary, placed him with W. H. Stedman, a minister in Urbana, Illinois.

Wassaja was tutored privately for two years, then was enrolled in a preparatory program for the University of Illinois, which he entered as a freshman the next year. He graduated with a bachelor of science degree in 1884. While working part time for a pharmacist, he attended the Chicago Medical College, graduating in 1889.

After having attempted a private practice for a short time in Chicago, Wassaja accepted an appointment in the Indian Service as physician-surgeon at the Fort Stevenson Indian School in North Dakota. After a year, he was transferred to the Western Shoshone Agency in Nevada. Three years later, he worked at the Colville Agency in Washington. Frustrated by the conditions on the western reservation, he began work in 1894 at the Carlisle Indian School in Pennsylvania. In 1896, Wassaja returned to Chicago to open a private practice. A specialist in stomach and intestinal diseases, he eventually was offered a teaching position at the College of Physicians and Surgeons and in the Postgraduate Medical School.

Wassaja became active in Indian affairs, giving lectures in which he criticized the Bureau of Indian Affairs and the reservation system and advocated citizenship for Indians. Although a proponent of Assimilation, he also called for pride in Indianness. He wrote three books, including *Let My People Go,* published in 1914, and founded the Indian magazine *Wassaja* in 1916. Presidents Theodore Roosevelt and Woodrow Wilson both offered him the position of Commissioner of Indian Affairs, but he refused and continued calling for the abolition of the bureau. He spent much of his time in his later years among his people on the Fort McDowell reservation, where he died.

YAZOO

The Yazoo lived along the lower Yazoo River, a tributary of the Mississippi River. Their main villages were located on the south side of the river near present-day Vicksburg, Mississippi. The Yazoo River parallels the Mississippi for about 175 miles before it joins the larger river, separated from it by natural levees, or dikes. So their tribal name, pronounced YAH-zoo and probably meaning "waters of the dead," is applied to any river that belatedly joins another. The Yazoo also have a county and city in Mississippi named after them.

A Tunican-speaking people, the Yazoo were villagers and farmers with lifeways in common with the TUNICA living near them. Yet it is known they were a group distinct from the Tunica because, unlike them, they used an *r* sound when speaking. Both tribes are classified as SOUTHEAST INDIANS.

It is possible that the Spanish expedition of Hernando de Soto that traveled throughout much of the Southeast had contact with the Yazoo in the 1540s. Yet most of what we know about the tribe comes from French records of the late 1600s and early 1700s. René-Robert Cavalier de La Salle, who claimed the Mississippi Valley for France in 1682, mentioned them. In 1718, the French established a military and trading post on the Yazoo River within the tribe's territory. And in 1729, a Jesuit missionary, Father Seul, settled among them.

That very year, however, the Yazoo joined the NATCHEZ, who lived to their south on the Mississippi, in the Natchez's Revolt. The Yazoo killed Father Seul and routed the French soldiers. Then a Yazoo warrior, dressed in the clothes of the missionary, traveled to the Natchez to offer them his people's support in driving the French from the area.

Yet with the defeat and dispersal of the Natchez, the Yazoo also departed from their ancestral homelands and joined other tribes in the area—probably the CHICKASAW and CHOCTAW—among whom they eventually lost their tribal identity.

YOKUTS

The name of the Yokuts, pronounced YO-kuts and generally written with an *s* whether singular or plural, means "person" or "people" in the various Yokutsan dialects of the Penutian language phylum spoken by different Yokuts bands. The Yokuts Indians occupied a wide expanse of ancestral territory now located in central California along the San Joaquin River valley and the foothills of the Sierra Nevada. They are discussed as Northern Valley, Southern Valley, and Foothills Yokuts.

Like other CALIFORNIA INDIANS, they were hunter-gatherers, depending on small mammals, fowl, fish, and wild plant foods, especially acorns, for their food. They constructed enclosures called blinds where they could hide to trap pigeons. They also hunted eagles. The following is a Yokuts prayer that was recited before killing an eagle:

Do not think that I will hurt you.
You will have a new body.
Now turn your head northward and lie flat.

The Yokuts made exquisite baskets, coiling thin bundles of grass stems upward in a spiral and binding them with marsh grass. They also drew elaborate picture messages, called pictographs, on rocks.

The Yokuts did not make up a unified tribe. Scholars sometimes use the word *tribelet* to describe the political or

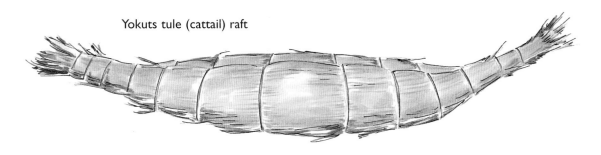
Yokuts tule (cattail) raft

territorial organization of the Yokuts and other California peoples, a category between a tribe and a village. The Yokuts had about 50 tribelets. A tribelet contained a main permanent village and several smaller satellite villages that were moved from time to time. Each tribelet had a chief and a shaman. A chief's messenger carried his commands to other villages. A village crier made announcements within his main village. These various positions were hereditary offices, passed to a younger brother or to a son. Each tribelet had a distinct name to differentiate it from other tribelets, and a distinct language dialect. Sometimes the different tribelets had disputes that led to violence.

The Yokuts, unlike most Indians, practiced cremation at death. When someone died, his or her possessions, even—in some instances—the entire house, were burned along with the body.

In 1818, the Yokuts, led by Chalpinich, stayed an uprising against the Spanish. In the late 1820s, following Mexico's independence from Spain, Yokuts under Stanislaus rebelled against the Mexicans. Yokuts also fought Americans in the Mariposa Indian War, which began in 1850 following the California gold rush when the number of non-Indians in the region radically increased. The Yokuts and neighboring MIWOK attacked miners and trading posts. The Mariposa Volunteer Battalion quelled the outbreak in 1851.

Yokuts groups presently hold one reservation and three rancherias. The Tule River Reservation has Yokuts descendants of the following bands: Koyati, Pankahlalchi, Wukchumni, Wuksachi, Yaudanchi, and Yawilmani. The Picayune Rancheria has mostly Chukchansi. Table Mountain Rancheria is mostly Chukchansi (and Mono Indians as well). The Santa Rosa Rancheria has mostly Tachi. Descendants of some other of the many Yokuts bands, such as the Choinumni, without reservation or rancheria lands also live in the San Joaquin valley and the Sierra Nevada foothills and have petitioned for federal recognition. The Yokuts continue to maintain strong community ties and meet to celebrate traditional customs, such as the annual renewal Spring Dance.

YUCHI

The language of the Yuchi is thought to have elements in common with dialects of the Siouan language family. Their ancestors perhaps long ago split off from other Siouan-speaking peoples. Their name, also spelled *Euchee* and pronounced YOO-chee, means "those far away."

The tribe's earliest known location was in what is now eastern Tennessee. But the Yuchi came to live in territory now part of many different states, including Georgia, Florida, and South Carolina. Scholars classify the Yuchi as SOUTHEAST INDIANS. They placed their villages and planted crops along river valleys and lived by farming, hunting, fishing, and collecting wild plant foods.

Spanish explorers recorded the earliest known history of the Yuchi. Hernando de Soto's expedition of 1539–43 encountered them. Other Spaniards mention various bands of Yuchi under different names in their historical accounts. Boyano, a member of Juan Pardo's expedition, claimed to have battled and killed many Yuchi on two different occasions in the mountains of either North Carolina or Tennessee. Because the explorers' maps were inexact, it is difficult to pinpoint the locations.

In the 1630s, various Yuchi bands swept south out of the Appalachian highlands to raid Spanish settlements

Yuchi Feather Dance wand

and missions in Florida. Some of these Yuchi settled in APALACHEE country.

In the 1670s, various Englishmen, exploring southwestward out of Virginia and the Carolinas, made contact with Yuchi still in Tennessee and North Carolina. In the following years, many Yuchi bands, probably because of pressure from hostile SHAWNEE, migrated from the high country, following the Savannah River toward the coastal country in Georgia. Some among those who previously had gone to Florida also migrated to Georgia. Both groups of Yuchi became allies of the English colonists and helped them in slave raids on mission Indians of Spanish Florida, including the Apalachee, CALUSA, and TIMUCUA.

By the mid-1700s, the Spanish military and mission systems in Florida were weakened. From that period into the 1800s, many Yuchi migrated southward and settled on lands formerly held by other tribes.

The Yuchi who stayed in Tennessee and North Carolina merged with the CHEROKEE; those who settled in Georgia joined the CREEK; and those who migrated to Florida united with the SEMINOLE.

The Yuchi among the Creek relocated to the Indian Territory with them in 1832. Although part of the Creek Nation legally, Yuchi descendants have maintained many of their own customs and presently hold ceremonies at three sacred sites in Creek County, Oklahoma: Polecat (the "mother ground"), Duck Creek, and Sand Creek. The Yuchi Nation has applied for federal recognition.

YUMA (Quechan)

The Yuma name has come to be applied to the Yuman language family spoken by many tribes in the region of western Arizona and southeastern California. The name, pronounced YOO-muh, probably means "people of the river." The various Yuman-speaking peoples are generally categorized as the Upland Yumans and the River Yumans. Upland Yumans include the HAVASUPAI, HUALAPAI, and YAVAPAI among others. River Yumans include the MOJAVE and the Yuma proper, or Quechan (pronounced kwuh-CHAN), in addition to other tribes not covered in this book. The Yuman-speaking peoples are classified by scholars as part of the Southwest Culture Area, although they border the California Culture Area (see SOUTHWEST INDIANS).

The Yuma proper lived on both sides of the Colorado River, near the mouth of the Gila River, not far from the present-day Mexican border. This is desert country, extremely hot and arid, with temperatures reaching as high as 105 to 120 degrees Fahrenheit. In order to survive this harsh environment, the Yuma placed their villages along the bottomlands of rivers. They lived in rectangular, open-sided structures, in rectangular, earth-covered pithouses, or in domed brush huts (wickiups). In the mosquito season, they burned dung at the doorway to keep the insects away. They fished the river and farmed the fertile soil of the riverbanks that flooded every year. They grew corn, beans, pumpkins, gourds, and tobacco. Both men and women tended the crops. The men also hunted small game, especially rabbits.

Yuma clothing was minimal. Men usually wore only rawhide sandals and sometimes a breechcloth. Women wore sandals and an apron made from willow-bark. In cool weather, both used blankets of rabbit skin or woven bark. Both men and women painted and tattooed themselves. The various Yuman peoples were tall and powerfully built. A Spanish explorer described them as "the tallest and the most robust that I have seen in all the provinces, and their nakedness the most complete."

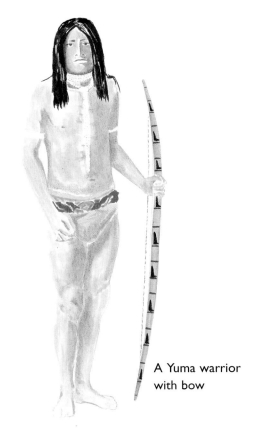

A Yuma warrior with bow

The River Yumans were generally more warlike than their Upland kinsmen. Warriors carried five-foot bows and long arrows, mallet-headed war clubs, or lances.

The Spanish were the first Europeans to visit the Yuma. Hernando de Alarcón reached their territory as early as 1540. The Jesuit Father Eusebio Francisco Kino visited them in 1698. The Franciscan Padre Francisco Garcés established two missions among them in 1780. Instead of founding a presidio with a garrison of soldiers to protect the missions, the Spanish stationed 10 soldiers at each. Within a year, the missions ran short of supplies and gifts for the Indians, who decided to reclaim control of their lands. In 1781, Chief Palma and his brother Ygnacio Palma led their warriors and allies in attacks on the missions, killing perhaps as many as 95 priests, soldiers, and settlers, and capturing 76 women and children. That year and the next, the Spanish launched several unsuccessful expeditions against the Yuma, who retained control of their homeland for years to come and continued their traditional way of life, unlike many tribes in California who were forced onto missions (see MISSION INDIANS).

During the mid-1800s, the Yuma frequently attacked travelers along the Southern Overland Trail (which later came to be called the Butterfield Southern Route). They raided wagon trains and stole supplies. The travelers for their part stole tribal crops. The numbers of migrants rose drastically in 1849 during the California gold rush. The Yuma controlled the Yuma Crossing, a natural passage of the Colorado River near the mouth of the Gila River. For a time, the Yuma provided a ferry service on rafts across the river. When a group of whites established their own ferry service in competition with that of the Indians, the Yuma became incensed and blocked passage.

In 1850, to keep the crossing open, the army built Fort Yuma on the California side of the Colorado. Warriors launched attacks on the fort and cut off its supplies. The soldiers had to abandon the post for a year. On returning, however, the soldiers were better equipped. A one-armed Irishman by the name of Thomas Sweeny, nicknamed "Fighting Tom," led expeditions against the militants. On one raid with only 25 men, he managed to take 150 prisoners. Before long, the rest of the Yuma ceased their hostilities.

The federal government created the Fort Yuma Reservation in California and Arizona for the Yuma in 1883. The tribe formally signed away most of its land in 1886. The Fort Yuma Indians use the tribal name Quechan. The Cocopah Reservation near Somerton, Arizona, formed in 1917, bears the name of another Yuman-speaking tribe, the Cocopah, but has Yuma and Maricopa descendants as well.

Tribally run gambling operations and trailer parks help generate income for modern-day Quechan.

YUROK

The Yurok were neighbors of the Karok, both peoples living in ancestral territory along the Klamath River in territory now mapped as part of northern California. The Karok, whose name, pronounced KAH-rock, translates as "upstream," lived farther inland up the river. The Yurok, whose name, pronounced YOUR-ock, means "downstream" in the Karok language, lived near the mouth of the river along the Pacific Coast.

It is interesting to note that even though these two peoples had similar cultures and that the Karok even gave the Yurok the tribal name that has lasted to modern times, the Karok language isolate is considered part of the Hokan language phylum, and the Yurok isolate is considered part of the Macro-Algonquian phylum. That would make the Yurok the westernmost ALGONQUIANS.

The Yurok, Karok, and HUPA, a neighboring people with a similar culture, are grouped by scholars in the California Culture Area. The northern CALIFORNIA INDIANS were hunter-gatherers, who depended heavily on acorns. They lived in villages in the winter and wandered in bands in the summer, like other California peoples. And like the tribes to their south, they crafted tightly woven baskets. But they also were influenced by the NORTHWEST COAST INDIANS to their north. For example, they fished the Klamath River for the staple food of the Northwest Coast tribes—salmon. They built rectangular houses with slanted roofs out of cedar planks. And they determined social status by an individual's wealth.

The Yurok practiced the annual World Renewal ceremonies, as did the Karok and Hupa, one more cultural trait used to distinguish northern California Indians from other California peoples. The purpose of the rituals

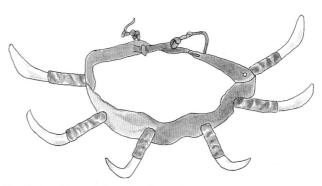

Yurok headdress of sea lion's teeth

was to renew the world, or "firm the earth," as the Indians described it, provide food, and perpetuate tribal well-being.

There is one cultural element, however, that the Yurok did not share with their neighbors, or with any other Indians in North America for that matter. For Native Americans, land was considered a source of life shared by the entire tribe. There was no such thing as private ownership of land. The Yurok individually owned land, measured wealth by it, and even sold it to one another, however.

But whites came to Yurok territory—British and American trappers starting in 1826–27, and a rush of settlers in 1849, after the California gold rush, leading to permanent settlement—and the Yurok eventually lost most of their land once and for all. The tribe presently holds several small rancherias, one of them adjoining Hupa lands. Many Yurok still live by hunting, fishing, and gathering, as their ancestors did. Migrant farm work also provides income as does a tribally run hotel and a bingo operation.

In 1983, the Yurok, along with the Karok and Tolowa (an Athapascan-speaking people) won a 10-year battle over a sacred site in the mountainous Six Rivers National Forest of northern California, just south of the Oregon border. Members of the three tribes climb into the unspoiled high country in order to be closer to the spirit world in which they believe.

ZUNI

Zuni, pronounced ZOO-nee or ZOON-yee, is the name of both a people and a pueblo, or village. The Zuni native name is A:shiwi, meaning "the flesh." Zuni people originally lived in seven pueblos along the north bank of the upper Zuni River, flowing out of the highlands of the Colorado Plateau. Zuni territory has since become a part of the state of New Mexico and lies in the state's western region near the present-day Arizona border. They are classified as SOUTHWEST INDIANS.

The Zuni language is unlike that of any other PUEBLO INDIANS. Some scholars now place this distinctive dialect of Zunian in the Penutian language phylum. Archaeological evidence indicates that two diverse cultural groups—one from the north and the other from the west or southwest—merged in prehistoric times to become the Zuni. Their ancestors might have been of the Mogollon culture and the Anasazi culture (see SOUTHWEST CULTURES). Much later, Indians from Mexico who served as bearers for the conquistadores, especially the Tlaxcalan, deserted the Spanish to settle among the Zuni.

The Zuni, like other Pueblo Indians, lived in multistoried houses interconnected by ladders. They used stone covered with plaster in their architecture, unlike the Rio Grande Pueblo Indians to the east who used adobe bricks.

Farming provided the primary source of food for the Zuni. They also hunted, fished, and foraged for wild plants. As is the case with the Hopi, another western Pueblo people living on the Colorado Plateau, kachinas, benevolent guardian spirits, played an important part in Zuni mythology.

Zuni buffalo-head altar carving

Early Spanish explorers believed the Zuni villages to be the legendary Seven Cities of Cibola (the Spanish word for "buffalo" and consequently for any buffalo-hunting Indians). Rumors of native cities filled with great riches in this Kingdom of Cibola had reached the ears of the conquistadores in the 1500s soon after the Spanish conquest of Mexico.

Frey Marcos de Niza, a Franciscan monk, set out with a contingent of soldiers and Indian bearers in 1539 to look for Cibola. He also took with him a black man from Barbary named Estevanico, sometimes called Estévan (Estéban) the Moor. Estevanico had had earlier experience dealing with Indians. He had participated in Cabeza de Vaca's expedition of 1528–36, which had met up with many native peoples along the Gulf of Mexico from Texas to northern Mexico. Some of the Indians thought the tall, dark-skinned Estevanico was a god. He wore ribbons, badges, feathers, rattles, and bells to call attention to himself. Marcos de Niza sent him ahead with a scouting party to offer presents to any Indians he met and to win them over.

Zuni men, angered by Estevanico's arrogance attacked and killed him. A messenger reported the incident to Marcos de Niza. The monk decided to continue on to see for himself whether these Indian cities were truly the Kingdom of Cibola. He advanced far enough to see Hawikuh, one of the Zuni pueblos. From a distance, the reddish brown adobe buildings must have glistened in the sunlight like gold, because Marcos de Niza returned to Mexico claiming he had found Cibola.

The following year, Francisco Vásquez de Coronado organized an expedition to conquer Cibola and claim its vast riches. To Coronado's disappointment, the Seven Cities of Cibola turned out to be ordinary Indian pueblos without streets of gold and without abundant jewels. After having defeating the Zuni in battle, Coronado pushed northeastward, still in search of wealth. On hearing rumors of the Kingdom of Quivira, Coronado explored as far north as Kansas. During his travels, he encountered many tribes, such as the WICHITA, and recorded information about them. He never made his fortune, however, and died in obscurity in Mexico City.

Other Spanish explorers visited the Zuni: Francisco Chamuscado in 1580; Antonio de Espejo in 1583; and Juan de Oñate, the colonizer of New Mexico, in 1598. The Spanish established their first mission in Zuni territory at Hawikuh in 1629. In 1632, the Zuni attacked and killed the missionaries. In 1672, APACHE warriors raided Hawikuh and forced the abandonment of the mission.

The Zuni participated in the Pueblo Rebellion of 1680. At that time, the Zuni lived in only three pueblos of their original seven—Halona (Halona: itiwanna), Matsa: Kya, and Kyakima. Villagers from three pueblos fled to a stronghold on the mesa of Iowa: yallane (Corn Mountain) to defend themselves from the Spanish troops approaching under Don Diego de Vargas. The Spanish negotiated with them to return to their village at Halona. Although a new church was built there in 1699, it was abandoned by the missionaries in the 1800s, who were for the most part unable to win over converts among the Zuni.

Zuni kachina mask of painted leather, showing earth and sky beings

The ancient site of Halona is the site of modern-day Zuni Pueblo, located in McKinley and Valencia counties near the Arizona border. Since their time of conflict with the Spanish, the Zuni have lived at this site peacefully through the Mexican period, from 1821 to 1848, and the subsequent American period.

The Zuni farm and raise livestock for a living. Some among them spend their summers in the neighboring farming villages, such as Pescado, Nutria, and Ojo. Zuni craftspeople have gained international reputations for their silver jewelry made with turquoise, shell, and other stones, often inlaid. Many Zuni participate in silversmithing and stonecutting. Zuni craftspeople are also known for their stone fetishes—usually small animals. Most of these animals have special meanings and supposed powers. Traditional pottery, weaving, and basketry are also still practiced. Zuni men also work as firefighters. The Forest Service frequently flies them to help battle the nation's worst forest fires.

Tourists can visit the Zuni Pueblo to watch the Shalako festival in late November or early December, part of the 48-day winter solstice festival. Part of the ceremonies include giant, birdlike kachina figures dancing in and around new homes to bless them.

Zuni silver and turquoise pin (modern)

GLOSSARY

activism Political involvement, sometimes militant. Used in reference to modern Indian organizations with political and social goals.

adobe A kind of brick made from mud and straw that is sun-dried (or a type of mud used as a mortar to hold stones together). Used by Pueblo Indians in their architecture.

adz A woodworking tool with an arched axlike blade at right angles to the handle.

Allotment A policy of the U.S. federal government, starting with the General Allotment Act of 1887 and lasting until 1934. Under the policy, Indian lands held by tribes were broken up and distributed to individual Indians. A large portion of lands held by Indians in Oklahoma was allotted.

appliqué A technique in decorating articles of clothing or other objects in which pieces of one material are applied to another. (See also **ribbonwork.**)

archaeology The recovery and study of objects remaining from early cultures.

artifact An object made by humans, especially a tool, weapon, ornament, or piece of pottery.

Assimilation A policy practiced by whites, especially in the late 1800s and early 1900s, in an effort to absorb Indians into mainstream culture. Also called "acculturation."

atlatl A spear-thrower that increases the leverage of the human arm and lets hunters throw spears harder and straighter. It was made by Prehistoric Indians from a stick about two feet long, with hide hoops to provide a firm grasp, a stone weight for balance, and a hook and groove to hold the spear shaft.

awl A pointed tool for making holes in wood or hide.

babiche Rawhide strips, used in toboggans, snowshoes, and other objects, for binding and support.

ball court An ancient playing field, sometimes sunken and sometimes paved, common in Mesoamerica, where games were played with a rubber ball.

balsa A type of raft or boat made with rushes, especially tule, tied in bundles in a cylindrical shape. The bundles would become water-logged after a period of use, but would dry out in the sun. Typical of California Indians.

band A subdivision or subtribe of an Indian tribe, often made up of an extended family living together, traveling together, and hunting and gathering together. Historically, the word *band* often appears when a part of a tribe breaks off from the main group under a new leader. In Canada, different self-governing groups, although sharing the same tribal descent, sometimes are referred to as *bands*. (See also **nation, tribe.**)

bannerstone A polished stone artifact, often in a winged, birdlike shape, used as a weight on an atlatl or on a staff as a symbol of authority. Sometimes called a birdstone. (See also **atlatl.**)

barabara A large communal house of the Aleut and some Inuit bands as well; a kind of pithouse. A square pit, about two-feet deep, is lined with planks that extend above the surface; planks and poles, often driftwood or whale ribs, are used to form a roof, which is covered with sod, except over a smokehole. The door faces east.

beadwork   Decorative work in beads, stitched on clothing, bags, and other items. Beadwork commonly replaced quillwork among Indians after Europeans brought glass beads to the Americas. (See also **quillwork.**)

bison   See **buffalo.**

Black Drink   A tea made by Southeast Indians, from *Ilex vomitoria,* tobacco, and other ingredients, for ceremonial purposes. The drink induced vomiting and was thought to purify the body.

bola   A hunting weapon made from two or more stone weights tied on thongs that are attached to a longer line. When thrown, it entangles the legs of mammals or the wings of birds.

Booger mask   A carved mask of the Cherokee, used in the Booger Dance. Booger masks have exaggerated features and expressions, often representing non-Indians, as well as animals. The names of the booger masks are often comical and obscene. The term *booger* is derived from the same European root as *boogie* in *boogieman* (*bogeyman*).

breechcloth   A cloth, usually made from deerskin, used to cover the loins. Also called "breechclout" or **loincloth.**

buffalo   (American bison, bison) A hoofed mammal with a dark-brown coat, shaggy mane, and short, curved horns. Buffalo, or bison, were essential to the Plains Indians for food, clothing, shelter, tools, and ceremonial objects.

bull boat   A circular, cup-shaped boat made from hide stretched over a wooden frame. Used by Indians of the upper Missouri River.

Bureau of Indian Affairs (BIA)   An agency of the U.S. federal government that handles Indian issues; part of the Department of the Interior. It was formed in 1824.

bustle   An attachment to clothing on the hind side, typically of feathers, for wearing in dances. Some tribes wore shields as bustles. In the Grass Dance, the bustle is a tail of braided grass.

cacique   A chief or headman. *Cacique* is from the Arawak term *kassequa,* applied by the Spanish to the rulers of various Caribbean, Mesoamerican, and South American Indians. The term was also passed via the Spanish to the Pueblo Indians, some of whom use the term in reference to priests.

calendar stick   A wooden stick with cuts and notches representing events in tribal history. Typical of the Tohono O'odham (Papago) tribe.

calumet   See **sacred pipe.**

camas   A plant having edible roots and bulbs, important in the diet of the Plateau Indians and northern Great Basin Indians.

camp circle   A circular formation of tipis, indicating kinship and political status.

canoe   A sleek boat with pointed ends, propelled by paddles. Some canoes were made of wood frames with bark coverings; others were dugouts, carved from a single log.

cassava   (manioc) A tropical plant with a large starchy root, important in the diet of the Arawak (Taino).

caste system   Social and political organization in which classes of society are separated by hereditary rank or profession. Common among Southeast Indians and Mesoamerican Indians.

catlinite   See **pipestone.**

celt   An ungrooved ax, used mainly without a handle, for woodworking.

ceremonial object   Any object used in religious rituals or with a sacred tribal meaning.

chert   A kind of rock, similar to flint, which can be shaped into tools or spear and arrow points. (See also **flaking.**)

chickee   A kind of house, raised on stilts and open on four sides, with a wood platform and thatched roof. The Seminole lived in chickees.

chiefdom   A tribe in which a chief has absolute power over other tribal members. Used in reference to some Southeast tribes.

chinampas   An artificial island made by piling silt and plant matter on wickerwork baskets. The Aztec used this technique to create additional land for their city of Tenochtitlán on Lake Texcoco.

city-state A city and its surrounding territory, with a government independent of other cities. Used in reference to Mesoamerican Indians. Some among the Mound Builders also lived in what might be called city-states.

clan A social group within a tribe, made up of several families who trace descent from a common ancestor.

cliff dwelling A dwelling along the walls of cliffs and canyons, on their ledges and in their caves and recesses. Modification of a natural structure was common through digging and the adding of stone or adobe walls. Typical of the Anasazi culture.

coiling A technique of making pottery in which rope-like coils of clay are built up from the bottom of the pot, then smoothed over to form the inner and outer walls. Also used to describe a similar technique of weaving baskets.

confederacy A political union of two or more tribes, often for military purposes. The terms *alliance, confederation,* and *league* also are used.

conquistador The Spanish word for "conqueror." Used in reference to Spanish explorers and soldiers who subjugated Indian peoples.

contact A term used to describe the first meetings between Indian peoples and Europeans or Euroamericans, with subsequent cultural changes among the Indians. *Precontact* refers to the period before Indians met whites (see also "pre-Columbian"). *Postcontact* refers to the period after Indians established communication and trade with whites. "Contact" for one tribe might have come at a different time than for another.

corral An enclosure made of stones, wood, or brush for trapping and confining animals.

council A gathering of tribal leaders for discussion of plans. Some councils are intertribal.

coup Touching an enemy in battle with the hand or an object to prove one's bravery. Plains Indians used "coup sticks" in some instances, rather than true weapons, and they "counted coup."

coureur de bois Literally, French for "runner of the woods." A fur trader of French descent who worked independently of the large trading compa-nies and who lived most of the time with Indians. (See also **voyageurs.**)

cradleboard A carrier for babies, usually made of wood and leather, worn on the back.

creation myth A tribal legend, recounting the supernatural origin of the tribe. Also called emergence myth.

culture area A geographical region where different Indian tribes had similar ways of life. The culture areas are a system of classification used to organize tribes.

culture hero A legendary figure, thought to have supernatural powers and usually considered a tribal ancestor.

deadfall A trap in which a heavy object, such as a log or a stone, is used to drop on the prey.

dialect A variation of a language, different from other dialects of the same language in vocabulary, grammar, or pronunciation.

digging stick A stick carved to a point, used to prepare soil for farming and to dig up wild edible roots and insects.

dugout A type of boat made by hollowing out a log. (See also **canoe.**)

earth lodge A large dwelling, usually dome-shaped, with a log frame covered with smaller branches or other plant matter, then packed with mud or sod. Typical of the Mandan and other Prairie and Plains tribes.

earthwork See **mound.**

emergence myth See **creation myth.**

False Face A wooden mask carved and worn by a member of the False Face Society of the Iroquois (Haudenosaunee). The masks, representing the forest spirits known as Faces of the Forest, are carved on a living tree; a ceremony of prayer and the offering of tobacco is held while cutting them out. They are believed to frighten away malevolent spirits that cause illness.

federal recognition The outcome of the process establishing a government-to-government trust relationship between an Indian tribe and the United States government, known as the "Federal Acknowledgment Process." Federally recognized tribes, or those with trust status, are entitled to special programs provided by the government. More than 300 tribal groups are now recognized by the federal government; many others are seeking recognition.

fetish   A small object, such as a carved-stone animal, believed to have power to protect or help its owner.

fire drill   A device for making fire in which one stick is twirled rapidly in a hole of another piece of wood, creating enough friction to ignite wood powder or shredded grass.

firing   The process of baking pottery to make it hard.

flaking   To remove chips of stone, usually from chunks of flint, chert, or obsidian, in order to shape tools or spear and arrow points. In percussion-flaking, the chips are removed by striking with a tool of stone, bone, or wood. In pressure flaking, the chips are removed by applying pressure with a tool of bone or antler.

flint   A kind of rock, a variety of quartz that can be worked into tools and points through flaking. (See also **flaking.**)

fluting   Grooves or channels in points. (See also **point.**)

Ghost Dance   An Indian religion of the late 19th century founded by the Paiute mystic Wovoka and popular for a number of years among many Plains tribes. The main ritual was a dance to bring about the restoration of traditional tribal ways.

glyph writing   See **pictograph.**

gorget   An ornament or piece of armor, usually made of shell or cooper, worn over the throat.

grass house   (grass lodge) A house covered with grass. Such a dwelling traditionally had long poles erected in a circle, usually 40 to 50 feet in diameter, with the tops meeting in a domed or conical shape; the framework was tied together with cordage, then covered with grass or thatch. Typical of the Caddo and Wichita.

hammock   A swinging bed or couch, a type of furniture, suspended between two trees or other supports. A Native American invention, adopted worldwide, becoming for centuries the dominant sleeping place on European ships. Typical of the Arawak (Taino).

hieroglyphics   See **pictograph.**

hogan   A dwelling with a log and stick frame covered with mud or sod (or occasionally made from stone). It can be cone-shaped, six-sided, or eight-sided. It traditionally faces east. The Navajo lived in hogans.

hunting-gathering   Obtaining food through hunting, fishing, and foraging for wild plants, without farming.

igloo   A dome-shaped dwelling made from blocks of ice. Also called a snow house. Some Inuit lived in igloos.

incising   A technique of decorating pottery by cutting a design in the still-wet clay with a sharp tool.

Indian Territory   A tract west of the Mississippi set aside as a permanent homeland for Indians in the 1830s, then diminished over the following years until it became the state of Oklahoma in 1907.

isolate   See **language isolate.**

jade   A kind of rock, usually pale green in color, used to make sculptures and jewelry.

jerky   Sun-dried strips of meat.

jimsonweed   A tall poisonous plant of the nightshade family, with large trumpet-shaped flowers and prickly fruit. Indians of California, the Southwest, and Mesoamerica made a tea from jimsonweed leaves, stems, and roots for ritualistic and medicinal purposes.

kachina (or katchina)   A supernatural being in the religion of the Hopi, Zuni, and other Pueblo Indians. Kachina masks are worn in tribal ceremonies. Kachina dolls are carved icons of the deities.

karmak   A type of earth-covered pithouse of the Inuit, about five to six feet underground and two to three feet above, with a frame of wood or whalebone. The entrance is an underground passageway.

kashim   A ceremonial house and clubhouse of the Inuit. In Alaska, these structures were typically rectangular; in eastern regions, circular *kashim* were generally found. They were constructed with post-and-beam framework and sod covering, as well as of ice blocks, like igloos. Many were semisubterranean with secret passageways.

kayak   A one- or two-person boat with an enclosed cockpit, made by stretching hide over a wooden frame. Typical of the Inuit.

kill site An archaeological site where remains of many animals have been found along with human artifacts.

kinnikinnik A mixture of tobacco and other plant matter, such as willow bark, for smoking. An Algonquian word.

kiva An underground ceremonial chamber or clubhouse. Typical of Southwest Indians.

labret An ornamental plug of shell, bone, or stone, worn in the lower lip (or sometimes in the chin).

lacrosse A game invented and played by eastern Indians, using long-handled rackets and a small ball. Lacrosse is now played all over the world.

land cession Land given up by Indians to whites through a treaty. Most land cessions were forced upon the Indians against their will. (See also **treaty.**)

land claim A tribe's legal assertion of rights to a particular tract of land based on ancestral use.

language family (language stock) A term used in linguistics to describe two or more languages, distinct but with elements in common and related historically in that they are descended (or assumed to be descended) from a common language.

language isolate A unique language with few or no elements in common with other languages.

language phylum (language superstock) A grouping of language families, based on elements in common, including vocabulary, grammar, and phonetics.

lean-to A temporary, open brush shelter, generally consisting of a single-pitched sloping roof. Some western Subarctic Indians constructed double lean-tos with two roofs meeting in a peak.

leister A three-pronged harpoon used for fishing by Arctic peoples.

lifeways Cultural traits or customs of a people.

Lithic Indians See **Paleo-Indians.**

longhouse A long dwelling, with a pointed or rounded roof and doors at both ends, made with a pole frame and usually covered with elm bark. The Iroquois (Haudenosaunee) lived in longhouses, several families to each one.

loom A device used to weave thread or yarn to make cloth.

maize Indian corn.

mammoth A large extinct mammal, similar to the elephant, once common in North America and hunted by Prehistoric Indians. The wooly mammoth was one variety. (See also **mastodon.**)

Manitou A supernatural being or force of nature in the religion of Algonquians. Known by other names in other Indian religions. Sometimes translated as "Great Spirit." (See also **Orenda** and **Wakenda.**)

mano and metate A set of millstones, with an upper and lower part, used to grind corn and other grains. (See also **mortar and pestle.**)

mastodon A large extinct mammal, similar to an elephant. (See also **mammoth.**)

matrilineal A term used to describe a social organization in which descent is traced through the female members, as is ownership of property. (See also **patrilineal.**)

medicine bundle A collection of various materials, often wrapped in leather or cloth, to which spiritual power and tribal meaning are assigned.

medicine man See **shaman.**

mesa A tableland, or flat-topped elevation with steep sides. Found in the American Southwest.

Mesoamerica The name of a culture area that is now part of Mexico and Central America. Some Indians in this part of the Americas lived in cities and had highly organized societies.

mesquite A spiny tree or shrub with sugar-rich pods, growing in the American Southwest.

Métis Literally, French for "mixed-blood." Many Canadian fur traders, especially French Canadian but also Scottish and Irish, lived among and intermarried with the Indians. They came to constitute a special class of people, like an Indian tribe but with a combined Indian-white culture. The word is capitalized when it identifies this special group. (See also **voyageur.**)

Midewiwin A secret society whose members supposedly have a link to the spirit world and strive to assure the well-being of the tribe. Typical of western Great Lakes tribes. Also called the "Grand Medicine Society."

military society See **secret society.**

Mission Indians   A phrase used to denote those Indians who gave up, or were forced to give up, their tribal way of life and came to live at missions. Used especially in reference to California Indians missionized by the Spanish.

moccasin   A soft leather shoe. Originally an Algonquian word, but now used in reference to footware of many different Indian peoples.

mocuck   A birch-bark container for holding sugar and other food, sometimes with a rawhide handle and carved design. Typical of the Chippewa (Ojibway).

moiety   A social group within a tribe. The word means "half." Some tribes with clans divided their clans into halves. The two halves were responsible for different chores and played against each other in games. (See also **clan.**)

mortar and pestle   A two-part milling tool, with a bowl-shaped stone, plus a club-shaped stone (or wooden bowl and wooden club), used for pulverizing plant or animal matter. (See also **mano and metate.**)

mosaic   A picture or design made from small, colorful pieces of stone, shell, or other material cemented together to form a design.

mound   A large earthwork made by ancient Indians for burials, to represent animals, or to contain or support temples or houses. The Native Americans who made these earthworks are known as Mound Builders.

mukluk   A soft and supple Inuit boot, usually made from sealskin.

nation   Originally a term applied by the French to tribes in Quebec. *Nation* was later applied by English-speaking peoples to large Indian confederacies, especially in the Southeast. It became the offical name for the Cherokee, Chickasaw, Choctaw, Creek, and Seminole tribal entities in the Indian Territory after their relocation in the 1830s. *Nation* is often used synonymously with *tribe;* it is favored by some Native Americans because the term implies the concept of sovereignty. In Canada, the phrase *First Nations* now is applied to Indian tribes.

nomadic   A way of life in which people frequently moved from one location to another in search of food. "Seminomadic" people had permanent villages, but left them in certain seasons to hunt, fish, or gather wild plant foods. (See also **hunting-gathering.**)

obsidian   Volcanic glass that is generally black and was prized by Indians because it could be readily flaked to a sharp point or edge. (See also **flaking.**)

Orenda   The supernatural force or "Great Spirit" in the Religion of the Iroquois (Haudenosaunee). (See also **Manitou** and **Wakanda.**)

paddling   A technique of decorating pottery by pressing a flat or curved wood paddle against the wet clay before firing. The paddle had a design carved in it or cords wrapped around it.

Paleo-Indians   The Paleolithic (Stone Age), prehistoric ancestors of modern Indians. The Paleo-Indians were known as makers of stone tools and hunters of now-extinct big game. Also called "Lithic Indians."

paleontology   The study of ancient life-forms and fossil remains.

palisade   A fence, usually made of upright logs and placed around a village, for purposes of defense. Also called a stockade.

pan-Indian   Having to do with all Indians and not just isolated tribes. Used in reference to cultural activities, common goals, and organizations relevant to all Indian peoples.

papoose   The Algonquian word for "baby," applied to infants of other Indians as well.

parfleche   A storage bag used to hold clothing, ceremonial objects, or meat and made from rawhide with the hair removed.

parka   A hooded outer garment, made by the Inuit and Aleut from the skin of mammals or birds. The length varies from people to people, from the hips to below the knees. Women's parkas are cut larger for carrying infants; they also are longer in back for insulation when sitting. Sometimes mittens are attached.

patrilineal   A type of social organization in which descent and property are passed along through the male line. (See also **matrilineal.**)

peace pipe   See **sacred pipe.**

pemmican   A concentrated food made by pounding together meat, fat, and berries and used especially on the trail.

percussion-flaking   See **flaking.**

permafrost   Permanently frozen subsoil, typical of the Arctic tundra. (See also **tundra.**)

peyote   A type of cactus eaten by some Indian peoples for its trance-like effect. Considered a sacrament by the Native American Church.

pictograph   A picture or sign representing a word or idea (as opposed to a sound, as in alphabet-writing or in syllabaries). When present, the colors in pictographs have symbolic meaning as well. The term *ideograph* (or *ideogram*) is used synonymously with *pictograph.* The terms *picture writing, hieroglyphics,* and *glyph writing* are used interchangeably with *pictography.* A petroglyph is a pictograph on rock.

piñon   A small pine tree producing edible nuts, growing in the American West and Southwest.

pipestone   A type of clay, usually red in color, used to make pipes. Also called catlinite, after the frontier painter George Catlin, who wrote about the Pipestone Quarry in Minnesota.

pithouse   A dwelling, placed over a hole, usually made with a log frame and walls and roof of saplings, reeds, and mud.

plaiting   A technique used in weaving baskets and cloth in which two different elements cross each other to create a checkerboard effect.

plank house   A dwelling made of hand-split planks over a log frame. Northwest Coast Indians built plank houses.

point   A stone spearhead or arrowhead.

potlatch   A tribal ceremony of feasting, speechmaking, and dancing during which possessions are given away to demonstrate wealth and rank. Typical of Northwest Coast Indians.

potsherd   (potshard, shard, sherd) A fragment of broken pottery. Potsherds, the most durable of archaeological evidence, are valuable in dating excavation sites.

powwow   A council or festival among Indians for socializing, trading, and dancing. Originally an Algonquian word.

pre-Columbian   The period of history in the Americas before Christopher Columbus's voyage of exploration.

prehistory   A general term applied to the cultural stage of a people before written records.

presidio   A Spanish "fort," typically built near missions.

pressure-flaking   See **flaking.**

promyshlenniki   The Russian term for fur traders.

pueblo   Originally, the Spanish word for an Indian village. Used for a particular type of architecture common among Southwest Indians—apartment-like, up to five stories high, interconnected by ladders, made from stone or adobe bricks. Also, with a capital *P,* when used in reference to the people living in pueblos.

pyramid   A massive stone monument with a rectangular base and four sides extending upward to a point. Found in Mesoamerica, where they were used to support temples.

rancheria   A small reservation, used in reference to Native American holdings in the state of California. The Spanish originally applied the term to nonmissionized Indian villages.

quarry site   A location where Indians went for workable stone such as flint and made stone tools. (See also **flaking.**)

quillwork   Decorative work on clothing, bags, and other items, made from porcupine quills dyed with vegetable colors. (See also **beadwork.**)

radiocarbon dating   A technique for dating ancient materials by measuring the amount of carbon 14 (a radioactive isotope) present. Also called carbon 14 dating.

Relocation   A term used to describe the forced removal of a tribe from one location to another. A common U.S. governmental practice in the 1800s. From the early 1950s into the 1960s, the federal government adopted a modern relocation policy, pressuring Indians to move from reservations to urban areas. (See also **Removal.**)

Removal   A term used to describe a 19th-century policy of the U.S. federal government in which eastern tribes were taken from their ancestral homelands and forced to live elsewhere, especially west of the Mississippi River in the Indian Territory. (See also **Indian Territory** and **Relocation.**)

Repatriation   The reacquisition by a tribe of human remains or sacred objects from the government, museums, or private owners, as defined in the Native American Graves Protection and Repatriation Act of 1990.

reservation   A tract of land set aside historically by the federal government or state governments for Indians. Reservations originally served as a kind of prison for Indians, who were not permitted to leave them. Nowadays, reservations are tribally held lands, protected by the government, where Indians are free to come and go as they choose. In Canada, the official term is *reserve.*

reserve   The Canadian equivalent of a reservation. In Canada, different bands typically have more than one reserve tract of land.

Restoration   A term used to describe cultural renewal, or a return to traditional ways and values. Often appearing as "tribal restoration," indicating a rediscovery of tribal identity and the establishment of tribal economic goals. Tribal restoration became widespread in the 1930s, when the U.S. federal government under President Roosevelt launched a "New Deal" for Indians.

ribbonwork   A kind of patchwork or appliqué in which ribbons or cutout designs of silk are sewn in strips on garments. Typical of the Seminole. (See also **appiqué.**)

roach   A construction of animal hair or fur worn on the top of the head as a hairstyle. Also, the featherwork part of a headdress. "Roach spreaders," usually carved of antler, held the featherwork erect.

saber-toothed tiger   A now-extinct mammal of the cat family with long upper teeth, hunted by early Indians.

sachem   The chief of a tribe. Originally an Algonquian word, but also used in reference to Iroquois (Haundenosaunee) chiefs. A "grand sachem" is the leader of a confederacy of tribes. (See also **sagamore.**)

sacred pipe   A pipe with a special meaning for a tribe; used in ceremonies. Usually with an intricately carved pipestone bowl and a long wooden stem and decorated with quills, beads, or feathers. Also called "calumet" or "peace pipe."

Sacred Shield   The paintings on shields had religious meanings to the Indians, supposedly serving as a link to the spiritual world and offering magical protection to the bearers.

sagamore   A subordinate chief of the Algonquian Indians, below a sachem in rank. (See also **sachem.**)

saguaro   A giant cactus, growing in the American Southwest. Used by the Akimel O'odham (Pima) and Tohono O'odham (Papago) for its edible fruit.

sandpainting   A design made by trickling colored sand onto plain sand for ceremonial purposes. A ritualistic art practiced by the Navajo.

scalplock   A lock of hair on an otherwise shaved head.

secret society   A sodality, or club, with exclusive membership, a common purpose, and particular rituals. Some tribes have many different societies. There are many variations on this term, including *ceremonial society, religious society,* and *shamans' society.* One also sees the term *dance society,* since secret societies typically have special dances. A *medicine society* involves healing rituals. A *military society, soldier society,* or *warrior society* is organized around rituals of war. Some Native American sodalities are open to all tribal members.

sedentary   A way of life in which people live in permanent villages. Most sedentary tribes practiced agriculture.

seine   A large net for fishing that hangs vertically in the water, with floats on top and weights on the bottom.

Self-Determination   A tribal and governmental policy calling for Indian self-government and cultural renewal.

seminomadic   See **nomadic.**

shaman   A member of a tribe who keeps tribal lore and rituals and interprets and attempts to control the supernatural. The shaman applies his or her powers to evoke visions, to cure the sick, and to bring success in food gathering and warfare. Also called medicine man.

sign language   A method of intertribal communication using hand signs. Typical of Plains Indians.

sipapu   A small round, shallow hole in the floor of early pithouses and later kivas, located between the firepit and the wall. In Pueblo Indian tradition, the opening symbolizes the center of the universe, leading to and from the Spirit World, through which the first humans emerged, deceased people pass, and legendary beings come and go.

slash-and-burn agriculture A type of farming in which the ground is cleared by cutting down and then burning trees and undergrowth. The resulting ashes help enrich the soil. Common in Mesoamerica.

sled A vehicle used for carrying people and possessions over snow and ice. A sled has runners and a raised platform. (See also **toboggan.**)

slip A thin mixture of fine clay and water applied to the surface of pottery before firing.

snare A device to trap game, mostly birds and small mammals, usually with a rope or leather noose.

snow pit A hole in the snow in which a hunter can hide to surprise game.

snowshoe A device for walking on top of deep snow, made from a racket-shaped wooden frame with leather webbing, and with thongs to attach it to the foot.

soapstone A kind of stone with a soapy texture; a variety of talc; used to make pots and sculptures. Also called steatite.

sodality A club, often with closed membership and secret rites.

soldier society See **secret society.**

soul-catcher A ceremonial object used by a shaman to hold the patient's soul in curing ceremonies.

sovereignty A term applied to Native American tribal self-determination, that is, control of a people over their own affairs without external interference. Many Indian tribes have made claims as sovereign nations, on an equal footing with other nations, but they in effect have "limited sovereignty." (See also **self-determination.**)

staple A basic food essential to survival. Corn, buffalo meat, deer meat, salmon, and acorns are examples of dietary staples for various Indian peoples.

steatite See **soapstone.**

stone-boiling A method of cooking in which pre-heated stones are placed inside containers of water.

Sun Dance The most famous of all the Indian ceremonies, an annual renewal rite, taking place in the summer and centered around the Sun. There were many rituals in the Sun Dance, the most dramatic of which involved self-torture by warriors. Typical of most Plains tribes.

sweathouse A structure used for sweating, a ritual purification through exposure to heat. Heat could be generated with a fire in an open fire pit or by pouring water onto hot stones and making steam. Sweathouses were generally dome-shaped. Large sweathouses are sometimes called sweatlodges and often doubled as clubhouses.

syllabary A list of language symbols, each one representing a syllable. Sequoyah, a Cherokee, invented a syllabary for his people so that their language could be written.

taiga The evergreen forests and swamplands of the subarctic region to the south of the treeless tundra.

temple A shrine or place of worship.

Termination A policy of the federal government practiced in the 1950s which sought to end the special protective relationship between the government and Indian tribes.

tipi (tepee) A conical tent with a pole frame and usually covered with buffalo hides. Typical of the Plains Indians.

tiswin (*tesguino, tulipai*) A beer made from corn. Corn stalks or green corn sprouts were pressed for the juices, which then were heated. Typical of the Apache.

toboggan A vehicle for transporting people or possessions over snow or ice. Toboggans, unlike sleds, have no runners; their platforms sit directly on the snow. (See also **sled.**)

tomahawk A type of warclub. *Tomahawk* is an Algonquian word. Unlike the more general word *warclub,* often applied to stone or wooden clubs, the term *tomahawk* is generally used to describe an axlike weapon with a metal head (which sometimes doubled as a pipe). Tomahawks were often made by Europeans for trade with Indians.

totem An animal or plant, or some other natural object or phenomenon, serving as the symbol or emblem of a family or clan. (See also **clan.**)

totem pole A post carved and painted with a series of figures and symbols, of special meaning with regard to tribal legends and history. Typical of Northwest Coast Indians.

travois   A device used for transporting people and possessions behind dogs (*dog travois*) or horses (*horse travois*). It consists of a wooden frame shaped like a V, with the closed end over the animal's shoulders, and the open end dragging on the ground, with a plank or webbing in the middle.

treaty   A formal agreement, pact, or contract negotiated between the federal government (or state government, or territorial government) and Indian tribes.

tribal government   The leadership of a tribe, sometimes hereditary and sometimes elected. May consist of a chief and/or tribal council.

tribal headquarters   The location where a tribal government meets, or simply the post office address of a tribe. It is a modern term commonly appearing with reservation names.

tribe   A general term applied to a number of different kinds of Indian social organization. Tribes usually have descent, territory, culture, and history in common and are made up of a number of bands or villages. (See also **band.**)

tribelet   A grouping of Indians with a main, permanent village and a number of temporary satellite villages. Applied to California Indians.

Trickster   A name for a recurring culture hero among various tribes, who symbolizes the unpredictable, absurd, and humorous nature of reality and fate. A Trickster figure represents both the sacred and the profane; he is a creator and a destroyer. Trickster is commonly depicted as a coyote or a magpie.

trust lands   Indian lands that are protected by the U.S. federal government and state governments but that are not true reservations. Applied especially to the allotted lands of Oklahoma tribes. (See also **Allotment** and **reservation.**)

tule   A bulrush or reed growing in California, the Southwest, and Mexico and used to make rafts, sandals, mats, and other items.

tundra   The treeless area of the Arctic, with a permanently frozen subsoil and low-growing vegetation, such as moss and lichens. (See also **permafrost.**)

umiak   A large, open, flat-bottomed boat made by stretching hide (usually walrus hide) over a wooden frame. Typical of the Inuit.

Vision Quest   Seeking visions or dreams through self-deprivation, exposure to the elements, or hallucinogenic drugs, usually for a rite of passage, such as from childhood to adulthood. Typical of Plains Indians.

voyageur   Literally, French for "traveler." A fur trader who traveled the rivers and backwoods for the large fur companies, such as the North West Company and Hudson's Bay Company. Many of the voyageurs were of mixed descent, especially French Canadian and Cree. (See also **coureur de bois** and **Métis.**)

Wakanda   The supernatural force or Great Spirit in the religion of the Sioux. Also spelled "Wakenda" and "Wakonda." (See also **Manitou** and **Orenda.**)

wampum   An Algonquian word, originally referring to strings or belts of small beads made from shells, especially purple and white quahog clam shells. Indians used "wampum belts" as tribal records and to communicate messages of peace or war to other tribes. After Europeans came to the Americas, the Indians began making wampum out of glass beads. The Europeans also made wampum for trade with the Indians. Wampum then became a form of money.

warbonnet   A headdress with different feathers representing feats in battle. Typical of Plains Indians.

warrior society   See **military society.**

wattle and daub   A type of construction using a pole framework intertwined with branches and vines and covered with mud and plaster. Found especially in the Southeast.

weir   A fenced-in enclosure placed in water for trapping or keeping fish.

wickiup   A conical or domed dwelling with a pole frame covered with brush, grass, or reeds. Typical of the Apache.

wigwam   A domed or conical dwelling with a pole frame overlaid with bark, animal skin, or woven mats. Typical of Algonquian tribes.

wild rice   A tall plant of the grass family, with an edible grain (not a true rice), growing especially along the western Great Lakes and gathered by Algonquian peoples.

SELECTED BIBLIOGRAPHY

Adams, Richard E.W. *Prehistoric Mesoamerica.* Norman: University of Oklahoma Press, 1991 (revised edition).

Axelrod, Alan. *Chronicle of the Indian Wars: From Colonial Times to Wounded Knee.* New York: Prentice Hall, 1993.

Baity, Elizabeth Chesley. *Americans Before Columbus.* New York: Viking, 1961.

Ballantine, Betty, and Ian Ballantine, eds. *The Native Americans: An Illustrated History.* Atlanta: Turner, 1993.

Bataille, Gretchen M., and Kathleen Mullen Sands. *American Indian Women: Telling Their Lives.* Lincoln: University of Nebraska Press, 1984.

Bear, Leroy Little, Menno Boldt, and J. Anthony Long, eds. *Pathways to Self-Determination: Canadian Indians and the Canadian State.* Toronto: University of Toronto Press, 1984.

Berkhofer, Robert F., Jr. *The White Man's Indian: Images of the American Indian from Columbus to the Present.* New York: Random House, 1979.

Bierhorst, John, ed. *The Sacred Path: Spells, Prayers, and Power Songs of the American Indian.* New York: William Morrow, 1983.

Boas, Franz. *Handbook of the American Indian Languages.* New York: Humanities Press, 1969 (reprint from 1911).

Brandon, William. *Indians.* New York: American Heritage; Boston: Houghton Mifflin, 1985.

Brown, Dee. *Bury My Heart at Wounded Knee: An Indian History of the American West.* New York: Holt, Rinehart, & Winston, 1970.

Burland, Cottie. *North American Indian Mythology.* New York: Peter Bedrick Books, 1985.

Ceram, C.W. *The First American: A Story of North American Archaeology.* New York: Harcourt Brace Jovanovich, 1971.

Champagne, Duane, ed. *Chronology of Native North American History: From Pre-Columbian Times to the Present.* Detroit: Gale Research, 1994.

Coe, Michael, Dean Snow, and Elizabeth Benson. *Atlas of Ancient America.* New York: Facts on File, 1986.

Collier, John. *Indians of the Americas.* New York: W.W. Norton, 1947.

Collins, Richard, ed. *The Native Americans: The Indigenous People of North America.* New York: Smithmark, 1992.

Cornell, Stephen. *Return of the Native: American Indian Political Resurgence.* New York: Oxford University Press, 1988.

Davis, Mary B., ed. *Native America in the Twentieth Century: An Encyclopedia.* New York: Garland, 1996.

Debo, Angie. *A History of the Indians of the United States.* Norman: University of Oklahoma Press, 1977.

Deloria, Vine, Jr. *Behind the Trail of Broken Treaties: An Indian Declaration of Purpose.* New York: Delacorte, 1974.

———.*Custer Died for Your Sins: An Indian Manifesto.* New York: Macmillan, 1969.

———.*God is Red.* New York: Grosset & Dunlap, 1973.

Dickason, Olive Patricia. *Canada's First Nations: A History of Founding Peoples from Earliest Times.* Norman: University of Oklahoma Press, 1992.

Dictionary of Daily Life of Indians of the Americas. 2 vols. Newport Beach, Calif.: American Indian Publishers, 1981.

Dockstader, Frederick J. *Great North American Indians: Profiles in Life and Leadership.* New York: Van Nostrand Reinhold, 1977.

Driver, Harold E. *Indians of North America.* Chicago: University of Chicago Press, 1969.

Eagle/Walking Turtle. *Indian America: A Traveler's Companion.* Santa Fe: John Muir Publications, 1991.

Edmonds, Margot, and Ella E. Clark. *Voices of the Winds: Native American Legends.* New York: Facts On File, 1989.

Edmunds, R. David, ed. *American Indian Leaders: Studies in Diversity.* Lincoln: University of Nebraska Press, 1980.

Embree, Edwin R. *Indians of the Americas.* New York: Collier, 1970 (reprint from 1939).

Fagan, Brian. *The Great Journey: The Peopling of Ancient America.* New York: Thames & Hudson, 1987.

Feder, Norman. *American Indian Art.* New York: Harry N. Abrams, 1965.

Feest, Christian F. *Native Arts of North America.* New York: Oxford University Press, 1980.

Fey, Harold E., and D'Arcy McNickle. *Indians and Other Americans: Two Ways of Life Meet.* New York: Harper & Row, 1970.

Fiedel, Stuart J. *Prehistory of the Americas.* Cambridge: Cambridge University Press, 1987.

Francis, Lee. *Native Time: A Historical Time Line of Native America.* New York: St. Martin's, 1996.

Gibson, Arrell Morgan. *The American Indian: Prehistory to the Present.* Lexington, Mass.: D.C. Heath, 1980.

Gonzales, Ray. *Without Discovery: A Native Response to Columbus.* Seattle: Broken Moon Press, 1992.

Hagan, William T. *American Indians.* Chicago: University of Chicago Press, 1979 (revised edition)

Hauptman, Laurence M. *Tribes and Tribulations: Misconceptions about American Indians and their Histories.* Albuquerque: University of New Mexico Press, 1996.

Hausman, Gerald. *Turtle Island Alphabet: A Lexicon of Native American Symbols and Culture.* New York: St. Martin's, 1992.

Highwater, Jamake. *Arts of the Indian Americas: Leaves from the Sacred Tree.* New York: Harper & Row, 1983.

———. *Ritual of the Wind: North American Ceremonies, Music, and Dances.* New York: Van Der Marck, 1984.

———, ed. *Words in the Blood: Contemporary Indian Writers of North and South America.* New York: New American Library, 1984.

Hirschfelder, Arlene, and Paulette Molin. *The Encyclopedia of Native American Religions.* New York: Facts On File, 1992.

Hirschfelder, Arlene, and Martha Kreipe de Montano. *The Native American Almanac: A Portrait of Native America Today.* New York: Prentice Hall, 1993.

Hodge, Frederick Webb, ed. *Handbook of American Indians North of Mexico.* 2 vols. Totowa, N.J.: Rowman & Littlefield, 1965 (reprint from 1907–1910).

Hoxie, Frederick E., ed. *Encyclopedia of North American Indians:* Boston: Houghton Mifflin, 1996.

Hultkrantz, Ake. *The Study of American Indian Religions.* New York: Crossroad, 1983.

Hunt, Norman Bancroft. *Native America Tribes.* Edison, N.J.: Chartwell Books, 1997.

Jaimes, M. Annette, ed. *The State of Native America: Genocide, Colonization, and Resistance.* Boston: South End Press, 1992.

Jenness, Diamond. *The Indians of Canada.* Toronto: University of Toronto Press, 1982 (reprint from 1932).

Jennings, Francis. *The Invasion of America: Indians, Colonialism, and the Cant of Conquest.* Chapel Hill: University of North Carolina Press, 1975.

Johnson, Michael G. *The Native Tribes of North America: A Concise Encyclopedia.* New York: Macmillan, 1994.

Josephy, Alvin, Jr. *The Indian Heritage of America.* New York: Knoft, 1970.

———. *The Patriot Chiefs: A Chronicle of American Indian Resistance.* New York: Viking, 1958.

———. *Red Power: The American Indians' Fight for Freedom.* New York: American Heritage, 1971.

Kelly, Lawrence C. *Federal Indian Policy.* New York: Chelsea House, 1990.

Klein, Barry T., ed. *Reference Encyclopedia of the American Indian.* 2 vols. West Nyack, N.Y.: Todd Publications, 1992 (revised edition).

Kopper, Philip. *The Smithsonian Book of North American Indians: Before the Coming of the Europeans.* Washington, D.C.: Smithsonian, 1986.

Kroeber, Alfred L. *Cultural and Natural Areas of Native North America.* Berkeley: University of California Press, 1963 (reprint from 1939).

La Farge, Oliver. *A Pictorial History of the American Indian.* New York: Crown, 1974.

Laubin, Reginald, and Gladys Laubin. *Indian Dances of North America.* New York, Viking, 1977.

Leitch, Barbara A. *A Concise Dictionary of Indian Tribes of North America.* Algonac, Mich.: Reference Publications, 1979.

Lesley, Craig, ed. *Talking Leaves: Contemporary Native American Short Stories.* New York: Dell, 1991.

Lincoln, Kenneth. *Native American Renaissance.* Berkeley: University of California Press, 1983.

Lurie, Nancy O. *North American Indian Lives.* Milwaukee: Milwaukee Public Museum, 1985.

Marquis, Arnold. *A Guide to America's Indians: Ceremonials, Reservations, and Museums.* Norman: University of Oklahoma Press, 1994 (revised edition).

Marshall, S.L.A. *Crimsomed Prairie: The Indian Wars.* New York: Scribner, 1972.

Mathews, Zena Pearlstone, and Aldona Jonaitis. *Native North American Art History: Selected Readings.* Palo Alto, Calif.: Peek Publications, 1982.

Matthiessen, Peter. *In the Spirit of Crazy Horse.* New York: Viking, 1980.

———. *Indian Country.* New York: Viking, 1984.

McLuhan, T.C. *Touch the Earth: A Self-Portrait of Indian Existence.* New York: Simon & Schuster, 1971.

McNickle, D'Arcy. *The Indian Tribes of the United States.* New York: Oxford University Press, 1962.

———. *Native American Tribalism: Indian Survivals and Renewals.* New York: Oxford University Press, 1973.

Moquin, Wayne, and Charles Van Doren. *Great Documents in American Indian History.* New York: Da Capo Press, 1995.

Moses, L.G., and Raymond Wilson. *Indian Lives: Essays on Nineteenth- and Twentieth Century Native American Leaders.* Albuquerque: University of New Mexico Press, 1985.

Nabokov, Peter, ed. *Native American Testimony: A Chronicle of Indian-White Relations from Prophecy to the Present, 1492–1992.* New York: Penguin, 1992.

Nabokov, Peter, and Robert Easton. *Native American Architecture.* New York: Oxford University Press, 1989.

Noble, David Grant. *Ancient Ruins of the Southwest.* Flagstaff, Ariz.: Northland Publishing, 1991 (revised edition).

O'Brian, Sharon. *American Indian Tribal Governments.* Norman: University of Oklahoma Press, 1989.

Parsons, Elsie Clews, ed. *North American Indian Life: Customs and Traditions of 23 Tribes.* New York; Dover, 1992 (reprint from 1922).

Paterek, Josephine. *Encyclopedia of American Indian Costume.* New York: W.W. Norton, 1994.

Patterson, E. Palmer II. *The Canadian Indian: A History Since 1500.* Don Mills, Ont.: Collier-Macmillan, 1972.

Prevar, Stephen L. *The Rights of Indians and Tribes.* Carbondale and Edwardsville: Southern Illinois University Press, 1992.

Prucha, Francis Paul. *Atlas of American Indian Affairs.* Lincoln: University of Nebraska Press, 1990.

———, ed. *Documents of United States Indian Policy.* Lincoln: University of Nebraska Press, 1990

———. *The Great Father: The United States Government and the American Indians.* Lincoln: University of Nebraska Press, 1984.

Roosevelt, Anna C., and James G.E. Smith, eds. *The Ancestors: Native Artisans of the Americas.* New York: Museum of the American Indian, 1979.

Ruoff, A. LaVonne Brown. *American Indian Literatures: An Introduction, Bibliographic Review, and Selected Bibliography.* New York: Modern Language Association, 1990.

Sauer, Carl. *Man in Nature: America Before the Days of the White Man.* Berkeley, Calif.: Turtle Island Foundation, 1975 (reprint from 1939).

Shaffer, Lynda Norene. *Native Americans Before 1492: The Moundbuilding Centers of the Eastern Woodlands.* Armonk, N.Y.: M.E. Sharpe, 1992.

Shanks, Ralph, and Lisa Woo Shanks. *The North American Indian Travel Guide.* Petaluma, Calif.: Costano Books, 1986.

Silverberg, Robert. *The Mound Builders.* Athens: Ohio University Press, 1970.

Snow, Dean R. *The Archaeology of North America: American Indians Their Origins.* New York: Thames & Hudson, 1980.

Starkey, Armstrong. *European and Native American Warfare, 1675–1815.* Norman: University of Oklahoma Press, 1998.

Steele, Ian K. *Warpaths: Invasions of North America:* New York: Oxford University Press, 1994.

Sturtevant, William C., general editor. *Handbook of North American Indians,* 20 vols. Washington D.C.: Smithsonian, 1970s–90s.

Swanton, John R. *The Indians of the Southeastern United States.* Washington, D.C.: Smithsonian, 1946.

———. *The Indian Tribes of North America.* Washington, D.C.: Smithsonian, 1952.

Symington, Fraser. *The Canadian Indian: The Illustrated History of the Great Tribes of Canada.* Toronto: McClelland & Stewart, 1969.

Taylor, Theodore W. *The Bureau of Indian Affairs.* Boulder, Colo.: Westview, 1984.

Tebbel, John, and Keith Jennison. *The American Indian Wars.* New York: Crown, 1960.

Turner, Geoffrey E.S. *Indians of North America.* Poole, Dorset: Blandford Press Ltd., 1979.

Tyler, S. Lyman. *A History of Indian Policy.* Washington, D.C.: U.S. Department of the Interior, 1973.

Underhill, Ruth M. *Red Man's America: A History of Indians in the United States.* Chicago: University of Chicago Press, 1971.

———. *Red Man's Religion: Beliefs and Practices of the Indians North of Mexico.* Chicago: University of Chicago Press, 1965.

Utley, Robert M. *Frontier Regulars: The United States Army and the Indian, 1866–1890.* New York: Macmillan, 1973.

———. *Frontiersmen in Blue; The United States Army and the Indian, 1848–1865.* New York: Macmillan, 1967.

Utley, Robert M., and Wilcomb E. Washburn. *Indian Wars.* New York: American Heritage; Boston: Houghton Mifflin, 1977.

Vanderwerth, W.C., ed. *Indian Oratory: Famous Speeches by Noted Indian Chieftains.* Norman: University of Oklahoma Press, 1971.

Versluis, Arthur. *The Elements of Native American Traditions.* Rockport, Me.: Element, 1993.

Vickers, Scott B. *Native American Identities: From Stereotype to Archetype in Art and Literature.* Albuquerque: University of New Mexico Press, 1998.

Wade, Edwin, L., ed. *The Arts of the North American Indian: Native Traditions in Evolution.* New York: Hudson Hill Press, 1986.

Walters, Anna Lee. *The Spirit of Native America: Beauty and Mysticism in American Indian Art.* San Francisco: Chronicle, 1989.

Weatherford, Jack. *Native Givers: How the Indians of the Americas Transformed the World.* New York: Crown, 1989.

———. *Native Roots: How the Indians Enriched America.* New York: Crown, 1991.

Weyler, Rex. *Blood of the Land: The Government and Corporate War Against the American Indian Movement.* New York: Everest House, 1982.

White, Robert H. *Tribal Assets: The Rebirth of Native America.* New York: Henry Holt, 1991.

Wissler, Clark. *Indians of the United States: Four Centuries of Their History and Culture.* Garden City, N.J.: Doubleday, 1966 (reprint from 1940).

Wright, Murial H. *A Guide to the Indian Tribes of Oklahoma.* Norman: University of Oklahoma Press, 1997 (revised edition).

INDEX

Page numbers in **boldface** indicate main articles. Page numbers in *italics* indicate illustrations. Page numbers followed by *g* indicate glossary entries; page numbers followed by *m* indicate maps.